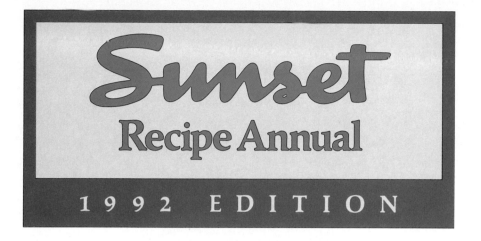

Sunset
Recipe Annual

1992 EDITION

Every *Sunset Magazine* recipe and
food article from 1991

By the *Sunset* Editors

Rosemary & Lemon Stretch Breadsticks (page 92)

Sunset Publishing Corporation ■ Menlo Park, California

Our Tribute to a Great 1991

Spiced Bell Pepper Soufflé (page 82)

Join us for our annual feast of culinary adventures—*Sunset's Recipe Annual*. Like the previous editions, this collection presents every food article from the past year's 12 issues of *Sunset Magazine*.

What's new from 1991? You'll find continuing efforts to reduce fat and calories in our recipes, the latest research on safe ways to use eggs, and ideas for festive parties.

Sample your way through the year, from spring's rhubarb and sweet onions to autumn's grapes and pistachios. Experiment with extra-long bread loaves, seaweed, herb-flavored ice cream, or pasta with flower "pictures."

What piques your interest? Stretch breadsticks? Assembly-line appetizers? Low-fat cooky cheesecake? Supper nachos? Halloween spider bread? A make-ahead fiesta? You'll find them all here, along with our ever-popular monthly features: *Sunset's Kitchen Cabinet*, *Chefs of the West*, and *Menus*.

Front cover: Tradewinds Cheesecake (recipe on page 122). Photography by Kevin Sanchez. Design by Susan Bryant. Food and photo styling by Susan Massey-Weil.

Back cover: Minestrone Genovese (recipe on page 232). Photography by Darrow M. Watt.

Sunset Magazine
   Editor: William R. Marken

Sunset Books
   Editor: Elizabeth L. Hogan

First printing March 1992

All material in this book originally appeared in the 1991 issues of *Sunset Magazine* and was created by the following editors, illustrators, photographers, and photo stylists:

Senior Editor (Food and Entertaining)
Sunset Magazine
Jerry Anne Di Vecchio

Food Writers
Sunset Magazine
Linda Lau Anusasananan, Senior Writer
Betsy Reynolds Bateson
Paula Smith Freschet
Bernadette Hart
Elaine Johnson
Karyn I. Lipman
Christine B. Weber

Illustrations
David Broad (*Chefs of the West*)
Alice Harth (*Sunset's Kitchen Cabinet*)

Photography
Glenn Christiansen
Peter Christiansen
Norman A. Plate
Darrow M. Watt
(See page 352 for individual credits)

Photo Styling
Carol Hatchard Goforth
Françoise Dudal Kirkman
Dennis W. Leong

Recipe Annual was produced by *Sunset Books*.

Contributing Editors
Cornelia Fogle
Helen Sweetland

Design
Williams & Ziller Design

Contents

A Letter from Sunset

DEAR READER,

When visitors come to *Sunset* and see the food editors busily working on stories in our test kitchens, the question they ask most often is: "Where do you get all those ideas?"

The answer isn't complicated. It's just a little involved.

First, many of our recipes and story ideas come directly from you, whether in our monthly *Kitchen Cabinet* or in features like "Rhubarb Pies" (February) and "A Make-ahead Fiesta" (June). Like every other recipe and party idea we publish, these reader contributions are of course thoroughly tested in *Sunset's* kitchens and evaluated by a taste panel.

Your growing interest in nutrition and fitness has been inspirational. In January, we chose 17 of our grand old recipes (we know they're favorites, since you've requested copies of them so often through the years), then trimmed them down to meet today's tastes and nutritional demands. The project was so much fun for us—and generated such an enthusiastic response from you—that a new monthly feature was born: "Lightening up *Sunset* Classics."

As we worked to streamline these recipes, we created a number of fat-reducing (and almost automatically cholesterol-trimming), flavor-adding steps using everyday foods. These steps are so effective and easy to use that we've incorporated them in many other recipes (even some of yours). Appealing examples include "A Lighter Beef Fondue" (February), "Summer Dinner Party for 12" (July), and "Skinny Gelato" (August). The two bonus recipe sections, "Good Foods of Summer" (June) and "Holiday Entertaining" (November) use these fat-lowering strategies to create delicious party foods you can enjoy without feeling guilty.

Because many of you have requested more information about fat in foods, all *Sunset* recipes (starting in July 1991) now include nutrition information on saturated fat as well as total fat.

Rallied round the famous life-size piggy bank in Seattle's Pike Place Market, Sunset's scouting food writers pause to ham it up (left to right): Jerry Di Vecchio, Betsy Bateson, Paula Freschet, Karyn Lipman, Christine Weber, Bernadette Hart, and Linda Anusasananan.

4

Situations that puzzle or worry you also provide us with topics, as in June's "Safe Ways to Use Eggs," for which we initiated new research.

We gather many wonderful story ideas while scouting both close to home and far afield. We sometimes work as a team; the photos on these pages were taken on a tasting trip to the Pacific Northwest. More often, though, we travel individually—interviewing good cooks and winemakers; trying out restaurant fare, plain and fancy; visiting with chefs; wandering through markets; touring farms, fisheries, and packing sheds; and talking with food producers and food scientists. Wherever we go, we're always on the alert for interesting recipes, entertaining ideas, and food news—and we share our successful finds with you. In this *Recipe Annual*, you'll find articles on Caribbean soups (February), hearty supper pies and Thai party appetizers (March), Dutch *Bosche bollen* (April), East-West fare from the Napa Valley (July), and holiday chili wreaths (December).

Because *Sunset's* food editors do their own shopping and recipe development, we're constantly in supermarkets, ethnic food markets, and all kinds of specialty food stores. As we shop, we keep a sharp eye out for new products, such as delicate tilapia (May) and out-of-the-ordinary dried fruits (November), then fill you in on good ways to use these foods.

We realize that there's a limit to the time you can spend cooking, so in each story, you'll find stopping points and make-ahead steps. Our monthly menus suggest quick, easy foods for everyday cooking. Sometimes, being in a hurry can even give you time to slow down, as in "Bake & Relax Dinners" (March).

We know you like foods with WOW, especially if those impressive results are easy to achieve. Skinny Stretch Breadsticks and broth-filled Surprise Dumplings (April), pasta "pictures" with fresh herbs and flowers (September), and Fila-wrapped Rum Cake Bundles (November) are all as straightforward to produce as they are stunning.

Chefs of the West has changed its rules. Now, women too can earn the tall white *Chef of the West* toque and lifetime membership in this organization.

Wine, as part of the good life, is suggested regularly. It also receives special attention in other stories, such as "Cooking with Fruit Wine" (March), "Autumn Teammates: Fresh Fruit, Cheese & Wine" (October), and "When the Chardonnay Makers Have Lunch" (October).

In this *Recipe Annual*, as in its four predecessors, recipes are grouped by the month in which they appeared in *Sunset Magazine*. For help in locating particular recipes easily, consult the three indexes on pages 339 to 352: an index of article titles, one of recipe names, and a longer, general index.

Whether you're putting together a family dinner or planning a gala for dozens, you'll find the *Recipe Annual* offers a bounty of helpful ideas: all the exciting, delicious, imaginative recipes from 1991's *Sunset Magazine*.

Enjoy them!

Jerry Di Vecchio

Jerry Anne Di Vecchio
Senior Editor (Food and Entertaining)
Sunset Magazine

Food writer Elaine Johnson (top) checks out melons with Kaan Gwee, our summer intern from UC Davis. Below, Sunset's food writers take a close look at live shellfish and fish on ice at Pike Place Market.

An Annual Tradition

1987 1988 1989 1990 1991

Starting with The Best of Sunset in 1987, each Recipe Annual that followed has been a keepsake edition of the previous year's food articles and recipes from Sunset Magazine.

TO USE OUR NUTRITION INFORMATION

Sunset recipes contain nutrition information based on the most current data available from the USDA for calorie count; grams of protein, total fat (including saturated fat, beginning in July), and carbohydrate; and milligrams of sodium and cholesterol.

This analysis is usually given for a single serving, based on the largest number of servings listed for the recipe. Or it's for a specific amount, such as per tablespoon (for sauces), or by a unit, as per cooky.

The nutrition analysis does not include optional ingredients or those for which no specific amount is stated (salt added to taste, for example). If an ingredient is listed with an alternative—such as unflavored yogurt or sour cream—the figures are calculated using the first choice. Likewise, if a range is given for the amount of an ingredient (such as ½ to 1 cup butter), values are figured on the first, lower amount.

Recipes using regular-strength chicken broth are based on the sodium content of salt-free homemade or canned broth. If you used canned salted chicken broth, the sodium content will be higher.

Pesto Cheese Torta (page 15)

Classic Sunset recipes
take on a leaner look as we start off the new year.
In a 14-page feature article, we trim and slim many of our
old favorites by reducing fat and using innovative techniques;
we also suggest ways you can lighten your own
special dishes. Prosciutto also gets a closer look, as you
learn more about how it's produced, how to judge quality,
and ways to use prosciutto in easy recipes. You'll also
find an imaginative solution to the challenge of
entertaining on a budget: for under $20, an elegant meal
that serves four people.

LIGHTENING UP SUNSET CLASSICS: **A Fresh Look at 17 Favorites**

HOW DO THREE DECADES *of Sunset recipes measure up to today's standards for a balanced diet? Though we've always put a priority on a well-balanced diet, we found many candidates that lent themselves beautifully to updating with trimmer ingredients.*

Here is a wide selection of old favorites we've lightened up by eliminating fat and using innovative techniques. Some dishes come surprisingly close to the originals; others are definitely different, though not necessarily less appealing. One interesting discovery: younger tasters on our staff— ones who tend to exercise regularly and avoid fatty foods—preferred the lighter versions.

Once upon a time, all a cook had to worry about was turning out pretty good food timed to appease appetites of the hard-working people who flocked to the table. Those were the days of creamy soups, juicy roasts, plenty of mashed potatoes, and lots of gravy.

Then life got easier and people didn't have to work so hard. But their eating habits changed very little. What had been thought of as good, nourishing food began to be linked with health problems like obesity, heart disease, high blood pressure, and more.

Reactionary fears focused on calories, fats, cholesterol, and sodium. But these weren't the basic problem—all are essential to our well-being. The true culprit is lack of balance. Variety and moderation are important for good health. This is not news, just reality. What and how much we eat are both dictated by individual needs (physical and genetic).

WHERE DO YOU START?

You should consume the basic nutrients (protein, carbohydrates, fats, vitamins, and minerals) in amounts that match your level of activity and physical needs. An effective diet emphasizes simply cooked meat, poultry, and fish with a wide variety of vegetables, grains, legumes, pastas, and fruits, with a little give for occasional extravaganzas.

For most people, calories are the best indicator of a balanced diet. But calories need to be scrutinized in terms of balance of the basic nutrients, particularly fat. Why focus on fat? It's a tool to make foods taste good with less effort, so we're inclined to use it freely. But by reducing fat, you automatically increase the proportion of other nutritional elements, except cholesterol. The bonus with less fat is that you aren't as tempted to overeat. Ways to lower fat in the following recipes are described in the six techniques on pages 20–21. Try them with other favorite recipes, too.

The American Heart Association advocates cutting calories from fat to 30 percent or less. But unless you're trying to lose weight or your doctor specifies this goal, it's reasonable to juggle 30 to 35 percent of your calories from fat, 50 to 55 percent from carbohydrates, and about 15 percent from protein.

MAIN DISHES

Favorite entrées over the past three decades include pasta, main-dish salads, and a cheese soufflé as well as hearty meat and fish recipes.

CARBONARA

Fat-marbled nuggets of pork butt, 1/4 cup butter, and 4 egg yolks are replaced by boned, fat-trimmed chicken thighs and braise-deglazed onions; the cheese has been reduced 25 percent.

  1 1/2 **pounds chicken thighs, boned, skinned, and trimmed of all fat**
  1 **large (1/2 lb.) onion, chopped**
  1/2 **teaspoon fennel seed**
  1 3/4 **cups regular-strength chicken broth**
  1 **cup minced parsley**
  1 **large egg**
  3 **large egg whites**
  3/4 **to 1 pound dry vermicelli**
  1 1/2 **cups (about 6 oz.) finely shredded parmesan cheese**
  Salt and pepper

Rinse chicken and pat dry. Cut in about 1/2-inch chunks.

In a 10- to 12-inch nonstick frying pan, combine onion, fennel seed, and 1 cup broth. Boil on high heat, uncovered, until liquid evaporates; stir occasionally. When browned bits accumulate in pan, add water, 2 tablespoons at a time, to release them; cook until mixture begins to brown again. Repeat deglazing step until onions are a pale golden brown color. Add 2 tablespoons more water and chicken; stir often until drippings begin to brown. Deglaze with 2 tablespoons water.

When pan is dry, add 3/4 cup broth and bring to boiling. Add parsley and keep warm. Meanwhile, pour 3 to 4 quarts water into a 5- to 6-quart pan; bring to boiling on high heat.

Whisk the whole egg and egg whites to blend well. When water boils, add pasta and cook, uncovered, until tender to bite, 8 to 10 minutes. Drain and at once pour into pan with chicken; pour eggs onto hot pasta and lift with 2 forks to mix well (eggs cook if you delay mixing pasta), adding 1 cup of the cheese. Pour onto a platter and continue to mix until most of the broth is absorbed. Offer remaining cheese and salt and pepper to add to taste. Makes 6 or 7 servings.

PER SERVING REVISED CARBONARA: 388 calories, 30 g protein, 41 g carbohydrates, 11 g fat, 97 mg cholesterol, 495 mg sodium

PER SERVING ORIGINAL CARBONARA (JUNE 1973, PAGE 160): 694 calories, 38 g protein, 38 g carbohydrates, 42 g fat, 263 mg cholesterol, 852 mg sodium

SALAD-IN-A-BOAT

One of Sunset's most popular food features a decade ago, this salad is served in a crisp cream puff shell. To lighten the pastry, we switched from butter to oil and used less; instead of 3 eggs, we used 1 egg and 3 egg whites.

  2/3 **cup water**
  1/4 **cup olive oil or salad oil**
  1/8 **teaspoon salt**
  2/3 **cup all-purpose flour**
  1 **large egg**
  3 **large egg whites**
  Cooking oil spray
  Chicken salad (recipe follows)

In a 1 1/2- to 2-quart pan, combine the water, olive oil, and salt. Bring to a boil on high heat. Add flour all at once; stir until dough holds together as a ball. Dump dough into a food processor (or leave in pan and remove from heat). Add egg and egg whites, 1 at a time, whirling (or beating) to incorporate smoothly.

(Continued on page 10)

Carbonara sauce features boned and trimmed chicken thighs, braise-deglazed onions, and a generous amount of parsley. Shredded parmesan clings to pasta with the help of lean egg whites. Cheese and egg yolks have been reduced, and butter has been eliminated.

With oil spray, lightly coat the interior of a 9-inch-wide cake pan with removable rim; dust pan with flour and shake out excess. Scrape dough into pan and smoothly spread over bottom and sides. Bake in a 400° oven until pastry is puffed and golden brown, about 40 minutes. Turn off oven.

Prick pastry with a toothpick in 10 to 12 places and leave in closed oven for about 10 minutes to dry, then remove pan from oven and cool completely. Use or, if made ahead, wrap airtight and keep at room temperature up until next day. To recrisp, unwrap and put crust in a 350° oven for about 15 minutes. Remove pan rim, set pastry on a plate, and fill with salad, as follows. Serves 6.

PER SERVING REVISED SALAD-IN-A-BOAT: 303 calories, 24 g protein, 24 g carbohydrates, 11 g fat, 80 mg cholesterol, 169 mg sodium

PER SERVING ORIGINAL SALAD-IN-A-BOAT (JULY 1980, PAGE 78): 451 calories, 29 g protein, 21 g carbohydrates, 27 g fat, 282 mg cholesterol, 325 mg sodium

Chicken salad. Mix 3 cups bite-size pieces boned and skinned **cooked chicken breast** with 2 teaspoons *each* minced **fresh cilantro** (coriander), minced **fresh ginger,** and **curry powder;** 3 tablespoons **seasoned rice vinegar** (or 3 tablespoons rice vinegar and 3/4 teaspoon sugar); 1 cup **nonfat yogurt;** 1 can (8 oz.) drained **sliced water chestnuts;** and **salt** to taste. If made ahead, cover and chill up until next day.

Pull stems and strings off 1/2 pound **edible-pod peas.** Drop peas into about 3 quarts rapidly boiling **water.** Cook, uncovered, just until peas are a brighter green, about 2 minutes; drain. Immerse peas in ice water; drain when cool. If made ahead, cover and chill up until next day.

To serve, put peas in pastry. Mix salad with 1/2 cup chopped **green onions** and pile onto peas. Garnish with **cilantro leaves.**

FISH WITH HORSERADISH SAUCE

The original version of this simple dish with Scandinavian heritage was relatively lean, but omitting 3 tablespoons butter and 2 tablespoons flour in the sauce is an easy way to lighten it up.

Popular Salad-in-a-Boat features crunchy chicken salad served in a slimmed-down shell of crisp cream puff pastry.

1 tablespoon **cornstarch**
1 cup **oven-poached fish liquid** (directions follow)
1 tablespoon **prepared horseradish**
Oven-poached fish (directions follow)
8 to 12 hot boiled **tiny potatoes**
About 3 **green onions,** ends trimmed, cut into 2-inch lengths and slivered

In a 1 1/2- to 2-quart pan, blend cornstarch smoothly with the fish liquid and horseradish. Bring to a boil on high heat, stirring. Spoon sauce evenly over poached fish, covering completely. If made ahead, cover and chill fish up until next day.

Bake fish, uncovered, in a 400° oven until sauce is bubbling and fish is warm in center, 15 to 20 minutes. Mound potatoes into dish; top with onions. Makes 4 servings.

PER SERVING REVISED BAKED FISH: 238 calories, 33 g protein, 20 g carbohydrates, 2.2 g fat, 89 mg cholesterol, 121 mg sodium

PER SERVING ORIGINAL BAKED FISH (JANUARY 1974, PAGE 82): 321 calories, 33 g protein, 20 g carbohydrates, 13 g fat, 119 mg cholesterol, 209 mg sodium

Oven-poached fish. Choose any one of the following **fish:** lingcod, halibut, rockfish, or sole. You will need a total of 1 1/2 pounds skinned and boned fish; fillets should be no more than 1 inch thick (fold in half fillets that are less than 1/2 inch thick), and steaks should be about 1 inch thick. Arrange pieces side by side in a shallow 8- to 9-inch-wide baking dish.

Pour 2/3 cup **regular-strength chicken broth** over fish. Cover and bake in a 400° oven until fish is opaque but still moist-looking in thickest portion (cut to test), 15 to 25 minutes depending on thickness of fish. Let cool slightly.

Holding fish in place with a wide spatula or pan lid, drain juices into a measuring cup; cover and chill fish. You should have about 1 cup liquid, but this varies with the fish; either boil juices in a 1- to 2-quart pan until reduced to 1 cup, or add more broth to make 1 cup. Use hot or cool.

SUPPER NACHOS

Our 15-year-old recipe for supper nachos used canned refried beans, prepared chorizo sausages, lots of cheese, and fried tortillas; this go-round, the beans aren't refried, but mashed and lightly seasoned with braise-deglazed onions; the chorizo mixture is homemade and very lean; cheese is cut back; and the tortillas for scooping are oven-crisped, not fried.

- ½ **pound fat-trimmed pork tenderloin**
- ½ **pound fat-trimmed beef sirloin steak**
- 2 **large (about 1 lb. total) onions, chopped**
- 2 **teaspoons *each* chili powder and dry oregano leaves**
- ¾ **teaspoon cumin seed**
- ½ **teaspoon crushed dried hot red chilies**
- ¼ **teaspoon ground cinnamon**
- 3 **cups regular-strength chicken broth**
- 6 **tablespoons cider vinegar**
  Salt
- 2 **cans (15 to 16 oz. each) pinto beans, drained**
- 1 **can (4 oz.) diced green chilies**
- 1 **cup shredded longhorn cheddar cheese**
  Toppings (directions follow)
  Water-crisped corn tortilla chips (directions follow)
- 2 **limes, cut in wedges**

Oven-poached fish yields juices to make the sauce. Serve with boiled tiny red potatoes and garnish with slivered green onions.

Cut pork and beef into chunks and whirl in a food processor just until minced (or grind through medium blade of a food chopper); set aside.

In a 10- to 12-inch nonstick frying pan, combine 1 chopped onion, chili powder, 1½ teaspoons oregano, ½ teaspoon cumin seed, crushed dried chilies, cinnamon, and 1 cup broth. Boil on high heat, uncovered, until liquid evaporates; stir often.

When browned bits stick in pan, add water, 2 tablespoons at a time, to release them; cook until mixture begins to brown again. Repeat deglazing step until onions are a rich brown color. Add 2 tablespoons more water, then meat; crumble meat and stir until drippings begin to brown. Repeat deglazing, using vinegar in 2-tablespoon portions and more water, if needed, until mixture is an attractive brown color.

Season to taste with salt. Pour mixture into a bowl and set aside; if made ahead, cover and chill up until next day.

Combine in frying pan the remaining onion, oregano, cumin, and 1 cup broth. Boil dry, brown, and deglaze as directed for first onion mixture until a light brown color. Add beans and 1 cup broth. Mash beans in pan, then stir over medium-high heat until mixture is thick enough to scoop. Season to taste with salt; if made ahead, cover and chill up until next day.

Scoop beans into a shallow, rimmed ovenproof dish (about 15 in. wide) and spread level. Top beans with meat mixture; sprinkle with green chilies, then cheese. Bake, uncovered, in a 400° oven until hot in center, 15 to 20 minutes.

Remove from oven and add toppings. Then tuck enough tortilla chips around edges of bean mixture for a petaled effect. Accompany with remaining tortilla chips.

Scoop bean mixture with tortilla chips; to keep nachos hot for leisurely dining, set platter on an electric warming tray while you eat. Season to taste with lime juice and salt. Makes 5 or 6 main-dish servings.

PER SERVING REVISED SUPPER NACHOS: 479 calories, 34 g protein, 53 g carbohydrates, 16 g fat, 68 mg cholesterol, 668 mg sodium

PER SERVING ORIGINAL SUPPER NACHOS (JANUARY 1976, PAGE 48): 1,059 calories, 37 g protein, 81 g carbohydrates, 68 g fat, 94 mg cholesterol, 1,670 mg sodium

Water-crisped tortilla chips surround no-fat bean and chorizo base for nachos.

Toppings. Peel and pit ½ of a small (5- to 6-oz. whole) firm-ripe **avocado**; cut in 6 wedges and moisten with **cider** or wine vinegar. Arrange slices on hot bean mixture. Sprinkle with ½ cup chopped **green onion,** ¼ cup **fresh cilantro** (coriander) **leaves,** and 3 or 4 **pitted large black ripe olives.** Mound in the center ¼ cup **unflavored nonfat yogurt** or light sour cream, and 1 **red pickled pepper.**

Water-crisped tortilla chips. Immerse 12 **corn tortillas** (10- to 12-oz. package, 6 to 7 in. wide), 1 at a time, in water. Let drain briefly, then lay flat. If desired, sprinkle tops lightly with **salt.** Cut each tortilla into 6 or 8 wedges.

Fill a 10- by 15-inch pan with a single layer of tortilla wedges, salt side up, placed close together (don't overlap). Bake in a 500° oven for 3 minutes. Turn with a wide spatula, then continue to bake until pale golden brown and crisp, 2 to 3 minutes more. Pour chips out and fill pan again; repeat until all are baked.

Serve warm or cool; if made ahead, store cool tortilla chips airtight at room temperature up to 2 weeks. Makes about 8 cups.

Simple steak and salad dinner cuts calories: meat is barbecued instead of pan-browned, and its juices flavor slimmed-down green peppercorn sauce. New version of Green Goddess dressing remains deliciously true to flavors of original.

STEAK & PEPPERCORN SAUCE

Braise-deglaze shallots with vinegar, water, and a few tablespoons whipping cream (down from 3/4 cup in the earlier version) to smooth flavors of sauce.

The meat is barbecued instead of pan-browned, but even though you lose tasty meat drippings, you can still enrich the sauce with meat juices. Let the cooked steak rest before slicing, then stir the accumulated meat juices into the sauce.

- 1/2 **cup minced shallots**
- 1/4 **teaspoon dry tarragon leaves**
- 1/4 **cup sherry vinegar or balsamic vinegar**
- 1 **tablespoon drained and rinsed canned green peppercorns**
- 1 **tablespoon Dijon mustard**
- 3 **tablespoons whipping cream**
- 3/4 **cup regular-strength beef broth**
- 1 **fat-trimmed beef sirloin steak (about 1½ lb.), cut about 1¼ inches thick; or 1 fat-trimmed flank steak (about 1½ lb.)**
- 2 **tablespoons brandy, warmed (optional)**
  Salt

In a 10- to 12-inch frying pan over medium-high heat, combine shallots, tarragon, vinegar, and 1/4 cup water; stir often, uncovered, until liquid evaporates. When browned bits stick to pan, add 2 tablespoons water and stir to free them; cook until browned bits begin to accumulate again. Deglaze with 2 more tablespoons water if you want more brown color in the sauce. When desired degree of brownness is achieved, add peppercorns, Dijon mustard, cream, and broth; stir often until reduced to 2/3 cup. Set aside.

Cook steak on a grill over a solid bed of hot coals (you can hold your hand at grill level only 2 to 3 seconds) until rare, 6 to 7 minutes on each side for a 1¼-inch-thick steak, about 10 minutes total for flank steak. Set steak on a platter and keep warm for 5 to 10 minutes.

Put brandy in a long-handled metal cup; set aflame and pour over meat.

Shake platter until flame dies (take care meat is *not* beneath the exhaust fan or flammable items). Drain juices from meat platter into the frying pan with sauce. Stir on high heat until hot. Slice meat thinly across grain and spoon sauce onto portions; add salt to taste. Makes 6 servings.

PER SERVING REVISED STEAK AND PEPPERCORN SAUCE: 188 calories, 25 g protein, 4.1 g carbohydrates, 7.5 g fat, 78 mg cholesterol, 146 mg sodium

PER SERVING ORIGINAL STEAK AND PEPPERCORN SAUCE (APRIL 1976, PAGE 95): 316 calories, 26 g protein, 4.9 g carbohydrates, 20 g fat, 105 mg cholesterol, 174 mg sodium

CANNELLONI

Retailored cannelloni retains its elegant delicacy even though it gives up more than 1/2 cup butter, a half-dozen egg yolks, and 3/4 pound high-moisture, mild teleme cheese; or you might try other mild-tasting, reduced-fat cheeses, such as jarlsberg lite, thinly sliced.

Not only is this recipe much leaner, it's also easier, faster, and uses fewer pans than its parent. The first shortcut replaces tediously produced egg-rich noodle wrappers with thin egg roll skins.

- 1 **large (8 oz.) onion, chopped**
- 1 **small clove garlic**
- 1 **teaspoon butter, margarine, or olive oil**
- 3/4 **pound boned and skinned chicken breast**
- 1/2 **pound boneless and skinless turkey breast fillet**
- 1/2 **pound low-fat ricotta cheese**
- 1/2 **cup freshly grated parmesan cheese**
- 1/8 **teaspoon ground nutmeg**
  Salt
- 1 **large egg white**
- 1 **tablespoon fine dry bread crumbs**
- 16 **egg roll wrappers (6 in. square, about 2/3 of a 1-lb. package)**
  Milk sauce (directions follow)
  Roasted tomato sauce (directions follow)
  About 3/4 pound teleme cheese

In a 9- by 13-inch pan, combine onion, garlic, butter, and 1/4 cup water. Bake, uncovered, in a 450° oven until onion begins to brown and liquid evaporates, about 15 minutes; stir often with a wide spatula. Add another 1/4 cup water to

pan and stir to scrape browned bits free; bake until liquid is almost gone, about 8 minutes.

Cut chicken and turkey into 1½-inch chunks and scatter in pan. Bake until thickest chunks are just white in the center, 8 to 10 minutes. Remove from oven and let stand until cool enough to touch. In a food processor, whirl about half the meat mixture with about half the ricotta and parmesan cheeses just until meat is minced. Scrape into a bowl. Repeat to mince remaining meat with cheeses. (Or grind meats and cheeses through fine blade of a food chopper.)

Season mixture with nutmeg and salt to taste, then beat in egg white, bread crumbs, and 2 tablespoons water. If made ahead, cover and chill up to 2 days.

Lay egg roll wrappers out flat in a single layer. Divide meat filling evenly among wrappers, placing along 1 edge. Shape filling into a log on each wrapper, then roll to enclose filling and set seam side down. If assembled ahead, cover and chill up to 6 hours. In a 1½- to 2-quart pan, combine milk sauce and roasted tomato sauce. Stir often over medium-high heat until hot.

To assemble, pour hot sauce into 1 oven-proof, shallow-rimmed serving container or equally into several smaller containers. For individual servings of 2 cannelloni each, use oval or rectangular dishes about 4 by 7 inches. For 8 servings, use a container about 16 by 20 inches, or use 2 containers, each about 7 by 10 inches.

Set cannelloni into sauce, leaving about 1/2 inch between them. Cut teleme into slices as thin as possible, then tear cheese pieces into sections and lay on cannelloni to cover fairly evenly; there will be bare spaces. Bake, uncovered, in a 425° oven until cheese melts and cannelloni are hot in the center, about 10 minutes. Use a long spatula and spoon to serve. Makes 8 servings, 2 each.

PER SERVING REVISED CANNELLONI: 439 calories, 39 g protein, 35 g carbohydrates, 16 g fat, 62 mg cholesterol, 496 mg sodium

PER SERVING ORIGINAL CANNELLONI (APRIL 1963, PAGE 181): 932 calories, 49 g protein, 61 g carbohydrates, 54 g fat, 498 mg cholesterol, 1,253 mg sodium

(Continued on next page)

Milk sauce. In a 1¹/₂- to 2-quart pan over medium-high heat, melt 2 teaspoons **butter** or margarine or warm 2 teaspoons olive oil. Add 1¹/₂ tablespoons **all-purpose flour** and stir until lightly toasted. Remove from heat and smoothly mix in 1 cup **skim milk** and 1¹/₂ cups **regular-strength chicken broth.** Stir over high heat until boiling, then boil gently, uncovered, until reduced to 1¹/₂ cups, about 20 minutes; stir often. If made ahead, cool, cover, and chill up to 2 days.

Roasted tomato sauce. Cut about 2 pounds **Roma-style tomatoes** in half lengthwise and lay skin side down in a 10- by 15-inch pan. Bake, uncovered, in a 450° oven until juices evaporate, leaving a dark brown residue, and edges of tomatoes are tinged with brown. Remove from oven and mix in 1 cup **regular-strength chicken broth** and 1 tablespoon **balsamic** or wine **vinegar.** Let cool; scrape browned bits free.

Whirl tomatoes and liquid, a portion at a time, in a food processor or blender until puréed. Pour into a 1¹/₂- to 2-quart pan and boil gently, uncovered, until reduced to about 1¹/₂ cups, about 30 minutes. If made ahead, cover and chill up to 2 days. Stir in ¹/₂ cup chopped **fresh basil leaves** or 2 teaspoons dry basil leaves.

CHORIZO ENCHILADAS

The messiest part of making enchiladas is frying the tortillas. In this recipe, we've modified the frying step considerably. Dampened tortillas pass through an oil slick, then are flipped in a dry frying pan. You make your own chorizo filling as a sure way to reduce fat.

It may seem elaborate to make the red chili sauce, but it's easy and adds considerably to the quality of the dish.

- 1 **pound fat-trimmed pork tenderloin**
- 1 **large (about ¹/₂ lb.) onion, chopped**
- 2 **teaspoons** *each* **chili powder and dry oregano leaves**
- 1 **teaspoon cumin seed**
- 1 **teaspoon crushed dried hot red chilies**

Lavish cannelloni cuts calories from fat to 32 percent—reduced from 52 percent. Not only is new recipe substantially leaner, but it is easier and faster to make.

- 1 **cup regular-strength chicken broth**
- ¹/₂ **cup cider vinegar**
  Red chili sauce (recipe follows)
- 2 **teaspoons cornstarch mixed with 1 tablespoon water**
  Salt
- 2 **teaspoons salad oil**
- 12 **corn tortillas (12-oz. package)**
- 1 **cup shredded cheddar cheese**
- ¹/₄ **cup light sour cream**
- 2 **or 3 pitted black ripe olives, sliced**
- ¹/₂ **small (5- to 6-oz.) firm-ripe avocado, pitted, peeled, and diced**

Cut pork into chunks. In a food processor, whirl about half at a time until finely chopped. Or grind through a food chopper with medium blade; set aside.

In a 10- to 12-inch nonstick frying pan, combine onion, chili powder, oregano, cumin seed, chilies, and broth. Boil on high heat, uncovered, until liquid evaporates; stir occasionally. When browned bits accumulate in pan, add water, 2 tablespoons at a time, to release them; cook until mixture begins to brown again.

Repeat deglazing step until onion is a rich brown color. Add 2 tablespoons more water, then meat; crumble meat and stir until drippings begin to brown. Repeat deglazing, using vinegar in 2-tablespoon portions and more water, if needed, until mixture is an attractive brown color.

Add ³/₄ cup of the red chili sauce, and cornstarch mixture. Stir until boiling; season to taste with salt. Use or, if made ahead, pour into a bowl, cover, and chill up until next day. Warm to use.

In a bowl at least 8 inches wide, put 2 to 3 inches water. Add salad oil. Dip a tortilla into water and lift out; a faint film of oil clings. Drop tortilla into a 10- to 12-inch nonstick frying pan over medium-high heat. Turn once to dry slightly, cooking about 15 seconds a side. Stack as heated. Spoon ¹/₁₂ of the meat mixture into center of each tortilla; roll to enclose filling and set seam side down in a 9- by 13-inch casserole. Spoon chili sauce over enchiladas; sprinkle with cheese.

Bake, uncovered, in a 375° oven until cheese melts and filling is hot, about 20 minutes. Remove from oven; top decoratively with light sour cream, olive slices, and avocado. Makes 6 servings.

PER SERVING REVISED CHORIZO ENCHILADAS: 425 calories, 29 g protein, 40 g carbohydrates, 19 g fat, 73 mg cholesterol, 312 mg sodium

PER SERVING ORIGINAL CHORIZO ENCHILADAS (MAY 1968, PAGE 174): 877 calories, 40 g protein, 37 g carbohydrates, 65 g fat, 163 mg cholesterol, 1,209 mg sodium

Red chili sauce. Lay 8 to 12 (about 3 oz. total) **dried red New Mexico** or California **chilies** in a 10- by 15-inch pan. Bake in a 300° oven just until aromatic, about 4 minutes. Let cool, then discard stems, seeds, and any veins. Rinse and drain chilies and put in a 2- to 3-quart pan. Add 2 cups **regular-strength chicken broth,** 2 cloves **garlic** (slivered), and 1 teaspoon **dry oregano leaves.** Bring to a boil. Cover and simmer gently until chilies are very soft, about 20 minutes.

Whirl mixture in a blender until smoothly puréed (or whirl chilies and 2 to 3 tablespoons of liquid in a food processor, then add remaining liquid). Pour chili mixture through a fine strainer into a bowl; rub with a spoon to extract liquid. Discard residue. You should have about 2 cups; if not, add **water** to make this amount. Or return to pan and simmer, uncovered, until reduced to 2 cups. Use warm or cool, or cover and chill up to 3 days.

Simplified chorizo filling lightens these enchiladas. Top with light sour cream, sliced olives, and avocado just before serving.

Cheddar flavors cheese soufflé; puff is lean because it's mostly egg whites.

CHEESE SOUFFLÉ

The butter and most of the egg yolks have been eliminated in this soufflé, but we kept all the cheese for its flavor and added extra egg whites for puffiness.

> Cooking oil spray
> About 2 tablespoons finely shredded parmesan cheese
> 2 tablespoons cornstarch
> 1/2 teaspoon dry mustard
> 1/8 teaspoon cayenne
> 1 cup skim milk
> 1 cup (4 oz.) shredded sharp cheddar cheese
> 2 large eggs, separated
> 4 large egg whites
> 1/2 teaspoon cream of tartar

Lightly coat the inside of a 1½-quart soufflé dish with oil spray. Add 1 tablespoon parmesan and rotate dish to coat interior with cheese; set aside.

Combine cornstarch, mustard, and cayenne in a 1½- to 2-quart pan. Smoothly blend in milk; stir over high heat until boiling. Add cheddar cheese and stir until melted. Remove pan from heat and at once stir in the egg yolks; set aside.

With an electric mixer, whip the 6 whites with cream of tartar in a large bowl until whites hold soft peaks. Stir about ¼ of the whites smoothly into the sauce. Gently fold sauce into remaining whites (mixture may be streaked), then scrape into prepared soufflé dish, mounding into center to avoid spillage as soufflé puffs.

Sprinkle with the remaining parmesan cheese. Bake at once in a 375° oven until well browned on top. For moist interior, allow 25 minutes; for firm interior, allow 30 minutes. Serves 4 or 5.

PER SERVING REVISED CHEESE SOUFFLÉ: 177 calories, 14 g protein, 6.2 g carbohydrates, 11 g fat, 112 mg cholesterol, 281 mg sodium

PER SERVING ORIGINAL CHEESE SOUFFLÉ (AUGUST 1962, PAGE 98): 259 calories, 13 g protein, 6.6 g carbohydrates, 20 g fat, 219 mg cholesterol, 504 mg sodium

APPETIZERS, SOUP & SALAD DRESSINGS

Next come leaner versions of two popular appetizers, a slimmed-down soup, and a pair of versatile salad dressings.

PESTO CHEESE TORTA

One of Sunset's most popular appetizers, it pops up at parties everywhere. Can its cool, delicate flavor and creamy texture be duplicated by less rich ingredients?

The original contained 1 pound each sweet butter and cream cheese. The revised recipe uses ricotta as the base with a reduced-oil pesto. The original recipe made 14 to 16 servings and kept longer; this one is quite flavorful but more perishable, so we scaled down the recipe. For best results, be sure dairy products are used well before their shelf-life date.

> 1 cup low-fat ricotta cheese
> 4 ounces neufchâtel (light cream cheese)
> Pesto filling (recipe follows)
> Fresh basil sprigs
> Thin baguette slices
> Crisp raw vegetables

With mixer, beat ricotta and neufchâtel until well blended. Smoothly line a clean, unused, tall 2-cup flower pot with a double layer of moistened and wrung dry cheesecloth (or 1 layer moistened muslin); cloth should drape over rim.

With a spoon, press ¼ of the cheese evenly into bottom of pot. Press ⅓ of the pesto onto the cheese; repeat, finishing with last layer of cheese. Fold edges of cloth smoothly over cheese. Cover airtight and chill at least 2 hours or until next day. Fold back cloth and invert torta onto a small plate. Gently lift off cheesecloth.

(Continued on next page)

Shredded beef in softly gelled juices substitutes for fat-marbled pork butt in this version of rillettes. Naturally lean beef shanks contain collagen, a protein that makes meat juices gel. Chill juices long enough to harden any fat, then lift off fat and discard.

If made ahead, cover airtight and chill up to 1 day. Garnish with basil sprigs. Spread on bread and vegetables. Makes about 2 cups, 7 or 8 appetizer servings.

Per Tablespoon Revised Cheese Torta: 34 calories, 2.5 g protein, 1.2 g carbohydrates, 2.4 g fat, 5.1 mg cholesterol, 74 mg sodium

Per Tablespoon Original Cheese Torta (July 1983, page 77): 79 calories, 1.3 g protein, 0.6 g carbohydrates, 8.2 g fat, 20 mg cholesterol, 46 mg sodium

Pesto filling. In a blender or food processor, whirl 2½ cups lightly packed **fresh basil leaves,** 1 cup (about 5 oz.) freshly grated **parmesan cheese,** 1 tablespoon **olive oil,** and enough **water** (1 or 2 tablespoons) to make a smooth paste. Stir in ¼ cup **pine nuts** and season with **salt** to taste.

BEEF RILLETTES

Naturally lean shanks are succulent and full of collagen, a protein that makes meat juices gel. Rillettes are made from all kinds of animals and cuts, usually with a big dose of butter or goose fat.

This recipe originally used fat-marbled pork butt, cooked until it fell apart. Then you mixed it with ½ cup butter; it spread very well, but you know where it was inclined to stick. These rillettes use beef shank and no butter, and capitalize on flavorful, softly gelled meat juices. Eat in Belgian endive leaves or small romaine leaves. Offer with mustard.

> About 1¼ pounds beef shanks, cut into 1-inch-thick slices, rinsed
> 1 clove garlic
> ½ teaspoon dry thyme leaves
> ½ teaspoon black pepper
> 1 dry bay leaf
> Salt

Oven method. Place meat in a 1- to 1½-quart casserole with 2 cups water, garlic, thyme, pepper, and bay leaf. Cover tightly with foil and bake in a 250° oven until meat is so tender it falls apart in shreds when prodded with a fork, about 4 hours.

With a slotted spoon, transfer meat to a bowl and let stand until cool enough to touch. Pull off and discard all fat, connective tissue, and gristle. Break meat into fine shreds; cover and chill. Chill juices long enough to harden fat, about 4 hours; lift off and discard fat. Juices should be softly gelled. If liquid, boil until reduced to 1½ cups. If rigid, add enough water to make 1½ cups and heat until melted. Add meat to liquid and heat until warm. Add salt to taste. Pour into a 2½- to 3-cup crock or jar.

Cover and chill until firm, at least 3 hours or up to 3 days; gelatin begins to weep if kept longer. Makes 2¼ cups.

Pressure cooker method. Place beef, 2 cups water, garlic, thyme, pepper, and bay leaf in a 4-quart pressure cooker. Bring cooker to 10 pounds pressure according to manufacturer's directions and cook for 1 hour. Reduce pressure under cold running water; open pan. Pour out and reserve the pan juices. Let meat cool, then shred and complete rillettes according to preceding directions.

PER TABLESPOON REVISED RILLETTES: 12 calories, 2 g protein, 0.1 g carbohydrates, 0.4 g fat, 4.6 mg cholesterol, 3.8 mg sodium

PER TABLESPOON ORIGINAL RILLETTES (MAY 1982, PAGE 202): 37 calories, 3.3 g protein, 0 g carbohydrates, 2.5 g fat, 15 mg cholesterol, 68 mg sodium

MARITATA SOUP

If excess were ever deserved, this soup could be justified for its delicacy and delectability. But we were surprised how well the flavor and texture translated using lighter ingredients. The exchange rate: ⅓ cup neufchâtel cheese, ⅔ cup grated parmesan cheese, and 3 egg whites for ¼ pound sweet butter, ¾ cup grated parmesan cheese, 4 egg yolks, and 1 cup whipping cream.

The deep color of the soup broth comes from dark-roasting the bones and vegetables before simmering with water. For a little showmanship, stir the seasoning mix into the very hot broth at the table.

Lighter ingredients in cheese mixture strip 277 calories per serving from this soup.

Smooth shallot dressing is water based, seasoned with Dijon mustard, shallots, and sherry vinegar. Thickened with arrowroot, it clings to salad greens.

6 cups richly flavored, fat-free broth (made with roasted bones and vegetables) or regular-strength beef broth
2 ounces (⅛ lb.) dry vermicelli, broken in short lengths
⅓ cup neufchâtel (light cream cheese)
⅔ cup grated parmesan cheese
3 egg whites

Bring broth to boiling in a 2- to 3-quart pan. Add pasta; simmer, covered, until tender to bite, 5 to 8 minutes.

With an electric mixer or in a blender, beat neufchâtel cheese with parmesan cheese and egg whites to blend well. Pour into a small bowl.

Pour boiling hot broth into a tureen. Stir the cheese-egg mixture into broth. Ladle into wide bowls. Makes 7 cups, 4 or 5 main-dish servings.

PER SERVING REVISED MARITATA SOUP: 156 calories, 11 g protein, 9.5 g carbohydrates, 7.8 g fat, 18 mg cholesterol, 334 mg sodium

PER SERVING ORIGINAL MARITATA SOUP (JANUARY 1967, PAGE 104): 433 calories, 11 g protein, 0 g carbohydrates, 39 g fat, 247 mg cholesterol, 303 mg sodium

SHALLOT DRESSING

Piquant and clinging, this oil-free dressing is surprisingly appealing on any salad greens. Arrowroot makes a very clean and neutral-tasting base so flavors shine through.

⅔ cup water
1 teaspoon arrowroot
1 tablespoon Dijon mustard
¼ cup finely slivered shallots
¼ cup sherry vinegar

In a 1- to 1½-quart pan, blend water smoothly with arrowroot. Bring to a boil, stirring. Chill (quickly, by setting pan in ice water) and add mustard, shallots, and vinegar. Use, or cover and chill up until next day. Makes about 1 cup.

PER TABLESPOON REVISED SHALLOT DRESSING: 4 calories, 0.1 g protein, 0.9 g carbohydrates, 0.1 g fat, 0 mg cholesterol, 28 mg sodium

PER TABLESPOON ORIGINAL SHALLOT DRESSING (SEPTEMBER 1966, PAGE 140): 94 calories, 0.1 g protein, 0.7 g carbohydrates, 10 g fat, 0 mg cholesterol, 98 mg sodium

GREEN GODDESS DRESSING

A classic in the West, Green Goddess Dressing was created (the oft-told story goes) at San Francisco's Palace Hotel in the early part of the century; this version is a revision of one we included in our first nothing-to-it party, published in April 1969.

Switching from a salad oil base was a challenge, but the flavors in this dairy-based mixture remain deliciously true to the original. Serve as a dip for vegetables, on salads, or as a sauce for grilled meat, fish, or poultry.

(Continued on next page)

1/3 cup coarsely chopped and lightly packed parsley

3 green onions, ends trimmed with about 3 inches of green tops

3/4 teaspoon dry tarragon leaves

1 tablespoon anchovy paste

1/2 cup low-fat cottage cheese

1/4 cup nonfat yogurt

2 tablespoons mayonnaise or reduced-calorie mayonnaise

In a blender or food processor, combine parsley, onions (cut in chunks), tarragon, anchovy paste, cottage cheese, yogurt, and mayonnaise. Whirl, pushing ingredients down into blade as needed, until smoothly puréed. Mixture will be thin; cover and let chill at least 30 minutes to thicken, or cover and chill up to 2 days. Makes about 1 cup.

PER TABLESPOON REVISED GREEN GODDESS: 23 calories, 1.5 g protein, 0.8 g carbohydrates, 1.5 g fat, 2 mg cholesterol, 83 mg sodium

PER TABLESPOON ORIGINAL GREEN GODDESS (APRIL 1969, PAGE 83): 111 calories, 1.1 g protein, 0.5 g carbohydrates, 12 g fat, 10 mg cholesterol, 91 mg sodium

DESSERTS

These four popular desserts have been reduced substantially in calories and fat without losing their appeal.

ANGEL PIE

To many tastes, a typical angel pie is way too sweet, so we cut the sugar. But because the sugar has been reduced in the meringue base, and the yolks and whipped cream omitted from the filling, this angel pie is too soft to cut.

Fresh citrus yogurt fills meringue crust in Angel Pie. Spoon from dish to serve.

Cooking oil spray

Flour

4 large egg whites

1/2 teaspoon cream of tartar

3/4 cup and 1/3 cup sugar

2 teaspoons grated lemon peel

1/4 cup lemon juice

1/3 cup orange juice

1 tablespoon cornstarch

1 pint nonfat unflavored yogurt

Citrus slices and fresh mint leaves

Lightly coat the interior of a 9-inch-wide pie pan or dish with oil spray, then coat with flour and shake out excess. Set aside.

In a large bowl with electric mixer, whip whites and cream of tartar at high speed until whites are foamy. Continue to beat and gradually add the 3/4 cup sugar until whites hold distinct peaks. Scrape into prepared pan and spread meringue evenly with the back of a spoon, pushing high on pan sides so it resembles a pie shell.

Bake in a 300° oven until meringue feels dry and is a pale gold color (a sweeter meringue feels firm), 30 to 35 minutes. Let cool. If made more than 2 hours ahead (or if it is raining), carefully wrap meringue airtight for up to 24 hours.

In a 1 1/2- to 2-quart pan, combine remaining 1/3 cup sugar, lemon peel, lemon juice, orange juice, and cornstarch. Mix until smooth, then bring to a boil, stirring. Set pan in ice water; stir often. When cool, stir yogurt into filling. Cover and chill up to 24 hours. Pour filling into meringue. Garnish with citrus slices and mint. Spoon from dish. Makes 8 servings.

PER SERVING REVISED ANGEL PIE: 155 calories, 5.1 g protein, 35 g carbohydrates, 0.2 g fat, 1.1 mg cholesterol, 73 mg sodium

PER SERVING ORIGINAL ANGEL PIE (MOST RECENTLY, JANUARY 1987, PAGE 64): 271 calories, 3.8 g protein, 39 g carbohydrates, 12 g fat, 139 mg cholesterol, 42 mg sodium

RUSSIAN CREAM

This cool, smooth dessert appears to be enjoying a revival; you'll see it called French cream, Italian panna cotta, or perhaps even Russian cream. It takes advantage of the increasing variety of dairy products with less milkfat.

Smooth and rich-tasting, molded Russian cream uses low-fat dairy foods to reduce calories, fat, and cholesterol from original version.

1/2 cup sugar

1 envelope unflavored gelatin

1/2 cup water

1 cup light sour cream

1 1/2 cups nonfat, unflavored yogurt

1 1/2 teaspoons vanilla

Orange twirls (recipe follows, optional)

In a 1- to 1 1/2-quart pan, mix sugar and gelatin. Stir in water and let stand about 5 minutes to soften gelatin. Bring to a full, rolling boil, stirring. Remove from heat. Scoop light sour cream into a bowl; quickly whisk hot gelatin mixture into it. Add yogurt and vanilla; whisk until blended. Pour into a decorative 4- to 5-cup mold. Cover and chill until set, at least 6 hours or up until next day.

To unmold, dip container up to its rim in hot-to-touch water just until edges begin to liquefy; it takes a few seconds. Quickly dry mold, and invert serving dish over it. Holding together, invert and let stand for dessert to slip free. If needed, dip in hot water again. Serve, or cover (without touching dessert) and chill up to a total of 24 hours from preparation time. Garnish with orange twirls. Makes 8 servings.

PER SERVING REVISED RUSSIAN CREAM: 142 calories, 4.2 g protein, 23 g carbohydrates, 3.7 g fat, 12 mg cholesterol, 46 mg sodium

PER SERVING ORIGINAL RUSSIAN CREAM (APRIL 1975, PAGE 210): 228 calories, 2.9 g protein, 22 g carbohydrates, 15 g fat, 39 mg cholesterol, 36 mg sodium

Orange twirls. Put 1 tablespoon finely slivered **orange peel** (orange part only) into a 1 1/2- to 2-quart pan. Add about 1/2 cup **water** and bring to a boil. Drain off water and add 2 tablespoons **sugar** and

½ cup **orange juice.** Boil until liquid is almost gone. Add another 3 tablespoons orange juice. Let cool and use, or pour into a jar and chill up to 1 week.

FROZEN PEPPERMINT PIE

Still somewhat of a splurge, a shift to purchased ingredients that include less fat helps bring this handsome dessert into perspective.

If you can't find peppermint-flavor frozen yogurt, whirl ½ cup hard peppermint candies with ¼ cup water in a blender or food processor until melted, then fold into slightly softened frozen yogurt. Refreeze to continue.

- ½ **gallon (about 2½ lb.) frozen peppermint-flavor or vanilla yogurt**
  Chocolate cooky crust (recipe follows)
- 3 **large egg whites**
- 1 **cup (4 oz.) marshmallow cream**
- 2 **teaspoons vanilla**
- 1 **ounce unsweetened chocolate**
- ¼ **cup sugar**
- ¾ **cup water**
- 2 **teaspoons arrowroot**

Spoon yogurt into crust, spreading smoothly and mounding toward center. Freeze until hard, at least 2 hours; wrap airtight if stored longer.

With a mixer on high speed, beat whites until stiff. Then beat in marshmallow cream, a large spoonful at a time, until whites hold soft peaks that curl slightly; blend in vanilla. Swirl meringue over yogurt, sealing to edge of crust. Bake in a 450° oven until meringue is lightly browned, 2 to 3 minutes. Return to freezer at once for at least 1 hour. When pie is frozen, wrap it lightly, airtight, if you plan to store it more than 24 hours.

Chop chocolate and put in a bowl with sugar. In a 1- to 1½-quart pan, blend water smoothly with arrowroot. Stirring, bring to a boil; then pour over chocolate. Stir occasionally until smooth. Pour into a small microwave-safe pitcher. Serve, or if made ahead, cover and chill up until next day. Rewarm in a microwave oven at half power (50 percent) for 15-second intervals; stir.

Unwrap pie and let stand at room temperature about 15 minutes. Cut into

Just one ounce unsweetened chocolate plus water, arrowroot, and a little sugar blend to make a smooth, warm sauce to pour over frozen peppermint yogurt pie.

wedges, using a sharp knife dipped often in hot water. Makes 8 to 10 servings.

PER SERVING REVISED PEPPERMINT PIE: 232 calories, 8.1 g protein, 43 g carbohydrates, 4.5 g fat, 8 mg cholesterol, 105 mg sodium

PER SERVING ORIGINAL PEPPERMINT PIE (JULY 1968, PAGE 97): 401 calories, 5 g protein, 42 g carbohydrates, 25 g fat, 56 mg cholesterol, 187 mg sodium

Chocolate cooky crust. In a food processor or with a rolling pin, finely crush enough **cookies** (such as cocoa-flavored biscotti or crisp almond macaroons, which typically have little or no added fat) to make 1½ cups crumbs. Whisk 1 **large egg white** until frothy, then mix with crumbs.

Lightly coat interior of a 9-inch pie pan with **cooking oil spray,** then dust lightly with flour. Press crumbs evenly over bottom and sides of pan. Bake in a 325° oven until crust feels dry and firm when pressed, about 20 minutes. Let cool, then chill at least 30 minutes; wrap airtight if held more than 2 hours.

LIQUEUR POUND CAKE

The original recipe was for a very buttery pound cake. In the new version, you use the same number of eggs, but only the whites, and omit ¾ pound butter. The finished cake is quite springy and holds up well when soaked with the apple-liqueur syrup. The rum and amaretto that flavor the syrup have ample time to boil off their caloric alcohol.

> Cooking oil spray
> 6 **large egg whites**
> 1¼ cups sifted powdered sugar
> 1 teaspoon vanilla
> 1 cup sifted cake flour
> 1 teaspoon baking soda
> ½ teaspoon baking powder
> **Apple-liqueur syrup (recipe follows)**

Lightly coat interior of a 4- by 8-inch loaf pan with oil spray; dust with flour and shake out extra. Set pan aside.

In a large bowl with electric mixer on high, whip egg whites until foamy. Then add sugar and beat until whites just barely hold soft peaks; add vanilla. Mix flour with baking soda and baking powder; add to whites. Beat just until well mixed.

Scrape batter into prepared pan. Bake in 300° oven until cake just begins to pull from pan sides and is golden brown, about 40 minutes. Run a knife between cake and pan sides. Invert cake onto rack. Pour ¼ cup apple-liqueur syrup into pan, then set cake into pan. With a slender skewer, pierce cake all over at 1-inch intervals. Slowly pour 6 or 7 tablespoons syrup over cake. Serve, or let cool and wrap airtight; chill up to 2

Techniques to Lighten Up Your Favorite Dishes

BELOW *are six ways to streamline your family's favorite recipes:*

Braise-deglaze. Recipes for soups, stews, sauces, and similar dishes often begin with chopped vegetables —such as onion, garlic, bell pepper, carrot, celery—cooked in fat to develop a flavor base. You can reduce or even eliminate the fat by using no-fat liquids.

For example, if a recipe calls for 3 to 4 tablespoons fat, omit it. Put vegetables in pan with enough liquid (one that will complement the finished dish, such as meat broth, dry wine, or just water) to almost cover them. Or you might add as little as 1 teaspoon fat to promote some sizzle.

water (or other selected liquid) in 2-tablespoon portions, stirring to release the browned mixture stuck in pan. Vegetables will soak up this color.

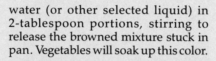

Repeat this step until the color is rich and appealing to your taste. Watch closely, however, as scorching is the next stage.

Boil on high or medium-high heat, uncovered, until liquid cooks away, stirring occasionally. When the liquid is gone and the vegetables begin to caramelize and stick in the pan, add

Then add remaining ingredients to the vegetable mixture and continue cooking as directed in preceding recipes such as Supper Nachos (page 11) and Carbonara (page 8).

Oven braise-deglaze. This works just like braise-deglaze, but you use a shallow pan in the oven, and the vegetables brown all over.

The cannelloni recipe uses this technique.

Oven-fry. Small pieces of food like meatballs, cut-up chicken or meat, or sliced vegetables (lightly coated with oil), arranged in a single layer with enough space around pieces to let moisture evaporate quickly, brown well in a very hot oven (between 400° and 500°, depending on the food).

Use more egg whites and fewer whole eggs or egg yolks. Egg whites function similarly to yolks in many dishes, and omitting all or most of the yolks is an easy way to reduce calories, fat, and cholesterol. For example, whites bind foods together (in the cannelloni filling), make airy foams (for cheese soufflé and angel pie), and give structural support (in the pastry shell for the chicken salad). Consider that in 1 large egg, the white has 18 calories and no fat or cholesterol. The egg yolk has 70 calories, 6 g fat, and 300 mg cholesterol.

Fill in with water. For cutting calories, nothing beats using water instead of fat. Fat makes sauces and dressings feel smooth and elegant in the mouth.

days. Invert onto platter; cut into ½ inch slices and offer remaining syrup to add to taste. Makes 16 servings.

PER SERVING REVISED LIQUEUR CAKE, INCLUDING SYRUP: 80 calories, 1.9 g protein, 19 g carbohydrates, 0.2 g fat, 0 mg cholesterol, 89 mg sodium

PER SERVING ORIGINAL LIQUEUR CAKE (DECEMBER 1986, PAGE 154): 528 calories, 4.1 g protein, 76 g carbohydrates, 19 g fat, 126 mg cholesterol, 489 mg sodium

Apple-liqueur syrup. In a 2- to 3-quart pan, combine 1 can (6 oz.) **apple juice concentrate,** ½ cup **rum,** 2 tablespoons **amaretto** (almond flavor liqueur), 1 tablespoon **lemon juice,** and 1 teaspoon **coriander seed.** Boil on high heat, uncovered, until reduced to 1 cup. Use hot or cool. If made ahead, cover and chill up to 2 days; reheat, if desired. Makes 1 cup syrup.

Texture of cake is fine and tender like a pound cake, but it's made without butter.

But if you replace some or all of it with slightly thickened water or other liquid (as appropriate to the dish), you preserve this smooth sensation and eliminate calories.

Thickeners include all-purpose flour, cornstarch, arrowroot, and potato starch. Flour takes the most heat without breaking down, but it makes an opaque sauce and requires simmering several minutes to get rid of the "raw" taste. The proportions to use for each cup of liquid are 1 tablespoon flour for a thin sauce, 2 tablespoons for a medium sauce, and 3 to 4 tablespoons for a thick sauce. With half as much cornstarch, you get the same kind of thickening, but the mixture will be clearer and is cooked as soon as it boils.

Arrowroot and potato starch (in supermarkets, arrowroot is usually found with spices, potato starch with flours or specialty foods) have thickening power equal to cornstarch, but they make very clear mixtures and are cooked just before coming to a boil. Very softly thickened mixtures remain liquid and do not develop unattractive rigidity.

When making sauces that combine flour (or other thickening starch) and melted fat, omit fat; simply dilute starch with some of the liquid you'll use in the sauce, then cook.

Recipes using this method include fish with horseradish sauce and shallot dressing.

Use low-fat and nonfat dairy foods. Dairy foods come with a wide range of fat profiles; many of the lighter versions can be used in place of a richer choice.

Percentages vary, in part because of local regulations, but generally *skim milk* has less than 0.25 percent milkfat, *low-fat milk* has 1 to 2 percent milkfat, and *homogenized whole milk* has about 3.25 percent milkfat. *Half-and-half* (homogenized), also called light cream, is usually 10 to 12 percent milkfat but can be 18 percent milkfat.

Some *whipping cream* is 30 percent milkfat (it's sometimes labeled light whipping cream); richer whipping cream is 36 percent (or more) milkfat, and sometimes it's labeled heavy whipping cream. Whipping cream is a favorite of cooks because, in addition to whipping to a fine fluff (up to a certain point, the higher the milkfat, the more stable the foam), it can be boiled, reduced, or mixed with acidic foods without curdling or separating (the higher the milkfat, the more stable the cream).

Sour cream has about 18 percent milkfat; *light sour cream* (sour half-and-half) usually has 10 to 12 percent milkfat. *Yogurt* comes in nonfat, low-fat, and whole-milk versions. *Ricotta cheese* comes as a low-fat or a whole-milk cheese. The light counterpart of *cream cheese* is *neufchâtel,* also called light cream cheese.

By nature, most *cheeses* have a fair amount of milkfat and lots of sodium (as salt, which regulates, among other things, bacterial growth that gives cheeses their characteristic flavor and texture). If you want to reduce calories or fat in a recipe, you may want to use the cheese as is for its flavor contribution, then cut fat from other ingredients. If you use cheeses or other products restructured by processing to lower a specific element, like cholesterol, check to be sure the product does not end up exceeding the food it is copying in other aspects, such as fat or sodium.

Commercial *ice cream* must contain at least 10 percent milkfat, and often it has much, much more, but it does not always contain eggs; *ice milk* has 2 to 7 percent milkfat. There are a host of other ice–cream–like products, including *frozen yogurts,* that are delicious alternatives to rich ice creams. And there are many fat-free frozen fruit mixtures.

Recipes using these alternatives include pesto cheese torta and Green Goddess dressing.

Rediscovering Prosciutto

BANISHED FROM THIS COUNTRY *for almost a quarter of a century, prosciutto from Italy is again available.*

This specially cured ham with its unique sweetness and texture can be sliced paper-thin, to be served as a cold meat or used as a flavor accent with other foods. We offer simple serving suggestions and some easy recipes.

But first, what is prosciutto and why is its return from Italy significant? This salt-cured, air-dried, and unsmoked ham is made from raw pork leg. It's made not only in Italy but also in the U.S. and other locations around the world.

Connoisseurs of Italian prosciutto credit the type of hog, the climate, the handling, and the long curing time for its character. The best is described as having a sweet, delicate flavor and smooth, silky texture.

To be sure, prosciuttos from different locales and producers, tasted side by side, display individual characteristics. And now you have a broader range of choices.

Bone-in prosciuttos keep aging in Milan delicatessen.

WHY WAS ITALIAN PROSCIUTTO BANISHED?

In 1967, the U.S. government banned importation of Italian-made prosciutto because of an outbreak of African swine fever on Sardinia, an island off mainland Italy. Even though the disease didn't affect animals used for prosciutto, the USDA required the Italian government to go through a lengthy research and testing program to prove that prosciutto was completely safe. Even now, only prosciutto from Parma, a province southeast of Milan, meets U.S. import specifications.

A LITTLE HISTORY

There is evidence that as early as the second century B.C., raw pork was cured in salt and air-dried in areas between the Alps and the Apennines (where Parma is). Prosciutto evolved from this method.

Today, for any prosciutto, the basic process involves salting raw pork legs, coating them with pepper, and air-drying them. The combination of the curing methods and the length of curing time destroys dangerous organisms, especially trichinae (rarely present if animals are correctly raised).

In this country, curing methods and times for prosciutto vary, but all are precisely controlled. Some producers fol-low techniques similar to those used in Italy; others have developed their own processes and timetables.

Parma prosciutto starts with pigs raised in a specific area, where they are fed grain and whey from the local Parmigiano-Reggiano cheese. Trimmed and salted, the legs dry in ventilated rooms. After several months, hams deemed worthy of further maturing for prosciutto have their cut surfaces coated with a mixture of softened lard and black pepper. In all, a Parma prosciutto cures about 400 days, losing 24 to 27 percent of its original weight.

HOW DO YOU JUDGE PROSCIUTTO?

To identify the qualities you prefer, sample several prosciuttos side by side. Eat both lean and fat. Compared to other prosciuttos, ones from Parma tend to taste less salty and have a deep rosy color, a more prominent layer of fat, and meat that is smooth and silky textured. Domestic versions are often much leaner and saltier and have pinker, moister meat.

You may find that you prefer different prosciuttos for different uses; price and availability can also influence your choice. Parma prosciutto costs from $20 to $25 a pound and is mostly limited to markets and delicatessens in metropolitan areas. A domestic prosciutto sells for $11 to $15 a pound. However, an ounce thinly sliced is a generous portion.

Although both imported and domes-tic prosciuttos are made from boned, skinned pork legs as well as from legs with bone and skin, currently only boned legs can be imported from Italy. Many cooks prefer a bone-in prosciutto because it can be hung in a cool, dry room and, if left uncut, will continue aging for many months (some claim years), slowly dispelling salt and growing progressively drier and sweeter. Italian cooks use all but the fabled squeal; they treasure bones, skin, and fat to enrich soup broth.

HOW TO USE PROSCIUTTO

Even though prosciutto is air-dried, once it has been cut, air and heat are its enemies and can quickly diminish the flavor and texture. To savor it at peak quality, use only freshly cut prosciutto. To store slices, wrap them airtight and chill up to 24 hours.

Prosciutto tastes best very thinly sliced, but thin slices tend to tear. To avoid this, ask to have layers separated by waxed paper—but you'll pay prosciutto prices for the paper's weight.

Eat both lean and fat; the fat gives prosciutto its tenderness and flavor.

SERVING SUGGESTIONS & EASY RECIPES

Here are some simple ways to try it.

Prosciutto plain. Drape thinly sliced **prosciutto** on a plate. Offer alone or with freshly ground **pepper** and **lemon** to add to taste. Serve as an appetizer.

Prosciutto and fruit. Drape thin slices of **prosciutto** over ripe **fig halves,** seeded ripe melon (especially good with cantaloupe or Persian), seeded papaya wedges, or sliced ripe pears.

Prosciutto and bread. For an appetizer, wrap thin slices of **prosciutto** around **breadsticks.** Or eat on chunks of crusty bread plain, with sweet butter, with cheese, or with extra-virgin olive oil.

Prosciutto and pasta. Cut sliced **prosciutto** into thin shreds and lightly sauté to season sauces. Also use to season fillings for pasta such as ravioli or tortellini.

Prosciutto and meat. Drape **prosciutto** slices over thin slices of browned **chicken** or veal. Use shreds to season sautés, stews, and braised meat.

Prosciutto and vegetables. Add thin shreds or julienned end pieces of **prosciutto** to **mixed greens;** dress with **oil** and **vinegar.** For a warm salad dressing, sauté thin shreds of prosciutto in olive oil, add vinegar to taste, and serve over Belgian endive spears or spinach leaves. For a hot salad, sauté thin shreds of prosciutto with sliced radicchio.

CHICKEN WITH PROSCIUTTO & CHEESE

- 6 **boned chicken breasts (about 2 lb. total), skinned**
- 2 **tablespoons olive oil**
- 1 **tablespoon minced fresh sage or 1 teaspoon dry rubbed sage**
- 1 **cup (4 oz.) shredded fontina or provolone cheese**
- 6 **thin slices (3 to 3½ oz. total) prosciutto**
  Fresh sage sprigs or parsley sprigs
  Salt and pepper

Rinse chicken and pat dry. Mix oil and minced sage; rub over chicken. Place on a rack in a 10- by 15-inch baking pan. Bake in a 450° oven until chicken is white in thickest part (cut to test), 12 to 16 minutes. Place ⅙ of the cheese and 1 slice prosciutto over each piece. Return to oven and bake just until prosciutto lightly browns, 2 to 4 minutes. Transfer to plates and garnish with sage sprigs. Add salt and pepper to taste. Makes 6 servings.

PER SERVING: 274 calories, 36 g protein, 0.4 g carbohydrates, 13 g fat, 101 mg cholesterol, 541 mg sodium

PROSCIUTTO & ASPARAGUS SALAD

- 12 **thick asparagus spears (total about 1 lb.), rinsed**
- 4 **thin slices (2 to 2½ oz. total) prosciutto**
- 3 **tablespoons extra-virgin olive oil**
  Lemon wedges
  Freshly ground pepper

In a 10- to 12-inch frying pan, bring about 1 inch water to a boil over high heat. Remove and discard tough ends of asparagus. Add spears to boiling water. Cook, uncovered, until asparagus is just tender when pierced, 4 to 6 minutes. Drain and immerse in ice water to cool. Drain.

Arrange 3 spears on each of 4 salad plates. Ripple a slice of prosciutto over each plate of asparagus. Offer olive oil, lemon, and pepper to season each serving. Makes 4 servings.

PER SERVING: 129 calories, 5 g protein, 2.2 g carbohydrates, 12 g fat, 8.4 mg cholesterol, 409 mg sodium

SHRIMP SAUTÉ WITH PROSCIUTTO

- 2 **tablespoons olive oil**
- ¾ **cup chopped shallots**
- 3 **ounces thinly sliced prosciutto, cut into thin slivers**
- 1 **pound medium-size (31 to 35 per lb.) shrimp, peeled and deveined**
- ⅔ **cup dry white wine**
- 2 **teaspoons chopped fresh tarragon leaves or ½ teaspoon dry tarragon**
- 1 **teaspoon finely shredded lemon peel**
  Freshly ground pepper

Place a 10- to 12-inch frying pan over medium-high heat. Add oil, shallots, and prosciutto; stir until shallots are soft, about 3 minutes. Add shrimp, wine, tarragon, and lemon peel; stir often until shrimp is opaque in thickest part (cut to test), about 2 minutes. Pour into a dish. Add pepper to taste. Makes 4 servings.

PER SERVING: 219 calories, 24 g protein, 24 g carbohydrates, 10 g fat, 152 mg cholesterol, 607 mg sodium

For a simple appetizer salad, drape a thin slice of prosciutto over lightly cooked asparagus. Add extra-virgin olive oil, lemon, and freshly ground pepper.

An Elegant Meal That Serves Four for Under $20

IT CAN BE DONE. *By thoughtfully selecting modestly priced foods, and with controlled splurges on a few costlier items (like Belgian endive and shrimp) to use in a showy way, you can assemble an elegant meal for four for a supermarket tab of less than $20.*

The price doesn't include recipe ingredients you likely already have in your pantry: vinegar, salad oil, sugar, salt, pepper, and the optional brandy or other spirit (here's the chance to use that miniature bottle saved from an airline flight). You still might be able to get all but the liqueur for $20 or less if you buy small units of the pantry items. Your meal beverage is not figured into the cost.

When you make your shopping list, include a total of 3 large oranges—1 for the salad, 2 for the dessert—and a standard supermarket chicken.

This meal saves time as well as money. You can organize the salad ingredients ahead or while the chicken and squash roast. You also can make the dessert sauce ahead and rewarm it.

CHIFFONADE OF GREENS ON ENDIVE

The French call salad greens cut into long shreds or slivers chiffonade.

- 2 **medium-size heads (about ½ lb. total) Belgian endive, leaves separated**
- 1 **small head (about ¾ lb., untrimmed) romaine lettuce**
- ¼ **pound shelled cooked tiny shrimp**

Citrus-cilantro dressing (recipe follows)
Salt and freshly ground pepper

Rinse endive and romaine; drain. Wrap loosely in towels; place in a plastic bag. Chill at least 30 minutes or up to 2 days.

Stack romaine leaves; cut into ⅛-inch-wide slivers. If done ahead, put in a plastic bag and chill up to 2 hours. Rinse shrimp with cold water; drain briefly on paper towels. Arrange equal portions of endive leaves, tips outward, on each of 4 salad plates. Mound slivered lettuce on endive, then sprinkle greens with shrimp. Spoon dressing equally onto each salad. Add salt and pepper to taste. Makes 4 servings.

PER SERVING: 156 calories, 8 g protein, 6.7 g carbohydrates, 11 g fat, 55 mg cholesterol, 187 mg sodium

Citrus-cilantro dressing. In a bowl, combine 1 tablespoon grated **orange peel;** ¼ cup **orange juice;** 2 tablespoons **red wine vinegar;** 3 tablespoons **salad oil;** 1 tablespoon **Dijon mustard;** 1 small **fresh jalapeño chili,** stemmed, seeded, and chopped; and 1 tablespoon minced **fresh cilantro** (coriander). Cover and let stand up to 4 hours.

ROASTED CHICKEN TERIYAKI

Juices from the roasted chicken season baked spaghetti squash (following).

- 1 **tablespoon salad oil**
- 1 **teaspoon anise seed**
- 3 **tablespoons** *each* **orange juice and soy sauce**

- 1 **tablespoon** *each* **sugar and dry sherry or any dry wine**
- 1 **clove garlic, minced or pressed**
- 1 **tablespoon minced fresh ginger**
- 1 **broiler-fryer chicken (4 to 4½ lb.)**

In a 1- to 1½-quart pan on medium heat, stir oil with anise seed until hot. Add orange juice, soy, sugar, sherry, garlic, and ginger; set teriyaki sauce aside.

Rinse chicken and pat dry; reserve giblets for other uses. Put chicken, breast up, on a rack in a 9- by 13-inch pan; coat generously with teriyaki sauce. Pour remaining sauce into cavity of bird. Roast, uncovered, in a 375° oven until chicken is no longer pink at thigh bone (cut to test), about 1¼ hours; after chicken has roasted 30 minutes, add ¼ cup water to pan.

Drain juices from chicken cavity into pan, then put bird on a platter and keep warm. Stir to free browned bits in pan. Measure juices; if more than ⅔ cup, place pan on high heat and boil until reduced to about ⅔ cup. Keep warm and save to use in the following recipe. Makes 4 servings.

PER SERVING WITH SPAGHETTI SQUASH: 804 calories, 60 g protein, 23 g carbohydrates, 51 g fat, 232 mg cholesterol, 1,030 mg sodium

SPAGHETTI SQUASH WITH ROASTED TERIYAKI SAUCE

- 1 **spaghetti squash, about 3 pounds**
  Warm juices from roasted chicken teriyaki (recipe precedes)
  Salt and pepper

Rinse squash. Pierce shell with tines of a fork in several places. Place in an 8- to 9-inch-wide baking pan. Bake, uncovered, in a 375° oven until shell gives slightly when gently pressed, about 1 hour. Halfway through baking, turn squash over.

Cut squash in half lengthwise; scoop out and discard seeds. With a fork, pull strands from shell halves onto a platter (beside chicken, preceding). Pour warm juices over squash; mix gently. Add salt and pepper to taste. Makes 4 servings.

Meal begins with salad of tiny shrimp and slivered romaine leaves on pale green Belgian endive spears. The tangy dressing has hints of citrus, mustard, and cilantro.

SPIRITED ORANGE BUTTER SAUCE SUNDAES

> 2 large (about 1¼ lb. total) oranges
> ⅓ cup sugar
> 3 tablespoons butter or margarine
> 2 tablespoons brandy or other spirit such as rum, whiskey, or Scotch (optional)
> 1 quart vanilla ice cream

With a vegetable peeler, pare colored peel from oranges; cut peel into very thin strips. Ream oranges; you should have about 1 cup juice.

In a 1- to 2-quart pan, combine orange juice, peel, and sugar. Bring to a boil on high heat, stirring often, until syrup is reduced to about ½ cup, 10 to 12 minutes. Remove from heat and stir in butter until melted; add brandy. Let sauce cool at least 10 minutes. If made ahead, cover and chill up to 2 days; reheat to use.

Divide ice cream among 4 individual dishes; spoon warm sauce equally onto ice cream and serve immediately. Makes 4 servings.

PER SERVING: 440 calories, 5.4 g protein, 55 g carbohydrates, 23 g fat, 83 mg cholesterol, 204 mg sodium

Anise-teriyaki sauce seasons main course of oven-cooked chicken and spaghetti squash. Serve with sweet-sour roasted onions.

For a dramatic finale, drizzle buttery orange sauce laced with brandy over vanilla ice cream; embellish with fresh mint.

SWEET-SOUR ROASTED ONIONS

> 2 large (about 1½ lb. total) red onions, peeled and quartered
> 2 tablespoons red wine vinegar
> 2 teaspoons sugar

In an 8- to 9-inch-wide baking pan, arrange onions evenly apart, cut side down. Mix vinegar with sugar; brush a little on the onions. Roast in a 375° oven until onions are well browned and tender when pierced, 1 to 1¼ hours; baste often with remaining vinegar mixture. Makes 4 servings.

PER SERVING: 61 calories, 1.8 g protein, 14 g carbohydrates, 0.4 g fat, 0 mg cholesterol, 3.1 mg sodium

Savory Spreads for Sandwiches or Dips

ENJOY THESE WHOLESOME *spreads in sandwiches or as dips. They get their flavor from oven-browned, puréed vegetables. The first combines eggplant and tomatoes, the second and third use zucchini as the base; extra-sweet onions are part of each roasted mixture. As the vegetables brown until just short of charring, their natural sugars caramelize, giving them a rich, sweet flavor.*

Offer with crisp vegetables as appetizers. Or serve in sandwiches with cheese or meat. The mixtures are also delicious condiments with grilled or roasted meats.

For even browning, alternate pan positions halfway through baking.

ROASTED TOMATO–EGGPLANT SPREAD

About 2 tablespoons olive oil
1 large (about ³/₄ lb.) red onion
About 2 tablespoons balsamic or red wine vinegar

1½ pounds (about 10 large) firm-ripe Roma-style tomatoes, cored
1 small (about 1 lb.) eggplant, stem trimmed
Salt and pepper

Line 2 baking pans, each 10 by 15 inches, with foil (or use nonstick pans). Oil foil or nonstick pans.

Cut onion into ½-inch-thick slices; place in a single layer in 1 pan. Brush generously with vinegar, then lightly with oil.

Cut tomatoes into slices about ¼ inch thick and overlap slightly on pan with onion; brush lightly with oil. Bake in a 475° oven until tomatoes are well browned on edges, 50 to 60 minutes.

Cut eggplant into ½-inch-thick slices and arrange in a single layer on second pan; brush lightly with oil. Bake in a 475° oven until browned and very soft when pressed, 30 to 40 minutes.

In food processor or blender, whirl tomatoes, onion, and eggplant until puréed to desired consistency. Add salt and pepper to taste. Serve warm or cool. If made ahead, cool, cover, and chill up to 3 days. Makes about 2 cups, 4 or 5 servings.

PER ½-CUP SERVING: 114 calories, 2.7 g protein, 15 g carbohydrates, 5.9 g fat, 0 mg cholesterol, 14 mg sodium

ZUCCHINI-MUSHROOM SPREAD

Follow recipe for **roasted tomato-eggplant spread** (preceding), but instead of tomatoes use 1¼ pounds **zucchini,** ends trimmed, cut lengthwise into ¼-inch-thick slices. Roast with onion until well browned, 30 to 40 minutes. Instead of eggplant, use 1¼ pounds **mushrooms,** rinsed, drained, and cut into ½-inch-thick slices. Roast until lightly browned, about 30 minutes. Makes about 3 cups, 5 or 6 servings.

PER ½-CUP SERVING: 118 calories, 4.7 g protein, 14 g carbohydrates, 6.2 g fat, 0 mg cholesterol, 9.8 mg sodium

ZUCCHINI-PARMESAN SPREAD

About 2 tablespoons olive oil
1 large (about ³/₄ lb.) red onion
About 2 tablespoons balsamic or red wine vinegar
2 pounds zucchini, ends trimmed
¼ cup reduced-calorie or regular mayonnaise
¼ cup grated parmesan cheese
2 teaspoons lemon juice
2 teaspoons Dijon mustard
Salt and pepper

Line 2 baking pans, each 10 by 15 inches, with foil (or use nonstick pans). Oil foil or nonstick pans.

Cut onion into ½-inch-thick slices; place in a single layer in 1 pan. Brush generously with vinegar, then lightly with oil.

Cut zucchini lengthwise into ¼-inch-thick slices. Arrange in single layers on pan with onion and on remaining pan. Brush zucchini lightly with oil. Bake in a 475° oven until vegetables are well browned on edges, 30 to 40 minutes.

In food processor or blender, whirl zucchini and onion with mayonnaise, cheese, lemon juice, and mustard until puréed to desired consistency. Add salt and pepper to taste. Serve warm or cool. If made ahead, cool, cover, and chill up to 3 days. Makes about 2 cups, 4 or 5 servings.

PER ½-CUP SERVING: 151 calories, 4.7 g protein, 12 g carbohydrates, 10 g fat, 7.1 mg cholesterol, 207 mg sodium

Hearty spread combines oven-roasted tomato, eggplant, and onion. Serve on bread with cheese and lettuce for open-face sandwich.

No-bake Cooky Cake

ALL AGES ENJOY THIS *New Year's Eve party. To keep the young ones busy, let them make the dessert—an easy no-bake cake put together from cookies and whipped cream. All the guests then get to decorate the simple cake by writing greetings or their signatures in chocolate.*

As the first guests arrive, let them begin assembling the cooky cake (allow at least 3 hours after assembly before serving the cake). You buy the cookies, so you just need to make a simple peppermint syrup and whip the cream. Each layer of the cake uses one package of cookies.

Once the cake is finished, the chocolate decorating can begin. Distribute pieces of parchment paper and plastic sandwich bags of melted chocolate among the guests, and let them experiment with writing their names and salutations for the New Year. Chill the decorations in the refrigerator or outdoors to firm before beginning to arrange them on the cake.

When the evening's cooking entertainment is complete, guests can choose from a serve-yourself soup and sandwich bar. Offer a hearty soup, such as a minestrone, either homemade or purchased from a delicatessen or restaurant, to serve in coffee mugs. For sandwiches, offer a selection of deli meats and rolls with all the fixings. Beverages can include champagne, sparkling cider, milk, or coffee.

Greet the New Year with this no-bake cake, assembled with cookies and whipped cream, then decorated with chocolate graffiti and crushed candy cane.

SIGNATURE COOKY CAKE

6 **cups whipping cream**
1/3 **cup powdered sugar**
2 **teaspoons vanilla**
4 **packages (5.6 oz. to 7 oz. each, 24 to 30 count) petit-beurre cookies**
   Peppermint syrup (recipe follows)
2 **packages (9 oz. each) chocolate wafer cookies**
   About 8 freezer zip-lock plastic sandwich bags
1 **large package (12 oz.) semi-sweet chocolate baking chips**
   Cooking parchment or waxed paper
   About 2 tablespoons crushed candy cane (optional)

In each of 2 large bowls, place half the cream, sugar, and vanilla. With an electric mixer, whip each batch at high speed until it holds soft peaks. Cover and chill up to 1 hour.

Dip 24 butter cookies (1 package), 2 or 4 at a time, completely in peppermint syrup; drain off excess, then arrange side by side on a large flat platter to form a rectangle about 9 by 16 inches. Spread evenly with about 1 1/2 cups whipped cream, to within 1/4 inch of cookies' edges. Arrange a second layer of syrup-dipped biscuits on the whipped cream; spread with about 1 1/2 cups cream. Use chocolate wafers for third and fourth layers; overlap wafers slightly to fit rectangle (you will have a few extras for snacking). Finish the cake with 2 more layers of butter cookies.

Frost top and sides of cake with remaining cream. Chill for at least 3 hours or up to 8 hours; you can prepare the chocolate decorations during this time.

Fill each sandwich bag with about 1/3 cup chocolate chips; zip shut. In a 6- to 8-quart pan over high heat, bring about 2 quarts of water to a boil. Remove pan from heat and fit a metal bowl snugly over pan. Lay bags in bowl to melt chocolate, 5 to 10 minutes (if bags are too hot to handle, cool briefly). Line baking sheets with parchment. Clip about 1/8 inch off one lower corner of each sandwich bag and squeeze the chocolate onto parchment to write (the stream of chocolate needs to be about 1/4 inch thick; if thinner, it's hard to transfer to the cake).

Chill chocolate messages until firm, at least 30 minutes. Gently peel paper from chocolate and place decorations on cake sides and top. Sprinkle with candy cane. Cut in pieces. Makes 20 to 24 servings.

PER SERVING: 509 calories, 5.4 g protein, 55 g carbohydrates, 30 g fat, 87 mg cholesterol, 281 mg sodium

Peppermint syrup. In a 1 1/2- to 2-quart pan over high heat, mix 1 cup **sugar** and 2 cups **water;** bring to a boil, stirring often, until sugar dissolves. Boil, uncovered, until reduced to 1 1/4 cups, 10 to 15 minutes. Remove from heat and stir in 1 1/2 teaspoons **peppermint extract.** Let syrup cool about 1 hour. (If made ahead, cover and chill up to 5 days.)

Infused with spices, muffins feature tiny marmalade-filled wells.

SIENA MUFFINS

- 1½ cups all-purpose flour
- 1 cup sliced almonds
- 1 teaspoon baking powder
- ½ teaspoon baking soda
- 1¼ teaspoons ground cinnamon
- ½ teaspoon *each* ground nutmeg and ground coriander
- ¼ teaspoon ground cloves
- ½ cup *each* honey and milk
- ¼ cup (⅛ lb.) butter or margarine, melted
- 1 large egg
- 1 teaspoon grated lemon peel
- ¼ cup orange marmalade
- 2 tablespoons sugar

Mix flour, almonds, baking powder, soda, 1 teaspoon cinnamon, nutmeg, coriander, and cloves. Make a well in center. Beat together honey, milk, butter, egg, and lemon peel. Pour mixture into the flour well; stir until just blended. Fill 10 buttered muffin cups (2¼ in. wide) ⅔ full. Using a teaspoon, gently press 1 rounded teaspoon marmalade into center of each muffin.

Bake in a 350° oven until golden and firm, about 20 minutes. Cool in pan 5 minutes; remove from pan onto a rack. Mix sugar and remaining cinnamon; dust tops of warm muffins. Makes 10. — *Dayle Doroshow Neal, Oakland.*

PER MUFFIN: 263 calories, 5 g protein, 39 g carbohydrates, 11 g fat, 35 mg cholesterol, 146 mg sodium

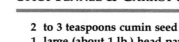

Cumin seed seasons crunchy fennel, carrot, and mint salad.

SPICY FENNEL & CARROT SALAD

- 2 to 3 teaspoons cumin seed
- 1 large (about 1 lb.) head partially trimmed fennel
- ⅓ cup minced parsley
- ¼ cup minced mint leaves
- ¼ cup salad oil
- ¼ cup lemon juice
- ¼ teaspoon ground allspice
- 2 cups (about ¾ lb.) shredded carrot
  Fresh mint sprigs (optional)

In a 6- to 8-inch frying pan set over medium-high heat, toast cumin, shaking pan often, until golden brown, about 4 minutes.

Trim off and discard tough stems, root end, and core of fennel. If desired, reserve some of the feathery wisps for garnish. Cut the fennel into thin slivers, about ¼ inch thick and 2 to 3 inches long, to make about 3 cups.

In a large bowl, mix together cumin, parsley, minced mint, oil, lemon juice, and allspice. Stir in fennel and carrot, thoroughly coating with dressing. Cover and chill for at least 2 hours or up until next day. Garnish with reserved wisps of fennel or mint sprigs. Serve cool or at room temperature. Makes about 6 servings.—*Roxanne E. Chan, Albany, Calif.*

PER SERVING: 122 calories, 1.7 g protein, 8.7 g carbohydrates, 9.5 g fat, 0 mg cholesterol, 91 mg sodium

Chicken cooks in chili-onion sauce; serve on bed of hot noodles.

DEVILISHLY SPICY CHICKEN

- 1 broiler-fryer chicken (about 4 lb.), cut up, skin removed
- 2 tablespoons butter or margarine
- 2 medium-size (about 1 lb. total) onions, chopped
- 1 can (12 oz.) beer or 1½ cups water
- ⅓ cup tomato-based chili sauce
- 3 tablespoons Worcestershire
- 1 tablespoon dry mustard
- 4 cups hot cooked egg noodles
- 1 package (10 oz.) frozen petite peas, thawed

Rinse chicken and pat dry; set aside. In a 10- to 12-inch frying pan set over medium-high heat, cook butter and onion, stirring often, until onion is golden brown, about 15 minutes. Stir in beer, chili sauce, Worcestershire, and mustard. Turn chicken, except breasts, in sauce to coat. Cover and simmer 20 minutes; turn pieces and add breasts. Continue simmering, covered, until meat at thigh is no longer pink (cut to test), about 20 minutes.

With a slotted spoon, lift out chicken and place on noodles; keep warm. Boil sauce, uncovered, until reduced to 2 cups, about 8 minutes. Stir in peas; spoon over chicken. Serves 4 to 6. —*Barbara Keenan, Fort Morgan, Colo.*

PER SERVING: 434 calories, 40 g protein, 43 g carbohydrates, 11 g fat, 147 mg cholesterol, 509 mg sodium

CRAB & RICE CHOWDER

- 2 tablespoons salad oil
- 1 small onion, chopped
- 1/2 pound mushrooms, rinsed and thinly sliced
- 2 cups (about 6 oz.) coarsely chopped broccoli
- 1 small red bell pepper, stemmed, seeded, and chopped
- 1/2 teaspoon dry thyme leaves
- 2 cups regular-strength chicken broth
- 2 cups milk
- 1 can (17 oz.) cream-style corn
- 1/3 pound shelled cooked crab
- 3 cups cooked long-grain rice
  Salt and pepper

In a 5- to 6-quart pan over medium-high heat, add oil, onion, and mushrooms. Cook, stirring often, until vegetables are tinged gold, about 8 minutes. Add broccoli, bell pepper, and thyme; stir frequently until broccoli turns bright green and is tender to bite, about 4 minutes more.

Stir in chicken broth, milk, and corn; cook, uncovered, just until hot, about 10 minutes. Stir in crab and rice. Simmer, uncovered, until hot, about 2 minutes. Ladle hot chowder into soup bowls. Add salt and pepper to taste. Makes 6 servings.—*Ellen S. Thomas, Portland.*

PER SERVING: 338 calories, 14.4 g protein, 52 g carbohydrates, 9 g fat, 36 mg cholesterol, 368 mg sodium

Vegetables and rice flavorfully accompany crab in winter soup.

PORK CHOPS IN SAKE MARINADE

- 2 cups sake or dry white wine
- 1/2 cup thinly sliced green onions
- 1/4 cup finely chopped fresh ginger
- 2 tablespoons soy sauce
- 2 cloves garlic, minced or pressed
- 4 shoulder pork chops (1 1/2 in. thick, about 2 lb. total), fat trimmed
- 2 tablespoons Oriental sesame oil or salad oil

In a 9- by 13-inch pan, mix sake, onion, ginger, soy, and garlic. Lay chops in marinade; cover and chill 2 hours or up until next day, turning occasionally.

Pour oil into a 10- to 12-inch frying pan over medium-high heat. Lift chops from marinade. Cook chops in a single layer, turning as needed, until browned, 8 to 10 minutes. Repeat if needed.

Return all chops and marinade to pan; bring to a boil. Cover and simmer, turning the chops occasionally, until tender when pierced, about 50 minutes. Transfer chops to a platter; keep warm. Skim fat from pan juices. Boil juices, uncovered, until reduced to 2/3 cup, about 10 minutes. Spoon over chops. Makes 4 servings.—*Robin Warren, Fort Bragg, Calif.*

PER SERVING: 334 calories, 33 g protein, 3.8 g carbohydrates, 20 g fat, 111 mg cholesterol, 648 mg sodium

Pork shoulder chops braise in a sake (rice wine) and ginger sauce.

LEMON-LIME OAT COOKIES

- 1 cup (1/2 lb.) butter or margarine, at room temperature
- 2 1/3 cups sugar
- 2 large eggs
- 1 teaspoon *each* grated lemon and lime peel
- 2 tablespoons *each* lemon and lime juice
- 2 1/2 cups all-purpose flour
- 1 cup regular rolled oats
- 2 teaspoons baking powder
- 1/2 teaspoon *each* ground cinnamon and ground nutmeg

In a bowl, blend butter and 2 cups sugar. Beat in eggs, lemon and lime peel, and lemon and lime juice. In a small bowl, mix flour, oats, baking powder, and 1/4 teaspoon *each* cinnamon and nutmeg. Gradually blend into butter mixture. Cover and chill until firm, at least 2 hours or until next day.

Mix 1/3 cup sugar and remaining cinnamon and nutmeg. Roll dough into 1 1/2-inch balls; coat in sugar. Place 2 inches apart on greased 12- by 15-inch baking sheets; with the bottom of a glass, press balls to 3/8 inch thick. Bake in a 350° oven until light gold, about 12 minutes. Cool on racks. Makes 4 dozen.—*Ruth O. Smith, White Salmon, Wash.*

PER COOKY: 105 calories, 1.2 g protein, 16 g carbohydrates, 4.2 g fat, 19 mg cholesterol, 60 mg sodium

Enjoy nutmeg- and citrus-scented oat cookies with a cup of coffee.

IN EARLIER, MORE FORMAL TIMES, *the arrival of salted nuts on the table meant that the meal was drawing to a close. Pleated paper cups in little openwork silver baskets held the nuts; the paper protected the silver from the salt. Because meals of this level of formality began with a soup, the expression "soup to nuts" came to signify completeness, the full treatment, or in the current language of fast-food gastronomy, the whole enchilada.*

Today's less formal service finds nuts performing more functions; adding richness to salads and garnishing fish are two of many.

Nuts have long been constituents of desserts, where their texture puts backbone in the soft richness of pecan pie or chocolate fudge.

Scotty Scott gives nuts the lead role in his recipe; the candy serves the nuts, not nuts the candy. The result is sweet and spicy, and the texture, though crunchy, is not so hard as to be a risk to high-priced dental work.

CANDY-COATED NUTS

    1   cup sugar
    ½   teaspoon ground cinnamon
    ¼   teaspoon *each* ground cloves
        and ground ginger
    ⅓   cup canned evaporated milk
    3   cups walnuts or pecans
    ½   teaspoon vanilla

In a 2- to 3-quart pan, stir together sugar, cinnamon, cloves, ginger, and milk. Stir over high heat until mixture reaches 238° (soft ball) on a thermometer, about 5 minutes.

Remove from heat and quickly stir in the nuts and vanilla until nuts are well coated. Spread out in an even layer on a sheet of foil or waxed paper. When cool, break candy into evenly sized chunks. Serve, or store airtight up to 3 days. Makes about 6 cups.

PER ¼ CUP: 134 calories, 2.4 g protein, 12 g carbohydrates, 9.5 g fat, 1 mg cholesterol, 5.3 mg sodium

"Scotty"

La Quinta, Calif.

BECAUSE WE ARE A NATION *of carnivores, in most places vegetables play supporting roles in menus. Eggplant seems to be one of the very few that attains star rank as a main dish. Cooks of the Mediterranean region handle it with special respect in such dishes as ratatouille or eggplant parmigiano, and grilled eggplant sandwiches have been turning up lately on the menus of modish Italian restaurants.*

Eggplant's virtue lies not in any strong, distinctive flavor but in its ability to absorb, complement, or heighten other flavors. It is the Great Cooperator.

Proving the point, Dr. Raoul Berke gives his eggplant entrée a Southwestern fillip with tomatoes, cumin, jalapeños, and pine nuts. Also try it as an appetizer on toast, just as you might serve another eggplant standard, caponata.

PIÑON EGGPLANT

    ¼   cup olive oil or salad oil
    ⅓   cup pine nuts
    1   medium-size (about 6 oz.) onion,
        chopped
    1   garlic clove, minced or pressed
    2   fresh jalapeño chilies, stemmed,
        seeded, and finely chopped
    ½   teaspoon ground cumin
    2   medium-size (about 1¼ lb. each)
        eggplants, stems trimmed, cut
        into ¾-inch cubes
    1   can (14½ oz.) cut-up tomatoes
        Salt and pepper

In a 5- to 6-quart pan over medium heat, stir oil and nuts until nuts are golden brown, about 4 minutes. Lift nuts from pan with a slotted spoon and set aside.

Add onion, garlic, chilies, and cumin to pan. Stir often until onion is limp but not browned, about 10 minutes. Stir in eggplant; cover and cook, stirring gently occasionally, until cubes are soft when pressed, about 30 minutes. Stir in tomatoes and their liquid. Continue to cook, uncovered, until most of the liquid has boiled away, about 15 minutes.

"Because formal meals began with a soup, the expression 'soup to nuts' came to signify completeness, the full treatment."

"Eggplant seems to be one of the very few that attains star rank."

Sprinkle each serving with nuts and add salt and pepper to taste. Makes about 7 cups, 4 to 6 main-dish servings.

PER SERVING: 196 calories, 5.1 g protein, 19 g carbohydrates, 14 g fat, 0 mg cholesterol, 121 mg sodium

Raoul Bede, MD

Albuquerque

THE POTATO HAS A RICH *and varied Old World history, considering that this root was delivered into the hands of cooks of that hemisphere a mere 499 years ago. Where would we be today without the grand heritage of these potato pancakes: latkes or kartoffelpuffer or kartoffel-pfannkuchen. But history marches on, and Chef Aulerich does not hesitate to improve on a good thing. For his sausage potato pancakes are very good, being plump and moist and spiced by sausage inside, crusty and aromatic on the outside.*

SAUSAGE POTATO PANCAKES

- 3 medium-size (about 1 lb. total) russet potatoes
- 5 large eggs
- 3/4 pound bulk pork sausage
- 1 small (3 to 4 oz.) onion, finely chopped
- 1/4 cup all-purpose flour
- 2 tablespoons chopped parsley
- 1/2 teaspoon pepper
- 1 tablespoon butter or margarine Salt

Peel and shred potatoes, then squeeze firmly to remove as much liquid as possible. Put potatoes in a large bowl and beat with eggs to blend. Stir in sausage, onion, flour, parsley, and pepper, mixing well.

In a 10- to 12-inch frying pan over medium-high heat, melt butter. Add batter in 1/3-cup portions, spreading into patties 1/2 inch thick; do not crowd pan. Cook patties until bottoms are well browned, about 7 minutes. Turn with a wide spatula and cook until other sides are browned, about 7 minutes. Drain pancakes on paper towels and keep warm until all are cooked. Add salt to taste. Makes 11 or 12.

PER PIECE: 129 calories, 6.3 g protein, 9.1 g carbohydrates, 7.3 g fat, 102 mg cholesterol, 213 mg sodium

Robert M J Aulerich

Gig Harbor, Wash.

WE ALL DREAM, *and some of us have made great discoveries in our dreams—only to forget them when we wake up. But there are notable exceptions. One such inspiration was the poetic fragment Kubla Khan, which Samuel Taylor Coleridge dreamed while dozing in a chair.*

Another is Johnny's Dream Bread, which was dreamed up (literally) by Chef Johnson. Fortunately, Mr. Johnson remembered his dream recipe in full, wrote it all down, and sent it off to us. This bread is great for toast or French toast.

JOHNNY'S DREAM BREAD

- 1 tablespoon butter, margarine, or vegetable shortening
- 1 cup half-and-half (light cream)
- 1 cup water
- 3/4 cup honey
- 1/2 teaspoon salt
- 2 packages active dry yeast
- 1 cup whole-wheat flour
- 2 cups oat flour
  About 2 1/2 cups all-purpose flour

In a 2- to 3-quart pan over medium heat, melt butter; then add half-and-half, water, honey, and salt. Heat to 110°. Pour into a large bowl and add yeast; let stand until yeast is softened, about 5 minutes. Add whole-wheat flour and oat flour and beat with a spoon or electric mixer until dough is stretchy. Then, with a spoon, stir in 2 cups all-purpose flour, 1/4 cup at a time. Scrape dough onto a lightly floured board. Knead until dough is smooth and elastic, about 10 minutes; add flour as required to prevent sticking.

Rinse, dry, and grease bowl. Place dough in bowl, turning it over to grease top. Cover with plastic wrap and let rise in a warm place until doubled in volume, about 45 minutes. Punch down, knead in bowl to expel air, then divide dough in half. Shape each half into a loaf to fit each of 2 well-greased 4 1/2- by 8 1/2-inch loaf pans. Cover pans with plastic wrap and let dough rise in a warm place until it almost fills pans, 35 to 40 minutes.

Bake, uncovered, in a 350° oven until loaves are richly browned, about 35 minutes. Invert loaves onto racks to cool. Serve warm or cool. To store, package airtight and hold up until next day; freeze to store longer. Makes 2 loaves, each 1 1/2 pounds.

PER OUNCE: 67 calories, 1.9 g protein, 14 g carbohydrates, 1.2 g fat, 2.5 mg cholesterol, 28 mg sodium

Johnny Johnson

Pleasanton, Calif.

"Fortunately, Mr. Johnson remembered his dream recipe in full."

January Menus

Enlist some outside help for meals this month. Purchased ready-to-eat foods can give you a quick start on preparation when time is short.

The weeknight egg supper and the sandwich lunch both use meats and cheeses from the deli. Pick up sausages for the make-ahead New Year's breakfast at a specialty meat market, delicatessen, or well-stocked supermarket.

EGGS FOR SUPPER

Mustard Seed Pineapple Salad
**Scrambled Eggs with
Salami & Onion**
Caraway Toast
Herbal Iced Tea

Scrambled eggs with cheese make a quickly prepared light meal after work.

Buy about 1 pound peeled and cored fresh pineapple for the salad. Slice the pineapple and dress with rice vinegar and mustard seed. While the salami-onion mixture cooks, toast English muffins, spread with butter, and sprinkle with caraway seed. Then quickly cook the eggs.

SCRAMBLED EGGS WITH SALAMI & ONION

- ¼ **pound thinly sliced cooked salami, cut into ⅛-inch-thick strips**
- 2 **large (about 1 lb. total) onions, minced**
- 10 **large eggs**
- 1 **tablespoon Dijon mustard**
- 1 **cup (4 oz.) shredded cheddar cheese**
- **Salt and pepper**
- **Fresh watercress sprigs**

In a 10- to 12-inch frying pan with a non-stick surface, stir salami and onion often over medium-high heat until salami is browned and onion is golden

Spoon golden-sweet onions and salami onto scrambled eggs laced with cheese. Accompany with caraway-flecked muffins and savory pineapple salad.

and sweet, about 20 minutes. Add 2 tablespoons water to pan, stirring often, to release accumulated juices from pan bottom. When liquid has evaporated and pan bottom is clean, transfer salami mixture to a bowl; set aside and keep warm.

Beat eggs to blend with mustard. Pour egg mixture into the frying pan (no need to wash pan) over medium-high heat; sprinkle with ⅔ cup cheese.

When edges of egg mixture begin to set, lift with spatula to let uncooked egg flow underneath; repeat until eggs are set as you like.

Spoon eggs onto 4 dinner plates; top equally with warm salami mixture and remaining cheese. Add salt and pepper to taste; garnish with watercress sprigs. Makes 4 servings.

Per Serving: 415 calories, 28 g protein, 11 g carbohydrates, 28 g fat, 579 mg cholesterol, 750 mg sodium

Popular deli favorites come together in these roast beef and cheese sandwiches filled with a savory-sweet onion relish.

Start the onion relish, then assemble the sandwiches. You can find crisp carrot or other vegetable chips in the snack or specialty food section at the supermarket.

ROAST BEEF & BRAISED ONION SANDWICHES

4 **onion rolls, each about 4 inches in diameter**
3/4 **pound thinly sliced roast beef or cooked turkey**
Onion relish (recipe follows)
1/4 **pound thinly sliced münster or gouda cheese**

Split rolls in half horizontally. Lay bottom halves, cut side up, on a 12- by 15-inch baking sheet. On each bottom, lay 1/4 of the beef; top with 1/4 of the relish and 1/4 of the cheese. Bake in a 500° oven until cheese begins to melt, about 3 minutes.

Place roll tops, cut side up, next to bottoms. Continue baking until cheese is bubbly and tops are toasted, 2 to 3 minutes more. Place roll tops over cheese and transfer to 4 dinner plates. Makes 4 servings.

PER SERVING: 459 calories, 37 g protein, 34 g carbohydrates, 18 g fat, 98 mg cholesterol, 550 mg sodium

Onion relish. In a 10- to 12-inch frying pan over medium-high heat, combine 2 tablespoons **water,** 2 teaspoons **salad oil,** 2 teaspoons **red wine vinegar,** 2 teaspoons **prepared horseradish,** and 1 large **onion,** thinly sliced. Stir often until onion is golden and liquid has evaporated, about 15 minutes. Makes 1 cup.

Party-givers often find on New Year's morning that they have inherited overnight guests who need breakfast. This menu makes it easy for hosts and guests.

For a completely make-ahead breakfast, the host cooks pancakes and sausages the day before. As guests rise the next morning, they can reheat single portions in a microwave oven. In a conventional oven, reheat single or group portions.

Or if you prefer, serve the pancakes and sausages freshly cooked in the morning.

The day before, brown 1 to 1½ pounds

sausages; choose from the variety available at a deli, meat market, or supermarket. Cut large sausages in half lengthwise; leave small sausages whole.

Also cook pancakes ahead, cool, and stack on a platter. Syrups can be quickly made in the morning or reheated.

To reheat sausages and pancakes in a microwave oven, place 1 serving sausage (about 1 large half or 3 small) on a microwave-safe plate. Cover with plastic wrap. Cook at full power (100 percent), checking at 30-second intervals until sausages are warm to touch, about 2 minutes.

Rotate plate halfway and add 1 serving pancakes (about 3); loosely cover and return to oven. Cook at full power (100 percent), checking at 30-second intervals until hot, about 2 minutes longer.

To reheat sausages and pancakes in a conventional oven, place 1 or more servings sausage and pancakes (see preceding for approximate serving size) on an ovenproof plate. Cover with foil and bake in a 350° oven until hot, 15 to 25 minutes.

(Continued on next page)

For a deli lunch, offer plump roast beef sandwiches with münster cheese and a savory-sweet onion relish. Serve with crunchy dill pickles and vegetable chips.

WHOLE-WHEAT GINGER PANCAKES

1⅓ cups all-purpose flour
1 cup whole-wheat flour
⅓ cup powdered sugar
3 tablespoons minced crystallized ginger
1½ teaspoons baking soda
1 teaspoon baking powder
1 teaspoon ground cinnamon
1 cup apple cider
1 cup vanilla yogurt
2 large eggs
2 tablespoons melted butter or margarine
   Salad oil
   Spiced apple or cherry–maple syrup (recipes follow)

In a large bowl, mix all-purpose and whole-wheat flours, sugar, ginger, baking soda, baking powder, and cinnamon. In a small bowl, beat cider, yogurt, eggs, and butter. Mix liquid ingredients into dry mixture until blended.

On a lightly oiled or nonstick griddle or 10- to 12-inch frying pan over medium heat, pour batter in ¼-cup portions at least 3½ inches apart. Spread batter to a 4-inch-diameter round. Cook until bubbles form on tops and bottoms are browned, about 1 minute. Turn with a wide spatula and cook until brown on bottoms, about 1 minute longer.

If made ahead, cool on racks, stack on a platter, cover, and chill up until the next day. To reheat, see preceding directions, page 33.

Serve hot with syrup to taste. Makes 20 to 24 pancakes, 7 or 8 servings.

PER PANCAKE: 86 calories, 2.4 g protein, 14 g carbohydrates, 2.2 g fat, 21 mg cholesterol, 92 mg sodium

SPICED APPLE SYRUP

½ cup purchased or homemade apple butter
1 cup maple syrup

To cook on the range: In a 1-quart pan over medium heat, stir apple butter and maple syrup until melted and hot, 3 to 5 minutes.

To cook in a microwave oven: In a 1-quart microwave-safe container, combine apple butter and maple syrup. Cook on full power (100 percent), stirring every 30 seconds, until melted and steaming, about 1½ minutes.

Serve warm. Makes about 1½ cups.

PER ¼ CUP: 176 calories, 0.1 g protein, 45 g carbohydrates, 0.2 g fat, 0 mg cholesterol, 5.7 mg sodium

CHERRY-MAPLE SYRUP

Follow recipe for **spiced apple syrup** (preceding) except substitute ¾ cup **cherry preserves** for the apple butter. Reduce syrup to ¾ cup. Makes about 1½ cups syrup.

PER ¼ CUP: 208 calories, 0.2 g protein, 54 g carbohydrates, 0 g fat, 0 mg cholesterol, 8.7 mg sodium

FEBRUARY

Rhubarb-Raspberry Pie (page 36)

Pink stalks of rhubarb appear
in Western markets in February. Show off this springtime
treat in your choice of five rosy-hued pies that rated top
marks from our tasters. Give a fresh twist to some old
favorites—meat loaf, canned seafood, root vegetables.
Other articles include a lighter version of beef fondue—
meat cooked by the bite in a ginger broth, then dipped in
flavorful sauces—and slimmed-down versions of three more
Sunset classics. You'll find surprising soups from the
West Indies and distinctive Mexican specialties from Puebla.

Rhubarb Pies

RHUBARB LOVERS *abound in the West. How do we know? When we asked readers to share with us their favorite recipes for summer fruit pies (see the June, 1990 Sunset), rhubarb was second only to peaches as the filling most mentioned.*

This was a bit of a surprise, considering that rhubarb's season isn't limited to summer (it begins in February), and it's actually a vegetable. But a small detail like botanical identity hasn't interfered with rhubarb's popularity, especially in pies, where sweetening balances its tart flavor.

Long, slender stalks of bright pink hothouse-grown rhubarb are in markets now through May. The green-tinged field-grown type appears later in spring and into summer. If you pick your own, trim stalks of all traces of the toxic green leaves.

What happened to those recipes for rhubarb pie? We tested, tasted, and rated, and here are five that came out on top. Three choices pair tart rhubarb with fruit: raspberries, strawberries, or spiced kumquats in pastry or shortbread crusts. In the other desserts, rhubarb bakes with cheesecake or a rich cream filling. A recipe for flaky pastry is on page 38.

RHUBARB-RASPBERRY PIE

> 1⅓ cups sugar
> ¼ cup quick-cooking tapioca
> 4 cups ½-inch pieces rhubarb
> 1 cup fresh or frozen raspberries
> 2 tablespoons lemon juice
> Raspberry vinegar pastry (recipe follows)

In a large bowl, stir together sugar and tapioca. Add rhubarb, raspberries, and lemon juice; mix gently but thoroughly. Let stand 15 minutes or up to 1 hour to soften tapioca; mix gently several times.

On a lightly floured board, roll half the pastry into a 12-inch-diameter round; ease into a 9-inch pie pan. Fill with rhubarb mixture. On floured board, roll remaining pastry into a 10-inch-diameter square. With a pastry wheel or knife, cut into 8 equal strips. Arrange strips on top of pie in lattice pattern; trim off as they lap over rim. Fold bottom crust over lattice, flush with pan rim; flute to seal.

Set pie in a foil-lined 10- by 15-inch pan (pie bubbles as it cooks). Bake in a 400° oven on the lowest rack until pastry is golden brown and filling is bubbly, 40 to 50 minutes. If rim begins to darken excessively before filling bubbles, drape with strips of foil.

Serve warm or at room temperature. If made ahead, let cool, then cover loosely and store at room temperature up until next day. Cut into wedges. Makes 8 or 9 servings.—*Michaela Rosenthal, Woodland Hills, Calif.*

PER SERVING: 412 calories, 3.8 g protein, 61 g carbohydrates, 18 g fat, 0 mg cholesterol, 64 mg sodium

Raspberry vinegar pastry. In a bowl, combine 2¼ cups **all-purpose flour** and ¼ teaspoon **salt.** With a pastry blender or your fingers, cut or rub in ¾ cup **solid vegetable shortening,** butter, or margarine until fine crumbs form. Sprinkle 2 tablespoons **raspberry vinegar** and 3 to 5 tablespoons **cold water** over crumbs. Stir with a fork until dough holds together. Divide dough in half and pat each portion into a smooth, flat round. Use or, if made ahead, seal in plastic wrap and chill up to 3 days.

RHUBARB-STRAWBERRY TART & ORANGE SHORTBREAD CRUST

> 4 cups strawberries
> 3 cups ½-inch pieces rhubarb
> ⅔ cup sugar
> 1 teaspoon grated orange peel
> ¼ cup cornstarch
> 2 tablespoons orange-flavor liqueur (optional)
> Orange shortbread crust (recipe follows)

Rinse and hull strawberries. Drain until dry on absorbent towels; cut berries in half. Set aside 1 cup of berries for garnish.

In a 2- to 3-quart pan over medium heat, combine remaining strawberries, rhubarb, sugar, and peel. Cover and stir occasionally until rhubarb is soft when pierced, about 5 minutes. Blend 2 tablespoons water with cornstarch; stir into rhubarb mixture, then stir over high heat until mixture reaches a rolling boil.

Rosy-hued rhubarb is available now in Western markets. Select crisp, brightly colored, unblemished stalks. Their toxic leaves have been trimmed off.

Mix liqueur with rhubarb mixture, then spread into baked tart shell. Chill until filling is cool and set, at least 1 hour; if made ahead, cover and chill up until next day. Top with reserved whole strawberries. Cut into wedges. Makes 8 or 9 servings.—*Ellen Nishimura, Fair Oaks, Calif.*

PER SERVING: 281 calories, 3.1 g protein, 43 g carbohydrates, 11 g fat, 51 mg cholesterol, 108 mg sodium

Orange shortbread crust. In a food processor or with your fingers, whirl or rub together 1¹/₃ cups **all-purpose flour;** 3 tablespoons **sugar;** ¹/₂ cup (¹/₄ lb.) **butter** or margarine, cut up; and 1¹/₂ teaspoons grated **orange peel.** Add 1 **large egg yolk;** process or stir with a fork until dough holds together. Press evenly over bottom and up sides of an 11-inch tart pan with removable bottom. Bake in a 325° oven until golden, 25 to 30 minutes; cool.

RHUBARB CHEESECAKE PIE

    1 **cup plus 3 tablespoons sugar**
    3 **tablespoons cornstarch**
    4 **cups 1-inch pieces rhubarb**
       Graham crust (recipe follows)
    2 **small packages (3 oz. each)**
       cream cheese
    2 **large eggs**
  ¹/₂ **teaspoon vanilla**
    1 **cup sour cream**

In a 2- to 3-quart pan, mix ³/₄ cup sugar and cornstarch; add rhubarb and 1 tablespoon water. Stir often over medium heat until mixture comes to a full boil. Pour rhubarb mixture into crust.

With a mixer or a food processor, smoothly blend cream cheese, eggs, vanilla, and 6 tablespoons sugar; pour over rhubarb.

Bake in 350° oven until filling appears set in center when pan is gently shaken, about 20 minutes. Mix sour cream with remaining 1 tablespoon sugar; spread evenly over filling. Bake until topping is set when gently shaken, about 5 minutes. Let cool, then cover and chill at least 2 hours or until next day. Cut into wedges. Makes 9 to 12 servings.—*Shirley Von, Glendora, Calif.*

PER SERVING: 262 calories, 4 g protein, 33 g carbohydrates, 14 g fat, 67 mg cholesterol, 165 mg sodium

Cradled in a graham cracker crust, triple-layer pie features tart rhubarb topped with layers of smooth cheesecake and sour cream.

Graham crust. In a blender or food processor, whirl 18 **graham cracker squares,** broken into pieces, to make fine crumbs (you should have about 1 cup). Pour crumbs into a 9-inch pie pan. Mix in 3 tablespoons melted **butter** or margarine. Press mixture firmly over bottom and up sides of pan. Bake in a 350° oven until darker brown at rim, 8 to 10 minutes.

RHUBARB CREAM PIE

    Pastry for a single-crust 9-inch pie
    (recipe on page 38)
    2 **cups ¹/₂-inch pieces rhubarb**
    3 **large eggs, separated**
  ¹/₂ **cup half-and-half (light cream) or**
       milk
    1 **cup sugar**
    2 **tablespoons all-purpose flour**
  ¹/₄ **teaspoon cream of tartar**
  ¹/₂ **teaspoon vanilla**

On a lightly floured board, roll pastry into a 12-inch-diameter round; ease into a 9-inch pie pan. Fold edges under; flute rim decoratively. Put rhubarb in pastry.

In a bowl, beat yolks, cream, ²/₃ cup sugar, and flour until smooth; pour over rhubarb. Bake in a 375° oven on lowest rack until pastry is golden brown and custard appears set in center when pie is jiggled, 40 to 45 minutes. If rim begins to brown excessively, drape with foil strips.

In a large bowl, beat whites and cream of tartar at high speed with an electric mixer until frothy. Gradually whip in remaining ¹/₃ cup sugar and vanilla, beating until whites hold stiff, glossy peaks.

(Continued on next page)

For lattice crust on spiced rhubarb-kumquat pie, lay pastry strips on top across filling, then weave additional strips in at right angles.

In a large bowl, stir together sugar, tapioca, cloves, nutmeg, cinnamon, and coriander. Add rhubarb, kumquats, and orange juice concentrate; mix well. Let mixture stand at least 15 minutes or up to 1 hour to soften tapioca; stir gently several times.

On a lightly floured board, roll half of pastry into a 12-inch-diameter round; ease into a 9-inch pie pan. Fill with rhubarb mixture. On a floured board, roll remaining pastry into a 10-inch square. With a pastry wheel or knife, cut into 8 equal strips. Arrange pastry strips on top of pie in lattice pattern; trim off strips as they lap over the rim. Fold bottom crust over lattice, flush with pan rim, and flute to seal.

Set pie in a foil-lined 10- by 15-inch pan (pie bubbles as it cooks). Bake in a 400° oven on the lowest rack until pastry is golden brown and filling is bubbly, 50 to 55 minutes. If rim begins to darken excessively, drape with strips of foil.

Serve warm or at room temperature. If made ahead, let cool, then cover loosely and store at room temperature up until next day. Cut into wedges. Makes 8 or 9 servings.—*Alan L. Fahrenbruch, Redwood City, Calif.*

PER SERVING: 658 calories, 7.1 g protein, 80 g carbohydrates, 35 g fat, 0 mg cholesterol, 248 mg sodium

PASTRY

Pastry for a double-crust 9-inch pie. In a bowl, combine 2 1/4 cups **all-purpose flour** and 1/2 teaspoon **salt.** With a pastry blender or your fingers, cut or rub 3/4 cup **solid vegetable shortening,** butter, or margarine until fine crumbs form. Sprinkle 5 to 7 tablespoons cold **water** over crumbs. Stir with a fork until dough holds together. Divide dough in half and pat each portion into a flat, smooth round. Use as specified in recipes; if made ahead, seal dough in plastic wrap and chill up to 3 days.

Pastry for a single-crust 9-inch pie. Follow preceding recipe, using 1 cup plus 2 tablespoons **all-purpose flour;** 1/4 teaspoon **salt;** 6 tablespoons **solid vegetable shortening,** butter, or margarine; and 2 to 3 tablespoons cold **water.**

Pile meringue onto hot filling. With a spatula, swirl meringue over filling and up against rim of pastry. Bake in a 400° oven until meringue is tinged with brown, 3 to 5 minutes (if you are concerned about undercooked eggs, continue to bake until temperature in center of meringue is 160°, about 7 minutes).

Serve warm or at room temperature. If made ahead, let cool completely, then cover without touching meringue and chill up until next day. Cut into wedges. Makes 8 or 9 servings.—*Janet Winner, Corvallis, Ore.*

PER SERVING: 406 calories, 6.1 g protein, 49 g carbohydrates, 21 g fat, 76 mg cholesterol, 148 mg sodium

SPICED RHUBARB-KUMQUAT PIE

- 1 **cup sugar**
- 1/4 **cup quick-cooking tapioca**
- 1/8 **teaspoon ground cloves**
- 1/4 **teaspoon ground nutmeg**
- 1/2 **teaspoon** *each* **ground cinnamon and ground coriander**
- 4 **cups 1/2-inch pieces rhubarb**
- 1/2 **cup kumquats, seeded and cut into quarters**
- 2 **tablespoons thawed frozen orange juice concentrate**
  Pastry for a double-crust 9-inch pie (recipe at right)

A Nutty Heart for Your Valentine

ROMANCE THAT EXTRA-SPECIAL PERSON *in your life with this caramel nut valentine. You can choose just one kind of nut or combine several kinds.*

It's easy to make—simply coat toasted nuts with a butter-sugar mixture and bake in a heart-shaped cake pan until the sugar caramelizes. Decorate, wrap, and give away your heart.

CARAMEL NUT VALENTINE

2¹/₂ **cups (8 to 10 oz.) unsalted whole almonds, hazelnuts, peanuts, or macadamia nuts, or pecan or walnut halves (choose 1 or a mixture)**
　　About ¹/₃ cup butter or margarine
¹/₃ **cup firmly packed brown sugar**
¹/₃ **cup light corn syrup**
¹/₄ **cup all-purpose flour**
1 **teaspoon vanilla**
　　Purchased decorating icing (in tubes or cans)

Place nuts in a 9-inch (measured from top center to bottom tip) heart-shaped cake pan; bake in a 350° oven until nuts are golden under skin, 10 to 15 minutes. Remove nuts from pan and set aside.

Line bottom and sides of the heart-shaped pan with foil. Coat foil with nonstick cooking oil spray or butter.

In a 1¹/₂- to 2-quart pan, melt ¹/₃ cup butter over low heat. Add sugar and syrup. Stirring, bring to a boil over high heat. Remove pan from heat and stir in flour and vanilla. Add nuts and mix well. Pour caramel–nut mixture into lined pan, spreading into an even layer.

Bake in a 325° oven until rich golden brown all over, about 30 minutes. Cool in pan on rack until firm but still slightly warm, 30 to 40 minutes. Invert a rack on pan; hold together and invert heart onto the rack.

Carefully peel the foil off the heart. Invert another rack onto heart; holding both racks, turn over so top of valentine is up. Remove rack on top. Cool heart completely.

If desired, with frosting write an inscription on the heart and decorate edges with more frosting. Let stand until frosting is dry and firm to touch, about 30 minutes.

Encase heart in plastic wrap, taping excess to back. If heart is not rigid, place decorated side up on a piece of lightweight cardboard cut in a matching heart shape; then overwrap with plastic wrap and secure with tape. Store at cool room temperature up to 5 days. Break apart or cut pieces. Makes 1 heart, about 1¹/₄ pounds.

PER OUNCE: 129 calories, 2.5 g protein, 11 g carbohydrates, 9 g fat, 8 mg cholesterol, 41 mg sodium

Offer heartfelt sentiments on a homemade edible valentine. Coat toasted nuts with caramel, then pour into foil-lined heart-shaped pan and bake.

A Lighter Beef Fondue

WELCOME A LIGHTER VERSION *of beef fondue: instead of sizzling oil, the fondue pot now contains flavorful broth. You poach beef by the morsel, then season it with one or more sauces, none even close in calories to butter-based béarnaise. The broth, which intensifies in flavor as the meat simmers, becomes in the end a soup to sip. With salad, crusty bread, and a mellow red wine, the fondue serves 6. To serve more, duplicate service at separate tables.*

For each group, you need a tabletop burner to keep broth simmering in an attractive 4- to 6-quart pan, a ladle, and a tray for bowls of sauces and vegetables. At each place, have a plate, a small bowl, a skewer or fondue fork, and a salad fork.

BEEF BROTH FONDUE

1³/₄ to 2 pounds beef tenderloin, trimmed of fat

    About 3 quarts regular-strength beef broth

2 tablespoons minced fresh ginger

¹/₂ pound edible-pod peas, ends and strings removed

    Purchased pub-style onions (optional)

    Shallot–tarragon sauce (recipe follows)

    Dried tomato–basil sauce (recipe follows)

    Mustard aïoli (recipe follows)

    Roasted carrot–herb cheese sauce (recipe follows)

    Herb–lime sauce (recipe follows)

1 cup thinly sliced green onions

Cut beef into about ³/₄-inch cubes; if done ahead, cover and chill up to 4 hours (meat darkens on standing).

In the kitchen, combine 3 quarts broth with ginger in an attractive 4- to 6-quart pan; heat to boiling. Meanwhile, put in individual bowls the peas, pub onions, shallot sauce, tomato sauce, mustard aïoli, carrot sauce, and herb sauce; add a spoon to each bowl. Group bowls on a tray for easy passing.

Transfer pan of boiling broth to a tabletop burner on serving table; adjust heat to keep bubbling and add the green onions. Also bring filled tray and meat in a bowl to the table.

To cook beef, spear 1 or 2 pieces at a time on a slender wooden skewer or fondue fork and immerse in simmering broth until cooked to the degree desired. For rare meat (gray on the surface, pink in the center, and soft when pressed), allow about 1¹/₂ minutes. Cook longer for less rare meat. Add sauce or sauces of choice (in sequence or blended) to individual bowls, and swirl meat through sauce. You can eat peas raw or spear and swish through hot broth and sauces. Accompany with pub onions.

If broth in the pan reduces to less than about 2 quarts, add additional broth to maintain this amount. When beef is cooked, add remaining peas to bowls, if desired, and ladle broth into bowls; season to taste with sauces. Sip soup and munch peas. Makes 6 servings.—*Anne Moller-Racke, Buena Vista Winery, Sonoma, Calif.*

PER SERVING OF BEEF, PEAS, AND BROTH WITHOUT SAUCES: 270 calories, 30 g protein, 9.5 g carbohydrates, 12 g fat, 82 mg cholesterol, 84 mg sodium

Shallot–tarragon sauce. Mince ¹/₃ pound (³/₄ cup) **shallots.** In a 10- to 12-inch frying pan over medium-high heat, boil shallots, ¹/₂ cup *each* **balsamic vinegar** and **regular-strength chicken broth,** and 1 teaspoon **dry tarragon leaves,** uncovered, until liquid is gone, 8 to 10 minutes. Cool. Stir into ¹/₃ cup *each* **sour cream** and **unflavored nonfat yogurt.** Cover and chill at least 1 hour, or up until next day. Makes about ³/₄ cup.

PER TABLESPOON: 37 calories, 1.3 g protein, 5.2 g carbohydrates, 1.4 g fat, 2.9 mg cholesterol, 13 mg sodium

Dried tomato–basil sauce. In a food processor or a blender, smoothly purée ¹/₂ cup drained **dried tomatoes packed in oil,** 2 tablespoons of the **tomato oil,** and ³/₄ cup **white wine vinegar.** Stir in 2 tablespoons finely chopped **fresh basil leaves** or 2 teaspoons dry basil leaves. Serve or, if made ahead, cover and chill up until next day. Makes about 1 cup.

PER TABLESPOON: 41 calories, 0.2 g protein, 1.4 g carbohydrates, 4 g fat, 0 mg cholesterol, 162 mg sodium

Mustard aïoli. Cut 1 large head **garlic** (about 3¹/₂ oz.) in half crosswise. Lay, cut side down, in an oiled 8-inch (round or square) pan. Bake in a 350° oven until garlic is soft when pressed, about 1

hour. Squeeze garlic cloves from peel into a small bowl. Mash cloves, then stir in ¹/₃ cup **coarse-ground mustard** and ¹/₄ cup *each* **mayonnaise** and **sour cream.** Mix well. Serve or, if made ahead, cover and chill up until the next day. Makes about 1 cup.

PER TABLESPOON: 47 calories, 0.8 g protein, 2.6 g carbohydrates, 3.8 g fat, 3.6 mg cholesterol, 72 mg sodium

Cook your own beef, bite by bite, in bubbling broth; choose from five sauces—some thick, some thin, all light—to season meat. Broth intensifies in flavor as meat simmers, becomes soup to sip at end of meal. Tabletop burner keeps broth hot.

Roasted carrot–herb cheese sauce. Peel and chop ½ pound **carrots** and 1 small **onion.** Mix with 2 tablespoons **olive** or salad **oil** in a 10- by 15-inch pan; spread vegetables level. Bake, uncovered, in a 350° oven until golden brown and very soft when pressed, about 45 minutes; turn the vegetables occasionally with a wide spatula. Let cool.

In a food processor, smoothly purée vegetable mixture with 1 package (4 oz.) **soft herb-flavored cheese** and ¼ cup **unflavored nonfat yogurt.** Serve or cover and chill up until next day. Makes about 1 cup.

PER TABLESPOON: 46 calories, 1.1 g protein, 2.4 g carbohydrates, 3.7 g fat, 7.1 mg cholesterol, 35 mg sodium

Herb–lime sauce. Mix together ½ cup *each* minced **fresh cilantro** (coriander) and **mint.** Use, or cover and chill up until next day. Add ¾ cup **lime juice** (herbs will darken after standing for about 2 hours). Makes about 1 cup.

PER SERVING: 2.9 calories, 0.1 g protein, 0.8 g carbohydrates, 0 g fat, 0 mg cholesterol, 2 mg sodium

CLASSIC DISHES *like moussaka have many variations, and when we published the original version of this Yugoslavian moussaka nearly 30 years ago, authenticity was our goal. But times —and tastes—have changed. In this modernized menu, the moussaka and two other long-time favorites with Sunset readers—a citrus salad and dove-shaped rolls—still satisfy a hankering for good, old-fashioned flavors but boast reduced calories and fat.*

MOUSSAKA DUBROVNIK

When this Yugoslavian version of moussaka was published, pan-frying was the way to go. In addition, you dipped eggplant slices in egg and flour before frying.

In this lightened up, less messy, and easier moussaka, we reduced ingredients by a quarter for realistic portions. You eliminate more than 1 cup fat; 7 eggs and 3 yolks have been usurped by cornstarch-thickened sauces.

Lean turkey breast replaces lamb, pork, and beef, but, if well trimmed, these meats would not be significantly fattier.

Light sour cream is once again available and adds a tangy smoothness to the butter-free sauce that tops the casserole.

- 2 **large (about 2¾ lb. total) eggplant, stems trimmed**
  Cooking oil spray
- 2 **large (about 1 lb. total) onions, finely chopped**
- 1 **clove garlic, minced or mashed**
- 2 **teaspoons olive oil**
- 1½ **pounds boneless and skinless turkey breast fillet, cut in chunks**
  About ⅛ teaspoon freshly grated or ground nutmeg
- ¼ **teaspoon *each* fennel seed, ground cinnamon, ground cumin, and ground cardamom**
- 3⅓ **tablespoons cornstarch**
- 3 **cups regular-strength chicken broth**
  Salt and pepper
- ½ **cup light sour cream (sour half-and-half) or unflavored nonfat yogurt**
- 2 **tablespoons freshly shredded parmesan cheese (optional)**

Multistep moussaka is an ideal make-ahead dish that loses calories with ease. Enjoy with refreshing salad and whole-wheat doves, both reduced in fat.

Cut eggplant lengthwise into ½-inch-thick slices. Lightly coat 2 baking pans (10 to 12 in. by 15 in.) with cooking spray. Lay slices in a single layer on pans (overlap slightly, if needed); spray eggplant very lightly with oil. Bake slices in a 450° oven for about 20 minutes, then turn over and bake until eggplant is lightly browned and very soft when pressed, about 10 minutes longer. Put slices from 1 pan in an even layer in a 2-inch-deep, 9- by 13- or 10- by 12-inch casserole. Set other pan with eggplant aside.

To empty pan add onions, garlic, the olive oil, and ½ cup water. Bake in the 450° oven until moisture evaporates and onions are darkly browned (take care not to scorch), about 35 minutes; stir often with a wide spatula and keep the onions in an even layer.

Meanwhile, in a food processor, whirl meat chunks, about half at a time, to mince. Or grind meat through fine blade of a food chopper.

Remove onions from oven, add another ½ cup water, and scrape browned bits free. Scatter turkey in small bits over onions; bake until meat is white throughout, about 6 minutes. Remove from oven.

In a 1½- to 2-quart pan, mix ⅛ teaspoon nutmeg, fennel seed, cinnamon, cumin, cardamom, and 4 teaspoons cornstarch. Blend in 1½ cups broth. Stir over high heat until boiling; mix with meat and onions. Add salt and pepper to taste.

Pour meat mixture over eggplant in casserole. Cover with remaining eggplant.

Rinse the 1½- to 2-quart pan; in it make a smooth paste of remaining 2 tablespoons cornstarch and a little broth. Smoothly mix in the light sour cream, then the remaining broth. Bring to a boil on high heat, stirring. Spoon evenly over eggplant. If made ahead, cover and chill up until next day.

Sprinkle sauce with parmesan cheese, then lightly with more nutmeg. Bake, uncovered, in a 425° oven until hot in the center, about 15 minutes (20 minutes if chilled). Or warm, uncovered, in a microwave oven on half-power (50 percent) until hot in center, reversing dish every 3 minutes, about 9 minutes total. Makes 8 to 10 servings.

PER SERVING REVISED MOUSSAKA DUBROVNIK: 172 calories, 19 g protein, 15 g carbohydrates, 4.3 g fat, 47 mg cholesterol, 73 mg sodium

PER SERVING ORIGINAL MOUSSAKA DUBROVNIK (OCTOBER 1960, PAGE 182): 667 calories, 26 g protein, 26 g carbohydrates, 52 g fat, 311 mg cholesterol, 685 mg sodium

ORANGE & OLIVE PATIO SALAD

Even when you're trying to eat "light" with a salad, it's surprising how quickly the calories build up. With water replacing oil in the dressing for this refreshing salad, calories drop readily and so does the percentage of calories from fat.

- ½ **cup water**
- 1 **teaspoon arrowroot**
- 4 **teaspoons honey**
- 2 **tablespoons finely chopped fresh mint leaves**
- 1 **small mild onion, thinly sliced crosswise**
- ¼ **cup wine vinegar**
- 6 **cups rinsed and crisped mixed leaves of butter lettuce and radicchio (or all of 1 kind)**
- 6 **cups rinsed and crisped watercress sprigs**
- 2 **medium-size (about 1 lb. total) oranges, peeled and thinly sliced crosswise**
- ¼ **cup pitted black ripe or niçoise olives**
- ¼ **cup lime juice**
  About ¼ cup *total* fresh basil leaves and fresh mint leaves
  Salt

In a 1- to 1½-quart pan, mix water with arrowroot, honey, and chopped mint leaves. Bring to a boil, stirring. Chill until cold, about 1 hour; if made ahead, cover and chill up until next day.

Put onion in a salad bowl; mix with vinegar. Let stand at least 15 minutes or up to 3 hours; drain and separate onion into rings.

To bowl add lettuce, radicchio, and watercress; mix. Top with orange slices and olives. Add lime juice to dressing mixture, then pour through a fine strainer onto salad; discard residue. Scatter basil and mint leaves on salad; season to taste with salt. Makes 8 to 10 servings.

PER SERVING REVISED ORANGE AND OLIVE SALAD: 39 calories, 1.3 g protein, 8.4 g carbohydrates, 0.6 g fat, 0 mg cholesterol, 42 mg sodium

PER SERVING ORIGINAL ORANGE AND OLIVE SALAD (OCTOBER 1962, PAGE 95): 168 calories, 1.7 g protein, 14 g carbohydrates, 13 g fat, 0 mg cholesterol, 127 mg sodium

SPRING DOVE BREADS

In the original recipe, the dough was buttery and full of eggs. These bird-shaped breads, however, work just as well with the leaner whole-wheat hearth bread from page 154 of the October 1976 Sunset. The rolls are generously sized; one is really big enough for two.

- 1 **package active dry yeast**
- 2 **cups warm water (110°)**
- 2 **tablespoons butter or margarine**
- 1 **tablespoon honey**
- 3 **cups whole-wheat flour**
  About 2 cups unbleached all-purpose flour
- 24 **raisins or currants**
- 12 **whole blanched almonds**
- 1 **large egg yolk beaten with 1 tablespoon water**

In a large bowl, mix yeast and warm water; let stand about 5 minutes to soften. Mix in butter and honey. Add whole-wheat flour and 2 cups all-purpose flour.

If mixing dough by hand, stir until moistened. Scrape dough onto a well-floured board and knead until dough feels velvety and smooth, about 10 minutes. Place in a greased bowl and turn over.

If using a dough hook, mix until dough pulls cleanly from bowl sides. Cover bowl with plastic wrap. Let dough rise in a warm place until nearly doubled in size, about 1 hour. Stir or knead dough to expel air, then divide into 12 equal portions; cover with plastic wrap.

Working with 1 portion at a time, pinch off a ¾-inch ball for dove head and put back under wrap. Roll large piece into a 9-inch-long tapering rope that measures about ½ inch in diameter at 1 end and 1 inch at the other. Loop thin end of rope to form an overhand knot. Set dough on a 12- by 15-inch nonstick baking sheet. For dove's tail, make 2 or 3 lengthwise cuts in wide end of rope and pull apart to resemble tail feathers. Cover with plastic wrap and chill while you shape each remaining large piece (minus a ball for head). Put on pan as formed, at least 2 inches apart; you'll need 2 baking sheets.

Now shape reserved balls of dough for heads, forming each into a smooth, tear-shaped drop. Settle heads into cavities of dough knots (poke a hole with your finger if needed); press down firmly to secure. Make a small slash on each side of head and insert raisins for eyes. Make a small slash at front of each head and insert wide end of an almond for beak. Cover with plastic wrap and let rise in a warm place just until puffy, about 30 minutes.

Before baking, push raisins and almonds back into head to secure. Brush rolls with egg yolk mixture. Bake in a 375° oven until golden, 12 to 15 minutes.

Serve hot; or cool, wrap airtight, and freeze. Thaw wrapped. To reheat, set on a baking sheet, cover with foil, and bake in a 375° oven until hot, about 10 minutes. Makes 1 dozen rolls, 1 or 2 servings each.

PER ROLL REVISED WHOLE-WHEAT SPRING DOVE BREADS: 201 calories, 6.5 g protein, 39 g carbohydrates, 2.7 g fat, 5.1 mg cholesterol, 22 mg sodium

PER ROLL ORIGINAL SPRING DOVE BREADS (APRIL 1982, PAGE 119): 285 calories, 6.7 g protein, 39 g carbohydrates, 11 g fat, 96 mg cholesterol, 188 mg sodium

Soup Surprises from the Caribbean

THE ISLAND OF ST. LUCIA, *in the West Indies, offers a cuisine that richly blends those of the Arawak Indians, Europeans, Africans, and East Indians. This diverse heritage, focused on locally harvested ingredients, produces delicious dishes to sample there or to make at home.*

In St. Lucia recently, we tasted many examples of the island's cuisine. Among the most flavorful were these homespun soups, which show off regional produce. Although some ingredients are difficult to find in the West, you can achieve similar results with alternatives.

CHAYOTE & WATERCRESS SOUP

This soup features two ingredients popular in St. Lucia. Its creator calls it Miss Helen Soup, referring to the island's nickname, Helen of the West Indies.

1¹/₃ **About 1¹/₃ pounds (2 medium-size) chayote**
¹/₂ **pound watercress, tough stems trimmed, rinsed and drained**
1 **tablespoon butter or margarine**
1 **large onion, coarsely chopped**
1 **stalk celery, chopped**
1 **clove garlic, minced or pressed**
2 **quarts regular-strength chicken broth**
  Salt and pepper

Pale green, pear-shaped chayote (called christophene in the Caribbean) and peppery watercress blend to make this light soup.

Peel chayote if skin is tough or spiny. Coarsely chop, cutting through the edible seed. Reserve a few sprigs of watercress for garnish; cover and chill until serving. Coarsely chop remaining watercress (you should have about 3¹/₂ cups).

In a 5- to 6-quart pan, combine butter, onion, celery, and garlic. Stir over medium-high heat until onion is limp, about 5 minutes. Add broth and bring to a boil. Add chopped chayote; cover and simmer 10 minutes. Add chopped watercress; cover and simmer until chayote is tender when pierced and watercress wilts, 5 to 10 minutes.

Purée soup, a portion at a time, in a blender or food processor. Return to pan and heat to simmering. Ladle into bowls. Garnish with reserved watercress. Add salt and pepper to taste. Makes 4 to 6 servings.—*Ivan Howell, Marigot Bay Resort.*

PER SERVING: 83 calories, 4.7 g protein, 5.5 g carbohydrates, 4.2 g fat, 5.2 mg cholesterol, 113 mg sodium

DASHEEN & LAMBIE SOUP
(Taro Leaves & Conch Soup)

Dasheen are young leaves from the taro root (we substitute collard greens or Swiss chard). Lambie is the island name for conch, the large marine mollusk inside yellow to pink spiral shells (we substitute clams).

2 **tablespoons butter or margarine**
1 **large onion, chopped**
4 **cloves garlic, minced or pressed**
1 **pound collard greens or Swiss chard, tough ends and stems trimmed, rinsed well and coarsely chopped**
1¹/₂ **quarts regular-strength beef broth**
2 **cups water**
¹/₂ **teaspoon dry thyme leaves**
5 **thin lime slices**
1 **cup thinly sliced celery**
4 **cans (6¹/₂ oz. each) chopped clams**
1 **can (14 oz.) coconut milk**
2 **tablespoons drained canned green peppercorns, rinsed and chopped**
¹/₄ **cup thinly sliced chives**

In a 5- to 6-quart pan, stir butter, onion, and garlic often over medium-high heat until onion is lightly browned,

about 15 minutes. Add greens; stir until wilted, 2 to 3 minutes. Remove from pan; set aside.

Add broth, water, thyme, lime, and celery to pan. Bring to a boil; cover and simmer 30 minutes. With a slotted spoon, lift out and discard sliced lime and celery. Add canned clams and their juices, coconut milk, green peppercorns, and cooked greens and onion mixture. Stir often over medium heat just until hot, 5 to 10 minutes. Ladle hot soup into bowls and sprinkle with chives. Makes 6 to 8 servings.—*St. Lucian Hotel.*

PER SERVING: 223 calories, 15 g protein, 9.7 g carbohydrates, 15 g fat, 40 mg cholesterol, 117 mg sodium

PUMPKIN & SPINACH SOUP
WITH BEEF

Islanders call all winter squash pumpkin.

1 **tablespoon butter or margarine**
1 **large onion, chopped**
1 **stalk celery, thinly sliced**
2 **quarts regular-strength chicken broth**
¹/₂ **pound boneless beef chuck, fat trimmed, cut into ¹/₂-inch cubes**
3¹/₂ **pounds Hubbard or banana squash, peeled, seeded, and cut into ¹/₂-inch cubes (about 10 cups)**
2 **large (about ¹/₂ lb. total) carrots, peeled and coarsely chopped**
¹/₂ **pound spinach, tough stems and wilted leaves discarded, rinsed well and drained**
  Salt and pepper

In a 6- to 8-quart pan, stir butter, onion, and celery over medium-high heat until onion is limp, about 5 minutes. Add broth and beef; cover and simmer for 30 minutes. Add squash and carrots; cover and simmer until squash and beef are very tender when pierced, 15 to 20 minutes. Cut spinach into ¹/₄-inch-wide strips.

With a slotted spoon, lift out about ³/₄ of the squash and coarsely mash. Return mashed squash to pan along with spinach. Bring to a boil; then simmer, uncovered, until spinach wilts, 3 to 4 minutes. Skim and discard fat. Ladle soup into bowls. Add salt and pepper to taste. Makes 6 to 8 servings.—*Pius Williams, Halcyon Beach Club.*

PER SERVING: 157 calories, 12 g protein, 18 g carbohydrates, 5 g fat, 21 mg cholesterol, 126 mg sodium

Cubes of golden winter squash, coarsely chopped carrots, shreds of spinach, and morsels of beef simmer together in chicken broth to make this popular Caribbean soup.

Puebla Stew

THE CUISINE OF PUEBLA *is a delightful fusion of tastes, ingredients, and techniques supplied by local Indians and transplanted Spanish, French, and other European settlers. A local specialty, mixiote, captures the spirit of these multiple infusions. (For another Puebla specialty, see the facing page.)*

Traditionally, paper-textured sheets of membrane from the leaf of the native agave plant are used to wrap chiliseasoned meat or poultry for steaming. Cooking parchment, sold in cookware stores and some supermarkets, or foil replaces the agave membrane. Folded back, the wrapper makes a bowl for each serving; accompany with guacamole seasoned with chopped tomatillos.

You can buy guajillo chilies in Mexican markets.

LAMB SHANKS MIXIOTE

6 ounces (about 24) dry guajillo chilies (or dry California or New Mexico chilies)

¾ pound (about 6 medium-size) Roma-style tomatoes, cored

8 cloves garlic

1 large (about ½ lb.) onion, chopped

1 tablespoon cumin seed

1 teaspoon pepper
  Salt

½ teaspoon ground cinnamon

8 lamb shanks (about 8 lb. total), cut through bone into 1½-inch-thick pieces (discard bony ends)

16 squares (15 in. each) cooking parchment or foil
  Lime wedges

Lay chilies in a 10- by 15-inch pan. Bake in a 300° oven until chilies smell lightly toasted and are soft, 4 to 5 minutes. Remove from oven. While warm, pull off stems; shake out and discard seeds. Rinse chilies, drain, and put into a bowl. Add 4 cups boiling water and let stand until soft, about 15 minutes.

In same pan, broil tomatoes 6 inches from heat until skins are dark brown and blistered, about 8 minutes; turn as needed.

With a slotted spoon, transfer chilies to a food processor or blender; save liquid. To chilies add tomatoes, garlic, onion, cumin, pepper, ½ teaspoon salt, and cinnamon. Whirl until smoothly puréed; add ½ cup soaking liquid to mix. Measure purée and add more soaking liquid to make 4 cups. Firmly rub sauce through a fine strainer into a bowl; discard residue.

In the center of double-layered parchment sheets, mound equal portions of lamb, then add equal portions of chili sauce. To seal each packet, bring together opposite sides of top sheet of parchment; fold edges over twice in ³/₄-inch-wide turns. Fold open ends up and compactly over meat. Repeat to fold outer sheet of parchment over meat, but bend last folds under meat. Tie shut with cotton string.

In a 12- to 14-quart pan (or 2 pans, 5 to 6 qt. each), position a steaming rack at least 1 inch above pan bottom. Add about 1 inch water. Set lamb packets (with flaps underneath) on rack, stacking as needed. Cover pan and bring water to boiling on high heat; boil gently for 2½ hours. Add boiling water as required to maintain water level. With a long slender skewer, pierce top of 1 packet of meat to test tenderness. If meat feels firm, continue to cook until it gives readily to skewer.

Set each packet on a dinner plate, with fold up. Snip string and fold parchment sheets back to form a bowl to contain juices. Add lime and salt to taste. Makes 8 servings.—*Patricia Quintana, Mexico City.*

PER SERVING: 782 calories, 69 g protein, 9.9 g carbohydrates, 51 g fat, 243 mg cholesterol, 214 mg sodium

Pueblan mixiote features lamb shanks steamed in a wrapper with a forthright chili sauce; parchment wrapper folded back creates a bowl.

Puebla's Celebrated Sandwich

PUEBLA'S RICH CULINARY STYLE *springs from its multicultural heritage. Built by the Spanish and visited by a smattering of other Europeans, the city developed a cuisine whose eclectic style sets it apart from Mexican food most Westerners are familiar with.*

The French introduced skilled baking with wheat and yeast. Among the many fine breads in Puebla, semitas, the top-hatted crusty rolls, stand out. Hats are lifted off to make way for sandwich fillings; the most common is breaded veal cutlets with pickled carrots and jalapeños.

If you visit Puebla, you can order a sandwich at a semitas stand. One of the best known is La Poblanita, in the Melchior Ocampo market, at 21 Poniente between 4 and 6 Sur. If you want to try the sandwich at home, here's the recipe.

Semitas dough, formed into oval rolls with 1 slash on top, becomes bolillos. If rolls have 2 slashes on top, Pueblans call them teleras. Teleras, filled with tinga (a long-simmered stew of flank steak), become sandwiches called tortas, a favorite evening snack.

Look for semolina flour and bread flour in some supermarkets or in natural-food stores. Semolina flour also shows up in Italian grocery stores and in fancy-food and cookware stores.

SEMITAS
(Top-hatted Puebla Rolls)

- 2 **cups warm water (110°)**
- 1 **envelope active dry yeast**
- 1 **tablespoon sugar**
- 2 **tablespoons salt**
- **About 2 cups** *each* **bread flour (or all-purpose flour) and semolina flour**
- 1/3 **cup** *each* **dehydrated masa flour (corn tortilla flour) and yellow or white cornmeal; or** 1/3 **cup** *each* **all-purpose bread flour and semolina flour**

In a bowl, combine water, yeast, sugar, and 1 1/2 teaspoons salt; let stand until yeast is softened, about 10 minutes. Mix together 2 cups *each* bread flour and semolina flour, the masa flour, and the cornmeal. Stir 3 cups flour mixture with yeast. Beat with a heavy spoon or an electric mixer until dough is stretchy.

Stir in remaining flour mixture, then beat with a dough hook or a heavy spoon until dough is elastic and only slightly sticky when lightly touched; scrape bowl often. Cover with plastic wrap. Let stand in a warm place until double in volume, about 1 hour. Beat air from dough with dough hook or spoon. With bread or all-purpose flour, lightly coat a board. Scrape dough onto it and divide into 8 equal pieces.

Working with 1 piece at a time, knead dough into a smooth ball. With a rolling motion and the side of your hand, press down on ball to form a figure 8, with 1/3 of the dough on 1 end (step 1, below) and a midriff about 1/2 inch wide. Flatten both balls to about 1/4 inch thick (step 2). Gently lift the smaller round, twist over, and lay it on larger section (step 3). Gently press top round to secure to base. Set rolls, as formed, about 2 inches apart on a nonstick 12- by 15-inch baking sheet (you'll need 2).

Let stand, uncovered, until puffy, about 45 minutes. When first pan of rolls is ready to bake, mix remaining salt with 3 tablespoons hot water and brush water over the rolls.

Set a large (about 12- by 15-in.) pan on lowest rack in a 450° oven; pour 1/2 inch boiling water into pan. Position remaining oven rack just above water and place pan of rolls on oven rack. Bake until richly browned, about 20 minutes. (If

Fill baked roll with ingredients of your choice. This one is layered with veal cutlet, pickled vegetable, cheese, and avocado. We substituted watercress for the green herb, popalo, used in Mexico.

you have 2 ovens, you can duplicate setup; otherwise, bake rolls in sequence.) Serve warm, or let cool on racks; rolls are best eaten when freshly baked. If made ahead, freeze when cool. Makes 8.

PER ROLL: 320 calories, 11 g protein, 65 g carbohydrates, 1.3 g fat, 0 mg cholesterol, 1,223 mg sodium

Roll dough and press with edge of hand to shape a figure 8, then flatten dough on floured board to make 1/4 inch thick. Twist small round, flip onto big one, and press to seal.

Calzone for Breakfast

A BIG ITALIAN TURNOVER, *calzone often boasts a savory filling similar to the topping found on pizza. Designed for breakfast, these untraditional versions use ingredients favored for a morning meal.*

Frozen bread dough—rolled into a circle, then folded—makes the crusty jacket. Choose fillings of scrambled eggs with sausage or poached apple slices with sharp cheddar cheese. Both mixtures can be made a day ahead; assemble and bake the turnovers in the morning.

BREAKFAST CALZONE

1 loaf (1 lb.) frozen white or whole-wheat bread dough, thawed
About 2 tablespoons salad oil
Apple or egg filling (recipes follow)
1 tablespoon beaten egg mixed with 1 teaspoon water (optional)

On a floured board, divide dough into 4 equal pieces and shape each into a ball. Roll out each ball into a 5- to 6-inch round. Brush 2 baking sheets (each 12 by 15 in.) with oil. Place 1 dough round on pan. With your hands, flatten round until about 1/8 inch thick and 7 to 8 inches wide.

Spoon 1/4 of the filling over half the dough round to within 1/2 inch of edge. Brush perimeter of round with water. Fold plain half over filling, pressing edges firmly together to seal. With a fork, prick top of turnover several times. Repeat with remaining dough and filling, placing 2 calzone on each pan. Brush calzone with beaten egg mixture. Bake in a 425° oven until richly browned, about 20 minutes, switching pans halfway if using 1 oven. Serve hot or warm. Makes 4 calzone.

PER APPLE CALZONE: 561 calories, 14 g protein, 82 g carbohydrates, 20 g fat, 52 mg cholesterol, 702 mg sodium

PER EGG CALZONE: 557 calories, 20 g protein, 58 g carbohydrates, 26 g fat, 212 mg cholesterol, 885 mg sodium

Apple filling. In a 10- to 12-inch frying pan over medium-high heat, combine 2 tablespoons **butter** or margarine, 3/4 teaspoon **anise seed**, and 1 large **onion**, thinly sliced. Stir often until onion begins to brown, about 8 minutes. Sprinkle 1 tablespoon **all-purpose flour** over onions; stir to mix. Add 1/2 cup **apple juice** and 3/4 pound **Golden Delicious** or Gala **apples** (about 2 medium size), peeled, cored, and thinly sliced. Reduce heat to medium; cook, covered,

Parmesan-dusted calzone holds creamy scrambled eggs speckled with Italian sausage, red pepper, and onion; serve with fresh fruit for breakfast.

stirring occasionally, until apples are tender when pierced, 10 to 15 minutes. Stir in 1/3 cup **raisins** and 1/2 cup coarsely chopped **sharp cheddar** or crumbled Roquefort **cheese.** Let cool. If made ahead, cover and chill up until the next day. Makes 2 to 2 1/2 cups.

After brushing dough with egg, sprinkle lightly with more **anise seed**, if desired.

Egg filling. In a bowl, beat 3 **large eggs** to blend with 3 tablespoons grated **parmesan cheese;** set aside. Remove casings from 1/4 pound **mild** or hot **Italian sausage.** Crumble sausage into a

10- to 12-inch frying pan over medium-high heat. Add 1 small **onion** (chopped) and 1 medium-size **red bell pepper** (stemmed, seeded, and chopped); stir often until onion and sausage are lightly browned, 8 to 10 minutes. Reduce heat to medium. Sprinkle 1 tablespoon **all-purpose flour** over onion mixture; stir until mixed. Stir in 1/4 cup **sour cream.** Add egg mixture to pan; stir gently until eggs are softly set. Add **salt** and **pepper** to taste. Let cool slightly. If made ahead, cover and chill up until the next day. Makes 2 to 2 1/2 cups.

After brushing dough with egg, sprinkle lightly with grated **parmesan cheese.**

Meat Loaf: New Ways with an Old Favorite

WITH RENEWED INTEREST *in old favorites, meat loaf has been elevated from its former status as standard fare. Instead, these days it's considered an ideal dish for blending contemporary flavors.*

Here we feature a beef loaf filled with a savory blend of Italian ingredients and a turkey herb loaf speckled with colorful vegetables. Both can be served hot or offered cold for make-ahead dining.

BEEF & PORCINI LOAF WITH BASIL SPIRAL

    1 ounce dry porcini mushrooms
    1 tablespoon olive oil
    1 large red onion, chopped
    2 to 3 slices sourdough bread, torn
       in pieces
 1¹/₂ pounds ground lean beef (such
       as sirloin or round)
  ¹/₂ pound mild Italian sausage,
       casings removed
    2 large eggs
    2 cloves garlic, minced or pressed
  ¹/₃ cup minced parsley
  ³/₄ cup grated parmesan cheese
  ¹/₄ teaspoon freshly ground pepper
       Filling (ingredients follow)

Soak mushrooms in ³/₄ cup hot water until soft, about 20 minutes. Squeeze and rub mushrooms to release any grit. Lift from water; chop finely and set aside. Without disturbing sediment in bottom of bowl, pour ¹/₄ cup of the water into a measuring cup; set aside. Discard remaining water.

In an 8- to 10-inch frying pan over medium-high heat, stir oil and onion often until onion begins to brown, 10 to 12 minutes; set aside.

Using parchment or waxed paper, wrap meat over layered filling jelly-roll style; to seal, pinch seam and ends closed.

In a blender or food processor, whirl enough bread to make 1¹/₄ cups crumbs. To a large bowl, add crumbs, mushrooms and reserved liquid, onions, beef, sausage, eggs, garlic, parsley, cheese, and pepper; mix until very well blended.

On a large sheet of parchment or waxed paper, pat meat mixture into a 10- by 15-inch rectangle. Distribute filling ingredients over meat in even layers to within 1 inch of edges.

Using paper to help roll meat, lift narrow end nearest you over filling and slowly roll meat to form a cylinder. Pinch seam and ends closed to seal in filling.

Using 2 wide spatulas, transfer loaf to a 9- by 13-inch baking dish. Bake, uncovered, in a 350° oven until well browned on top, about 1¹/₄ hours. Carefully transfer to a platter with spatulas. Serve hot or cool, or cover and chill until next day and serve cold. Cut into slices. Makes 8 to 10 servings.

PER SERVING: 478 calories, 29 g protein, 12 g carbohydrates, 35 g fat, 143 mg cholesterol, 1,006 mg sodium

Filling. Assemble 3 ounces thinly sliced **prosciutto**, ¹/₂ pound thinly sliced **fontina cheese**, 1¹/₄ cups lightly packed **fresh basil leaves**, and ¹/₂ cup drained and finely chopped **dried tomatoes packed in oil**.

TURKEY LOAF WITH VEGETABLE CONFETTI

    2 tablespoons olive oil
    1 medium-size zucchini (ends
       trimmed), diced
    1 medium-size carrot (ends
       trimmed), peeled and diced
    1 medium-size ear of corn (husks
       removed), kernels cut off
    1 small red bell pepper, stemmed,
       seeded, and diced
    2 to 3 slices white or wheat bread,
       torn in pieces
    2 pounds ground turkey
    2 large eggs
  ¹/₄ cup minced parsley
    1 tablespoon *each* minced fresh
       savory leaves and minced fresh
       thyme leaves, or 1 teaspoon
       each dry savory leaves
       and dry thyme leaves
       Salt and pepper
       Confetti sauce (recipe follows)

A slice of the cooked loaf—here served cold—reveals the savory prosciutto, cheese, basil, and tomato filling.

To a 10- to 12-inch frying pan over medium heat, add oil, zucchini, carrot, corn, and bell pepper. Stir often until vegetables begin to brown, about 15 minutes.

In a blender or food processor, whirl enough bread to make 1¹/₄ cups crumbs. In a large bowl, mix crumbs, ³/₄ of the vegetable mixure, turkey, eggs, parsley, savory, and thyme until well blended.

In a 9- by 13-inch baking pan, shape meat mixture into a 5- by 11-inch loaf. Bake, uncovered, in a 350° oven until browned and no longer pink in center (cut to test), about 1 hour.

Using 2 wide spatulas, transfer loaf to a platter. Serve hot or cool; or cover, chill until next day, and serve cold. Slice and add salt and pepper to taste. Spoon sauce equally over portions. Makes 8 to 10 servings.

PER SERVING WITH SAUCE: 211 calories, 19 g protein, 7.6 g carbohydrates, 11 g fat, 110 mg cholesterol, 143 mg sodium

Confetti sauce. Mix 1 cup **unflavored yogurt**, ¹/₂ teaspoon minced **fresh thyme leaves**, remaining **cooked vegetables** (preceding), and **pepper** to taste.

Lobster Stretchers

THE SWEET, RICH TASTE *of lobster brings a note of luxury to a meal. Unfortunately, lobster also commands a premium price.*

For more affordable dining, buy tails. They have less waste than the whole shellfish. Cut meat into thin slices and combine with other ingredients to stretch the number of servings. Sliced fresh fruit brightens the first recipe we offer here; in the second, slices of lobster float flowerlike in broth to give the soup its name.

The tails, usually sold frozen, come from Australia, New Zealand, Southern California, Hawaii, and Florida. A 6- to 8-ounce tail can cost $10 to $12.

LOBSTER SALAD WITH GINGER DRESSING

- ½ **pound edible-pod peas, strings removed**
- 2 **lobster tails (6 to 8 oz. each), thawed if frozen**
- 3 **quarts (about 9 oz.) rinsed, crisped, bite-size pieces butter lettuce**
- 2 **large (about 5 oz. each) firm-ripe kiwi fruit, peeled and thinly sliced**
- 4 **preserved kumquats, thinly sliced**
   Ginger dressing (recipe follows)

In a 5- to 6-quart pan, bring about 3 quarts water to a boil. Add pea pods and cook just until tender-crisp to bite, about 2 minutes. Lift out with a slotted spoon and immerse in ice water.

Return water in pan to a boil. Add lobster tails. Simmer, covered, until meat is opaque when cut in center, 7 to 9 minutes. Drain lobster and immerse in the ice water to cool. Drain peas and lobster.

With kitchen scissors, clip fins from edges of each tail's undershell. Then cut along undershell; peel back undershell and discard. Working from body end, carefully remove meat from shell in 1 piece. Thinly slice meat crosswise. If made ahead, cover and chill pea pods and lobster up until the next day.

On 4 dinner plates, arrange equal portions of lettuce, kiwi fruit, kumquats, lobster, and pea pods. Spoon ginger dressing equally over each serving. Makes 4 servings.

PER SERVING: 199 calories, 13 g protein, 37 g carbohydrates, 0.9 g fat, 34 mg cholesterol, 220 mg sodium

Ginger dressing. Mix 1 teaspoon finely shredded **orange peel,** ¾ cup **orange juice,** 2 tablespoons **sherry** or red wine **vinegar,** and 2 tablespoons minced **crystallized ginger.** If made ahead, cover and chill up until the next day.

LOBSTER FLOWER SOUP

- 1 **tablespoon butter or margarine**
- ½ **cup minced shallots**
- 1 **cup dry white wine**
- 1 **quart regular-strength chicken broth**
- ½ **teaspoon dry tarragon leaves**
- 3 **thin strips (about ½ by 3 in.) lemon peel, yellow part only**
- 2 **lobster tails (6 to 8 oz. each), thawed if frozen**
- ½ **pound spinach, ends and tough stems trimmed, rinsed and drained**
- 4 **thin lemon slices**

In a 5- to 6-quart pan, combine butter and shallots over medium heat. Stir often until shallots are limp, about 5 minutes. Add wine, broth, tarragon, and lemon peel. Cover and simmer 30 minutes.

With kitchen scissors, clip fins from edges of each tail's undershell. Cut along undershell; peel back undershell and discard. Working from body end, carefully remove meat from shell in 1 piece. Thinly slice meat crosswise.

When broth is ready, discard lemon peel. Stir in spinach and lobster; simmer, uncovered, until lobster is opaque, about 1½ minutes. Ladle into bowls. Float lemon slices on soup. Makes 4 or 5 servings.

PER SERVING: 105 calories, 11 g protein, 7 g carbohydrates, 3.9 g fat, 33 mg cholesterol, 239 mg sodium

Lobster slices add dressy touch to salad laced with fruit and ginger-spiced dressing. Remove meat from lobster tail in one piece and cut into thin slices.

Cooking with Canned Seafood

ANNED SEAFOOD *has a major advan-tage: you can always have it around. The challenge is finding novel ways to use it. Here we present three possibilities: clam or shrimp won tons, a dill-salmon quiche, and a sardine pâté.*

CLAM OR SHRIMP POUCHES

2 cans (6½ oz. each) chopped clams, rinsed and drained; or 1 can (4¼ oz. drained weight) tiny shrimp, rinsed and drained
1 small package (3 oz.) cream cheese
6 tablespoons minced chives or green onion
2 teaspoons minced fresh ginger
½ teaspoon pepper
16 won ton or pot sticker skins (a partial package of either)
4 or 5 large lettuce leaves, rinsed

Mix clams, cream cheese, 4 tablespoons chives, ginger, and pepper until blend-ed. In center of 1 won ton skin, mound 1 tablespoon fish mixture. Gather skin around filling, pressing skin to filling so it sticks; leave top of filling exposed (skin should not extend more than ¼ inch above filling). Place pouch, open end up, on a plate; cover with plastic wrap. Repeat to fill remaining skins. If made ahead, chill up to 4 hours.

Position a flat steamer rack at least 1 inch above bottom of a 5- to 6-quart pan; add about ¾ inch water. Cover a 7- to 8-inch plate with lettuce. (Or use an Oriental bamboo steamer set above 1 inch of water in a wok, lining tiers with lettuce.) Set filled pouches, open ends up and slightly apart, on leaves (if using 1 rack, steam half at a time). Bring water to boil on high heat; cover and steam until wrappers are tender to bite, about 20 minutes. Replenish water with boiling water if needed. Serve hot pouches sprinkled with remaining chives. Makes 16.

PER CLAM POUCH: 65 calories, 4.4 g protein, 6.6 g carbohydrates, 2.2 g fat, 14 mg cholesterol, 30 mg sodium

PER SHRIMP POUCH: 56 calories, 3.1 g protein, 6 g carbohydrates, 2 g fat, 19 mg cholesterol, 29 mg sodium

Sardine pâté, flavored with mustard and lemon juice, is served on fish-shaped crackers. Prepare it as a quick appetizer when unexpected company arrives.

SALMON QUICHE

1 can (15½ oz.) pink salmon, drained
1 cup shredded mild cheddar cheese
½ cup thinly sliced green onion
½ teaspoon pepper
1 baked 9-inch pie shell
3 large eggs
1 cup milk or half-and-half (light cream)
2 tablespoons madeira or dry sherry
1 tablespoon minced fresh dill or 1 teaspoon dried dill weed

Break salmon into about ½-inch pieces. Mix with cheese, onion, and pepper; spoon mixture into pie shell.

Beat to blend eggs, milk, madeira, and dill. Pour into crust. Bake in a 350° oven until center is firm to touch and doesn't jiggle when gently shaken, about 55 minutes. Let quiche cool for about 10 minutes before cutting. Makes 6 servings.—*Wendy Brody, Berkeley.*

PER SERVING: 379 calories, 24 g protein, 16 g carbohydrates, 24 g fat, 186 mg cholesterol, 652 mg sodium

SARDINE PÂTÉ

2 cans (3¾ oz.) sardines packed in oil, drained
2 tablespoons mayonnaise
1 tablespoon Dijon mustard
1 tablespoon drained capers
1 teaspoon lemon juice
¼ teaspoon pepper
1 tablespoon minced parsley Crackers

Finely mash sardines, mayonnaise, and mustard. Stir in capers, lemon juice, and pepper. Spoon into a bowl; sprinkle with parsley. Spread on crack-ers. Makes about 1¼ cups.—*Jane Cross, Albuquerque.*

PER TABLESPOON: 32 calories, 2.4 g protein, 0.2 g carbohydrates, 2.3 g fat, 15 mg cholesterol, 93 mg sodium

Winter's Root Vegetables

THERE WAS A TIME *when perishable vegetables weren't available year-round, and only root vegetables appeared on the winter table. Just the opposite is true now, so we thought it time to take a fresh look at those all-but-forgotten standbys.*

We've mellowed their sometimes assertive pungency by serving them scalloped in a simple white, cream, or cheese sauce. For mildest flavor, choose firm, smooth, small- to medium-size vegetables.

Spoon hot brie sauce over layers of duxelles and sticks of golden rutabaga and potato before baking. Top vegetables with grated parmesan during final minutes.

SCALLOPED RUTABAGA WITH DUXELLES

- 2 tablespoons butter or margarine
- ³/₄ cup thinly sliced green onion
- 1 pound mushrooms, finely chopped
- 1 teaspoon *each* dry marjoram and dry tarragon leaves
- 1 tablespoon *each* dry white wine and brandy, optional
- 1 pound (about 2 medium-size) rutabagas, peeled and cut into ¹/₄-inch-thick sticks
- ³/₄ pound (about 2 medium-size) russet potatoes, peeled and cut into ¹/₄-inch-thick sticks
  Brie sauce (recipe follows)
- ¹/₄ cup grated parmesan cheese

In a 10- to 12-inch frying pan over medium-high heat, combine butter, onion, mushrooms, marjoram, tarragon, wine, and brandy; stir often until liquid evaporates, 8 to 12 minutes.

Butter a shallow 2¹/₂- to 3-quart baking dish. Arrange ¹/₂ the rutabaga and potato sticks to cover bottom of dish in an even layer. Cover evenly with ¹/₂ the mushroom mixture and ¹/₂ the sauce. Repeat; finish with mushroom mixture, then sauce.

Bake, covered, in a 400° oven for 30 minutes; remove cover, sprinkle evenly with parmesan. Continue baking until cheese is lightly browned and rutabagas are tender when pierced, 20 to 30 minutes longer. Makes 4 to 6 servings.

PER SERVING: 340 calories, 13 g protein, 27 g carbohydrates, 21 g fat, 65 mg cholesterol, 372 mg sodium

Brie sauce. In a 1¹/₂- to 2-quart pan over medium-high heat, stir ¹/₄ cup (¹/₈ lb.) **butter** or margarine with ¹/₄ cup **all-purpose flour** until mixture is smooth and bubbling. Off heat, whisk in 2 cups **milk;** stir on medium heat until boiling. Off heat, add 4 ounces ripe **brie** cheese, cut into small chunks; stir until smooth. Add **salt** and **pepper** to taste.

SCALLOPED CARROTS & TURNIPS WITH THYME

- ³/₄ pound (about 2 medium-size) carrots, peeled and thinly sliced
- 1 pound (about 3 medium-size) turnips, peeled and thinly sliced
- 1 large Golden Delicious apple, peeled, cored, and thinly sliced
  White sauce (recipe follows)
- 1 cup (4 oz.) shredded cheddar cheese

Butter a shallow 2¹/₂- to 3-quart baking dish. Arrange ¹/₂ the carrot slices to cover bottom of dish in an even layer. Cover evenly with ¹/₂ the turnips and ¹/₂ the apple; spoon ¹/₂ the white sauce over these layers. Repeat; finish with apple, then sauce.

Bake, covered, in a 400° oven for 30 minutes; remove cover, sprinkle evenly with cheese, and continue baking until cheese begins to brown and vegetables are tender when pierced, 25 to 30 minutes longer. Makes 4 to 6 servings.

PER SERVING: 265 calories, 9.1 g protein, 21 g carbohydrates, 17 g fat, 52 mg cholesterol, 294 mg sodium

White sauce. In a 1¹/₂- to 2-quart pan over medium-high heat, stir ¹/₄ cup (¹/₈ lb.) **butter** or margarine with ¹/₄ cup **all-purpose flour** until mixture is smooth and bubbling. Off heat, whisk in 2 cups **milk** and ¹/₂ teaspoon **dry thyme leaves.** Stir over medium heat until boiling. Add **salt** and **pepper** to taste.

PARSNIPS & PEARS IN GINGER CREAM

- 1 cup half-and-half (light cream) or milk
- 1 tablespoon minced fresh ginger
- ¹/₂ teaspoon anise seed
- 1¹/₄ pounds (about 3 medium-size) parsnips, peeled and thinly sliced
- 1 small ripe Bosc or Comice pear, peeled, cored, and thinly sliced
- 1 medium-size onion, thinly sliced
  Crumbs (directions follow)
  Minced parsley
  Lemon wedges

Bring cream, ginger, and anise to steaming in a 1- to 1¹/₂-quart pan over high heat. Butter a shallow 2¹/₂- to 3-quart casserole. Layer half each of the parsnips, pear, and onion in dish; pour half the cream mixture over them. Repeat.

Bake, covered, in a 400° oven for 30 minutes; remove cover, sprinkle evenly with crumbs. Bake until crumbs are toasted and parsnips are tender when pierced, about 15 minutes longer. Sprinkle with parsley; offer lemon to taste. Makes 4 to 6 servings.

PER SERVING: 200 calories, 3.5 g protein, 28 g carbohydrates, 9.2 g fat, 26 mg cholesterol, 124 mg sodium

Crumbs. In a blender, whirl 2 cups (2¹/₂ oz.) soft **white bread** cubes until fine crumbs form. Stir in 2 tablespoons melted **butter** or margarine until well mixed.

More February Recipes

OTHER FEBRUARY ARTICLES *present recipes for two unusual salads, a festive rice and chicken platter from Persia, and flavorful popcorn snacks.*

HEART TO HEART SALAD

During the romantic month of February, salute the heart with a salad of canned hearts of artichoke, celery, and palm. Valued for their delicacy, mild flavor, and succulence, these hearts mingled in a mint-accented dressing make an inviting valentine offering. Brighten the combination with tomatoes (the love fruit) and tender romaine.

Look for the hearts in the canned vegetable section of most supermarkets. They cost $1.50 to $2.75 for a 14-ounce can.

    2 cans (7 oz. each) small artichoke
       hearts or 1 can (14 oz.) artichoke
       hearts, drained
 1/2 cup seasoned rice vinegar (or 6
       tablespoons white wine vinegar
       mixed with 2 tablespoons water
       and 2 teaspoons sugar)
    3 tablespoons salad oil
    2 tablespoons minced fresh mint
       leaves or 2 teaspoons dry mint
    1 tablespoon lemon juice
    2 teaspoons Dijon mustard
    1 can (14 oz.) celery hearts, drained
       and cut into 1-inch pieces
    1 can (14 oz.) palm hearts, drained
       and cut into 1-inch pieces
    1 cup cherry tomatoes, rinsed,
       stemmed, and cut in half
    2 small heads (about 1 1/4 lb. total)
       romaine lettuce, rinsed and
       crisped
       Fresh mint sprigs (optional)
       Salt and pepper (optional)

Cut large artichoke hearts into halves; leave small ones whole. In a bowl, mix rice vinegar, oil, minced mint, lemon juice, and mustard. Add artichoke hearts, celery hearts, palm hearts, and tomatoes; gently mix to coat vegetables. Cover and chill for at least 4 hours or up until next day.

Reserve large romaine leaves for another use. Arrange small leaves on 4 to 6 dinner or salad plates and evenly spoon vegetables and marinade over romaine. Garnish with mint sprigs; if desired, add salt and pepper to taste. Makes 4 to 6 servings.—*Pamela Dhno, Maple Valley, Wash.*

PER SERVING: 128 calories, 4.3 g protein, 13 g carbohydrates, 7.5 g fat, 0 mg cholesterol, 121 mg sodium

SESAME NOODLE & SHRIMP SALAD

Toasted noodles, crisp nuts, and crunchy sesame seed make pleasing texture and flavor foils for tender butter lettuce and tiny shrimp in this luncheon salad. A distinctive Oriental-style dressing lightly coats ingredients.

    1 tablespoon butter or margarine
    1 package (3 oz.) ramen noodles,
       broken into small pieces (reserve
       seasoning packet for other uses)
 1/2 cup slivered almonds
 1/3 cup sesame seed
   16 cups (about 1 1/4 lb.) rinsed and
       crisped bite-size pieces butter
       lettuce
    1 cup chopped green onion
    1 pound shelled cooked tiny
       shrimp
       Oriental dressing (recipe
       follows)

In an 8- to 10-inch frying pan, melt butter over medium-high heat until it sizzles. Add noodles and almonds; stir to coat evenly with butter. Cook, stirring often, until a light golden color, 4 to 5 minutes. Add sesame seed and stir until mixture is toasted, about 1 minute. Pour onto a paper towel to cool.

Combine in a large bowl the lettuce, onion, shrimp, noodle mixture, and dressing; stir gently to mix. Spoon onto individual plates. Makes 6 to 8 main-dish servings.—*Sharon A. Norton, Everett, Wash.*

PER SERVING: 354 calories, 17 g protein, 21 g carbohydrates, 23 g fat, 114 mg cholesterol, 278 mg sodium

Oriental dressing. Combine 1/4 cup firmly packed **brown sugar,** 1/2 cup **rice vinegar** or cider vinegar, 1/2 cup **salad oil,** 1 tablespoon **soy sauce,** 1/2 teaspoon **pepper,** and 1/2 teaspoon **Oriental sesame oil** (optional). Stir before using. Makes 1 1/4 cups.

(Continued on next page)

Mint dressing coats hearts of celery, palm, and artichoke combined with halved cherry tomatoes. Salad is served on bed of crisp inner romaine leaves.

CHICKEN WITH JEWEL RICE

Jewel-like fruits brighten this festive rice and chicken platter from Persia. The candied orange peel and tart barberries (tiny berries similar to cranberries) make an enticing combination of flavors.

Look for the dried barberries in Middle Eastern markets; store in the refrigerator to preserve their color. If unavailable, use dried, fresh, or frozen cranberries.

3 cups white basmati or white long-grain rice

3/4 cup dried barberries, or dried, fresh, or thawed frozen cranberries

3 large (about 1½ lb. total) oranges

½ cup sugar

2 small (about ¼ lb. total) carrots, peeled and cut into matchstick pieces about 3 inches long

¼ cup (⅛ lb.) butter or margarine

1 large onion, chopped

3/4 cup golden raisins

¼ teaspoon crushed saffron threads mixed with ¼ cup hot water

Braised chicken (recipe follows)

2 tablespoons chopped pistachios Salt

Rinse rice in a bowl with water to cover; repeat, changing water, until water is clear. Drain. Rinse barberries well, removing any stems and debris; drain. (Rinse cranberries and coarsely chop.)

With a vegetable peeler, pare all orange skin from oranges. Cut enough peel into julienne strips to make about ½ cup. Reserve fruit for another use.

In a 1- to 1½-quart pan, combine orange peel and 2 cups water. Bring to a boil; simmer, uncovered, 2 to 3 minutes. Drain. Return peel to pan and add ½ cup water, sugar, and carrots. Bring to a boil; simmer, uncovered, until carrots are tender to bite and peel is translucent, 12 to 14 minutes. Set aside.

In a 10- to 12-inch frying pan, combine 2 tablespoons butter and the onion. Stir often over medium-high heat until onion is golden, about 8 minutes. Add raisins, drained barberries, and carrot mixture with syrup. Stir often over medium heat just until syrup evaporates and raisins begin to brown, 8 to 10 minutes. If made ahead, cover and chill up until next day.

In a deep, heavy 6- to 8-quart pan, bring about 2 quarts water to a boil. Stir in rinsed rice and boil, uncovered, until rice is slightly translucent on surface but still firm to bite, 5 to 8 minutes. Pour into a colander (lined with cheesecloth, if holes are large). Rinse rice with cool water; drain well.

Rinse pan and dry; add 2 tablespoons butter and melt over low heat. In pan, spread ⅓ of the rice, then ¼ of the barberry mixture; repeat once, then mound last ⅓ of rice on top to form a pyramid. Reserve the remaining half of the barberry mixture for chicken, following.

Distribute saffron mixture evenly over rice. Set a double layer of paper towels over the pan, then cover it tightly with lid. Cook on high heat just until steam begins to escape, 6 to 8 minutes, then reduce heat to very low and cook until rice is tender to bite, 10 to 15 minutes.

Braised chicken encircles saffron-colored rice cooked with barberries, carrots, and raisins; plate of crisp rice chunks completes Persian dish. Serve with radishes and fresh mint.

Mix whipped egg white quickly into popcorn.

Then stir to distribute seasonings; dry in oven.

No butter, but this lean popcorn is tasty. Whipped egg white coats the kernels, making seasonings stick.

Mound loose rice from pan on a large platter; spoon chicken beside rice and garnish with pistachios. If rice crust on pan bottom is crisp, use a wide spatula to remove crust chunks; place on a plate. If crust is soft, cook, uncovered, over low heat until crisp (keep chicken warm). Add salt to taste to both. Makes 8 to 10 servings.—*Niloufar Farzaneh, Palo Alto, Calif.*

PER SERVING: 517 calories, 28 g protein, 71 g carbohydrates, 13 g fat, 107 mg cholesterol, 154 mg sodium

Braised chicken. In a 5- to 6-quart pan, combine 2 tablespoons **salad oil** and 2 large (about 1 lb. total) **onions,** chopped. Stir often over medium-high heat until faintly browned, about 10 minutes. Cut 2½ pounds **skinned and boned chicken thighs** into 1-inch chunks. Add to onions. Simmer, covered, stirring occasionally, until chicken is no longer pink in thickest part (cut to test), 20 to 25 minutes. Skim and discard fat. Stir in **barberry mixture** (reserved from rice, preceding). Add **salt** and **pepper** to taste. If made ahead, cool, cover, and chill up until the next day. Simmer, covered, to reheat.

PARMESAN POPCORN

Whipped egg white—instead of butter—coats this lean, flavorful popcorn, making seasonings stick. You dry the seasoned kernels in the oven until crisp. Since moisture in the egg whites can make the kernels deflate somewhat, work fast during mixing to minimize shrinkage.

- ¼ **cup grated parmesan cheese**
- 1 **tablespoon chicken-flavor instant bouillon granules**
- 1 **teaspoon garlic powder (optional)**
- 1 **large egg white**
- ⅛ **teaspoon cream of tartar**
  About 4 quarts air-popped or oil-popped popcorn (directions follow)

Use 2 nonstick 12- by 17-inch pans, or coat pans lightly with cooking spray.

In a small bowl, stir together parmesan cheese, bouillon, and garlic powder.

In a large bowl, whip egg white and cream of tartar until egg white holds soft peaks. Working quickly, stir white into popcorn until fairly well distributed. Kernels that get the wettest shrink the most. At once, pour equally into pans; sprinkle and mix with parmesan mixture. Bake, uncovered, in a 350° oven until popcorn is crisp and dry, 10 to 15 minutes; stir often, and alternate pans after 5 minutes.

Serve warm or cool. Store airtight at room temperature up to 4 days. Makes about 8 cups.

PER ½ CUP WITH AIR-POPPED POPCORN: 31 calories, 1.6 g protein, 4.8 g carbohydrates, 0.7 g fat, 1 mg cholesterol, 207 mg sodium

Air-popped popcorn. Pop ½ cup **popcorn** in an air popcorn maker, following manufacturer's directions. Makes about 4 quarts.

Oil-popped popcorn. Pour 2 tablespoons **salad oil** into a 5- to 6-quart pan. Add ⅔ cup **popcorn;** cover and place on high heat. When kernels begin to pop, shake pan often until popping almost stops. Remove from heat. Makes about 4 quarts.

ONION POPCORN

Follow directions for **parmesan popcorn** (preceding), but instead of parmesan cheese and garlic powder, use 2 tablespoons **dry buttermilk,** 1 tablespoon finely ground **instant minced onion,** and ½ teaspoon ground **cumin.**

PER ½ CUP WITH AIR-POPPED POPCORN: 30 calories, 1.4 g protein, 5.4 g carbohydrates, 0.4 g fat, 0.7 mg cholesterol, 189 mg sodium

BREAKFAST TEA BREAD

For Valentine's Day, try this orange-laced bread filled with raisins and nuts.

3 large eggs
¾ cup sugar
½ cup (¼ lb.) butter or margarine
1 tablespoon finely shredded orange peel
1 cup sour cream
2 cups all-purpose flour
1 teaspoon baking powder
2 cups dark raisins
2 cups golden raisins
½ cup chopped almonds

In a large bowl, beat eggs, sugar, butter, and peel until blended. Stir in sour cream. In a small bowl, mix flour with baking powder; add to egg mixture and beat to blend. Stir in dark and golden raisins and almonds. Pour into a greased or nonstick 5- by 9-inch loaf pan. Spread batter in pan; smooth top.

Bake in a 325° oven until a wooden skewer inserted in center comes out clean and loaf begins to pull away from sides of pan, 1 hour to 1 hour and 15 minutes. Cool in pan on a rack 15 minutes. Invert onto rack and cool thoroughly. If made ahead, wrap airtight and store at room temperature up to 4 days. Thinly slice loaf. Makes 1 loaf, about 2½ pounds.—*Rebecca Armstrong, Orem, Utah.*

PER OUNCE: 161 calories, 2.6 g protein, 26 g carbohydrates, 6 g fat, 31 mg cholesterol, 55 mg sodium

BAVARIAN APPLE SPREAD

Mix apple, cheese, currants, onion, and parsley for a quick appetizer spread.

¼ cup mayonnaise
1 tablespoon prepared horseradish
1 teaspoon cider vinegar
½ teaspoon ground allspice
1 large Golden Delicious apple
½ cup small-curd cottage cheese
¼ cup currants
¼ cup chopped parsley
1 green onion, ends trimmed, finely chopped
1 to 2 teaspoons sugar
Salt and pepper
About 6 cups vegetables, such as cucumber slices and celery sticks
Round butter crackers

In a large bowl, mix mayonnaise, horseradish, vinegar, and allspice to blend. Core apple; peel, if desired. Working quickly, coarsely chop apple and stir into horseradish sauce to coat. Add cottage cheese, currants, chopped parsley, ⅔ of the green onion, and sugar to taste; mix until well blended.

Mound apple mixture into a serving bowl; sprinkle remaining onion on top. Serve, or cover and chill up to 4 hours. Add salt and pepper to taste. Serve with the raw vegetables and crackers. Makes about 2 cups, 6 to 8 servings.—*Roxanne Chan, Albany, Calif.*

PER ¼ CUP: 92 calories, 2 g protein, 8 g carbohydrates, 6 g fat, 6 mg cholesterol, 95 mg sodium

SHRIMP & WHITE BEAN SOUP

Tiny pink shrimp and chopped parsley garnish puréed white bean soup.

1 tablespoon salad oil
2 large (about 8 oz. each) onions, chopped
1 cup thinly sliced celery
3 cloves garlic, minced or pressed
2 cans (15 oz. each) cannellini beans, drained
1 quart regular-strength chicken broth
¼ cup catsup
2 tablespoons dry sherry (optional)
⅓ pound shelled cooked tiny shrimp
¼ cup chopped parsley
Salt and pepper

In a 4- to 5-quart pan, combine oil, onion, celery, and garlic. Cook over high heat, stirring frequently, until golden brown, about 25 minutes.

Transfer onion mixture to a food processor or blender. Add half the beans and half the broth. Whirl to a smooth purée. Return mixture to pan. Purée remaining beans and broth; add to pan. Stir in catsup and sherry. If made ahead, cover and chill until next day. Stir over medium heat until hot. Ladle soup into bowls and top equally with shrimp and parsley. Add salt and pepper to taste. Makes 4 or 5 servings.—*Carol Arne, Oakland.*

PER SERVING: 243 calories, 14 g protein, 35 g carbohydrates, 5.4 g fat, 58 mg cholesterol, 658 mg sodium

FISH WITH CAPERS

- ¼ cup (⅛ lb.) butter or margarine
- 1 teaspoon grated lemon peel
- 1½ pounds skinless white-flesh fish fillets (each about 1 in. thick), such as Chilean sea bass, lingcod, or rockfish
- 1 cup plain or seasoned fine dry bread crumbs
- 2 tablespoons drained capers
  Lemon wedges
  Salt and pepper

Place butter in a 9- by 13-inch baking pan and set in a 425° oven until melted, about 5 minutes. Remove from oven and stir in lemon peel. Rinse fish and pat dry. Turn fillets in butter, then in bread crumbs, to coat all sides. Arrange fillets in a single layer in baking pan. Bake, uncovered, until crumbs are golden brown and fish is opaque but still moist-looking in thickest part (cut to test), 12 to 17 minutes.

Using a wide spatula, carefully transfer fish to a platter. Sprinkle capers evenly over fish. Offer lemon wedges, salt, and pepper to add to taste. Makes 4 or 5 servings.—*Sandee Nagayama, Clovis, Calif.*

PER SERVING: 295 calories, 28 g protein, 15 g carbohydrates, 13 g fat, 83 mg cholesterol, 425 mg sodium

Coat fish fillets in lemon butter and bread crumbs, then bake. Capers go on last.

BROILED REUBEN MUFFINS

- 1 can (8 oz.) sauerkraut, well drained
- ¼ cup mayonnaise
- 1 tablespoon sweet pickle relish
- 1 tablespoon catsup
- 1 tablespoon Dijon mustard
- 1 teaspoon caraway seed
- 4 English muffins, split in half
- ¾ pound thinly sliced cooked corned beef
- ¼ pound thinly sliced Swiss cheese
- 2 tablespoons thinly sliced green onion

In a bowl, mix sauerkraut, mayonnaise, relish, catsup, mustard, and caraway until blended. Place muffin tops and bottoms cut side up on a 12- by 15-inch baking sheet. Bake in a 375° oven until golden, about 10 minutes. Place ⅛ of the beef on each muffin half; top equally with sauerkraut mixture and cheese. Arrange muffins in a single layer on baking sheet.

Broil muffins about 6 inches below heat until cheese is bubbly and lightly browned, 2 to 4 minutes. Garnish sandwiches with onion. With a spatula, transfer 2 halves to each of 4 plates. Serve warm. Makes 4 servings.—*Dorothea Kent, Port Angeles, Wash.*

PER SERVING: 571 calories, 28 g protein, 32 g carbohydrates, 36 g fat, 118 mg cholesterol, 1,719 mg sodium

Serve warm Reuben sandwiches for lunch or dinner with crisp carrot sticks.

BROWN CHEWS

- 2 cups all-purpose flour
- 1 cup quick-cooking rolled oats
- ½ teaspoon *each* baking powder and baking soda
- 1 cup coarsely chopped dates
- 1 cup coarsely chopped pecans
- 1 cup (½ lb.) butter or margarine, cut into chunks
- 1 cup firmly packed light brown sugar
- 1 teaspoon vanilla
- 1 cup sour cream
  Powdered sugar (optional)

In a bowl, mix flour, oats, baking powder, soda, dates, and pecans.

In a large bowl, beat butter, brown sugar, and vanilla until well blended. Stir in sour cream. Add flour mixture to sugar mixture; stir to moisten well. Spread batter into a greased 9-inch square baking dish or pan.

Bake in a 325° oven until a toothpick inserted in center comes out clean, about 45 minutes. Let cool in pan on a rack, then cut into roughly 2-inch squares. Sprinkle lightly with powdered sugar. Serve cookies or store airtight up to 3 days. Makes 16 squares. —*Margie Denton and Wally Harbin, Los Alamos, N.M.*

PER PIECE: 338 calories, 3.7 g protein, 39 g carbohydrates, 20 g fat, 37 mg cholesterol, 169 mg sodium

Tuck chewy cooky bars into lunch boxes or pack for a hike.

ONCE CONSIDERED ODD *if not actually subversive, a vegetarian diet has a multitude of nuances and an ever-widening group of followers who have found many vegetable dishes to be quite appealing—even without the intrusion of moral issues. Certainly the success of an increasing number of vegetarian restaurants shows that people will not only eat but even buy vegetable-based meals.*

For his vegetarian tostadas, Michael McCarroll beautifully blends Middle Eastern bulgur with the techniques and ingredients of Mexico, home of one of the world's great vegetable-focused cuisines.

BULGUR MEXICANA

  2 **tablespoons salad oil**
  1 **large (about ½ lb.) onion, chopped**
  ¾ **cup bulgur (cracked wheat)**
  2 **cans (10 oz. each) enchilada sauce**
  1 **can (14½ oz.) Mexican-style stewed tomatoes**
  ⅔ **cup toasted wheat germ**
  1 **package (10 oz.) frozen chopped Swiss chard or spinach**
  2 **fresh jalapeño chilies, stemmed, seeded, and finely chopped**
  ½ **teaspoon dry oregano leaves**
  1 **can (8 oz.) kidney beans, drained**
  6 **flour tortillas (about 8 in. wide)**
     Fresh cilantro (coriander) sprigs
     Purchased salsa
     Unflavored yogurt

Pour oil into a 12-inch frying pan over medium heat; add onion and bulgur. Stir often until onion is limp, about 10 minutes. Mix in enchilada sauce, tomatoes, wheat germ, Swiss chard, chilies, oregano, and beans. Cover and simmer until liquid is absorbed, 10 to 15 minutes; stir several times to break up the chard.

Meanwhile, wrap tortillas in foil and heat in a 350° oven until hot, about 15 minutes. Or, to heat in a microwave oven, wrap tortillas in paper towels and loosely enclose in plastic wrap; warm on full power (100 percent) until hot to touch, 30 to 45 seconds.

Pour bulgur mixture into a bowl and garnish with cilantro sprigs. To each portion, add salsa and yogurt to taste. Accompany with warm tortillas. Makes 6 servings.

PER SERVING: 362 calories, 13 g protein, 65 g carbohydrates, 6.9 g fat, 0 mg cholesterol, 1,516 mg sodium

Michael McCarroll

Los Altos, Calif.

NOT SO LONG AGO, *cheesecake was a relatively simple and predictable dessert. It was made either with cottage cheese (the spartan version) or cream cheese (the sybaritic version). Its flavor*

"Michael McCarroll beautifully blends Middle Eastern bulgur with the techniques and ingredients of Mexico."

"Cheesecake was enrobed in virginal sour cream."

was usually lemon or vanilla, and it was enrobed in virginal white sour cream. But then—as must happen to all desserts—elegant variation came forth.

Leonard Cohen from Avila Beach, California, sends us a truly nouvelle cheesecake—toffee cheesecake with caramel sauce. The filling is conventional, but the creamy caramel sauce contributes a flavor that only empty calories can confer. What makes it nouvelle? The "gravy" is under the "meat," as in the very best restaurants.

LEONARD'S CARAMEL CHEESECAKE

- 1 **cup graham cracker crumbs**
- 2 **tablespoons firmly packed brown sugar**
- 1/4 **cup (1/8 lb.) melted butter or margarine**
- 2 **large packages (8 oz. each) cream cheese**
- 1 1/4 **teaspoons *each* lemon juice and vanilla**
- 3/4 **cup granulated sugar**
- 3 **large eggs**
  Caramel sauce (recipe follows)

In a 9-inch cheesecake pan with removable rim, mix together graham cracker crumbs, brown sugar, and butter until well blended. Press crumb mixture over the bottom and about 1 inch up the sides of pan. Chill until ready to use.

With a mixer or in a food processor, smoothly blend cream cheese, lemon juice, vanilla, and granulated sugar. Add eggs, 1 at a time, beating mixture well after each. Pour cheese mixture into prepared crust. Bake in a 350° oven until cake jiggles only slightly in the center when gently shaken, about 45 minutes. Let cool; if made ahead, cover and chill up to 2 days.

Ladle warm caramel sauce equally onto 12 dessert plates; cut cheesecake into 12 wedges and set a piece on each plate. Makes 12 servings.

PER SERVING: 456 calories, 5.6 g protein, 45 g carbohydrates, 29 g fat, 138 mg cholesterol, 274 mg sodium

Caramel sauce. In a 2- to 3-quart pan over high heat, melt 1/4 cup (1/8 lb.) **butter** or margarine. Add 1 1/4 cups **sugar** and 1 teaspoon **vanilla**; stir until sugar is melted and amber-colored, about 4 minutes. Remove mixture from heat and slowly pour in 1 cup **whipping cream,** stirring constantly. Keep warm or, if made ahead, cover and chill up to 2 days; reheat, stirring. Makes about 1 3/4 cups.

Avila Beach, Calif.

EVERY GARDENER KNOWS *that good drainage is essential to the health of most crops. Cranberries are one exception to the rule. These rhododendron relatives thrive in soils too acidic for most plants. They perform best with a water table a few inches below the soil surface and are flooded periodically to control pests and weeds, to protect plants from frost, and to aid in harvest. Because the plants are only a few inches tall, many berries would be lost beneath the vines if they couldn't be skimmed from the water surface after being shaken loose by a rake or harvesting machine.*

Although once associated only with Thanksgiving and Christmas, cranberries freeze well and can be had over a fairly long season—check the freezer case in your market. No one willingly eats the berries raw, but their acidity and rich color bring zest to salads, sauces, quick breads, and desserts.

Eric Lie comes from cranberry country in Washington. He likes his cranberry sauce spicy and adds cinnamon, cloves, allspice, orange juice, and (surprise!) cider vinegar to the berries.

SPICY CRANBERRY SAUCE

- 1 **bag (12 oz., or 3 cups) fresh or frozen cranberries**
- 2/3 **cup cider vinegar**
- 1 **teaspoon grated orange peel**
- 1/3 **cup orange juice**
- 2 **cups sugar**
- 1 **tablespoon ground cinnamon**
- 3/4 **teaspoon ground allspice**
- 1/4 **teaspoon ground cloves**

Pick out and discard any bruised or spoiled cranberries; rinse and drain the remainder.

Place fruit in a 4- to 5-quart pan and stir in the vinegar, orange peel, orange juice, sugar, cinnamon, allspice, and cloves. Bring mixture to a boil on high heat; reduce heat and simmer gently, stirring often, until reduced to about 3 1/2 cups, 30 to 45 minutes. As sauce thickens, reduce heat and stir more frequently to prevent sticking.

Spoon cranberry sauce into jars or plastic freezer containers (about 1-cup size), let cool, then cover and chill for up to 3 weeks or freeze for longer storage. Makes about 3 1/2 cups.

PER TABLESPOON: 32 calories, 0 g protein, 8.3 g carbohydrates, 0 g fat, 0 mg cholesterol, 0.2 mg sodium

Edmonds, Wash.

"Cranberries freeze well and can be had over a fairly long season."

February Menus

To keep away *the harsh winter chill, we offer these warming and easy-to-prepare meals for February.*

For a quick week-night meal, oven-fry chicken legs and potatoes. On Valentine's Day, make crab cakes for an elegant but cozy dinner for two. A hearty open-faced sandwich suits a casual lunch for company or family on the long Presidents' Day weekend.

WEEK-NIGHT OVEN SUPPER

Spicy Oven-fried Chicken & Potatoes
Cauliflower with
Toasted Mustard Seed
Sundaes with
Hot Apricot–Nutmeg Sauce
Gewürztraminer   Milk

Coat chicken and potato wedges in a spicy cornmeal mixture, then bake until crusty and golden brown.

You can prepare the cauliflower while the chicken and potatoes bake, or up to 4 hours ahead. For dessert, stir ¼ teaspoon ground nutmeg into ½ cup apricot jam. Warm mixture in the microwave or over low heat on the stove, then spoon over individual dishes of vanilla ice cream.

SPICY OVEN-FRIED CHICKEN & POTATOES

³/₄ cup yellow cornmeal
2 tablespoons all-purpose flour
1 tablespoon chili powder
1 teaspoon crushed dried hot red chilies
4 large (about 10 oz. each) chicken legs with thighs attached
2 tablespoons salad oil
1¼ pounds (about 2 large) russet potatoes, scrubbed

In a wide, shallow bowl, mix together cornmeal, flour, chili powder, and crushed red chilies. Brush chicken evenly with 1 tablespoon oil. Roll chicken legs in cornmeal mixture, coating them completely. Place chicken, skin side up, on a rack in an 11- by 13-inch broiler pan (or on a rack set in a 10- by 15-inch baking pan).

Week-night supper features spicy cornmeal-crusted chicken and potato wedges, and cool cauliflower salad with mint and mustard seed.

Cut each potato lengthwise into 8 wedges. In a 10- by 15-inch baking pan, mix wedges with remaining oil. Add potatoes to cornmeal mixture, stirring to coat. Arrange potatoes in a single layer in the baking pan.

Bake chicken and potatoes in a 400° oven until potatoes are tender when pierced, chicken is crusty, and meat near thigh bone is no longer pink (cut to test), about 45 minutes. Transfer to a serving platter. Makes 4 servings.

Per Serving: 615 calories, 42 g protein, 50 g carbohydrates, 26 g fat, 128 mg cholesterol, 152 mg sodium

CAULIFLOWER WITH TOASTED MUSTARD SEED

- 3 tablespoons mustard seed
- 1 large (about 2 lb.) head cauliflower, stem and leaves trimmed
- 1½ cups unflavored low-fat or nonfat yogurt
- ¼ cup minced fresh or 2 tablespoons crumbled dry mint leaves
- 2 teaspoons sugar
- 1 teaspoon ground cumin
- 1 small (about ½ lb.) head romaine lettuce, rinsed and crisped
  Fresh mint sprigs (optional)

Pour mustard seed into a 6- to 9-inch frying pan over medium heat. Cook, shaking pan often, until seed turns gray, about 5 minutes. Set aside.

Cut the cauliflower into bite-size flowerets. Place flowerets on a rack over 1 inch of boiling water in a 5- to 6-quart pan. Cover and steam until cauliflower is tender when pierced, about 8 minutes. Immerse the cauliflower in ice water and let it stand until cold. Drain well on paper towels.

In a large bowl, stir together the yogurt, minced mint, sugar, cumin, and 2 tablespoons of the mustard seed. Add cauliflower and mix well. If made ahead, cover and chill up to 4 hours.

Arrange romaine leaves on a serving platter. Spoon cauliflower alongside romaine. Sprinkle remaining mustard seed over cauliflower. If desired, garnish salad with mint sprigs. Makes 4 servings.

PER SERVING: 123 calories, 8.4 g protein, 15 g carbohydrates, 4 g fat, 5.1 mg cholesterol, 72 mg sodium

---

VALENTINE DINNER FOR TWO

Crab Cakes with Tomato Chutney
Mesclun Salad with Vinaigrette
Crusty Breadsticks
Chocolate Truffles   Strawberries
Champagne   Sparkling Grape Juice

This festive and cozy meal for two can easily be put together after a busy workday. Purchased mixed greens, tomato or other fruit chutney, and chocolate truffles are real time savers.

Festive Valentine dinner for two stars delicate crab cakes with tomato chutney, mesclun salad with vinaigrette dressing, and breadsticks.

Buy about 4 ounces torn salad greens mix (sometimes called mesclun mix) or other lettuce of your choosing. Rinse the greens, tear into bite-size pieces if needed, and drain and crisp in the refrigerator while you make the crab cakes. Just before serving, dress the greens with your favorite oil-and-vinegar dressing.

CRAB CAKES WITH TOMATO CHUTNEY

- 2 tablespoons butter or margarine
- 1 small onion, chopped
- ⅓ pound shelled cooked crab
- ½ cup fine dry bread crumbs
- ¼ cup finely chopped green onion
- 1 large egg, beaten to blend
- ¼ cup nonfat or low-fat milk
  Tomato or other fruit chutney (purchased or homemade)

In a 10- to 12-inch nonstick frying pan, melt 2 teaspoons of the butter over medium heat. Add onion and cook, stirring often, until onion is lightly browned and sweet to taste, about 20 minutes.

In a bowl, combine cooked onion, crab, bread crumbs, green onion, egg, and milk; mix well. Divide crab mixture into 6 equal parts and shape each into a patty about 3 inches in diameter. If made ahead, place patties on a plate in a single layer, cover, and chill up to 2 hours.

In the frying pan, melt the remaining butter over medium-high heat. Cook the patties in a single layer until bottoms are lightly browned, 4 to 5 minutes. With a wide spatula, carefully turn patties over and cook to brown other sides, about 4 minutes. Transfer to a plate and keep warm. If needed, repeat to cook remaining patties.

Arrange 3 patties on each dinner plate. Offer tomato chutney to add to taste. Makes 2 servings.

PER SERVING: 334 calories, 23 g protein, 22 g carbohydrates, 16 g fat, 214 mg cholesterol, 558 mg sodium

(Continued on next page)

**HOLIDAY WEEKEND
LUNCH**

Lemon-touched Bouillon
Ham & Fontina Sandwiches
with Spiced Pears
Radishes   Carrot Sticks
Sliced Oranges   Gingersnaps
Fumé Blanc   Apple Cider

Spiced, sautéed pears add a fresh accent to broiled open-faced ham and cheese sandwiches. Offer with fresh raw pear slices for munching.

For the bouillon, add 1 to 2 tablespoons grated lemon peel to 1 quart regular-strength beef broth (canned or home-made); cook until hot. Serve bouillon as a first course or along with the sandwiches.

HAM & FONTINA SANDWICHES WITH SPICED PEARS

3 large (about 1¼ lb. total) firm-ripe pears (such as Anjou or Comice)
2 tablespoons butter or margarine
½ teaspoon *each* ground cinnamon and ground coriander
¼ teaspoon ground ginger
4 thin slices pumpernickel bread
½ pound thinly sliced cooked ham
3 ounces (about 1 cup) grated fontina or Swiss cheese

Core, peel, and cut 2 of the pears lengthwise into ¼-inch-thick slices. In a 10- to 12-inch frying pan, melt the butter over medium heat. Stir in cinnamon, coriander, and ginger. Add pear slices; cook gently, turning often, until lightly browned, 10 to 12 minutes. Remove from heat and set aside.

Arrange bread slices on a 12- by 15-inch baking sheet. Top each with ¼ of the ham, ¼ of the pear slices, and ¼ of the cheese. Broil sandwiches 4 inches below heat until cheese is bubbling, about 5 minutes.

Core and thinly slice remaining pear. Transfer sandwiches to 4 dinner or salad plates. Place the raw pear slices alongside. Makes 4 servings.

PER SERVING: 382 calories, 21 g protein, 35 g carbohydrates, 18 g fat, 73 mg cholesterol, 1,241 mg sodium

MARCH

Apricot Turban Bread (page 72)

Serve this handsome
golden loaf for a spring brunch—it's a sugar-spangled,
turban-shaped bread with a tunnel of dried apricots,
marzipan, and raisins. To simplify meal planning this
month, select one of the bake-and-relax dinners or prepare a
flavorful main-dish pie. For more elegant entertaining,
you might choose one of the entrées cooked with
fruit wine and finish with a handsome caramel dessert.
You'll also find a potpourri of Asian-inspired recipes—party
appetizers from Thailand, a Chinese shortcut to filled
pastas, savory rice soups, and Sichuan pickles.

Supper Pies

SUPPER UNDER A CRUST *is an old-fashioned concept enjoying a revival in the West. You can either buy main-dish pies to take home and heat or create make-it-yourself versions offering preparation and reheating options that stretch over 3 days.*

Three flavorful choices follow: beef, chicken, and spinach. With a green salad, one makes a quick dinner.

GREEN CHILI & BEEF PIE

        Green chili and beef filling
        (recipe follows)
    1   cup (4 oz.) shredded cheddar
        cheese
        Cream cheese pastry (recipe
        follows) or 1 unbaked crust
        for a 9-inch pie, laid flat
    1   large egg, beaten to blend

Pour filling into a 9-inch pie pan or dish. If made ahead, cover and chill up until next day; sprinkle with cheese.

On a lightly floured board, roll pastry into a 10-inch-diameter round. With a cooky cutter, cut 1 or 2 pieces from center of pastry or unbaked pie crust; reserve cutouts. Lay pastry over filling, fold edges under and flush with pan rim, and flute firmly against rim; top with cutouts. If made ahead, cover and chill up to 2 days if filling is fresh, 1 day if filling was made a day ahead.

Set pie in a 10- by 15-inch baking pan. Brush pastry and cutouts with egg.

Bake in a 400° oven on the lowest rack until pastry is well browned and filling is hot in center, 40 to 55 minutes. If pastry rim or cutouts darken excessively before center is brown, drape rim and cover cutouts with foil.

If baked pie is made ahead, cool, cover airtight, and chill up until next day. Reheat pie, uncovered, in a 350° oven until filling is hot in center, 30 to 40 minutes; lay foil over crust if it begins to darken too much. Spoon from dish. Makes 8 or 9 servings.

PER SERVING: 447 calories, 30 g protein, 27 g carbohydrates, 24 g fat, 155 mg cholesterol, 684 mg sodium

Cream cheese pastry. In a food processor or bowl, combine 1¼ cups **all-purpose flour**; ½ cup (¼ lb.) **butter** or margarine, in chunks; and ⅓ cup (about 3 oz.) **neufchâtel** (light cream) **cheese.** Whirl or rub with fingers until coarse crumbs form. Add 1 **large egg;** whirl or stir with a fork until dough holds together. Pat into a ball. If made ahead, chill airtight up to 3 days.

GREEN CHILI & BEEF FILLING

    2   pounds beef skirt steak or
        boned chuck, trimmed of
        excess fat, cut into 1-inch
        pieces
    1   large onion, coarsely chopped
    2   tablespoons soy sauce
    2   cloves garlic, minced or pressed
    1   teaspoon dry oregano leaves
    1   package (10 oz.) frozen corn
        kernels
    1   can (7 oz.) diced green chilies
    3   tablespoons cornstarch
    ¾   cup regular-strength beef broth

Place meat, onion, soy, 2 tablespoons water, garlic, and oregano in a 4- to 5-quart pan. Cover and bring to a boil over medium heat; let simmer 30 minutes. Uncover; boil over high heat until juices evaporate. When meat sizzles, add ¼ cup water and stir to release browned bits; when liquid evaporates, repeat procedure once. Then add 1 cup water, cover, and simmer until meat is very tender when pierced, about 30 minutes. Stir in corn and chilies.

Mix cornstarch with broth. Add about ⅔ of the mixture to meat and stir until boiling. Let cool; stir in remaining mixture. Use to fill pie, preceding.

CHICKEN POT PIE

    1   tablespoon butter or margarine
    1   large (8 oz.) onion, finely
        chopped
    1   teaspoon dry thyme leaves
    1   dry bay leaf
    ¾   cup regular-strength chicken
        broth
    3   tablespoons cornstarch
    5   cups cooked chicken thigh
        chunks (2 lb. raw boned and
        skinned chicken thighs)
    1½ cups thinly sliced carrots
    1   package (10 oz.) frozen
        petite peas
    1   cup unflavored nonfat yogurt

In a 4- to 5-quart pan over medium-high heat, combine butter, onion, thyme, and bay leaf. Stir often until onion is lightly browned, about 15 minutes. Add ⅓ cup water; stir to release browned bits and cook until liquid evaporates.

Mix broth with cornstarch. To pan, add chicken, carrots, peas, yogurt, and ⅔ of cornstarch mixture; stir until boiling. Let cool; stir in remaining cornstarch mixture.

Follow recipe for green chili and beef pie (preceding) but use this filling. Makes 8 or 9 servings.

PER SERVING: 489 calories, 37 g protein, 26 g carbohydrates, 26 g fat, 178 mg cholesterol, 397 mg sodium

SPINACH MUSHROOM PIE

    1   large (8 oz.) onion, finely
        chopped
    ½   pound mushrooms, thinly
        sliced
    2   slices (about 2 oz. total)
        bacon, finely chopped
    3   large cloves garlic, minced
        or pressed
    2   tablespoons chopped fresh or
        1 teaspoon dry tarragon leaves
    2   packages (10 oz. each) frozen
        chopped spinach, thawed and
        moisture squeezed out
    1   cup part-skim ricotta cheese
    1   cup soft bread crumbs
    2   large eggs
    ½   cup grated parmesan cheese
    ⅓   cup finely chopped parsley

In a 12-inch frying pan or 4- to 5-quart pan over medium heat, stir onion, mushrooms, bacon, garlic, and tarragon often until liquid evaporates and onion is golden brown, about 20 minutes.

Remove pan from heat. Crumble spinach and add to pan along with the ricotta cheese, bread crumbs, eggs, parmesan cheese, and parsley; beat to mix well.

Follow the recipe for green chili and beef pie (preceding) but use this filling and omit the cheddar cheese. Makes 8 or 9 servings.

PER SERVING: 351 calories, 14 g protein, 24 g carbohydrates, 23 g fat, 146 mg cholesterol, 404 mg sodium

Rustic Western flavors—beef, corn, and chilies—fill this satisfying make-ahead dinner pie. Savory base bakes under a cream cheese pastry crust; use a cooky cutter to cut decorative design. Pie can be assembled ahead and refrigerated unbaked for last-minute cooking, or baked and reheated.

Party Appetizers from Thailand

CALLED THE CHARCUTERIE of Thailand, Chiang Mai produces fine sausages and other pork specialties known throughout the country. Many visitors to this city make it a point to sample dishes made from the favored pig.

At the Kettawa Restaurant, Prapitpong Ketkarn and Akkadej Nakballung serve northern Thai favorites. Here we offer some of their pork dishes that you can make at home. Serve them for a first course or a party appetizer, or as part of an Asian meal.

Offer spicy meatballs flavored with curry paste and chunks of peppery roast pork to dip in a green chili sauce. With this sauce, you might also present traditional accompaniments such as cucumber slices, cabbage wedges, whole green onions, cauliflower flowerets, and purchased fried pork rinds.

Another popular snack is ground pork seasoned with chilies and herbs, eaten with bites of crisp raw vegetables, lightly browned small dry red chilies, and raw shallots. These fiery starters taste best with an icy glass of beer, water, or tea to quench the heat.

With the improved distribution of Southeast Asian ingredients in the West, you'll find fresh lemon grass, fish sauce, dark soy sauce, and oyster sauce in well-supplied supermarkets and Asian grocery stores. If you can't find them in your area, use the readily available substitutes.

THAI SPICY SAUSAGE
(Si Uah)

Traditionally, this pork mixture is forced into sausage casings, sliced, and grilled. To save time, shape it into small meatballs and brown in a hot oven.

- 1 pound ground lean pork
  Red curry paste (recipe follows)
- 1 tablespoon fish sauce (nam pla or nuoc mam) or soy sauce
  Roasted chili sauce (recipe follows)

Mix the pork, curry paste, and fish sauce until well blended. Roll mixture into 1-inch balls and place about 1 inch apart in 10- by 15-inch baking pans. (If made ahead, cover and chill up until next day.)

Bake in a 450° oven until browned and no longer pink in center (cut to test), 10 to 15 minutes. Place on a serving dish. Accompany with chili sauce for dipping. Makes 35 to 40, enough for 8 appetizer servings.

PER SERVING: 120 calories, 11 g protein, 1.6 g carbohydrates, 7.6 g fat, 42 mg cholesterol, 44 mg sodium

Red curry paste. Trim root end, tough tops, and outer leaves from 2 stalks fresh **lemon grass**. Mince tender portion to make about 3 tablespoons. (Or use 1 teaspoon grated lemon peel instead of lemon grass.)

Combine minced lemon grass, 4 teaspoons **ground dry New Mexico** or California **chilies**, 1 tablespoon minced **garlic**, 1 tablespoon minced **fresh ginger**, 1/4 teaspoon **ground coriander**, and 1/8 teaspoon **ground turmeric**; mix well.

PORK WITH PEPPER
(Moo Tod)

Coat pork chunks generously with black pepper and garlic and a combination of sweet dark soy sauce (contains sugar or molasses), salty fish sauce, and richly flavored oyster sauce; then oven-brown.

- 1 1/2 pounds boned country-style pork ribs or shoulder, fat trimmed
- 1 teaspoon ground coriander
- 1 1/2 tablespoons black peppercorns or 1 tablespoon coarse-ground pepper
- 2 tablespoons minced garlic
- 1 tablespoon dark soy sauce (or soy sauce plus 1/2 teaspoon sugar)
- 1 tablespoon oyster sauce or soy sauce
- 1 teaspoon fish sauce (nam pla or nuoc mam) or soy sauce
  Roasted chili sauce (recipe follows)

Cut pork into about 3/4-inch chunks. In a mortar, combine the coriander, black peppercorns, and garlic; grind with pestle to a paste. (Or mix the ground coriander, ground pepper, and garlic.) In mortar or a bowl, add dark soy sauce, oyster sauce, fish sauce, and meat; mix well. Cover and chill at least 2 hours or up until the next day; stir occasionally.

Purée chilies, garlic, and shallots to make sauce for meatballs and vegetables.

Place pork in a 10- by 15-inch baking pan. Bake in a 450° oven until no longer pink in center (cut to test), 15 to 20 minutes. Serve hot or warm with chili sauce. Makes 8 to 10 appetizer servings.

PER SERVING: 115 calories, 14 g protein, 1.8 g carbohydrates, 5.4 g fat, 46 mg cholesterol, 227 mg sodium

ROASTED CHILI SAUCE
(Nam Prik Hnum)

- 1/2 pound (about 5 medium-size) fresh Anaheim green chilies, rinsed
- 1 or 2 large (1 to 2 oz. total) fresh jalapeño chilies, rinsed
- 12 large (about 2 1/2 oz. total) cloves unpeeled garlic
- 3 medium-size (about 3 1/2 oz. total) unpeeled shallots
- 3 tablespoons lime juice
  Fish sauce (nam pla or nuoc mam) or salt

Place Anaheim and jalapeño chilies, garlic, and shallots in a 10- by 15-inch baking pan. Broil 4 inches from heat, turning until pieces are charred all over; remove each one as done, 10 to 15 minutes.

Remove and discard stems, skins, and seeds from chilies. Peel garlic and shallots. In a food processor or blender, whirl chilies, garlic, and shallots until finely chopped. Add lime juice and fish sauce to taste. (If made ahead, cover and chill up until the next day.) Makes 1 cup.

PER TABLESPOON: 16 calories, 0.7 g protein, 3.8 g carbohydrates, 0 g fat, 0 mg cholesterol, 2.8 mg sodium

MINCED PORK APPETIZER
(Laab)

To this highly seasoned ground pork mixture, Thai cooks add thin slivers of chewy boiled pork skin and velvety liver for textural contrast. Since these special parts aren't widely available in the West, we converted the meat to all ground pork.

   1 **pound ground lean pork**
   1 **stalk fresh lemon grass or**
      ¹/₂ teaspoon grated lemon peel
 ¹/₂ **cup thinly sliced green onion**
 ¹/₂ **cup chopped fresh cilantro**
      (coriander)
 ¹/₄ **cup lime juice**
 ³/₄ **to 1 teaspoon crushed dried**
      hot red chilies
 ¹/₂ **teaspoon fennel seed**
 ¹/₄ **teaspoon ground coriander**
   1 **to 2 tablespoons fish sauce**
      (nam pla or nuoc mam) or
      soy sauce
      Garnishes (suggestions follow)

Crumble pork into a 10- to 12-inch frying pan over medium heat; stir until crumbly and no longer pink, about 6 minutes. Drain off fat. Meanwhile trim root end, tough tops, and outer leaves from lemon grass. Mince tender part.

Into pan with meat, stir lemon grass, onion, cilantro, lime juice, crushed chilies, fennel seed, ground coriander, and fish sauce to taste. Pour into a dish. Offer 4 to 8 garnishes to eat with the hot or warm mixture. Makes 8 appetizer servings.

PER SERVING: 118 calories, 11 g protein, 1.4 g carbohydrates, 7.4 g fat, 42 mg cholesterol, 33 mg sodium

Garnishes. Fresh cilantro (coriander) **sprigs; tomato** slices; **green leaf lettuce** leaves, rinsed and crisped; **cucumber** slices; **cauliflower** flowerets; whole **green onions,** ends trimmed; small **shallots,** peeled; **small dried hot red chilies,** lightly browned in salad oil.

In northern Thailand, restaurateur presents pork appetizers (clockwise from clay water jug): minced pork; sausage slices (similar to garlic sausages); and platter with (clockwise from rice basket) spicy sausage, pork and pepper, raw vegetables, fried pork rinds, and fried pork strips to dip in roasted green chili sauce (center).

Cooking with Fruit Wine

THE INTENSE ESSENCE *of fruit in some dessert wines marries surprisingly well with certain main dishes. In these entrées, the wines' fruity character complements hot, spicy, sweet, and tart notes. Use a little of the wine in cooking the dish, then sip small glasses of the same wine—ice cold—with the entrée.*

A black muscat or berry wine glazes and flavors fresh fennel, onions, and spicy Italian sausages as they bake. Apricot wine echoes the same fruit found in a warmly spiced couscous with braised lamb shanks. Golden orange muscat wine mellows a chili- and cocoa-thickened chicken stew. Spoon a little orange muscat wine over chèvre-topped oven-glazed pork chops.

MUSCAT-GLAZED SAUSAGES, FENNEL & ONION

- 1/3 **cup black muscat or berry dessert wine**
- 1/3 **cup red wine vinegar**
- 2 **medium-size (about 1½ lb. total) heads partially trimmed fennel**
- 2 **small (about ¾ lb. total) unpeeled onions, cut in half lengthwise**
- 4 **mild or hot Italian sausages (about 1 lb. total)**

In a 9- by 13-inch baking dish, mix wine and vinegar. Trim tough stems, any bruises, and root ends from fennel; reserve feathery green leaves. Cut each fennel head in half lengthwise through core. Set fennel, cut side down, in pan. Cover and bake in a 400° oven for 30 minutes.

Remove from oven and set onion halves, cut side down, in pan. Turn sausages in the wine mixture to coat and lay in pan in a single layer.

Bake, uncovered, in a 400° oven, turning sausages once, until vegetables are soft when pressed, sausages are browned, and most of the liquid has evaporated, about 1 hour. Transfer to serving dish. Garnish with green fennel leaves. Makes 4 servings.

PER SERVING: 457 calories, 19 g protein, 14 g carbohydrates, 36 g fat, 86 mg cholesterol, 970 mg sodium

LAMB SHANKS WITH APRICOT COUSCOUS

- 2 **tablespoons salad oil**
- 4 **lamb shanks (¾ to 1 lb. each), bones cracked if desired**
- 1 **large (½ lb.) onion, chopped**
- 1½ **teaspoons ground coriander**
- 1 **teaspoon ground ginger**
- ½ **teaspoon ground cumin**
- ¼ **teaspoon ground allspice**
- 1 **cinnamon stick (about 3 in.)**
- 2 **cups regular-strength chicken broth**
- ¼ **cup apricot or orange muscat dessert wine**
- 1 **cup (about 6 oz.) dried apricots**
- 1¾ **cups couscous**
  Fresh mint sprigs (optional)

Pour oil into a deep 12-inch frying pan or a 5- to 6-quart pan over medium-high heat. Add as many lamb shanks as will fit without crowding, and brown well, turning often, 8 to 10 minutes total. Remove from pan and repeat with any remaining lamb. Set aside lamb.

Add onion to pan and stir often until limp, about 5 minutes. Add coriander, ginger, cumin, allspice, cinnamon, broth, and lamb. Bring to a boil, cover, and simmer for 45 minutes. Turn over lamb in juices. Cover and continue simmering until lamb is tender when pierced, about 1 hour longer. (If made ahead, cool, cover, and chill up until the next day; reheat to continue.) Lift out lamb and place on a serving dish; keep warm.

Skim off and discard all fat from pan juices. Measure juices; you need 2⅓ cups. If not enough, add water; otherwise boil, uncovered, until reduced to 2⅓ cups. Add wine and apricots; bring to a boil. Stir in couscous. Cover and remove from heat. Let stand until liquid is absorbed, 5 to 7 minutes. Stir with a fork to fluff, and mound couscous alongside lamb. Garnish with mint sprigs. Makes 4 servings.

PER SERVING: 809 calories, 59 g protein, 96 g carbohydrates, 18 g fat, 142 mg cholesterol, 180 mg sodium

BRAISED CHICKEN IN CHILI-ORANGE SAUCE

- About 2 **tablespoons salad oil**
- 3 **pounds boned and skinned chicken thighs, cut into 1½-inch chunks**
- 1 **large (½ lb.) onion, chopped**
- 2 **cloves garlic, pressed or minced**
- 2 **tablespoons ground dry New Mexico or California chilies**
- 2 **tablespoons unsweetened cocoa**
- 1 **teaspoon sugar**
- 1 **teaspoon ground cumin**
- ½ **teaspoon ground cinnamon**
- 1 **cup regular-strength chicken broth**
- 2 **large (about 1½ lb. total) oranges**
- ¼ **cup orange muscat dessert wine**
  Salt

Pour 2 tablespoons oil into a 5- to 6-quart pan over high heat. Add about half of the chicken and cook, turning, until lightly browned on all sides, 6 to 8 minutes. Remove chicken from pan and repeat, adding a little more oil if needed. Set aside the chicken.

Add onion and garlic to pan, stirring often over medium heat until limp, about 5 minutes. Mix ground chilies, cocoa, sugar, cumin, and cinnamon; stir to coat onion. Add broth to pan. Scrape free browned bits. Add chicken.

Grate enough peel from 1 orange to make ½ teaspoon; ream this orange to make about ½ cup juice. Add orange peel and juice to pan. Cover and simmer for 10 minutes to blend flavors.

Meanwhile cut peel and white membrane from remaining orange. Thinly slice the orange crosswise; set aside.

When chicken is done, skim fat. Add wine and bring to a boil. Add salt to taste. Pour into a dish and garnish with reserved orange slices. Makes 6 servings.

PER SERVING: 391 calories, 47 g protein, 15 g carbohydrates, 15 g fat, 188 mg cholesterol, 232 mg sodium

Orange muscat wine, mixed with mustard and honey, glazes baked pork chops. Topping is chèvre cheese, mint, and more wine. Sip the same wine with the pork to savor the merging of flavors.

PORK & CHÈVRE WITH ORANGE WINE

- ½ **cup orange muscat dessert wine**
- 1 **tablespoon Dijon mustard**
- 1 **teaspoon honey**
- 6 **loin pork chops, each 1 inch thick (about 3 lb. total)**
- 5 **ounces unripened chèvre cheese, thinly sliced or crumbled**
- ⅓ **cup finely shredded or chopped fresh mint leaves or fresh cilantro (coriander)**
  Fresh mint or cilantro sprigs (optional)
  Salt and pepper

In a bowl, combine 2 tablespoons wine, mustard, and honey. Brush mixture all over chops and set on a greased rack in a foil-lined 12- by 15-inch broiler pan.

Bake in a 500° oven until lightly browned, 15 to 18 minutes. Distribute cheese equally over chops. Return chops to oven and continue cooking until meat is no longer pink at bone (cut to test) and cheese is hot, 3 to 5 minutes longer. Transfer chops to 6 warm dinner plates. Drizzle remaining wine equally over chops and sprinkle with shredded mint. Garnish with fresh mint sprigs. Add salt and pepper to taste. Makes 6 servings.

PER SERVING: 525 calories, 40 g protein, 4.4 g carbohydrates, 36 g fat, 148 mg cholesterol, 276 mg sodium

Caramel Desserts

THE GOLD THAT ENRICHES *these elegant desserts begins with sugar heated until it melts and turns a deep amber color. When cool, hard, and crushed to a fine powder, this caramel gives glowing color, intense flavor, and velvety texture to ice cream, flan, and mousse. Reserve some of the hardened caramel for decorating the desserts, or make a batch just for this purpose. Store as for caramel powder.*

Brittle amber sheet of caramel (melted sugar) whirls to a fine powder in food processor. Use powder to sweeten and flavor desserts.

CARAMEL VELVET ICE CREAM

1½ cups whipping cream or half-and-half (light cream)
1½ cups milk
 1 batch caramel powder (recipe follows)
 4 large egg yolks
 2 teaspoons vanilla
   Salt and crushed ice (optional)

In a 3- to 4-quart pan, combine cream, milk, and caramel powder; stir often over medium-high heat until caramel melts (it hardens first). In a small bowl, whisk a little of the hot liquid with yolks, then stir back into pan. Reduce heat to low; stir until mixture is thick enough to coat a metal spoon in a smooth, velvety layer, about 8 minutes. At once, set pan in a bowl of ice water. Add vanilla; stir often until mixture is lukewarm to cold, then remove from water. Cover and chill until cold, or up until next day.

Freeze mixture in a self-refrigerated ice cream maker (or in an ice cream maker with 1 part salt to 6 parts ice) until dasher is hard to turn. Serve, or store in freezer for up to 1 week. Makes about 1½ quarts, 12 servings of ½-cup size.

PER ½ CUP: 257 calories, 2.6 g protein, 36 g carbohydrates, 12 g fat, 108 mg cholesterol, 28 mg sodium

CARAMEL POWDER

Line a 10- by 15-inch baking pan with a single sheet of foil, folding up at edges.

Pour 2 cups **sugar** into a 10- to 12-inch nonstick frying pan; place over medium-high heat. Shake pan often until most of the sugar liquefies, about 10 minutes. Reduce heat to medium; tilt pan to mix hot caramel with sugar until all is melted and the color is deep amber, 3 to 5 minutes.

Immediately pour hot caramel into foil-lined pan. Using hot pads to protect hands (mixture is very hot), tilt pan to spread caramel in thin layer. Set aside until hard and completely cool, about 30 minutes.

When cool, lift foil from pan; peel foil from caramel. Break caramel into chunks. To make powder, whirl chunks in a blender or food processor fitted with metal blade (container must be completely dry). If you use a blender, you may need to make powder in several batches. Use, or store airtight at room temperature up to 1 month. Makes about 1¾ cups.

PER TABLESPOON: 55 calories, 0 g protein, 14 g carbohydrates, 0 g fat, 0 mg cholesterol, 0 mg sodium

DOUBLE CARAMEL FLAN

⅓ cup sugar
 2 cups milk
⅔ cup caramel powder (recipe precedes)
 6 large eggs
 1 teaspoon vanilla
   Caramel chunks (optional)

In a 10- to 12-inch nonstick frying pan, frequently shake sugar over medium heat until all is melted and the color is deep amber, 3 to 5 minutes. Immediately pour into an 8- to 9-inch-diameter straight-sided baking dish or pan (at least 1-qt. size). Quickly rotate dish to coat bottom.

In a 1- to 1½-quart pan over medium-high heat, stir milk and caramel powder until all the caramel melts (it hardens first), about 7 minutes. In a bowl, whisk some hot liquid with eggs and vanilla; stir back into pan. Remove from heat.

Pour mixture into prepared baking dish. Set dish in a larger rimmed pan; pour 1 inch boiling water into outer pan. Bake in a 350° oven until center of flan jiggles only slightly when gently shaken, 35 to 45 minutes.

Remove dish with flan from water. Let cool, then cover and chill at least 4 hours or up to 2 days. To serve, run a thin knife between flan and dish. Invert platter over flan; holding together, invert. Lift off pan. Garnish with small chunks of caramel, if desired. Cut into wedges. Makes 8 servings.

PER SERVING: 200 calories, 6.7 g protein, 30 g carbohydrates, 5.8 g fat, 167 mg cholesterol, 77 mg sodium

CARAMEL-ORANGE MOUSSE

1 **envelope (2 teaspoons) unflavored gelatin**
2 **cups milk or half-and-half (light cream)**
1 **cup caramel powder (recipe precedes)**
4 **large eggs, separated**
1 **tablespoon orange-flavor liqueur**
 Whipped cream (optional)

In a 2- to 3-quart pan, sprinkle gelatin over milk. Let stand until softened, about 5 minutes. Add ½ cup caramel powder and stir often over medium-high heat until caramel melts (it hardens at first).

Meanwhile, in a bowl, beat whites with a mixer on high speed until soft peaks form. Gradually beat in remaining caramel until whites hold stiff, moist peaks.

In a small bowl, whisk yolks with a little hot liquid, then stir back into pan. Stir over low heat until mixture coats a metal spoon in a smooth layer, about 10 minutes. Remove from heat; at once whisk ⅓ of the whites into custard.

Pour custard into remaining whites, add liqueur, and fold gently until whites are just incorporated. Cover and chill until mixture just begins to set, 1½ to 2 hours; gently whisk every 20 minutes. Spoon into 6 to 8 individual dishes (about 1-cup size). Cover and chill until set, about 45 minutes, or up until next day. Add whipped cream to taste. Makes 6 to 8 servings.

PER SERVING: 192 calories, 5.9 g protein, 32 g carbohydrates, 4.5 g fat, 114 mg cholesterol, 62 mg sodium

Golden ice cream has silken texture and deep, rich caramel flavor. While some ice creams turn grainy in freezer, the high proportion of sugar in this one keeps it soft.

Glistening chunks of golden caramel and sauce of melted caramel accent flavoring in fragile flan. Cut into wedges to serve.

Easter Bonnet Bread

CROWN YOUR BREAKFAST TABLE *with its own Easter bonnet—a sugar-spangled turban-shaped bread. A tunnel of dried apricots, marzipan, and raisins spirals its way through the sweet, golden loaf.*

The bread is easy to shape, but you need space to roll out the dough. Start with a butter- and egg-enriched yeast dough. Roll it into a long, thin strip, and sprinkle the filling down the middle. Seal the edges of the strip together, forming a tube, then loosely coil the tube to make the turban.

APRICOT TURBAN BREAD

1 package active dry yeast
¼ cup warm water (110°)
½ cup milk
3 tablespoons granulated sugar
½ teaspoon salt
¼ cup (⅛ lb.) butter or margarine, cut into ½-inch pieces
About 3¼ cups all-purpose flour

3 large eggs, beaten to blend
¾ teaspoon ground coriander or ground mace
¾ teaspoon grated lemon peel
1 cup (about 6 oz.) chopped dried apricots
7 ounces (about 1⅓ cups) marzipan or almond paste, in ½-inch chunks
⅓ cup golden raisins
14 cocktail sugar cubes, coarsely crushed (about 2 tablespoons)

In a large bowl, sprinkle yeast over warm water to soften, about 5 minutes.

Meanwhile, in a 1- to 1½-quart pan, combine milk, granulated sugar, salt, and butter. Heat, stirring occasionally, until mixture reaches 110° on a thermometer (butter doesn't need to melt). Or, in a 1-cup glass measure, combine milk, sugar, salt, and butter and heat in a microwave oven at full power (100 percent) until mixture reaches 110° on oven's temperature probe or a thermometer, about 35 seconds.

Stir milk mixture into yeast mixture. Add 1½ cups of the flour and stir to moisten evenly. Reserve 1 tablespoon of the beaten egg; cover and chill until bread is ready to bake. Add remaining egg, coriander, and lemon peel to dough; beat with an electric mixer until well blended. Add 1½ cups of the flour and beat at low speed until flour is incorporated.

To knead by hand, sprinkle board and dough generously with flour, using ¼ cup total. Scrape dough onto the floured board. Knead dough until smooth and no longer sticky, adding more flour, about 1 tablespoon at a time, as required. Return dough to bowl.

To knead with a dough hook, add ¼ cup flour to bowl. Beat on low speed until flour is incorporated, then on medium speed until dough is smooth, not sticky, and pulls cleanly from bowl sides. Add flour, 1 tablespoon at a time, as required. Kneading dough takes about 5 minutes.

Cover dough with plastic wrap. Let rise in a warm place until almost doubled, 1 to 1½ hours.

Punch dough down and knead briefly on a lightly floured board to release air. With your hands, roll and stretch dough into a log 15 to 18 inches long. With a rolling pin, evenly roll and stretch dough into a thin strip, 5 to 6 inches wide and about 36 inches long; keep board floured under strip. Let dough rest a few minutes between rolling and stretching if it's too elastic to stay in place.

Evenly sprinkle the apricots, marzipan, and raisins down the center of the strip. Brush long edges of dough strip with water. Bring long edges of strip together and pinch to seal. To create the base of the bread, shape 1 end of the dough tube into a circle about 7 inches across, turning tube so seam faces inside of circle. Coil remaining dough tube onto the base, gradually making it narrower and higher, forming a slouchy turban shape.

Carefully transfer turban to a greased 12- by 15-inch baking sheet. Lightly cover with plastic wrap and let rise in a warm place until puffy, 20 to 30 minutes.

Brush bread with the reserved 1 tablespoon beaten egg. Sprinkle crushed sugar cubes over the loaf. Bake in a 325° oven. After 30 to 35 minutes, check loaf;

Pinch edges of long, thin dough strip together to seal in fruit and marzipan filling.

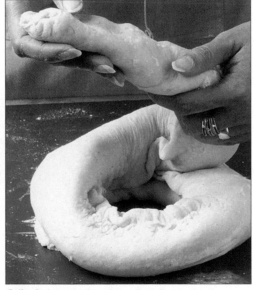

Coil tube into a turban shape. Start by creating a 7-inch circle at one end, forming the bread's base, then curl rest of tube inward and upward.

Sparkling chips of crushed sugar cubes crust golden, shiny, turban-shaped yeast loaf. Filling of dried apricots, marzipan, and golden raisins spirals through interior. Bread can be served warm or cool; cut into wedges to serve.

if it's already a rich golden brown, cover lightly with foil. Continue baking until a long, slender wooden skewer inserted in thickest part (not in the marzipan) comes out clean, 50 to 55 minutes. Transfer bread from pan to a rack.

Serve bread warm or cool. If made ahead, cool on a rack, wrap airtight, and store at room temperature up until next day or freeze up to 2 weeks. To reheat, thaw (allow at least 4 hours) if frozen. Bake, lightly covered, in a 325°

oven until warm in center, 20 to 25 minutes.

With a serrated knife, cut bread into wedges. Makes 1 loaf, about 2³/₄ pounds.

PER OUNCE: 86 calories, 1.9 g protein, 16 g carbohydrates, 1.7 g fat, 18 mg cholesterol, 42 mg sodium

Bake & Relax Dinners

IF TODAY'S VERSION *of fast cooking has you checking your watch from the time you hit the kitchen running until, breathlessly, you leave the table, we say it's about time to relax.*

Try quick cooking the slow way.

How? The secret to these no-fuss menus is quick assembly of ingredients in 1 pan (or sometimes 2) that you just pop into the oven to bake. If the cooking times—which vary from 1½ to 3 hours— sound extreme for a weeknight, consider that if you get home at 5 and take 15 to 20 minutes to get ingredients into the oven, dinner can be ready between 6:45 and 8:15.

If time allows, organize ingredients the night before (or in the morning); then the first person home can slide foods in to bake. This gives you at least an hour of duty-free time (you'll need to stir foods occasionally) for a little civilized relaxation—listening to music, reading the paper, catching up on the news, or perhaps conversing. NOTE: *It is essential to cover pans tightly with foil as directed; otherwise, moisture cooks away and foods are apt to scorch.*

Even if the baking times are longer than your workweek schedule permits, try these dinners on weekends when you have chores about the house and garden.

A special attraction of these oven meals is that they broaden the horizon to ingredients that seem to take too much time and effort for weekdays—shanks of veal and lamb, roasts of beef or pork, as well as risotto, polenta, and other tasty companions. Another benefit: few dirty dishes.

HONEY-PEPPER PORK WITH GLAZED APPLES & ONIONS, HOMINY & GREENS

Moist heat, achieved with covered baking, converts pork shoulder into a succulent roast. After the meat, fruit, onion, and hominy are done, use the roasting juices to wilt the greens.

- 1 **boned pork shoulder roast (3 to 3½ lb.), excess fat trimmed**
- ½ **cup honey**
- 3 **tablespoons Dijon mustard**
- 2 **teaspoons pepper**
- 2 **large (about 1⅓ lb. total) onions, sliced**
- 4 **large (about 2 lb. total) firm, tart apples (such as Granny Smith, Idared, Melrose, or Newtown Pippin)**
- 2 **cans (14½ oz. each) white or yellow hominy (or 1 of each), drained and rinsed**
- 2 **pounds mustard greens or Swiss chard, rinsed, tough stems discarded, cut into bite-size pieces**

Place pork in an 11- by 17-inch roasting pan. Mix together honey, mustard, and pepper. Brush or spoon mixture all over meat, then arrange onion around pork. *Cover pan tightly with foil.* Bake in a 350° oven for 2 hours; baste meat and onion 2 or 3 times with pan juices.

Remove pan from oven and skim fat from juices. Core and quarter apples and arrange around meat; spoon juices over meat, apples, and onion. *Cover pan tightly with foil.* Bake in a 450° oven, basting once with juices, until apples are just tender when pierced, about 15 minutes.

Uncover pan and bake until meat is well browned, 15 to 20 minutes longer; baste meat and apples often with juices. Gently push apples and onion to 1 end of pan; mix hominy with juices in cleared space. Bake until hominy is hot, about 10 minutes. With a slotted spoon, transfer meat, apples, onion, and hominy to a large platter; keep warm.

Place roasting pan with juices on high heat. Add greens and stir until just wilted, about 4 minutes. With a slotted spoon, transfer greens to platter with meat. Boil juices, uncovered, until reduced by about a quarter, 3 to 5 minutes. Spoon juices over meat. Makes 6 servings.

PER SERVING: 679 calories, 49 g protein, 76 g carbohydrates, 20 g fat, 152 mg cholesterol, 706 mg sodium

OSSO BUCO WITH RISOTTO

First, brown veal shanks the nonmessy way—in the oven at a high temperature —then cover and bake. When meat is very tender, stir rice into the pan juices. As the rice bakes, the grains absorb the flavorful liquid and become risotto the easy way.

- 2 **tablespoons butter or margarine**
- 5 **to 6 pounds meaty veal shanks, cut 2 inches thick**
- 4 **cups regular-strength chicken broth**
- 2 **tablespoons grated lemon peel**
- 1 **teaspoon dry thyme leaves**
- ¼ **teaspoon ground ginger**
- ¼ **teaspoon ground cinnamon**
- 2 **cups water**
- 2 **cups medium-grain or short-grain (pearl) white rice**
- ¼ **cup minced parsley**
- 2 **cloves garlic, minced or pressed**
- ¼ **cup grated parmesan cheese Lemon wedges and parsley sprigs (optional)**

Place butter in an 11- by 17-inch roasting pan. Heat in a 475° oven until butter sizzles, about 2 minutes. Lay shanks in pan in a single layer.

Bake shanks, uncovered, for 30 minutes, then turn them over and continue baking until the meat is browned, about 30 minutes more. To pan, add broth, 1 tablespoon of the lemon peel, thyme leaves, ginger, and cinnamon; stir and scrape to release any browned bits.

Cover pan tightly with foil. Bake until meat is tender enough to pull apart easily, about 1½ hours.

Uncover pan and stir water and rice into broth. Bake, uncovered, stirring rice and turning shanks occasionally, until liquid is absorbed and rice is tender to bite, 20 to 25 minutes.

Mix together remaining lemon peel, minced parsley, and garlic; set aside. Remove shanks from pan and transfer to a large platter. Sprinkle meat with parsley mixture. Stir cheese into rice and spoon it onto platter alongside meat or into a separate bowl. Garnish with lemon wedges and parsley sprigs. Makes 4 to 6 servings.

PER SERVING: 568 calories, 55 g protein, 52 g carbohydrates, 13 g fat, 190 mg cholesterol, 297 mg sodium

RUMP ROAST WITH OVEN RATATOUILLE & SMALL POTATOES

While the beef roasts in 1 pan, tomatoes bake in a second pan until they begin to brown. More vegetables are baked with the tomatoes to make a hearty ratatouille. Then you transfer meat to pan with vegetables and add little potatoes to bake, using meat juices to baste the browning beef. Remaining meat juices mixed with vegetable juices from the ratatouille are thickened to make a rich-tasting brown gravy.

1 **beef rump roast (2³/₄ to 3 lb.),**
   excess fat trimmed
1 **teaspoon coarse-ground pepper**
1½ **cups regular-strength beef broth**
½ **cup dry red wine**
1½ **pounds (about 10 medium-size)**
   firm-ripe Roma-type tomatoes,
   cored and halved lengthwise
2 **tablespoons olive oil**
1 **medium-size (about 1¹/₃ lb.)**
   eggplant, stem trimmed, cut
   into 2-inch chunks
4 **medium-size (about 1¹/₄ lb. total)**
   zucchini, ends trimmed, cut
   into 2-inch chunks
1 **large red bell pepper, stemmed,**
   seeded, and cut into strips
2 **large (about 1¹/₃ lb. total) onions,**
   chopped
¼ **cup minced fresh or**
2 **tablespoons dry basil leaves**
2 **tablespoons finely chopped**
   fresh or 2 teaspoons dry
   oregano leaves
2 **cloves garlic, minced or pressed**
3 **tablespoons balsamic or red**
   wine vinegar
8 **small (about 1½ lb. total)**
   thin-skinned potatoes,
   rinsed and scrubbed
   Fresh basil sprigs (optional)
1 **tablespoon cornstarch mixed**
   with ¼ cup water
   Salt and pepper

Sprinkle beef with pepper and place in a 10- by 14-inch roasting pan; add broth and wine. *Cover pan tightly with foil.*

Place tomatoes, cut side up, in an 11- by 17-inch roasting pan. Sprinkle evenly with 1 tablespoon oil. Place tomatoes, uncovered, on the top rack and foil-covered meat on a lower rack of a 425° oven. Bake until the tomatoes are well browned, about 1 hour.

Reduce oven temperature to 375° and turn meat over. *Cover tightly with foil.* Scrape tomatoes free in pan and add remaining oil, eggplant, zucchini, bell pepper, onion, minced basil, oregano, and garlic; mix well. *Cover tightly with foil.* Bake until meat is very tender when pierced and ratatouille mixture is very soft when pressed, about 1½ hours.

Uncover ratatouille, stir in vinegar, and push to 1 end of pan. Put roast in cleared space; reserve meat pan juices.

Arrange potatoes around meat and the vegetables. *Cover tightly with foil.* Bake in a 375° oven until potatoes are

(Continued on next page)

Four no-fuss dinners (clockwise from top): Veal shanks and risotto oven-simmer in fragrant broth, then are topped with parsley, garlic, and lemon peel. Beef rump bakes tender with potatoes and ratatouille; cooking juices make a richly browned gravy. Oven-braised lamb shanks, mint-accented lentils, carrots, and onion all roast in same pan; a splash of cider vinegar adds pleasing tartness. Glazed pork, onions, caramelized apples, hominy, and mustard greens all cook in one roasting pan.

just tender when pierced, about 30 minutes. Uncover, baste meat with reserved juices, and bake until potatoes are very tender when pierced and meat is well browned, 15 to 20 minutes longer; baste meat often with pan juices.

With a slotted spoon, transfer meat, potatoes, and ratatouille to a large platter; garnish with basil sprigs.

Add reserved meat juices to pan with vegetable juices; add cornstarch mixture. Stir until boiling. Pour sauce into a bowl; offer with salt and pepper to add to taste to meat, potatoes, and ratatouille. Makes 6 servings.

PER SERVING: 501 calories, 52 g protein, 39 g carbohydrates, 15 g fat, 120 mg cholesterol, 144 mg sodium

LAMB SHANKS WITH MINTED LENTILS & CARROTS

After the shanks and carrots brown, uncovered, in the oven, add the seasonings, lentils, and broth. Tightly covered, all bake moist and tender.

   4 **lamb shanks (about 1 lb. each), bones uncracked**
1½ **pounds (about 6 medium-size) carrots, peeled and thinly sliced on the diagonal**
   1 **large onion (about ½ lb.), chopped**
   2 **tablespoons salad oil**
   ¼ **cup cider vinegar**
   ½ **cup minced fresh or 2 tablespoons dry mint leaves**
   1 **tablespoon grated lemon peel**
1½ **cups lentils, sorted for debris and rinsed**
   3 **cups regular-strength beef broth**
   1 **teaspoon coarse-ground pepper Fresh mint sprigs (optional)**

Arrange shanks in 1 end of an 11- by 17-inch roasting pan. Pile carrots and onion in other end. Drizzle all evenly with oil, then turn shanks and stir vegetables to mix with oil. Bake, uncovered, in a 450° oven until shanks are browned, about 1 hour; turn shanks and stir vegetables occasionally to brown evenly.

Mix vinegar, mint, and lemon peel into vegetables; push vegetables aside. Pour lentils onto pan bottom, then scatter vegetables over them and add broth

Oven supper bakes with little attention. Sausages and grapes brown together in pan as polenta bakes in dish; sausage drippings can be part of dressing for green salad.

and pepper (mixture runs over into meat area); lentils need to be covered with liquid.

Cover pan tightly with foil. Bake in a 350° oven until meat is very tender when pierced, about 1½ hours; 2 or 3 times, mix vegetables and lentils, and baste shanks with pan juices.

Transfer shanks and vegetables with lentils to a platter. Garnish with mint sprigs. Makes 4 servings.

PER SERVING: 853 calories, 65 g protein, 62 g carbohydrates, 38 g fat, 152 mg cholesterol, 195 mg sodium

OVEN-BRAISED SAUSAGES WITH GRAPES & POLENTA

To complete this meal, make a salad of rinsed, crisped mesclun or other mixed greens (½ to ¾ lb.) dressed with 3 tablespoons of the warm pan drippings and balsamic or red wine vinegar to taste.

   1 **quart (about 1½ lb.) seedless green grapes, rinsed and drained**
   1 **tablespoon minced fresh or 1½ teaspoons dry rosemary leaves**
   8 **(about 2 lb. total) mild Italian sausages**
   6 **cups regular-strength chicken broth**
1½ **cups polenta or yellow cornmeal Fresh rosemary sprigs (optional)**

Pour grapes into an 11- by 17-inch roasting pan. *Cover tightly with foil.* Bake on a rack in the upper third of a 400° oven until grapes begin to feel soft when pressed, about 25 minutes.

Stir minced rosemary into grapes. Pierce sausages several times with a fork, then lay them in a single layer on top of the grapes. Return pan to oven and bake, uncovered, until sausages begin to brown, about 20 minutes.

Meanwhile, in a 3- to 4-quart shallow baking dish, mix the broth and polenta. Place polenta on a rack in lower third of oven. Turn sausages and stir grapes, then continue baking until sausages have browned well, grapes have caramelized, and polenta has absorbed all the liquid but is still soft—45 to 55 minutes longer. Turn sausages and stir grapes and polenta occasionally during baking.

Spread polenta in a thick layer on a large platter. With a slotted spoon, transfer sausages and grapes onto polenta; if you like, use drippings to dress salad greens (see directions above). Garnish platter with rosemary sprigs. Makes 8 servings.

PER SERVING: 477 calories, 21 g protein, 38 g carbohydrates, 27 g fat, 70 mg cholesterol, 823 mg sodium

A Chinese Shortcut to Filled Pastas

PURCHASING *eggroll wrappers and gyoza skins gives you a shortcut when you make these filled main-dish pastas. A flour-and-water paste seals them securely.*

AGNOLOTTI WITH SHRIMP & AVOCADO

Pickled scallions are sold in Asian markets. Round gyoza skins make agnolotti; square won ton skins make raviolini.

- ³⁄₄ **pound shelled, cooked tiny shrimp**
- ¹⁄₂ **cup pickled scallions, minced**
- ¹⁄₄ **cup minced green onion**
- 2 **tablespoons grated lemon peel**
  About 5 dozen gyoza (potsticker) or won ton skins
- 2 **tablespoons all-purpose flour mixed with ¹⁄₄ cup water**
- ¹⁄₄ **cup (¹⁄₈ lb.) butter or margarine**
- ¹⁄₃ **cup lemon juice**
- 3 **small (about 1¹⁄₄ lb. total) firm-ripe avocados**
  Lemon wedges

In a bowl, mix together shrimp, scallions, 2 tablespoons green onion, and lemon peel. Lay 1 gyoza skin flat. Place about 1 teaspoon shrimp mixture in the center. With your finger, lightly brush flour paste around the edge of half the wrapper. Fold plain side over filling and press edges together firmly to seal. Lay on lightly floured 12- by 15-inch baking sheets and cover with plastic wrap to prevent drying. Repeat until all filling is used, placing filled wrappers slightly apart. If made ahead, chill up to 4 hours.

In a 5- to 6-quart pan, bring 3 quarts water to a boil over high heat. While water heats, melt butter with ¹⁄₄ cup lemon juice (in microwave oven or over direct heat). Pit, peel, and halve or slice avocados; sprinkle with remaining lemon juice.

Add pasta to boiling water and cook, uncovered, until just tender to bite, about 2 minutes. Gently drain pasta, then return to pan and place over low heat. At once, add lemon butter and mix gently. Divide pasta among 6 dinner plates. Sprinkle with remaining onion. Place an avocado half (or slices) on each plate. Offer lemon wedges to squeeze onto pasta. Makes 6 servings.

PER SERVING: 428 calories, 22 g protein, 43 g carbohydrates, 20 g fat, 131 mg cholesterol, 415 mg sodium

CANDY-WRAP PASTA WITH CHEESE & BLACK BEAN SAUCE

- 8 **ounces feta cheese**
- 8 **ounces part-skim ricotta cheese**
- ¹⁄₂ **cup firmly packed fresh cilantro (coriander)**
- 2 **tablespoons milk**
- 2 **tablespoons grated parmesan cheese**
- 18 **eggroll (springroll) wrappers**
- 2 **tablespoons all-purpose flour mixed with ¹⁄₄ cup water**
  Black bean sauce (recipe follows)

In a food processor or blender, smoothly whirl feta with ricotta, ¹⁄₃ cup cilantro, milk, and parmesan. Lay 1 wrapper flat. Place 1 heaping tablespoon cheese mixture in center along edge of 1 side (a narrow side if rectangular). Pat cheese into log shape about ³⁄₄ inch wide and 1¹⁄₂ inches long. With a finger, lightly rub flour paste along each side of filling to opposite edge of wrapper. Also rub paste along edge opposite filling.

Starting at edge with the cheese, gently roll up the wrapper and press edge to seal. Firmly squeeze dough together at both ends of the filling where flour paste is painted, making the pasta look like a candy twisted in paper. Lay pasta on lightly floured 12- by 15-inch baking sheets. Cover with plastic wrap to prevent drying. Repeat to use all filling. If made ahead, cover and chill up to 4 hours. Or freeze on pan until solid, then transfer to containers to freeze up to 1 month.

Chop remaining cilantro; set aside.

In a deep 10- to 12-inch frying pan, bring about 2 inches water to boiling over high heat. Reduce heat to maintain a gentle boil. Carefully add about half the pasta to water and cook, uncovered, just until pasta is tender to bite, 2 to 3 minutes (5 to 6 if frozen). Lift out with a slotted spoon and lay in a single layer on a clean baking sheet; keep warm. Cook remaining pasta.

Quickly spoon sauce evenly on 6 rimmed plates. Arrange pasta equally onto plates; sprinkle with cilantro. Makes 6 servings.

PER SERVING: 474 calories, 25 g protein, 48 g carbohydrates, 14 g fat, 52 mg cholesterol, 827 mg sodium

Black bean sauce. In an 8- to 10-inch frying pan over medium heat, stir often 1 tablespoon **butter** or margarine and 1 small, chopped **onion** until onion is lightly browned, about 8 minutes. Put onion in a food processor or blender with 1 can (about 15 oz.) **black beans** and liquid, and 1 cup **regular-strength chicken broth.** Whirl smooth. Pour into a 1¹⁄₂- to 2-quart pan; add **salt** and **pepper** to taste. If made ahead, cover and chill up until next day. Stir over medium heat until hot; use hot.

Half-moon shrimp pasta goes with avocado, cheese pasta with black bean sauce. Purchased eggroll wrappers and gyoza skins speed up preparation time.

Lightening Up Sunset Classics: Three Satisfying Choices

As WE CONTINUE TO EXPLORE *ways to lighten up Sunset's long-time favorite recipes, we seek flavorful alternatives for steps where fat is used. Trimming down three challenging choices—a pub pie, an oil-and-vinegar dressing, and a buttery fruit sauce—produced these results.*

TURKEY, KIDNEY & OYSTER PIE

Turkey replaces beef; all butter browning is omitted. The fat-free sauce gets its rich flavor and color from braised-deglazed vegetables. Half as much pastry is used (made with less than half the fat).

- 1 **large (¹/₂ lb.) onion, finely chopped**
- ¹/₂ **pound mushrooms, rinsed and cut into about ¹/₂-inch-thick pieces**
- 1 **teaspoon dry thyme leaves**
- ¹/₂ **teaspoon pepper**
- 2¹/₂ **cups regular-strength chicken broth**
- 3 **tablespoons balsamic vinegar**
- 4 **tablespoons cornstarch**
- 2 **lamb kidneys (¹/₄ lb.)**
- 1¹/₂ **pounds boneless, skinless turkey breast fillets**
- 1 **can (8 oz.) small oysters**
- ¹/₂ **cup minced parsley**
  Pastry (directions follow)
  Salt

Pub pie, pine nut salad, and pears with orange sauce make light, handsome menu.

In a 10- to 12-inch nonstick frying pan, combine onion, mushrooms, thyme, pepper, and 1 cup broth. Boil on high heat, uncovered, until liquid evaporates; stir occasionally. When browned bits accumulate in pan, add 2 tablespoons water and stir to release; boil until mixture begins to brown again. Repeat this deglazing step until onions are a rich, dark brown. Add vinegar; boil until evaporated. Blend 1¹/₂ cups broth with 3 tablespoons cornstarch. Mix into pan; stir until boiling. Set aside.

Cut kidneys in half lengthwise; trim out and discard tubes and fat. Rinse kidneys and slice thin. Cut turkey across the grain into about ¹/₄-inch-wide slices. If made ahead, cover and chill meats and sauce separately until the next day. Blend smooth remaining 1 tablespoon cornstarch and juice drained from oysters; mix with kidneys, turkey, and parsley, then stir mixture into sauce. Pour into a shallow oval or rectangular casserole about 9 by 12 inches. Scatter oysters over filling, then gently push down into sauce.

Roll pastry out on a floured board until about 1 inch longer and wider than casserole. Cut pastry into ³/₄-inch-wide strips. Weave as a lattice on the filling; trim ends, reroll scraps, cut strips, and crimp on casserole rim to anchor lattice in place.

Bake, uncovered, in a 400° oven until pastry is browned and filling is bubbling, 40 to 45 minutes. Scoop into wide bowls; add salt to taste. Makes 8 or 9 servings.

PER SERVING REVISED PIE: 265 calories, 26 g protein, 16 g carbohydrates, 9.2 g fat, 107 mg cholesterol, 204 mg sodium

PER SERVING ORIGINAL BEEFSTEAK, KIDNEY, AND OYSTER PIE (MARCH 1977, PAGE 182): 533 calories, 28 g protein, 28 g carbohydrates, 34 g fat, 242 mg cholesterol, 361 mg sodium

Pastry. In a bowl, stir together 1¹/₄ cups **all-purpose flour,** ¹/₂ teaspoon **baking powder,** and ¹/₄ teaspoon **salt.** Beat to blend 1 **large egg white,** 2 tablespoons **water,** and ¹/₄ cup **olive** or salad **oil.** Stir into flour until dough holds together. Pat into a ball. If made ahead, cover and chill up until next day. Use at room temperature.

PINE NUT SALAD DRESSING

Nuts give a rich flavor to this dressing, a favorite on tender spinach. We've cut out ¹/₂ cup salad oil and ²/₃ of the nuts.

- ¹/₄ **cup pine nuts**
- 1 **teaspoon arrowroot**
- ¹/₂ **teaspoon dry tarragon leaves**
- ¹/₄ **teaspoon grated lemon peel**
- ¹/₈ **teaspoon ground nutmeg**
- ²/₃ **cup water**
- ¹/₃ **cup seasoned rice vinegar (or rice vinegar plus 1 teaspoon sugar)**

In a 6- or 7-inch frying pan, stir nuts over medium heat until golden. Pour from pan. To pan add arrowroot, tarragon, lemon peel, and nutmeg; blend in water until smooth. Stir until boiling. Chill until mixture is cold, about 45 minutes; if made ahead, cover and chill up until next day. Add vinegar and nuts. Makes 1 cup.

PER TABLESPOON REVISED DRESSING: 17 calories, 0.5 g protein, 1.7 g carbohydrates, 1.1 g fat, 0 mg cholesterol, 1 mg sodium

PER TABLESPOON ORIGINAL PINE NUT DRESSING (JANUARY 1967, PAGE 103): 59 calories, 1 g protein, 0.8 g carbohydrates, 6.3 g fat, 0 mg cholesterol, 42 mg sodium

PEAR FANS WITH ORANGE SYRUP

We deleted ¹/₄ cup each sugar and butter.

- ¹/₄ **cup sugar**
- 1¹/₂ **cups orange juice**
- 2 **teaspoons finely shredded orange peel**
- 1 **teaspoon arrowroot**
- 3 **medium-size firm-ripe red or golden pears**
- 2 **tablespoons lemon juice**

In a 2- to 3-quart pan over high heat, combine sugar, 1 cup orange juice, and peel. Boil, uncovered, until juice is almost gone; *do not scorch.* Dilute arrowroot with remaining juice. Stir into pan; heat until boiling. Serve hot, warm, or cool.

Cut pears in half lengthwise. Core and trim out stem and blossom ends; rub with some of lemon juice. Lay fruit cut side down and, from blossom end, slice each pear half into ¹/₄-inch-wide strips, keeping stem end intact. Drizzle cuts with lemon juice.

With a wide spatula, transfer fruit, flat side down, to dessert plates. With your palm, lightly press cut portion of fruit down and away from you to fan slices. Spoon syrup over fruit. Makes 6 servings.

PER SERVING REVISED PEAR FAN: 98 calories, 0.7 g protein, 25 g carbohydrates, 0.3 g fat, 0 mg cholesterol, 1.8 mg sodium

PER SERVING ORIGINAL PEAR FAN (SEPTEMBER 1983, PAGE 86): 177 calories, 0.5 g protein, 28 g carbohydrates, 7.9 g fat, 21 mg cholesterol, 80 mg sodium

Simple & Savory Soups from the Far East

ASIAN PEOPLES *eat rice all day long in many different forms. A favorite for breakfast or a late-night snack is a soup based on rice. These simple, savory soups are also delicious for supper.*

In the Chinese version, rice simmers in broth until it falls apart, imparting creaminess and thickness. Pour the hot soup over thin slices of raw fish; the soup's heat gently cooks the fish. Lettuce shreds and seasonings add texture and flavor.

A faster version, from Thailand, starts with leftover cooked rice or raw long-grain rice. Cook the rice in broth just until tender, then add ground pork, green onion, and cilantro. Condiments of garlic oil and a chili sauce enliven the soup.

CHINESE CREAMY RICE SOUP
(Jook)

- 8 **cups regular-strength chicken broth**
- 3/4 **cup short- or medium-grain white rice**
- 6 **thin slices (each about the size of a quarter) fresh ginger**
- 1/2 **pound boned and skinned lean white-flesh fish such as rockfish, cut into very thin slices**
- 2 **tablespoons dry sherry**
  Soy sauce
- 1 **tablespoon Oriental sesame oil**
- 2 **cups (about 6 oz.) finely shredded iceberg lettuce**
- 1/2 **cup fresh cilantro (coriander) leaves**
- 2 **tablespoons finely shredded fresh ginger**
  White pepper

In a 3- to 4-quart pan, combine the broth, rice, and sliced ginger. Bring to a boil; cover and simmer, stirring occasionally, until rice almost disintegrates, 1½ to 2 hours. If soup becomes so thick it starts to stick to the bottom of the pan, add a little water. Discard ginger slices, if desired.

Mix together the fish, sherry, 1 tablespoon soy sauce, and sesame oil. In each of 6 bowls, place an equal portion of fish mixture. Ladle simmering rice soup over fish. (Or, if you prefer, stir marinated fish slices into hot soup in pan and cook until fish turns opaque; ladle into bowls.) Sprinkle equal portions of lettuce, cilantro, and shredded

Ladle simmering rice soup over thinly sliced raw fish in bowl to cook gently. Add iceberg lettuce shreds, fresh ginger, soy sauce, cilantro, and white pepper to season.

ginger onto each serving. Offer additional soy sauce and white pepper to add to taste. Makes 6 servings.

PER SERVING: 197 calories, 12 g protein, 24 g carbohydrates, 5.1 g fat, 13 mg cholesterol, 269 mg sodium

THAI RICE SOUP
(Kao Tom)

Instead of the raw rice, you can use 3 cups cooked rice. Omit the water and bring the broth, cooked rice, and ginger to a boil, then add pork and continue as directed.

- 6 **cups regular-strength chicken broth**
- 2 **cups water**
- 1 **cup long-grain white rice**
- 1 **tablespoon minced fresh ginger**
- 1 **pound ground lean pork**
- 1/2 **cup thinly sliced green onion**
- 1/3 **cup chopped fresh cilantro (coriander)**
- 1/4 **teaspoon pepper**
  Fish sauce (nam pla or nuoc mam) or soy sauce
- 4 **to 6 medium-size eggs (optional)**
  Garlic oil (recipe follows)
  Chili sauce (recipe follows)

In a 5- to 6-quart pan, combine broth, water, rice, and ginger; bring to a boil. Reduce heat; cover and simmer, stirring occasionally, until rice is tender to bite,

occasionally, until rice is tender to bite, about 20 minutes. Crumble pork into broth; simmer, uncovered, until meat is no longer pink, about 5 minutes. Skim off and discard fat. Stir in onion and cilantro. Add pepper and fish sauce to taste.

If desired, break an egg into each serving bowl. Ladle simmering soup into bowls. Each diner can stir egg into soup; residual heat in the soup gently cooks egg. Offer garlic oil and chili sauce to add to taste. Makes 4 to 6 servings.

PER SERVING: 271 calories, 19 g protein, 27 g carbohydrates, 8.7 g fat, 52 mg cholesterol, 109 mg sodium

Garlic oil. In a 6- to 8-inch frying pan, cook 2 tablespoons minced **garlic** in 1/3 cup **salad oil** over low heat, shaking pan often, just until garlic is light gold and crisp, about 5 minutes. Use warm or cool. Makes about 6 tablespoons.

PER TABLESPOON: 111 calories, 0.2 g protein, 1.1 g carbohydrates, 12 g fat, 0 mg cholesterol, 0.6 mg sodium

Chili sauce. Mix 3 tablespoons **fish sauce** (*nam pla* or *nuoc mam*) or soy sauce, 2 tablespoons **lime juice,** and 1 tablespoon minced **fresh hot chili.** Makes 1/4 cup.

PER TABLESPOON: 31 calories, 8.9 g protein, 2.9 g carbohydrates, 1.3 g fat, 0 mg cholesterol, 1.4 mg sodium

Oven-roasting a Pot Roast

OVEN-ROASTING *is the easy way to a juicy and flavorful pot roast, especially when you brown a collection of root vegetables in the oven at the same time. As the heat draws out the vegetables' moisture, the roots' naturally sweet flavors intensify.*

NEW-FASHIONED POT ROAST

About ⅓ cup all-purpose flour
2 teaspoons coarse-ground pepper
1 boned beef chuck roast (4½ to 5 lb.), rolled and tied
½ cup (¼ lb.) butter or margarine
6 tablespoons olive or salad oil
1½ pounds (about 6 large) carrots, peeled
2 large (1 lb. total) onions, chopped
2 cups regular-strength beef broth

2 cups dry red wine
2 dry bay leaves
4 fresh thyme sprigs (about 3 in. long), or 1 teaspoon dry thyme leaves
1 pound (about 4 medium-size) parsnips, peeled and cut into ⅜-inch-thick sticks
1½ pounds (about 4 medium-size) beets, peeled and cut into ⅜-inch-thick sticks
1½ pounds (about 4 medium-size) turnips, peeled and cut into ⅜-inch-thick sticks
1 pound (about 2 medium-size) rutabagas, peeled and cut into ⅜-inch-thick sticks
¾ pound (about 2 medium-size) thin-skinned potatoes, scrubbed and cut into ⅜-inch-thick sticks
Parsley sprigs (optional)
Salt and pepper

Mix 2 tablespoons flour with pepper; pat over meat. In a 500° oven, melt 2 tablespoons butter with 3 tablespoons oil in a pan about 10 by 14 inches and 2 inches deep. Bake meat in pan, turning to brown evenly, about 12 minutes.

Chop 2 carrots; mix with onion in pan. Bake until vegetables are limp, about 10 minutes. Add broth, wine, bay leaf, and thyme. Cover tightly with foil. Reduce heat to 350°; bake until meat is tender when pierced, about 2½ hours. After 1 hour, turn meat over.

Meanwhile, in a 12- by 17-inch pan, or in 2 pans, each 10 by 15 inches, mix the remaining oil and 2 tablespoons butter (if using 2 pans, divide equally). Cut the remaining carrots into ⅜-inch-thick sticks. In pan, mix the carrots, parsnips, beets, turnips, rutabagas, and potatoes.

If using 1 pan, place in oven after roast has cooked 1 hour; turn vegetables with wide spatula every 15 to 20 minutes until tinged with brown, about 1½ hours. For 2 pans, bake in sequence; combine to finish. Put 1 batch in with roast when oven is turned to 350°; bake 1¼ hours. Remove and add second batch; bake 1¼ hours. When roast is done, combine vegetables in 1 pan and bake in 450° oven until vegetables are tinged with brown, about 20 minutes. Keep warm until meat is ready.

Transfer roast to a large platter and keep warm. Pour juices through a fine strainer into bowl; discard residue. Skim and discard fat from juices; measure juices. If more than 4 cups, boil down to this amount over high heat in roasting pan; if less, add water to make 4 cups. Pour juices into the measure and set aside.

In roasting pan, melt remaining ¼ cup butter over medium heat. Add 3 tablespoons flour and stir until bubbling; remove from heat. With a whisk, smoothly mix in reserved juices. On high heat, stir until gravy boils rapidly; pour into a small bowl. Spoon vegetables around meat; snip and pull off string. Moisten with a little gravy. Garnish with parsley. Serve meat and vegetables with gravy, salt, and pepper to taste. Makes 9 or 10 servings.
—*Bradley Ogden, Larkspur, Calif.*

PER SERVING: 533 calories, 40 g protein, 38 g carbohydrates, 25 g fat, 123 mg cholesterol, 315 mg sodium

Spoon rich, brown gravy over tender, oven-cooked pot roast slices and root vegetables. Parsnips, carrots, potatoes, turnips, rutabagas, and beets are good partners for roast.

Sichuan Pickles

I**N THE USUAL** *vinegary sense, these aren't pickles. They're fresh vegetables that draw their spicy flavor as well as a crunchy texture from soaking in a seasoned brine. If you want tartness, sprinkle with vinegar.*

Unlike typical pickles, Sichuan pickles are best eaten within a week. Serve as you would any pickles, or try them in these hearty Chinese dishes.

Daikon is available in supermarkets; you may have to shop at an Oriental market for the fragrant Sichuan peppercorns.

SICHUAN PICKLES

- 1 **pound napa cabbage, stem end trimmed**
- 1 **daikon (Oriental radish), about 8 inches long and 1½ to 2 inches in diameter, peeled and cut in half lengthwise**
- 2 **medium-size cucumbers, cut in half lengthwise, seeds removed**
- 2 **large carrots, peeled**
- 4 **cups water**
- 2 **tablespoons salt**
- 2 **tablespoons thinly sliced fresh ginger**
- 3 **cloves garlic, crushed**
- 1 **teaspoon Sichuan peppercorns or black peppercorns, crushed**
- ½ **to 1 teaspoon crushed dried hot red chilies**

Cut cabbage crosswise into ½-inch-thick slices. Cut daikon, cucumbers, and carrots into ⅛-inch-thick slices. Combine the cabbage, daikon, cucumbers, and carrots and mix well. Firmly pack vegetables into a 1-gallon jar or bowl.

In a 2- to 3-quart pan over high heat, bring water to a boil. Remove from heat; add salt, ginger, garlic, peppercorns, and chilies. Stir to dissolve salt. Cool to room temperature; pour over vegetables. Cover and chill overnight, then serve. To store, put pickles into 2 jars (1-qt. size), pressing down to fill compactly; cover with liquid.

Cover the jars with lids and chill up to 1 week. Makes 2 quarts.—*Rose Brosseau, Coupeville, Wash.*

PER ¼-CUP SERVING: 9.5 calories, 0.4 g protein, 2.1 g carbohydrates, 0 g fat, 0 mg cholesterol, 418 mg sodium

STEAMED PORK WITH SICHUAN PICKLES

- 2 **tablespoons dry sherry**
- 1 **tablespoon soy sauce**
- ½ **teaspoon pepper**
- 2 **green onions, thinly sliced**
- 1 **pound boneless pork such as shoulder or butt**
- 1 **teaspoon Oriental sesame oil (optional)**
  Salt
- ½ **cup Sichuan pickles (recipe precedes)**

In a shallow 8- to 9-inch rimmed serving dish or pie pan, mix sherry with soy, pepper, and half of the sliced onions.

Trim and discard excess fat from pork; cut meat into thin strips about 1 by 3 inches. Add to sherry mixture and stir to mix well.

In a 5- to 6-quart pan (at least 9 in. wide) with lid, position a rack about 1 inch above the bottom. Add water to pan almost up to the rack. Bring water to a boil on high heat. Set dish of meat on rack and lay a piece of foil on dish, covering it completely. Cover pan and boil gently until meat in center of dish is no longer pink (cut to test), about 40 minutes. Add boiling water to the pan as needed to maintain the water level.

(Or put covered dish of meat in a bamboo steamer basket, cover, and cook over gently boiling water.)

Sprinkle meat with sesame oil, remaining green onions, and salt to taste. Mound Sichuan pickles on pork, or serve to accompany the meat. Makes 3 or 4 servings.

PER SERVING: 325 calories, 19 g protein, 2.9 g carbohydrates, 26 g fat, 82 mg cholesterol, 608 mg sodium

Peppery-cool crunch of pickled vegetables perks up soy-seasoned steamed pork.

Crisp refrigerator pickles are easy to make: you pack sliced cucumber, cabbage, daikon, and carrot into a jar of salt water seasoned with ginger, garlic, peppercorns, and chilies.

BARLEY SOUP WITH SICHUAN PICKLES

- 1 **tablespoon salad oil**
- ½ **pound boneless lean beef such as chuck or bottom round, cut into thin strips about 3 inches long**
- 1 **small onion, chopped**
- 2 **cloves garlic, pressed or minced**
- 6 **cups regular-strength beef broth**
- ½ **cup pearl barley, rinsed**
- 1 **bay leaf**
- ⅓ **cup sliced green onions**
  About 1½ cups Sichuan pickles (recipe precedes)

Pour oil into a 4- to 5-quart pan over medium-high heat. Add beef and cook, stirring occasionally, until beef is lightly browned, about 5 minutes. Add onion and garlic and stir often until onion is limp but not browned, about 3 minutes.

Add broth, barley, and bay leaf; bring to a boil. Reduce heat, cover, and simmer until barley is tender, about 40 minutes. Pour soup into a tureen; stir in green onions. Serve with Sichuan pickles to add to taste. Makes 5 or 6 servings.

PER SERVING: 174 calories, 10 g protein, 18 g carbohydrates, 6.8 g fat, 25 mg cholesterol, 454 mg sodium

Bell Pepper or Onion Soufflé

SHINY BELL PEPPERS *and aromatic* onions *make handsome containers for individual soufflés. The pepper soufflé has polenta and jack cheese. The onion wells hold a sweet onion puff. These airy creations are well suited to brunch or a light supper.*

SPICED BELL PEPPER SOUFFLÉS

Rather than elongated peppers, choose squarish ones that stand upright.

- 4 **large (6 to 7 oz. each) red, yellow, or green bell peppers**
- 3 **tablespoons minced, seeded fresh jalapeño chilies**
- 2 **teaspoons dry oregano leaves**
- 3 **tablespoons butter or margarine**
- ¼ **cup polenta or cornmeal**
- 1 **cup milk**
- ¾ **cup shredded jack or cheddar cheese**
- 3 **large egg yolks**
- 4 **large egg whites**
  Salt

If peppers tip when set on their bottoms, trim a thin sliver from base (without piercing wall) so they sit solidly. Cut off tops about ½ inch below bottom of stems. Seed peppers, rinse, then set upright in a 9- by 13-inch pan. Trim stem from tops and chop the pepper scraps.

In a 2- to 3-quart pan over medium-high heat, frequently stir chopped peppers, chilies, and oregano in butter until vegetables are limp, about 10 minutes. Add polenta; stir 1 minute. Add milk. Stirring, bring sauce to a boil and simmer for 5 minutes. Remove from heat; add cheese and stir until melted, then stir in egg yolks. If made ahead, cover and chill until next day. Reheat to simmering, stirring.

In a deep bowl, whip egg whites with a mixer until they hold firm, moist peaks. Stir about ¼ of whites into sauce, then fold all of sauce into whites.

Gently pile soufflé into peppers. Bake, uncovered, in a 375° oven until soufflés are well browned and puffed, 35 to 40 minutes. Season with salt to taste. Makes 4 servings.

PER SERVING: 324 calories, 15 g protein, 19 g carbohydrates, 22 g fat, 210 mg cholesterol, 296 mg sodium

Crusted soufflé rises dramatically above golden bell pepper. Filling contains polenta and jack cheese seasoned with oregano and fresh jalapeño chilies.

ONION SOUFFLÉS IN ONION CUPS

- 4 **large (about 10 oz. each) onions**
- 2 **tablespoons balsamic or red wine vinegar**
- 2 **teaspoons sugar**
- 2 **tablespoons butter or margarine**
- 2 **tablespoons all-purpose flour**
- ¾ **cup milk**
- ½ **cup grated parmesan cheese**
- 2 **large eggs, separated**
  Salt and pepper

Halve onions horizontally, then trim rounded ends to sit flat. Place onions, cut side up, in a 9- by 13-inch pan. Spoon vinegar evenly over cut surfaces; sprinkle with sugar. Cover with foil and bake in a 350° oven until very tender when pierced, about 1 hour. Let stand in pan until cool enough to handle. If made ahead, cover and chill up until next day.

Pull centers from onions, leaving a ⅛-inch shell (it's all right if there's a hole in the bottom). Finely chop centers.

In a 3- to 4-quart pan, melt butter over medium-high heat. Add chopped onion; stir often until very limp, about 10 minutes. Add flour and stir for 1 minute. Add milk, stirring until sauce boils rapidly. Remove from heat; mix in cheese, then egg yolks. If made ahead, cover everything and chill up until next day. Reheat sauce to simmering, stirring frequently.

In a deep bowl, whip egg whites with a mixer until they hold firm, moist peaks. Stir about ¼ of whites into sauce, then fold all of sauce into whites.

Gently pile soufflé mixture into onion shells. Bake, uncovered, in a 375° oven until soufflés are well browned and puffed, about 35 minutes. Transfer with a wide spatula to plates. Season with salt and pepper. Makes 4 servings.

PER SERVING: 281 calories, 13 g protein, 29 g carbohydrates, 14 g fat, 136 mg cholesterol, 304 mg sodium

More March Recipes

OTHER MARCH ARTICLES *feature a shrimp curry cooked in the microwave oven and chocolate chip cookies to present as a gift.*

MICROWAVE SHRIMP CURRY

The good cook further simplifies this easy microwave curry by making it in the serving bowl.

- 2 tablespoons butter or margarine
- 1/2 cup *each* chopped celery and green onion
- 1 clove garlic, minced or pressed
- 1 teaspoon minced fresh ginger
- 2 tablespoons all-purpose flour
- 1 tablespoon curry powder
- 1/8 teaspoon cayenne
- 2/3 cup half-and-half (light cream) or milk
- 1/3 cup dry sherry or regular-strength chicken broth
- 1 pound medium-size shrimp (31 to 35 per lb.), peeled and deveined
  Hot cooked rice
  Condiments (suggestions follow)

Place butter in a 1- to 1½-quart microwave-safe bowl. Heat in a microwave oven on full power (100 percent) until melted, about 1 minute. Stir in celery, onion, garlic, and ginger; cook, uncovered, until vegetables are soft, 4 to 5 minutes. Stir in flour, curry, and cayenne; cook at full power 1 minute.

Smoothly stir half-and-half and sherry into flour mixture. Cook on full power for 2 minutes; stir, then cook until boiling, 2 to 3 more minutes. Add shrimp, cook 2 minutes, stir, then cook until shrimp are just opaque in thickest part (cut to test), 3 to 4 minutes. Spoon curry onto rice; add condiments to taste. Makes 4 servings.—*Russell Crawford, Fairfield, Calif.*

PER SERVING WITHOUT RICE AND CONDIMENTS: 236 calories, 21 g protein, 10 g carbohydrates, 12 g fat, 170 mg cholesterol, 228 mg sodium

Condiments. Offer 1 or all of the following: 1/4 cup **salted cashews,** 1/4 cup **raisins,** 1/4 cup thinly sliced **green onion.**

CHOCOLATE CHIP COOKIES ON A STEM

Why bake cookies on a stick? For no reason but fun, and to give them a festive look. Presented in a florist's box, they're bound to evoke a smile.

- 1 cup (½ lb.) butter or margarine, at room temperature
- 3/4 cup firmly packed brown sugar
- 3/4 cup granulated sugar
- 1 large egg
- 2 teaspoons vanilla
- 2 cups all-purpose flour
- 1 teaspoon baking soda
- 1/2 teaspoon baking powder
- 2 1/3 cups quick-cooking rolled oats
- 12 ounces semisweet chocolate, or 6 ounces *each* semisweet and white chocolate, coarsely chopped
- 24 pieces hardwood dowel (sold in home centers and lumberyards), 1/4 inch in diameter and cut about 12 inches long

In a bowl, cream butter and brown and granulated sugars with a mixer. Beat in egg and vanilla. Mix together flour, baking soda, baking powder, and oats. Blend with butter mixture. Stir in chocolate.

Shape dough into 24 walnut-size balls. Assemble 1 at a time on an oiled 12- by 15-inch baking sheet. Set ball at 1 of the narrow ends, insert a dowel into center of ball, then pat dough into 2½-inch round; keep dowel in center of round and covered by dough. Repeat, placing rounds about 2 inches apart. At opposite end of sheet, center dough between dowels (see top right). A pan holds 5 or 6 cookies. Keep dough covered until ready to shape.

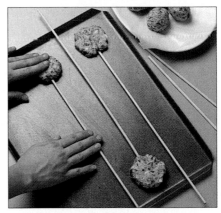

Gently flatten cooky dough around dowel, making sure wood is completely covered.

Deliver a bouquet of long-stemmed cookies in see-through florist's box.

Bake cookies in a 375° oven until golden brown, about 15 minutes (if using 1 oven, alternate pan positions after 8 minutes). Slide a spatula under each cooky to release from pan; leave in place for 5 minutes. Then carefully lay cookies with dowels flat on racks (supported the full length on racks of equal height) until cool.

To wrap, enclose each cooky with plastic wrap and tie wrap to dowel with a ribbon (green for "leaves") to keep cooky airtight. Serve, or store wrapped cookies up to 3 days at room temperature. Freeze to store longer. Makes about 24.

PER COOKY: 262 calories, 3.3 g protein, 34 g carbohydrates, 13 g fat, 29 mg cholesterol, 126 mg sodium

Spoon spicy, golden shrimp curry, cooked quickly in the microwave, over hot steamed rice; garnish with cashews.

SUMMER-WINTER PEACH COFFEE CAKE

- 6 medium-size (about 2¼ lb.) fresh firm-ripe peaches, peeled, pitted, and halved; or 2 cans (16 oz. each) peach halves in light syrup, drained
- 1 small package (3 oz.) cream cheese
- ⅔ cup sugar
- 6 tablespoons butter or margarine
- 1 large egg
- ½ teaspoon almond extract
- 1½ cups all-purpose flour
- 1 teaspoon baking soda
- 1 teaspoon baking powder
- 2 tablespoons finely chopped almonds
- 1 teaspoon ground cinnamon

Top cake with fresh peaches (this month, from the Southern Hemisphere) or canned fruit.

In a food processor or blender, whirl 3 peach halves, cheese, ½ cup sugar, 5 tablespoons butter, egg, and extract until smooth. Mix flour, soda, and baking powder and add to batter; whirl to blend. Pour into a buttered 9-inch-wide cake pan with removable rim.

Lay remaining peaches, cut side down, on batter; dot with 1 tablespoon butter. Sprinkle remaining sugar, nuts, and cinnamon over fruit. Bake in a 350° oven until cake is well browned and pulls from pan sides, 45 to 60 minutes. Serve warm or cool; remove pan rim. Makes 8 servings.—*Patricia Sigmen, Tacoma.*

PER SERVING: 314 calories, 4.9 g protein, 43 g carbohydrates, 14 g fat, 61 mg cholesterol, 284 mg sodium

ZUCCHINI BURGERS

- 1½ pounds zucchini, ends trimmed, coarsely shredded
- 2 tablespoons butter or margarine
- 1 large (about ½ lb.) onion, finely chopped
- ¼ cup fine dry bread crumbs
- 2 large eggs
- ¼ cup grated parmesan cheese
- 6 onion-flavor bagels, split and toasted
  Tartar sauce or catsup

Drain zucchini in a colander for 30 minutes; squeeze to remove moisture.

Meanwhile, in a 10- to 12-inch nonstick frying pan over medium heat, stir 2

Gold-green zucchini cakes fill bagels to make hearty sandwiches.

teaspoons butter with onion often until onion is lightly browned, about 15 minutes. In a bowl, mix the onion, zucchini, crumbs, eggs, and cheese.

In pan, melt remaining butter over medium-high heat. Ladle 3 mounds zucchini mixture, each about ¼-cup size, into pan, spreading to make 3-inch-wide cakes. Cook until bottoms are lightly browned, about 3 minutes. With a wide spatula, turn cakes over and brown bottoms, about 3 minutes; keep warm. Repeat to cook remaining zucchini. Serve cakes on bagels, and season with tartar sauce to taste. Makes 6 servings. —*Val Gehrisch, San Diego.*

PER SERVING: 278 calories, 13 g protein, 40 g carbohydrates, 7.9 g fat, 84 mg cholesterol, 476 mg sodium

RED & BLUE DRESSING

- 2 tablespoons extra-virgin olive oil or salad oil
- ¼ cup red wine vinegar
- 1 tablespoon catsup
- 1 teaspoon sugar
- ½ teaspoon Worcestershire sauce
- ¼ teaspoon liquid hot pepper seasoning
- ⅔ cup crumbled Roquefort or other blue cheese
  Crisped salad greens

In a bowl, mix oil, vinegar, catsup, sugar, Worcestershire sauce, hot pepper seasoning, and cheese.

Blue cheese in red-hued dressing goes on salad or makes a dip.

Serve or, if made ahead, cover and chill up to 2 days. Stir just before using. Spoon over salad greens. Makes 1 cup.— *Romaine Hon, Boise.*

PER TABLESPOON DRESSING: 37 calories, 1.2 g protein, 0.8 g carbohydrates, 3.4 g fat, 4.8 mg cholesterol, 111 mg sodium

Red Roquefort dip. Stir or whirl **dressing** (preceding) in a blender with 1 cup **low-fat** or nonfat **cottage cheese.** Serve or, if made ahead, cover and chill up to 2 days. Offer as a dip for **carrot sticks, celery, broccoli flowerets,** and **cauliflowerets.** Makes 1½ cups.

PER TABLESPOON DIP: 32 calories, 1.9 g protein, 0.8 g carbohydrates, 2.4 g fat, 3.6 mg cholesterol, 112 mg sodium

Spinach with Sesame & Garlic

1½ tablespoons sesame seed
1 tablespoon seasoned rice vinegar (or 1 tablespoon rice vinegar and ½ teaspoon sugar)
2 teaspoons soy sauce
1 tablespoon Oriental sesame oil or salad oil
3 large cloves garlic, minced
1½ pounds spinach, roots trimmed and yellowed leaves discarded; leaves rinsed, drained, coarsely chopped

Place seed in a 5- to 6-quart pan over medium-high heat. Shake pan often until seed is lightly browned, about 7 minutes. Pour from pan and set aside. Mix vinegar and soy sauce; set aside.

In the pan over low heat, combine sesame oil and garlic. Stir often until garlic is barely golden, about 4 minutes; take care not to scorch. Add spinach. Turn heat to high and stir until leaves wilt and most of liquid has evaporated, 4 to 5 minutes. With a slotted spoon, transfer spinach to a platter. Sprinkle with sesame seed and drizzle with vinegar-soy mixture. Makes 4 servings.— *Rhonda Gee, Arrowbear, Calif.*

Per Serving: 88 calories, 4.7 g protein, 7.5 g carbohydrates, 5.5 g fat, 0 mg cholesterol, 612 mg sodium

Tender leaves of quick-cooking spinach get Japanese-style seasoning.

Snowy Day Stew

1½ pounds ground lean beef
1 large egg
¼ cup seasoned fine dry bread crumbs
2 teaspoons dry thyme leaves
1 tablespoon olive or salad oil
1 small onion, chopped
¾ pound mushrooms, sliced
2 medium-size (about ⅓ lb. total) carrots, peeled
1 to 1¼ pounds thin-skinned potatoes, scrubbed
1 can (14 oz.) stewed tomatoes
1 cup regular-strength beef broth
½ cup dry red wine
1 package (10 oz.) frozen peas
Salt

Mix beef, egg, crumbs, and 1 teaspoon thyme. Shape into 30 equal-size balls.

Pour oil into a 4- to 5-quart pan over medium-high heat. Add remaining thyme, onion, and mushrooms; stir often until vegetables are well browned, about 20 minutes. Cut carrots and potatoes into chunks; add to pan with tomatoes and their liquid, broth, and wine. Bring to a boil; add meatballs. Cover and simmer until potatoes are tender when pierced, about 35 minutes. Stir in peas; heat through. Add salt to taste. Serves 6.—*Toby Rubel, Golden, Colo.*

Per Serving: 510 calories, 28 g protein, 37 g carbohydrates, 27 g fat, 121 mg cholesterol, 465 mg sodium

Meatballs poach in stew among colorful chunks of vegetables.

Triple Ginger Cake

2¼ cups all-purpose flour
2 teaspoons baking powder
1 teaspoon ground ginger
¾ cup (⅜ lb.) butter or margarine
2 cups sugar
1 cup ginger ale or water
4 large egg whites
Frosting (recipe follows)
½ cup finely chopped crystallized ginger

Mix flour, baking powder, and ground ginger. In a bowl, beat butter and sugar until fluffy. Add flour mixture and ginger ale; stir until evenly moistened. In deep bowl, whip whites on high speed until they hold stiff, moist peaks. Gently fold whites into batter.

Divide batter between 2 greased and flour-dusted 9-inch-diameter cake pans. Bake in a 350° oven until cake springs back when lightly pressed in center, about 35 minutes. Invert onto racks to cool. Spread layer tops with frosting. Set 1 layer on the other; sprinkle with chopped ginger. Makes 8 to 10 servings.—*Joanne Eglash, Sunnyvale, Calif.*

Per Serving: 438 calories, 4.5 g protein, 75 g carbohydrates, 14 g fat, 37 mg cholesterol, 258 mg sodium

Frosting. Beat together 1 large package (8 oz.) **cream cheese,** ¼ cup (⅛ lb.) **butter** or margarine, 2 cups **powdered sugar,** and ½ cup minced **crystallized ginger.**

Three kinds of ginger flavor this old-fashioned layer cake.

LEGEND HAS IT *that the sandwich was invented by the Fourth Earl of Sandwich, an inveterate gambler rumored to have spent 24 hours a day at a gaming table with no sustenance except cold beef between slices of bread. He simply couldn't bear to quit his gambling for the dining room, but we have better reasons for eating a sandwich. It is marvelously portable, it economizes on china and silverware, and it reminds us to eat our bread.*

Some nations look down on us for our love of sandwiches, considering us fastfood addicts, but even the fastidious French have their croque-monsieurs and Italians their tostas. Nearer home is the taco, quite possibly of more ancient lineage than any of the others. But a Thai sandwich? David Yingling's Thai Tuna Sandwiches may very well be a first. He uses cilantro, mint, cayenne, and peanut butter to put a Southeast Asian spin on an American favorite that has something of a reputation for blandness. The combination seems strange at first to the Yankee palate but is easy to get used to.

"Thai Tuna Sandwiches put a Southeast Asian spin on an American favorite."

THAI TUNA SANDWICHES

1 **can (6½ oz.) chunk-style albacore tuna packed in water, drained**
2 **green onions (ends trimmed), chopped, including tops**
1½ **tablespoons lemon juice**
3 **tablespoons mayonnaise**
¼ **cup chopped fresh cilantro (coriander)**

2 **tablespoons chopped fresh mint leaves**
¼ **to ½ teaspoon cayenne**
4 **slices thin-sliced bread, toasted**
4 **to 6 tablespoons chunk-style peanut butter**
Fresh cilantro sprigs
Major Grey chutney (optional)

In a bowl, mix tuna, onion, lemon juice, mayonnaise, cilantro, mint, and cayenne.

Spread each toasted bread slice with peanut butter, then equally spoon tuna mixture on top; garnish with cilantro sprigs. Serve with knife and fork, and offer chutney to add to taste. Makes 4 servings.

PER SERVING: 297 calories, 18 g protein, 17 g carbohydrates, 18 g fat, 25 mg cholesterol, 431 mg sodium

David Yingling

Long Beach, Calif.

HAVING BEEN ELECTED *chief cook of a multiethnic family in Hawaii, Don Gibson was faced with a problem: the Japanese side of the family favored stir-fry while the Irish side wanted Mexican food. His solution combines Asian technique with ingredients that are basically Mexican, although a bed of cooked rice is certainly Oriental in provenance, while the sherry and cornstarch are Oriental by adoption. The seasonings—cumin, oregano, and basil—and the salsa are distinctly Mexican.*

For a firmer Japanese grip, Mr. Gibson might substitute ginger and soy for cumin and oregano, omit the salsa, and serve a perfectly respectable main-line stir-fry.

STIR-FRY MEXICANA

> About 1 pound pork tenderloin, fat trimmed
> 1 medium-size onion
> 2 tablespoons salad oil
> 4 cloves garlic, minced or pressed
> 1/2 pound mushrooms, sliced
> 1 medium-size red or green bell pepper, stemmed, seeded, and cut into thin strips
> 1/2 teaspoon *each* ground cumin, dry oregano leaves, and dry basil leaves
> 3/4 cup *each* prepared salsa and regular-strength chicken broth
> 2 tablespoons cornstarch blended with 1/4 cup dry sherry
> Hot cooked rice
> Lemon wedges or rice vinegar

Thinly slice pork, then cut slices into pieces that are about 3/4 by 3 inches. Cut onion lengthwise into thin, crescent-shaped slices.

Place a wok or 12-inch frying pan over medium-high heat. When hot, add oil, then pork and garlic; stir-fry until pork is no longer pink, 3 to 4 minutes. Lift from pan with a slotted spoon and set aside.

To wok, add onion, mushrooms, and bell pepper; stir-fry until tender-crisp to bite, 3 to 4 minutes. Individually stir in cumin, oregano, basil, pork mixture (and juices), salsa, broth, and cornstarch mixture. Stir until juices boil. Serve over rice. Season to taste with lemon. Makes 4 to 6 servings.

PER SERVING: 184 calories, 17 g protein, 10 g carbohydrates, 6.9 g fat, 49 mg cholesterol, 228 mg sodium

Don Gibson

Kaneohe, Hawaii

READERS OF MURDER *mysteries know that the scent of bitter almonds means the victim has met his doom by hydrocyanic (or prussic) acid. Bitter almonds contain a substance very like prussic acid, and the aroma and flavor of these almonds expressed in almond extract are familiar to most of us in almond macaroons and marzipan. Almond is also the characteristic flavor and perfume of a liqueur known as amaretto. Why are we telling you this? Because amaretto is the mystery ingredient in Gary Fauskin's recipe.*

Dr. Fauskin enlivens the beans with crunchy pistachios and employs almond liqueur to deliciously baffle the palate. Green beans will never be the same again.

GREEN BEANS WITH PISTACHIOS & ALMOND LIQUEUR

> 1 pound green beans, ends and strings removed
> 1 tablespoon butter or margarine
> 2 tablespoons finely chopped dry-roasted, salted pistachios
> 1/8 teaspoon pepper
> 1 can (5 oz.) nonfat evaporated milk or 3/4 cup light cream (half-and-half)
> 2 to 3 teaspoons almond-flavor liqueur
> 1 teaspoon cornstarch blended with 2 teaspoons water
> Salt

Rinse beans and cut into 1-inch lengths.

Position a steaming rack above at least 1 inch of water in a 4- to 5-quart pan; bring water to boiling. Set beans on rack, cover, and boil gently until beans are tender-crisp when pierced, 10 to 15 minutes.

Meanwhile, melt butter in a 1- to 1 1/2-quart pan over medium heat. Add pistachios and stir 2 to 3 minutes. Add pepper, milk, 2 teaspoons almond liqueur, and cornstarch mixture; stir on high heat just until boiling. Taste and add more almond liqueur, if desired; keep sauce warm.

Put beans in a bowl and pour sauce over them. Season to taste with salt. Makes 4 servings.

PER SERVING: 113 calories, 5.3 g protein, 13 g carbohydrates, 5 g fat, 9.2 mg cholesterol, 76 mg sodium

Gary M. Fauskin

El Cajon, Calif.

"Amaretto is the mystery ingredient in his recipe for green beans."

March Menus

SPRING BRINGS *the freshness of a new season to this month's menus.*

Celebrate Easter with a picnic brunch featuring asparagus, avocado, and strawberries. The oven supper takes advantage of artichokes and thin-skinned potatoes coming into the market. In the third meal, Swiss chard adds a bright note to a warming lentil and pasta main dish.

EASTER BRUNCH PICNIC

Pastrami-cloaked Asparagus Spears
Easter Eggs   Avocado Dip
Bread Blossoms   Butter
Whole Strawberries
Sparkling Wine   Orange Juice

For this portable brunch, dip asparagus and shelled eggs in avocado mixture.

Wrap cooked thick asparagus spears (allow 3 per person) with thin pastrami slices. Assemble the asparagus, bake the bread, and make the dip the night before or in the morning. Serve sparkling wine and juice solo or mixed together.

AVOCADO DIP

  1 **medium-size (about ½ lb.)
     ripe avocado, peeled and pitted**
 ½ **cup light or regular sour cream**
 ⅓ **cup chopped fresh cilantro
     (coriander)**
 ¼ **cup chopped green onion**
  3 **tablespoons lemon juice**
  1 **clove garlic
     Salt and pepper**

In a blender or food processor, whirl the avocado, sour cream, cilantro, onion, lemon juice, and garlic until mixture is smooth. Add salt and pepper to taste. If made ahead, cover and chill up until the next day. Makes 1 cup.

PER TABLESPOON: 31 calories, 0.7 g protein, 1.6 g carbohydrates, 2.6 g fat, 2.5 mg cholesterol, 1.8 mg sodium

Tempting enough to divert the Easter bunny from his egg-delivering tasks, brunch features pastrami-wrapped asparagus, avocado dip, and blossom-shaped rolls.

BREAD BLOSSOMS

1 loaf (1 lb.) frozen whole-wheat
   or white bread dough, thawed
2 tablespoons beaten egg
1/2 teaspoon sesame seed

On a floured board, cut loaf into 6 equal pieces. Roll each piece into a ball. Place ball in a greased 2 1/2-inch-wide muffin cup. Cover lightly with plastic wrap and set in a warm place. Let rise until almost doubled, about 30 minutes. With scissors, make 4 cuts in top half of ball to form a cross; separate cuts to form petals. Brush dough gently with egg and sprinkle center of cuts with sesame seed.

Bake in a 375° oven until golden brown, about 25 minutes. Serve warm or cool. If made ahead, wrap airtight and store up to 8 hours. Makes 6 rolls.

PER ROLL: 212 calories, 6.3 g protein, 36 g carbohydrates, 4.4 g fat, 25 mg cholesterol, 371 mg sodium

---

DOWN-HOME OVEN SUPPER

**Artichokes with Mayonnaise
Roasted Game Hens
with New Potatoes
Apple Pie
Dry Sauvignon Blanc**

Offer whole artichokes, hot or cold, with the oven-cooked entrée.

Boil artichokes (1 large per serving) up to 1 day ahead. Accompany with your favorite flavored mayonnaise. While the potatoes bake, prepare the hens.

Split Cornish hens, baked in a honey-wine glaze, cook in the same oven with baby new potatoes; serve with whole artichokes.

ROASTED GAME HENS WITH NEW POTATOES

8 to 12 small (about 2-in. diam.)
   thin-skinned potatoes, scrubbed
2 Cornish game hens (1 1/4 to
   1 1/2 lb. each)
2 tablespoons Dijon mustard
2 tablespoons honey
1/4 cup dry white wine or apple juice
1 tablespoon minced fresh or
   1 teaspoon dry thyme leaves
   Salt and pepper

Place potatoes in an 8- to 9-inch-square pan and set on a rack in upper third of a 425° oven. Bake 20 minutes.

Meanwhile, with kitchen scissors or a knife, split hens in half, cutting along backbone and breastbone. Rinse and pat dry. Reserve neck and giblets for another use. Mix mustard, honey, wine, and thyme. Rub all over hens. Place hens, skin up, on a rack in a foil-lined 12- by 15-inch broiler pan.

Set hens in bottom third of the oven. Bake until potatoes are tender when pierced and meat is no longer pink at thigh bone (cut to test), 25 to 30 minutes. Add salt and pepper to taste. Makes 4 servings.

PER SERVING: 412 calories, 36 g protein, 25 g carbohydrates, 17 g fat, 110 mg cholesterol, 224 mg sodium

(Continued on next page)

VEGETABLE PASTA SUPPER

Roasted Red Peppers   Olives
Pasta with Lentils
Crusty Bread   Butter
Ice Cream with Pistachios

This family meal focuses on vegetables.

As lentils cook, assemble antipasto: drain 1 jar (12 to 14 oz.) roasted red bell peppers; place on a platter and drizzle with extra-virgin olive oil. Garnish with calamata olives. For dessert, top vanilla ice cream with honey and chopped pistachios.

PASTA WITH LENTILS

- 1 cup lentils
- 3 cups regular-strength chicken broth
- 1 teaspoon cumin seed
- 1 pound Swiss chard, rinsed
- 2 tablespoons olive oil
- 1 large (1/2 lb.) onion, chopped
- 2 cloves garlic, pressed or minced
- 1/2 teaspoon crushed dried hot red chilies
- 12 ounces dry linguini
- 2 small packages (3 oz. each) neufchâtel cheese, diced
  Salt and pepper

Sort lentils to remove debris; rinse and drain. In a 5- to 6-quart pan, bring 2 cups broth to a boil. Add lentils and cumin. Simmer, covered, until lentils are tender to bite, about 30 minutes; pour into bowl.

Meanwhile, trim stems from chard. Separately, slice stems and leaves crosswise into 1/4-inch-wide strips.

To pan, add oil, chard stems, onion, garlic, and chilies. Stir often over medium heat until onion is tinged with brown, 15 to 20 minutes. Add the chard leaves; stir until limp, about 3 minutes. Add lentils and remaining 1 cup broth; simmer, uncovered, until hot, about 3 minutes.

Meanwhile, in another 5- to 6-quart pan, bring 3 quarts water to a boil. Add the linguini and cook, uncovered, until pasta is tender to bite, about 7 minutes. Drain; pour pasta into a wide bowl. Add lentil mixture, cheese, and salt and pepper to taste; mix to blend. Makes 6 servings.

PER SERVING: 478 calories, 22 g protein, 68 g carbohydrates, 13 g fat, 22 mg cholesterol, 310 mg sodium

APRIL

Fresh Onion Rings with Mint (page 95)

As spring slides toward summer, it's the season to enjoy fresh salmon and the mild-flavor sweet onions now appearing in Western markets. Enjoy them together (page 94) or separately in a variety of dishes this month. A noted chef shares his roasting technique for intensifying the flavor of fresh vegetables. Other suggestions to perk up April menus include stir-fry salads, new make-ahead versions of lasagne, quick one-pan dinners, easy breadsticks, and a California variation of the Mediterranean favorite, bouillabaisse.

Stretch Breadsticks

THRILLED WITH THE CRUNCH *of bread-sticks but put off by the thought of laboriously hand-shaping them? These need no rolling—just a cut and tweak and they're ready to bake.*

After kneading the yeast dough, pat it into a square. Let rise, then cut dough into pieces and stretch them into rustically irregular, skinny breadsticks. Season the sticks Italian-style with rosemary, or try the lively chili powder version with a cornmeal coating.

ROSEMARY & LEMON STRETCH BREADSTICKS

If you're watching your sodium intake, use the smaller amount of salt.

- 1 **package active dry yeast**
- 1 **cup warm water (110°)**
- 1 **teaspoon sugar**
- 1 **teaspoon grated lemon peel**
- 1/2 **to 1 teaspoon salt**
- 1 1/2 **teaspoons dry rosemary leaves**
- 2 **tablespoons plus 1 teaspoon olive oil**
  About 2 3/4 cups all-purpose flour

In a large bowl, combine yeast, water, and sugar; let stand until yeast is softened, about 5 minutes. Add lemon peel, salt, rosemary, 2 tablespoons olive oil, and 1 1/2 cups of the flour. Beat with a heavy spoon or an electric mixer until dough is stretchy, 1 to 2 minutes.

Mix in enough additional flour to make a soft dough, about 1 cup. Turn dough out onto a floured surface and knead until smooth and springy, about 10 minutes; add flour as required to prevent sticking.

Generously flour work surface. Set dough on floured area and pat into a 6-inch square. Brush dough with 1 teaspoon oil, lightly cover with plastic wrap, and let stand until puffy, about 45 minutes.

Grease 3 baking sheets, each 12 by 15 inches. Gently rub dough with 2 tablespoons flour. With a sharp knife, cut dough lengthwise into quarters. Working with 1 section at a time, cut lengthwise again into 8 equal pieces. Pick up 1 piece and stretch it to the length of the pan. Repeat to make each stick; arrange at least 1/2 inch apart.

Bake breadsticks in a 350° oven until crisp to bite, 20 to 25 minutes; if using 1 oven, chill 1 pan of sticks while baking the other 2—switch pan positions halfway through baking. Lift sticks from pans. Serve or let cool on racks, then store airtight up to 3 days. Freeze for longer storage. Makes 32.

PER STICK: 49 calories, 1.2 g protein, 8.4 g carbohydrates, 1.1 g fat, 0 mg cholesterol, 35 mg sodium

CHILI-CORNMEAL STRETCH BREADSTICKS

Follow preceding directions for **rosemary and lemon stretch breadsticks** but omit rosemary and use 2 tablespoons **chili powder.** After dough rises, sprinkle with 2 tablespoons **cornmeal** instead of flour. Makes 32.

PER STICK: 52 calories, 1.3 g protein, 9.1 g carbohydrates, 1.1 g fat, 0 mg cholesterol, 39 mg sodium

Let dough rise on work surface, then cut it into skinny strips and gently stretch each piece to length of baking sheet. No rolling is needed to shape these easy breadsticks.

Crisp, flour-spattered rosemary breadsticks and sparkling drinks make refreshing appetizers for summer parties.

Fresh Sweet Onions

DID YOU EVER *eat a raw onion as sweet as an apple? This is the time to try, as the season for fresh onions begins.*

Fresh onions look almost like the more durable storage onions, with similar colors and sizes, yet they have opposite seasons and different characteristics.

Certain fresh onions (producers sometimes call them designer onions) are particularly known for their mild, even sugary taste. These onions contain more sugars and fewer sulfur-containing compounds than other onions do.

They are often identified by geographic origin and described as being sweet. Best known are Maui, Walla Walla, Vidalia, Texas Spring, California Imperial, and New Mexico Carzalia. A popular sweet red variety from the San Joaquin Valley is called California Italian Red.

Fresh sweet onions come to market from April to August. Because their individual seasons are short and their supplies limited, these onions often command premium prices. Maui sweets appear sporadically throughout the year, and some fresh sweet onions come from Chile in winter.

All fresh onions have a paper-thin skin and a high proportion of water and sugar, which cause them to deteriorate rapidly, especially when bruised. They can be stored in the refrigerator for up to 2 weeks but shouldn't touch each other or moisture. Wrap them in paper towels or, for a large quantity, encase them in clean old nylons, separated by knots, and hang them in a cool, dry, dark place.

Storage onions, harvested from August through March, are the tear-producers with the most robust to hot tastes, but even the hottest is converted to mellow sweetness when cooked long and slowly. Their thick skins and significantly lower moisture content endow these onions with long life—up to 10 months—for year-round availability.

To play up the flavor of sweet fresh onions to best advantage, use them raw or lightly cooked, as in these recipes.

BARBECUED SALMON WITH SWEET ONIONS

- 1/2 **cup sugar**
- 3 **tablespoons salt**
- 2 **dry bay leaves**
- 2 **teaspoons coarse-ground pepper**
- 1 **salmon fillet (2 to 2 1/2 lb.)**
- 1 **cup hickory chips**
- 1 **pound (about 1 large or 2 medium-size) fresh sweet onions, sliced thin**
  Lemon wedges
  Parsley sprigs

In a 9- by 13-inch baking dish, combine sugar, salt, bay leaves, pepper, and 3 cups water; stir until salt dissolves. Place salmon fillet, skin side down, in sugar solution. Cover and chill 1 to 2 hours.

Soak hickory chips in warm water to cover, 30 minutes to 1 hour. Ignite 50 charcoal briquets on firegrate of a barbecue with a lid. When coals are well spotted with gray ash, about 30 minutes, push equally to opposite sides of grate.

Drain fish and rinse well with cool water; pat dry. Lay fillet, skin down, on 2 layers of foil. Fold or trim foil to fit fish.

Top brined salmon fillet with sliced fresh onion as it cooks on the grill. The mild onion cooks lightly and picks up delicate smokiness.

When charcoal is completely covered with gray ash, drain hickory chips and distribute equally over briquets. Set grill about 6 inches above firegrate. Put fish, on foil, in center of grill (not over coals). Distribute onion evenly over fish. Cover barbecue, open dampers, and cook until fish is moist-looking but opaque in thickest part (cut to test), 25 to 30 minutes.

Transfer fish and onions, using foil as support, to a platter. Garnish with lemon wedges and parsley sprigs. Makes 6 to 8 servings.

PER SERVING: 191 calories, 23 g protein, 7 g carbohydrates, 7.3 g fat, 62 mg cholesterol, 369 mg sodium

Make a sandwich of sweet onions, arugula, and gjetost cheese on pumpernickel.

Young man proudly displays big sweet onions from Walla Walla County, Washington.

ONION & TOMATO SALAD

- 1 pound (about 1 large or 2 medium-size) fresh sweet onions
  Basil dressing (recipe follows)
- 1 large (about 3/4 lb.) firm-ripe tomato, cored and cut crosswise into 1/4-inch-thick slices
- 4 to 6 canned anchovies, drained (optional)
  Fresh basil sprigs (optional)
  Salt and pepper

Cut onions crosswise into thin slices and separate rings into a bowl. Pour dressing over onions and gently mix. On 3 or 4 dinner or salad plates, arrange equal portions of the tomato. Top with equal portions of onions and dressing. Garnish with anchovies and basil sprigs. Add salt and pepper to taste. Makes 3 or 4 servings.

PER SERVING: 185 calories, 2.7 g protein, 15 g carbohydrates, 14 g fat, 0 mg cholesterol, 19 mg sodium

Basil dressing. Mix 1/4 cup **extra-virgin olive oil**, 3 tablespoons **red wine vinegar,** and 1/4 cup chopped **fresh basil leaves** or 1 tablespoon dry basil leaves.

SWEET ONION SANDWICH

- 1/3 cup sour cream
- 4 or 8 slices dark, dense-texture pumpernickel bread
- 4 ounces thin-sliced Swiss or gjetost cheese
- 12 to 16 (1 to 2 oz. total) tender arugula leaves or watercress sprigs, rinsed and crisped
- 1 medium-size (about 8 oz.) fresh sweet onion, sliced thin
  Salt and pepper

Spread sour cream equally over 1 side of 4 slices bread. Equally distribute cheese, arugula, and onion over sour cream. Add salt and pepper to taste. Eat open-faced or cover sandwich filling with another bread slice. Makes 4 servings.

PER SERVING: 250 calories, 13 g protein, 24 g carbohydrates, 12 g fat, 35 mg cholesterol, 275 mg sodium

Sliced Italian Reds from Fresno, California, make icy-crisp onion rings in a marinade seasoned with fresh mint leaves and dried hot red chilies.

FRESH ONION RINGS WITH MINT

- 1 pound (about 1 large or 2 medium-size) fresh sweet onions
- 1/3 cup seasoned rice vinegar (or rice vinegar plus 1 teaspoon sugar)
- 1 tablespoon chopped fresh mint leaves
- 1/8 teaspoon crushed dried hot red chilies
- 1 cup small ice cubes or coarsely crushed ice
  Salt

Cut onions crosswise into 1/4-inch-thick slices; separate into rings. In a bowl, mix onion rings, vinegar, mint, chilies, and ice; cover and chill 10 to 15 minutes, stirring occasionally. Serve with the unmelted ice. Add salt to taste. Makes 4 to 6 servings.

PER SERVING: 36 calories, 1.2 g protein, 8.2 g carbohydrates, 0.1 g fat, 0 mg cholesterol, 10 mg sodium

Marin Bouillabaisse

A WELL-STRUCTURED BROTH *lends subtle dimensions to a good fish soup. Fred Halpert learned this lesson in France when he studied to become a professional chef. Now he applies the lesson and adds a Western touch to create his own version of bouillabaisse.*

Halpert makes the aromatic broth in advance and brings it to the table in the pan—with partially cooked potatoes—to simmer over a portable burner. Then he adds the tender chunks of white fish to cook quickly while guests sip wine and develop appetites.

You need fresh fish trimmings to make the broth; it's a good idea to let the fish market know several days in advance what you want. Be sure to rinse trimmings well to get rid of fishy aromas.

The broth and aïoli (garlic mayonnaise) can be made a day ahead. Several hours before dinner, toast baguette slices and prepare salad greens; use an oil-and-vinegar salad dressing. If you prefer red wine, consider a soft French Bandol or a dry California rosé; the soup can stand up to it.

FRED'S HOME-STYLE BOUILLABAISSE

   Bouillabaisse broth (recipe follows)
2 **dozen small (about 1 1/2-in.-wide) thin-skinned potatoes, scrubbed**
3 **pounds skinned and boned firm white-flesh fish, such as halibut, sea bass, lingcod, monkfish, or rockfish (choose 1 or several)**

Vegetable medley, fish scraps, lemon, and saffron infuse the broth with flavors essential to bouillabaisse.

2 **dozen small (about 3-in.-long; about 3/4 lb. total) mussels, well scrubbed, with beards pulled off**
   Aïoli (recipe follows)
   Toasted baguette slices (1-lb. loaf)

Bring broth to boiling over high heat. Cut potatoes in half and add to broth. Cover and simmer until just tender when pierced, about 20 minutes.

Meanwhile, rinse fish, drain, and cut into 1-inch chunks. When potatoes test just tender, add fish and mussels to pan. Cover and continue to cook until mussels pop open and fish is no longer translucent but is still moist-looking in center of thickest part (cut to test), 8 to 10 minutes.

Ladle soup into wide bowls. Offer aïoli to add to taste to soup and, if desired, to spread on toast. Makes 8 to 10 servings.

PER SERVING WITHOUT AÏOLI: 479 calories, 39 g protein, 52 g carbohydrates, 12 g fat, 52 mg cholesterol, 475 mg sodium

Bouillabaisse broth. Cut 4 medium-size (about 2 lb. total) **onions** in quarters and put in a 10- to 12-quart pan with 1/3 cup **extra-virgin olive oil.**

Trim stems and discolored areas from 2 heads **fennel** (about 2 lb. total); rinse fennel and chop. Add to pan along with 6 cloves **garlic,** minced or pressed; 1 cup minced **parsley;** and 1 teaspoon **saffron threads** or 1/2 teaspoon powdered saffron. Stir often over medium-high heat until onion is limp, about 25 minutes.

Rinse, core, and quarter 8 medium-size firm-ripe **tomatoes** (about 4 lb. total); add to pan. Stir often until tomatoes are very soft, about 20 minutes.

Rinse well and drain about 3 pounds **fish bones, fish trimmings,** and **fish heads** (gills removed) from **lean white-flesh fish** such as rockfish, lingcod, or perch. Add fish pieces to pan with 2 quarts **water,** 1 cup **dry white wine,** and 3 or 4 thin slices of **lemon.** Boil, uncovered, until liquid is reduced by about a third, about 1 1/2 hours.

Let stand until mixture is cool enough to touch. Set a colander in a large bowl; line colander with damp cheesecloth and pour broth mixture into cloth. Gather cloth edges and twist tightly to squeeze out as much liquid as possible; discard residue.

Skim and discard any fat on broth; measure broth and pour into a 4- to 5-quart pan. If needed, add water to make 10 cups; or boil, uncovered, over high heat until reduced to 10 cups. If made ahead, cool, cover, and chill broth in pan up until next day; discard any remaining fat. Reheat to continue.

Aïoli. Immerse 1 **large egg** in water heated to just below boiling point (about 200°); hold at this temperature for 3 minutes. Break egg and scoop into a blender or food processor; let stand until cool.

Add 2 cloves **garlic** and 1 1/2 tablespoons **lemon juice;** whirl smooth. With motor on, add 3/4 cup **extra-virgin olive oil** in a thin, steady stream. As mixture thickens, add oil faster. If mayonnaise gets too thick to mix, stir in remaining oil. Add **salt** to taste. Serve or, if made ahead, cover and chill up to 4 days. Makes about 1 cup.

PER TABLESPOON: 96 calories, 0.4 g protein, 0.4 g carbohydrates, 11 g fat, 13 mg cholesterol, 4.3 mg sodium

From simmering pot on tabletop burner, he serves Westernized version of bouillabaisse featuring fish, mussels in the shell, and small potatoes. Offer aïoli (garlic mayonnaise) to season soup and to spread on toast. Most of the preparations can be completed in advance.

Fresh Salmon as the Norwegians Enjoy It

KING (CHINOOK) SALMON *are running; silver (coho) and sockeyes (red) are on their way. But with advancing technology in aquaculture, fresh salmon of fine quality and reliable supply are available every month of the year. They come from ocean pens worldwide—Norway to the Pacific Northwest to Chile.*

Can you use wild and farmed interchangeably? Yes, though some tasters find farmed salmon has milder flavor and softer texture than the wild fish. As in the wild, the color of the flesh varies according to species and what the fish eat.

In Norway recently, we sampled salmon as Norwegians enjoy it most. The following examples are both handsome and simple to prepare at home.

One main dish is grilled and the other presents salmon in a light broth. The elegant first course on the facing page is enhanced by inexpensive fish caviars in the sour cream sauce.

CHARRED SALMON

About 1 cup tender watercress sprigs, rinsed and crisped
1/3 cup mayonnaise
2 tablespoons milk
1/2 pound fresh chanterelles or oyster mushrooms
1 tablespoon butter or margarine
4 salmon fillets (6 to 7 oz. each) with skin on, 1 to 1 1/2 inches thick
About 2 tablespoons extra-virgin olive oil
Lemon wedges (optional)

In a blender or food processor, combine 1 cup watercress, mayonnaise, and milk. Whirl until smooth. If made ahead, cover and chill up until next day.

Rinse chanterelles and drain well. If stems are thicker than 1/2 inch, cut chanterelles in half lengthwise. In an 8- to 10-inch frying pan, melt butter over medium-high heat. Add chanterelles and stir often until lightly browned, 10 to 15 minutes. Remove chanterelles from heat; keep warm.

Brush skin side of salmon with 1 tablespoon oil. Place salmon, skin side down, on a well-oiled grill 4 inches above a solid bed of very hot coals (you can hold your hand at grill level only 1 to 2 seconds). Cover grill; cook salmon until skin is charred and crisp and meat is just opaque on top, 5 to 7 minutes. Loosen skin from rack with a wide spatula and remove salmon.

Cut each salmon fillet in half. On each of 4 dinner plates, arrange one fillet half skin side down, and one half skin side up. Divide chanterelles and watercress mayonnaise among plates, spooning the mayonnaise along edge of salmon. Drizzle salmon evenly with remaining oil. If desired, garnish with lemon wedges and watercress sprigs. Makes 4 servings.—*Eyvind Hellstrøm, Oslo, Norway.*

PER SERVING: 477 calories, 36 g protein, 3.6 g carbohydrates, 35 g fat, 113 mg cholesterol, 219 mg sodium

For delicious contrast of crisp, blackened skin and moist meat, salmon fillets are grilled only on one side over very hot coals; sautéed chanterelles and a watercress mayonnaise accompany the fish.

SALMON IN BROTH WITH VEGETABLES

1 large (about 1/3 lb.) zucchini, ends trimmed
1 large (about 1/4 lb.) carrot, trimmed and peeled
1 small (about 1/4 lb.) red bell pepper, stemmed and seeded
2 skinned salmon fillets (6 to 7 oz. each), about 1 inch thick
5 cups regular-strength chicken broth
1/4 cup lemon juice
1 tablespoon grated lemon peel
1 tablespoon minced fresh or 1 teaspoon crumbled dry thyme leaves
Fresh thyme sprigs (optional)

Cut the zucchini, the carrot, and the pepper into very thin matchstick slivers about 2 inches long. Divide the vegetables evenly among 4 wide, shallow

Delicate, lime-scented salmon fillets float in a pool of luxurious caviar-speckled sour cream sauce for an elegant first course. Garnish with thin lime slices and chives.

soup bowls. Place bowls in a warm (150° to 200°) oven until vegetables are hot, about 8 minutes.

Meanwhile, cut the fillets in half horizontally and set aside. Also cut 4 pieces of foil large enough to cover each bowl.

In a 3- to 4-quart pan, combine broth, lemon juice, lemon peel, and thyme; bring to a rolling boil on high heat. Set a piece of salmon in each bowl and quickly but gently ladle hot broth over the fish. Cover the bowls with foil and return them to oven until salmon is just opaque and still moist-looking in thickest part (cut to test), 10 to 12 minutes. Remove the foil and garnish salmon with fresh thyme sprigs. Makes 4 servings.—*Arne Brimi, Lom, Norway.*

PER SERVING: 182 calories, 20 g protein, 7.4 g carbohydrates, 7.5 g fat, 47 mg cholesterol, 117 mg sodium

SALMON WITH CAVIAR SAUCE

Look for the flying fish roe (tobiko) at Asian markets.

- 2 skinned salmon fillets (6 to 7 oz. each), 1 to 1½ inches thick
- 2 tablespoons extra-virgin olive oil
- ⅓ cup lime juice
- ½ teaspoon coarse-grind pepper
- 1 cup light sour cream or unflavored low-fat yogurt
- ⅓ cup regular-strength chicken broth
- 2 tablespoons flying fish roe (tobiko), rinsed and well drained
- 2 tablespoons black lumpfish caviar, rinsed and well drained
  Chives (optional)
  Thin lime slices (optional)

Cut each fillet lengthwise into 6 equal slices. Carefully place in a shallow bowl. Combine oil, lime juice, and

pepper; pour over salmon. Cover and chill, turning occasionally, at least 1 hour or up to 4 hours.

In an 8- to 10-inch nonstick frying pan over medium-high heat, cook ⅓ of salmon slices until bottoms are lightly browned, about 1 minute. Turn slices over and cook other side until lightly browned, about 1 minute. Remove from pan and keep warm. Repeat to cook remaining salmon.

Whisk sour cream with broth until smooth. Gently fold in tobiko. In the center of each of 4 dinner plates, spoon ¼ of the sauce; tilt plates to spread sauce. Set 3 slices salmon on each plate. Spoon black caviar in small dots equally around salmon. Garnish with chives and lime. Makes 4 servings.—*Henning Stordal, Oslo, Norway.*

PER SERVING: 316 calories, 24 g protein, 6 g carbohydrates, 22 g fat, 134 mg cholesterol, 151 mg sodium

Roasting Vegetables

ONE SECRET to making food taste good is to intensify the flavors. Bradley Ogden, a proprietor and chef of The Lark Creek Inn in Larkspur, California, has made an art of intensifying the taste of vegetables by roasting them.

Ogden gets help from a large wood-burning brick oven at the restaurant—but you can achieve similar results at home by cooking at high temperatures in a conventional oven. Vegetables will be sweet and have intense flavor. Once in the oven, the vegetables need little attention. All the recipes have make-ahead options.

One surprise from the oven is arti-chokes, first steamed, then roasted. Concentrated seasonings blended with vinegar and oil form a flavorful marinade. The artichokes are served cool or at room temperature.

Apples and onions roasted with winter squash, then whirled with broth and juice, create a smooth, golden soup.

Roasted onions are real winners because they are so versatile; Ogden cooks them by the panful and serves them plain to go with meats or to use in a variety of dishes. Here, we show ways to incorporate them in soup, in a ham and cheese appetizer salad, and in a butter relish.

ROASTED ARTICHOKE SALAD

- 4 large (4- to 4½-in.-diameter) artichokes
- 2 cups regular-strength chicken broth
- 1 teaspoon *each* dry rosemary leaves, dry oregano leaves, mustard seed, and chili powder
- ½ cup balsamic vinegar
- ¼ cup extra-virgin olive or salad oil
- 4 medium-size (about ¾ lb. total) Roma-type tomatoes, cored, seeded, and chopped
- ⅓ cup minced red onion
- 2 tablespoons chopped Italian parsley

Break small coarse outer leaves from artichokes. With a sharp knife, cut off thorny top; with scissors, snip any remaining thorny tips off leaves. Using same knife, peel stem and trim base. Immerse artichokes in water, swishing up and down; shake from stem end to remove water.

Place artichokes in a 10- by 14-inch roasting pan. Mix broth, 1 cup water, rosemary, oregano, mustard seed, and chili powder; pour into pan. Cover pan tightly with foil. Bake in a 450° oven until artichoke bottoms are tender when pierced, about 50 minutes. Uncover and bake artichokes until just tinged with brown, 8 to 10 minutes longer.

Lift out the artichokes, draining, and put in a rimmed dish; reserve juices in pan. When the artichokes are cool enough to touch, ease the center of each open and pull out a few of the tiny thorn-tipped center leaves. Then scoop out the fuzzy choke in the center with a teaspoon. Discard tiny center leaves and choke.

Over high heat, boil pan juices, uncovered, until reduced to ½ cup. Remove from heat, stir in vinegar and oil, and pour liquid over artichokes. Cover and chill at least 2 hours or up until next day.

Lift artichokes onto individual rimmed plates. Mix tomato, onion, and parsley into artichoke juices. Spoon about 2 tablespoons of the liquid into the center of each artichoke, then divide remaining mixture among the plates. Serve cool or at room temperature. Makes 4 servings.

PER SERVING: 245 calories, 6.4 g protein, 26 g carbohydrates, 16 g fat, 0 mg cholesterol, 168 mg sodium

Oven-roasted artichoke rests in a dressing of seasoned cooking juices, balsamic vinegar, tomatoes, red onion, and parsley.

ROASTED GOLDEN SQUASH BISQUE

About 2¹/₂ pounds yellow-fleshed winter squash, such as a whole butternut or piece of banana squash

2 tablespoons *each* butter or margarine and extra-virgin olive or salad oil

2 medium-size (about 1 lb. total) Newtown Pippin or other tart apples, cut in half and cored

2 small (about ³/₄ lb. total) onions, unpeeled and cut in half

¹/₂ cup hazelnuts

3 cups regular-strength chicken broth

1 cup apple juice or cider

If squash is whole, cut it in half lengthwise; if shell is hard, tap the blunt edge of the knife with a mallet to drive it through. Scoop out and discard seeds and strings.

Melt butter and oil in a 10- by 15-inch rimmed pan in a 400° oven. Lay squash, skin down, in pan; put apple and onion halves beside squash. Bake until squash is very tender when pierced and the flesh is tinged with brown, about 1¹/₂ hours.

Meanwhile, in an 8- to 9-inch-wide pan, bake hazelnuts in the same oven until golden under skin, about 10 minutes; shake occasionally. Place nuts in a towel and rub to remove as much of the brown skin as possible. Lift nuts from towel, chop coarse, and set aside.

Let squash stand until cool enough to touch, then scoop flesh from shell. Also scrape apple from skins and pull off onion skins; discard shell and skins. Put squash, apple, and onion in a blender or food processor. Add enough chicken broth to help make a very smooth purée.

Pour purée, remaining broth, and juice into a 3- to 4-quart pan. Stir over medium-high heat until steaming. If made ahead, cover and chill up to 3 days; reheat to continue. Ladle into bowls and sprinkle with nuts. Makes 6 servings.

PER SERVING: 281 calories, 4.5 g protein, 36 g carbohydrates, 16 g fat, 10 mg cholesterol, 74 mg sodium

Chopped hazelnuts float on soup made from roasted and puréed butternut squash, onions, and apples.

OVEN-ROASTED ONIONS

The onions taste good as is, or in some of the following recipes.

18 small (2-in.-diameter, about 5 lb. total) onions, peeled

**2 tablespoons *each* butter or margarine, extra-virgin olive or salad oil, and balsamic vinegar
Salt and pepper**

In a 10- by 14-inch roasting pan, combine onions, butter, oil, and vinegar. Bake, uncovered, in a 400° oven, gently turning onions over about every 20 minutes, until they are very soft when pressed and cut edges are richly browned, about 1¹/₂ hours.

Serve onions hot or at room temperature, adding salt, pepper, and pan juices to taste. Or use onions and juices in following recipes (you'll need 2 tablespoons of the juice for ham and cheese with oven-roasted onions). If made ahead, cover and chill up to 1 week. Makes 6 to 9 servings.

PER ONION: 63 calories, 1.3 g protein, 8.4 g carbohydrates, 3.1 g fat, 3.4 mg cholesterol, 15 mg sodium

(Continued on next page)

Shiny with glaze of balsamic vinegar and olive oil, roasted onions go with thin-sliced ham and shaved parmesan cheese to make first course.

OVEN-ROASTED ONION SOUP

- 1 or 2 ham hocks (about 1 lb. total), sawed in half lengthwise, rinsed
- 4 slices French bread, each about ½ inch thick and 4 inches wide
  About 2 tablespoons extra-virgin or regular olive oil
- 8 oven-roasted onions (recipe precedes)
- 1 tablespoon balsamic vinegar
  About 2 ounces parmesan cheese, shaved thin with a cheese slicer
  Salt and pepper

In a 3- to 4-quart pan, combine ham hock and 5 cups water. Bring to a boil, cover, and simmer until the meat is very tender when pierced, about 2 hours. If made ahead, let cool, then cover and chill up to 2 days; reheat until warm to continue.

Meanwhile, lightly brush baguette slices with olive oil and place in a 10- by 15-inch baking pan. Bake in a 400° oven until golden, about 5 minutes; let cool, then package airtight up to 8 hours.

Lift hock from pan, reserving liquid. When meat is cool enough to touch, pull it from bone. Set meat aside; discard bone, gristle, skin, and any fat.

In a blender or food processor, whirl meat, onions, and enough reserved liquid to make as smooth a purée as possible. Pour purée through a fine strainer into pan with remainder of reserved liquid. Rub mixture through strainer with a flexible spatula to extract as much liquid as you can. Discard residue.

Bring soup to boiling on high heat and stir often, uncovered, until reduced to about 4½ cups. Stir in balsamic vinegar. Ladle into 4 wide soup bowls. Accompany soup or top with toasted bread and the shaved cheese. Add salt and pepper to taste. Makes 4 servings.

PER SERVING: 392 calories, 20 g protein, 29 g carbohydrates, 22 g fat, 51 mg cholesterol, 1,143 mg sodium

HAM & CHEESE WITH OVEN-ROASTED ONIONS

Serve as a first course or a light meal; it's the equivalent of a sandwich.

- 8 oven-roasted onions (recipe precedes), at room temperature
- ¼ pound thin-sliced cooked ham
  About ¼ pound parmesan cheese, shaved thin with a cheese slicer
- 1 slender baguette (1 lb.), broken into 4 equal pieces
  Coarse-grind pepper
  Watercress sprigs or parsley (optional)
- 2 tablespoons *each* balsamic vinegar and reserved oven-roasted onion juices or extra-virgin olive oil (optional)

On each of 4 salad or dinner plates, arrange 2 onions, equal amounts of the ham and cheese, and a piece of the bread.

Sprinkle a little pepper onto each portion and garnish with watercress. Mix vinegar and reserved onion juices and add to taste. Makes 4 servings.

PER SERVING: 618 calories, 30 g protein, 81 g carbohydrates, 20 g fat, 46 mg cholesterol, 1,569 mg sodium

ROASTED ONION BUTTER

Spoon onto simply cooked hot meats, poultry, or fish.

- 2 oven-roasted onions (recipe precedes), minced
- 3 tablespoons butter or margarine, at room temperature
- 1 tablespoon *each* balsamic vinegar and dry red wine
  About 1 teaspoon coarse-grind pepper

Stir onion, butter, vinegar, wine, and pepper together until well blended. Makes about ¾ cup. Allow 1 to 2 tablespoons for each serving.

PER TABLESPOON: 37 calories, 0.3 g protein, 1.6 g carbohydrates, 3.4 g fat, 8.3 mg cholesterol, 32 mg sodium

The New Thermal-Microwave Ovens

HIGH TECH HAS ENTERED the kitchen, as is apparent to anyone shopping for appliances. And one of the latest innovations is an oven that provides two kinds of energy—thermal (radiant and convection heat) and microwave—at once. This thermal-microwave unit comes in three formats: built-in, free standing, and countertop. At $1,400 to $3,000, the two larger formats are intended to replace your regular oven (regular ovens typically run from $600 to $900). Countertop versions cost $350 to $500, plug into any outlet, and can supplement your regular oven.

How does a new thermal-microwave oven differ from older bake-microwave oven combinations? Instead of switching back and forth between kinds of energy, the new kind can use both simultaneously. This way, it combines the microwave's timesaving advantages with a thermal oven's browning and crisping abilities.

Like bake-microwave ovens, simultaneous thermal-microwave ones are available with radiant heat, convection heat, or both together. Radiant heat is supplied from a heating coil. An oven using only radiant heat has a coil on the bottom for baking and one on top for broiling. A convection oven has an upper coil for broiling; to bake, a fan circulates hot air from the back of the oven. (Convection ovens cook faster than radiant-heat ones, and manufacturers recommend lower temperatures or adjusted cooking times.)

All thermal-microwave ovens can be used for baking or microwave cooking and combination cooking. Most offer a micro-broil option, so foods can microwave and broil at the same time—great if you like meats well done and not heavily browned.

In addition, thermal-microwave ovens let you readily preprogram cooking methods. For example, you can set the oven to bake for 20 minutes and then do combination baking (microwave energy plus thermal heat) for 10 minutes. Most models also offer adjustable microwave power levels (you can bake at a selected temperature with a selected level of microwave power). This makes it much easier to control the quality and evenness of the cooking.

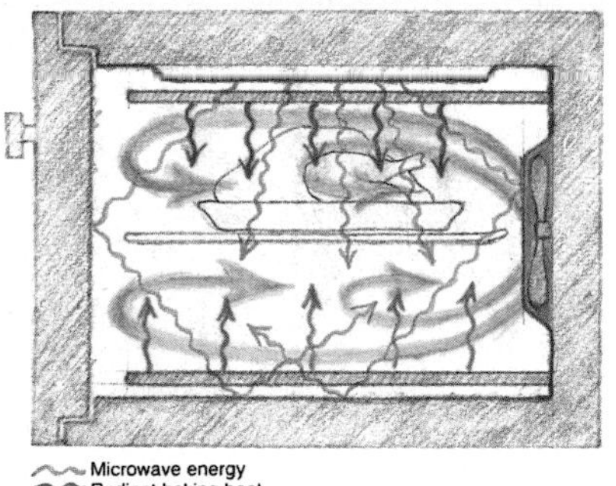

ADJUSTMENTS FOR SUCCESSFUL COOKING

It takes practice to strike a good balance when combining thermal and microwave energy, but you can check and test as you proceed, making adjustments. The most manageable combination to start with is the recommended baking temperature plus 75 percent microwave power. Begin checking for doneness after about a third of the suggested cooking time, and frequently thereafter.

Use the chart below as a guide. To develop it, we tested foods in both

~ Microwave energy
~ Radiant baking heat
▬ Convection heat
~ Radiant broiling heat

conventional and thermal-microwave ovens.

Poultry, meat, fish, most casseroles. We found that these cooked well with thermal and microwave energy used together the whole time. But if microwave level is too high, foods may be tough or overcooked.

Baked goods. Ones that change shape or need to develop a specific texture—such as breads, cookies, cakes, pastries—should be cooked with thermal heat until they have risen and developed the desired texture. Then you can add microwave energy to finish the cooking faster.

Tougher cuts of meat, dishes containing eggs. Such foods, which need to be cooked more gently, do best at the prescribed baking temperature with 50 percent (or less) microwave power.

Any time you cook with microwave energy, the size (mass) and shape of the food affect the evenness of the cooking. The more food, the longer the cooking time required (2 potatoes take more time than 1). The more irregular the food's shape, the more uneven the cooking (roasts with bones cook less evenly than boned ones). But convection heat, with its fan-driven circulation, helps even the cooking.

What cookware to use. In a thermal-microwave, you need cookware that works with both thermal *and* microwave energy, such as glass or ceramic.

Thermal-Microwave Baking Versus Conventional Baking

Food	Time saved (%)	Energy used
Poultry (whole)	40 to 60	Thermal-microwave bake
Fish (steaks, fillets)	30 to 40	Thermal-microwave bake
Meat (boned, tied roasts)	30 to 50	Thermal-microwave bake
Vegetables and casseroles	35 to 40	Thermal-microwave bake
Egg dishes (custards, soufflés, Dutch babies)	30 to 50	Thermal-microwave bake with 50 percent or less microwave setting
Breads, cakes, cookies, pies	40 to 60	Thermal bake, then thermal-microwave bake

Stir-fry Salads

H OT SALADS *featuring stir-fried meat and pungent sauce poured over cool, crisp greens make convenient entrée-size dishes for two. Add a bowl of hot rice or warm sesame rolls to complete the meal.*

First rinse and crisp the greens. As they chill, mix the sauce and slice the meat. Once ingredients are assembled, it takes only minutes to cook the meat.

In the first recipe, pork and a honey-thyme sauce top escarole studded with apple slices. In the second, lamb and chili-garlic dressing adorn iceberg lettuce.

STIR-FRIED PORK & ESCAROLE SALAD

    6 cups (5 to 7 oz.) bite-size pieces
       rinsed and crisped escarole or
       spinach leaves
 1/3 cup cider vinegar
    4 teaspoons honey
    1 medium-size Red Delicious
       apple, cored and sliced thin
    2 teaspoons cornstarch
 1/2 cup regular-strength chicken
       broth
    1 teaspoon Dijon mustard
 1/4 teaspoon dry thyme leaves
 1/2 pound lean boneless pork loin,
       loin end, or leg
    1 tablespoon salad oil
    1 large shallot, chopped
       Salt and pepper

On 2 dinner plates, equally mound escarole. In a small bowl, mix vinegar, honey, and apple slices. Lift out slices with a slotted spoon and scatter on escarole. Blend with vinegar mixture the cornstarch, chicken broth, mustard, and thyme.

Trim fat from pork. Cut meat into paper-thin strips about 1/2 by 3 inches.

Place a wok or 10- to 12-inch frying pan over high heat; when hot, add oil and tilt pan to coat. Add shallot and pork; stir-fry until pork is lightly browned, about 2 minutes. Push meat to 1 side of pan; add vinegar mixture and stir until it boils, about 1 minute. Stir meat into sauce. Spoon mixture equally over escarole. Add salt and pepper to taste. Makes 2 servings.

PER SERVING: 388 calories, 28 g protein, 36 g carbohydrates, 16 g fat, 72 mg cholesterol, 194 mg sodium

Hot out of the wok, stir-fried pork and thyme dressing go over escarole and sliced apples for salad entrée.

STIR-FRIED SPICY LAMB SALAD

    2 large iceberg lettuce leaves,
       rinsed and crisped
    4 cups (10 to 12 oz.) fine-shredded
       iceberg lettuce
 1/2 pound boneless lean lamb leg
       or loin
    1 tablespoon salad oil
    1 teaspoon minced garlic
       Chili dressing (recipe follows)
 3/4 cup cherry tomatoes, stems
       removed, cut in half
    2 tablespoons thin-shredded fresh
       mint leaves or chopped fresh
       cilantro (coriander)

On each of 2 dinner plates, place 1 lettuce leaf. Mound shredded lettuce equally on leaves. Trim fat from lamb; cut meat into paper-thin strips about 1/2 by 3 inches.

Place a wok or 10- to 12-inch frying pan over high heat; when hot, add oil and tilt pan to coat. Add garlic and lamb; stir-fry until lightly browned, about 2 minutes. Push meat to 1 side of pan; add dressing and stir until boiling. Stir meat into dressing and spoon equally onto lettuce; top with tomatoes and mint. Makes 2 servings.

PER SERVING: 319 calories, 26 g protein, 17 g carbohydrates, 15 g fat, 75 mg cholesterol, 1,130 mg sodium

Chili dressing. Mix 2 teaspoons **cornstarch** with 1 teaspoon **sugar**. Stir in 1/2 cup **water** or regular-strength chicken or beef broth, 2 tablespoons **sherry** or cider **vinegar**, 2 tablespoons **soy sauce,** and 1/4 teaspoon **crushed dried hot red chilies.**

Surprise Dumplings

DECEPTIVELY AUSTERE, *these plain-looking dumplings, floating in a pool of classic made-from-scratch roasted-bone broth, conceal a delectable treasure.*

Inside each thin-skinned packet is an intense concentration of broth enhanced by madeira. How do you get soup inside a dumpling? It's really quite easy; just follow the steps we outline here for elegant results that make a first course for a few special guests. You might want to warn your guests that dumplings will squirt when they release their savory interiors—it's best to pop dumplings in the mouth whole.

Although soup dumplings aren't complicated or expensive to make, you do have to allow time for the broth and filling to cook (untended).

Use bones and meat scraps collected over a period of time in the freezer, or buy an assortment. Roast until richly browned, then simmer about 4 hours in water. Strain broth and save some for the soup. Boil down the rest with madeira until thick; it will be very rigid when chilled.

The thin wrappers couldn't be simpler: they're won ton skins. Seal cubes of concentrated broth into the skins with a flour-and-water paste. You can store them in the refrigerator for a few hours or in the freezer for a couple of weeks. They take only minutes to cook.

CONSOMMÉ DUMPLINGS

Don't crowd dumplings in pan when cooking; they can stick and tear.

- 1 tablespoon all-purpose flour
- 16 won ton skins
  Consommé (recipe follows)
- 2 to 2½ cups homemade broth (recipe follows)
  Salt
- 2 tablespoons freshly grated parmesan cheese
- 2 tablespoons thin-sliced chives

Mix flour and 2 tablespoons water until smooth. Cut won ton skins in half lengthwise to make pieces about 1¾ by 3¼ inches; keep them covered with plastic wrap until ready to fill. Brush edges of 1 won ton piece with flour paste. On 1 half of the skin, place a cube of consommé; press edges of skin together to seal completely. Lay dumplings, slightly apart, in flour-dusted 10- by 15-inch pans; cover with plastic

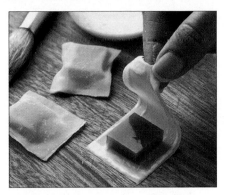

Enclose consommé cube in half of a won ton skin, edges brushed with flour-water paste. Press edges of skin to seal completely.

wrap. If made ahead, wrap dumplings airtight and chill up to 8 hours or freeze up to 2 weeks.

In a 1½- to 2-quart pan, bring broth to a simmer. Add salt to taste; cover and keep hot. In a 5- to 6-quart pan or deep 10- to 12-inch frying pan, bring 2 to 3 inches water to a boil (to cook dumplings all at once, cook half in each of 2 pans). Add half the dumplings (do not thaw if frozen) to water; spoon boiling water over tops, or gently turn, until won ton skins become translucent and fillings liquefy, about 2 minutes. Reduce heat to low.

Ladle hot broth into 6 to 8 warm shallow soup bowls. With slotted spoon, carefully transfer 1 or 2 dumplings at a time to bowls, putting 3 to 5 in each; keep warm. Repeat until all are cooked. Dust with cheese and chives. Makes 6 to 8 first-course servings.

PER SERVING: 83 calories, 2.7 g protein, 13 g carbohydrates, 1.9 g fat, 1.2 mg cholesterol, 34 mg sodium

Consommé. In a 6- to 8-quart pan or 10- to 12-inch frying pan over high heat, bring 3½ to 4 cups **homemade broth** (recipe follows) and ½ cup dry **madeira** to a boil. Boil broth and madeira, uncovered, until reduced to ⅔ cup, 20 to 30 minutes. Pour into a 4- by 8-inch loaf pan; cool, cover, and chill until firm, at least 1½ hours or up to 1 week. Cut into 32 equal pieces, about ¾ by 1 inch.

Homemade broth. Cut and break about 6 pounds **poultry** and/or **meat bones** and **scraps** (cooked or raw, including poultry skin and giblets, but omitting liver; limit bare beef bones to no more than ⅓ of the total) into pieces so they will fit into a 6- to 8-quart pan. Spread out pieces in a 12- by 17-inch roasting

pan. Bake them, uncovered, in a 400° oven until well browned, 1¼ to 1½ hours.

Transfer browned pieces and drippings to the 6- to 8-quart pan. With a little water, rinse all browned bits from baking pan and add to bones and scraps. Add 8 **black peppercorns;** 2 **dry bay leaves;** 2 sprigs **parsley;** 2 large (about 1 lb. total) **onions,** cut into chunks; and 2 large (about 10 oz. total) **carrots,** cut into chunks. Add enough **water** (2 to 2½ qt.) to almost cover ingredients.

Bring to a boil, cover, and simmer for about 4 hours. With a slotted spoon, remove and discard big pieces. Pour broth and residue into a colander lined with a double thickness of damp cheesecloth, catching broth in a container.

Cool, cover, and chill broth until firm, at least 3 hours or up until next day. Lift off and discard fat. Cook broth over high heat just until liquid; measure. If you have more than 1½ quarts, boil, uncovered, to reduce. If you have less than this amount, add water to make 1½ quarts. Remove 2 to 2½ cups broth; cover and chill until ready to use, up to 1 week, or freeze airtight up to 1 month. Use the remaining broth for consommé (recipe precedes).

Savor each dumpling in one bite so flavorful broth filling doesn't leak.

Lasagne with a Twist

FOR A PARTY *or the family, lasagne is an ideal dish because it serves a crowd and can be completely assembled up to a day ahead. Here we offer two twists on the traditional beef-and-tomato version. Serve with a green salad and bread.*

Hearty vegetable lasagne brims with black beans, roasted tomatoes, and ricotta and jack cheeses. Casserole can be assembled a day ahead, ready for last-minute baking.

BLACK BEAN LASAGNE

- 4 pounds Roma-type tomatoes, cored and cut in half lengthwise
- 1½ tablespoons olive or salad oil
- 2 cloves garlic, minced or pressed
- 1 cup firmly packed fresh cilantro (coriander), chopped
- 10 dry wide lasagne noodles (about 5 oz. total)
- 3 cans (15 oz. each) black beans, drained and rinsed
- ¼ cup regular-strength chicken broth
- 1 teaspoon ground cumin
- ½ teaspoon chili powder
- 2 cartons (15 oz. each) part-skim ricotta cheese
- ¾ pound jack cheese, shredded (about 4 cups)
  Salt

Arrange tomatoes cut side up in a 10- by 15-inch baking pan (a few tomatoes can rest on top of each other). Sprinkle evenly with oil and garlic. Bake tomatoes in a 425° oven until well browned, about 1¼ hours. Set aside until cool enough to handle. Peel off and discard skins. Place tomatoes in a colander and press them lightly to drain off watery liquid.

Whirl tomatoes in a blender or food processor with cilantro until smooth. If made ahead, cover and chill tomatoes up to 2 days.

Bring 3 quarts water to a boil in a 5- to 6- quart pan over high heat. Add noodles and cook, uncovered, until just tender to bite, about 8 minutes. Drain and immediately immerse noodles in cold water.

In a bowl, combine beans, broth, cumin, and chili powder. With a potato masher or the back of a large spoon, coarsely mash beans until liquid is incorporated. In another bowl, mix the ricotta and 2½ cups of the jack cheese.

Drain noodles; blot dry. Arrange 5 noodles, slightly overlapping, to cover the bottom of a lightly oiled 8- by 12-inch or 9- by 13-inch baking dish. Top with half each of the beans, ricotta mixture, and tomato sauce. Repeat layers to use remaining noodles, beans, ricotta, and sauce. Sprinkle top with remaining jack cheese. If made ahead, cover and chill up until next day.

Bake lasagne, uncovered, in a 375° oven until top is browned and casserole is bubbling, about 40 minutes (45 to 50 minutes if chilled). Let stand 10 minutes before serving. Add salt to taste. Makes 8 servings.

PER SERVING: 582 calories, 36 g protein, 55 g carbohydrates, 25 g fat, 70 mg cholesterol, 996 mg sodium

LASAGNE WITH ROASTED ONIONS, TURKEY & THYME

- 3½ pounds (about 5 large) red onions, sliced thin
- 3 slices bacon, diced
- 3 tablespoons balsamic or red wine vinegar
- 1 pound ground turkey
- 3 tablespoons minced fresh or 3 teaspoons crumbled dry thyme leaves
- 10 dry wide lasagne noodles (about 5 oz. total)
- 2 cups regular-strength chicken broth
- 1½ cups low-fat milk
- 2 tablespoons cornstarch dissolved in ¼ cup water
- 1 cup (4 oz.) shredded parmesan cheese

In an 11- by 17-inch roasting pan, mix together onions, bacon, and vinegar. Bake in a 400° oven, stirring occasionally, until onions and bacon are well browned, about 55 minutes. Sprinkle with turkey and 1 tablespoon fresh or 1 teaspoon dry thyme and bake until turkey just turns white, 8 to 10 minutes. Transfer onion-meat mixture to a bowl; reserve pan.

Meanwhile, bring 3 quarts water to a boil in a 5- to 6-quart pan over high heat. Add noodles and cook, uncovered, until just tender to bite, about 8 minutes. Drain and immediately immerse in cold water.

To reserved roasting pan, add broth, milk, and remaining thyme. Place over high heat and bring to a boil, stirring to free browned bits. Add cornstarch mixture; stir until boiling. Remove from heat.

Drain noodles; blot dry. Slightly overlap 5 noodles over bottom of a lightly oiled 8- by 12-inch or 9- by 13-inch baking dish. Top with half each of the meat, sauce, and cheese. Repeat layers to use remaining noodles, meat, sauce, and cheese. If made ahead, cover and chill up until next day.

Bake lasagne, uncovered, in a 375° oven until top is browned and casserole is bubbling, about 40 minutes (45 to 50 minutes if chilled). Let stand 10 minutes before serving. Makes 8 servings.

PER SERVING: 342 calories, 21 g protein, 33 g carbohydrates, 14 g fat, 57 mg cholesterol, 339 mg sodium

Little Lamb Chops

LITTLE LAMBS *produce diminutive chops, each just a few tender bites. The small size means the chops cook especially fast—and care must be taken to get good browning as well as moist meat.*

Two techniques work well: barbecuing over hot coals and sautéing in a pan. The barbecued chops are seasoned before grilling, then served with a salad and citrus dressing, which flavors the meat and greens. The pan-browned lamb with wine sauce is easiest to cook in rack form; to serve, slice between bones into chops.

Australia and New Zealand produce the bulk of our "little lamb" supply. These countries prefer smaller cuts of meat and market a lighter-weight animal. Although American lamb cuts tend to be up to twice as big, occasionally meat from smaller domestic lambs is available.

Lamb for small chops is generally sold fresh or frozen as racks. Some markets regularly carry small lamb racks; others may have them by special order. The price will be higher than for larger chops, up to $12 per pound.

Buy 2 racks that each have about 8 ribs and weigh 1½ to 1¾ pounds before trimming, about 1 pound afterward.

Ask the meat cutter to trim off the chine (backbone) and feather bones, and to French-cut the ribs (French-cutting means trimming the little amount of meat and fat from the ribs, cleaning the bones).

HOT LAMB CHOP & CITRUS SALAD

- 2 **pounds trimmed small lamb racks (fat, chine, and feather bones removed and ribs French-cut)**
- 4 **large cloves garlic**
- 2 **tablespoons salad oil**
- 1½ **tablespoons ground coriander**
- 1 **large pink grapefruit**
- 2 **large oranges**
  About ½ cup orange juice
- 1 **teaspoon cornstarch**
- ¾ **pound escarole, torn into pieces, rinsed and crisped**
  Salt and pepper

Cut lamb between ribs into chops.

In a food processor or with a mortar and pestle, whirl or mash garlic, oil, and coriander into a paste. Rub meat with ¾ of paste.

Cut off peel and white membrane from grapefruit and oranges. Working over a bowl, cut between inner fruit membranes to release segments. Squeeze juice from membranes into bowl and discard membranes. Drain juice into a measuring cup and add enough orange juice to make 1 cup; stir in cornstarch. Mix escarole with fruit segments; set aside.

In a 1- to 2-quart pan over medium-high heat, stir remaining garlic mixture until slightly softened, 2 to 3 minutes. Stir in juice mixture. Bring to a boil over high heat, stirring. Set aside to cool.

Cook chops on a greased grill 4 to 6 inches above a solid bed of hot coals (you can hold your hand at grill level only 2 to 3 seconds). Turn chops frequently until they're done to your liking (cut to test), about 5 minutes for rare.

Mix salad with half of juice dressing and arrange on plates with chops. Offer remaining dressing and salt and pepper to add to taste. Makes 4 or 5 servings.

PER SERVING: 341 calories, 26 g protein, 23 g carbohydrates, 17 g fat, 77 mg cholesterol, 101 mg sodium

RACK OF LAMB IN SPICED WINE SAUCE

- 2 **pounds trimmed small lamb racks (fat, chine, and feather bones removed and ribs French-cut)**
- 1 **teaspoon salad oil**
- ⅓ **cup minced shallots**
- ½ **teaspoon ground allspice**
- 1 **teaspoon ground cinnamon**
- ¼ **cup currants**
- 1½ **cups dry red wine**
- 1 **cup regular-strength beef broth**
- 2 **tablespoons whipping cream**
- ½ **teaspoon cornstarch**
  Salt and pepper

Cut racks into 4-rib sections. In a 10- to 12-inch frying pan over medium-high heat, brown meat and bones in oil on all

Petite grilled chops and escarole salad share coriander, garlic, and citrus seasonings.

sides, turning, until meat is done to your liking (cut to test), 12 to 14 minutes total for rare. Transfer meat to a platter; keep warm in a 150° oven.

Add shallots to frying pan and stir often until limp, 4 to 5 minutes. Stir in allspice, cinnamon, currants, wine, and broth. Boil over high heat until reduced to 1¼ cups, about 7 minutes. Stir cream and cornstarch until smooth; add to wine mixture with any juices from meat platter. Stir until boiling.

Spoon sauce onto warm plates. Slice ribs apart and arrange in sauce. Season with salt and pepper. Makes 4 or 5 servings.

PER SERVING: 262 calories, 24 g protein, 9.6 g carbohydrates, 14 g fat, 84 mg cholesterol, 93 mg sodium

French Duck & Bean Stew

WHERE THE GREEN *Dordogne River valley snakes through limestone cliffs dotted with ancient chateaux, duck and goose reign supreme. Foie gras is the best-known food of this area of southwestern France. But among the locals, a rustic duck and bean stew is equally celebrated.*

Simple, rich ingredients make the stew special: roasted, simmered duck; white beans; earthy vegetables; hearty croutons.

We enjoyed the stew at La Ferme, a restaurant in Montfort specializing in home-style food of the region. Complete the meal the Dordogne way, with green salad dressed with wine vinegar and walnut oil, and an inky Cahors wine (of Malbec grapes) or a robust Zinfandel.

DORDOGNE DUCK, BEAN & RYE STEW

- 1 **duck, 4 to 5 pounds, thawed if frozen**
- 2 **large (1 lb. total) leeks, roots and tough leaves trimmed, sliced**
- 1 **cup chopped shallots**
- 3½ **quarts water or regular-strength chicken broth (or equal parts of each)**
- 1 **pound (2⅓ cups) dry Great Northern beans, sorted of debris and rinsed**
- 1 **teaspoon pepper**
- ½ **to ¾ pound unsliced coarse, dense rye bread (preferably sourdough rye), torn into 1½-inch chunks**
- 1 **pound slender carrots, cut into 2-inch lengths**
- ¾ **pound thin-skinned potatoes, peeled and sliced ½ inch thick**
  Chopped parsley
  Salt

Pull out duck giblets; reserve liver for other uses. Rinse bird and giblets and pat dry. Pull off and discard lumps of fat. With poultry shears or a sharp knife, quarter the duck. Place bird and giblets in a 12- by 15-inch roasting pan. Bake in a 500° oven until duck is well browned, 30 to 35 minutes. Twice during cooking, spoon or siphon fat from pan into a bowl. Lift duck from roasting pan and set aside.

Drain all but ¼ cup fat from pan into bowl. Stir leeks and shallots into roasting pan. Bake until vegetables are limp, about 5 minutes. Add 1 cup water to vegetables and stir to loosen browned bits. Scrape mixture into an 8- to 10-quart pan. Add remaining water, then beans, then duck and pepper.

Bring to a boil over high heat; cover and simmer until beans are tender to bite, about 2 hours.

Meanwhile, brush bread with about 2 tablespoons reserved duck fat; discard extra fat. Put bread in a 10- by 15-inch pan; bake it in a 325° oven until lightly toasted, about 15 minutes. (If made ahead, store uncovered up to 1 day.)

Lift duck from pan; when cool enough to handle, pull off and discard skin and bones; discard giblets. Tear meat into chunks and return to pan. (At this point, you can let stew cool, then cover and chill up to 1 day. Reheat to simmering.)

Add carrots and potatoes to stew. Bring to a boil over high heat, then cover and simmer until potatoes are tender to bite, 20 to 30 minutes; stir occasionally.

Put bread in wide soup bowls and fill with stew. Sprinkle with parsley and season with salt. Makes 4½ quarts, 8 servings.

PER SERVING: 565 calories, 32 g protein, 72 g carbohydrates, 18 g fat, 62 mg cholesterol, 239 mg sodium

Outdoors in California or in France, this rustic duck and bean stew satisfies hearty appetites. Complete the meal with green salad and robust red wine.

Quick One-pan Dinners

USE ONE PAN *and keep it simple. This way, dinner is easy to prepare. These four dishes—corn stew, polenta soup, a thick bean soup, and paella—go together quickly.*

TRIPLE CORN STEW

- ³/₄ **pound chorizo sausage, casings removed**
- 1 **can (14¹/₂ oz.) golden hominy, drained**
- 1 **can (17 oz.) cream-style corn**
- 1 **can (16 oz.) corn kernels, drained, or 1 package (10 oz.) frozen corn kernels**
- 1 **teaspoon cornstarch**
- ¹/₂ **cup regular-strength chicken broth**
  Thin-sliced red radishes

Coarsely chop or crumble sausage. In a 4- to 5-quart pan over medium heat, stir sausage until well browned, 15 to 20 minutes. Discard drippings. Add hominy, cream-style corn, and corn kernels. Cook, uncovered, stirring occasionally until hot, about 5 minutes.

Mix cornstarch with broth; stir into pan and continue stirring until mixture boils. Ladle stew into 4 wide bowls. Garnish with radishes. Makes 4 servings.

PER SERVING: 260 calories, 17 g protein, 53 g carbohydrates, 0.5 g fat, 18 mg cholesterol, 129 mg sodium

POLENTA SOUP

- ³/₄ **pound mild Italian sausage**
- 3¹/₂ **cups (2 cans, each 14¹/₂ oz.) regular-strength chicken broth**
- 2 **cups water**
- ³/₄ **cup polenta or yellow cornmeal**
- 3 **ounces thin-sliced fontina cheese**
  Fresh basil leaves (optional)

Remove sausage casings and discard. Crumble sausage into a 4- to 5-quart pan over medium heat and stir often until well browned, about 20 minutes. Discard drippings. Add broth, water, and polenta to pan. Bring mixture to a boil and stir often until polenta is creamy to bite, 7 to 10 minutes. Ladle soup into 4 bowls; top equally with cheese, then with basil. Makes 4 servings.

PER SERVING: 405 calories, 22 g protein, 23 g carbohydrates, 24 g fat, 73 mg cholesterol, 791 mg sodium

Chorizo seasons this three-corn stew blending hominy, creamed corn, and whole kernels. Crisp radish slices make peppery garnish.

BLACK BEAN SOUP

Look for the instant refried black beans at natural-food stores.

- 2 **teaspoons salad oil**
- 1 **large onion, chopped**
- 1³/₄ **or 2³/₄ cups regular-strength chicken broth**
- 1 **can (28 oz.) tomatoes**
- 3 **cans (15 oz. each) black beans, drained and puréed, or 1 package (7 oz.) instant refried black bean mix**
- 1 **fresh jalapeño chili, stemmed, seeded, and minced**
- 2 **teaspoons whole cumin seed**
  Condiments (choices follow)

In a 5- to 6-quart pan over medium heat, stir oil and onion often until golden, about 20 minutes. Add 1³/₄ cup broth (or 2³/₄ cup if using instant beans), tomatoes and their liquid, beans, jalapeno, and cumin; break up tomatoes with a spoon. Bring to a boil; simmer, uncovered, until thick and flavors blend, 7 to 10 minutes. Ladle into bowls; offer condiments. Makes 4 servings.

PER SERVING: 273 calories, 15 g protein, 43 g carbohydrates, 5.2 g fat, 0 mg cholesterol, 855 mg sodium

Condiments. Shredded **cheddar cheese, sour cream, fresh cilantro** (coriander), **tortilla chips,** and **lime** wedges.

COUSCOUS PAELLA

- 1 **large (about ¹/₂ lb.) onion, chopped**
- ¹/₂ **pound linguisa sausage, sliced thin**
- 1 **bottle (8 oz.) clam juice**
- 1¹/₄ **cups regular-strength chicken broth**
- 2 **teaspoons cumin seed**
- 1¹/₂ **cups couscous**
- 1 **small red bell pepper, stemmed, seeded, and chopped**
- ¹/₃ **pound shelled cooked tiny shrimp, rinsed and drained**

In a 10- to 12-inch frying pan over medium heat, stir onion and sausage often until browned, 10 to 15 minutes. Add clam juice, broth, and cumin. Bring to a boil; stir in couscous. Cover pan; remove from heat. Let stand until liquid is absorbed, about 5 minutes. Stir in bell pepper and top with shrimp. Makes 4 to 6 servings.

PER SERVING: 573 calories, 25 g protein, 60 g carbohydrates, 25 g fat, 112 mg cholesterol, 619 mg sodium

New Versions of French Toast

A VERSATILE DISH, *French toast needn't be limited to breakfast. It can easily lend itself to supper or even a decadent dessert.*

All three of these recipes call for baking the toast instead of pan-frying it. This not only eliminates excess fat but also makes cleanup easy.

TROPICAL FRENCH TOAST

>   3 large eggs
>   3/4 cup orange juice
>   3 tablespoons lime juice
>   1/4 cup powdered sugar
>   1/2 teaspoon coconut extract
>   8 slices French bread (cut diagonally
>   from loaf), each about 1/2 inch thick
>   3/4 cup sweetened flaked coconut
>   Tropical topping (recipe follows)
>   Whole strawberries, rinsed and
>   drained (optional)

Colorful glow of strawberries, papaya, and bananas tops French toast soaked in orange and lime juice and baked with coconut.

In a wide bowl, beat together eggs, orange juice, lime juice, powdered sugar, and coconut extract until well blended.

Dip each piece of bread in egg mixture, turning to saturate both sides. Arrange slices in a single layer on a lightly greased 12- by 15-inch baking sheet. Sprinkle tops of slices evenly with half the coconut. Lightly press coconut onto bread.

Bake bread in a 400° oven until coconut is lightly browned, about 10 minutes. With a wide spatula, turn slices over. Sprinkle evenly with remaining coconut. Continue baking until slices are puffed and coconut and bread are lightly browned, about 10 minutes longer.

Transfer slices to individual plates; allow 2 per serving. Spoon topping over bread, dividing it evenly among plates. Garnish with whole strawberries. Makes 4 servings.

PER SERVING: 276 calories, 8.6 g protein, 40 g carbohydrates, 9.3 g fat, 160 mg cholesterol, 288 mg sodium

Tropical topping. Peel, seed, and coarsely chop 1 large (about 1 lb.) ripe **papaya.** Peel and slice 2 medium-size (about 3/4 lb. total) firm-ripe **bananas.** In a bowl, gently mix papaya, banana, 1 1/2 cups hulled and sliced **strawberries,** 2 tablespoons **sugar,** 1 1/2 tablespoons **lime juice,** and 1 tablespoon **orange-flavor liqueur** (optional). If made ahead, cover and chill up to 2 hours.

CHILI-CHEESE FRENCH TOAST WITH SALSA

>   3 large eggs
>   1 cup nonfat or low-fat milk
>   8 slices French bread (cut diagonally
>   from loaf), each about 1/3 inch
>   thick and about 3 by 6 inches
>   1/3 pound jack cheese, shredded
>   1 can (4 oz.) diced green chilies
>   1/4 cup minced fresh cilantro
>   (coriander)
>   About 2 cups purchased salsa

In a wide bowl, beat together eggs and milk until well blended. Dip 4 slices of bread into egg mixture; turn to saturate both sides. Arrange slices on a lightly greased 12- by 15-inch baking sheet.

Top bread evenly with cheese, chilies, and cilantro. Dip remaining slices in egg mixture, coating both sides. Top cheese-covered bread with plain slices to form 4 sandwiches.

Bake sandwiches in a 400° oven until they begin to brown, about 12 minutes. With a wide spatula, turn sandwiches over and continue baking until they are puffed and evenly browned, about 10 minutes longer. Cut sandwiches in half crosswise. Transfer 2 halves to each of 4 plates; overlap one half over the other. Offer salsa to add to taste. Makes 4 servings.

PER SERVING: 323 calories, 18 g protein, 26 g carbohydrates, 16 g fat, 194 mg cholesterol, 1,308 mg sodium

SINFUL FRENCH TOAST SUNDAES

>   2 slices French bread (cut diagonally
>   from loaf), each about 2 1/2 inches
>   thick and about 3 by 6 inches
>   1/4 cup peanut butter, smooth or
>   chunk-style
>   1/4 cup semisweet chocolate chips
>   3 large eggs
>   1/2 cup nonfat or low-fat milk
>   3 tablespoons powdered sugar
>   1 teaspoon vanilla
>   1/2 teaspoon ground cinnamon
>   Vanilla or chocolate ice cream or
>   frozen yogurt

Cut bread slices in half crosswise. In the cut side of each piece, carefully tear or cut out a pocket about 1 1/2 inches long, 3/4 inch wide, and 2 1/2 inches deep. In each one, gently spread about 1 tablespoon peanut butter, then add 1 tablespoon chocolate chips. Push chocolate toward the back of the pocket with a spoon.

In a bowl, beat together eggs, milk, 2 tablespoons sugar, vanilla, and cinnamon until well blended. Dip each stuffed bread slice into egg mixture, turning to saturate both sides. Arrange slices on a lightly greased 12- by 15-inch baking sheet.

Bake in a 400° oven until tops are lightly browned, about 12 minutes. Turn slices over and continue baking until bread is browned, about 10 minutes longer.

Sift remaining powdered sugar evenly over bread. Transfer to dessert plates. Serve warm with scoops of ice cream or frozen yogurt. Makes 4 servings.

PER SERVING: 371 calories, 15 g protein, 42 g carbohydrates, 16 g fat, 161 mg cholesterol, 392 mg sodium

Muffins without Bottoms

MUFFIN FANS *are of two types: conformists who enjoy the whole thing and oddballs who eat only the tops. How do you make an oddball happy? You bake muffins without bottoms, like big, thick cookies.*

These three flavorful batters meet the challenge well. Choose from citrus and spice, apple-raisin-bran, and raspberry streusel; or try all three. Instead of using muffin tins, you mound the batter on flat baking sheets.

To bake muffin tops, put baking sheets with batter in a 350° oven until well browned, 20 to 22 minutes (if using 2 pans in 1 oven, switch pan positions after 10 minutes). Remove the muffin tops from pans with a wide spatula and serve, or let cool on racks. Serve warm or cool.

To store, wrap airtight and hold at room temperature up until next day; freeze to store longer (thaw wrapped).

To reheat, return muffin tops to baking sheets, cover with foil, and warm in a 350° oven for 15 to 18 minutes.

CITRUS & SPICE MUFFIN TOPS

- 2 cups all-purpose flour
- 1 cup sugar
- 1½ teaspoons baking powder
- ½ teaspoon baking soda
- ½ teaspoon *each* ground nutmeg and ground coriander
- ¼ teaspoon ground cloves
- 1 large egg
- ¼ cup regular or nonfat milk
- ¼ cup (⅛ lb.) butter or margarine, melted
- 1 tablespoon grated orange peel
- 1 teaspoon *each* grated lemon and lime peel
- 3 tablespoons *each* lemon and lime juice

In a bowl, stir together flour, sugar, baking powder, baking soda, nutmeg, coriander, and cloves. Make a well in center and add egg; milk; butter; orange, lemon, and lime peel; and lemon and lime juice. Beat liquids to blend, then stir to incorporate dry ingredients until evenly moistened.

Spoon batter in ⅓-cup-size mounds about 2 inches apart on lightly greased baking sheets, 12- by 15-inch size.

To bake, store, or reheat muffin tops, see preceding. Makes 8.

PER PIECE: 283 calories, 4.4 g protein, 51 g carbohydrates, 7.2 g fat, 44 mg cholesterol, 205 mg sodium

APPLE-RAISIN-BRAN MUFFIN TOPS

- 1 large egg
- 1½ cups bran cereal (not flakes)
- ⅓ cup *each* salad oil and water
- 1 cup regular or nonfat milk
- 1 large (about ½ lb.) tart apple (such as Granny Smith or Newtown Pippin), peeled, cored, and diced
- ½ cup raisins
- 1½ cups all-purpose flour
- ¼ cup *each* granulated sugar and firmly packed brown sugar
- 2 teaspoons baking powder
- 1 teaspoon *each* baking soda and ground cinnamon
- ¼ teaspoon ground allspice
- ¼ teaspoon salt

In a large bowl, beat until well blended the egg, bran cereal, oil, water, milk, apple, and raisins.

Mix flour, granulated sugar, brown sugar, baking powder, baking soda, cinnamon, allspice, and salt. Add to the bran mixture and stir until evenly moistened.

Spoon batter in ⅓-cup-size mounds about 2 inches apart on lightly greased baking sheets, 12- by 15-inch size.

To bake, store, or reheat muffin tops, see preceding. Makes 12.

PER PIECE: 211 calories, 4.5 g protein, 37 g carbohydrates, 7 g fat, 18 mg cholesterol, 301 mg sodium

RASPBERRY STREUSEL MUFFIN TOPS

- 2⅓ cups all-purpose flour
- 1 cup firmly packed brown sugar
- ½ cup chopped almonds
- ½ teaspoon ground nutmeg
- ¾ cup (⅜ lb.) butter or margarine
- 2 teaspoons baking powder
- 1 teaspoon baking soda
- 1 large egg
- ⅔ cup regular or nonfat milk
- 1 cup raspberries, fresh or unsweetened frozen (thawed)

In a bowl, combine flour, sugar, almonds, and nutmeg. With your fingers, rub in butter until the mixture forms coarse crumbs; set aside ¾ cup of this mixture.

To bowl add baking powder and baking soda. Stir to mix thoroughly, then make a well in center; add egg and milk and beat to blend, then stir to incorporate and evenly moisten dry ingredients. Gently stir raspberries into batter.

Spoon batter in ⅓-cup-size mounds about 2 inches apart on lightly greased baking sheets, 12- by 15-inch size. Firmly squeeze the reserved crumb mixture to form large lumps, then coarsely break lumps into chunks about the size of peanuts. Scatter chunks evenly over batter mounds.

To bake, store, or reheat muffin tops, see preceding. Makes 10 or 11.

PER PIECE: 341 calories, 5 g protein, 43 g carbohydrates, 17 g fat, 56 mg cholesterol, 302 mg sodium

Where's the bottom? If you like muffin tops best, toss the muffin pan and bake the batter on a baking sheet for a flat cooky shape.

Scaled-down Foods for Toddlers

ATISFYING TODDLERS at meals or snacktime with scaled-down wholesome foods not only makes eating more appealing and manageable but can also eliminate waste and scattered scraps.

Here, we feature nutritious foods to fit both small hands and small appetites. Try the fruit-filled mini-muffins or petite yogurt-based frozen juice bars. Vegetables offer some fanciful choices, too: diminutive "trees" of cooked broccoli and cauliflower, and "grass," as one of our toddler tasters dubbed her spear of asparagus.

Tiny apple-raisin muffin is just the right size for two-year-old appetites.

APPLE, CINNAMON & RAISIN MINI-MUFFINS

- 1 cup all-purpose flour
- 1 cup quick-cooking rolled oats
- 3 tablespoons firmly packed brown sugar
- 2 teaspoons baking powder
- ½ teaspoon ground cinnamon
- 1 large egg
- ½ cup apple juice
- 3 tablespoons salad oil
- 1 medium-size tart apple (such as Granny Smith or Newtown Pippin), peeled, cored, and shredded
- ½ cup raisins

In a small bowl, stir together flour, oats, sugar, baking powder, and cinnamon.

In another bowl, beat to blend egg, juice, oil, apple, and raisins. Add the dry ingredients; stir just until moistened throughout.

Spoon batter equally into 24 greased tiny muffin pans (about 1½-in. diameter). Bake in a 400° oven until well browned, 20 to 25 minutes. Remove from pans; serve warm or cool. If made ahead, package cool muffins airtight and hold at room temperature up until next day; freeze to store longer. Makes 24.

PER MUFFIN: 71 calories, 1.4 g protein, 12 g carbohydrates, 2.2 g fat, 8.9 mg cholesterol, 39 mg sodium

FROZEN YOGURT & JUICE BARS

Look for plastic popsicle molds in houseware departments or from companies selling plastic houseware goods.

- ½ cup unflavored nonfat yogurt
- ½ cup (1 bottle, 4-oz. size) mixed fruit juice for babies
- 1 small ripe banana, peeled and sliced
- ½ teaspoon vanilla
- 1 tablespoon apricot jam (optional)

In a food processor or blender, smoothly purée yogurt, juice, banana, vanilla, and jam. Pour equally into 6 plastic popsicle molds, 2 ounces each. Cover and freeze until solid, about 2 hours. Serve or freeze up to 2 weeks.

To remove 1 bar at a time, wrap mold base with a small hot, wet cloth or drizzle mold with hot water about 5 seconds. Lift out bar. Makes 6.

PER JUICE BAR: 36 calories, 1.3 g protein, 7.5 g carbohydrates, 0.1 g fat, 0.4 mg cholesterol, 15 mg sodium

TREE FOOD

Broccoli and cauliflower flowerets have easy-to-hold "trunks." Budding gourmets might use trees with party dips, too.

Broccoli trees. Cut flower heads and about 3 inches of stem from about ½ pound **broccoli.** Peel stems if skin is tough. Break or cut vertically through broccoli flowerets and stems to create trees with trunks no more than about ¾ inch wide. Drop into about 1½ inches boiling **water;** cook on high heat just until stem is barely tender when pierced, 4 to 5 minutes. Drain and at once immerse in ice water; when cool, drain. Serve, or cover and chill up to 2 days.

PER ⅛ POUND: 17 calories, 1.8 g protein, 3.1 g carbohydrates, 0.2 g fat, 0 mg cholesterol, 16 mg sodium

Cauliflower trees. Remove and discard outer leaves from ½ of a small head (about 1¼ lb. total) **cauliflower.** Cut flowerets from core and split stems up through floweret tops to make trunks no more than ¾ inch wide. Drop into about 1½ inches boiling **water;** cook on high heat until stems are barely tender when pierced, 4 to 5 minutes. Drain. Serve cool, or cover and chill up to 2 days.

PER ⅛ POUND: 14 calories, 1.8 g protein, 3 g carbohydrates, 0.1 g fat, 0 mg cholesterol, 8.9 mg sodium

BLADES OF GRASS

Snap off and discard tough ends from ¼ to ½ pound **asparagus;** peel stalks with a vegetable peeler. Fill a 10- to 12-inch frying pan with 1 to 1½ inches **water;** bring to a boil. Add asparagus and cook just until tender when pierced, 2 to 4 minutes. Drain and immerse asparagus in ice water; when cool, drain. Serve, or cover and chill up until next day.

PER ⅛ POUND: 13 calories, 1.8 g protein, 2.2 g carbohydrates, 0.1 g fat, 0 mg cholesterol, 1.2 mg sodium

A Deliciously Messy Dutch Treat

NO ONE COULD FINISH *a chocolate éclair this big and decadent. Or so we thought, eyeing a Bosche bol on a recent trip to the Netherlands. A few mouthfuls later, the rich whipped cream–filled puff, enrobed in dark chocolate, was gone.*

Two bakeries in the town of 's-Hertogenbosch, 50 miles southeast of Amsterdam, make this dessert their specialty. Jan de Groot bakery claims to have taken the first puff from the oven more than 40 years ago. Now it does a brisk business of about 2,000 "bollen," or balls, per day. The name Bosche bollen is taken from a local, more pronounceable version of the town's name: Den Bosch.

At home, make Bosche bollen with a classic egg-rich cream puff paste. Spoonfuls of the paste rise dramatically in the oven, leaving hollow pockets that you fill with the heaviest whipping cream you can justify. The icing is chocolate and more cream.

BOSCHE BOLLEN

If undercooked, the shells may soften and collapse.

- ½ cup water
- ¼ cup (⅛ lb.) butter or margarine
- ½ cup all-purpose flour
- 2 large eggs
  Whipped cream (recipe follows)
  Dark chocolate glaze (recipe follows)

In a 2- to 3-quart pan over medium-high heat, bring water and butter to a boil. When butter melts, add flour all at once and stir until mixture holds together and pulls from side of pan, 15 to 30 seconds.

Remove pan from heat; you can put mixture in a food processor or leave in pan. Let cool for 2 minutes.

Add eggs, 1 at a time, whirling or beating vigorously after each addition until egg is incorporated and mixture is glossy.

Evenly space 6 equal mounds of dough on a greased 10- by 15-inch baking sheet. Bake in a 425° oven until puffs are deep golden, and firm and dry to touch, about 35 minutes. Transfer puffs to a rack and let cool completely.

If made ahead, store puffs airtight up to 2 days or freeze. If they soften, reheat on baking sheet in a 400° oven

Decadent and deliciously messy, this supersize, super-rich Dutch version of a chocolate éclair has sweet cream inside a crisp shell.

until puffs are crisp to touch, about 5 minutes.

With a serrated knife, gently cut the upper fourth from each puff. Pull out and discard eggy webs, then fill with whipped cream. Replace puff lids. Place puffs on a wire rack set over a rimmed pan. Spoon chocolate glaze over puffs, covering tops and sides as well as you can. Lift rack from pan and scrape chocolate drips from pan back into double boiler; return rack to rimmed pan and spoon chocolate over puffs to finish coating.

Chill puffs until chocolate is set, about 30 minutes. Serve, or chill up to 2 hours longer. Makes 6.

PER PUFF: 494 calories, 7 g protein, 29 g carbohydrates, 43 g fat, 170 mg cholesterol, 127 mg sodium

Whipped cream. In the bowl of an electric mixer, beat 1¼ cups **whipping cream,** ¼ cup **powdered sugar,** and 1 teaspoon **vanilla** until mixture holds soft peaks.

Dark chocolate glaze. Over hot water in the top of a double boiler, combine ½ cup **whipping cream** and 6 ounces (¾ cup) chopped **bittersweet chocolate** or semisweet chocolate baking chips. Stir over medium heat until chocolate melts and mixture is smooth. Use warm.

Purée spinach and dry basil for pesto pasta salad.

SPINACH PESTO PASTA SALAD

- 1 pound dry linguine
- 1 cup (about 2 oz.) firmly packed rinsed, drained, and chopped spinach leaves
- 3 tablespoons dry basil leaves
- 1 or 2 cloves garlic
- 1/3 cup grated parmesan cheese
- 1/3 cup olive oil
- 1/2 cup drained chopped dried tomatoes packed in oil (optional)
- 1 can (2 1/4 oz.) sliced ripe olives, drained
- 2 cups (about 1 lb.) cherry tomatoes, rinsed, stemmed, and cut in half

  Salt and pepper

In a 5- to 6-quart pan, bring about 3 quarts water to a boil. Add linguine and cook until barely tender to bite, about 7 minutes. Drain, rinse with cold water until cool, and drain again.

In a food processor or blender, combine spinach, basil, garlic, cheese, and oil. Whirl, scraping bowl as needed, until mixture is puréed.

In a large bowl, combine the cooked linguine, spinach mixture, dried tomatoes, sliced olives, and cherry tomatoes. Mix well. Add salt and pepper to taste. Makes 8 to 10 servings.—*Lois Dowling, Tacoma.*

PER SERVING: 265 calories, 7.7 g protein, 38 g carbohydrates, 9.5 g fat, 2.1 mg cholesterol, 117 mg sodium

Chicken-pineapple kebab makes easy, attractive dinner.

CHICKEN KEBABS SHANGHAI

- 3/4 teaspoon grated orange peel
- 1/3 cup orange juice
- 3 tablespoons firmly packed brown sugar
- 2 tablespoons soy sauce
- 4 teaspoons minced fresh ginger
- 4 teaspoons wine vinegar
- 1 tablespoon Oriental sesame oil or salad oil
- 1/2 teaspoon ground coriander
- 1 1/2 pounds skinned and boned chicken breast
- 3/4 pound peeled and cored pineapple

In a bowl, mix the orange peel, juice, sugar, soy sauce, ginger, vinegar, sesame oil, and coriander. Cut chicken into 1 1/2-inch chunks and stir into orange juice mixture. Cover and chill at least 30 minutes or up to 2 hours. Cut pineapple into about 1-inch chunks.

On thin skewers, thread chicken and pineapple, alternating 2 pieces chicken with 1 piece pineapple. Brush remaining marinade over pineapple. Place skewers on a rack in a 12- by 15-inch broiler pan. Broil about 4 inches from heat, turning once, until chicken is white in thickest part (cut to test), 12 to 14 minutes. Makes 4 or 5 servings.—*Susan Robin Kelso, La Costa, Calif.*

PER SERVING: 251 calories, 32 g protein, 19 g carbohydrates, 4.7 g fat, 79 mg cholesterol, 504 mg sodium

Fill blanched Swiss chard with rice, cheese, chilies.

CHARD-RICE PACKETS

- 8 large (1 to 1 1/2 lb. total, with green sections about 6 by 8 in.) Swiss chard leaves, rinsed
- 1 1/2 cups cooked rice
- 1 can (7 oz.) diced green chilies or 1 jar (11 oz.) cactus (nopales), drained and chopped
- 6 ounces (1 1/2 cups) diced or crumbled kuminost cheese
- 3 tablespoons chopped fresh cilantro (coriander)

  Salt and pepper

In a 5- to 6-quart pan, bring about 3 quarts water to a boil. Cut chard stems from leaves. Plunge stems into water; cook until tender when pierced, 4 to 5 minutes. Lift out of water and drain. Add leaves to water and cook until limp, 1 to 2 minutes. Drain.

Coarsely chop the chard stems. In a bowl, mix stems, rice, chilies, cheese, cilantro, and salt and pepper to taste. Place 1/8 of rice mixture in center of each chard leaf. Wrap leaf sides and ends around filling to enclose. Place packets seam down in a shallow 3-quart baking dish. Bake, covered, in a 400° oven until hot in center (cut to test), about 20 minutes. Makes 8 servings.—*Janet M. Maney Quiroz, Tempe, Ariz.*

PER SERVING: 146 calories, 7.5 g protein, 15 g carbohydrates, 6.7 g fat, 19 mg cholesterol, 387 mg sodium

Banana Buckwheat Muffins

1 cup all-purpose flour
½ cup buckwheat flour
½ cup whole-wheat flour
2 tablespoons poppy seed
2 teaspoons baking powder
1 teaspoon baking soda
¾ teaspoon ground nutmeg
3 medium-size (about 1 lb. total) ripe bananas
2 large eggs
¼ cup salad oil
¼ cup honey

In a small bowl, mix all-purpose flour, buckwheat flour, whole-wheat flour, poppy seed, baking powder, baking soda, and nutmeg. Peel bananas and break them into 1-inch chunks.

In a food processor or blender, combine bananas, eggs, oil, and honey; whirl until puréed. Pour banana mixture into flour mixture; mix lightly just to blend.

Spoon the batter equally into 12 greased or paper-lined muffin cups (2½ in. wide).

Bake in a 375° oven until golden and top springs back when lightly touched in center, about 20 minutes. Remove from pans and cool on racks. Serve warm or cool. Makes 12 muffins.—*Linda Hiatt, Arcata, Calif.*

PER MUFFIN: 177 calories, 4 g protein, 27 g carbohydrates, 6.5 g fat, 35 mg cholesterol, 152 mg sodium

Offer banana muffins for breakfast treat.

Trout with Dill-Mushroom Sour Cream Sauce

4 trout (½ to ¾ lb. each), cleaned
1 tablespoon butter or margarine
½ pound mushrooms, sliced thin
½ cup thin-sliced green onion
1 tablespoon all-purpose flour
1 cup regular-strength chicken broth
2 tablespoons lemon juice
2 tablespoons minced fresh dill or ½ teaspoon dry dill weed
½ cup light or regular sour cream
Salt and pepper

Remove heads from trout, if desired. Rinse fish, pat dry, and lay in an oiled 10- by 15-inch baking pan. Bake, uncovered, in a 400° oven until fish looks opaque but is still moist in thickest part (cut to test), 12 to 16 minutes.

Meanwhile, in a 10- to 12-inch frying pan, combine butter, mushrooms, and onion; stir often over high heat until mushrooms are browned, about 10 minutes. Stir in flour. Add broth, lemon juice, and dill; stir until sauce boils rapidly. Reduce heat to low, add sour cream; stir until hot. Pour into a bowl.

With wide spatulas, transfer trout to a serving platter. Offer sauce to spoon over fish. Add salt and pepper to taste. Makes 4 servings.—*Shanti Adamson, Oregon City, Ore.*

PER SERVING: 274 calories, 27 g protein, 7.7 g carbohydrates, 15 g fat, 82 mg cholesterol, 105 mg sodium

Bake trout; serve with dill-mushroom sauce.

Dessert Nachos with Fruit Salsa

⅓ cup sugar
1 teaspoon ground cinnamon
10 flour tortillas (7 to 8 in. wide)
1 large package (8 oz.) neufchâtel or cream cheese
½ cup orange juice
3 tablespoons honey
Fruit salsa (recipe follows)

Mix sugar and cinnamon in a shallow bowl. Working with 1 tortilla at a time, brush both sides lightly with water, then cut into 6 equal wedges. Dip 1 side of each wedge in sugar mixture. Arrange in a single layer, sugar up, on oiled, foil-lined 12- by 15-inch baking sheets. Bake in a 500° oven until crisp and golden, 4 to 5 minutes.

In a 1- to 2-quart pan, combine the cheese, orange juice, and honey. Whisk over low heat until sauce is smooth, about 3 minutes. Mound chips on a platter. Offer sauce and salsa to spoon onto chips. Makes 10 to 12 servings. —*Lisa Sturgis, Temecula, Calif.*

Fruit salsa. Peel and dice 2 large (about 8 oz. total) **kiwi fruit.** Hull and rinse 2 cups **strawberries;** dice into a bowl. Add kiwi and 1 can (11 oz.) **mandarin oranges,** drained. Makes 3 cups.

PER SERVING: 220 calories, 5.1 g protein, 40 g carbohydrates, 4.6 g fat, 14 mg cholesterol, 253 mg sodium

Spoon fruit salsa and cheese sauce onto sweet tortilla crisps.

IN MANY PARTS of the world, breakfast is a lightweight affair, designed primarily to wake you up and fuel you until you have a substantial lunch. In France and Italy, for instance, breakfasts feature just bread and coffee, but the bread comes in many forms and flavors and the coffee is strong enough to float a nail.

In colder climates, and especially among hardworking rural folk, breakfast is heartier, with meat, cheese, eggs, potatoes, or all the above added to the basics. The German farmer's breakfast (Bauernfrühstück) is a super-omelet with eggs, potatoes, onions, and bacon. To Pennsylvania Dutch farmers, breakfast scarcely differs from lunch or dinner and very likely will include dessert.

From chilly Juneau, John St. Martin sends us a breakfast taco that will wake you up and keep you awake until lunch—maybe even dinner. It has the sustaining elements of a German breakfast—though with a lighter touch—and the warmth of Mexican spices.

BREAKFAST TACOS

1 medium-size (about ½ lb.) russet potato
1 pound bulk pork sausage
1 small onion, chopped
1 teaspoon *each* chili powder and ground cumin
  Cayenne
1 large egg
6 flour tortillas (7 to 8 in. wide)
1 cup (¼ lb.) shredded sharp cheddar cheese
  Homemade or prepared salsa
  Unflavored nonfat yogurt or sour cream

In a 1- to 1½-quart pan, cook potato, covered, in boiling water to cover until tender when pierced, 30 to 35 minutes. Drain. When cool enough to handle, peel and cut into ½-inch cubes.

Into a 10- to 12-inch frying pan over medium-high heat, crumble sausage and add onion, chili powder, and cumin, then sprinkle lightly with cayenne. Stir often until browned, 10 to 15 minutes. Spoon out and discard fat. Add potato and let cook 2 to 3 minutes. Beat egg to blend, pour into pan, and stir until it is set.

Stack and wrap tortillas in foil; place in a 350° oven until hot, about 10 minutes. (Or wrap in paper towels and heat in a microwave oven on full power—100 percent—until warm, about 2 minutes.)

Spoon equal amounts of the hot sausage mixture down the center of each tortilla, top with cheese, and roll to enclose filling. Accompany with salsa and yogurt to add to taste. Makes 6 servings.

PER SERVING: 323 calories, 16 g protein, 20 g carbohydrates, 20 g fat, 85 mg cholesterol, 739 mg sodium

John St. Martin

Juneau

SPAGHETTI SQUASH *has been around for a long time, but its popularity is fairly recent. Years ago, it skulked in the rear sections of seed catalogs along with other suspect novelties like the bush huckleberry (a sort of nightshade, whose only virtue was not being poisonous) and the chufa (whose imperishable nut-like tubers made it a noxious lawn weed). Spaghetti squash showed up as an object resembling an elongated football cut in half and spilling a great tangle of pasta onto its plate. The representation was not a photograph, but the sort of over-inked steel engraving that makes everything seem improbable as well as shabby.*

A few years ago, this squash made a reappearance. With diligent (and honest) promotion, it has become a familiar sight on produce counters. It does not, of course, contain real spaghetti, but the tender-crisp strands look like pasta and have its genius for blending with sauces. Robert Martin dresses it with a classic Italian sauce based on sausage, tomatoes and tomato paste, herbs, and wine.

SPAGHETTI SQUASH WITH SAUSAGE SAUCE

3 to 4 pounds spaghetti squash
1 pound mild Italian sausage
1 medium-size onion, sliced thin
1 clove garlic, minced or pressed
¼ cup finely chopped parsley
2 medium-size (about ⅓ lb. total) Roma-type tomatoes, cored and chopped
½ teaspoon *each* dry basil leaves and dry oregano leaves
1 tablespoon tomato paste or catsup
1 cup dry white wine
¾ cup shredded provolone cheese

Rinse squash, then pierce shell with a sharp fork in 10 to 12 places. Place squash on a paper towel in a microwave

"From chilly Juneau, John St. Martin sends us a breakfast taco that will wake you up."

oven; cook on full power (100 percent) for 14 to 20 minutes, turning squash over every 4 minutes. Loosely cover the squash and set it aside.

Meanwhile, remove sausage casings and crumble meat into a 10- to 12-inch frying pan over medium-high heat. Add onion and garlic; stir often until sausage is browned, 10 to 15 minutes. Discard drippings. Add to meat the parsley, tomatoes, basil, oregano, tomato paste, and wine. Stir, then bring to a boil on high heat. Reduce heat and boil gently, uncovered, until most of the liquid has evaporated, about 10 minutes; stir often.

While sauce simmers, press squash shell; if shell does not give easily to pressure, cook in microwave oven at full power for 1½ minutes at a time until it does give under pressure.

Cut squash in half lengthwise; scoop out and discard seeds. Pull strands free with a fork, leaving them in the shell halves. Evenly top with sauce, then sprinkle with cheese. Heat squash halves in microwave oven on full power just until cheese melts, 3 to 4 minutes. Makes 4 to 6 servings.

PER SERVING: 296 calories, 16 g protein, 16 g carbohydrates, 19 g fat, 53 mg cholesterol, 688 mg sodium

Graham, Wash.

M OST CUISINES *worth investigating have in their repertoires recipes for what might generically be called "things in broth." The Chinese have their won ton, the Russians pelmeni, Spain and Mexico albóndigas, and Jewish tables kreplach.*

The Italians bear the palm away with a host of lovely morsels—agnollotti and tortellini, for instance—luxuriating in steaming broths of chicken, beef, or veal. Less renowned are gnocchi, for which dumplings is an inadequate, even stingy, translation. Usually served with a sauce, these delicacies are entirely at home in a rich beef broth.

John Macchia has drawn inspiration from all these Italian morsels and perhaps also from passatelli, an egg, cheese, and bread crumb mixture pressed through a sieve in strands into hot broth. The cheese puffs in his soup have the shape of gnocchi and the ingredients of passatelli— with significant alterations.

"Tender-crisp strands look like pasta and have its genius for blending with sauces."

CHEESE PUFF SOUP

1⅓ cups low-fat ricotta cheese
1½ cups (6 oz.) shredded fontinella cheese
1 cup (¼ lb.) shredded light or regular Jarlsberg cheese
1¼ cups all-purpose flour
1 large egg
8 cups or 4 cans (14½ oz. each) regular-strength beef broth plus water to make 8 cups
Pepper
Grated parmesan cheese

In a bowl, mix well the ricotta, fontinella, Jarlsberg, and ¾ cup of the flour. Beat in the egg to blend thoroughly.

Spread ¼ cup flour on a board; scrape cheese mixture onto board, dust with ¼ cup flour, and knead to incorporate most of the flour. Form into a ball, cover, and let rest for 30 minutes. Divide ball into 4 equal portions, then shape each into a log about ¾ inch thick. Cut each log into ¾-inch pieces; with the tines of a fork, flatten each piece slightly, leaving grooves in dough; transfer to a flour-dusted platter.

In a 5- to 6-quart pan, bring broth to boiling on high heat. Add dough pieces (take care not to cluster in a lump) and cook until puffs come to the surface, about 1½ minutes. As they float up, lift from pan with a slotted spoon and put in a tureen, then pour broth into tureen. Ladle into bowls and season to taste with pepper and grated cheese. Makes 8 to 10 first-course servings.

PER SERVING: 205 calories, 14 g protein, 15 g carbohydrates, 9.7 g fat, 51 mg cholesterol, 231 mg sodium

Morgan Hill, Calif.

A SOMEWHAT FATUOUS *pre–World War II song celebrated a sandwich of bygone days in impassioned though vague terms. We know only that it was a sentimental sandwich the singer had shared with his inamorata and that he was hungry for it, not for lobster, wine, or stew. If we just knew what that sandwich contained to unleash such a flow of song, we might feel more sympathy for the singer. We hope that it might have been as good as Ralph Pujolar's Cordon Bleu Sandwich.*

Cordon Bleu—French for blue ribbon— is a name that recalls the distinguished cooking school and a style of veal or chicken preparation. With a name like that, it has to be good.

CORDON BLEU SANDWICH

About 2 teaspoons butter or margarine, at room temperature
2 slices French bread or rye bread
1 slice (about 1 oz.) cooked chicken or turkey breast
1 slice (about 1 oz.) cooked ham
Prepared mustard (optional)
1 slice (about 1 oz.) Swiss cheese
1 thin slice large firm-ripe tomato
Dill pickle spears

Butter 1 side of each bread slice; place 1 slice, buttered side down. Top with chicken and ham; spread ham with mustard, then add cheese and tomato. Top with remaining bread, buttered side up.

Place a 7- to 8-inch frying pan over medium heat; when hot, add sandwich and cook until golden brown, about 6 minutes. Turn over and continue to cook until golden brown and cheese is melted, about 5 minutes longer. Serve hot with pickle. Makes 1 serving.

PER SERVING: 440 calories, 29 g protein, 33 g carbohydrates, 21 g fat, 89 mg cholesterol, 929 mg sodium

San Francisco

April Menus

Golden start: breakfast combines anise-cornmeal dollar pancakes, strawberries, and orange wedges with honey-sweetened bacon.

GIVE THE FAMILY *a fresh outlook with a seasonal focus on menus for April. Top pancakes with strawberries, feature asparagus at supper, and fire up the barbecue to cook a complete meal.*

SPRING BREAKFAST

Anise-Cornmeal Dollar Cakes
with Strawberries
Vanilla Yogurt
Baked Honey Bacon
Coffee   Apple Juice

Tiny spiced pancakes complement the sweet red berries.

Assemble ingredients for pancakes, then put bacon in the oven to bake while you mix and cook the cakes on a griddle. Eat the yogurt from small bowls or on fruit.

ANISE-CORNMEAL DOLLAR CAKES WITH STRAWBERRIES

- ³/₄ cup all-purpose flour
- ¹/₄ cup yellow cornmeal
- 1 teaspoon baking powder
- ¹/₄ teaspoon salt
- ³/₄ teaspoon anise seed
- 2 large eggs, separated
- 1 cup milk
  Salad oil
  Strawberries (directions follow)
  Orange wedges

In a bowl, mix flour, cornmeal, baking powder, salt, and anise seed. In another bowl, beat to blend egg yolks and milk. Pour liquid into dry ingredients; stir just to evenly moisten.

With an electric mixer, beat egg whites on high speed until soft peaks form. Gently fold whites into batter.

Place a lightly oiled or nonstick griddle or 10- to 12-inch frying pan over medium heat. When griddle is hot, pour batter onto it in 2-tablespoon portions at least 2 inches apart. Spread batter into 3-inch rounds. Cook until bubbles form on tops and the bottoms are brown, about 2 minutes. Turn with a spatula and cook until brown on bottoms, about 1 minute longer; serve, or keep warm until all are cooked. Repeat to cook remaining pancakes. Accompany with strawberries, and orange wedges to squeeze onto fruit. Makes 4 servings.

PER SERVING: 246 calories, 8.8 g protein, 33 g carbohydrates, 8.6 g fat, 115 mg cholesterol, 305 mg sodium

Strawberries. Rinse and drain 2 cups **strawberries;** hull and slice into a bowl. Sweeten to taste with **powdered sugar.** Use, or cover and chill up until next day.

BAKED HONEY BACON

8 to 12 slices thick-cut bacon
3 tablespoons honey

Line a 10- by 15-inch baking pan with foil. Lay bacon slices side by side (or overlapping if necessary) on foil. Bake, uncovered, in a 350° oven until edges begin to brown, 10 to 15 minutes. Remove from oven; drain off and discard fat.

Brush honey evenly on bacon. Bake in a 350° oven until bacon is well browned, 15 to 20 minutes. Let stand until cool enough to pick up with your fingers, or serve cool. Makes 4 servings.

PER SLICE: 140 calories, 4.9 g protein, 13 g carbohydrates, 7.8 g fat, 13 mg cholesterol, 254 mg sodium

Plump rigatoni and fontina cheese are baked and topped with shrimp; serve with fresh asparagus.

BAKED PASTA SUPPER

**Baked Rigatoni & Fontina
with Shrimp**
Steamed Asparagus
Chocolate Cake with Toffee Cream
Sauvignon Blanc   Sparkling Water

This contemporary macaroni-and-cheese casserole makes a delicious background for mounds of fresh asparagus.

Cook asparagus just before the casserole comes out of the oven.

For dessert, top slices of homemade or purchased chocolate cake with soft whipped cream, then scatter crushed brittle toffee candy over cream.

BAKED RIGATONI & FONTINA WITH SHRIMP

8 ounces dry rigatoni (tube pasta)
1 tablespoon butter or margarine
¼ cup all-purpose flour
2 cups regular-strength chicken broth
1 or 1½ cups nonfat, low-fat, or whole milk
2 cups (8 oz.) shredded fontina cheese
2 teaspoons minced fresh or ¾ teaspoon dry tarragon leaves Fresh-ground pepper
⅓ cup fresh-grated parmesan cheese
½ pound shelled cooked tiny shrimp
¼ cup thin-sliced green onion

In a 4- to 5-quart pan, bring 2 to 3 quarts water to boiling on high heat. Add pasta and boil, uncovered, just until barely tender to bite. Drain well.

In the same pan on medium-high heat, stir butter with flour until smooth. Off the heat, stir in broth and 1 cup milk (if making ahead, use 1½ cups milk); stir on heat until boiling. Remove from heat, then add fontina, tarragon, and pepper to taste; stir until cheese melts. Mix in rigatoni.

Pour mixture into a shallow 2-quart baking dish; sprinkle evenly with parmesan cheese. (If made ahead, cover and chill up until next day.) Bake, uncovered, in a 400° oven until top is bubbly and center of casserole is hot, 20 to 25 minutes (30 to 35 minutes if chilled). Scatter shrimp and onion over casserole. Makes 6 servings.

PER SERVING: 418 calories, 28 g protein, 37 g carbohydrates, 17 g fat, 129 mg cholesterol, 548 mg sodium

(Continued on next page)

LAZY-COOK BARBECUE

Rosemary-Garlic Lamb Patties
Skewered Shallots, Tomatoes
& Zucchini
Minted Couscous
Chilled Cooked Sugar Snap Peas
Frozen Peach Yogurt
with Raspberries
Pinot Noir   Milk

Move out of the kitchen for this menu.

You can use the grill to cook patties, vegetables, and even couscous all at the same time. You'll need 1½ cups couscous. Follow package directions, but use a shallow pan so liquid heats quickly; season with fresh mint. For dessert, top scoops of frozen peach yogurt with raspberries.

ROSEMARY-GARLIC LAMB PATTIES

1½ pounds ground lean lamb
⅓ cup dry bread crumbs
1 clove garlic, minced or pressed
¾ teaspoon dry rosemary leaves
¼ teaspoon *each* crushed dried hot red chilies and ground cloves
2 tablespoons minced parsley
½ cup dry red wine
   Salt and pepper

In a bowl, combine lamb, crumbs, garlic, rosemary, chilies, cloves, parsley, and wine. Mix with your hands or a spoon until thoroughly blended. Shape lamb mixture into 6 patties about ¾ inch thick.

Place patties on a grill 4 to 6 inches above a solid bed of hot coals (you should be able to hold your hand at grill level only 2 to 3 seconds); cook, turning once, until browned outside and pink in center (cut to test), about 10 minutes for medium-rare. Add salt and pepper to taste. Makes 6 servings.

PER SERVING: 280 calories, 22 g protein, 4.8 g carbohydrates, 17 g fat, 83 mg cholesterol, 112 mg sodium

SKEWERED SHALLOTS, TOMATOES & ZUCCHINI

½ pound small shallots, peeled
½ pound cherry tomatoes, stemmed
2 medium-size (about ½ lb.) zucchini, ends trimmed, cut into ½-inch-thick slices
2 tablespoons olive oil
   Salt

Using 6 metal skewers (9 to 10 in. long), thread each kind of vegetable separately on 2 skewers. Brush evenly with oil.

Place on grill 4 to 6 inches over a solid bed of hot coals (you can hold your hand at grill level only 2 to 3 seconds). Cook, turning as needed, until vegetables are browned: 8 to 10 minutes for tomatoes; 10 to 15 minutes for shallots; 10 to 15 minutes for zucchini. To serve, push vegetables off skewers. Add salt to taste. Makes 6 servings.

PER SERVING: 80 calories, 2.0 g protein, 9.2 g carbohydrates, 4.7 g fat, 0 mg cholesterol, 8.9 mg sodium

MAY

Tradewinds Cheesecake (page 122)

Tropical fruits—mangoes, bananas, papayas, pineapples—star in desserts this month during the lull between peak seasons of winter and summer fruits. A professional baker shares secrets to help you duplicate Europe's crusty country breads. We experiment with nori, a seaweed surprise, and learn about tilapia, a relative newcomer to American fish markets. You'll find new, leaner versions of lasagne and other Italian favorites. For special dinners, try one of our tongue-tingling appetizers or ice cream flavored with aromatic herbs.

Tropical Treats

Like understudies *to a lead player, many tropical fruits are discovered only when the star disappears.*

During this lull between the peak seasons of winter and summer fruits, look at the choices from the warm, lush tropics. Sweet, juicy pineapples, creamy bananas, fragrant, melon-like papayas, and luscious, delicate mangoes take top billing in the marketplace now. Their flavors shine through in the four striking desserts presented here.

Store tropical fruit at room temperature until ripe. Mangoes and papayas are ready when they give slightly when gently pressed. A golden color indicates ripeness in pineapples and bananas.

Crisp-fried egg roll fritter contains banana slices. Serve with coconut sauce and chopped peanuts.

TRADEWINDS CHEESECAKE

    2 large packages (8 oz. each)
       neufchâtel or cream cheese,
       at room temperature
    ³/₄ cup sugar
    4 large eggs
    1 cup light or regular sour cream
    2 tablespoons orange-flavor
       liqueur (or ¹/₂ teaspoon grated
       orange peel)
    1 teaspoon vanilla
       Crust (recipe follows)
       Orange sauce (recipe follows)
    1 pound (about 1 large) firm-ripe
       mango
       Fresh mint sprigs (optional)

In a large mixing bowl, beat cheese and sugar until creamy. Add eggs, 1 at a time, beating well after each addition. Add sour cream, liqueur, and vanilla; beat until blended. Pour over crust.

Bake in a 325° oven until center of cake jiggles only slightly when gently shaken, 45 to 50 minutes. Cool completely on a rack. (If made ahead, cover and chill up until next day.)

Spoon about ¹/₃ of the lukewarm orange sauce over cheesecake, to within 1 inch of sides. Peel mango. Cut fleshy cheeks off each side of pit, then cut off remaining fruit. Cut mango into thin slices 4 to 5 inches long. Arrange over cheesecake, overlapping slightly. Spoon remaining sauce over fruit and cake to within about ¹/₄ inch of sides. Cover; chill until sauce is set, about 30 minutes, or up to 8 hours.

Run a knife around inside edges of pan. Remove pan rim. Garnish with mint. With a sharp knife, cut cake into wedges. Makes about 12 servings.

PER SERVING: 363 calories, 8.2 g protein, 36 g carbohydrates, 28 g fat, 132 mg cholesterol, 217 mg sodium

Crust. Mix 1¹/₂ cups finely crushed **crisp coconut macaroon cookies** with ¹/₄ cup (¹/₈ lb.) melted **butter** or margarine. Press mixture over bottom and about 1 inch up sides of a 9-inch cheesecake pan with removable rim. Bake in a 325° oven until lightly browned, about 15 minutes.

Orange sauce. In a 2- to 3-quart pan, mix 3 tablespoons **sugar** and 4 teaspoons **cornstarch.** Stir in ²/₃ cup **orange juice** and 3 tablespoons **orange-flavor liqueur** (or orange juice). Stir over high heat until boiling. Cool to lukewarm.

BANANA PACKETS WITH COCONUT SAUCE

    2 medium-size (about ³/₄ lb. total)
       firm-ripe bananas
    8 egg roll wrappers
    1 tablespoon flour mixed with
       1¹/₂ tablespoons water
       Salad oil
    ¹/₄ cup chopped salted
       roasted peanuts
       Coconut sauce (recipe follows)

Peel bananas and cut them crosswise into ¹/₄-inch-thick slices. Working with 1 egg roll wrapper at a time (keep remaining ones covered), place ¹/₈ of the banana slices (about 4) on 1 triangular half of wrapper. Brush edges of wrapper with flour paste and bring them together to form a triangle; press to seal. Lay packet on 1 of 2 flour-dusted 10- by 15-inch baking pans; cover. Repeat to form 8 packets, arranging on pans in a single layer. Hold, covered, up to 30 minutes.

In a deep 10-inch frying pan or wok, heat about 1¹/₂ inches oil to 350°. Carefully lift packets from pans and add to hot oil, 1 or 2 at a time; cook until golden on both sides, about 2 minutes total. Lift out with a slotted spoon and drain on paper towels. Repeat to cook all. Keep cooked ones warm in a 200° oven up to 20 minutes.

Place banana packets on dessert plates. Sprinkle with chopped peanuts; offer hot coconut sauce to add to taste. Makes 8 servings.

PER SERVING: 145 calories, 3.9 g protein, 21 g carbohydrates, 5.9 g fat, 0 mg cholesterol, 45 mg sodium

Coconut sauce. In a 1- to 1¹/₂-quart pan, mix 2 tablespoons **sugar** and 2 teaspoons **cornstarch.** Stir in 1 can (14 oz.) **coconut milk;** cook over medium-high heat, stirring, until it thickens. Serve hot. Makes 1¹/₂ cups.

PER TABLESPOON: 37 calories, 0.3 g protein, 1.7 g carbohydrates, 3.5 g fat, 0 mg cholesterol, 2.1 mg sodium

HOT PAPAYA SUNDAES

    2 small (about 1 lb. each) firm-ripe
       papayas
    1 tablespoon melted butter or
       margarine
    ¹/₂ teaspoon fine-shredded
       lime peel
    ¹/₃ cup rum or water
    ¹/₄ cup lime juice
    3 tablespoons honey
       About 1 pint vanilla ice cream

Cut papayas in half lengthwise and remove seeds. In a 9- by 13-inch baking

Baked papaya holds ice cream. Drizzle with warm lime-rum-honey sauce to taste.

For a dramatic dessert, squeeze wedge of orange over cut pineapple spangled with pieces of crystallized ginger.

dish or pan, combine the butter, lime peel, rum, lime juice, and honey. Lay papayas cut side down in pan. Bake in a 375° oven until papayas are hot and sauce begins to bubble, about 15 minutes.

Transfer warm fruit, cut side up, to 4 dessert plates. Let cool about 5 minutes. Fill each papaya half with a scoop of ice cream. Pour pan juices into a small pitcher or bowl and offer as topping. Makes 4 servings.

PER SERVING: 313 calories, 3.4 g protein, 45 g carbohydrates, 10 g fat, 38 mg cholesterol, 95 mg sodium

PINEAPPLE PLUMES WITH GINGER

- **1 large (4 to 5 lb.) pineapple**
- **6 tablespoons minced crystallized ginger**
- **1 tablespoon finely shredded orange peel (optional)**
  Orange wedges

With a heavy, sharp knife, cut pineapple lengthwise into sixths through crown and fruit (if needed, use a hammer or mallet to help push knife through fruit).

With a grapefruit knife, cut fruit away from shell. Remove fruit and cut away core; reserve core to eat, or discard. Cut fruit in each section lengthwise. Return fruit to its shell; cut fruit crosswise down to shell into about 1/3-inch slices. Sprinkle evenly with ginger and orange peel. Offer orange wedges to squeeze over each section. Makes 6 servings.

PER SERVING: 132 calories, 0.7 g protein, 33 g carbohydrates, 0.7 g fat, 0 mg cholesterol, 11 mg sodium

Baking Crusty French Breads

To the frustration of many bakers, the rustic good looks, coarse porous texture, and crisp, chewy crusts of many breads sold in Italian and French bakeries seem difficult to reproduce at home.

Joe Ortiz of Gayle's Bakery in Capitola, California, looked for a solution at the source—bakeries in Italy and France. Now he duplicates many of those traditional country breads and, here, shares two of his most popular recipes, pane francese (Italian for French bread) and French bread started with biga (an overnight "sponge," which gives the bread a slightly tangy flavor, depending on fermentation time).

In many bread recipes, dough is kneaded until it is no longer sticky and easy to handle, holds its shape when baked, and boasts a fine, even texture. The secret to

Ortiz's breads is wet dough and a hot oven, which yield flatter, crisp loaves.

To begin, you mix and knead the dough in a food processor or bowl (if you like a more porous texture or are mixing the dough by hand, add a little more water). To prevent sticking when handling the wet mass, coat dough and board with lots of flour; very little actually goes into the gently worked dough.

After shaping the loaves, you let them rest, then transfer them to baking sheets, stretching them slightly in the process. This step also adds texture, elongating the air cells in the bread.

These breads taste best freshly baked. If you hold them more than 8 hours, wrap and freeze. Thaw and reheat, uncovered, in a 350° oven just until warm, 5 to 10 minutes.

ORTIZ'S FRENCH BREAD
(Pane Francese)

- 1 envelope active dry yeast
- ¼ cup warm water (110°)
  About 3 cups all-purpose flour
- 1 teaspoon sugar
- 1 teaspoon salt
- 1 to 1¼ cups ice-cold water

In a small bowl, sprinkle yeast over warm water. Let the mixture stand until it starts to bubble, about 10 minutes.

If using a food processor, mix 3 cups flour, sugar, and salt. With the processor running, add the yeast mixture and gradually pour in 1 cup of ice-cold water. Process, scraping bowl occasionally, until flour and water are incorporated (if dough is dry or difficult to whirl, add more water, 1 to 2 teaspoons at a time). Whirl dough until shiny, elastic, and slightly sticky, 3 to 4 minutes (if machine stops, wait a few minutes for motor to cool, then resume, or transfer to a bowl and beat by hand). To test for elasticity, stretch apart a small piece of dough with your hands; if it forms a thin skin you can see through, the dough is ready.

Sprinkle dough with about 2 tablespoons flour to make it easier to handle. Scrape the soupy dough into a large bowl.

If using an electric mixer and dough hook or mixing by hand, mix 3 cups flour, sugar, and salt in a large bowl. Add yeast mixture and 1 cup of the cold water. Beat on medium speed or with a heavy spoon until well blended. Change to a dough hook or use a spoon and beat until dough is shiny, elastic, and slightly sticky, about 5 minutes with mixer, 10 to 20 minutes by hand (if the dough is dry or difficult to beat, add more water, 1 to 2 teaspoons at a time). To test elasticity, stretch apart a small piece of dough with your hands; if it forms a thin skin you can see through, the dough is ready.

Let dough rise, covered with plastic wrap, in a warm place until it doubles in size, 1½ to 2 hours.

To shape the loaves, sprinkle about 2 tablespoons flour over dough and scrape out onto a well-floured board. Divide the dough in half. With floured hands, lightly pat each portion of dough into a 7- by 8-inch rectangle. Starting on a short side, roll dough jellyroll fashion (step 2 above right); with

Crisp, flour-dusted crust and porous, chewy interior—trademarks of rustic breads from Italian bakeries—are duplicated in homemade loaf from professional baker Joe Ortiz.

2 *With your hands, gently pat dough into a rectangle, then use fingertips to ease rectangle into a log.*

3 *With each turn of log, press rolled edge against unrolled dough to seal. Flour board under loaf, cover, and let rest.*

4 *Gently stretch loaves to a length of 12 to 14 inches while transferring them to baking sheets. Let rise until puffy, then bake.*

1 *To create soft, wet dough, knead ingredients in a food processor until shiny, elastic, and slightly sticky.*

each turn of the roll, press rolled edge against unrolled portion with heel of hand (step 3). Repeat, pressing the last exposed side to loaf. Transfer loaves to floured area of board, seam side down; sprinkle flour lightly over top. Let loaves rest, lightly covered with plastic wrap, on the board for 30 minutes.

Carefully pick up ends of each loaf and transfer to a greased or cooking parchment–lined 14- by 17-inch baking sheet, stretching each loaf to a length of 12 to 14 inches in the move (if loaf sticks to board, gently scrape free with a spatula). Place loaves 4 to 5 inches apart. Cover loosely with plastic wrap; let rise in a warm place until loaves are slightly puffy, 10 to 15 minutes.

Place in a 475° oven, then immediately turn heat down to 425°. Bake until golden brown all over, 20 to 30 minutes. For a crisper crust, turn oven off, prop oven door ajar slightly, and leave loaves in oven for about 10 minutes. Remove from pans and cool on racks. Makes 2 loaves, each about 11 ounces.

PER OUNCE: 63 calories, 1.8 g protein, 13 g carbohydrates, 0.2 g fat, 0 mg cholesterol, 100 mg sodium

ORTIZ'S FRENCH BREAD WITH SPONGE

Biga (recipe follows)
1½ teaspoons salt
About ¼ cup ice-cold water
About 1¼ cups all-purpose flour

If using a food processor, mix the biga and salt. Add ¼ cup cold water and whirl until shiny and smooth, about 30 seconds. Add 1¼ cups flour, ¼ cup at a time, pulsing 3 or 4 times after each addition. If dough is too dry to incorporate flour, add more water (1 to 2 teaspoons at a time), whirling until water is blended. Then process until dough is shiny, elastic, and slightly sticky, 1 to 2 minutes (if machine stops, wait a few minutes for motor to cool, then continue, or transfer to a bowl and beat by hand). To test elasticity, stretch apart a small piece of dough with your hands; if it forms a thin skin you can see through, the dough is ready.

If using a dough hook or mixing by hand, place the biga and salt in a large bowl; stir to mix. Add ¼ cup cold water and

beat at medium speed or with a heavy spoon until well blended. Add 1¼ cups flour, ¼ cup at a time, beating well after each addition. If dough is too dry to incorporate flour, add more water, 1 to 2 teaspoons at a time, beating until blended and dough is shiny, elastic, and slightly sticky, about 5 minutes with a dough hook, 20 to 25 minutes by hand. To test elasticity, stretch apart a small piece of dough with your hands; if it forms a thin skin that you can see through, the dough is ready.

Let rise, shape, and bake loaves as directed for French bread (preceding). Makes 2 loaves, each 9 to 10 ounces.

PER OUNCE: 79 calories, 2.4 g protein, 16 g carbohydrates, 0.2 g fat, 0 mg cholesterol, 174 mg sodium

Biga. In a 2- to 3-quart bowl, soften 1 teaspoon **active dry yeast** in 1⅛ cups warm **water** (110°), about 5 minutes. Gradually add 2 cups **all-purpose flour;** stir the mixture until smooth. Cover and let stand in a warm place at least 8 hours or up until the next day.

Moist, Delicate Tilapia

ALTHOUGH A RELATIVE NEWCOMER *to American fish markets, tilapia is actually not a new fish at all. This small, perch-like fish is a native of Africa and has been known to man since Biblical times.*

Tilapia is extremely hardy. Because it's a warm-water fish, its only essential requirement seems to be temperatures above 55°. It survives in fresh, salt, or brackish water and with no supplemental food, eating only algae present in the water. Tilapia also needs very little oxygen, which enables it to withstand crowded conditions. Its main drawback is a tendency to act like a sponge and pick up flavors from the water it lives in. In the past, this characteristic gave tilapia a bad name; the wild fish often had a muddy flavor.

Farm-raised tilapia, on the other hand, has a clean, delicate flavor (similar to that of petrale sole). Although a lean fish, it maintains a moist, tender texture when cooked.

Tilapia's hardiness makes it an ideal fish for farming. And today, tilapia is farmed worldwide, in such places as the Middle East, Mexico, and Taiwan, as well as in the United States.

In this country, there are tilapia farms in several states, including California, Arizona, and Hawaii. These farms raise the fish in tanks with clean water and use population control methods and nutritionally balanced feed to ensure high quality.

A farm-raised tilapia weighs 1½ to 2 pounds. Fish farmers have developed

A whole, dressed tilapia—baked on a bed of ginger-spiked onion and lemon slices—is just the right size for two diners.

Sweet-smoky mixture of roasted onion and bacon tops crusty, cornmeal-coated tilapia fillets. Garnish with lemon wedges.

hybrids that range in color from red-gold to silver-blue. (In the wild, the fish is gray-black.)

Tilapia is available whole, dressed (gutted, with head and tail attached), and as fresh or frozen fillets weighing between 4 and 7 ounces each. The retail price ranges from $6 to $8 per pound.

WHOLE TILAPIA WITH ONION & LEMON

1¼ **pounds (about 2 large) red onions, cut into ⅛-inch slices**

3 **tablespoons lemon juice**

1 **tablespoon minced fresh ginger**

1 **whole tilapia (about 1½ lb.), dressed (gutted, with head and tail attached)**

1 **tablespoon extra-virgin olive oil**

2 **large (about ½ lb. total) lemons**

3 **tablespoons minced fresh cilantro (coriander)**

Salt and pepper

In a large bowl, mix onion with lemon juice and ginger. Arrange all but 1 or 2 onion slices in the bottom of a 9- by 13-inch or shallow 4- to 5-quart baking dish. Rinse tilapia; pat dry. Brush both sides with oil, then lay fish on top of the onion mixture.

Cut off ½ inch from each end of lemons. Stuff fish cavity with reserved onion, lemon ends, and half the cilantro. Cut remaining lemon into thin slices; tuck slices around fish. Sprinkle remaining cilantro over onion and lemon in dish.

Bake, uncovered, in a 400° oven until fish registers 135° on a thermometer inserted into the thickest part and flesh is opaque but still moist-looking (cut to test), 20 to 25 minutes. To serve, gently pull off skin and serve fish with onion. Add salt and pepper to taste. Makes 2 servings.

PER SERVING: 344 calories, 37 g protein, 35 g carbohydrates, 10 g fat, 81 mg cholesterol, 149 mg sodium

OVEN-FRIED TILAPIA WITH ROASTED ONION

3 **large (about 1¾ lb. total) onions, sliced thin**

4 **slices (about 3½ oz. total) bacon, minced**

½ **cup cornmeal**

½ **teaspoon pepper**

1 **large egg white, beaten to blend**

1½ **to 1¾ pounds tilapia fillets, rinsed**

2 **tablespoons salad oil**

Lemon wedges (optional)

Place onion slices in an 11- by 17-inch roasting pan. Sprinkle with bacon. Bake onion in a 500° oven, stirring occasionally, until onion and bacon are browned, about 35 minutes; keep warm.

Meanwhile, mix cornmeal and pepper in a wide, shallow dish or bowl. Pour egg white into another wide, shallow bowl. Dip each fillet in egg white, then roll in cornmeal, coating all sides evenly.

Pour oil into a 10- by 15-inch baking pan; swirl to coat pan. Place pan in a 500° oven for 5 minutes. With a wide spatula, transfer cornmeal-coated fillets to pan. Bake for 4 minutes. Turn fish over and bake until lightly browned and flesh is opaque but still moist-looking in thickest part (cut to test), 3 to 5 minutes more.

Transfer fish to 4 dinner plates and spoon the bacon and onion equally over fillets. Garnish with lemon wedges. Makes 4 servings.

PER SERVING: 468 calories, 38 g protein, 28 g carbohydrates, 22 g fat, 96 mg cholesterol, 301 mg sodium

POACHED TILAPIA WITH LEMON & BASIL

- ¼ **cup regular-strength chicken broth**
- 3 **tablespoons orange juice**
- 2 **tablespoons lemon juice**
- 2 **tablespoons fruity extra-virgin olive oil**
- 1½ **to 1¾ pounds tilapia fillets, rinsed**
  About 8 whole fresh basil leaves
- 1 **tablespoon shredded lemon peel**

In a 10- to 12-inch frying pan, combine the broth, orange juice, lemon juice, and oil over high heat. Cover and bring to a boil. Add tilapia in a single layer to pan, cover, and simmer gently for 4 minutes.

Lay 1 or 2 basil leaves diagonally across each fillet. Cover pan and simmer until fish is opaque but still moist-looking in thickest part (cut to test), 1 to 2 minutes more. Transfer fillets with a slotted spatula to 4 individual plates; keep warm.

Boil the pan juices, uncovered, over high heat until reduced to about ¼ cup, 2 to 3 minutes. Spoon equal amounts of sauce over fillets, then sprinkle each equally with lemon peel. Makes 4 servings.

PER SERVING: 225 calories, 32 g protein, 2.3 g carbohydrates, 9.1 g fat, 81 mg cholesterol, 143 mg sodium

Moist, delicate tilapia fillets poached with citrus juices and fruity olive oil have accents of fresh basil and lemon peel.

PRESERVING THE ESSENCE *of flavor—while cutting back on fat-rich ingredients—was the goal in lightening up these favorite Sunset Italian classics. Our new versions of lasagne, sausage soup, and frozen chocolate tartufo pass the test with flying colors.*

LEANER LASAGNE

The original Lasagne al Forno included extravagant amounts of cheese, butter, and meat, adding up to more than 900 calories per portion and almost 50 grams of protein (a woman's recommended protein intake for an entire day).

We've eliminated the beef and butter, used no-fat sausage, and cut the cheese in half. Tasters were amazed to learn that such a good lasagne was so lean.

- 2 **large (about 1½ lb. total) onions, chopped**
- 2 **large stalks (about ½ lb. total) celery, chopped**
- 2 **medium-size (about ⅓ lb. total) carrots, chopped**
- 5 **cups regular-strength beef broth**
  No-fat Italian sausage (recipe follows)
- 1 **can (6 oz.) tomato paste**
- 1½ **teaspoons dry basil leaves**
- ½ **teaspoon dry rosemary**
- ¼ **teaspoon ground nutmeg**
- 3 **tablespoons cornstarch**
- 1½ **cups nonfat milk**
- 2 **cups (½ lb.) shredded fontina cheese**
- 12 **ounces dry lasagne noodles**
- ½ **cup grated parmesan cheese**

In a 5- to 6-quart pan (nonstick if possible), combine onion, celery, carrots, and 1½ cups of the broth. Boil, uncovered, on high heat, stirring occasionally, until liquid evaporates and vegetables start to brown, 12 to 15 minutes. To deglaze, stir in ¼ cup water to release browned bits. Stir occasionally until liquid evaporates and mixture begins to brown again, 1 to 3 minutes. Repeat deglazing step 3 more times, until mixture is richly browned.

Add sausage and ½ cup more water. Stir often until liquid evaporates and meat starts to brown, about 10 minutes. Add ⅓ cup water and stir often until meat is brown, 2 to 4 more minutes.

Over medium-low heat, add 2½ cups more broth; stir to loosen browned bits. Mix in tomato paste, basil, rosemary,

Beneath crusted cheese topping, swirled—not layered—lasagne combines wide noodles with slimmed-down tomato-meat sauce.

and nutmeg. Simmer covered, stirring occasionally, until flavors blend, about 20 minutes.

Stir remaining 1 cup broth with cornstarch and milk. Add to meat mixture; stir over medium-high heat until the sauce bubbles and thickens. Stir in 1 cup fontina; remove from heat.

Fill a 6- to 8-quart pan half-full of water. Bring to a boil over high heat, add lasagne noodles, and cook until barely tender to bite, about 8 minutes; drain. Stir noodles into sauce and mix gently to coat. Loosely swirl pasta in a 3-quart shallow baking dish; sprinkle with parmesan and remaining fontina. If

made ahead, cool, cover, and chill up until next day.

Bake, uncovered, in a 375° oven until bubbling, 25 to 30 minutes. Makes 8 servings.

PER SERVING LEANER LASAGNE: 457 calories, 31 g protein, 53 g carbohydrates, 13 g fat, 75 mg cholesterol, 585 mg sodium

PER SERVING ORIGINAL LASAGNE (OCTOBER 1971, PAGE 193): 913 calories, 48 g protein, 44 g carbohydrates, 60 g fat, 192 mg cholesterol, 1,280 mg sodium

No-fat Italian sausage. Cut 1 pound fat-trimmed **pork tenderloin** or loin into 1-inch chunks. In a food processor, whirl about half at a time until coarsely chopped (or put through a food chopper with medium blade). In a bowl, mix meat with ¼ cup **dry white wine**, 2 tablespoons chopped **parsley**, 1½ teaspoons crushed **fennel seed,** 1/2 teaspoon **crushed dried hot red chilies,** and 2 cloves minced **garlic.** If made ahead, chill airtight up until next day.

ITALIAN SAUSAGE SOUP

By making our own sausage and braising-deglazing the vegetables, we eliminated almost all the fat.

- 2 **large onions, chopped**
- 2 **cloves garlic, minced or pressed**
- 5 **cups regular-strength beef broth**
  No-fat Italian sausage (recipe precedes)
- 1 1/2 **cups dry red wine**
- 1 **can (28 oz.) Italian-style tomatoes, broken up**
- 1 **tablespoon dry basil**
- 1 **tablespoon sugar**
- 1 **medium-size (about 1/3 lb.) green bell pepper, stemmed, seeded, and chopped**
- 2 **medium-size (about 1/2 lb. total) zucchini, sliced 1/4 inch thick**
- 2 **cups (5 oz.) dry bow-tie pasta, 1 1/2-inch size**
- 1/2 **cup chopped parsley**
  Salt and pepper

In a 5- to 6-quart pan (nonstick if possible), combine onions, garlic, and 1 cup broth. Boil on high heat, stirring occasionally, until liquid evaporates and vegetables start to brown, 10 to 14 minutes. To deglaze, stir in 3 tablespoons water to release browned bits. Cook, uncovered, until liquid evaporates and mixture begins to brown again, about 1 minute. Repeat deglazing step 3 more times until mixture is richly browned.

Add sausage and 1/2 cup more water. Stir gently until liquid evaporates and meat begins to brown, 8 to 10 minutes.

Add remaining 4 cups broth. Stir to loosen browned bits. Then add wine, tomatoes and their liquid, basil, sugar, bell pepper, zucchini, and pasta. Cover and bring to a boil over high heat. Simmer until pasta is just tender to bite, about 15 minutes. Serve hot, with parsley, and salt and pepper to taste. (If made ahead, let cool, then cover and chill up until next day. Reheat to simmering.) Makes 6 servings.

PER SERVING REVISED SOUP: 260 calories, 23 g protein, 36 g carbohydrates, 2.9 g fat, 49 mg cholesterol, 269 mg sodium

PER SERVING ORIGINAL SOUP (JANUARY 1973, PAGE 104): 436 calories, 23 g protein, 34 g carbohydrates, 23 g fat, 87 mg cholesterol, 997 mg sodium

Plenty of vegetables, pasta, and ultra-lean Italian sausage make a satisfying, low-calorie soup.

FROZEN ITALIAN CHOCOLATE TARTUFO

Revamped tartufo retains its sleek texture despite losing 3 egg yolks, a cup of cream, and 6 ounces of chocolate.

- 1 **cup sugar**
- 1/2 **cup unsweetened cocoa**
- 1 **tablespoon cornstarch**
- 1 **cup nonfat milk**
- 1/2 **cup water**
- 3 **large egg whites**
- 1/2 **cup semisweet chocolate baking chips**
  Powdered sugar

Place 1/2 cup sugar, cocoa, and cornstarch in a 1- to 1 1/2-quart pan and stir until no lumps remain. Add milk; whisk until smooth. Over medium heat, stir until mixture boils and thickens, 8 to 11 minutes. Place plastic wrap directly touching pudding. Cool completely, but don't chill.

Combine remaining sugar and water in a 1- to 1 1/2-quart pan. Bring to a boil over high heat and boil uncovered, without stirring, until a thermometer reaches 260° (tip pan to cover thermometer base when reading), 8 to 12 minutes.

About 2 minutes before sugar syrup is ready, beat egg whites in large bowl of an electric mixer at high speed until stiff peaks form. Pour in syrup in a slow stream, beating with the mixer (or a spoon, if beaters spray syrup all over bowl sides). Beat on high speed, scraping bowl occasionally, until stiff peaks form. With a rubber scraper, gently fold pudding into whites until well blended. Cover and freeze until firm, at least 4 hours or up until next day.

Meanwhile, grind chocolate chips until fine in a blender or food processor; place in a mound on waxed paper.

Scoop frozen mixture into 6 equal portions, and use your hands or two large spoons to quickly shape each portion into a rough ball. Roll in ground chocolate to coat. Place slightly apart in a chilled 9-inch pan and freeze until firm, at least 1 hour or up to 2 weeks (cover if stored longer than a few hours). Just before serving, sprinkle each tartufo with powdered sugar. Makes 6 servings.

PER PORTION REVISED FROZEN CHOCOLATE: 250 calories, 5.4 g protein, 49 g carbohydrates, 5.4 g fat, 1 mg cholesterol, 49 mg sodium

PER PORTION ORIGINAL FROZEN CHOCOLATE (FEBRUARY 1982, PAGE 153 N, 156 S, D; JULY 1982, PAGE 122 C): 368 calories, 3.6 g protein, 42 g carbohydrates, 24 g fat, 128 mg cholesterol, 11 mg sodium

Hot & Cold Appetizers: Bold Fillings in Cool Leaves

WRAP COOL LEAVES *around warm, savory mixtures for tongue-tingling appetizers. Use tender butter lettuce, crisp cabbage, or Belgian endive as wrappers. Ground pork, turkey (or chicken), and fish—all boldly seasoned with Southeast Asian flavors—become the intriguing fillings.*

Offer these hot-and-cold duos as appetizers or, supplemented with hot rice, as a casual supper. Accompany with tall glasses of iced lemonade or beer to cool some of their fiery heat.

PORK & PEANUTS IN LETTUCE CUPS

- 1/2 **cup sweetened shredded dry coconut**
- 1 **tablespoon salad oil**
- 1/2 **cup chopped shallots**
- 1/4 **cup chopped fresh ginger**
- 2 **tablespoons chopped garlic**
- 1 **pound ground lean pork**
- 1/3 **cup lime juice**
- 1/4 **cup chopped fresh mint leaves**
- 1/2 **cup chopped roasted peanuts**
- 3 **to 4 tablespoons minced fresh hot chilies**
- 2 **to 3 tablespoons fish sauce (nam pla or nuoc mam) or soy sauce**
  Fresh mint sprigs
- 2 **small heads (about 1/2 lb. each) butter lettuce, rinsed and crisped**

In a 10- to 12-inch frying pan, stir coconut over medium-low heat until golden and crisp, 5 to 10 minutes. Remove from pan and set aside.

Add oil to pan and place over medium heat. Add shallots, ginger, and garlic; stir often until shallots are soft, about 5 minutes. Add pork; stir until meat is crumbly and no longer pink, about 5 minutes. Spoon off and discard fat. Add lime juice, chopped mint, peanuts, coconut, chilies, and fish sauce to taste; mix to blend.

Pour into a dish and garnish with mint sprigs. Accompany with lettuce leaves. To eat, spoon warm meat mixture onto a leaf, then roll to enclose. Makes 8 to 10 appetizer or 4 or 5 entrée servings.

PER APPETIZER SERVING: 224 calories, 11 g protein, 7.7 g carbohydrates, 17 g fat, 33 mg cholesterol, 42 mg sodium

SPICED TURKEY IN CABBAGE WRAPS

- 1/4 **cup short- or long-grain white rice**
- 1 **tablespoon salad oil**
- 3 **cloves garlic, pressed or minced**
- 1 **pound ground turkey or chicken**
- 1/2 **cup thinly sliced green onion**
- 1/4 **cup chopped fresh cilantro (coriander)**
- 1 **teaspoon sugar**
- 1/3 **cup lemon juice**
- 2 **to 3 tablespoons minced fresh hot chilies**
- 2 **to 3 tablespoons fish sauce (nam pla or nuoc mam) or soy sauce**
  Fresh cilantro sprigs (optional)
- 1 **medium-size (1 1/2 lb.) cabbage, cut into quarters through the core; or 3 heads (about 5 oz. each) radicchio, separated into leaves and rinsed and crisped**

In a 10- to 12-inch frying pan, stir rice often over medium heat until golden, 5 to 8 minutes. Pour rice into a blender or food processor and whirl until finely ground. Set aside.

Add oil to pan and place over medium heat. Add garlic and turkey; stir often until turkey is crumbly and white, about 5 minutes. Remove from heat and add onion, chopped cilantro, sugar, ground rice, lemon juice, chilies, and fish sauce to taste; mix to blend.

Pour into a dish and garnish with cilantro sprigs. Set cabbage wedges alongside. To eat, pull off a cabbage leaf and place a spoonful of turkey mixture onto leaf; roll to enclose. Makes 8 appetizer or 4 entrée servings.

PER APPETIZER SERVING: 156 calories, 12 g protein, 12 g carbohydrates, 6.7 g fat, 41 mg cholesterol, 57 mg sodium

LEMON FISH WITH ENDIVE SCOOPS

- 4 **teaspoons sugar**
- 4 **teaspoons cornstarch**
- 1 **teaspoon grated lemon peel**
- 1/2 **cup lemon juice**
- 1 **cup chopped red onion**
- 1/2 **teaspoon crushed dried hot red chilies**
- 1 **pound boned and skinned white-flesh fish such as rockfish or lingcod**
- 2 **tablespoons salad oil**
- 3 **tablespoons minced fresh ginger**
- 2 **cloves garlic, pressed or minced**
- 2 **to 3 tablespoons fish sauce (nam pla or nuoc mam) or soy sauce**
  Thin lemon slices or red onion rings
- 2 **large heads (about 3 oz. each) Belgian endive, rinsed and crisped**

In a small bowl, mix together the sugar and cornstarch. Stir in lemon peel, lemon juice, chopped onion, and crushed chilies; set aside.

With a food processor or knife, finely chop fish. Pour oil into a 10- to 12-inch frying pan over medium heat. Add ginger and garlic and stir until garlic is soft, about 3 minutes.

Add fish and stir just until opaque and crumbly, about 3 minutes. Add onion mixture and stir over high heat just until mixture boils, about 2 minutes. Add fish sauce to taste.

Pour fish mixture into a bowl and garnish with lemon slices or onion rings. Separate endive and arrange leaves beside fish. Spoon hot or warm fish mixture onto leaves. Makes 8 appetizer or 4 entrée servings.

PER APPETIZER SERVING: 122 calories, 12 g protein, 7.8 g carbohydrates, 4.8 g fat, 20 mg cholesterol, 40 mg sodium

In these tongue-tingling appetizers, cool leaves enclose boldly seasoned fillings. Spoon ground lean pork mixture—generously laced with toasted shredded coconut, peanuts, shallots, fresh ginger, fresh mint, and hot chilies—into tender butter lettuce cups.

Seaweed Surprises

MORE THAN A TOE-TICKLER *for swim-mers, seaweed also tickles diners' fancies. You may know Japanese nori as seaweed wrappers for sushi. But have you tried nori and its Chinese counterpart in other ways? These seaweed sheets—sold in Asian markets and many supermarkets —add salty, nutty flavor to simple Asian and Western dishes.*

Plain nori works well snipped or crumbled to top plain or seasoned rice, green salads, baked potatoes, and grilled fish, and to tuck into omelets. You can also sauté nori shreds for extra crispness, then mix with sesame seed; serve as suggested for plain nori or as an appetizer. Teriyaki and horseradish nori are interchangeable with unseasoned nori in these recipes.

Chinese seaweed sheets are thicker than nori and have a more pronounced flavor. They make excellent soup seasoning.

Most nori comes preroasted. If not, you can lightly toast it to bring out its flavor. You don't need to toast seaweed for soup.

Eat nori immediately after mixing with food, since it softens on standing. Store opened packages of either kind airtight; recrisp as directed below if sheets soften.

For a fascinating appetizer, snip nori into strips, sauté briefly in a wok, and mix with sesame seed. Sautéed mixture also makes an unusual crisp topping for many dishes.

SWEET & SOUR GREEN RICE

- 3/4 **ounce plain or seasoned nori**
- 1/3 **cup rice vinegar**
- 2 **tablespoons sugar**
- 4 **cups hot cooked pearl rice**
  Salt

If nori isn't preroasted, toast as directed (following). With scissors, snip sheets into 1/8- by 3-inch strips to make 1 1/2 cups lightly packed. Set aside.

Seaweed sheets include, from left, green seasoned Japanese nori, larger plain nori, and purple Chinese seaweed.

Stir vinegar and sugar until sugar dissolves. Pour over rice and lightly mix. Spoon onto plates and sprinkle with nori. Add salt to taste. Makes 6 servings.

PER SERVING: 204 calories, 4 g protein, 45 g carbohydrates, 0.3 g fat, 0 mg cholesterol, 48 mg sodium

Toasted nori. If **plain** or seasoned **nori** is preroasted and package is just opened, use as is. To toast or recrisp:

Over a gas burner, hold each sheet with tongs; pass 1 side about 1 inch over flame, just until nori goes limp, 5 to 10 seconds.

Over an electric burner, cook 1 sheet at a time in a 10- to 12-inch frying pan over medium-high heat just until nori bubbles slightly, 5 to 10 seconds.

CRISP FRIED SEAWEED

- 1 3/4 **ounces plain or seasoned nori**
- 1 **tablespoon sesame seed**
- 1 **tablespoon salad oil**

Snip nori into 1/8- by 3-inch strips to make 1 quart lightly packed. In a wok or 12-inch frying pan over medium-high heat, stir sesame seed until golden, 2 to

3 minutes. Scrape into a bowl. Pour oil into wok. When hot, add nori. Stir rapidly just until it crisps, 1 to 2 minutes. Mix with sesame. Serve, or store airtight up to 2 days. Makes 1 quart, 6 servings.

PER SERVING: 40 calories, 1.3 g protein, 2.4 g carbohydrates, 3.1 g fat, 0 mg cholesterol, 61 mg sodium

FLOTSAM & JETSAM SOUP

- 4 **cups regular-strength chicken broth**
- 3 **tablespoons rice vinegar or 2 tablespoons distilled white vinegar**
- 1/3 **cup 1-inch torn pieces Chinese seaweed sheets or nori**
- 1/2 **cup fine-shredded carrots**
- 1/2 **cup fine-shredded red radishes**
- 2 **tablespoons sliced green onion**

In a 3- to 4-quart pan, bring broth and vinegar to a boil over high heat. Add seaweed; simmer 1 minute. Arrange separate mounds of carrots and radishes in wide soup bowls. Ladle broth into empty sections. Sprinkle with onion. Makes 4 servings.

PER SERVING: 43 calories, 2.7 g protein, 4.5 g carbohydrates, 1.6 g fat, 0 mg cholesterol, 71 mg sodium

Quick & Light One-pot Meals

SOUP OR STEW? *In these examples, the difference between the two is muted. Like stew, they're substantial enough to make one-pot meals, but they sport a clear broth akin to many light soups. With spring vegetables, these soup-stews make handsome warm-weather suppers.*

CHICKEN, SHIITAKE & BOK CHOY SOUP-STEW WITH GINGER-GARLIC PASTE

1½ tablespoons Oriental sesame oil or salad oil

⅓ pound fresh shiitake or common mushrooms, rinsed, drained, and sliced thin

8 green onions, ends trimmed, coarsely chopped (including tops)

3 cups regular-strength chicken broth

4 boned and skinned chicken breast halves (about 6 oz. each)

2 large (about ⅔ lb. total) carrots, peeled and sliced thin on the diagonal

8 baby bok choy (about ¾ lb. total), coarse outer leaves discarded

2 cups hot cooked short- or medium-grain rice

3 tablespoons minced fresh cilantro (coriander)

Ginger-garlic paste (recipe follows)

Place oil in a 4- to 5-quart pan over medium heat. Add mushrooms and half the onion; cook, stirring often, until mushrooms are lightly browned, about 10 minutes. Add broth and scrape free any browned bits. Cover pan and bring to a boil over high heat.

Add chicken and carrots; arrange so that they are covered with liquid and cover tightly. Simmer over low heat until chicken is no longer pink in the thickest part (cut to test), about 15 minutes.

Remove chicken and transfer to a cutting board. Add bok choy and remaining green onion to pan; cover and simmer over medium heat until bok choy is bright green and just tender when pierced, about 5 minutes. Meanwhile, cut chicken crosswise on the diagonal into ½-inch slices.

Place a ½-cup scoop of rice off center in each of 4 wide, shallow soup bowls. Arrange 1 sliced chicken breast around each rice mound. With a slotted spoon, distribute vegetables evenly among

bowls. Stir cilantro into broth; gently pour into bowls over meat and vegetables. Offer ginger-garlic paste to stir into broth. Makes 4 servings.

PER SERVING: 442 calories, 46 g protein, 42 g carbohydrates, 8.9 g fat, 98 mg cholesterol, 214 mg sodium

Ginger-garlic paste. In a blender or food processor, whirl together ¾ cup (about 3 oz.) peeled and coarsely chopped fresh **ginger,** 3 cloves **garlic,** and 3 tablespoons **seasoned rice vinegar** (or 3 tablespoons rice vinegar mixed with 1 teaspoon sugar) until very smooth. If made ahead, cover and chill the paste up to 4 hours. Makes about ½ cup.

PER TEASPOON: 4 calories, 0 g protein, 0.8 g carbohydrates, 0 g fat, 0 mg cholesterol, 0.8 mg sodium

SEAFOOD & SPINACH SOUP-STEW

4 cups regular-strength chicken broth

1 tablespoon shredded lemon peel

¼ cup minced fresh basil leaves or 2 tablespoons crumbled dry basil

1 tablespoon minced fresh thyme leaves or 1 teaspoon crumbled dry thyme leaves

1 pound small (about 1½-in. diameter) thin-skinned potatoes, scrubbed

½ pound spinach leaves, rinsed and drained, stems trimmed

¾ pound firm-textured white-flesh fish (such as halibut, sea bass, or shark), cut into 1½-inch pieces

¾ pound large shrimp (31 to 35 per pound), shelled and deveined

1 pound Roma-type tomatoes, coarsely chopped

In a 4- to 5-quart pan, combine the broth, lemon peel, basil, thyme, and potatoes over high heat. Bring to a boil; cover tightly and simmer until potatoes are just tender when pierced, about 20 minutes.

Meanwhile, cut spinach leaves lengthwise into slivers about ⅛ inch wide; set aside.

Return broth to a rolling boil over high heat and add the fish. Cover pan tightly and simmer over low heat for 2 minutes. Stir in shrimp, tomatoes, and half the spinach. Cover and continue simmering until fish and shrimp are opaque but still moist-looking in the thickest part (cut to test), 3 to 5 minutes more.

Divide mixture among 6 wide, shallow bowls. Garnish tops with the remaining spinach slivers. Makes 6 servings.

PER SERVING: 218 calories, 26 g protein, 20 g carbohydrates, 3.5 g fat, 88 mg cholesterol, 168 mg sodium

Light soup-stew pairs chicken with tender-crisp vegetables and rice in a clear broth; add intensely flavored ginger-garlic paste to taste.

Herby Ice Creams

AROMATIC HERBS *give a clean, refreshing taste to homemade ice cream. Just simmer rosemary or mint in milk to infuse its flavor, then mix with eggs and cream. Churn the old-fashioned way with ice and salt, or use an ice-free cylinder or self-refrigerated ice cream freezer.*

ROSEMARY–DESSERT WINE ICE CREAM

1½   **cups milk**
¾   **cup sugar**
1   **teaspoon minced fresh or dry rosemary leaves**
2   **large eggs**
1   **cup whipping cream**
½   **cup late-harvest wine such as Johannisberg Riesling or Semillon**
1   **teaspoon vanilla**
   Crushed ice and salt (use 8 parts ice to 1 part salt), optional

In a 2- to 3-quart pan over medium heat, frequently stir milk, sugar, and rosemary until mixture just comes to a boil.

In a bowl, whisk hot milk mixture into eggs. Mix in cream, wine, and vanilla (mixture may look slightly curdled). Cover and chill until mixture is cold, about 2 hours, or up until next day.

Pour mixture into a 1-quart or larger ice cream freezer container (frozen cylinder, self-refrigerated, or with ice and salt). Freeze according to manufacturer's directions or until dasher is hard to crank. Serve ice cream softly frozen. (Or, if made ahead, pack ice cream in a container and freeze airtight up to 1 week.) Makes about 1 quart.

PER ½-CUP SERVING: 218 calories, 3.7 g protein, 22 g carbohydrates, 12 g fat, 93 mg cholesterol, 49 mg sodium

MINT ICE CREAM

2   **cups milk**
¾   **cup sugar**
1   **cup (about 2 oz.) minced fresh mint leaves, or 1 teaspoon mint extract**
2   **large eggs**
1   **cup whipping cream**
1   **teaspoon vanilla**
   Crushed ice and salt (use 8 parts ice to 1 part salt), optional

In a 2- to 3-quart pan over medium heat, frequently stir milk, sugar, and mint until mixture just comes to a boil.

Flecks of rosemary are frozen throughout rich, creamy ice cream.

In a bowl, whisk hot milk mixture into eggs. Mix in whipping cream and vanilla. Cover and chill until cold, about 2 hours, or up until next day.

Pour mixture through a fine strainer into a 1-quart or larger ice cream freezer container (frozen cylinder, self-refrigerated, or with ice and salt); discard mint pieces. Freeze according to manufacturer's directions or until dasher is hard to crank. Serve ice cream softly frozen. (Or, if made ahead, pack ice cream in a container and freeze airtight up to 1 week.) Makes about 1 quart.

PER ½-CUP SERVING: 220 calories, 4.4 g protein, 23 g carbohydrates, 13 g fat, 95 mg cholesterol, 56 mg sodium

Perfect Chocolate Curls

HAVE PERFECT CHOCOLATE *curls eluded you? With these tricks, success is assured.*

The secrets are the tool—a standard flexible-blade vegetable peeler—and the technique—getting chocolate to just the right temperature. Dark chocolate can be finicky, though it's not too difficult to work with; white and milk chocolate curl most readily.

EASY CHOCOLATE CURLS

For a quantity of curls, warm each bar as you need it. Use a regular oven if your microwave oven is 500 watts or less; low-wattage microwaves can heat unevenly.

1 or more bars semisweet, white, milk, or bittersweet chocolate without nuts or filling, each 3 to 4 ounces and about ¼ inch thick, unwrapped

Place chocolate, scored side down, on a sheet of cooking parchment or foil, about 8 by 10 inches.

In a microwave oven, heat chocolate on parchment, uncovered, at full power (100 percent) until edges of chocolate give slightly to gentle fingertip pressure. Warm for 15 seconds, check, then warm for 5 seconds at a time until chocolate tests as indicated. Total time will be 15 to 40 seconds, depending on oven's wattage and the kind of chocolate.

In a conventional oven, place chocolate on foil on oven rack in a 150° oven until edges give slightly to gentle fingertip pressure, 1 to 1½ minutes.

If chocolate gets too soft, let it cool for a few minutes.

Set chocolate on paper or foil on a counter, aligning a long side of bar with counter edge; let paper or foil hang over edge. Stand with your hip to the counter. With 1 hand, gently hold end of chocolate bar closest to you. With the other, hold peeler perpendicular to edge and rest blade on opposite end of bar. Firmly and evenly, pull peeler toward you along bar, peeling off chocolate to make a curl.

If chocolate strip splays out instead of curling, neaten it up with your fingers. Some curls will wrap around themselves; others break off into short sections.

With tip of peeler, lift each curl to a flat surface to cool and firm. Turn paper

Three colors of curls add drama to cake cloaked in dark chocolate. To make curls, pull peeler (one with handle and blade in line) across bar of warm chocolate.

180° and repeat to make curls from opposite long side of bar. As chocolate bar gets thin, it's inclined to break; just pull peeler over smaller pieces.

If chocolate is too firm to curl smoothly, or if it firms as you work, rewarm in a microwave oven on full power (100 percent) for 5 to 10 seconds at a time, or in a conventional oven at 150° for 30 seconds.

Save chocolate scraps for other uses. If made ahead, store curls airtight up to 1 week. A 3-ounce bar makes 1¾ to 2¼ ounces (1½ to 2 cups) curls.

PER OUNCE SEMISWEET: 144 calories, 1.2 g protein, 16 g carbohydrates, 10 g fat, 0 mg cholesterol, 0.6 mg sodium

PER OUNCE WHITE: 154 calories, 1.4 g protein, 18 g carbohydrates, 8.5 g fat, 4.8 mg cholesterol, 23 mg sodium

PER OUNCE MILK: 147 calories, 2.2 g protein, 16 g carbohydrates, 9.2 g fat, 5.7 mg cholesterol, 27 mg sodium

Fila Dough Sandwiches

THESE FLAKY SANDWICHES, *made of paper-thin fila dough baked around a savory meat filling, are patterned after buttery appetizer favorites. Coated sparingly with oil or butter, fila dough provides a light, crisp, layered wrap.*

Find fila in the refrigerated or frozen foods section of supermarkets. Thaw frozen dough airtight in the refrigerator at least 8 hours. Carefully remove the number of sheets you need, then rewrap remaining sheets airtight and freeze. Keep sheets covered until ready to use; they become brittle when allowed to dry out.

DELI FILA SANDWICHES

- 6 ounces thin-sliced pastrami
- 4 teaspoons Dijon mustard
- 1/4 cup thin-sliced green onion
- 6 ounces thin-sliced Swiss cheese
- 8 sheets fila dough (each about 12 by 17 in.), thawed if frozen
- 2 tablespoons olive oil or melted butter

Lay pastrami flat in 8 portions. Spread with mustard, and top equally with onion and cheese. Fold meat into triangles (about 4-in. sides, 5-in. base) to enclose filling.

To assemble sandwiches, lay fila, 1 sheet at a time, on work surface (keep remaining fila covered airtight). Lightly brush with oil. Place 1 meat bundle at 1 end of fila in center of dough, setting a short side of meat triangle along base.

Fold sides of fila over filling. Fold covered filling over into a triangle. Continue folding flag-style to completely enclose filling in a triangular packet. Tuck loose ends under.

Place about 1 inch apart, seam side down, on an ungreased 10- by 15-inch baking pan. Cover with plastic wrap. Repeat with remaining fila and filling. (If made ahead, cover and chill up until the next day.)

Bake sandwiches, uncovered, in a 350° oven until golden brown, 25 to 35 minutes. Let sandwiches cool 5 minutes. Serve warm. Makes 8 sandwiches, 4 servings.

PER SERVING: 396 calories, 24 g protein, 32 g carbohydrates, 20 g fat, 56 mg cholesterol, 969 mg sodium

GINGER-TURKEY FILA SANDWICHES

- About 3 tablespoons olive oil or melted butter
- 3/4 pound ground turkey
- 1 large onion, chopped
- 2 tablespoons minced fresh ginger
- 1 teaspoon cornstarch
- 1/4 cup regular-strength chicken broth
- 3 tablespoons seasoned rice vinegar (or 3 tablespoons rice vinegar and 1 teaspoon sugar)
- 3 tablespoons drained capers
- 1 tablespoon grated lemon peel
- 8 sheets fila dough (each about 12 by 17 in.), thawed if frozen

In an 8- to 10-inch frying pan over medium-high heat, cook 2 teaspoons oil, turkey, onion, and ginger; stir often until meat and onion are tinged with brown, about 20 minutes. Mix cornstarch, broth, and vinegar; add to pan. Stir until boiling. Mix in capers and lemon peel. Let cool.

Assemble and bake sandwiches following the preceding recipe for deli fila sandwiches. Mound filling into a triangular shape (about 4-in. sides, 5-in. base) on fila, so 1 short side of triangle lies along base of sheet at center. Makes 8 sandwiches, 4 servings.

PER SERVING: 353 calories, 20 g protein, 32 g carbohydrates, 16 g fat, 62 mg cholesterol, 419 mg sodium

Light lunch features warm sandwiches enclosed in crisp fila dough. Filling is thinly sliced pastrami or seasoned ground turkey.

More May Recipes

OTHER MAY ARTICLES *featured a stir-fry entrée from Hawaii—shrimp in a savory black bean sauce—and a deceptively rich-tasting, no-fat chocolate cake.*

SHRIMP WITH BLACK BEAN SAUCE

Savory contrasts enhance the flavors of this light, quick main dish. Sweet shrimp, savory Chinese black beans, and mellow pork are stir-fried together, then served hot on cold slivers of napa cabbage.

- 2 **tablespoons fermented Chinese black beans (sold in Asian markets)**
- ¼ **pound ground lean pork**
- 3 **cloves garlic, minced or pressed**
- 1 **tablespoon minced fresh ginger**
- 1½ **cups regular-strength chicken broth**
- 2 **tablespoons oyster sauce**
- 1 **tablespoon cornstarch**
- 2 **tablespoons salad oil**
- 1 **pound medium-size shrimp (43 to 50 per lb.), peeled and deveined**
- 4 **green onions, ends trimmed, sliced thin**
- 6 **cups finely shredded napa cabbage**

Rinse beans in a fine strainer under cool running water; drain. Mix beans with pork, garlic, and ginger. Stir broth and oyster sauce with cornstarch.

Place wok or a 10- to 12-inch frying pan over medium-high heat and add oil. When oil is hot, add shrimp. Stir-fry just until shrimp are opaque in center (cut to test), about 3 minutes. Lift from pan.

To pan, add pork mixture. Stir-fry until crumbly and lightly browned, about 5 minutes. Add broth mixture and stir until boiling. Mix in shrimp and onions. On a platter, mound cabbage; top with shrimp mixture. Makes 4 to 6 servings.—*Raymond Chau, Won Kee Seafood, Honolulu.*

PER SERVING: 173 calories, 18 g protein, 6 g carbohydrates, 8 g fat, 106 mg cholesterol, 506 mg sodium

NO-FAT CHOCOLATE CAKE

Deceptively rich tasting, this cake is less than meets the eye. It packs in flavor without fat. Whipped egg whites and non-fat yogurt lighten up this version of the classic chocolate cake.

Contrasts in flavor and temperature add pleasing dimensions to this quick entrée. Spoon hot shrimp stir-fry with black beans onto cold, crisp shreds of napa cabbage.

- 1 **cup sifted cake flour**
- ⅓ **cup unsweetened cocoa**
- 1 **teaspoon *each* baking soda and baking powder**
- 6 **large egg whites**
- 1⅓ **cups firmly packed brown sugar**
- 1 **cup unflavored nonfat yogurt**
- 1 **teaspoon vanilla**
  Powdered sugar

Mix flour, cocoa, baking soda, and baking powder. In a large bowl, beat whites, brown sugar, yogurt, and vanilla until well blended. Stir in flour mixture and beat until evenly moistened.

Pour batter into a nonstick 8-inch-square pan (or coat an unfinished pan lightly with cooking-oil spray or salad oil, and dust with flour). Bake in a 350° oven until cake springs back when lightly pressed in center, 30 to 40 minutes. Let the cake cool for 15 minutes, then invert it onto a serving plate.

Sift powdered sugar over cake (if desired, use a doily as stencil for sugar pattern). Serve warm or cool. If made ahead, wrap airtight and store in a cool place up to 2 days. Cut into squares. Makes 8 servings.

PER SERVING: 220 calories, 5.8 g protein, 49 g carbohydrates, 0.8 g fat, 0.6 mg cholesterol, 230 mg sodium

Green chili, cheese, and egg bake on flour tortilla until crisp; top with condiments.

TWO-CHILI BRUNCH TOSTADA

- 1 cup chopped tomatoes
- 1 large (about ½ lb.) firm-ripe avocado, peeled, pitted, and diced
- 1 small jalapeño chili, stemmed, seeded, and minced
- 1 tablespoon lime juice
- 4 flour tortillas (7- to 8-in. size)
- 1 can (7 oz.) whole green chilies
- 1 cup (4 oz.) shredded cheddar cheese
- 4 large eggs
- 2 cups shredded iceberg lettuce
  Sour cream (optional)

In a bowl, mix tomatoes, avocado, jalapeño, and lime juice; set aside.

Immerse 1 tortilla at a time in water; drain briefly. Lay tortillas in 2 lightly oiled baking pans, each 10 by 15 inches; bake in a 500° oven until pale gold, 3 or 4 minutes. Remove from oven and place 1 green chili, split open, on each tortilla; sprinkle each with ¼ of the cheese. Break an egg onto center of each tortilla; stir yolk with a knife to blend with white slightly. Bake until whites are firm, 5 to 7 minutes.

Transfer tortillas to dinner plates. Offer lettuce, tomato mixture, and sour cream to add to taste. Makes 4 servings.—*Mickey Strang, McKinleyville, Calif.*

PER SERVING: 354 calories, 17 g protein, 23 g carbohydrates, 23 g fat, 242 mg cholesterol, 693 mg sodium

---

Make-ahead salad layers spinach, celery, water chestnuts, peas, bacon, and creamy blue cheese dressing.

LAYERED SPINACH SALAD

- 1 pound spinach, rinsed well
- 1 small (about ¼ lb.) red onion, sliced thin
- ½ cup thin-sliced celery
- 1 can (8 oz.) water chestnuts, drained and sliced
- 1 cup frozen petite peas, thawed
- 2 hard-cooked eggs, chopped fine
- ½ cup *each* mayonnaise and unflavored yogurt
- 1 tablespoon mustard seed
- 2 ounces blue-veined cheese, crumbled, about ⅓ cup
- ¾ pound bacon, cooked crisp
  Coarse-grind pepper

Remove and discard stems and wilted or yellow leaves from spinach. Wash and drain. Place leaves in a shallow 3- to 4-quart glass serving dish. Top with even layers of onion, celery, water chestnuts, peas, and egg. In a small bowl, mix mayonnaise, yogurt, mustard seed, and cheese. Spread evenly over egg layer. Cover and chill for at least 2 hours, or up until next day.

Just before serving, crumble bacon evenly over salad. Use a fork and spoon to lift out servings, including portions of each layer and some of the dressing. Add pepper to taste. Makes 6 servings.—*Debra Nelson, Ellensburg, Wash.*

PER SERVING: 357 calories, 14 g protein, 14 g carbohydrates, 28 g fat, 103 mg cholesterol, 610 mg sodium

---

Watercress purée adds color and flavor to spiced carrot soup.

SPICED PURÉE OF CARROT SOUP

- 1 tablespoon olive oil
- 1½ pounds carrots (about 6 medium-size), sliced thin
- 1 pound onions (about 2 medium-size), chopped
- 1 cup chopped celery
- 1 pound russet potatoes (about 2 medium-size), peeled
- 1 teaspoon ground cumin
- 1 teaspoon curry powder
- 6 cups regular-strength chicken broth
- 3 tablespoons lemon juice
  Cress purée (recipe follows)

In a 4- to 5-quart pan over medium-high

heat, combine oil, carrots, onion, and celery. Cook, covered, stirring often, until vegetables begin to brown, 12 to 15 minutes. Cut potatoes into ½-inch cubes; add to pan with cumin, curry, and broth. Simmer, covered, until potatoes are tender when pierced, 10 to 15 minutes. Add lemon juice. Purée soup, a portion at a time, in a blender or food processor. Pour into 5 or 6 bowls and drizzle with cress purée. Makes 5 or 6 servings.—*Karil Frohboese, Park City, Utah.*

Cress purée. In a blender, purée 1 cup lightly packed **watercress** sprigs and ¼ cup **unflavored yogurt.**

PER SERVING: 194 calories, 6.5 g protein, 33 g carbohydrates, 4.6 g fat, 0.5 mg cholesterol, 129 mg sodium

VERMICELLI WITH TURKEY, BASIL & DRIED TOMATOES

- 8 ounces dry vermicelli
- 1/3 cup dried tomatoes packed in oil (reserve oil)
- 2 cloves garlic, minced or pressed
- 1 small onion, chopped
- 1 small (about 1/2 lb.) yellow or red bell pepper, chopped
- 3/4 pound zucchini (about 2 medium-size), ends trimmed, sliced thin
- 1 cup regular-strength chicken broth
- 2 cups shredded cooked turkey
- 1/2 cup chopped fresh basil leaves or 3 tablespoons dry basil
  Grated parmesan cheese

In a 5- to 6-quart pan, cook vermicelli in 3 quarts boiling water until just tender to bite, 5 to 6 minutes; drain well and set aside.

Cut tomatoes into slivers. In the same pan over medium-high heat, combine slivered tomatoes, 2 tablespoons oil from tomatoes, garlic, onion, bell pepper, and zucchini. Stir often until vegetables begin to brown, 8 to 10 minutes.

Add pasta, broth, turkey, and basil; stir occasionally until hot. Transfer to a large serving bowl. Offer cheese to add to taste. Makes 4 servings.—*Carolyn Morrow Ocheltree, Fresno, Calif.*

PER SERVING: 493 calories, 31 g protein, 53 g carbohydrates, 18 g fat, 54 mg cholesterol, 501 mg sodium

Mix stir-fried vegetables with cooked pasta, turkey, and basil for one-dish meal.

GRILLED GAME HENS WITH CILANTRO MARINADE

- 2/3 cup minced fresh cilantro (coriander)
- 1 teaspoon dry mustard
- 4 cloves garlic, minced or pressed
- 2 tablespoons soy sauce
- 3 tablespoons honey
- 1/4 cup marsala or apple juice
- 4 Rock Cornish game hens (1 1/4 to 1 1/2 lb. each), rinsed

In a 1- to 2-quart pan on high heat, bring 1/2 cup cilantro, mustard, garlic, soy, honey, and marsala to a boil. Cool.

Reserve hen necks and giblets for other uses. With poultry or kitchen shears, split birds lengthwise through breastbones. Open hens; press, skin up, to crack bones so birds lie flat. Place hens and marinade in a large plastic bag. Seal bag and rotate; set in a large pan. Chill for 1 hour or up until next day.

Place hens, skin up, on grill 4 to 6 inches above a solid bed of medium coals (you can hold your hand at grill level only 4 to 5 seconds). Cook, turning often, for 20 minutes. Baste with marinade and turn often until meat at thigh bone is no longer pink (cut to test), 15 to 20 minutes more. Sprinkle with remaining cilantro. Makes 4 to 6 servings.—*Karen Bennett, Seaside, Calif.*

PER SERVING: 343 calories, 35 g protein, 11 g carbohydrates, 17 g fat, 110 mg cholesterol, 448 mg sodium

Split game hens with shears. Marinate in cilantro, garlic, honey, and marsala; then grill.

CHOCOLATE-MACAROON SQUARES

- 1/3 cup butter or margarine, cut up
- 3/4 cup sugar
- 1 1/4 cups all-purpose flour
- 4 large egg whites
- 1 1/2 teaspoons vanilla
- 3 cups sweetened shredded dry coconut
- 1 1/2 cups (9 oz.) semisweet chocolate baking chips

In a food processor or with your fingers, whirl or rub butter, 1/4 cup sugar, and 1 cup flour until dough begins to hold together. Press evenly over bottom of a 9-inch-square pan. Bake crust in a 350° oven until golden, 10 to 15 minutes.

In a large bowl, beat egg whites until frothy. Add vanilla and remaining 1/2 cup sugar and 1/4 cup flour; mix until smooth. Stir in coconut.

Sprinkle chocolate in an even layer over pastry. Spoon coconut mixture evenly over chocolate; use a spatula to cover chocolate completely. Continue baking until macaroon topping is golden and slightly wet-looking, about 25 minutes.

Cool in pan on a rack. Using a very sharp knife, cut into 1 1/2-inch squares. Makes 36 squares.—*Rebecca Lowe-Warren, Portland.*

PER SQUARE: 116 calories, 1.6 g protein, 15 g carbohydrates, 5.7 g fat, 4.6 mg cholesterol, 39 mg sodium

Indulge Mother on her day with delectable chocolate-coconut macaroon morsels.

THANKS TO THE MARVEL *of modern transportation, we now have zucchini—and other tender squash—all year. They are certainly welcome. In times of limited supply, we are happy to have them with just a little butter. In summer and fall, though, they can become a problem because of their rampant abundance. When they darken the earth with their fecundity, we look for novel ways to use them up.*

Noel Damon has a preparation that is both delicious and attractive. It begins, like the Italian peperonata, with a simple sauté of onion, green or red pepper, and tomato. It adds zucchini and yellow crookneck squash and, for a Mexican fillip, green chili and cumin. The result is as colorful as the flag of Bolivia and infinitely more flavorful.

SQUASH MEDLEY

1 **tablespoon butter or margarine**
1 **medium-size (about 6 oz.) onion, chopped**
1/2 **teaspoon cumin seed**

1 **medium-size (about 6 oz. total) red or green bell pepper, stemmed, seeded, and cut into thin strips**
1 **fresh Anaheim (California) green chili, stemmed, seeded, and chopped; or 1/2 cup diced canned green chilies**
2 **medium-size (about 3/4 lb. total) firm-ripe tomatoes, cored, peeled, and chopped**
2 **medium-size (about 1/2 lb. total) zucchini, ends trimmed, cut into 1/4-inch-thick slices**
2 **medium-size (about 1/2 lb. total) yellow crookneck squash, ends trimmed, cut into 1/4-inch-thick slices**
Salt and pepper

Melt butter in a 12-inch frying pan or 4- to 5-quart pan over medium heat. Add onion and cumin seed and stir often until onion is limp, 8 to 10 minutes. Then add the bell pepper and chili; stir often for 3 minutes.

Add the chopped tomatoes and stir often until hot; then add zucchini and crookneck squash. Cover and simmer until squash is just tender to bite, 6 to 8 minutes. Season to taste with salt and pepper. Makes 4 to 6 servings.

PER SERVING: 57 calories, 1.9 g protein, 8.6 g carbohydrates, 2.4 g fat, 5.2 mg cholesterol, 27 mg sodium

Noel Damon

Colorado Springs, Colo.

"In summer and fall, zucchini can become a problem because of their rampant abundance."

MEAT LOAF, *often thought of as the most pedestrian of dishes, is capable of almost limitless variation. The old Viennese meat loaf had a core of hard-cooked eggs. When sliced, each piece displayed a golden disk that needed only a few capers and a curved sliver of truffle to counterfeit the well-known happy face. You could almost hear "Have a nice day!"*

Still, not all the changes have been rung. John Young moistens his loaf with applesauce and throws in a few raisins for visual and gustatory attention. The result is not mincemeat, as you might think, but a moist meat loaf that slices well and tastes great.

MUSHROOM-RAISIN MEAT LOAF PLUS

- ³/₄ **pound ground lean beef**
- ¼ **pound bulk pork sausage**
- ½ **cup fine dry bread crumbs**
- 1 **large egg**
- ¼ **cup applesauce**
- ⅓ **cup fine-chopped onion**
- 2 **tablespoons raisins**
- ¼ **pound mushrooms, chopped**
- 1 **tablespoon Worcestershire**
- ½ **teaspoon dry rubbed sage**
- ¼ **teaspoon dry oregano leaves**
- ½ **teaspoon** *each* **salt and pepper**
- 2 **tablespoons catsup**
- 2 **slices bacon**

In a large bowl, thoroughly mix the beef, sausage, crumbs, egg, applesauce, onion, raisins, mushrooms, Worcestershire, sage, oregano, salt, and pepper. Lightly press mixture evenly

"Charles Ploof's cookies are fairly loaded with surprises."

into a 4½- by 8½-inch loaf pan. Spread top with catsup, then lay bacon slices lengthwise on loaf.

Bake in a 350° oven until meat in center is no longer pink (cut to test), about 1 hour. Let stand about 10 minutes.

Invert loaf onto a platter; turn baked side up, and cut into thick slices. Makes 6 servings.

PER SERVING: 350 calories, 16 g protein, 15 g carbohydrates, 25 g fat, 96 mg cholesterol, 560 mg sodium

Scottsdale, Ariz.

MOST CULINARY EFFORTS *offered as surprises promise more than they produce. But Charles Ploof's cookies are fairly loaded with surprises—chewy rolled oats, crunchy nuts, and, as a climax, candy-coated chocolate bits that are certain to melt not in your hand but in your mouth.*

CHUCK'S COOKY SURPRISES

- 1 **cup (½ lb.) butter or margarine**
- 1 **cup firm-packed brown sugar**
- 1 **cup granulated sugar**
- 2 **large eggs**
- 2 **tablespoons water**
- 1 **tablespoon vanilla**
- 3 **cups all-purpose flour**
- 1½ **teaspoons** *each* **baking soda and cream of tartar**
- 1 **cup regular rolled oats**
- 1 **cup oven-toasted rice cereal, crushed**
- 1 **cup coarse-chopped nuts**
- 1 **package (8 oz.) plain candy-coated chocolate candies**

In a bowl, beat together butter and the sugars. Beat in eggs, water, and vanilla. Mix flour, soda, and cream of tartar. Add to butter mixture with oats, cereal, nuts, and candies.

Drop the mixture by 2-tablespoon mounds, about 2 inches apart, on greased 12- by 15-inch baking sheets. Bake in a 350° oven until tops are golden brown and firm to the touch, about 20 minutes. Transfer to racks and let cool. Serve or, if made ahead, store airtight up to 3 days; freeze to store longer. Makes about 40.

PER COOKY: 177 calories, 2.5 g protein, 24 g carbohydrates, 8.1 g fat, 24 mg cholesterol, 96 mg sodium

Mukilteo, Wash.

May Menus

MILD WEATHER *is in the air—it's time for menus that suit outdoor dining. Serve either of these meals for brunch, lunch, early supper, or late dinner.*

The first takes advantage of convenience foods. The second streamlines a flavorful main-dish salad into easy steps.

GARDEN PIZZAS

Insalata with Caper Vinaigrette
Individual Yellow Pepper Pizzas
Melon Wedges with Berry Liqueur
Campari & Soda with Lime
Milk

Individual pizzas made from purchased frozen bread dough sport a spicy topping of pickled hot yellow chilies and sweet yellow bell pepper. If you're sensitive to chilies, use the smaller quantity (or none).

For variety in the salad, use several different types of Italian salami or mortadella. The salad platter can be assembled a couple of hours before mealtime.

For dessert, splash wedges of honeydew or cantaloupe with a berry liqueur.

INSALATA CAPER VINAIGRETTE

- 1/2 to 3/4 **pound thin-sliced salami or mortadella (choose 2 or 3 kinds)**
- 1 **can (2 oz.) anchovies, drained (optional)**
- 4 **large (about 3/4 lb. total) firm-ripe Roma-type tomatoes, cored and sliced thin**
- 6 **to 12 butter lettuce leaves, rinsed and crisped**
  Caper vinaigrette (recipe follows)

Roll sliced meats. Arrange meats, anchovies, tomatoes, and lettuce on a platter. (If made ahead, cover and chill up to 2 hours.) Drizzle with caper vinaigrette. Makes 4 servings.

PER SERVING: 345 calories, 17 g protein, 7 g carbohydrates, 27 g fat, 51 mg cholesterol, 1,588 mg sodium

Caper vinaigrette. Mix 1/4 cup **red wine vinegar**, 2 tablespoons **olive oil**, 2 tablespoons drained **capers**, 1 tablespoon **lemon juice**, and 1/2 teaspoon ground **pepper**.

INDIVIDUAL YELLOW PEPPER PIZZAS

- 1 **loaf (1 lb.) frozen white bread dough, thawed**
- 1 1/2 **cups (6 oz.) firmly packed shredded mozzarella cheese**
- 1 **medium-size (about 7 oz.) yellow bell pepper, stemmed, seeded, and sliced thin**
- 2 **to 4 medium-size pickled hot yellow chilies, drained, stemmed, seeded, and sliced thin (optional)**
- 8 **teaspoons grated parmesan cheese**
  About 1/2 cup fresh cilantro (coriander) leaves, rinsed and crisped

Cut dough into quarters; shape into balls. On a lightly floured board, roll out each ball to make a 6- to 7-inch-diameter round. Place rounds, about 1 inch apart, on 2 lightly oiled baking sheets, each 12 by 15 inches. With your hands, flatten rounds to about 1/4 inch thick and 7 inches wide, making outside edges slightly thicker. Let stand, uncovered, at room temperature until puffy, about 20 minutes.

Sprinkle each round to within 1/4 inch of edge with 1/4 cup mozzarella cheese. Cover with equal amounts of bell pepper and hot chilies. Evenly sprinkle equal amounts of remaining

Colorful but casual, outdoor supper features salami and tomato salad, individual pizzas, and sweet melon wedges with berry liqueur.

Individual cilantro-garnished pizzas with yellow chilies and bell pepper are cut into quarters for hand-held eating.

mozzarella cheese and parmesan cheese over vegetables on each round.

Bake pizzas in a 400° oven until crust is brown on bottom (lift to check), 16 to 18 minutes; if using 1 oven, rotate pan positions after 8 minutes. Cut rounds into quarters, top with cilantro leaves, and serve. Makes 4 servings.

PER PIZZA: 449 calories, 19 g protein, 57 g carbohydrates, 16 g fat, 41 mg cholesterol, 770 mg sodium

---

ASIAN PASTA SALAD WITH GRILLED SALMON

Barbecued Salmon & Asian-style Noodles on Mixed Greens & Herbs
Crusty Bread   Butter
Chocolate-topped Cookies
Mango Slices
Dry Sauvignon Blanc
Sparkling Water

With a few make-ahead steps, this meal can be ready in about 10 minutes—the time it takes to cook thin salmon fillets on the barbecue or under the broiler.

Buy mixed greens or combine your own. Look for seasoned rice vinegar, chili oil, and sesame oil in the Asian section of your supermarket (or use alternatives).

To ensure ripeness, choose mangoes that give slightly when gently pressed.

You can cook the noodles, crisp the greens, and peel and slice the mangoes 1 to 2 hours ahead. To barbecue fish, ignite briquets about 1 hour before dining.

BARBECUED SALMON & ASIAN-STYLE NOODLES ON MIXED GREENS & HERBS

6 to 8 ounces dry capellini

5 tablespoons seasoned rice vinegar (or 4 tablespoons distilled vinegar mixed with 1 tablespoon water and 1 tablespoon sugar)

3 tablespoons lime juice

6 teaspoons Oriental sesame oil

2 teaspoons hot chili oil or 1/4 teaspoon cayenne

2 teaspoons soy sauce

1/2 cup thin-sliced green onion

4 thin boned and skinned baby salmon fillets (about 1 1/2 lb. total)

1/3 pound (about 8 cups) mixed salad greens, rinsed and crisped

1 cup *each* firmly packed fresh cilantro (coriander) leaves and basil leaves, chopped

1 medium-size (about 3/4 lb.) cucumber, peeled, seeded, and sliced thin

Lime wedges (optional)

Salt and pepper

Bring about 2 quarts water to a boil in a 4- to 5-quart pan over high heat. Add noodles and cook just until tender to bite, about 4 minutes. Drain, rinse with

(Continued on next page)

Barbecued salmon fillet goes atop a mound of cool Asian-spiced noodles and salad greens mixed with chopped basil and cilantro.

cold water, and drain again. In a bowl, mix 3 tablespoons seasoned rice vinegar, the lime juice, 4 teaspoons sesame oil, the hot chili oil, the soy sauce, and the green onion. Stir in noodles, cover, and chill until noodles are cool, at least 30 minutes or up to 2 hours.

Coat both sides of fish with remaining 2 teaspoons sesame oil.

To barbecue fish, set fillets on a grill 4 to 6 inches above a solid bed of hot coals (you can hold your hand at grill level only 2 to 3 seconds).

To broil fish, set fillets on a rack in a 12- by 15-inch broiler pan and place 4 inches from heat.

Barbecue or broil fillets, turning them once, until fish is opaque but still moist-looking in thickest part (cut to test), 4 to 6 minutes total.

Mix together salad greens, cilantro, basil, and remaining 2 tablespoons rice vinegar. On 4 dinner plates, evenly divide the greens and arrange equal amounts of cooked noodles and sliced cucumber on greens. Lay a hot fillet on each mound of noodles. Offer lime wedges, salt, and pepper to add to taste. Makes 4 servings.

PER SERVING: 581 calories, 43 g protein, 56 g carbohydrates, 21 g fat, 94 mg cholesterol, 269 mg sodium

JUNE

Fiesta Party (page 146)

Join us this month in a salute to the good foods of summer and to meals that are easy on the cook! You'll find quick-to-make dishes to brighten barbecues and picnics, simple one-pot main dishes, ideas for camp cooking at home, and an expandable Mexican fiesta party menu that feeds a crowd. Experiment with refreshing cool beverages, bold dips for appetizers, delicious make-ahead salads, and simple desserts that showcase summer's ripe fruits. We also present the latest research on safe ways to use eggs and how to test for egg safety.

THE GOOD FOODS OF SUMMER: A Make-ahead Fiesta

DINNER FOR 150? *No problem! Nine years' experience gives Jeanette Navarro and Becky and Bobby Betancourt of Santa Barbara plenty of savvy for hosting their big Mexican fiesta every year.*

We've scaled their recipes down to a party for 25. For a larger group, make several batches of each dish.

What are the Santa Barbarans' secrets? First, they keep records and lists from year to year. A few friends (not enough to cause a traffic jam) help with food preparation, decoration, service, and cleanup. Nearly all the food is made in stages, weeks ahead, and frozen.

The party dishes are all simple, good-tasting Mexican classics. Some start with purchased components (such as salsa) to which you add fresh ingredients and seasonings.

Two basic recipes—one for simmered beef and one for pork—become four when you divide the cooked meat and season it differently to make taquitos, beans, tamales, and chili verde.

You make one large batch of the doctored salsa. Use some with chips as an appetizer, some in the taco salad and guacamole, the rest with entrées.

FIESTA PARTY FOR 25 TO 150

Tortilla Chips with Red Salsa
Guacamole   Bean Dip
Bite-size Chicken Flautas
Taco Salad   Cheese Enchiladas
Cecy's Tamales   Chili Verde
Beans from the Pot
Beef Taquitos
Oranges & Plums
Assorted Cookies & Cakes
Mexican Pastries
Sparkling Water   Mexican Beer
Margaritas   Citrus Sours

Advance preparation makes it possible for just a few people to assemble this party. For help planning, refer to the time schedule on the facing page.

To streamline efforts, do similar tasks—like frying taquitos and flautas, and simmering pork and beef—together.

You may need to line up some auxiliary refrigerator space at a friend's.

For 25 people, buy 3 large packages (16 oz. each) tortilla chips to offer with salsa, guacamole, and bean dip.

RED SALSA

Use about 6 cups salsa with chips, the rest with guacamole, salad, and entrées. Most markets sell refrigerated salsa.

- 1 gallon (16 cups) purchased fresh red salsa, mild to hot
- 1 cup chopped fresh cilantro (coriander)
- 1 cup sliced green onions
- 4 cloves garlic, minced or pressed

In a 5- to 6-quart bowl, mix salsa, cilantro, onions, garlic. Use, or cover and chill up to 3 days. Makes 1 gallon.

PER TABLESPOON: 11 calories, 0.2 g protein, 0.9 g carbohydrates, 0.9 g fat, 0 mg cholesterol, 1.2 mg sodium

GUACAMOLE

Use about 6 cups with chips, the rest with flautas, enchiladas, and taquitos.

- 7 pounds (14 large) ripe avocados, pitted and peeled
- 1³/₄ cups red salsa (recipe precedes)
- ¹/₂ cup lemon juice
- 4 cloves garlic, minced or pressed
- 4 to 6 fresh jalapeño chilies, stemmed, seeded, and minced
  Salt

In a large bowl or (part at a time) a food processor, coarsely mash or purée avocados. Stir or whirl in salsa, juice, garlic; add chilies and salt to taste. If made ahead, smooth plastic over guacamole; chill up to 1 day. Makes 13 cups.

PER TABLESPOON: 22 calories, 0.3 g protein, 1.1 g carbohydrates, 2 g fat, 0 mg cholesterol, 1.6 mg sodium

BEAN DIP

- 2 cans (2¹/₄ oz. each) sliced black ripe olives, drained
- 3 cans (1 lb. each) chili with beans
- 1 large package (8 oz.) and 1 small package (3 oz.) cream cheese
- 4 to 6 fresh jalapeño chilies, stemmed, seeded, and minced
  Chopped onion (optional)

Set aside 2 tablespoons olives. Place remaining olives, chili, and cream cheese (in chunks) in a 3- to 4-quart pan. Stir often over medium heat until hot, about 20 minutes. Add chilies to taste. (If made ahead, chill up to 2 days. Reheat to simmering; thin with water.) Pour into 1 or more bowls.

Dancers entertain at big annual party engineered by just three people. To help you plan your own fiesta, we offer planning tips and a menu of make-ahead Mexican favorites.

Garnish bean dip with onion and reserved olives. Serve warm. Makes about 6 cups, 25 servings.

PER TABLESPOON: 30 calories, 1.1 g protein, 1.9 g carbohydrates, 2.1 g fat, 6 mg cholesterol, 94 mg sodium

BITE-SIZE CHICKEN FLAUTAS

- 3 medium-size onions, chopped
- 2 cloves garlic, minced or pressed
- 5 to 6 cups salad oil
- 2 large (about 1 lb. total) ripe tomatoes, cored, peeled, and chopped
- 2 medium-size green bell peppers, stemmed, seeded, and chopped
- 2 fresh jalapeño chilies, stemmed, seeded, and minced
- 1/2 cup minced fresh cilantro (coriander)
- 3 1/2 cups shredded cooked chicken (use meat from a 3 1/2-lb. chicken or from 2 1/2-lb. chicken breasts) Salt and pepper
- 25 to 30 flour tortillas (7- to 8-in. size) Red salsa and guacamole (recipes precede)

In a 5- to 6-quart pan over medium-high heat, frequently stir onions and garlic in 2 tablespoons oil until limp, 12 to 15 minutes. Add tomatoes, bell peppers, and jalapeños. Stir often until bell pepper is limp, 10 to 15 minutes more. Remove from heat; stir in cilantro, chicken, and salt and pepper to taste.

Stack 6 tortillas in a plastic bag; leave open. Heat in a microwave oven on full power (100 percent) until warm, about 1 minute. Repeat as needed. (Or stack all tortillas, wrap in foil, and put in a 350° oven until warm, about 20 minutes.)

A few at a time, lay warm tortillas flat. Place 1/4 cup of chicken mixture in a band down a side of each tortilla, leaving about a 1-inch margin on each end. Fold ends over filling; roll to enclose. Fasten each flauta shut with 2 toothpicks. Repeat to use all filling.

Pour 1 inch salad oil into a 10- to 12-inch frying pan and set on medium-high heat. When oil reaches 350°, add about 5 flautas at a time. Cook, turning once, until well browned, 3 to 5 minutes total. Lift out and drain on paper towels. Remove toothpicks. If serving immediately, cut diagonally in half.

If made ahead, let whole flautas cool completely, then freeze airtight up to 1 month. To reheat, thaw flautas in refrigerator, cut diagonally in half, place slightly apart in 2 baking pans (each 10 by 15 in.), and bake in a 400° oven until hot, about 20 minutes; turn over halfway through baking. Serve hot flautas with salsa and guacamole. Makes 50 to 60 pieces, 25 servings.

PER PIECE: 95 calories, 3.8 g protein, 11 g carbohydrates, 3.9 g fat, 7.3 mg cholesterol, 95 mg sodium

TACO SALAD

- 3/4 pound ground lean beef
- 2 to 3 teaspoons ground dry New Mexico or California chilies, or chili powder Salt
- 1/2 pound cheddar cheese, shredded
- 4 medium-size (about 1 1/2 lb. total) ripe tomatoes, cored and chopped
- 3 pounds (about 3 large heads) iceberg, butter, or romaine lettuce (or combination), rinsed and crisped
- 3 cans (2 1/4 oz. each) sliced black ripe olives, drained
- 1 package (12 oz.) corn tortilla chips, slightly crushed Fiesta dressing (recipe follows) Salt

In a 10- to 12-inch frying pan over medium-high heat, stir beef often until browned, about 10 minutes. Spoon out and discard fat. Stir ground chilies and salt to taste into meat. Let cool completely. If made ahead, cover and chill up to 2 days, or freeze airtight up to 1 month.

To serve, divide beef, cheese, tomatoes, lettuce (in bite-size pieces), olives, and chips between 2 large bowls (6- to 8-qt. size); add dressing equally and mix gently. Add salt to taste. Makes 25 servings.

PER SERVING: 293 calories, 6.7 g protein, 14 g carbohydrates, 24 g fat, 20 mg cholesterol, 229 mg sodium

Fiesta dressing. Place 1 1/2 cups **salad oil** in a blender with 3 tablespoons **sugar,** 2 tablespoons **ground dry New Mexico** or California **chilies** (or use chili powder), and 1 1/2 teaspoons **dry oregano leaves.** Whirl, gradually adding 3/4 cup **red salsa** (recipe precedes) and 3/4 cup **white wine vinegar.** If made ahead, chill, covered, up to 3 days.

Getting Organized

GOOD PLANNING *makes a party this size run smoothly. Here's the hosts' time and work checklist.*

One month ahead. Send out invitations. Arrange to borrow or rent tables and folding chairs.

Two weeks ahead. Prepare and freeze flautas, enchiladas, tamales, chili verde, beans, taquitos.

One week ahead. Make the margarita mix.

Two or three days ahead. Make salsa, bean dip, taco salad meat.

One day ahead. Set up tables and chairs; decorate. Slice oranges. Rinse and crisp salad lettuce. Thaw frozen food in the refrigerator. Buy desserts; make guacamole.

On the party day. Before guests arrive, put beverages in large tubs with ice. Set out chips, salsa, guacamole, and bean dip. Post friends to direct parking.

During the party. Make margaritas. Reheat food; for large groups, set out some of each dish at a time, then replenish dishes as the guests help themselves.

CHEESE ENCHILADAS

If you're making several batches of enchiladas, disposable 7- by 11-inch aluminum pans are handy as containers.

- 6 cans (10 oz. each) enchilada sauce
- 2 tablespoons dry oregano leaves
- 25 corn tortillas (about 7-in. size)
- 2 1/4 pounds cheddar cheese, shredded
- 2 1/2 cups sliced green onions Red salsa and guacamole (recipes precede)

Pour 2 cans enchilada sauce into a 10- to 12-inch frying pan over medium-high heat; add 2 teaspoons oregano. Stir often until simmering. Reduce heat to low. Dip 1 tortilla at a time in sauce just to soften, about 30 seconds; lift with tongs and transfer to 7- by 11-inch or 9-by 13-inch pans (you'll need 3 dishes of either size).

In a band down center of each tortilla, sprinkle 1/4 cup cheese and 1 table-spoon onions. Roll to enclose; place, seam side down, in dish. Repeat to make remaining enchiladas, placing side by side. As you use up sauce, heat 2 more cans at a time with 2 more teaspoons oregano. Pour remaining sauce evenly over filled tortillas. Sprinkle with remaining cheese.

If made ahead, cover and chill up to 3 days. Or wrap airtight in foil and freeze up to 1 month (thaw in refrigerator).

Sprinkle enchiladas with remaining onions. Bake, uncovered, in a 350° oven until hot in center, 20 to 30 minutes. Serve with salsa and guacamole. Makes 25 enchiladas, 25 servings.

PER ENCHILADA: 262 calories, 13 g protein, 21 g carbohydrates, 15 g fat, 43 mg cholesterol, 960 mg sodium

CECY'S TAMALES

For small husks, use a little masa to paste 2 together, overlapping slightly. Steam only 1 batch of tamales at a time.

- 3 **pounds prepared masa, purchased or homemade (recipe follows)**
- 1/3 **cup pork broth (from simmered pork, recipe follows), if needed**
  Soaked corn husks (directions follow)
  Pork filling (recipe follows)

In a large bowl, beat purchased masa with broth until smooth and easy to spread. (Omit this step with home-made masa.) If made ahead, cover and chill up to 24 hours.

For each tamale, lay a drained husk flat. Evenly spread about 3 tablespoons masa in a 3- by 5-inch rectangle on husk, with 3-inch side flush against 1 long edge of husk; leave a bare border at least 1 inch wide on opposite edge. Also leave at least 1 inch bare between masa and husk tip and 3 inches bare at base.

Spoon 2 tablespoons pork filling in the center of the masa. Fold husk lengthwise so masa on 1 side meets masa opposite to enclose filling; wrap plain edge of husk around tamale. Fold both ends of husk over filled portion, pressing lightly along creases to seal.

Lay tamale folds down; cover with plastic wrap. Repeat to use up filling, stacking tamales as shaped.

You'll need an 8- to 12-quart pan with a rack for steaming. Set rack on supports at least 1 inch above bottom of pan. Pour 1 inch of water into pan. Stand tamales upright on rack with large folded edges down; arrange so steam can circulate.

Cover pan; bring water to a boil over high heat. Reduce heat but maintain boil (replenish water as needed) until masa is firm to touch and no longer sticks to husk (open a tamale to test), about 1 hour. Serve, or keep in steamer over low heat up to 1 hour.

If made ahead, remove from steamer and let cool. Cover and chill up to 3 days. To freeze, lay tamales in a single layer on baking sheets, freeze solid, then store in freezer bags. To reheat, steam chilled or frozen tamales as directed, preceding, until hot in the center, 20 to 30 minutes. Makes 25 to 30 tamales, 25 servings.

PER TAMALE: 239 calories, 8.1 g protein, 15 g carbohydrates, 16 g fat, 35 mg cholesterol, 62 mg sodium

Prepared homemade masa. Whip 1 1/4 cups **lard** or solid shortening and 1 teaspoon **salt** (optional) with an electric mixer until fluffy. Blend in 4 cups **dehydrated masa flour** (corn tortilla flour) and 3 cups **pork broth** (from simmered pork recipe, following) until evenly mixed. Use the masa at room temperature; if made ahead, cover and chill up to 2 days. Makes 5 3/4 cups (about 3 lb.), enough for 25 tamales.

Soaked corn husks. Place 1 package (about 8 oz.) **dried corn husks** in a large bowl and cover with hot water. Let stand until pliable, at least 20 minutes or as long as overnight. You need 25 to 30 large outer husks; as ready to use, lift from water, discard silk and other debris, and pat dry. Discard remaining corn husks.

Pork filling. Let 2 1/3 cups **simmered pork** (recipe follows) stand until cool enough to handle. Shred with fingers and return to 5- to 6-quart pan; set aside.

In a blender or food processor, whirl smooth 6 cloves **garlic**; 1 small **onion,** in chunks; 2/3 cup **purchased red chili sauce** (Mexican-style, not type used for hamburgers); 1/2 cup **water;** and 1 tablespoon **ground dry New Mexico** or California **chilies** or chili powder. Stir

into meat. Bring to a simmer over medium heat. Simmer, uncovered, for 15 minutes to blend flavors, stirring often.

Remove from heat and stir in 2 cans (2 1/4 oz. each) drained **sliced black ripe olives.** Let stand until cool. If made ahead, chill, covered, up to 24 hours.

SIMMERED PORK

Cut 6 pounds **boned pork butt** or shoulder (fat trimmed) into 2-inch chunks. In a 5- to 6-quart pan over high heat, combine meat and 3/4 cup **water.** Cover and simmer on medium-high heat for 30 minutes. Uncover; stir occasionally until liquid evaporates and juices turn a rich brown and stick to pan, about 30 minutes. Spoon off and discard fat. Add 1 quart **water,** scraping brown bits free. Add 6 cloves **garlic** and 2 medium-size **onions,** quartered. Bring to a boil over high heat; cover and simmer until meat is tender when pierced, 1 3/4 to 2 hours. Drain meat; reserve broth.

Skim any remaining fat from broth, then measure broth. You should have at least 3 cups; if not, add **regular-strength beef broth** to equal this amount. Use for tamales (recipe precedes).

Lift 2 1/3 cups meat from pan and use to make pork filling for tamales. Use remaining meat for chili verde (recipe follows). Makes 7 to 8 cups.

CHILI VERDE

Use purchased salsa if you haven't already made the red salsa.

- 4 2/3 **cups meat from simmered pork (recipe precedes)**
- 1 **large can (7 oz.) diced green chilies**
- 1 **large can (13 oz.) tomatillos**
- 1 1/2 **cups red salsa (recipe precedes) or purchased salsa**
- 2 **teaspoons ground cumin**
- 2 **teaspoons dry oregano leaves**
  White and green onions (optional)

Put meat in a 2 1/2- to 3-quart casserole. In a blender, purée chilies, tomatillos and liquid, salsa, cumin, and oregano until smooth. Stir into meat.

Bake, uncovered, in a 350° oven until bubbling, 30 minutes. If made ahead,

Ready for a crowd, buffet features Mexican classics. Clockwise from taco salad at top, fiesta menu includes beans, chili verde, tamales, enchiladas, guacamole, salsa, bean dip, chips, flautas, citrus sours, beef taquitos. Many of the dishes can be prepared in stages, weeks ahead, and frozen.

let cool, then cover and chill up to 2 days or freeze up to 1 month (thaw in refrigerator). Reheat, covered, in a 350° oven until hot in center, 20 to 30 minutes. Top with onions. Makes 8 cups, 25 servings.

PER SERVING: 137 calories, 13 g protein, 1.3 g carbohydrates, 8.7 g fat, 50 mg cholesterol, 102 mg sodium

SIMMERED BEEF

- 6 **pounds boned beef chuck (fat trimmed), cut into 2-inch chunks**
- 2 **large onions, coarsely chopped**
- 4 **cloves garlic, chopped**
- 2 **tablespoons ground dry New Mexico or California chilies, or chili powder**
- 1 **tablespoon ground cumin**

Put beef, onions, garlic, and 3/4 cup water in a 5- to 6-quart pan. Cover and simmer on medium-high heat for 30 minutes. Uncover; stir occasionally until liquid evaporates and juices turn a rich brown and stick to pan, 30 to 45 minutes.

Add ground chilies and cumin; stir for about 30 seconds. Stir in 4 cups water, scraping browned bits free.

Cover and simmer until meat is almost tender when pierced, about 1 hour. With a slotted spoon, lift 5 cups of meat from pan and reserve for use with beans (recipe follows). Simmer remaining meat, covered, until very tender when pierced, about 30 minutes longer. With a slotted spoon, lift meat from pan and set aside.

Boil juices over high heat, uncovered, until reduced to 1 1/2 cups, about 10 minutes; stir often. Remove from heat; skim off and discard fat. With 2 forks, tear the meat into long shreds. Return to pan and mix with juices. Measure mixture; you need 3 1/2 cups. If necessary, take from or add to meat saved for the beans. Use shredded beef in beef taquitos (recipe follows). If made ahead, chill, covered, up to 1 day. Makes 8 1/2 to 9 1/2 cups.

BEANS FROM THE POT

- 2 **pounds (5 cups) dry pinto beans, sorted of debris and rinsed**
- 4 **large cloves garlic**
- 2 **medium-size onions, chopped**

- 3 **tablespoons ground dry New Mexico or California chilies, or chili powder**
- 5 **cups simmered beef (recipe precedes)**
  Salt

In an 8- to 10-quart pan over high heat, bring beans, garlic, onions, chilies, and 3 quarts water to a boil over high heat. Cover and simmer until beans are almost tender to bite, about 2 hours.

Break beef into 1/2- to 1-inch pieces. Add to beans and simmer, uncovered, until beans and meat are very tender to bite, about 30 minutes; stir often.

If made ahead, let cool; cover and chill up to 2 days. Or freeze airtight up to 1 month (thaw in refrigerator). Reheat to simmering. If beans are stiff, thin with 1 to 1 1/2 cups water. Season to taste with salt. Makes about 16 cups, 25 servings.

PER SERVING: 205 calories, 17 g protein, 22 g carbohydrates, 5.4 g fat, 33 mg cholesterol, 54 mg sodium

BEEF TAQUITOS

- 3 1/2 **cups shredded simmered beef (recipe precedes)**
- 2 **teaspoons dry oregano leaves**
- 1/2 **teaspoon ground cinnamon Salt**
  About 5 cups salad oil
- 25 **to 27 corn tortillas (7-in. size) Red salsa and guacamole (recipes precede)**

Mix beef with oregano, cinnamon, and salt to taste.

Pour 1 inch oil into a 10- to 12-inch frying pan over medium-high heat. Heat oil to 350°. Dip tortillas in oil, 1 at a time, until small blisters form on surface, about 5 seconds. Let drain on paper towels. Remove oil from heat.

For each taquito, spread about 2 tablespoons meat in a thin band about 1 inch from edge of a tortilla. Roll up tightly. Fasten with 2 toothpicks. Repeat to use up filling. Bring oil to 350° on medium-high heat. Add taquitos, 5 or 6 at a time, and cook, turning once, until golden, 3 to 5 minutes. Drain on paper towels; remove picks. Serve hot with salsa and guacamole.

If made ahead, let taquitos cool, then chill airtight up to 2 days; or freeze up to 1 month (thaw in refrigerator). Place thawed taquitos in 2 pans, each about 10 by 15 inches. Bake in a 400° oven until

hot to touch, about 20 minutes. Makes 25 to 27 taquitos, 25 servings.

PER SERVING: 200 calories, 9.9 g protein, 13 g carbohydrates, 12 g fat, 26 mg cholesterol, 86 mg sodium

ORANGES & PLUMS

Slice 7 large unpeeled **oranges** crosswise and arrange on a platter with 25 small ripe **plums** (about 3 lb. total). You can chill, covered, up to 1 day. Makes 25 servings.

PER SERVING: 54 calories, 0.8 g protein, 13 g carbohydrates, 0.4 g fat, 0 mg cholesterol, 0 mg sodium

ASSORTED COOKIES, CAKES & MEXICAN PASTRIES

Bake or purchase cookies, brownies, cakes, Mexican pastries, and candies. Allow at least 1 cooky and 1 piece of cake, pastry, or candy per person. Cut cakes before setting them out.

SPARKLING WATER, MEXICAN BEER

For 25 people, you'll need 12 quarts of cold **sparkling water** and 10 large **limes,** sliced thin; allow 1 lime slice per glass. If you serve cold **Mexican beer,** allow 1 or 2 bottles per person, plus margaritas.

MARGARITAS OR CITRUS SOURS

- 11 **cans (12 oz. each) frozen limeade concentrate, thawed**
- 5 1/2 **quarts water**
- 2 **quarts tequila or orange juice**
- 1 **quart orange-flavor liqueur**
- 15 **pounds small ice cubes**
- 1/2 **cup lime juice (optional) Kosher or cocktail salt (optional)**
- 10 **large limes, sliced thin crosswise**

Divide the limeade, water, tequila, and orange-flavor liqueur equally among 3 containers, each at least 1 gallon; stir. Chill up to 1 week.

To make margaritas, stir lime mixture, then put 2 1/2 cups of it and 2 cups ice at a time in a blender. Whirl until smooth. Dip rims of glasses in lime juice, then in salt. Add margarita mixture; place 1 lime slice in each glass. Makes 91 cups; 100 servings, about 1 cup each.

PER 1 CUP: 135 calories, 0.1 g protein, 23 g carbohydrates, 0 g fat, 0 mg cholesterol, 0.3 mg sodium

The Good Foods of Summer: Cool Blends for Sipping

COOL OFF WITH SIPS *of these refreshing beverages. Two are based on berries; the other two start with vegetables and could also pass as cold first-course soups.*

For the smoothest mixtures, use a blender. If using a food processor, whirl fruit or vegetables as smooth as you can with the ice, then add the liquids.

STRAWBERRY SHRUB

Because strawberries' sweetness varies, taste shrub and add the sugar you want.

- 1 cup hulled and rinsed strawberries
- 1 cup orange juice
- 1 tablespoon balsamic vinegar
  About ¹/₂ cup small ice cubes or crushed ice
  Sugar
  Chilled sparkling water (optional)

Reserve 2 pretty berries. Put the remainder in a blender; add juice, vinegar, and ¹/₂ cup ice cubes. Purée smooth. Add sugar to taste. Pour into tall glasses; for a version with half the calories, fill glasses halfway, then fill the rest of the way with sparkling water. To decorate glasses, slash reserved berries about halfway through and perch 1 on each glass rim (or cut berries in half, slash, and slip onto rim). Makes 2 servings, 4 with sparkling water.

PER UNDILUTED SERVING: 180 calories, 1.3 g protein, 19 g carbohydrates, 0.4 g fat, 0 mg cholesterol, 2 mg sodium

BUTTERCUPS

To turn this into a rosy sunrise, use red bell peppers alone or with yellow or orange bells. For a shortcut, use 1 jar (12 to 14 oz., or 2 cups) canned red bell or other sweet peppers or pimientos.

- 2 large (about 1 lb. total) yellow or orange bell peppers
- 2 cups small ice cubes or crushed ice
- 1 cup buttermilk
- 2 tablespoons lemon juice
- ¹/₂ teaspoon cumin seed (optional)
  Salt
- 1 tablespoon minced fresh dill or 1 teaspoon dry dill weed
- 4 green onions, ends trimmed

Cut peppers in half lengthwise. Lay cut side down in a foil-lined 10- by 15-inch pan. Broil peppers about 4 inches from heat until skin is charred, about 10 minutes. Remove from oven, cover with foil, and let cool. Pull off and discard skins, stems, and seeds. Drain liquid from peppers into a blender. Add peppers, ice cubes, buttermilk, and lemon juice. Whirl until puréed smooth. Stir in cumin seed and salt to taste. Pour into glasses and sprinkle with dill; add a green onion as a stirrer to each glass. Makes about 3²/₃ cups, 4 servings.

PER SERVING: 54 calories, 3.2 g protein, 9.3 g carbohydrates, 1 g fat, 2.5 mg cholesterol, 70 mg sodium

FLAMING SUNSET SIPPING BORSCHT

Sip, or serve in wide bowls as soup for a summer supper first course or for a cool lunch with a sandwich.

- 1 can (about 1 lb.) sliced pickled beets
- 1 pint (2 cups) nonfat yogurt
- 1 cup small ice cubes or crushed ice
- 1 cup rinsed and drained blackberries
- ¹/₂ cup orange juice
- 2 tablespoons lemon juice
  Salt
  Bread-and-butter pickles

Cranberries, raspberries, and the perfume of roses blend delicately for sipping.

In blender (at least 6-cup capacity), combine beets and liquid, yogurt, ice cubes, berries, orange juice, and lemon juice. Whirl until puréed smooth. Add salt to taste and pour into tall glasses; garnish each glass with a pickle slice. Makes about 6 cups, 6 servings.

PER SERVING: 114 calories, 5.3 g protein, 24 g carbohydrates, 0.3 g fat, 1.5 mg cholesterol, 259 mg sodium

SUMMER ROSE

Look for rose flower water with supermarket fancy foods or at liquor stores.

- 1 cup cranberry juice cocktail
- ¹/₂ cup raspberries, rinsed and drained
- 1 teaspoon rose flower water
  Seed from 1 cardamom pod
- 1 cup small ice cubes or crushed ice
  Thin orange slices; or small rosebuds (free of pesticides), rinsed and drained

In a blender, combine juice, raspberries, rose flower water, cardamom seed, and ice. Whirl until puréed smooth. Pour into tall glasses and garnish with orange slices or float a rosebud in each. Makes about 2¹/₂ cups, 2 or 3 servings.

PER SERVING: 58 calories, 0.2 g protein, 15 g carbohydrates, 0.2 g fat, 0 mg cholesterol, 1.7 mg sodium

Buttercup drink's golden color comes from yellow bell peppers, smoothness from buttermilk.

The Good Foods of Summer: Refreshing New Dips

REFRESHING AS A SPLASH *in the pool, these dips and sauces add zest to all manner of nibbling foods—from crisp vegetables to savory bites of meat. All have make-ahead steps.*

THYME–HONEY–LEMON RELISH

Rather like a marmalade, but less sweet and slightly bitter, this relish is a particularly good complement to meats. Try it as a dip with roasted chicken wings, grilled pork ribs, tiny lamb chops, or small chunks of sausage.

- 1 medium-size (about 5 oz.) lemon
- 1/4 cup honey
- 1 teaspoon dry thyme leaves

Put lemon in a deep 1½- to 2-quart pan and cover with water. Bring to a boil on high heat, uncovered; let simmer 5 minutes. Drain. When cool, cut in chunks into a blender or food processor (to catch juice); pick out and discard seeds, then whirl to chop fine.

Return lemon and juices to pan. Add honey, thyme, and 1 cup water. Boil on high heat, stirring often, until almost dry, 10 to 12 minutes. Be careful not to scorch. Stir in 1/2 cup more water and boil until reduced to 2/3 cup. Serve warm or cool. If made ahead, cover and chill up to 1 week. Makes about 2/3 cup.

PER TABLESPOON: 29 calories, 0.2 g protein, 8.6 g carbohydrates, 0.1 g fat, 0 mg cholesterol, 0.9 mg sodium

Chinese salted black beans add surprise punch to potato appetizer.

CHINESE BEAN & BLUE CHEESE SAUCE

Pungent fermented salted black beans are a popular Chinese seasoning, used frequently with meats. Equally pungent blue cheese marries extremely well with the beans; in this topping they give eye-opening interest to plain steamed potato slices, hot or cool.

- 1 tablespoon fermented salted black beans
- 1 clove garlic, minced or pressed
- 1 tablespoon salad oil
- 2 tablespoons rice vinegar
- 1 medium-size firm-ripe Roma-style tomato, cored and diced
- 1/4 cup coarsely crumbled blue cheese
- 2 tablespoons fine-chopped green onions (including tops)
- 5 cooked thin-skinned potatoes (each about 3 in. long), hot or cool

Carefully sort through beans to remove debris (such as tiny rocks), then put beans in a fine strainer and rinse well with water. Let drain. In a bowl, mash beans with garlic. Mix in the oil and rice vinegar, then add tomato, cheese, and onions. Stir to blend. If made ahead, cover and let stand up to 6 hours; mix to use.

Cut potatoes crosswise into about 3/8-inch-thick slices. Spoon about 1 teaspoon bean mixture onto each slice; pick up to eat. Makes 1/2 cup sauce, or 24 portions.

PER PORTION WITH POTATOES: 27 calories, 0.7 g protein, 3.8 g carbohydrates, 1 g fat, 1.1 mg cholesterol, 39 mg sodium

INDONESIAN GADO GADO DIP

Companionable foods to scoop through smooth sauce include crisp Belgian endive leaves, cool cucumber slices, tender-crisp raw asparagus tips, cauliflowerets, and grilled bites of chicken, beef, or pork on tiny skewers.

- 1/3 cup peanut butter
- 2 tablespoons *each* rice vinegar, Oriental sesame oil, and sugar
- 1 tablespoon soy sauce

In a small bowl, stir together the peanut butter, vinegar, oil, sugar, and soy until smooth. If made ahead, cover and chill up to 1 week. Makes 1/2 cup.

PER TABLESPOON: 81 calories, 2 g protein, 4.6 g carbohydrates, 6.5 g fat, 6 mg cholesterol, 286 mg sodium

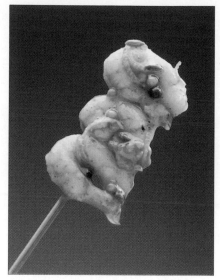

Lean dip with curry flavors clings to tiny shrimp.

CURRY SEED SAUCE

This lightly clinging, aromatic sauce sticks just enough to flavor any food with curry seasonings.

- 1½ teaspoons mustard seed
- 1 teaspoon sugar
- 1/2 teaspoon *each* curry powder and coriander seed
- 1/4 teaspoon dry thyme leaves
  Seed from 1 cardamom pod
- 1/2 teaspoon grated lemon peel
- 2 teaspoons cornstarch or arrowroot
- 1 cup regular-strength chicken broth
- 2 tablespoons lemon juice

In an 8- to 10-inch frying pan, combine mustard seed, sugar, curry powder, coriander seed, thyme leaves, and cardamom seed. Stir over medium heat until spices smell lightly toasted, 2 to 3 minutes.

Remove pan from heat and add lemon peel, cornstarch, and chicken broth, mixing to blend until smooth. Stir over high heat until boiling. Let cool (to speed, set pan in ice water), then add lemon juice. If made ahead, cover and chill up to 2 days. Makes about 1¼ cups.

PER TABLESPOON: 5.4 calories, 0.2 g protein, 0.8 g carbohydrates, 0.2 g fat, 0 mg cholesterol, 3.1 mg sodium

GENOVESE GREEN SAUCE

Delicate but not timid, this subtle pistachio–tarragon sauce makes a fine bath for fennel stalks, mushroom slices, and broccoli flowerets.

- ½ cup shelled, salted pistachios
- 2 teaspoons arrowroot or cornstarch
- ½ teaspoon dry tarragon leaves
- 1 cup regular-strength chicken broth
- ¼ cup packed parsley
- 2 tablespoons drained capers

Rub nuts in a towel to remove as much of the brown membrane as possible. Lift nuts from towel and discard residue. Chop ¼ cup of the nuts until fine.

In a 1- to 1½-quart pan, mix arrowroot, tarragon, and broth. Stirring, bring to a boil on high heat. Let cool (to speed, set pan in ice water).

Put unchopped nuts and parsley in a blender or food processor. Whirl with enough seasoned broth to make a coarse purée. Mix purée with broth, capers, and chopped nuts. Pour sauce into a bowl and serve. If made ahead, cover and chill up to 2 days. Makes about 1¼ cups.

PER TABLESPOON: 21 calories, 0.8 g protein, 1.2 g carbohydrates, 1.6 g fat, 0 mg cholesterol, 25 mg sodium

CAESAR CREAM

All the vibrant good tastes of a Caesar salad are captured in this smooth, pale green mixture. Naturally, crunchy romaine leaves are used for dipping. So are the crusty croutons.

- ½ cup fresh-grated parmesan cheese
- 2 to 3 drained canned anchovy fillets
- 2 or 3 tablespoons lemon juice
- ½ cup packed parsley
- 1 cup light or regular sour cream
  A few strands fine-shredded parmesan cheese
- 1 to 2 quarts small inner romaine lettuce leaves, rinsed and crisped
  Parmesan toast (directions follow)

In a blender or food processor, combine the ½ cup cheese, 2 anchovy fillets, 2 tablespoons lemon juice, and the parsley.

Whirl to purée smooth; you may have to add 3 to 4 tablespoons of sour cream to help the mixture purée well. Mix purée with remaining sour cream in a small bowl; add more lemon juice, if desired. If made ahead, cover and chill up to 2 days.

Garnish cream with remaining anchovy and shreds of cheese. Place cream on a tray and arrange lettuce leaves and toast alongside for dipping. Makes 1¼ cups, 8 to 10 servings.

PER TABLESPOON CREAM: 73 calories, 4.7 g protein, 3.3 g carbohydrates, 48 g fat, 12 mg cholesterol, 127 mg sodium

PER APPETIZER SERVING: 157 calories, 7.2 g protein, 16 g carbohydrates, 7.2 g fat, 14 mg cholesterol, 282 mg sodium

Parmesan toast. Cut ½ slender **baguette** (8-oz. size) in about ⅜-inch slices. Arrange in a single layer in a 10- by 15-inch pan. Bake in a 350° oven until lightly toasted, 10 to 15 minutes; turn the slices over once or twice.

Remove from oven and lightly brush slices with 1 tablespoon (total) **olive oil** and sprinkle lightly with 2 tablespoons **fresh-grated parmesan cheese.**

Return seasoned slices to the oven and bake until golden, 3 to 5 minutes. Serve warm or cool. If made ahead, package airtight and hold at room temperature up until next day.

Caesar salad inspired the flavors of this pale green dip; serve with crunchy romaine leaves and crisp croutons for dipping.

JUST BRING A SALAD! *When an invitation to a picnic includes this often-made request, these durable and delicious legume and grain salads are ideal. Even after standing for a few warm hours, they keep their looks without wilting, and they don't spoil. If the surface dries, freshen it with a stir.*

These high-carbohydrate salads contain a mix of ingredients that form complete protein. In addition, they are very low in fat.

Bullets indicate make-ahead steps (see footnotes).

BULGUR & HOMINY SALAD

- 2 **cups regular-strength chicken broth**
- 1 **tablespoon mustard seed**
- 1 **teaspoon dry thyme leaves**
- 1/2 **teaspoon fennel seed**
- 1 **cup bulgur (cracked wheat)**
- 1/4 **cup sherry vinegar or red wine vinegar**
- 1 **tablespoon rinsed and drained green peppercorns**
- 2 **cans (about 14 1/2 oz. each) golden hominy, drained**
- 1/4 **cup lightly packed minced parsley**
  Salt
  Napa cabbage leaves, rinsed and drained (optional)
- 1/2 **to 1 cup thin-sliced red radishes**
- 1 **to 1 1/2 cups stemmed and rinsed seedless green grapes**

In a 1- to 1 1/2-quart pan, bring chicken broth to boil with mustard seed, thyme leaves, and fennel seed. Stir in bulgur, vinegar, and green peppercorns.

Cover pan, remove from heat, and let mixture stand until bulgur is tender to bite, about 30 minutes. Pour the seasoned bulgur into a bowl and mix with hominy; cover and chill.•

Mix salad with parsley; season to taste with salt. Mound onto a platter or in a bowl lined with cabbage leaves; top with radishes and grapes. Serve.•• Makes 8 to 9 cups, 6 to 8 servings.

PER SERVING: 168 calories, 4.9 g protein, 34 g carbohydrates, 2.1 g fat, 0 mg cholesterol, 236 mg sodium

BEAN SALAD WITH PICKLED ONIONS

- 3 **large (about 3/4 lb. total) carrots**
- 1 **chicken or beef bouillon cube**
- 3/4 **pound kale**
- 1 **jar (about 4 3/4 oz., or drained, 1/2 cup) pickled onions or scallions**
- 2 **cans (about 15 oz. each) cannellini (white kidney) beans, drained**

Peel carrots and cut into 1/4-inch dice. In a 10- to 12-inch frying pan, combine carrots, bouillon cube, and 1/2 cup water. Cook over high heat until liquid boils away and a dark brown film forms in pan; stir often. Add 2 to 3 tablespoons water and stir to free brown film. Continue to cook until film forms again. Repeat rinsing and boiling dry until carrots are dark brown, 3 or 4 more times, 15 to 20 minutes total.

Meanwhile, trim off and discard tough kale stems. Rinse leaves; set aside 2 or 3 leaves and sliver remainder. Mix slivered kale and 2 tablespoons water into carrots; stir just until leaves wilt, about 2 minutes. Let cool.•

Drain onions; save liquid. Add onions and 3 tablespoons of their liquid to beans; taste and add more liquid, if desired. Mound onto kale in a platter or a bowl; garnish with reserved kale leaves. Serve.•• Makes 6 cups, 4 to 6 servings.

PER SERVING: 113 calories, 6.2 g protein, 22 g carbohydrates, 0.6 g fat, 0.1 mg cholesterol, 804 mg sodium

Hearty kale stays bright green; it seasons mellow canned beans with pickled onions and diced carrots.

WHEAT BERRY SATAY SALAD

- 2 large (about 1 lb. total) onions, sliced thin
- 2 cups wheat berries, rinsed and drained
- 3 cups regular-strength chicken broth
- 1/2 teaspoon crushed dried hot red chilies
- 1 tablespoon minced fresh ginger
- 2 tablespoons peanut butter
- 2 tablespoons fruit or berry jam or jelly
- 2 tablespoons rice vinegar
  About 1 tablespoon soy sauce
- 1 cup *each* chopped cilantro and green onions (including tops)
- 1/4 cup minced salted peanuts

In a 4- to 5-quart pan, cook onions in 1/2 cup water over high heat until juices boil away and a dark brown film forms in pan, 15 to 20 minutes; stir often. Add 2 to 4 tablespoons water and stir to free brown film.

Continue to cook until brown film forms again. Repeat rinsing and boiling dry until onions are dark brown, 3 or 4 more times, about 10 more minutes.

Add wheat berries, chicken broth, dried chilies, and minced ginger. Bring to a boil on high heat. Cover and simmer until wheat berries are just tender to bite, 50 to 60 minutes; stir occasionally. Remove from heat; drain and reserve cooking liquid.

In a small bowl, stir together until smooth 1/4 cup of reserved cooking liquid, peanut butter, and jam. Stir into the wheat berries along with the vinegar. Add soy sauce to taste. Cover salad and let stand until cool.•

Stir about 2/3 of the chopped cilantro and green onions into wheat berry mixture; pour salad into a bowl. Moisten to taste with reserved cooking liquid. Mix remaining chopped cilantro and green onions and sprinkle onto salad, then top with peanuts and serve.•• Makes 6 cups, 4 to 6 servings.

PER SERVING: 329 calories, 13 g protein, 54 g carbohydrates, 8.7 g fat, 0 mg cholesterol, 287 mg sodium

Mint and tangy goat cheese mingle with pink onions and tender lentils in red cabbage leaf frame.

MINTED LENTILS WITH GOAT CHEESE

- 1 package (12 oz. or 1¾ cups) lentils, sorted for debris and rinsed
- 3 cups regular-strength chicken broth
- 1/2 teaspoon dill seed
- 1 teaspoon dry thyme leaves
- 2 to 3 tablespoons olive oil
- 3 tablespoons wine vinegar
  Red cabbage leaves (optional)
  Rosy onion rings (directions follow)
  About 1/4 pound goat cheese, such as montrachet or bûcheron, coarsely crumbled
- 1/4 cup chopped fresh mint leaves
  Fresh mint sprigs

In a 2- to 3-quart pan, combine lentils, broth, dill seed, and thyme; bring to a boil on high heat. Cover and simmer just until lentils are tender to bite, 15 to 20 minutes; stir once or twice. Drain, reserving liquid. Let lentil mixture and liquid cool; if made ahead, cover and chill both.•

Mix lentils with 4 to 6 tablespoons reserved liquid (just to moisten), then add 1 tablespoon oil and the vinegar. Pour lentils onto a platter or into a bowl lined with cabbage leaves. Top lentils with onion, cheese, and chopped mint; drizzle with 1 to 2 tablespoons more oil. Garnish with mint sprigs. Serve.•• Makes about 7 cups, 6 or 7 servings.

PER SERVING: 290 calories, 18 g protein, 34 g carbohydrates, 10 g fat, 15 mg cholesterol, 130 mg sodium

Rosy onion rings. Peel and slice thin 1 large (about 3/4 lb.) **red onion.** Bring 3 cups **water** and 2 tablespoons **vinegar** to boil in a 2- to 3-quart pan over high heat. Push onion into liquid. When boil resumes, drain. Use, or cover and chill.•

• Chill at least 2 hours or up to 2 days.
•• Holds up to 4 hours at 70° to 80°.

THE GOOD FOODS OF SUMMER: A Flexible Barbecue Strategy

SUMMER MEALS *that focus on simple, hearty meats sizzling on the barbecue work best if companion dishes like vegetables or salads are designed to wait patiently while the chef performs.*

Meals with this relaxed structure have several pluses. Cooking times aren't crucial, dishes can be made ahead, duties are readily delegated, and—with all this flexibility—it's about as easy to serve 16 as 6. Bullets indicate make-ahead steps (see footnotes).

First settle on the entrée. For all-round popularity, spareribs or sausages are hard to top; some suggestions follow. Then choose companion dishes from the five vegetables on these pages; for grain and legume choices, see "Picnic Salads", page 154. They stay fresh and colorful for hours with no temperature monitoring.

You might also include baked potatoes (kept hot up to 2 hours in an insulated chest) or steamed rice (kept hot in a rice cooker or in a steamer).

BARBECUE-READY SPARERIBS

Use your own favorite sparerib preparation or try the seasoned, cooked, ready-to-heat spareribs now sold. To prevent flareups, cook spareribs over indirect heat (a solid border of hot coals arranged around perimeter of meat, but not beneath). If ribs are already cooked, heating and browning them takes about 20 minutes on a grill over a solid bed of medium coals (you can hold your hand at grill level only 4 to 5 seconds). Allow 3/4 to 1 pound for each serving.

MIXED SAUSAGE GRILL

Offering a mixture of sausages—frankfurters, robust Italian, spiced chicken or turkey—is one of the easiest ways to satisfy diverse tastes.

Cooked sausages, like frankfurters or garlic or Polish sausages, need only to be heated through on the grill.

Fragile uncooked sausages like bockwurst or boudin should be firmed before grilling: cover (by at least 2 in.) with boiling water; let stand 15 minutes. Drain. Grill, or chill until ready to heat.

Raw meat sausages that require cooking, like Italian, stay juicier with this pre-grill treatment: put sausages in a pan and cover generously with water; bring to a boil on high heat; remove from heat and let stand 10 minutes. Drain. Grill, or chill until ready to heat.

One adequate serving is 1/4 pound meat, or, more generously, 1 or 2 sausages.

HONEY CARROTS WITH CURRANTS

- 6 to 8 large (about 1 1/2 lb. total) carrots, peeled and cut into 1/8-inch-thick sticks, each 3 to 4 inches long
- 2 tablespoons honey
- 2 tablespoons lemon juice
- 1/4 cup dried currants
- 1/4 cup Major Grey chutney, minced
- 1/4 cup orange juice
  Fine-slivered orange peel
  Salt

In a 4- to 5-quart pan, bring 1 1/2 cups water to boiling; add carrots, honey, and lemon juice. Stir often until carrots are barely tender to bite, about 3 minutes. Drain carrots, reserving liquid. Put carrots in a rimmed serving dish; set aside.•

Return liquid to pan and boil over high heat, uncovered, until only about 1/4 cup liquid remains, about 10 minutes. Add currants; stir until mixture begins to caramelize and currants puff. Stir in chutney and let cool.• Mix orange juice with currants, then spoon mixture over carrots. Top carrots with orange peel and add salt to taste.•• Makes 6 to 8 servings.

PER SERVING: 86 calories, 1.1 g protein, 22 g carbohydrates, 0.2 g fat, 0 mg cholesterol, 45 mg sodium

SEARED CORN WITH COCONUT & GRAPEFRUIT

- 1/2 cup sweetened shredded dry coconut
- 4 ears corn (each about 8 in. long), husks and silks removed
- 2 large (about 1 lb. each) pink grapefruit
  Thai sauce (recipe follows)
- 1 can (4 oz.) diced green chilies
- 1/2 cup slivered shallots

In a 10- to 12-inch frying pan, stir coconut over medium-high heat until golden, about 6 minutes. Pour from pan; set aside.•

Lay corn in the same pan and cook on high heat, rolling ears as needed to lightly singe most of the kernels with brown, about 30 minutes. Remove from heat and let cool. With a sharp knife, cut kernels from cob;• discard cobs.

With the knife, also cut peel and white membrane from grapefruit, then cut between membrane wedges to release segments. Squeeze juice from membrane into a bowl and add the Thai sauce.•

In a wide, rimmed bowl, arrange in separate mounds the coconut, corn, grapefruit, chilies, and shallots. Pour dressing evenly over the salad.•• Mix gently. Makes 6 to 8 servings.

PER SERVING: 81 calories, 2.3 g protein, 15 g carbohydrates, 2.3 g fat, 0 mg cholesterol, 105 mg sodium

Precooked spareribs (100 lb. total) brown quickly for hungry crowd at Marti and Phil Caires' annual basketball tournament.

Thai sauce. In a small bowl, mix together 3 tablespoons **lime juice,** 2 tablespoons **fish sauce** (*nam pla* or *nuoc mam*), 1 tablespoon minced **fresh ginger,** and 1 teaspoon **sugar.**

ONIONS WITH ONIONS

  2 **pounds small (about 1¼-in. diameter) onions, peeled**
     About ¼ cup olive or salad oil
  ½ **cup balsamic or sherry vinegar**
  2 **teaspoons sugar**
  1 **large (about ¾ lb.) red onion, sliced thin**
 12 **green onions, ends trimmed**
     Salt and pepper

Put small whole onions in a 9- by 13-inch metal pan with 1 tablespoon oil, ¼ cup vinegar, and sugar. Bake, uncovered, in a 400° oven until juices in pan begin to turn dark brown, about 25 minutes. Add ½ cup water and stir to free all brown bits. Repeat baking step 2 or 3 times, scraping free browned drippings, until onions are tender when pierced, about 35 minutes total.

Remove onions from oven; if pan is dry, add 2 to 3 tablespoons water and stir to free brown bits. Pour onions and drippings into a bowl or rimmed platter.•

As whole onions bake, bring 1 quart water and 2 tablespoons vinegar to a boil in a 2- to 3-quart pan over high heat. Push sliced red onion into water; cook until boil resumes. Remove pan from heat and let stand 5 to 10 minutes. Drain and mound in center of onions in bowl; set aside.•

Cut green onions into about 2-inch lengths; sliver lengthwise. If serving within 1 hour, scatter half the green onions onto onions in bowl. Otherwise, wrap green onions airtight; chill up to 4 hours.

Heat 3 tablespoons oil in an 8- to 10-inch frying pan until hot enough for a drop of added water to sizzle. Add remaining green onions to pan and stir until lightly browned, about 30 seconds. Drain on towels; if made ahead, let stand up to 4 hours. Scatter over onions in bowl. Mix in remaining vinegar and salt and pepper to taste.•• Makes 6 to 8 servings.

PER SERVING: 115 calories, 1.7 g protein, 12 g carbohydrates, 7.1 g fat, 0 mg cholesterol, 3 mg sodium

Onions prepared four ways—sweet-roasted, tart-poached, sautéed, and raw—complement grilled meats.

BRAISED RADICCHIO & CAMBOZOLA

If you like the bitter bite of braised radicchio, this dish will please you.

     About 1¾ pounds (3 heads, about 3 in. wide) radicchio
  1 **tablespoon olive oil**
  2 **tablespoons lemon juice**
  ¼ **pound cambozola or gorgonzola cheese, sliced thin**
     Salt and pepper
     Lemon wedges

Trim bruised or discolored portions from radicchio, then cut heads in half.

Lay cut side down in a 10- to 12-inch frying pan (edges may overlap, but radicchio will shrink). Add oil, lemon juice, and ½ cup water. Cover and simmer on medium heat until limp on top, about 15 minutes. Remove lid, turn heat to medium-high, and cook until liquid evaporates and radicchio browns lightly, about 5 minutes. Turn pieces over; add 2 tablespoons water. Cover and cook until water evaporates and radicchio browns lightly, about 2 minutes.

Turn heat to low, add 2 tablespoons water, and lay cheese on vegetables; cover and heat just until cheese melts. Transfer to a platter, season with salt and pepper, and garnish with lemon wedges.•• Makes 6 servings.

PER SERVING: 112 calories, 5.8 g protein, 5.4 g carbohydrates, 8.1 g fat, 14 mg cholesterol, 277 mg sodium

SHERRIED GREEN BEANS & PEAS

 1½ **pounds tender green beans, ends and strings removed**
  2 **cups (1 package, 10 oz.) frozen petite green peas**
  2 **teaspoons cornstarch**
  1 **tablespoon minced fresh ginger**
  2 **tablespoons soy sauce**
  ¼ **cup dry sherry**
  1 **tablespoon Oriental sesame oil**
  ¼ **cup finely diced red bell pepper**

Bring about 2 quarts water to boiling on high heat in a 4- to 5-quart pan. Add beans and cook, uncovered, until just tender to bite, 4 to 8 minutes. Stir in peas, then drain well. Cover with ice water; when cool, drain and pour into a wide serving bowl or rimmed platter.•

In pan, blend cornstarch, ginger, soy, sherry, and ½ cup water; stir over high heat until boiling. Let cool; stir in sesame oil.• Pour over vegetables; garnish with bell pepper. Mix gently.•• Makes 8 to 10 servings.

PER SERVING: 63 calories, 2.6 g protein, 9.2 g carbohydrates, 1.5 g fat, 0 mg cholesterol, 248 mg sodium

• If made ahead, cover and chill up until next day.

•• Mixture holds 4 hours at 70° to 80°.

THE GOOD FOODS OF SUMMER: Fresh Fruit Options

ONE OF SUMMER'S *most delicious hallmarks is the abundance of fresh fruits. And desserts inspired by their grand spectrum of flavors and colors make the season all the more memorable. Your choices range from fruit sorbets in crisp cooky cones to purple plum mousse on an orange torte.*

PRALINE LACE CONES WITH SORBET

> About ¼ cup (⅛ lb.) melted butter or margarine
> ½ cup firmly packed brown sugar
> 1 large egg
> ¼ cup fine-chopped pecans
> 1 tablespoon all-purpose flour
> 1 to 1½ cups lemon sorbet
> 1 to 1½ cups raspberry sorbet
> Fresh mint sprigs

In a bowl, beat together butter, sugar, egg, nuts, and flour.

Cut 8 pieces of cooking parchment or foil, each 6 inches square. Butter squares lightly on 1 side, then draw a 5-inch circle in the center of each. Set buttered side up on 2 baking sheets, 12- by 15-inch size. Divide batter equally among circles; spread batter smooth to fill circles. Bake 1 pan at a time in a 300° oven until cookies are light gold in center and edges darken slightly, about 15 minutes.

Let cool on pan about 1 minute; then, working quickly while cookies are still flexible but not soft, peel off parchment or foil. (If cookies harden, return briefly to oven to soften.) At once, cut each cooky in half and overlap cut edges to form cones. Set cones, tip down, in muffin cups until cool and rigid, about 10 minutes. At once, put in an airtight container. Repeat to prepare remaining cookies. Serve or store up until next day. Spoon sorbet equally into cones. Put a cone of each sorbet on each plate; garnish with mint. Serves 8.—*Sharon and Jim Wilson, Molly and Walt Person, Great Falls, Mont.*

PER SERVING: 195 calories, 1.4 g protein, 29 g carbohydrates, 8.9 g fat, 43 mg cholesterol, 79 mg sodium

RASPBERRY SUNDAES WITH BLACK RASPBERRY LIQUEUR

> 3 cups raspberries, rinsed and drained
> ¼ cup black raspberry–flavor or cassis-flavor liqueur

Lace cooky cornucopias show off raspberry and lemon sorbets.

> 2 tablespoons sugar
> 1 pint rich vanilla ice cream
> ½ cup whipping cream, softly whipped

In a 1- to 1½-quart pan, combine 1½ cups raspberries, berry liqueur, and sugar. Place over medium-high heat just until fruit is warm and begins to fall apart; stir gently once or twice.

Remove fruit from heat and gently mix in remaining raspberries. Scoop ice cream into 4 dessert bowls. Spoon warm berry mixture into bowls, and add dollops of whipped cream. Serve at once. Makes 4 servings.

PER SERVING: 372 calories, 3.5 g protein, 38 g carbohydrates, 22 g fat, 77 mg cholesterol, 64 mg sodium

CANDIED LEMONS

Serve this tart-sweet sauce over wedges of melon such as green honeydew.

> 2 medium-size (about 5 oz. each) lemons, ends trimmed
> 2 teaspoons finely shredded orange peel
> ½ cup sugar
> ¾ cup orange juice
> 2 tablespoons orange-flavor liqueur such as curaçao

Slice lemons thin and put in a 10- to 12-inch frying pan with orange peel, sugar, ½ cup orange juice, and ¼ cup water.

Boil, uncovered, on high heat until liquid is almost gone, about 8 minutes; shake pan occasionally and watch closely to avoid scorching. Add remaining juice and liqueur; bring to a rolling boil. Use warm or cool. If made ahead, cover and chill up to 1 week. Makes about ⅔ cup.

PER TABLESPOON: 60 calories, 0.4 g protein, 15 g carbohydrates, 0.1 g fat, 0 mg cholesterol, 1 mg sodium

HONEYDEW MELON DESSERT BOWL

Melon shells keep the fruit fresh-tasting at least 3 hours at room temperature.

> 2 medium-size (2½ to 3½ lb. each) honeydew melons
> 1 can (20 oz.) or 2 cans (11 oz. each) litchis
> Strawberry sauce (recipe follows)
> 10 to 16 strawberries, rinsed, hulled, drained, and cut in half

Set melons on side that rests steadiest, then cut off the top 1/3 of each. Scoop out and discard seeds, then scoop melon in balls or chunks from shells and lids, using as much melon as you can.

Spoon fruit into a bowl. Drain the litchis; save syrup for strawberry sauce (following). Add litchis and strawberries to the melon pieces; mix gently, then spoon the fruit into large sections of melon shells. If made ahead, cover and chill up to 4 hours. Ladle into bowls and add strawberry sauce to taste. Makes 8 to 10 servings.

PER SERVING WITHOUT SAUCE: 85 calories, 0.7 g protein, 23 g carbohydrates, 0.2 g fat, 0 mg cholesterol, 32 mg sodium

Strawberry sauce. Rinse, hull, and drain 3 cups **strawberries.** In a blender or food processor, whirl berries with 1/2 cup **reserved litchi syrup** (see preceding), 2 tablespoons **lemon juice,** and **sugar** (about 1 tablespoon) to taste. If made ahead, cover and chill up to 4 hours. Sauce holds well at room temperature up to 3 hours. Makes about 3 cups.

PER TABLESPOON: 11 calories, 0.1 g protein, 2.8 g carbohydrates, 0 g fat, 0 mg cholesterol, 0.3 mg sodium

PLUM MOUSSE ON ORANGE TORTE

1/2 cup (1/4 lb.) butter or margarine
1/4 cup powdered sugar
   About 1 cup all-purpose flour
1/2 teaspoon baking powder
 1 cup granulated sugar
 2 large eggs
1/2 of 1 medium-size (8-oz.) orange
   Plum mousse (directions follow)

Cut butter in chunks into a food processor or bowl. Add powdered sugar and 1 cup flour. Whirl, or rub with fingers, until dough holds together. Squeeze into a ball, then pat over bottom of a 9-inch cheesecake pan with removable rim. Bake in a 350° oven until light golden brown, about 20 minutes.

Meanwhile, in food processor combine 2 tablespoons flour, baking powder, sugar, eggs, and orange, cut in chunks; whirl until orange is finely ground. (Or put ingredients in a bowl, squeezing juice from orange into it; then mince orange and beat to blend.)

Honeydew melon shell makes handsome, protective bowl for melon balls, litchis, and halved strawberries.

Pour mixture into hot or cool crust. Return to oven and bake until top is golden brown, about 20 minutes. Let cool, then cover and chill until cold, at least 1 hour or up to 1 day.

Spoon plum mousse onto torte; cover and chill until mixture is softly set, at least 4 hours or up until next day. Slide a knife between dessert and pan rim, then remove rim. Makes 10 to 12 servings.

PER SERVING: 206 calories, 2.5 g protein, 30 g carbohydrates, 8.6 g fat, 56 mg cholesterol, 107 mg sodium

Plum mousse. Pit and dice 4 or 5 medium-size (about 1 1/2 lb. total) firm-ripe **red-skin plums.** In a 1 1/2- to 2-quart pan, mix 1/2 cup **sugar** and 1 envelope **unflavored gelatin.** Add plums and 2 tablespoons **water.** Cook over medium heat, stirring often, until fruit is soft enough to fall apart, about 25 minutes.

Let cool until gelatin begins to thicken mixture (to speed, set pan in ice water). Beat 1 cup **whipping cream** until it holds soft peaks. Fold into plums and spoon onto orange torte (preceding).

The Good Foods of Summer: Breakfast for a Crowd

IT'S SCRAMBLED EGGS, *as many as 4 dozen at a crack, buried under a blanket of toppings (including some of everyone's favorites) that kick the Magill family reunion into gear.*

About 20 years ago, this family first gathered to honor patriarch Grandfather Magill on his 80th birthday; the reunion was such a success it's been repeated annually. From 50 to 100 of the 200-plus clan attend. The first event is a big breakfast. The way they manage the eggs translates well for any breakfast or brunch, big or small, indoors or out.

The method described here gives good results even under quite primitive conditions. Testing facilities were campfires at public campgrounds.

Spoon through a patchwork of flavorful toppings—such as cheeses, meats, bell pepper, avocado, green onions—into 3 dozen scrambled eggs.

Cooking Eggs for 2 to 48

The secret of the eggs' moist quality and tender texture is thickened chicken or beef broth beaten into them before they are cooked. The sauce also extends the heat tolerance of the eggs.

Select quantity of ingredients and pan size to match. Blend broth with cornstarch until smooth in a pan that's at least 2 to 4 cups bigger than the amount of liquid. Bring mixture to a boil, stirring often. Let cool slightly (if made ahead, cover and chill up until next day). Break eggs into a bowl; whisk broth mixture into eggs to blend well.

Place pan over medium heat (on a range, use 2 burners if pan overlaps 2). Add butter; when melted, pour eggs into pan. Let cook until eggs begin to turn opaque against pan bottom and sides. With a wide spatula, ripple cooked egg from pan, letting raw egg flow beneath. For creamiest texture, do not stir eggs, just push them aside. Cook until eggs are firm but still shiny-looking on top (they will be a salmonella-proof 160°); 1/2 dozen eggs take about 5 minutes, 4 dozen eggs up to 20 minutes.

When eggs are cooked, quickly arrange toppings separately on them. To serve, spoon egg and toppings desired from pan. If kept warm over very low heat, eggs stay moist up to about 45 minutes.

Toppings

For each 6 eggs, allow a maximum of 2 cups toppings; 12 eggs, 4 cups; 18 eggs, 6 cups; 24 eggs, 8 cups; 30 eggs, 10 cups; 36 eggs, 12 cups; 42 eggs, 14 cups; 48 eggs, 16 cups.

Choose from the following (or add your own favorites): **cheese** such as shredded mild to sharp cheddar, jack, fontina, asiago, or crumbled gorgonzola, cambozola, or domestic blue; **browned meats** such as cooked chopped bacon or Italian sausage; **cold meats** such as slivered prosciutto, cooked ham, cooked turkey or chicken; diced **avocado;** diced red, yellow, orange, or green **bell peppers;** slivered or chopped **onions** such as green onions, shallots, mild sweet onions, or chives; sliced **ripe olives; salsa** or diced tomatoes; **sour cream** or yogurt; inexpensive **caviars;** cooked **mushrooms;** fresh **herbs** like basil, tarragon, or parsley.

Scrambled Eggs for 2 to 48

Large eggs	Broth*	Cornstarch	Butter or margarine	Pan size (in.)
6	5 tablespoons	1 1/2 teaspoons	1 1/2 teaspoons	8 to 10
12	2/3 cup	1 tablespoon	1 tablespoon	10 to 12
18	1 cup	1 1/2 tablespoons	1 1/2 tablespoons	12 to 14
24	1 1/2 cups	2 tablespoons	2 tablespoons	12 to 14
30	1 3/4 cups	2 1/2 tablespoons	2 1/2 tablespoons	12 to 14
36	2 cups	3 tablespoons	3 tablespoons	14 to 16
42	2 1/2 cups	3 1/2 tablespoons	3 1/2 tablespoons	12- to 14- by 18-inch roasting pan
48	3 cups	4 tablespoons	4 tablespoons	12- to 14- by 18-inch roasting pan

ALLOW 1 TO 3 EGGS PER SERVING. Without toppings, a 1-egg portion contains 87 calories, 6.4 g protein, 1.3 g carbohydrates, 6 g fat, 215 mg cholesterol, 76 mg sodium.

*Use regular-strength chicken or beef broth.

THE GOOD FOODS OF SUMMER: One-pot Meals

ONE-POT MEALS *that cook quickly are a sailor's most reliable way to deal with cooking in a limited space, with limited equipment, and in small galleys that get hot fast. The ease of preparation of these kinds of dishes also translates very well to underequipped vacation-home kitchens or just to easy dinners for a busy family.*

These three one-pot main dishes fit the bill; ingredient lists are simple, preparation is basic, and cooking time is brief.

For a fine dinner, serve with green salad, an interesting bread (like focaccia, onion bagels, or even toasted English muffins), and fresh fruit for dessert.

WINE-STEAMED CLAMS

- 2 tablespoons butter or margarine
- 2 small (about ½ lb. total) leeks, white parts only, rinsed well and sliced thin; or 1 medium-size (5- to 6-oz.) onion, diced
- 1 clove garlic, pressed or minced
- 1 cup dry white wine
- 1 tablespoon chopped fresh or 1 teaspoon dry thyme leaves
- ½ teaspoon pepper
- 6 pounds clams in shells, suitable for steaming, scrubbed
- 1 lemon, cut into wedges

Melt butter in a 6- to 8-quart pan over medium-high heat; add leeks and garlic. Stir often until leeks are limp, about 5 minutes. Add 2 cups water, wine, thyme, and pepper.

Cover and bring to boiling over high heat. Add clams; cover and cook until shells open, 8 to 10 minutes. Discard any unopened clams.

Ladle into bowls; offer lemon to season to taste. Makes 4 to 6 servings.

PER SERVING: 101 calories, 9.3 g protein, 6.8 g carbohydrates, 4.6 g fat, 34 mg cholesterol, 83 mg sodium

BASIL VEGETABLE SOUP

- 6 to 8 green onions, ends trimmed
- 1 clove garlic, minced or pressed
- 1 tablespoon olive oil
- 6 cups regular-strength chicken broth
- 2 medium-size (about ¾ lb. total) yellow or green zucchini or crookneck squash, ends trimmed, sliced thin
- 1 jar (about 7 oz.) roasted red peppers, coarsely chopped
- 4 or 5 medium-size (about 1 lb. total) Roma-type tomatoes, cored and chopped
- ¼ cup chopped fresh or 1 tablespoon dry basil leaves
- 2 tablespoons balsamic vinegar
  About 1 cup shredded parmesan cheese

Slice green tops of onions thin and set aside. Chop white part of onions; put in a 5- to 6-quart pan with garlic and oil. Stir over medium-high heat until onions are limp, about 3 minutes.

Add broth to the pan, cover, and bring to boiling over high heat. Stir zucchini, peppers, and tomatoes into broth; cover and simmer until zucchini is tender when pierced, about 5 minutes. Stir in reserved green onions, basil, and vinegar. Ladle into bowls and add parmesan to taste. Makes 5 or 6 servings.

PER SERVING: 160 calories, 11 g protein, 9.8 g carbohydrates, 9 g fat, 13 mg cholesterol, 372 mg sodium

GROUND BEEF CHOWDER

- 1 pound ground lean beef
- 1 medium-size (5- to 6-oz.) onion, diced
  About 1 pound (4 large) carrots, sliced thin
  About 1 pound (2 medium-size) thin-skinned potatoes, scrubbed and diced
- ¼ cup chopped fresh dill or 1 tablespoon dry dill weed
- 1 dry bay leaf
- 6 cups (or 1 large, 49-oz. can) regular-strength chicken broth
- 1 tablespoon cornstarch mixed with 2 tablespoons water
- 1 cup nonfat unflavored yogurt

In a 5- to 6-quart pan, crumble beef and stir often over medium-high heat until lightly browned, about 8 minutes. Add onion and stir often until limp, about 5 minutes. Add carrots, potatoes, dill, bay leaf, and broth. Stir to scrape browned bits free from pan.

Cover and bring to a boil over high heat; simmer until potatoes are tender to bite, about 15 minutes.

Mix cornstarch and water with yogurt; stir into soup. Stir over high heat until boiling. Ladle into bowls. Makes 5 or 6 servings.

PER SERVING: 360 calories, 20 g protein, 29 g carbohydrates, 18 g fat, 58 mg cholesterol, 168 mg sodium

Steamed clams, salad, wine, and bread are easy to manage, whether cooked at home or in a one-burner galley.

MAKING BREAD AND JAM *outdoors keeps children busily occupied for several hours as they work toward payoff with a favorite activity—eating something good.*

A reflector oven, organized for cooking in the garden, bakes the bread; sunshine gets put to work to make the sweet-smelling strawberry jam.

Gray day? Both recipes have kitchen options.

Depending on the weather, sunshine jam can be ready to eat in as little as 2 hours or up to 6, so let its production set your pace (if needed, finish the next day). Getting ready to bake bread outdoors fills a couple of those hours.

Reflector ovens are modestly priced and found in camping supply stores.

For back-yard baking in a reflector oven, build fire in foil-lined pan.

STRAWBERRY SUNSHINE JAM

  2 **cups strawberries, hulled and rinsed**
1¹/₂ **cups sugar**
  1 **tablespoon lemon juice**

Cut strawberries in half. Put into a 10- to 12-inch frying pan and sprinkle with sugar and lemon juice. Let stand about 30 minutes for the fruit to get juicy. Cook over medium heat until the mixture begins to bubble, about 5 minutes. Stir gently several times. Turn heat to high and cook for 5 minutes, stirring often; jam is very hot, so an adult should supervise. (On a gray day, boil until juices form fine, wispy strands when dripped from a lifted spoon, about 8 minutes.) Remove jam from heat. Let stand until pan is cool to touch (jam for a gray day is ready to eat).

Pour fruit and all the liquid into a 9- by 13-inch glass dish. Cover dish snugly with plastic wrap, leaving a gap about 1 inch wide at 1 end of the dish. Set jam in bright sunshine (make sure shade doesn't fall on the spot later). About every hour or so, uncover dish and turn over each piece of fruit, then replace plastic wrap.

After 2 to 6 hours, depending on how hot the day is (jam thickens faster with more heat), liquid around edges of dish should be as thick as corn syrup and fruit should be plump. The jam tastes best when warm and sweet from the sun. Spoon extra into a jar; cover and chill up to 2 weeks. Makes about 1¹/₂ cups.

PER TABLESPOON: 52 calories, 0.1 g protein, 13 g carbohydrates, 0 g fat, 0 mg cholesterol, 0.4 mg sodium

SETTING UP A REFLECTOR OVEN

Place reflector oven outdoors in a draft-free location on hard-packed soil, gravel, tiles, or lawn (well away from flammable materials, like dry grass or bushes). For safety, have a big bucket of water nearby.

To protect garden from fire damage, line an old baking pan (at least 10 by 15 in.) with foil and set it on 4 bricks, making sure they're steady. Set directly in front of oven; build fire in pan. Let ashes cool completely before disposing of them.

You'll need about half a large grocery bag of small wood scraps (3 to 4 gal.).

CAMP BREAD

       About 3 tablespoons salad oil
  1 **large egg**
  1 **cup milk**
  3 **tablespoons firm-packed brown sugar**
  1 **cup whole-wheat flour**
  1 **cup all-purpose flour**
1¹/₂ **teaspoons baking powder**
  1 **teaspoon baking soda**
¹/₄ **teaspoon salt**

Make a double layer of foil slightly larger than reflector oven shelf (at least 10 by

12 in.). Fold edges of foil under to make piece slightly smaller than oven shelf. Lay foil on a flat pan (rimless on at least 1 side). Rub foil lightly with oil.

In a bowl, beat to blend egg, milk, sugar, and 3 tablespoons oil. In another bowl, mix whole-wheat flour, all-purpose flour, baking powder, soda, and salt.

Bring both bowls, foil on pan, and a flexible spatula out to where oven is set up (preceding).

Crumple several newspapers in fire pan; arrange wood scraps on paper tepee fashion. Ignite paper. Set oven directly in front of fire.

Add dry ingredients to bowl with egg mixture. Stir with spatula to moisten evenly, then scrape batter into center of foil prepared for the oven. Spread dough into a round that is at least 1¹/₂ inches away from foil edges.

With potholders, pull oven away from fire. Slide foil with dough onto oven shelf and move oven back to face fire (see photo). For steady heat, add a handful of wood whenever flames start to die down.

Keep an eye on bread as it cooks (and watch fire to make sure sparks don't land on anything that might burn). The front bottom edge should begin to brown in 10 to 15 minutes. If it browns faster, use potholders to pull oven a few inches away from heat; if it browns too slowly, build up fire quickly with a few small pieces of wood.

As an edge starts to brown, rotate foil ¹/₄ turn. Bake until bread springs back when lightly pressed on top; after edges firm, slide a spatula under loaf about every 15 minutes to check bottom browning. If it starts to scorch, pull oven slightly away from fire. Because of heat variations, allow 50 minutes to 1¹/₂ hours. Pull oven from heat (carefully, so oven doesn't collapse); slide bread onto a tray. Break into chunks. Serve warm or cool. Makes 1 loaf, about 1¹/₂ pounds; serves 6.

PER SERVING: 267 calories, 7.3 g protein, 39 g carbohydrates, 9.6 g fat, 41 mg cholesterol, 368 mg sodium

Gray-day bread. Mix batter, then spread in an oiled 8-inch-square pan. Bake in a 350° oven just until bread begins to pull from pan sides and edges are a darker brown, 35 to 40 minutes.

Readers Share Their Potato Salads

A STANDARD FOR SUMMER MEALS, *potato salad can be simple, exotic, or anything in between. Here, three Sunset readers offer wholesome and refreshing variations on this popular dish.*

VIENNESE POTATO SALAD

    1/2 cup pecan or walnut pieces
    2 1/2 pounds cooked red thin-skinned
         potatoes (directions follow)
    3 large (about 1 1/2 lb. total) red
         apples such as Red Gravenstein
         or Red Delicious
    1/2 cup chopped green onions
    1/3 cup raisins or currants
    1/3 cup late-harvest Gewürztraminer
         or Johannisberg Riesling
    1/3 cup cider vinegar
    2 tablespoons salad oil
    1 tablespoon grated lemon peel
    2 teaspoons poppy seed

In a 7- to 8-inch frying pan, stir the pecans over medium-high heat until lightly browned and toasted, 2 to 3 minutes. Pour nuts from pan, let cool, then coarsely chop. Set aside.

Cut potatoes into 1-inch cubes. Remove cores from 2 of the apples and cut the fruit into 1-inch chunks. In a large bowl, combine nuts, potatoes, apples, onions, raisins, wine, vinegar, oil, lemon peel, and poppy seed; mix gently. If made ahead, cover and chill up to 6 hours.

Mound salad onto a serving platter. Core remaining apple and cut into slices; fan slices out along the salad on 1 side of the platter. Makes 6 to 8 servings.—*Roxanne Chan, Albany, Calif.*

PER SERVING: 267 calories, 3.8 g protein, 44 g carbohydrates, 8.8 g fat, 0 mg cholesterol, 13 mg sodium

CITRUS GROVE POTATO SALAD

    2 tablespoons grated orange peel
    1/2 cup orange juice
    6 tablespoons lemon juice
    1/3 cup mayonnaise
    3 pounds cooked small thin-
         skinned potatoes (directions
         follow), peeled

    3 large (about 1 3/4 lb. total) oranges
    1 large (about 3/4 lb.) red onion,
         chopped
    1 large (about 1/2 lb.) firm-ripe
         avocado
    2 tablespoons minced fresh cilantro
         (coriander)
       Salt and pepper

In a large bowl, stir together orange peel, orange juice, 5 tablespoons lemon juice, and mayonnaise. Cut potatoes into 1-inch cubes and add to bowl; mix gently. Cover and chill at least 1 hour or up to 6 hours.

With a knife, cut peel and white membrane from oranges. Cut oranges crosswise into 1/4-inch-thick slices; arrange slices on 1 side of a serving platter. Stir onion into potato mixture, then mound potatoes in the center of platter.

Peel, pit, and slice avocado into thin wedges. Sprinkle with remaining 1 tablespoon lemon juice. Fan avocado on platter beside salad and opposite the oranges. Sprinkle salad with cilantro. Season individual portions to taste with salt and pepper. Makes 6 to 8 servings.—*Barbara J. Morgan, Concord, Calif.*

PER SERVING: 295 calories, 4.9 g protein, 46 g carbohydrates, 11 g fat, 5.3 mg cholesterol, 69 mg sodium

TRI-MUSTARD POTATO SALAD

    1 jar (6 oz.) marinated artichokes
    3 tablespoons balsamic vinegar
    3 pounds cooked red thin-skinned
         potatoes (directions follow)
    5 cups (about 5 oz.) loosely packed
         watercress sprigs, rinsed and
         crisped
    1 cup black ripe pitted olives
    1/4 cup (about 5 slices) crumbled
         cooked bacon
    2 tablespoons minced parsley
       Tri-mustard dressing (recipe
         follows)

Drain artichokes, reserving 3 tablespoons of marinade; mix marinade with vinegar. Cut potatoes into 1/2-inch-thick slices. Layer slices in a 9- by 13-inch dish, sprinkling each layer with marinade mixture. Let stand at least 30 minutes; if made ahead, cover and chill up to 4 hours.

Poppy seed–speckled potato salad also includes apples, pecans, and raisins; in dressing, fruitiness of late-harvest wine balances cider vinegar.

Arrange potatoes and marinade, artichokes, watercress, and olives on a platter; sprinkle with bacon and parsley. Offer dressing to add to taste. Makes 6 to 8 servings.—*J. Hill, Sacramento.*

PER SERVING: 203 calories, 5.5 g protein, 33 g carbohydrates, 5.7 g fat, 3.3 mg cholesterol, 341 mg sodium

Tri-mustard dressing. Mix together 1/2 cup **mayonnaise**, 1 tablespoon **honey mustard**, 1 tablespoon **Dijon mustard**, 1/2 teaspoon **dry mustard**, 1 tablespoon **water**, and 1 tablespoon **lemon juice**.

PER TABLESPOON: 53 calories, 0.1 g protein, 1 g carbohydrates, 5.6 g fat, 4 mg cholesterol, 72 mg sodium

COOKED POTATOES FOR SALADS

Scrub **thin-skinned potatoes,** then put them in a 4- to 5-quart pan. Add water to barely cover the potatoes. Over medium-high heat, bring water to just below boiling, then cover pan; barely simmer until potatoes are tender when pierced, 30 to 45 minutes, depending on thickness. Drain potatoes; let cool. If done ahead, let stand up to 3 hours. For best flavor, season before chilling.

Asparagus Salad from the Barbecue

DOMESTICALLY GROWN *asparagus is widely available and well priced now. Celebrate its season with this salad; both asparagus and shallots cook on the barbecue.*

You start by grilling a generous amount of shallots until they are golden and sweet. Purée them with broth and balsamic vinegar for a thick, rich-tasting, but low-fat dressing. Last, grill the asparagus spears over the waning coals. Pair warm spears with lettuce for an elegant salad that could begin a dinner party or star as a light luncheon salad.

GRILLED ASPARAGUS & SHALLOT SALAD

- 3 tablespoons extra-virgin olive oil or salad oil
- 2 cloves garlic, minced or pressed
- 1 to 1¼ pounds asparagus, tough ends trimmed
- 1¾ pounds shallots, peeled
- ¾ cup regular-strength beef broth
- ¼ cup balsamic or red wine vinegar
- ⅓ pound (about 8 cups) bite-size pieces mixed salad greens (a combination of lettuces or mesclun), rinsed and crisped
  Salt and pepper

Mix oil and garlic. With a vegetable peeler, pare stems of asparagus. Brush asparagus with half the oil mixture, then set aside.

Thread shallots on 3 or 4 metal skewers (about 12-in. size). Brush with remaining oil mixture. Lay skewers on a grill 6 inches above a solid bed of medium-hot coals (you can hold your hand at grill level only 3 to 4 seconds). Cook, turning often, until shallots are well browned and tender when pierced, about 15 minutes.

Lightly grilled asparagus and sweet, golden shallots team up with mixed greens for a refreshing salad.

Reserve 12 large, nice-looking shallots. Trim scorched bits from remaining shallots and put them in a blender or food processor with broth and vinegar. Whirl until smooth; set aside.

By now the coals should be medium to medium-low (you can hold your hand at grill level 4 to 5 seconds). Grill the asparagus spears over the coals, turning them often, until they are lightly browned and just tender when pierced, 5 to 7 minutes; keep warm.

Mix about ½ of the shallot dressing with salad greens; divide mixture evenly among 4 or 6 dinner plates. Divide asparagus among plates, fanning spears beside salad. Garnish each with 2 or 3 of the reserved shallots. Offer with remaining dressing, salt, and pepper to add to taste. Makes 4 servings as a main dish, 6 servings as a first course.

PER SERVING: 161 calories, 4.6 g protein, 23 g carbohydrates, 7.3 g fat, 0 mg cholesterol, 18 mg sodium

LIGHTENING UP SUNSET CLASSICS: Picnic Salami

CAN SALAMI BE LEAN *but still taste good? We looked at our popular beef salami recipe from June 1977 to see how it could be lightened up. The original used marbled beef. Here, we switch to lean turkey, chicken breast, and pork tenderloin.*

Frankly, these lean sausages are not as moist-tasting as the original. But our tasters liked their flavors, rated their firm-chewy texture as pleasant and salami-like, and were quite surprised to learn how little fat they contained.

Though curing salt contains nitrates, it gives the meat a moister, firmer texture than does the salt-and-sugar substitute. Curing salt can also be difficult to find. You can order Tender-Quick curing salt from Cumberland General Store, Route 3, Box 81, Crossville, Tenn. 38555; (800) 334-4640. A 2-pound bag costs $3.92, plus shipping.

cool. Serve, or wrap airtight; with salt and sugar, chill up to 1 week; with curing salts, chill up to 2 weeks. Freeze up to 1 month. Slice thin. Makes 2, each about 12 ounces.

PER OUNCE:
SMOKED TURKEY SALAMI: 46 calories, 8.8 g protein, 0.6 g carbohydrates, 0.6 g fat, 23 mg cholesterol, 117 mg sodium

ITALIAN CHICKEN SALAMI: 48 calories, 9 g protein, 1 g carbohydrates, 0.6 g fat, 22 mg cholesterol, 172 mg sodium

ASIAN PORK SALAMI: 46 calories, 8 g protein, 0.8 g carbohydrates, 1 g fat, 25 mg cholesterol, 107 mg sodium

PER OUNCE ORIGINAL SMOKY BEEF PICNIC SALAMI (JUNE 1977, PAGE 98): 84 calories, 6.7 g protein, 0.4 g carbohydrates, 6 g fat, 24 mg cholesterol, 586 g sodium

Seasoned meat mixtures:

Smoked turkey. Cut 2 pounds **boned and skinned turkey breast** into 1-inch chunks; or use 2 pounds ground turkey breast. Mix well with 1 teaspoon **salt** and 1 tablespoon firmly packed **brown sugar** (or use instead 1 tablespoon curing salt),

1 teaspoon **liquid smoke**, 1 teaspoon **pepper**, and 1/2 teaspoon **garlic powder**.

Italian chicken. Cut 2 pounds **boned, skinned chicken breast** into 1-inch chunks. Mix well with 1½ teapoons **salt** and 1 tablespoon firmly packed **brown sugar** (or use instead 1 tablespoon curing salt); 2 tablespoons *each* grated **parmesan cheese** and **dry minced onion;** and 2 teaspoons *each* **dry oregano leaves, dry basil leaves,** and **dry marjoram leaves.**

Asian pork. Trim fat from 2 pounds **pork tenderloin;** cut meat into 1-inch chunks. Mix well with 1/2 teaspoon **salt** and 1 tablespoon firmly packed **brown sugar** (or use instead 1 tablespoon curing salt), 1 tablespoon **soy sauce**, 2 teaspoons **crushed dry hot red chilies,** 1½ teaspoons **ground ginger,** and 1/2 teaspoon **garlic powder.**

LEAN PICNIC SALAMI

If you use a food chopper, grind meat with a medium blade, then season.

Seasoned meat mixture (choices follow)
2 sheets foil, each 12 by 18 inches

Put meat mixture in a food processor. Whirl, pulsing on and off, until mixture is finely ground. Cover mixture and refrigerate 2 hours or up until next day for flavors to blend. Divide mixture in half. Shape each portion into a compact 8-inch log. Place each log on a foil sheet. Roll snugly in foil; fold ends shut. Using a 2-pronged fork or a skewer, pierce all over at about 1-inch intervals, just breaking through foil. Set rolls in a pan (at least 9 in. square). Bake in a 225° oven for 3 hours; rolls should feel firm when pressed.

While salami is still warm to touch, gently peel off foil, removing any tiny bits. Blot salami with towels. Chill until

Baked logs of well-seasoned, very lean ground poultry or pork make slimmed-down salami. Slice thin to nibble or enjoy in sandwiches. Salami keeps well in refrigerator. Sausages are (left to right) smoked turkey, Asian pork, and Italian chicken.

Different Basils, Different Flavors

A FAVORITE CHOICE both in the kitchen and in the garden, basil is a versatile and aromatic addition to many dishes. Use it fresh in salads, or add it to recipes for soup, fish, and sauces.

Each variety of fragrant basil imparts a distinctive scent and flavor to foods. You can try almost any kind (see photo below) with these recipes. The results depend on which kind you choose.

In 19th-century Europe, more than 60 varieties of basil were in cultivation. Although most have disappeared, garden catalogs feature more than a dozen kinds you can grow from seed—special Italian varieties, dwarf basil from Greece, and ones scented in lemon, licorice, or clove.

All of these types have the herb's typical perfumy fragrance and pungent flavor, but they vary significantly in richness. For the intense taste that's perfect for pestos, use 'Genovese', 'Genova Perfumatissima', or 'Lettuce Leaf'.

Scented basils are milder in basil taste but have pungent overtones of whatever their name describes, such as cinnamon or lemon; 'Tulsi' has a clove fragrance. Use the leaves to season vegetables and fruit salads, as garnishes, and for tea.

Dwarf basils, such as 'Greek Mini', 'Bush Green', and 'Spicy Globe' have tiny, fragrant leaves that are good for garnishes. Grow these in pots, as small hedges along borders, or on a kitchen windowsill.

Purple-leaf basils are spicier and more pungent but not as sweet as other kinds. They're striking in salads, as a garnish, and in vinegar for flavor and color.

Basil Salsa

Serve on toasted baguette slices with olive oil or as a condiment with grilled fish, chicken, or beef.

- 1 large (about 10 oz.) firm-ripe tomato, cored, coarsely chopped
- 1/3 cup chopped fresh basil leaves
- 1 to 2 tablespoons balsamic or red wine vinegar
  Salt and pepper

In a bowl, mix tomato and basil. Add vinegar and salt and pepper to taste. Makes about 1½ cups.

PER TABLESPOON: 3.1 calories, 0.1 g protein, 0.7 g carbohydrates, 0 g fat, 0 mg cholesterol, 1 mg sodium

Mix one or several varieties of basil with lettuce to make this easy salad; dress greens with extra-virgin olive oil and wine vinegar.

Broth with Basil & Tofu

- 1½ quarts regular-strength chicken broth
- 6 thin slices (about the size of a quarter) fresh ginger
- 1 small dried hot red chili
- 3 strips lemon peel (each about 4 in., yellow part only)
  About 1 pound soft tofu, rinsed, drained, and cut in 1-inch cubes
- 3 tablespoons lemon juice
- 3 cups (about 3 oz.) lightly packed fresh basil leaves; cut leaves in half if larger than 2 inches
  Lemon wedges

In a 2½- to 3-quart pan, combine broth, ginger, chili, and lemon peel. Cover and bring to a boil; simmer for 20 minutes.

Add tofu; cover and simmer until tofu is hot, about 5 minutes. Add lemon juice and basil; cook just until basil wilts, about 30 seconds. Remove and discard ginger, chili, and lemon peel, if desired. Ladle into bowls. Accompany with lemon wedges. Makes 4 to 6 servings.

PER SERVING: 84 calories, 6.4 g protein, 6.7 g carbohydrates, 3.8 g fat, 0 mg cholesterol, 62 mg sodium

Basil leaf shape, size, and color can vary widely. Shown clockwise from top left are 'Tulsi' ('Holy' or 'Sacred'), 'Bush Green', 'Lettuce Leaf', 'Thai' ('Anise'), 'Opal', and 'Purple Ruffles'.

BASIL & LETTUCE SALAD

2 cups (about 2 oz.) lightly packed
  fresh basil leaves; use 1 or several
  varieties
8 cups butter or leaf lettuce, rinsed
  and crisped, in bite-size pieces
3 to 4 tablespoons extra-virgin olive
  oil
2 to 3 tablespoons wine vinegar
  Salt and pepper

In a salad bowl, mix basil, lettuce, olive
oil, and vinegar. Add salt and pepper to
taste. Makes 6 to 8 servings.

PER SERVING: 65 calories, 1.0 g protein, 2.6 g carbohydrates, 6.3 g
fat, 0 mg cholesterol, 3.4 mg sodium

GRILLED FISH WITH BASIL

1½ pounds boned and skinned
  firm-flesh fish such as halibut,
  mahimahi, or swordfish
2 cups (about 2 oz.) lightly packed
  fresh basil leaves (about
  1½ in. long)
¼ cup extra-virgin olive oil
¼ cup lemon juice
  Salt and pepper

Rinse fish and pat dry. Cut into about
1-inch chunks. On thin wooden skewers, alternate pieces of fish with basil
leaves, then chop remaining leaves. Mix
the chopped basil, oil, and lemon juice.
Reserve ⅓ cup of the mixture. Brush
remaining basil mixture over the skewered fish.

Lay fish on a grill 4 to 6 inches above
a solid bed of hot coals (you can hold
your hand at grill level only 2 to 3
seconds), turning to cook evenly until
fish is still moist-looking but opaque in
thickest part (cut to test), about 10
minutes. Arrange skewers on a platter
and evenly spoon reserved basil mixture over fish. Add salt and pepper to
taste. Makes 4 to 6 servings.

PER SERVING: 213 calories, 24 g protein, 2.1 g carbohydrates, 12 g
fat, 36 mg cholesterol, 64 mg sodium

*Clear, light syrup flecked with anise basil bathes fresh berries and melon. Other
scented basils have pungent overtones of cinnamon, lemon, or cloves.*

BASIL-SCENTED SYRUP

*Serve this flavored syrup over melon, berries,
peaches, or plums. Anise, cinnamon, and
lemon basil each add delightful nuances.*

½ cup sugar
½ cup water
2 tablespoons lemon juice
¼ cup chopped fresh basil leaves

In a 1- to 2-quart pan, mix the sugar and
water. Bring to a boil, stirring, until
sugar dissolves. Let cool about 5
minutes. Add lemon juice and basil.
Cool. If made ahead, cover and chill up
until the next day. Makes about ¾ cup.

PER TABLESPOON: 34 calories, 0.1 g protein, 8.7 g carbohydrates, 0 g
fat, 0 mg cholesterol, 0.7 mg sodium

Fish Marinade from Old Japan

THE RESIDUE OF SAKE (*rice wine*) *production, known as sake lees or sake kasu, gives foods a rich, slightly fermented, and pungent flavor. Although it's new to the Western palate, the Japanese have used it for centuries to preserve foods.*

In the traditional mixture, the cook combines lees with mirin (sweetened sake), water, sugar, and sometimes secret seasonings to make a marinade frequently used on fish; the fish is first soaked in brine to give it succulence and longevity.

Here, we have simplified the recipe and reduced the salt and sugar to give a milder flavor. When you shop, look for fish with a high fat content, such as Chilean sea bass, salmon, or sablefish (also called black cod, found in Asian markets). You can find the sake lees, generally sold in 1-pound bags, in Japanese markets. If you have to buy a 5-pound bucket, freeze what you don't need for future use. Price varies from 50 cents to $2 a pound.

For a stronger, more authentic flavor, look for ready-to-cook marinated salmon

Generously spread sake kasu marinade over fish fillets, then chill at least 6 hours.

and black cod; the fish names will be followed by the word kasu. Prices range from $10 to $12 a pound. You can find the fish in Japanese markets and in some supermarkets serving an Asian clientele.

Sake lees (sake kasu) and mirin (sweet sake) are the base of a historical Japanese marinade. You'll find the sake lees in paste or sheet form in the refrigerator at Japanese markets. There, you can also buy ready-to-cook marinated fish. The mirin is available at most supermarkets in the Asian food section.

SAKE KASU ON FISH & VEGETABLES

> 3 pounds boned Chilean sea bass, salmon, or sablefish (black cod) fillets
> Sugar-salt brine (recipe follows)
> 1 pound sake lees, paste or sheets
> ³/₄ cup *each* mirin and water
> ¹/₄ cup sugar
> 3 medium-size (about 1¹/₄ lb. total) red bell peppers, stemmed, seeded, and each cut into 8 equal-size wedges
> 9 small (about 1¹/₄ lb. total) yellow or green patty pan squash

Place fish in the sugar-salt brine. Cover and chill 1 hour, turning occasionally.

Meanwhile, in a blender or food processor, whirl together sake lees, mirin, water, and sugar until smooth. Cover and chill until ready to use, up to 1 week; or freeze up to 3 months.

Drain fish, discarding brine; rinse and pat dry. Place fish in a 9- by 13-inch baking dish; spread about 2 cups of the sake lees marinade over fish, coating all sides. Cover and chill at least 6 hours or up to 3 days, turning occasionally.

Meanwhile, in a 3- to 4-quart pan, bring about 2 quarts water to a boil over high heat. Add pepper wedges and cook just until tender, about 3 minutes. Lift from water with a slotted spoon; set aside. Add squash and cook until tender when pierced with a fork, about 6 minutes; drain, cool, and cut in halves. If made ahead, cover and chill up until next day.

In a bowl, mix pepper and squash with 1 cup sake lees marinade. To grill the vegetables, you'll need 12 slender wooden skewers, each about 10 inches long. With each pair of skewers spaced about 1¹/₂ inches apart, alternately thread 4 pepper wedges and 3 squash halves. If made ahead, cover and chill up to 2 hours.

Marinade of sake lees and mirin gives barbecued sea bass and skewered vegetables distinctively pungent flavor. The Japanese have used it for centuries to preserve foods.

An hour before serving, ignite about 60 charcoal briquets on firegrate of a barbecue (use a covered one) with lid off and with drafts open. When covered with gray ash, 30 to 40 minutes, spread briquets into a single solid layer. Spray grill with nonstick cooking spray and place about 6 inches above briquets.

When coals are medium (you can hold your hand 4 to 5 seconds at grill level), set vegetable skewers on grill, cover barbecue, and cook until browned on grill side, about 5 minutes. Turn skewers and cook until browned on other side, about 5 minutes more. Place vegetables on a platter; cover to keep warm. Lift fillets from marinade, brushing off excess, and place on grill. Cover barbecue and cook until browned, about 6 minutes. Turn fish over, cover barbecue, and cook until fish is opaque and moist-looking in thickest part (cut to test), about 7 minutes longer. Place on platter with vegetables. Makes 6 servings.

ESTIMATED PER SERVING (WITHOUT SAKE KASU MARINADE): 275 calories, 44 g protein, 12 g carbohydrates, 5.2 g fat, 93 mg cholesterol, 818 mg sodium

Sugar-salt brine. In a 9- by 13-inch baking dish, combine 1/2 cup **sugar,** 3 tablespoons **salt,** and 3 cups warm **water;** stir until sugar and salt dissolve.

Safe Ways to Use Eggs

ONE OF NATURE'S *most effectively packaged foods, the egg, has taken a lot of hard cracks of late. It has been pinpointed as the source of outbreaks of salmonella poisoning and has been the subject of much discussion in the press.*

News is breaking about safe ways to use eggs in old favorite recipes.

What is salmonella? How does it get into foods? Must we avoid eggs to avoid it? Are there ways to safeguard foods?

In a months-long research project, both in our kitchens and in an independent research laboratory, we have cracked and cooked a lot of eggs to come up with some answers to the big question: can you still use eggs raw or lightly cooked in your favorite dishes?

WHAT IS SALMONELLA?

Very common and widely present, salmonella bacteria (of which there are numerous strains) can cause food poisoning and gastrointestinal distress. Under certain conditions—including a combination of time and temperature—salmonella can thrive in many foods, most typically those that contain protein—not only eggs but also others such as fish, meat, and poultry. The bacteria can also multiply on less obvious foods like fruits and vegetables if they come in contact with the bacteria and are held under conditions that are sufficiently warm and moist.

Cooking to sufficient heat levels destroys salmonella. Acid is another way to control salmonella; see details on the facing page.

If salmonella-free solid meat, like beef steak or chicken breast, comes in contact with the bacteria, only the surface will be contaminated. When cooked enough to be browned and flavorful, these foods will be much hotter on the surface than needed to kill salmonella.

Until the last few years, home cooks had little cause to worry about the safety of well-handled eggs. But serious outbreaks of salmonella illness in the Eastern states were traced to eggs. (So far, no comparable incidents have occurred in the West.)

HOW DOES SALMONELLA GET INTO EGGS? HOW DO YOU DEAL WITH IT?

How eggs become contaminated is at the center of the widespread alarm. Some salmonella found in eggs got there before the shell formed; the current concern is that this appears to be happening more often in some areas of the country.

Yolks are most susceptible to salmonella growth. According to current research, egg whites have natural defenses against salmonella; they're designed to protect the nutrient-rich yolk in which bacteria, given opportunity, can thrive. Even though egg whites are less vulnerable, however, contamination is still a possibility.

Avian (poultry and egg) scientists are divided about how to deal with eggs. Some recommend that eggs be totally cooked or that pasteurized eggs (not readily available to consumers) be used. Others feel that properly handled eggs can be enjoyed in recipes even without cooking.

Bear in mind that raw and lightly cooked eggs have never been advised for certain people: young children; the aged; and individuals taking medications that alter the immune system, such as treatments for cancer.

Unfortunately, unless your kitchen is equipped with laboratory tools (rare in homes) needed to spot salmonella, you can't tell if it is present.

THE BASIC RULE OF FOOD SAFETY: PROCEED AS IF A PROBLEM EXISTS

The following procedures—recommended by food scientists, lab-tested for *Sunset*, and double-checked in our kitchens—will give trouble-free results. The tools and techniques are simple: they have to do with cleanliness, temperature, time, and acidity. We have used the procedures with raw and lightly cooked eggs. You can also use them with your own recipes.

First, choose and handle eggs with care. Be sure the eggs you buy are fresh (most cartons are dated) and have always been refrigerated below at least 50° (this is difficult to confirm). Then keep the eggs in the refrigerator until you use them. Salmonella grow and quickly reach danger levels within hours when the temperature is 60° or warmer.

If you use eggs raw or lightly cooked, observe these precautions.

1. Use only eggs that have been refrigerated at all times. Do not let eggs stand at room temperature more than a total of 2 hours at any time before consuming (some authorities feel this is overcautious and are comfortable with a total of 4 hours).

2. Serve any foods with lightly cooked eggs immediately, or chill at once to serve cold. Do not let these chilled foods stand at room temperature long enough to warm up.

3. Wash hands with soap and water. Do this before handling foods and between foods that can cross-contaminate, like raw chicken or fish, then an egg.

4. Keep work areas clean. Wash with hot soapy water, then rinse when you change foods, like meats to salad greens—or eggs. To avoid cross-contamination, keep tools and equipment clean.

5. If using whipped raw egg whites, be sure to keep foods containing them chilled at all times. These include fluffy desserts like mousses, soufflés, and bavarians. (When we tried making meringues with hot sugar syrups instead of sugar, they did not reach salmonella-killing temperature without becoming too sweet.)

TWO SALMONELLA KILLERS: HEAT & ACID

To enjoy eggs soft or lightly cooked, gentle heat is important. Two heat-killing methods work: either cook food to 140° and hold at that temperature for 3½ minutes, or cook to 160° (no holding time required).

For some mixtures, like mayonnaise or dressing for a Caesar salad, that rely on raw egg to form an emulsion or give the dressing a clinging quality, we have found that egg white works as effectively as whole egg. When using raw egg whites, a few steps taken to lower their acid level to 3.5 will ensure they're safe to consume.

To be sure foods are hot enough or acidic enough to kill salmonella, you need some simple measuring tools.

Temperature. An accurate **quick-read thermometer** is indispensable for determining the internal temperature (in the center) of cooked foods. Occasionally verify the thermometer's accuracy by dipping it in boiling water (212° at sea level, 208.4° at 2,000 feet, 203° at 5,000 feet). To avoid any possible contamination, dip the thermometer in boiling water before using it to test eggs. Also, the thermometer's ability to register rapidly (important with quick-cooking

eggs) is enhanced if you dip it first in hot water.

Acid. To measure acidity, buy **pH indicator strips** at a scientific supply store. A package of 100 usually costs less than $10. Choose strips that indicate pH between 3 and 6 (the lower the number, the greater the acidity).

To use, moisten a strip with the food, then check the color the paper turns against color guides on the package. When pH measures 3.5 or lower, the food's acid level is adequate, under refrigeration, to stop growth of salmonella and then kill it within 48 hours.

SOFT-COOKED EGGS

Once you've seen how eggs look at a salmonella-safe temperature, you can judge the internal temperature fairly accurately by eye. Serve softly cooked at once; otherwise, yolks continue to firm.

Poached. Put **large eggs** (at refrigerator temperature) into individual poaching cups. Cook, covered, over simmering water until 140° in the center of the yolks, then hold at that temperature (over water but off heat) for 3½ minutes. Yolks will still be semiliquid in center. Eggs cooked just to 160° at the center are still moist but not liquid.

In the shell. Put up to 6 **large eggs** (at refrigerator temperature) in a 2- to 3-quart pan; add cold water to cover them by about 1 inch. Bring water to 200° over high heat; remove from heat and let stand 1 minute. Remove 1 egg and plunge a thermometer into center of yolk; the temperature should be 140° (if

Testing for Egg Safety

TO DETERMINE *how to cook eggs to salmonella-safe temperatures, or to acidify egg whites to eat uncooked, Sunset food editors did extensive research over many months, converted what they learned to workable kitchen procedures, and then had the results checked by leading authorities and an independent food laboratory.*

In our kitchens, we could evaluate processes that used heat to kill salmonella. Sunset food editor Karyn Lipman cooked hundreds of eggs by a number of methods, each time checking the internal temperature of the egg or food containing eggs. Thermometers were checked often for accuracy; to do the same, see temperature section, at left.

For whole eggs, she found the texture of the just-cooked yolk to be an accurate way to gauge its internal temperature —even without a thermometer.

ENLISTING THE HELP OF A LABORATORY

To test how effectively acid killed salmonella, we needed scientific help. Authorities assured us that salmonel-

la bacteria don't grow in an acid medium, and that the acid also probably killed them—under controlled temperatures. But they did not know whether this was true when acid was at low enough levels to be palatable.

We focused on testing ratios of lemon juice and egg white that would work well to make the flavorful mayonnaise and the Caesar dressing (page 173). Then we contracted with an independent laboratory to run tests on egg white–lemon juice mixtures with these proportions.

In the lab, some mixtures were left salmonella-free; the rest were inoculated with varying amounts (some very large) of the bacteria. Also tested were egg whites without lemon juice, plain and salmonella-inoculated. Mixtures were refrigerated. Samples taken at 1, 4, 24, and 48 hours were cultured. Salmonella in the acid mixtures began to decline significantly and were less than detectable after 48 hours.

At home, to be assured that you have a safe amount of acid, you can use testing paper (above).

Safe: 140° for 3½ minutes
Pan-poached yolk is still semiliquid at minimum salmonella-safe temperature.

Safe: scalding milk on raw eggs
For uncooked ice cream, scalding milk heats raw eggs to safe temperature.

not, check after 1 more minute). Once yolks are 140° in center, let remaining eggs stand in water for 3½ minutes longer; yolks will be semiliquid.

To bring eggs to 160° in the center, leave them in water 7 minutes after removing from heat.

Once you've achieved the results you want, you can duplicate them with the same amount of water and 1 to 6 eggs, and skip the thermometer.

Fried. Break refrigerated **eggs** into frying pan and cook over low to medium heat, turning once; when yolks begin to firm all around but are still semiliquid in center, the temperature will be 140° (as shown for poached egg, above); keep warm in pan on lowest heat for 3½ minutes. Or continue to cook to doneness desired.

Omelets. Omelets (not the puffy kind) that are still shiny and moist-looking on the surface will be, when folded or rolled over, more than 160° in the center.

Scrambled. Test with your thermometer to make sure they are cooked to 140° and held at that temperature for 3½ minutes; or cook to a firmer 160°.

ICE CREAM

Ice cream is often made by beating together milk, sugar, and flavoring with uncooked eggs. A simple precaution that does not alter the quality of the finished product is to heat the milk and sugar to 200°, then whisk this mixture into a deep metal bowl with eggs (at least 1 cup **milk** and ¼ cup **sugar** for each 3 refrigerator-temperature **large eggs**). Check temperature; if 160°, heat no further. If between 140° and 160°, set bowl in a container of 150° water and stir for 3½ minutes. Chill mixture, add **flavoring,** and continue as your recipe directs.

STIRRED & BAKED CUSTARDS

By the time either of these mixtures is hot enough to thicken, it exceeds 160°. Serve hot or warm; or cover, chill, and serve cold.

HOLLANDAISE & BÉARNAISE SAUCES

You can make cooked or uncooked versions of either sauce salmonella-proof by heating butter to a specific temperature.

For 1 **large egg** or 3 large egg yolks (all refrigerator temperature) and 1 tablespoon **lemon juice** or vinegar (add more later, to taste), you need 1 cup (½ lb.) **butter** or margarine heated to 220°.

Either whisk hot butter in a rapid steady stream into eggs over hot water or very low heat, or pour into whirling eggs in a blender or food processor. If the temperature of the sauce is not at least 160° when all the butter is added, set container in a bowl of 150° water and stir or whisk for 3½ minutes. Remove sauce from heat, mix in **seasonings,** and serve.

Safe: center of meringue is 140°
Golden meringue on lemon pie is baked for 25 to 30 minutes to reach safe temperature.

Safe: acid with uncooked egg white
Egg white with lemon juice makes a safe but thick mayonnaise (acid in lemon kills salmonella in 48 hours).

ZABAGLIONE

Start with at least **4 large egg yolks** plus 1/2 cup **wine** or fruit juice, and **sugar** to taste. By the time you have whisked the mixture over direct heat or simmering water until it is thick enough to mound slightly, it is usually at least 160°. If not, continue to whisk in pan in a bowl of 150° water for 3 1/2 minutes.

SOFT MERINGUE FOR PIE

Sugar in whipped egg whites makes meringues even less hospitable to salmonella but does not destroy it. To be salmonella-proof, the meringue must be baked on the pie longer and at a lower temperature than typical, so the heat penetrates. Chill meringue pies until served.

For an 8- to 9-inch pie, whip **4 large egg whites** (at refrigerator temperature) with 1/4 teaspoon **cream of tartar** on high speed until frothy; gradually beat in 1/4 cup **sugar,** whipping until whites hold soft peaks.

Pour **hot cooked pie filling** (such as chocolate or lemon) into **baked pie shell.** At once swirl meringue over filling, sealing to pie shell. Bake in a 325° oven until meringue is evenly browned and temperature in meringue center is 140° or above, 25 to 30 minutes. Chill (warm filling also needs to firm) and serve cold.

ACIDIFIED EGG WHITE

Mix 1 **large egg white** with 2 tablespoons **lemon juice.** Check *p*H; it should be 3.5. If not, add more lemon juice, 1 tablespoon at a time, checking with each addition until *p*H is 3.5. Cover airtight and refrigerate at least 48 hours or up to 4 days (on longer standing, the egg begins to solidify); use as directed, following.

ACIDIFIED EGG WHITE MAYONNAISE

Put 1 **acidified egg white** (directions precede) in a blender, food processor, or deep bowl of an electric mixer. Add 2 tablespoons **water** and 2 teaspoons **Di-jon mustard.** Whirling or beating at high speed, add 1 cup **salad oil** or olive oil in a slow stream until mixture starts to thicken, then add faster, incorporating smoothly. Add more **lemon juice** and **salt** to taste. Serve, or cover and chill up to 4 days. Makes about 1 1/4 cups.

PER TABLESPOON: 98 calories, 0.2 g protein, 0.2 g carbohydrates, 11 g fat, 0 mg cholesterol, 18 mg sodium

ACIDIFIED CAESAR SALAD DRESSING

In a blender, food processor, or deep bowl of an electric mixer, whirl or beat 1 **acidified egg white** (directions precede) with 2 tablespoons **lemon juice,** 1/4 cup **olive oil** or salad oil, 2 teaspoons **Worcestershire,** and 1/8 teaspoon freshly ground **pepper.** Finely chop 6 to 8 drained **canned anchovy fillets** and add to dressing. Makes about 3/4 cup.

In a large salad bowl, put 8 to 9 cups rinsed and crisped bite-size pieces **romaine lettuce.** Pour dressing over salad; as you mix, sprinkle greens with 2 to 4 tablespoons freshly grated **parmesan cheese.** Makes 7 or 8 servings.

PER SERVING: 80 calories, 2.3 g protein, 2.1 g carbohydrates, 7.2 g fat, 1.7 mg cholesterol, 137 mg sodium

OAT GRANOLA

Enjoy oat granola with berries and milk for a healthy breakfast.

- 4 **cups (1 lb.) oat bran**
- 4 **cups (¾ lb.) regular rolled oats**
- ¼ **cup unsalted shelled sunflower seeds**
- ¼ **cup slivered almonds**
- ⅓ **cup salad oil**
- ¼ **cup water**
- ¾ **cup firmly packed brown sugar**
- 2 **teaspoons ground cinnamon**
- 1 **teaspoon coconut extract**
- 1 **teaspoon almond extract**
  Milk
  Fresh blueberries and hulled strawberries (optional)

In a deep 12- by 14-inch roasting pan, combine oat bran, oats, sunflower seeds, and almonds. Set aside.

In a 1- to 2-quart pan over high heat, bring oil, water, sugar, and cinnamon to a boil. Remove from heat and stir in coconut and almond extracts; pour over oat mixture. Let cool briefly, then mix with your hands to coat evenly.

Spread oat mixture in roasting pan and bake in a 325° oven, stirring occasionally, until almonds are golden and crisp, about 1 hour. Serve warm, with milk and berries, or let cool completely and store airtight for up to 2 weeks. Makes 8 cups, or 16 servings.—*Sheryl Kindle Fullner, Everson, Wash.*

PER SERVING: 257 calories, 9.2 g protein, 44 g carbohydrates, 10 g fat, 0 mg cholesterol, 5.4 mg sodium

GRILLED BEEF POCKET SANDWICHES

Skewers of grilled beef and red bell pepper go into pocket bread for sandwiches.

- 1½ **pounds tender beef steak, such as loin, about 1 inch thick**
- 1 **large clove garlic**
- ½ **small onion, cut into chunks**
- 2 **tablespoons *each* sugar, water, salad oil, and lemon juice**
- ⅓ **cup soy sauce**
- 2 **large (½ lb. each) red bell peppers, stemmed and cut into 1½-inch squares**
- 12 **pocket bread halves**
- 2 **cups fresh cilantro (coriander) sprigs, rinsed and crisped**

Trim fat from steak; cut meat into long, ¼-inch-thick slices. In a blender or food processor, purée garlic, onion, sugar, water, oil, lemon juice, and soy; mix with peppers and beef. Cover and chill 30 minutes or until next day. Drain off and save marinade. On thin skewers, alternately thread beef and peppers.

Place skewers on a grill 4 to 6 inches above a solid bed of medium-hot coals (you should be able to hold your hand at grill level for 3 to 4 seconds). Turn often, basting with marinade, until meat is medium-rare (cut to test), 4 to 5 minutes. Fill bread with meat, peppers, and cilantro. Makes 6 servings.—*Annie Windrem, San Diego.*

PER SERVING: 425 calories, 33 g protein, 46 g carbohydrates, 11 g fat, 76 mg cholesterol, 1,329 mg sodium

ZUCCHINI SALSA

Whirl zucchini, pepper, tomatoes, and cilantro to make salsa for tortilla chips.

- 2 **medium-size zucchini (about ½ lb. total), sliced**
- ¼ **cup minced green bell pepper**
- ½ **cup minced firm-ripe tomato**
- 3 **tablespoons minced red onion**
- 3 **tablespoons lime juice**
- ½ **teaspoon ground cumin**
  About 2 tablespoons minced fresh cilantro (coriander)
  Salt
  Tortilla chips or raw vegetables, such as cherry tomatoes, bell pepper and carrot strips, and peeled jicama wedges

In a blender or food processor, whirl zucchini (a portion at a time if using a blender) until coarsely ground; or finely mince zucchini with a knife.

In a bowl, mix together the zucchini, bell pepper, tomato, onion, lime juice, and cumin. Season vegetable mixture to taste with cilantro and salt. Transfer to a small serving bowl. (If made ahead, cover and chill up until the next day.)

Offer tortilla chips or raw vegetables for scooping up the zucchini salsa. Makes about 2 cups.—*Diane Nebel, Rosalia, Wash.*

PER TABLESPOON: 2.5 calories, 0.1 g protein, 0.5 g carbohydrates, 0 g fat, 0 mg cholesterol, 0.8 mg sodium

DEEP-DISH PESTO PIZZA

1 loaf (1 lb.) frozen whole-wheat
    bread dough, thawed
    Cornmeal
2 cups (½ lb.) shredded
    mozzarella cheese
⅓ cup grated parmesan cheese
⅔ cup canned marinara sauce
    Pesto (recipe follows)
⅓ cup drained dried tomatoes
    packed in oil, sliced

Place dough in a greased bowl, cover,
and let rise in a warm place until it has
doubled, 1 to 1½ hours; divide in half.
On a floured board, roll each piece into
a 12-inch circle. Lightly grease 2 metal pie
pans, 9-inch size; sprinkle with cornmeal. Line pans so the dough extends ¾
of the way up sides.

Mix mozzarella and parmesan; scatter
¼ of it over bottom of each pan. Put ½ of
the marinara sauce, pesto, and tomatoes
over cheese in each pan. Sprinkle with
remaining cheese. Bake on bottom rack
of a 450° oven until crust is browned, 15
to 18 minutes. Makes 8 servings.—*Donna
Higgins, Halfway, Ore.*

PER SERVING: 433 calories, 15 g protein, 34 g carbohydrates, 27 g
fat, 32 mg cholesterol, 901 mg sodium

Pesto. In a blender or food processor,
purée 2 cups (about 2 oz.) lightly packed
fresh basil leaves, ⅓ cup **olive oil**, ¼ cup
walnuts, 2 cloves **garlic**, and ½ cup
grated **parmesan cheese**.

*Slip pizza topped with pesto
and marinara sauce out of
the pan to serve.*

WARM GOAT CHEESE SALAD

¾ pound mixed salad greens such as
    red-leaf, oak-leaf, and butter
    lettuces, rinsed and crisped
¼ cup walnut oil or olive oil
¼ cup white wine vinegar
1 tablespoon Dijon mustard
¾ cup walnut halves or pieces
3 rounds (2 oz. each) goat cheese
    with rind, such as crottin or
    chavignol; or 1 log (about 8 oz.)
    soft goat cheese, such as
    montrachet
    Salt and pepper

Tear lettuce into large pieces and arrange
on 6 salad plates. Whisk oil, vinegar, and
mustard until smooth; pour into a small
pitcher and set aside. Place nuts on a 10-
by 15-inch baking pan and bake in a 400°
oven until dark golden brown, about 8
minutes. Cut cheese into 6 equal pieces
and place on pan. Broil about 3 inches below heat until cheese is speckled brown
and slightly melted, 2 to 4 minutes.

Transfer 1 piece of cheese onto each
salad. Sprinkle nuts over salads. Add
dressing, salt, and pepper to taste. Makes
6 servings.—*Jane Cross, Albuquerque.*

PER SERVING: 270 calories, 7.8 g protein, 6.6 g carbohydrates, 25 g
fat, 26 mg cholesterol, 255 mg sodium

*Warm goat cheese lies on a
bed of salad greens, topped
with mustard dressing.*

CHERRY CHOCOLATE CHEESECAKE PIE

    Pastry for a single-crust 9-inch pie
1 large package (8 oz.) cream cheese,
    cut into chunks
¾ cup sugar
¼ cup unsweetened cocoa
2 large eggs
1 cup unflavored low-fat yogurt
⅛ teaspoon almond extract
1½ cups pitted fresh or thawed frozen
    sweet dark cherries

Roll out pastry, ease into a 9-inch pie pan,
and flute onto rim. Prick pastry all over
with a fork and bake on the bottom rack
in a 350° oven until golden, 20 to 25
minutes.

In a bowl with an electric mixer, beat the
cream cheese, sugar, and cocoa until mixture is creamy. Beat in the eggs until
blended. Then add yogurt and almond
extract to the mixture; beat until smooth.
Stir in cherries. Scrape into the pastry.

Bake in a 350° oven until the center of
cheesecake jiggles only slightly when
gently shaken, about 40 minutes. Let
cake cool on a rack, then cover and chill
in the refrigerator until cold, at least 3
hours or up to 1 day. Makes 9 or 10 servings.—*Babette Holliday, Berthoud, Colo.*

PER SERVING: 284 calories, 5.6 g protein, 32 g carbohydrates, 16 g fat,
69 mg cholesterol, 220 mg sodium

*Whole cherries fill
creamy interior of
chocolate cheesecake pie.*

I**F YOU NAME A DISH** *Pork Enchiladas Maximilian and Carlota, it had better have a history. Thanks to chef Walter Matera, this one does. It's a Mexican variation on a recipe for pork chops with crispy potatoes from the Sunset book French Cooking Country-style—but with*

tortillas filling in for potatoes. The result is a happier mix than the effort at collaboration Napoleon III undertook when he set up the Austrian Archduke Maximilian and his Belgian wife, Carlota, as emperor and empress of Mexico. Napoleon's attempt to wed France and Mexico lacked the consent of the bride, and Maximilian ended up before a firing squad in 1867.

Tequila is a novel fuel for incendiary chefs, but it works well here.

PORK ENCHILADAS MAXIMILIAN & CARLOTA

About 2 pounds pork shoulder chops or steaks
Salt and pepper
1/2 teaspoon ground cumin
1 teaspoon dry oregano leaves
1 clove garlic, minced or pressed
1 medium-size (about 6 oz.) onion, chopped
3 tablespoons tequila
8 corn or flour tortillas (6- to 8-in. size)
Sour cream
Homemade or prepared salsa
Shredded lettuce
Shredded sharp cheddar cheese

Trim and discard bone and excess fat from chops, then cut meat into bite-size pieces. Sprinkle lightly with salt, pepper, cumin, and oregano; then mix with garlic. Put meat mixture in a 10- to 12-inch frying pan over high heat; add 1/2 cup water. Cover and cook 10 minutes. Uncover and stir often until pan is dry and browned bits stick. Add onion and another 1/2 cup water, stirring to loosen browned bits. Cook, uncovered, until liquid evaporates and meat begins to brown; stir often.

Pour tequila into pan (not beneath exhaust fan or flammables) and carefully ignite (tequila is far more explosive than brandy). Shake pan until flames die.

"Tequila is a novel fuel for incendiary chefs, but it works well here."

Meanwhile, stack and wrap tortillas in foil; heat in a 350° oven until hot throughout, 10 to 15 minutes.

Evenly spoon meat and juices into tortillas. To taste, add sour cream, salsa, lettuce, and cheese; roll tortillas to enclose filling. Set filled tortillas, seam side down, on plates, adding more sour cream, salsa, lettuce, and cheese as desired. Makes 4 servings, 2 enchiladas each.

PER SERVING: 437 calories, 37 g protein, 29 g carbohydrates, 19 g fat, 111 mg cholesterol, 233 mg sodium

Lakewood, Calif.

A CLASSIC WAY *to roast a leg of lamb is to give it a crust of mustard or bread crumbs and garlic. And, of course, an addition of mint is very familiar. But Earl Howe has figured out how to crust the leg, perfume it with mint, and get the flavors deep inside the meat with a single blend of ingredients that he calls mint pesto. In effect, he makes a lamb jelly roll.*

CRUSTED LAMB WITH MINT PESTO

  2 **cups loosely packed fresh mint leaves**
 1/2 **cup loosely packed chopped parsley**
  3 **large cloves garlic, halved**
 1/4 **cup olive oil**
 1/3 **cup neufchâtel (light cream) cheese**
 1/4 **cup pine nuts or walnuts**
1 1/2 **tablespoons lemon juice**
 1/8 **teaspoon pepper**
  1 **leg of lamb (6 to 7 lb.), boned and butterflied**

In a food processor or blender, combine mint, parsley, 2 cloves garlic, oil, cheese, pine nuts, lemon juice, and pepper. Whirl to make a coarse paste; scrape container sides often.

Trim and discard excess fat from lamb. Sliver remaining garlic clove; with tip of a knife, make small cuts in lamb and insert garlic slivers. Spread the boned side of the lamb with about 2/3 of the mint mixture. Roll meat to enclose filling and tie securely. Spread remaining mint pesto mixture over outside of meat.

Ignite 50 charcoal briquets on firegrate in a barbecue with a lid. When coals are covered with gray ash, 30 to 40 minutes, push an equal number to opposite sides of the grate. Set a foil drip pan on grate between coals. Place grill 4 to 6 inches over coals, then set lamb over drip pan.

Put lid on barbecue and open dampers. Cook lamb until a meat thermometer inserted in thickest portion registers 130° for rare (about 1 hour) or 140° for medium (about 1 1/4 hours). Let roast rest on a carving board for 10 to 15 minutes, then cut in thin slices. Makes 8 to 10 servings.

PER SERVING: 324 calories, 39 g protein, 1.9 g carbohydrates, 17 g fat, 122 mg cholesterol, 145 mg sodium

Napa, Calif.

THE DUTY OF AN APPETIZER *is to arouse the gastric juices and keep them flowing as dinner makes its way to the table. But to be effective, tidbits should not be so filling as to take the edge off the appetite.*

In that respect, mushrooms make admirable starters, but they need a little help to escape the charge of blandness. A vinaigrette marinade is often used to sharpen the flavor, but Steven Scott has a special approach: quick browning, followed by a soak in hot white zinfandel and an eventual finish in the broiler with cheese and sage topping.

"Mushrooms make admirable starters."

MUSHROOM APPETIZERS

1 1/2 **pounds large (about 2-in.-wide caps) mushrooms, rinsed and stem ends trimmed**
  1 **tablespoon olive oil**
  1 **clove garlic, minced or pressed**
  1 **cup white zinfandel or other moderately dry white wine**
  1 **cup (1/4 lb.) shredded jalapeño-flavor jack cheese**
    Chopped fresh sage leaves (optional)

Quarter mushrooms vertically through stems. In a 10- to 12-inch frying pan on high heat, combine mushrooms, oil, and garlic. Stir until mushrooms are lightly browned, about 5 minutes.

Add wine and boil, uncovered, until about half the liquid evaporates. If made ahead, cover and let stand up to 2 hours.

Transfer mushrooms and juices to 6 individual heatproof ramekins (about 2/3-cup size); evenly sprinkle with cheese. Broil 3 to 4 inches from heat until cheese melts, 5 to 6 minutes. Sprinkle with sage and serve at once. Makes 6 servings.

PER SERVING: 123 calories, 7 g protein, 6.3 g carbohydrates, 8.7 g fat, 20 mg cholesterol, 133 mg sodium

Seattle

June Menus

CELEBRATE FATHER'S DAY *with a light, wholesome lunch featuring pasta and a cucumber salad—simple enough for young cooks to manage. For a hot summer night, make a meal out of a main-dish salad. And for an afternoon treat, bake cream cheese cookies to serve with fresh summer fruit.*

FATHER'S DAY LUNCH

Arugula & Red Cherry Tomatoes with Noodles
Red Onion & Cucumber Salad
Crusty Bread
Extra-virgin Olive Oil
Zinfandel   Sparkling Water
Watermelon Wedges

This spicy meal can be whipped up in just about a half-hour.

You can make the salad and rinse and trim the arugula hours ahead of time. Accompany the pasta and salad with bread to dip into a small dish of olive oil.

ARUGULA & RED CHERRY TOMATOES WITH NOODLES

2/3 **pound arugula (about 12 cups), bare stems cut off and yellow or bruised leaves discarded; or 12 cups watercress**

2 **to 4 tablespoons olive oil**

1 **large onion, coarsely chopped**

2 **cloves garlic, minced or pressed**

1 **package (14 oz.) fresh Chinese noodles (about 1/8 in. wide), 9 ounces fresh fettuccine, or 11 ounces dry fettuccine**

3 **cups (about 1 lb.) red cherry tomatoes, stemmed and halved**

About 1/2 cup freshly grated parmesan cheese

About 1/4 teaspoon crushed dried hot red chilies

Salt

Lemon wedges

Rinse and drain arugula; coarsely chop and set aside.

In a 12-inch frying pan or a 5- to 6-quart pan, combine 2 tablespoons oil, onion, and garlic. Stir frequently over high heat until the onion is lightly browned, about 10 minutes. Keep mixture warm.

Tantalize dad on Father's Day with the fresh garden tastes of arugula and bright cherry tomatoes in this easy-to-make noodle dish. Serve it with crusty bread.

Meanwhile, bring about 4 quarts of water to a boil in a 6- to 8-quart pan on high heat. Add noodles and cook, uncovered, just until tender to bite, 3 to 5 minutes (about 8 minutes for dry pasta).

When pasta is almost done, turn heat to high under onions and stir in arugula until leaves wilt, 2 to 4 minutes.

Pour noodles into a colander. As they drain, stir tomatoes with the onion and arugula mixture over high heat until the tomatoes are barely warm. Put noodles on a warm rimmed platter; add the vegetable mixture and the remaining oil, if desired. Mix the noodles with 2 forks. Sprinkle with cheese and chilies; mix again. Season portions with salt and lemon to taste. Makes 5 or 6 servings.

PER SERVING: 299 calories, 14 g protein, 43 g carbohydrates, 8.8 g fat, 84 mg cholesterol, 197 mg sodium

RED ONION & CUCUMBER SALAD

¼ cup minced mild red onion
1 large (about 1¼ lb.) European cucumber, sliced thin
3 tablespoons red wine vinegar
1 tablespoon sugar
  Salt

Mix onion with cucumber, vinegar, and sugar. If made ahead, cover and chill up to 4 hours. Add salt to taste. Makes 5 or 6 servings.

PER SERVING: 24 calories, 0.6 g protein, 5.6 g carbohydrates, 0.1 g fat, 0 mg cholesterol, 2 mg sodium

SUMMERTIME SALAD

Oriental Turkey Salad
Sesame Breadsticks
Lemon Sorbet Gingersnaps
Iced Green Tea

Sliced turkey breast, cabbage, and tangy peanut sauce make a filling salad that's just right for a warm summer night.

Use leftover turkey or buy it cooked, plain or smoked. Also buy the sorbet and gingersnap cookies. Tender napa cabbage leaves hold salad. A piquant peanut dressing adds Asian flair.

ORIENTAL TURKEY SALAD

1 large head (about 1¾ lb.) napa cabbage, rinsed and drained
1 cup lightly packed fresh cilantro (coriander) leaves
½ cup thinly sliced green onion, including tops
½ cup drained pickled shallots or onions, coarsely chopped
  Peanut dressing (recipe follows)
¼ cup dry-roasted peanuts, coarsely chopped
¾ pound boned and skinned cold cooked or smoked turkey

Discard bruised cabbage leaves. Arrange 4 to 8 large outer leaves on 4 plates. Finely shred remaining cabbage and mix gently with cilantro, green onion, pickled shallots, and ⅔ of the dressing. Mound salad equally on leaves; sprinkle with nuts. Thinly slice turkey and place beside salads. Add remaining dressing to taste. Makes 4 main-dish servings.

PER SERVING: 234 calories, 30 g protein, 9.7 g carbohydrates, 8.9 g fat, 66 mg cholesterol, 451 mg sodium

Peanut dressing. Mix ¼ cup **creamy peanut butter**, ¼ cup **hoisin sauce** (or 3 tablespoons peanut butter, 2 tablespoons water, 1 tablespoon soy sauce, 2 teaspoons *each* cider vinegar and sugar), 3 tablespoons **seasoned rice vinegar** (or 3 tablespoons rice vinegar and 1 teaspoon sugar), and ½ teaspoon **Oriental sesame oil**.

PER TABLESPOON: 55 calories, 2.1 g protein, 4.4 g carbohydrates, 3.6 g fat, 0 mg cholesterol, 235 mg sodium

(Continued on next page)

Wide napa cabbage leaf cradles a salad that mingles spicy-sweet Asian flavors—a fine complement to cold sliced turkey. Accompany with crisp sesame breadsticks.

SWEET SNACK TIME

Cream Cheese Cookies
Bowls of Raspberries or
Clusters of Seedless Red Grapes
Milk   Iced Coffee

Fill the cooky jar for a quick treat to accompany the fruits of summer.

Arrange the foods on a tray and carry out into the garden to enjoy.

CREAM CHEESE COOKIES

1 **cup (½ lb.) butter or margarine, cut into chunks**
¾ **cup sugar**
1 **small package (3 oz.) cream cheese, cut into chunks**
1 **large egg**
½ **teaspoon vanilla**
2 **cups all-purpose flour**

In a food processor or with a mixer, whirl or beat butter, sugar, cream cheese, egg, and vanilla until smooth. Whirl or mix in the flour.

Drop dough in 1-tablespoon mounds, about 1 inch apart, on 2 baking sheets, each 12 by 15 inches.

Bake in a 325° oven until cookies are golden brown, about 20 minutes; switch pan positions halfway through baking. Cool on racks. If made ahead, store airtight up to 3 days. Makes about 3½ dozen.—*Marilyn Lipton, Belmont, Calif.*

PER COOKY: 83 calories, 1 g protein, 8.2 g carbohydrates, 5.3 g fat, 19 mg cholesterol, 52 mg sodium

JULY

Barbecued Pork Spareribs (page 189)

Casual summer meals should be easy on the cook. This month we offer a summer party buffet for 12, featuring Mediterranean chicken and other make-ahead dishes. Wine enthusiasts will enjoy the elegantly simple East-West menu created to show off Napa Valley wines. For barbecue chefs, the latest word on grilling ribs includes new cooking techniques and bold sauces. Other July articles highlight unusual cabbage salads, colorful fruit pies, dishes using fresh sweet corn, and other treats that show off summer's superb produce.

Summer Dinner Party for 12

PROFESSIONAL FOOD STYLISTS—*who are paid to make food look beautiful and appetizing—quickly learn which foods stay fresh-looking and good-tasting over periods of time. Stevie Bass of Food Concepts takes her extensive food-styling knowledge to its logical conclusion in creating this attractive, easy-to-duplicate dinner party she served recently in her Mill Valley, California, home.*

SUMMER DINNER PARTY

Mediterranean Chicken
Fruited Quinoa Salad
Tomatoes with Herb Vinaigrette
Citrus Sauce   Basil-Jicama Pesto
Chocolate Fondue
Fresh Fruit Basket

Citrus sauce and pesto go with chicken, quinoa, and tomatoes. The day before, you can cook the chicken and quinoa, and make the sauce.

For fondue fruit, buy watermelon (about 5-lb. piece), pineapple (2, each 2 to 3 lb.), and strawberries (6 to 8 cups), or any single fruit. Early on party day, cut watermelon and pineapple into bite-size cubes; rinse and drain strawberries. Cover and cool; to serve, mound on a platter.

MEDITERRANEAN CHICKEN

Grate orange peel to flavor citrus sauce before you peel fruit for the chicken.

- 1/2 **cup orange marmalade**
- 2 **teaspoons prepared horseradish**
- 12 **boned and skinned chicken breast halves (each 4 to 5 oz.), rinsed and patted dry**
- 4 **large (about 2 lb. total) oranges**
- 3 **large (about 1 lb. total) blood oranges, or 2 small (about 1 1/4 lb. total) pink grapefruit**
- 3 **large (about 10 oz. each) firm-ripe avocados**
- 1/4 **cup lemon juice**

In a bowl, mix marmalade and horseradish with chicken. Place chicken in 2 greased 10- by 15-inch pans. Bake, uncovered, in a 450° oven until meat is white in thickest part (cut to test), 12 to 15 minutes; switch pan positions halfway through cooking. Let cool. If made ahead, cover and chill up to next day. Arrange chicken on a large platter.

Cut peel and white membrane from oranges and blood oranges. Slice fruit crosswise into 1/4-inch-thick rounds; arrange beside chicken. (For grapefruit, cut segments from membrane; discard membrane.) Peel, pit, and slice avocados; coat with lemon juice and place beside chicken. Makes 12 servings.

PER SERVING: 349 calories, 41 g protein, 24 g carbohydrates, 10 g fat (1.8 g saturated), 99 mg cholesterol, 120 mg sodium

FRUITED QUINOA SALAD

- 1/4 **cup pine nuts or slivered almonds**
- 2 **to 2 1/2 cups (about 1 lb.) dried apricots**
- 3 **cups quinoa or 2 cups bulgur (cracked wheat)**
- 1 **tablespoon olive or salad oil**
- 4 **to 6 cups regular-strength chicken broth**
- 4 **teaspoons grated lemon peel**
- 1/4 **cup lemon juice**
- 1 1/2 **to 2 cups currants**
  Salt

In a 6- to 8-inch frying pan, stir nuts often over medium heat until golden brown, 3 to 5 minutes. Remove from pan; set aside. Coarsely chop 1 cup apricots; set aside.

Place quinoa in a fine strainer and rinse with cool water (bulgur needs no rinsing). Pour oil into a 12-inch frying pan or 4- to 5-quart pan over medium heat. Add quinoa or bulgur; stir often until it turns a slightly darker brown, 8 to 10 minutes.

To pan, add broth (6 cups for quinoa, 4 cups for bulgur), peel, and juice. Bring to a boil on high heat. Cover and simmer until grain is just tender to bite, 10 to 15 minutes. Drain any liquid from grain; reserve for soup or discard. Stir chopped apricots and 1 cup currants into grain. Let stand until warm or cool. If made ahead, cover and chill up until next day.

Mound salad in center of a large rimmed platter. Garnish with remaining apricots, currants, and nuts. Season to taste with salt. Serve warm or cool. Makes 12 servings.

PER SERVING: 299 calories, 8.6 g protein, 57 g carbohydrates, 5.7 g fat (0.8 g saturated), 0 mg cholesterol, 49 mg sodium

TOMATOES WITH HERB VINAIGRETTE

- 1/4 **cup olive oil**
- 1/4 **cup red wine vinegar**
- 1/2 **teaspoon *each* dry marjoram leaves and dry thyme leaves**
- 3 1/2 **pounds (9 to 10 cups total) firm-ripe cherry tomatoes (red or yellow, any size), stemmed, rinsed, drained, and halved**

In a large shallow bowl, mix oil, vinegar, marjoram, and thyme. Add tomatoes; mix gently. Serve or, if made ahead, cover and chill up to 4 hours. Makes 12 servings.

PER SERVING: 64 calories, 1.1 g protein, 5.5 g carbohydrates, 4.8 g fat (0.6 g saturated), 0 mg cholesterol, 9.7 mg sodium

CITRUS SAUCE

- 1 **cup light or regular sour cream**
- 3 **tablespoons orange marmalade**
- 1 **teaspoon grated orange peel**
- 2 **teaspoons prepared horseradish**
  White pepper

In a bowl, mix sour cream, marmalade, peel, and horseradish. Add pepper to taste. Use, or cover and chill up until next day; stir before serving. Makes 1½ cups.

PER TABLESPOON: 23 calories, 0.7 g protein, 2.5 g carbohydrates, 1.3 g fat (0.7 g saturated), 3.3 mg cholesterol, 0.8 mg sodium

BASIL-JICAMA PESTO

- 2 cups lightly packed fresh basil leaves
- 1 cup coarsely chopped jicama
- ½ cup grated parmesan cheese
- ⅓ cup regular-strength chicken broth
- 2 tablespoons olive oil
- 2 tablespoons drained canned capers
- 2 garlic cloves

In a blender or food processor, purée basil, jicama, parmesan, broth, oil, capers, and garlic. Serve, or cover and chill up to 8 hours. Makes about 1½ cups.

PER TABLESPOON: 26 calories, 1.1 g protein, 2 g carbohydrates, 1.7 g fat (0.5 g saturated), 1.3 mg cholesterol, 51 mg sodium

CHOCOLATE FONDUE

In the top of a double boiler over barely simmering water, combine 3 cups **semi-sweet chocolate baking chips,** ½ cup **nonfat milk,** and 3 tablespoons **orange-flavor liqueur** or nonfat milk. Stir often until smoothly melted.

Transfer to serving bowl or chafing dish. Keep warm up to 4 hours in bowl on an electric warming tray or in the hot water jacket of a chafing dish over a low flame; stir occasionally. Spear **fruit** (for kinds and amounts, see facing page) with skewers and dip into fondue. Makes 12 servings.

PER TABLESPOON FONDUE: 49 calories, 0.7 g protein, 5.8 g carbohydrates, 2.4 g fat (0 g saturated), 0.1 mg cholesterol, 1.1 mg sodium

Make-ahead party features fruited quinoa, tomato salad, Mediterranean chicken; pesto and citrus sauce season the dishes. Dessert combines fruit and chocolate fondue.

Ultimate Ribs

GRILLED RIBS, *dripping with sauce, rank high as a favorite summer meal.*

This year as you shop for the meat, you may be surprised at the range of options: some are old standbys, others are new. Leaner cuts, cuts from different parts of the animal, and new ways of cutting all add to the choices. A recent innovation presents precooked marinated ribs that require only reheating.

On the following pages, we offer charts to guide you through shopping for and preparing ribs. Choose the cut you plan to use and follow the suggested methods of cooking (details for each method are on pages 186–190). To give extra flavor or a shiny glaze, add sauce from choices on page 190; use sauces interchangeably on any meat you select.

LOIN VERSUS BELLY CUTS

Imagine an X-ray view of a cow, pig, or lamb to see where ribs come from. From the shoulder back to the rump or leg is the rib-loin section. These ribs attach to the backbone and fall to the stomach area. Ribs along the upper back section of the loin are lean and tender. Those cut from the center of this section (back or prime ribs are best known) have the leanest meat and most uniform size. In pork, they are a by-product of center-cut loin roasts and commonly called baby back pork ribs.

Ribs along the upper back closer to the shoulder or rump have more irregular bone structure and more fat marbling in the meat; they can be slightly chewier and more flavorful. One new pork choice, Danish-cut pork loin back ribs, comes from the blade end near the shoulder. Beef cross-cut back ribs are cut across the bones of a three- to four-rib section to form thin strips with oval cross-sections of bones.

As the bones move lower, closer to the belly, more fat marbles the meat, providing juicy, flavorful eating. Some cuts, especially those near the shoulder or leg, tend to be thicker. Popular names for some of these cuts include beef short ribs, country-style pork ribs, pork spareribs, and lamb riblets.

Where the cut was taken and the way the ribs are cut, as well as the names by which they are sold, vary by store. If you're confused, ask at the meat counter what part of the animal the piece came from.

COOKING RIBS—ON THE GRILL, IN THE OVEN

Back ribs and spareribs (from the center) are generally sold in whole racks; others are often presliced into serving-size pieces. For juicier meat, leave racks whole for cooking; cut ribs apart if you want sauce to completely coat the meat.

Some people swear by the technique of precooking ribs before grilling. It involves simmering or oven-braising the ribs first, then glazing and finishing them on the barbecue. It's an effective technique for fatty cuts; the first cooking renders much of the fat, reducing flare-ups on the grill. Precooking also can tenderize chewier cuts and reduce grill time for thick cuts.

If you have more ribs than you can fit on the grill at one time, you might precook them to shorten barbecue time. However, double-cooking can also draw out more meat juices, resulting in a drier texture in lean or thin cuts.

Barbecuing gives ribs rich browning, a mild smokiness, and a crusty exterior that many connoisseurs favor. Thin pieces and precooked thicker cuts cook well over direct heat. Use indirect heat for thick, raw pieces, fatty cuts, and meats that need more thorough cooking, such as pork.

Oven-barbecuing can glaze meat but can't give charcoal's smokiness and crustness. It's best suited to thicker, fattier pieces that need more cooking time to develop a deep brown color. Thin lean cuts may dry out before they brown.

For complete cooking instructions, see pages 186–190.

To precook ribs on range, place rack or serving-size pieces into pan with water. Cover and simmer until meat is tender.

To precook in oven, lay rack or pieces in baking pan. Add a little water; cover tightly and bake until meat is tender.

On grill, cook raw or precooked ribs until well browned, then brush both sides with sauce of your choice to add flavor.

Barbecued pork spareribs, crusty and shiny with a sticky, sweet, and spicy sauce, are the focus of this ultimate summer meal. Serve the glazed ribs with your favorite potato salad and wedges of juicy watermelon.

Sunset's Guide to Ribs & Best Ways to Cook Them

	Name of cut	Characteristics
BEEF	**Back ribs** (1) (also called prime ribs)	Long to short bony ribs with meat between them. From the center loin, the meat is naturally tender. Allow about 1 pound ribs for each serving.
	Cross-cut back or short ribs (2) (flanken-, Hawaiian-, or Korean-style; or barbecue ribs)	Thin cut enhances tenderness. Fattiness depends on whether cross-cut is from well-marbled short ribs or leaner back ribs. Easiest to find at Asian markets. Allow 1/2 to 3/4 pound ribs per serving.
	Short ribs (3) **English-cut short ribs** (4)	Meaty, fat, juicy pieces have wide, flat rib bones that can be cut at 2- to 3-inch intervals. Short ribs come from the back end of the lower center rib section, English-cut ribs from the front of it. Some short ribs are cut from the chuck and fattier short plate. Allow about 1/2 pound per serving.
LAMB	**Lamb riblets** (5, 6)	This cut, from the belly, is naturally fatty. Have riblets cut to any size; good for finger food. Allow about 1/2 pound per serving.
	Breast of lamb ribs (7)	A breast is a perfect size for 2; however, it's work to find the meat—a real finger dinner. From the belly, the breast is quite fatty. Allow about 3/4 pound per serving.

Best ways to cook, cooking times	Nutrition information

Precooking not needed.

To barbecue over direct heat, cook raw ribs until browned, about 5 minutes a side. Baste with sauce; cook, turning once, until meat between bones is slightly pink (cut to test) and sauce browns, about 4 minutes a side longer.

To barbecue over indirect heat, cook raw ribs until browned, about 10 minutes. Baste with sauce; cook until meat between bones is slightly pink (cut to test) and sauce browns, about 4 minutes a side longer.

To oven-barbecue, cook raw ribs until browned, about 15 minutes. Baste with sauce; cook until meat between bones is slightly pink (cut to test) and sauce browns, about 15 minutes longer.

ESTIMATED PER 1-POUND SERVING WITHOUT SAUCE: 507 calories, 32 g protein, 0 g carbohydrates, 41 g fat (17 g saturated), 119 mg cholesterol, 89 mg sodium

---

Precooking not needed.

To barbecue over direct heat, baste and cook raw ribs, turning often, until well browned, about 10 minutes total.

To oven-barbecue, baste and cook raw ribs, turning often, until well browned, about 20 minutes total.

ESTIMATED PER ½-POUND SERVING WITHOUT SAUCE: 254 calories, 16 g protein, 0 g carbohydrates, 21 g fat (8.5 g saturated), 60 mg cholesterol, 44.5 mg sodium

---

Precooking is necessary.

To precook on the range, simmer until tender when pierced, about 1 hour.

To precook in the oven, bake until tender when pierced, about 1 hour.

To barbecue over direct heat, cook precooked ribs until browned, about 5 minutes a side. Baste with sauce; continue cooking until sauce browns and bubbles, about 4 minutes a side longer.

To barbecue over indirect heat, cook precooked ribs until browned, about 10 minutes. Baste with sauce; continue cooking until sauce browns and bubbles, about 8 minutes longer.

To oven-barbecue, cook precooked ribs until browned, about 10 minutes. Baste with sauce; continue cooking until sauce browns and bubbles, about 8 minutes longer.

ESTIMATED PER ½-POUND SERVING WITHOUT SAUCE: 757 calories, 35 g protein, 0 g carbohydrates, 67 g fat (29 g saturated), 152 mg cholesterol, 80 mg sodium

---

Precooking is necessary.

To precook on the range, simmer until tender when pierced, about 15 minutes.

To precook in the oven, bake until tender when pierced, about 20 minutes.

To barbecue over indirect heat, cook precooked ribs until well browned, about 10 minutes. Baste with sauce; continue cooking until sauce browns and bubbles, about 3 minutes a side longer.

To oven-barbecue, cook precooked ribs until well browned, about 8 minutes a side. Baste with sauce; continue cooking until sauce browns and bubbles, about 6 minutes a side longer.

NUTRITION INFORMATION NOT AVAILABLE

Precooking is necessary.

To precook on the range, simmer until tender when pierced, about 30 minutes.

To precook in the oven, bake until tender when pierced, about 40 minutes.

To barbecue over indirect heat, cook precooked ribs until well browned, about 15 minutes. Baste with sauce; continue cooking until sauce browns and bubbles, about 5 minutes a side longer.

To oven-barbecue, cook precooked ribs until well browned, about 10 minutes a side. Baste with sauce; continue cooking until sauce browns and bubbles, about 3 minutes a side longer.

NUTRITION INFORMATION NOT AVAILABLE

PORK

Name of cut	Characteristics
Pork loin back ribs (8) (baby back ribs)	With less fat and smaller than the traditional pork sparerib, these ribs from the center loin have tender, lean meat. Allow about 3/4 pound per serving.
Danish-cut pork loin back ribs (9)	These ribs, from blade end of the loin near the shoulder, are not uniform in shape; they're less meaty than baby back ribs. Allow about 1 pound per serving.
Spareribs (10)	These are the largest ribs; cut from the belly, they're fattier, juicier, meatier. Slabs come with and without the breast bone. The breast bone meat is not as tender and makes the ribs look chunky. Allow about 3/4 pound per serving.
Country-style pork ribs (11)	Most often from the blade end of the loin, near the shoulder, these are very meaty and fatty; however, amount of fat depends on where the piece is cut from. Allow about 1/2 pound per serving.

Best ways to cook, cooking times	Nutrition information

Precooking is not needed.

To barbecue over direct heat, cook raw ribs until browned, about 8 minutes a side. Baste with sauce; continue cooking until meat between bones is no longer pink (cut to test) and sauce browns, about 5 minutes a side longer.

To barbecue over indirect heat, cook raw ribs until browned, about 20 minutes. Baste with sauce; continue cooking until meat between bones is no longer pink (cut to test) and sauce browns, about 10 minutes a side longer.

To oven-barbecue, cook raw ribs until browned, about 10 minutes a side. Baste with sauce; continue cooking until meat between bones is no longer pink (cut to test) and sauce browns, about 20 minutes longer.

NUTRITION INFORMATION NOT AVAILABLE

Cooking directions are the same as for the pork loin back ribs.

NUTRITION INFORMATION NOT AVAILABLE

Precooking is not necessary but reduces fat.

To precook on the range, simmer until tender when pierced, about 40 minutes.

To precook in the oven, bake until tender when pierced, about 1 hour.

To barbecue over indirect heat, cook raw ribs until browned, about 20 minutes a side (for precooked ribs, about 8 minutes a side). Baste with sauce; continue cooking until meat between bones is no longer pink (cut to test) and sauce browns, about 10 minutes a side longer (for precooked ribs, about 5 minutes a side longer).

To oven-barbecue, cook raw ribs until browned, about 20 minutes a side (for precooked ribs, about 10 minutes a side). Baste with sauce; continue cooking until meat between bones is no longer pink (cut to test) and sauce browns, about 10 minutes a side longer (for precooked ribs, about 5 minutes a side longer).

ESTIMATED PER ¾-POUND SERVING WITHOUT SAUCE: 836 calories, 60 g protein, 0 g carbohydrates, 64 g fat (24 g saturated), 256 mg cholesterol, 196 mg sodium

---

Precooking is advised if grilling over direct heat, optional for indirect or oven barbecuing.

To precook on the range, simmer until tender when pierced, about 1 hour.

To precook in the oven, bake until tender when pierced, about 1 hour.

To barbecue over direct heat, cook precooked ribs until browned, about 5 minutes a side. Baste with sauce; continue cooking until sauce browns and bubbles, about 5 minutes a side longer.

To barbecue over indirect heat, cook raw ribs until browned, about 25 minutes a side (for precooked ribs, about 5 minutes a side). Baste with sauce; continue cooking until meat is no longer pink in thickest part (cut to test) and sauce browns and bubbles, about 8 minutes a side longer (for precooked ribs, about 5 minutes a side longer).

To oven-barbecue, cook raw ribs until browned, about 25 minutes a side (for precooked ribs, about 10 minutes a side). Baste with sauce; continue cooking until meat in thickest part is no longer pink (cut to test) and sauce browns and bubbles, about 10 minutes a side longer (for precooked ribs, about 5 minutes a side longer).

ESTIMATED PER ½-POUND SERVING WITHOUT SAUCE: 312 calories, 17 g protein, 0 g carbohydrates, 27 g fat (10 g saturated), 78 mg cholesterol, 103 mg sodium

To precook ribs on the range. Place 3 to 4 pounds **ribs** (whole racks or serving-size pieces; see chart for choices), trimmed of excess fat, in a 6- to 8-quart pan. Add **water** to cover. Cover pan and simmer just until tender when pierced (see chart for times). Lift out ribs. Reserve pan juices for broth, or discard. (If made ahead, cool, cover, and chill ribs up until next day.) Barbecue ribs (directions follow).

To precook ribs in the oven. Place 3 to 4 pounds **ribs** (whole racks or serving-size pieces; see chart for choices), trimmed of excess fat, in an 11- by 17-inch roasting pan. Add ¾ cup **water.** Cover tightly; bake in a 425° oven until tender when pierced (see chart for times). Lift out ribs. Reserve pan juices for broth, or discard. (If made ahead, cool, cover, and chill ribs up until next day.) Barbecue ribs (directions follow).

To barbecue over direct heat. Place 3 to 4 pounds raw or precooked **ribs** (whole racks or serving-size pieces; see chart for choices), trimmed of excess fat, on a grill 4 to 6 inches above a solid bed of medium coals (you can hold your hand at grill level only 4 to 5 seconds). For thin beef cross-cut ribs, use hot coals (you can hold your hand at grill level only 2 to 3 seconds). Cook as directed on chart.

To barbecue over indirect heat. Mound 50 to 60 charcoal briquets on firegrate in a barbecue with a lid; open the bottom dampers. Ignite and let burn until charcoal is covered with gray ash, about 30 minutes. Using long-handled tongs, bank the briquets on opposite sides of firegrate. Position grill 4 to 6 inches above coals; lightly grease the grill.

Set 3 to 4 pounds raw or precooked **ribs** (whole racks or serving-size pieces; see chart for choices) in the middle of the grill without coals beneath ribs. Add 5 or 6 briquets to each mound of coals. Cover barbecue and adjust dampers to maintain an even heat. Cook as directed on chart.

To oven-barbecue. Place 3 to 4 pounds raw or precooked and drained **ribs** (whole racks or serving-size pieces; see chart for choices) in a single layer in a foil-lined 11- by 17-inch roasting pan. Bake, uncovered, in a 450° oven as directed in chart.

Great Sauces for Ribs

DRESS UP RIBS *with a flavorful sauce. Choose from a sticky spicy glaze, a penetrating marinade that can be thickened for a baste, and a thick pesto topping. All the sauces can be used interchangeably on beef, pork, or lamb ribs.*

STICKY SPICY BARBECUE SAUCE

This sweet sauce browns to a thick sticky glaze as it cooks. Generously baste ribs; it coats 5 to 6 pounds.

Look for hoisin sauce in the Asian food section of your supermarket.

- ½ cup *each* **catsup and hoisin sauce**
- ¼ cup *each* **lemon juice and sugar**
- 4 **cloves garlic, minced or pressed**
- ½ teaspoon *each* **ground cinnamon and ground allspice**
- ¼ teaspoon **cayenne**
- ⅛ teaspoon **ground cloves**

Mix together catsup, hoisin sauce, lemon juice, sugar, garlic, cinnamon, allspice, cayenne, and cloves. If made ahead, cover and chill up to 4 days. Makes 1½ cups.

PER TABLESPOON: 23 calories, 0.4 g protein, 5.5 g carbohydrates, 0.1 g fat (0 g saturated), 0 mg cholesterol, 230 mg sodium

ASIAN-SEASONED BARBECUE SAUCE

This sauce doubles as a marinade and baste. Use it to marinate about 4 pounds raw or precooked ribs in a heavy plastic bag set in a baking pan; chill at least 30 minutes or up until the next day. Lift ribs from marinade, reserving marinade. If desired, cook marinade with cornstarch to make a barbecue baste or thickened sauce to spoon over cooked ribs.

Check an Asian market to find the mirin (sweetened sake) and miso (fermented soy bean paste) or bean sauce used in this recipe.

- ½ cup mirin or cream sherry
- 1 tablespoon grated orange peel
- ½ cup *each* orange juice and soy sauce
- ¼ cup shiro miso or bean sauce (optional)
- ¼ cup firmly packed brown sugar
- 3 tablespoons minced fresh ginger
- 2 teaspoons cornstarch (optional)

To make marinade, mix mirin, peel, juice, soy sauce, miso, sugar, and ginger.

To make a baste or thickened sauce, mix fresh or reserved marinade (preceding) with cornstarch. In a 1- to 1½-quart pan, stir mixture over high heat until it boils, about 4 minutes. Use hot or cool. If made ahead, cover and chill up to 4 days. Makes about 2 cups.

PER TABLESPOON: 22 calories, 0.3 g protein, 4.1 g carbohydrates, 0 g fat, 0 mg cholesterol, 258 mg sodium

HERB PESTO SAUCE

Thickly spread this green sauce on about 3 pounds well-browned ribs. Just before serving, brush with more sauce.

- 2 cups (about 3 oz.) packed fresh basil leaves
- ½ cup chopped green onion
- ⅓ cup loosely packed fresh oregano leaves or 1 tablespoon dry oregano leaves
- ¼ cup grated parmesan cheese
- ¼ cup red wine vinegar
- 2 tablespoons salad oil
- 2 tablespoons fresh rosemary leaves or 1 tablespoon dry rosemary
- ½ teaspoon pepper

In a food processor or blender, whirl basil, green onion, oregano, parmesan, vinegar, oil, rosemary, and pepper until smooth. If made ahead, cover and chill up until the next day. Makes about 1 cup.

PER TABLESPOON: 26 calories, 0.7 g protein, 1.2 g carbohydrates, 2.2 g fat (0.5 g saturated), 1 mg cholesterol, 24 mg sodium

Surprising Coleslaws

COLESLAW IS STUCK WITH *a stolid name and a reputation to match. But don't write it off as a summer standby. With an array of cabbages and seasonings to choose from, it's easy to give this familiar union of shredded cabbage and dressing an element of surprise.*

Here you find napa cabbage with chunks of tart apple, pickled ginger, and caraway seed. The color of red cabbage is echoed and its flavor enhanced by the addition of red onion, pickled beets, sweet red cherries, and crystallized ginger. Humble green cabbage goes sophisticated with fresh spinach, tiny shrimp, and a tart, light yogurt and lemon dressing.

All these salads share the virtues of make-ahead steps and resistance to wilting.

KIM'S CABBAGE SLAW

1 small (about 7 oz.) tart green apple, such as Granny Smith, cored and diced
1/4 cup rice vinegar
1 small (about 6 oz.) onion, thinly sliced
1/2 cup mayonnaise
1/4 cup drained pickled, slivered ginger
1 tablespoon sugar
1 to 2 teaspoons caraway seed
1/2 teaspoon pepper
8 cups (about 1 1/2 lb.) shredded napa cabbage
Thin apple slices dipped in rice vinegar (optional)

In a large bowl, mix diced apple, rice vinegar, onion, mayonnaise, ginger, sugar, caraway seed (to taste), and pepper. Add cabbage and mix well. Pour into serving dish. Garnish with apple slices, if desired. Serve, or cover and chill up to 4 hours. Makes 8 servings. —*Kim Haworth, Brisbane, Calif.*

PER SERVING: 145 calories, 1.6 g protein, 11 g carbohydrates, 11 g fat (1.7 g saturated), 8.1 mg cholesterol, 102 mg sodium

GINGERED RED SLAW

1/2 cup finely chopped red onion
1/3 cup red wine vinegar
1/4 cup salad oil
1/4 cup minced parsley
1/4 cup minced crystallized ginger

1 can (15 or 16 oz.) pickled beets, drained and diced
2 cups pitted sweet red cherries or frozen pitted sweet red cherries
6 cups (about 1 lb.) finely shredded red cabbage
Parsley sprigs (optional)
Salt and pepper

In a large bowl, mix together onion, vinegar, oil, minced parsley, ginger, beets, and cherries. Add cabbage and mix well. Serve, or cover and chill up to 6 hours, then mix again. Garnish slaw with parsley sprigs; offer salt and pepper to season to taste. Makes 8 servings.—*Roxanne E. Chan, Albany, Calif.*

PER SERVING: 169 calories, 1.8 g protein, 26 g carbohydrates, 7.4 g fat (0.9 g saturated), 0 mg cholesterol, 152 mg sodium

SHRIMP & SPINACH SLAW

4 cups (about 1/2 lb.) finely shredded green cabbage
3 cups (about 1/4 lb.) thinly sliced spinach leaves
1 medium-size (about 10 oz.) cucumber, peeled and thinly sliced
2 medium-size celery stalks, rinsed and thinly sliced
Yogurt-lemon dressing (recipe follows)
About 12 large spinach leaves, rinsed and crisped (optional)
3/4 to 1 pound shelled cooked tiny shrimp
Lemon wedges (optional)
Salt and pepper

In a large bowl, combine cabbage, slivered spinach, cucumber, and celery; if made ahead, cover and chill up until the next day.

Add dressing to salad and mix well. Either garnish salad with spinach leaves, or arrange leaves on rim of a platter and mound salad in the center. Sprinkle shrimp onto slaw and add, to taste, juice from lemon wedges and salt and pepper. Makes 8 servings.—*Beth Scherman, Milwaukie, Ore.*

PER SERVING: 97 calories, 12 g protein, 8.3 g carbohydrates, 2.2 g fat (0.5 g saturated), 85 mg cholesterol, 176 mg sodium

Yogurt-lemon dressing. Stir together to blend well 2/3 cup **unflavored nonfat yogurt**, 3 tablespoons **reduced calorie** or regular **mayonnaise**, 1/2 cup thinly sliced **green onion**, 1 teaspoon grated **lemon peel**, 2 tablespoons **lemon juice**, and 1 tablespoon **sugar**. If made ahead, cover and chill up until next day.

Crisp salads for summer barbecues combine napa cabbage with apples (top), red cabbage with beets and cherries, and green cabbage with spinach and shrimp.

Fruit Pies as Works of Art

ARBLING *is the technique used to transform these summer pies into works of art. Intensely flavored fruit purées intertwine in decorative swirls, streaks, and zigzags.*

Start with brightly hued, cooked fruit mixtures, cool to thicken, and spoon into a baked crust. Then pull a chopstick from one color into another to marble.

You can make pies a day ahead, but the designs grow less distinct on standing.

MARBLED SUMMER FRUIT PIE

    9 tablespoons sugar
    ⅓ cup cornstarch
    2 cups peeled, pitted, chopped
       nectarines
    3 tablespoons lemon juice
    2½ cups raspberries, rinsed
       and drained
    2½ cups blackberries or
       boysenberries, rinsed and
       drained
       Press-in lemon crust (recipe
       follows)

Mix sugar and cornstarch; divide into 3 equal portions. In blender or food processor, purée nectarines, 1 tablespoon lemon juice, and a portion of sugar mixture until smooth; pour into a 1- to 3-quart pan. Rinse blender; purée raspberries with 1 tablespoon lemon juice and a portion of sugar mixture until smooth. Press through a fine strainer into another 1- to 3-quart pan; discard seeds. Rinse blender and strainer. Purée blackberries with remaining lemon juice and sugar mixture until smooth; press through strainer into another 1- to 3-quart pan. Discard seeds.

Stir mixtures 1 at a time over medium-high heat, starting with nectarines (which darken), until bubbling vigorously, 3 to 5 minutes. As cooked, place pans in larger bowls of ice water. Stir often until mixtures are thick enough to flow heavily when pans are tilted, 5 to 10 minutes.

Spoon mixtures in alternating, parallel bands into crust, making 2 or 3 bands of each flavor. (Pile more of the same flavor onto each band if you have extra.) Pull tip of a chopstick or knife across bands, drawing 1 color into the next. Wipe tip of tool between pulls; you can alternate direction of pulls, or make all in 1 direction (for pie shown on facing page, we made 12 alternating pulls).

Chill pie, uncovered, until set to touch, at least 3 hours. If made ahead, cover and chill until next day. To serve, push from rim and set on a platter. Makes 8 to 10 servings.

PER SERVING: 280 calories, 3.4 g protein, 45 g carbohydrates, 10 g fat (5.9 g saturated), 46 mg cholesterol, 102 mg sodium

Press-in lemon crust. In a food processor or bowl, mix 1½ cups **all-purpose flour,** ¼ cup **sugar,** and 1½ teaspoons **grated lemon peel.** Add ½ cup (¼ lb.) **butter** or margarine, cut into small pieces; whirl or rub with your fingers until fine crumbs form. Add 1 **large egg;** whirl or stir with a fork until dough holds together. Pat into a smooth ball. Press dough over bottom and up sides of a greased and floured 10½- to 11-inch tart pan with removable rim. Bake in a 300° oven until pale gold, about 35 minutes; let cool.

SHOOTING STAR STRAWBERRY–LEMON CURD PIE

    ⅓ cup butter or margarine
    ½ teaspoon grated lemon peel
    ⅓ cup lemon juice
    1 cup sugar
    3 large eggs
       Press-in lemon crust (recipe
       precedes)
    ⅓ cup cornstarch
    1½ quarts hulled strawberries,
       rinsed and drained

In the top of a double boiler over simmering water, melt butter with lemon peel, lemon juice, and ⅔ cup sugar. Whisk in eggs until blended, then stir until mixture thickly coats a spoon, about 5 minutes. Set aside ¼ cup lemon curd. Spread remaining curd into crust; chill uncovered.

In a blender or food processor, purée remaining sugar, cornstarch, and strawberries (a portion at a time, if needed) until smooth. Pour into a 2- to 3-quart pan. Stir over medium-high heat until boiling rapidly, 6 to 7 minutes. Place pan in a larger bowl of ice water. Stir often until thick enough to flow heavily when pan is tilted, 15 to 20 minutes. Spoon into crust.

Drop 6 or 7 spoonfuls of reserved lemon curd, well apart, on strawberry filling. With tip of a chopstick or knife, draw lemon curd in swirls into strawberry mixture. Chill, uncovered, until set to touch, at least 3 hours. If made ahead, cover and chill until next day. To serve, push from rim and set on a platter. Makes 8 to 10 servings.

PER SERVING: 372 calories, 5.2 g protein, 50 g carbohydrates, 18 g fat (10 g saturated), 126 mg cholesterol, 184 mg sodium

CHERRY-CHOCOLATE SWIRL PIE

    4 cups pitted Bing cherries
    ¼ cup sugar
    2 tablespoons lemon juice
    6 tablespoons cornstarch
    ⅓ cup kirsch
    ¼ teaspoon almond extract
    ½ cup whipping cream
       Chocolate crust (recipe follows)

In a blender or food processor, purée cherries, sugar, lemon juice, and cornstarch until smooth. Pour into a 2- to 3-quart pan. Add kirsch. Bring to a boil over medium-high heat, stirring often; boil and stir for 2 minutes.

Stir almond extract into cherry mixture. Place pan in a larger bowl of ice water. Stir often until mixture flows heavily when pan is tilted, about 20 minutes. Whip cream until soft peaks form. Fold in 1¼ cups of the cherry mixture to blend.

Drop alternating spoonfuls of cream mixture and plain cherry mixture into crust. With tip of a chopstick or knife, swirl streaks of 1 mixture into the other, starting in center and spiraling to edge. Chill, uncovered, until set to touch, at least 3 hours. If made ahead, cover and chill up until next day. To serve, push from rim and set on a platter. Makes 8 to 10 servings.

PER SERVING: 288 calories, 2.4 g protein, 38 g carbohydrates, 13 g fat (6.2 g saturated), 30 mg cholesterol, 203 mg sodium

Chocolate crust. In a blender or food processor, whirl enough **dark chocolate wafer cookies** (about 34) to make 1⅔ cups fine crumbs. Mix with ⅓ cup melted **butter** or margarine and 2 tablespoons **sugar.** Press over bottom and up sides of a 10½- to 11-inch tart pan with a removable rim. Bake in a 300° oven for 30 minutes. Let cool.

Marbling technique transforms fruit purée fillings into artistic masterpieces: (clockwise from top) Marbled Summer Fruit Pie, Cherry-Chocolate Swirl Pie, and Shooting Star Strawberry–Lemon Curd Pie. To create marbling, pull chopstick through bands of purées, drawing one color into another. Chill to set fillings.

East Meets West in the Napa Valley

REFRESHING CONTRASTS *in tastes, textures, and cuisines mark this dinner created by Japanese-born Mitsuko Shrem, who deftly weaves Asian ingredients into a contemporary Napa Valley meal.*

In three dishes—chilled tofu, won ton ravioli, and beef fillet—relatives of the onion family enhance the compatibility of the foods with wines made by her husband, Jan, at Clos Pegase in Calistoga. Strawberries form the base of a light dessert.

Simple recipes with make-ahead steps, coupled with ready-to-use items like tofu and won ton skins, help the meal come together smoothly.

Appetizer. Soft cold tofu flavored with olive oil, lemon juice, salt, and chives tastes like a delicate, savory custard. Serve with a dry Sauvignon Blanc or Fumé Blanc.

Pasta course. Cheese and leeks fill ravioli made with won ton skins. They nestle in a paprika cream sauce with sautéed shallots. Chardonnay complements the flavors.

CHILLED TOFU TIMBALE WITH CHIVES

- 4 tablespoons lemon juice
- 2 tablespoons olive oil
  Coarse salt
- 1 pound cold soft tofu, drained and rinsed
- 2 tablespoons chopped chives
  Chive spears (optional)

On 4 rimmed salad plates, spoon equal amounts of lemon juice and oil; swirl together and sprinkle liberally with salt. Cut tofu into 8 equal pieces; set 2 on each plate. Garnish with chives. Makes 4 servings.

PER SERVING: 124 calories, 5.4 g protein, 4.1 g carbohydrates, 9.8 g fat (0.9 g saturated), 0 mg cholesterol, 11 mg sodium

WON TON RAVIOLI WITH PAPRIKA CREAM

- 1/2 cup minced shallots or onion
- 2 teaspoons *each* olive oil and butter or margarine
- 1/2 cup whipping cream
- 2 tablespoons lemon juice
- 2 to 3 tablespoons water
  About 1/2 teaspoon paprika
  Won tons (directions follow)
  Thin leek or green onion slices

In a 10- to 12-inch frying pan over medium-high heat, frequently stir shallots with oil and butter until limp, about 5 minutes. Add cream, juice, 2 tablespoons water, and paprika. Stir until bubbling; set aside and keep warm.

Meanwhile, bring 2 quarts water to boiling in a 4- to 5-quart pan. Add won tons and cook on high heat, uncovered, until dough is tender to bite, about 2 minutes. Thin sauce to original consistency with water, if needed; spoon equally onto 4 warm plates. With a slotted spoon, lift out won tons; put 3 on each plate. Garnish with leeks and paprika. Makes 4 servings.

PER SERVING: 239 calories, 6.2 g protein, 18 g carbohydrates, 17 g fat (7.2 g saturated), 47 mg cholesterol, 91 mg sodium

Won tons. Lay 12 **won ton skins** flat. In center of each, mound equal portions of 1/4 cup shredded **jack cheese** and 2 tablespoons minced **leeks**. Rub rims with a paste of 1 tablespoon *each* **all-purpose flour** and **water**. Fold won tons over filling, aligning edges and pressing to seal. If made ahead, cover and chill up to 8 hours.

Entrée. Soy-seasoned grilled beef tenderloin, served hot or cold, is strewn with warm wilted green onions; accompany with steamed cauliflower. Offer with Cabernet Sauvignon.

TATAKI FILLET

> 1 **piece (1 to 1½ lb.) fat-trimmed beef tenderloin**
> 3 **tablespoons soy sauce**
> **About 3 tablespoons olive oil**
> 1 **to 1½ cups thinly sliced green onions**

Mix meat with soy and 1 tablespoon of the oil. Cover and chill at least 30 minutes or until the next day.

Cook meat on a grill 4 to 6 inches above a solid bed of medium-hot coals (you can hold your hand at grill level only 3 to 4 seconds) just until very rare (cut to test), about 15 minutes; turn to brown evenly. Put meat on a platter and keep warm in a 150° oven up to 30 minutes. Or, if made ahead, cover and chill up until next day.

Just before serving, slice meat. Also place a 10- to 12-inch frying pan on high heat. Add remaining oil; when hot, add onions. Stir just until slightly wilted,

about 30 seconds. Spoon over meat. Makes 4 servings.

PER SERVING: 267 calories, 25 g protein, 2.7 g carbohydrates, 17 g fat (4.3 g saturated), 72 mg cholesterol, 441 mg sodium

STRAWBERRY FOAM

In a food processor or blender, purée 2½ cups sliced **strawberries;** add **sugar** to taste. In a 1- to 2-cup pan, mix 1 envelope (2 teaspoons) **unflavored gelatin** with ½ cup **water;** let stand until liquid is absorbed, then stir over medium heat until melted. Whirl into strawberries.

Pour mixture into a bowl; cover and chill until thickened but not firm, about 30 minutes. With a mixer, beat mixture until foamy; pour into a 4- by 8-inch pan (or individual bowls). Cover; chill until firm, 2 hours or until next day. To unmold, dip pan in hot water until edges barely melt; invert onto plate. Cut in 4 pieces; put in bowls. Garnish with whole **strawberries.** Makes 4 servings.

PER SERVING: 71 calories, 2.1 g protein, 16 g carbohydrates, 0.4 g fat (0 g saturated), 0 mg cholesterol, 2.6 mg sodium

Dessert. Whipped, strawberry-rich gelatin dessert makes cool finale to dinner.

LIGHTENING UP SUNSET CLASSICS: Navajo Tacos

IN KEEPING WITH *the worthy goal of eating well but lighter, we've modified our popular recipe for Navajo tacos (August 1988, page 54) to trim fat but retain the wholesome flavors and satisfying bulk.*

The fried taco shell is now baked or pan-toasted. Braise-deglazing gives the chili rich flavor. Yogurt replaces sour cream, and salsa is naturally low in calories.

LIGHTENED-UP NAVAJO TACOS

    Taco shells (recipe follows)
²/₃ cup shredded cheddar cheese
    Chili beans (recipe follows)
¹/₂ **pound iceberg lettuce, finely shredded** (about 4 cups)
    Fresh salsa (recipe follows)
¹/₂ cup **unflavored nonfat yogurt**

Lay 1 taco shell on each of 6 dinner plates. Top equally with cheese, chili, and lettuce. Spoon ¹/₄ cup salsa and 1 tablespoon yogurt onto each taco; add remaining salsa and yogurt to taste. Makes 6 servings.

PER REVISED SERVING: 525 calories, 33 g protein, 62 g carbohydrates, 16 g fat (5.6 g saturated), 70 mg cholesterol, 458 mg sodium
PER ORIGINAL SERVING: 815 calories, 43 g protein, 65 g carbohydrates, 42 g fat (18 g saturated), 106 mg cholesterol, 1,112 mg sodium

Taco shells. Mix 2 cups **all-purpose flour,** ¹/₂ cup **instant nonfat dry milk,** and 1 tablespoon **baking powder.** Add 2 tablespoons **shortening.** Rub with fingers into coarse crumbs. Add ³/₄ cup **water** and stir with a fork until dough clings together. Knead on a well-floured board until dough feels smooth, 2 to 3 minutes. Divide into 6 equal portions; cover with plastic wrap. Shape 1 portion into a ball, then roll or pat it on a floured board to make a 6- to 7-inch round. Cover with plastic wrap; repeat to shape remaining dough.

For crisp shells, place rounds on 2 lightly greased baking sheets (12- by 15-in. size). Bake in a 450° oven until puffed and browned, about 12 minutes.

For soft shells, place an 8- to 10-inch nonstick frying pan over medium heat. When pan is hot enough to make a drop of water sizzle, lay 1 dough round in pan. Cook until speckled brown on bottom, about 1¹/₂ minutes. Turn over and cook until bottom is speckled brown, 1 to 1¹/₂ minutes longer. Transfer to a platter and keep warm in a 150° to 200° oven. Repeat until all are cooked.

Use shells warm. If made ahead, let cool, then wrap airtight. Store at room temperature up until next day. To reheat, lay in a single layer on baking sheets; bake in a 375° oven until hot, about 5 minutes.

Chili beans. Sort and discard debris from 1 cup **dry Great Northern beans** or pinto beans; rinse well. Place beans and 1 quart **water** in a 3- to 4-quart pan over high heat; bring to a boil. Cook, uncovered, for 10 minutes. Remove from heat, cover, and let stand 1 hour. Drain beans; set aside.

Into pan on medium heat, crumble 1 pound **ground turkey breast;** add 1 large **onion,** chopped. Cover tightly and simmer until meat and onions exude juices, 15 to 20 minutes; stir occasionally. Uncover and boil over high heat, stirring often, until liquid evaporates and browned bits stick to pan. Stir in ¹/₄ cup water, scraping to release browned bits. Boil, stirring often, until liquid is gone and browned bits stick. Add ¹/₄ cup water and repeat.

Add 3 cups **regular-strength chicken broth** to pan; stir to free browned bits. Add beans; 1 tablespoon **chili powder;** 2 cloves **garlic,** pressed or minced; and 2 teaspoons *each* **ground cumin, dry oregano leaves,** and **dry basil leaves.** Bring to a boil over high heat. Cover; simmer until beans are tender to bite, 1¹/₂ to 2 hours. Boil, uncovered, on high heat until reduced to 4 cups, 5 to 7 minutes; stir often. Use; or cool, cover, and chill up to 3 days. To reheat, stir often over medium heat until simmering. Add **salt** to taste.

Fresh salsa. Mix 1 pound cored and chopped **Roma-type tomatoes,** ¹/₂ cup minced **cilantro** (coriander), 4 minced **green onions,** ¹/₄ cup **lime juice,** and 1 or 2 (to taste) minced **fresh jalapeño chilies.** Makes about 3 cups.

PER ¹/₄ CUP: 10 calories, 0.5 g protein, 2.4 g carbohydrates, 0.1 g fat (0 g saturated), 0 mg cholesterol, 4.3 mg sodium

Piled high with cheddar cheese, seasoned chili, shredded lettuce, fresh salsa, and yogurt, revised Navajo tacos are about 35 percent leaner than original version.

Turkey Burger in a Pocket

FOR A DIFFERENT VERSION *of meat on a bun, tuck turkey burgers into pita bread with tomatoes, onion, and cucumber.*

TURKEY BURGERS WITH SALAD

- 1 medium-size red onion
- 1 teaspoon salad oil
- 1/2 pound ground turkey
- 1/2 teaspoon ground cumin
  Fresh-ground pepper
- 1/4 cup water
- 2 tablespoons white wine vinegar or sherry vinegar
- 2 whole-wheat pocket breads (each about 6 in. wide)
- 1 small (about 6 oz.) cucumber, peeled and thinly sliced
- 2 small tomatoes, sliced
  Yogurt sauce (recipe follows)

Cut onion in half horizontally. Chop half; thinly slice remaining half, separate into rings, and set aside.

In a 12- to 14-inch nonstick frying pan, combine chopped onion and oil. Stir often over medium-high heat until onion is limp, about 7 minutes. Transfer to a bowl. Let cool slightly; mix with turkey, cumin, and a generous sprinkling of pepper. Shape mixture into 2 patties.

Place patties in pan and cook over medium-high heat to brown both sides, about 8 minutes total; turn once. Drain and discard fat. Add water and vinegar. Reduce heat, cover, and simmer until almost all liquid has evaporated and patties are no longer pink in center (cut to test), about 7 minutes.

Meanwhile, wrap pocket breads in foil and place in a 250° oven until hot, about 15 minutes. In a bowl, mix together cucumber, onion rings, tomatoes, and half the yogurt sauce.

Offer turkey patties with pocket breads, cucumber mixture, and remaining yogurt sauce; assemble elements into sandwiches. Makes 2 servings.

PER SERVING: 498 calories, 35 g protein, 57 g carbohydrates, 15 g fat (4 g saturated), 59 mg cholesterol, 539 mg sodium

Yogurt sauce. In a small bowl, stir together 1 cup **unflavored nonfat yogurt**, 1/4 cup **white wine vinegar** or sherry vinegar, and 2 tablespoons **dry dill weed.**

Pan-browned turkey burger tucks into whole-wheat pocket bread with yogurt-dressed cucumbers, sliced tomatoes, and rings of red onion. Corn on the cob and fresh fruit are good accompaniments.

Cooking with Corn, Fresh off the Cob

THE SEASON'S BEST *fresh corn on the cob is available now. Here are three recipes designed to take advantage of its delicate sweetness and textural quality.*

Salads highlighting corn off the cob make up two of the recipes—one is part of a main dish from the grill with shrimp, and the other is a simple first course with cheese. In the third, a creamy risotto is laced with corn and fresh sage.

GRILLED CORN & BLACK BEAN SALAD WITH SHRIMP & CORNBREAD TRIANGLES

To make cornbread triangles, use your favorite cornbread recipe (based on about 1 cup each cornmeal and flour) or an 8- to 13-ounce mix and bake bread in an 8-inch-square baking pan.

- 16 colossal-size shrimp (about 15 per lb.), shelled, deveined, and rinsed
  Honey-lime marinade (recipe follows)
- 6 tablespoons olive oil
- 3 medium-size ears (about 1½ lb. total) yellow or white corn, husks and silk removed
- 1 can (15 oz.) black beans, drained
- ½ cup thinly sliced green onion
- 1 tablespoon minced fresh cilantro (coriander)
- 1 baked cornbread square (see preceding)
- 1 large (about ½ lb.) firm-ripe avocado
  Fresh cilantro sprigs

Place shrimp in a heavy plastic bag; pour ⅓ cup marinade over shellfish. Seal bag and rotate. Chill at least 30 minutes or up to 6 hours; turn occasionally. Blend remaining marinade with oil; set aside.

Place corn on a grill 4 to 6 inches above a solid bed of medium coals (you should be able to hold your hand at grill level only 4 to 5 seconds). Cover barbecue, open dampers, and cook, turning corn occasionally, until lightly browned on all sides, 10 to 15 minutes. Remove from grill and let cool. Add 6 to 8 briquets to the fire.

Meanwhile, thread 4 shrimp on each of 4 slender wooden skewers. Cut corn off cob and place kernels in a large bowl. Add beans, onion, minced cilantro, and reserved marinade mixture; blend well.

Cut cornbread into 4 equal squares; cut each piece diagonally, then split

horizontally. When coals are medium-hot (you should be able to hold your hand at grill level only 3 to 4 seconds), lay ½ of bread cut side down on grill until toasted, about 1 minute; turn and toast other side, about 1 minute longer. Remove from grill; keep warm. Repeat to grill remaining bread.

Place shrimp on grill and cook, brushing with excess marinade in bag and turning once, until opaque but moist-looking in center (cut to test), 7 to 8 minutes total. Remove from grill and keep warm.

Cut avocado in half; pit and peel. Cut each half lengthwise in half. Mound equal portions of the corn salad on each of 4 dinner plates. Arrange shrimp skewers, cornbread triangles, and avocado wedges alongside. Garnish with cilantro sprigs. Makes 4 main-dish servings.

PER SERVING: 866 calories, 38 g protein, 84 g carbohydrates, 44 g fat (6.9 g saturated), 179 mg cholesterol, 699 mg sodium

Honey-lime marinade. Combine 1 teaspoon grated **lime peel**; ⅓ cup **lime juice**; 2 tablespoons **distilled white vinegar**; 1 tablespoon **honey**; 2 teaspoons **Dijon mustard**; 1 teaspoon **ground cumin**; 2 cloves **garlic**, minced; and 1 fresh **jalapeño chili**, stemmed, seeded, and minced.

FRESH CORN ON ROMAINE WITH PARMESAN

- 2 medium-size ears (about 1 lb. total) yellow or white corn, husks and silk removed
- 2 small heads (about 1¼ lb. total) romaine lettuce, rinsed and crisped
- 1 small (about 5 oz.) red bell pepper, stemmed, seeded, and cut into slivers
- 1 piece (about 2 oz.) imported or domestic parmesan cheese
  Balsamic-mustard dressing (recipe follows)

In a 5- to 6-quart pan, bring about 2 quarts water to a boil on high heat. Add corn and cook, covered, until hot, 4 to 6 minutes. Drain and let cool. Cut kernels from cob with a sharp knife.

Reserve large romaine leaves for another use. Arrange small leaves on 4 salad plates. Scatter equal portions bell pepper slivers and corn kernels over greens.

Pull a cheese-shaving slicer or vegetable peeler over the cheese to make thin strips; gently lay cheese on salads. Drizzle the dressing equally onto each salad. Makes 4 servings.

PER SERVING: 263 calories, 9.1 g protein, 14 g carbohydrates, 20 g fat (4.6 g saturated), 14 mg cholesterol, 297 mg sodium

Balsamic-mustard dressing. Combine 3 tablespoons **olive oil** with 2 tablespoons **balsamic** or red wine **vinegar,** 2 tablespoons **mayonnaise,** 1 teaspoon **coarse-grain mustard,** 1½ teaspoons minced **shallots,** and **pepper** to taste.

CORN RISOTTO WITH SAGE

- 3 medium-size ears (about 1½ lb. total) yellow or white corn, husks and silk removed
- 1 tablespoon butter or margarine
- 1 large onion, finely chopped
- 1 cup short-grain white rice (such as arborio or pearl)
- 3½ cups regular-strength chicken broth (if salted, use half broth and half water)
- ¼ cup grated parmesan cheese
- ¼ cup shredded fontina cheese
- 3 tablespoons chopped fresh sage leaves or 2 teaspoons dry sage leaves
  Fresh sage leaves

With a sharp knife, cut kernels from cobs; set aside kernels and cobs.

In a 10- to 12-inch frying pan, melt butter over medium heat. Add onion and cook, stirring often until limp, about 5 minutes. Add rice and stir until opaque and milky-looking, about 2 minutes. Stir in about ¾ of the corn kernels.

Mix in broth. Bring to a boil, stirring often. Reduce heat and simmer, uncovered, stirring occasionally until rice is tender and most of the liquid is absorbed, 20 to 25 minutes. Lower heat and stir more often as mixture thickens.

Remove rice from heat. Holding cobs over rice, with dull side of knife scrape them lengthwise so corn juices fall into rice mixture. Gently stir in parmesan, fontina, and chopped sage; let stand until cheese melts, about 2 minutes.

Transfer to a warm rimmed platter or shallow bowl. Scatter remaining corn over risotto; garnish with sage leaves. Makes 4 or 5 servings.

PER SERVING: 279 calories, 9.3 g protein, 45 g carbohydrates, 7.2 g fat (3.7 g saturated), 16 mg cholesterol, 189 mg sodium

Grapes as Team Players

ALTHOUGH DELICIOUS UNADORNED, sweet, crisp grapes flaunt their virtues to an even greater degree when they're mixed with other foods.

Combine the grapes' natural sugars with a few tart tomatillos for a sweet-sour fruit relish to complement smoked pork chops. Grapes also add a cool moistness to the jicama salad's crunchy snap. And the grapes' natural acidity balances the sweetness in the chocolate bonbon dessert.

You'll find grapes in good supply now. Look for plump ones firmly attached to fresh, pliable stems.

GRAPES WITH SMOKED PORK CHOPS

- 3 cups (about 1 lb.) green seedless grapes, rinsed
- 1½ cups (6 to 7 oz.) small tomatillos, husks removed, rinsed and cut in half
- 4 smoked pork chops (about 1¾ lb. total)
  Small clusters of green seedless grapes

Put the 3 cups of grapes and the tomatillos in a 10- to 12-inch frying pan. Cover and cook over medium heat until grapes are soft, 10 to 15 minutes. Add pork chops and cook, uncovered, over high heat; turn chops and stir grapes occasionally. As liquid reduces, lower heat to medium; stir often until chops are lightly browned and grapes are soft and lightly browned, 12 to 18 minutes. Transfer chops to platter and spoon the grape mixture over the meat. Garnish with grape clusters. Makes 4 servings.

PER SERVING: 380 calories, 29 g protein, 27 g carbohydrates, 18 g fat (5.6 g saturated), 91 mg cholesterol, 2,095 mg sodium

JICAMA & GRAPE SALAD

- 1¼ pounds jicama, peeled and cut into matchstick-size sticks (about 4 cups)
- ¾ pound (about 2 cups) green, red, or black seedless grapes, rinsed and cut in half
  Mint dressing (recipe follows)
  Fresh mint sprigs (optional)

Crisp sticks of jicama and juicy red seedless grapes team up with a mint dressing for a refreshing light salad. Garnish with a sprig of fresh mint.

In a bowl, mix jicama, grapes, and mint dressing. Pour onto a platter. Garnish with mint sprigs. Makes 6 servings.

PER SERVING: 89 calories, 1.7 g protein, 21 g carbohydrates, 0.6 g fat (0.1 g saturated), 0 mg cholesterol, 8.8 mg sodium

Mint dressing. Mix ⅓ cup **lime juice,** 2 tablespoons chopped **fresh mint leaves** or 1 tablespoon dry mint leaves, 2 tablespoons **water,** 1 tablespoon **sugar,** ½ teaspoon **cumin seed** (crushed), and **fish sauce** (*nuoc mam* or *nam pla*) or salt to taste.

CHOCOLATE GRAPE BONBONS

- 1 cup semisweet or white chocolate baking chips
- 2 teaspoons shortening
- 2 dozen large (5 to 7 oz.) green, red, or black seedless grapes, rinsed and patted dry
- 1½ tablespoons minced crystallized ginger

In the top of a double boiler, combine chocolate and shortening; place over simmering water. Stir often until chocolate is melted and smooth, about 2 minutes.

Or, in a microwave oven, combine chocolate and shortening in a small microwave-safe bowl. Cook on half-power (50 percent), stirring occasionally, just until chocolate is melted and smooth, 3 to 4 minutes. (If white chocolate begins to firm up and doesn't appear to melt, let cool for a few minutes, then stir until smooth.)

On a waxed paper–lined, 12- by 15-inch baking sheet, drop 1-teaspoon portions of melted chocolate about 1½ inches apart. Set 1 grape on each puddle; place equal portions of ginger on chocolate. Chill until firm, at least 10 minutes or up until the next day; cover when chocolate is firm. Remove from paper and serve. Makes 24.

PER SERVING: 50 calories, 0.6 g protein, 6.8 g carbohydrates, 2.4 g fat (0.9 g saturated), 0.1 mg cholesterol, 0.8 mg sodium

Nectarines, blueberries, and sour cream bake to make a pie that's good for brunch or dessert.

BLUEBERRY & NECTARINE CREAM PIE

- 1 frozen 9-inch deep-dish pie shell
- 2 cups blueberries
- 1 cup sour cream
- 2 teaspoons cornstarch
- 4 cups peeled and sliced firm-ripe nectarines (about 2 lb. total)
- 1 teaspoon vanilla
- 1/2 cup granulated sugar
- 3 tablespoons quick-cooking tapioca
- 1/3 cup firmly packed brown sugar
- 1/2 cup all-purpose flour
- 3 tablespoons butter or margarine, melted

Bake pie shell in a 350° oven until deep golden, about 35 minutes.

Rinse blueberries and drain. Smoothly blend sour cream and cornstarch, then mix with blueberries, nectarines, and vanilla. Stir granulated sugar with tapioca, then stir into the fruit mixture; pour into warm pie shell and set aside.

With a fork or your fingers, combine the brown sugar, flour, and butter. Squeeze to form a ball, then crumble in almond-size pieces over filling.

Bake pie in a 350° oven until filling is bubbling in center and topping is well browned, about 1 hour. Cool at least 3 hours; if made ahead, cover and chill up until next day. Makes 6 to 8 servings. —*Sandy Wesoky, Englewood, Colo.*

PER SERVING: 419 calories, 4.4 g protein, 62 g carbohydrates, 19 g fat (8.3 g saturated), 24 mg cholesterol, 202 mg sodium

---

Golden mango dressing tops salad of shredded carrot, bean sprouts, fresh basil.

CARROT & BEAN SPROUT SALAD

- 1 medium-size (about 11 oz.) firm-ripe mango, peeled
- 1/2 cup orange juice
  About 2 teaspoons fish sauce (nuoc mam or nam pla) or soy sauce
- 1 clove garlic, minced or pressed
- 1/4 teaspoon curry powder
- 4 medium-size (about 1/2 lb. total) carrots
- 4 cups (about 3/4 lb.) bean sprouts, rinsed
- 1/4 cup minced fresh basil leaves
- 1 tablespoon lemon juice
  About 12 large leaves of red-leaf lettuce, rinsed and crisped

Cut mango from pit into a food processor or blender. Add orange juice, 1 teaspoon fish sauce, garlic, and curry; purée until smooth. Scrape into a serving bowl or individual bowls; serve, or cover and chill up until next day.

Peel and finely shred carrots; mix with bean sprouts, basil, lemon juice, and fish sauce to taste.

On a platter or salad plates, arrange lettuce leaves. Evenly divide carrot mixture among leaves. Spoon mango dressing over salad to taste. Makes 6 servings.—*Sydni Rozenfeld, San Francisco.*

PER SERVING: 75 calories, 3.1 g protein, 17 g carbohydrates, 0.5 g fat (0.1 g saturated), 0 mg cholesterol, 19 mg sodium

---

Green tomatillos make a tart sauce to layer with tortillas and cheeses.

CHICKEN TORTILLA CASSEROLE

  Green sauce (recipe follows)
- 8 corn tortillas (6 to 7 in. wide), cut into 1-inch-wide strips
- 1/2 pound shredded jack cheese
- 2 cups shredded cooked chicken
- 2 cups low-fat cottage cheese
- 1/4 cup milk
- 1/4 cup grated parmesan cheese

Spread 1/3 of the sauce in a 9- by 13-inch baking dish. Layer with 1/2 the tortillas, 1/2 the jack cheese, all the chicken, and 1/2 the remaining sauce. Make layers of remaining tortillas, jack cheese, and sauce. In a blender or food processor, purée cottage cheese and milk; spread on top. Sprinkle with parmesan. Bake in a 400° oven until bubbling in center, about 25 minutes. Makes 6 to 8 servings.—*J. Hill, Sacramento.*

PER SERVING: 324 calories, 29 g protein, 20 g carbohydrates, 14 g fat (1.7 g saturated), 1 mg cholesterol, 520 mg sodium

Green sauce. Husk and rinse 1 1/2 pounds **tomatillos.** Cook, shaking often, in a 10- to 12-inch frying pan over medium-high heat until tinged with brown and tender, 4 to 6 minutes; pour into a blender or food processor. In pan, boil 3/4 cup **regular-strength chicken broth;** 1 small **onion,** chopped; and 4 cloves **garlic,** chopped, until the liquid evaporates. Purée with tomatillos and 2 cups **fresh cilantro** (coriander).

Summer Fruit & Almond Salad

- ½ cup sliced almonds
- ½ pound jicama
- ¼ cup orange juice
- 2 tablespoons lemon juice
- 1 teaspoon *each* poppy seed and sugar
- ¼ teaspoon almond extract
- 2 cups cubed, seeded watermelon
- 2 cups cubed cantaloupe
- 1 cup seedless grapes, halved
- 1 cup strawberries, rinsed, hulled, and sliced
- 12 to 16 large lettuce leaves, rinsed and crisped
- 1 large (about ¼ lb.) kiwi fruit

In a 10- to 12-inch frying pan, shake almonds often over medium-high heat until toasted, about 3 minutes; pour from pan and set aside.

Peel jicama; rinse and cut into matchstick pieces. Mix in a large bowl with orange and lemon juices, poppy seed, sugar, and almond extract. Add watermelon, cantaloupe, grapes, and strawberries; gently mix.

Arrange lettuce on 6 to 8 salad plates, then evenly mound fruit on leaves. Peel and thinly slice kiwi fruit. Sprinkle salad with kiwi fruit and almonds. Makes 6 to 8 servings—*Dianne Percefull, Lake Forest, Calif.*

PER SERVING: 118 calories, 3.2 g protein, 20 g carbohydrates, 3.9 g fat (0.3 g saturated), 0 mg cholesterol, 13 mg sodium

Citrus juices and almonds flavor colorful fruit and jicama salad.

Salmon with Chive & Herb Sauce

- 1 cup regular-strength chicken broth
- 2 teaspoons *each* minced fresh tarragon leaves and fresh thyme leaves, or ½ teaspoon *each* of the dry herbs
- 4 salmon steaks, each about 6 ounces and 1 inch thick
- 1 clove garlic, minced or pressed
- 1 teaspoon cornstarch
- 3 tablespoons thinly sliced chives
- Salt and pepper
- Lemon wedges

In a 10- to 12-inch frying pan over high heat, bring broth, tarragon, and thyme to a boil. Lay salmon in pan and reduce heat to simmering; cover pan. Cook until fish is opaque but still moist-looking in thickest part (cut to test), 10 to 15 minutes. Lift steaks onto a platter; cover and keep warm.

Add garlic to pan; boil on high heat, uncovered, until liquid is reduced to ½ cup, 3 to 4 minutes. Mix the cornstarch with 2 tablespoons of water and stir into pan; stir until boiling. Mix in chives and pour sauce over the salmon. Season servings individually with salt, pepper, and juice from the lemon wedges. Makes 4 servings.—*Eleanor Strowbridge, Corvallis, Ore.*

PER SERVING: 254 calories, 35 g protein, 1.5 g carbohydrates, 11 g fat (1.7 g saturated), 94 mg cholesterol, 89 mg sodium

Salmon steaks have lean sauce from herb-seasoned poaching broth.

Hilary's Do-it-yourself Candy Bars

- 2 cups semisweet chocolate baking chips
- ½ cup raisins
- ½ cup sweetened shredded dry coconut
- ½ cup chopped salted peanuts
- ½ cup oven-toasted rice cereal

In a microwave-safe bowl, heat the chocolate in a microwave oven on full power (100 percent) for 1 minute; stir. Repeat until the chocolate is melted and smooth, 3 to 4 minutes total. Stir in the raisins, coconut, peanuts, and rice cereal.

Cover a flat tray with waxed paper. Spoon chocolate mixture onto paper into 8 bars, each about 1 inch wide and 5 inches long; smooth with a spatula. Chill until firm to touch, about 1 hour. Eat, or wrap each bar in plastic wrap and chill up to 2 weeks. Makes 8.—*Hilury Golden, Lakeport, Calif.*

PER BAR: 332 calories, 5.8 g protein, 40 g carbohydrates, 18 g fat (2 g saturated), 0.5 mg cholesterol, 114 mg sodium

Candy bars are full of nuts, cereal, coconut, raisins.

SALMON IS NOT AS EXPENSIVE as truffles or the finest Strasbourg pâté, but it is seldom inexpensive enough to warrant taking chances. For some people, though, fortune smiles and they have access to goodly quantities of salmon. Such a person is Mark Crain, whose uncle gave him 600 pounds of the fish—and with it a free rein to experiment.

"His uncle gave him 600 pounds of salmon..."

Crain reports that simpler preparations produce the best results, then sends this recipe as an example. Drunken salmon (the term is poetic rather than literal) starts off a little like gravlax, with dill, pepper, and a bit of liquor, but it ends up as barbecued salmon with a sauce based on the marinade. Such simplicity should be encouraged.

DRUNKEN SALMON

- 4 **salmon steaks, each about 1 inch thick (1¼ to 1½ lb. total)**
- ½ **teaspoon dry dill weed or dry tarragon leaves**
- 1 **teaspoon coarsely ground pepper**
- 1 **teaspoon salad oil**
- 2 **tablespoons lemon juice**
- ¼ **cup Scotch or Bourbon**
  Lemon wedges
  Salt

Rinse salmon, drain, and lay in a dish about 9 by 13 inches. Mix dill, pepper, oil, lemon juice, and Scotch; pour evenly over salmon. Cover and chill for 1 to 3 hours. Lift salmon from dish, draining. Pour marinade into a 1- to 1½-quart pan.

Place steaks on a lightly greased grill 4 to 6 inches above a solid bed of medium-hot coals (you can hold your hand at grill level only 3 to 4 seconds). Cook for 4 minutes. Brush salmon with marinade, turn with a wide spatula, and brush again.

Continue to cook until salmon is opaque but still moist-looking in center of thickest part (cut to test), about 6 minutes longer.

When you turn salmon, set pan with marinade on grill beside fish. Transfer salmon to a platter. Pour hot marinade over fish. Accompany with lemon wedges and salt to add to taste. Makes 4 servings.

PER SERVING: 232 calories, 28 g protein, 0.9 g carbohydrates, 10 g fat (1.5 g saturated), 78 mg cholesterol, 65 mg sodium

Pine Grove, Calif.

MARK KEMP KNOWS *about the calories, fats, and sugars that most of us consume, but his attitude toward dessert is sensible: when he indulges, he will yield only to major temptation. His chocolate cheesecake is certainly that, combining the delights of butter cookies, cheesecake, and chocolate. There is no skimping on calories here. (Well, neufchâtel cheese is a bit lower in calories than cream cheese, but you wouldn't know by its taste.)*

CHOCOLATE CHEESECAKE

- 1 **package (about 7¼ oz.) butter cookies**
- ¼ **cup (⅛ lb.) butter or margarine, melted**
- 2 **cups (12-oz. package) semisweet chocolate baking chips**
- ⅔ **cup sugar**
- 1 **tablespoon all-purpose flour**
- 2 **large packages (8 oz. each) neufchâtel (light cream) cheese**
- 2 **large eggs**
- 1 **tablespoon vanilla**
- 1 **tablespoon sweet marsala or sweet sherry**

In a food processor or blender, whirl cookies to make fine crumbs. Pour into a 9-inch cheesecake pan with removable rim. Add butter, mix well, then press crumbs evenly over pan bottom and about 1 inch up pan sides; set aside.

In a food processor or blender, whirl ½ the chocolate chips. In processor or a mixer bowl, combine ground chocolate, sugar, and flour; whirl or stir to mix. Add cheese cut into chunks, then eggs, vanilla, and marsala. Whirl or beat until well mixed.

Scatter ½ the remaining chocolate into crust, then pour cheesecake batter into pan; spread batter level. Sprinkle remaining chocolate over batter.

Bake in a 300° oven until cake jiggles only slightly in the center when gently shaken, 1¼ to 1½ hours. Let cool; then cover and chill until cold, at least 4 hours or up to 2 days. Makes about 16 servings.

PER SERVING: 318 calories, 6 g protein, 33 g carbohydrates, 18 g fat (7.2 g saturated), 66 mg cholesterol, 205 mg sodium

Eugene, Ore.

RESPECT FOR VEGETABLES *is one mark of a good cook, and Floyd Paige is a fast learner. In just four months of married life, he's leaned away from meat and potatoes toward a more creative approach to what appears on the dinner plate. He devised this green bean, almond, bacon, and cheddar cheese combination to impress his bride.*

FLOYD'S ZESTY GREEN BEANS

- 1/3 **cup sliced almonds**
- 4 **slices bacon**
- 1 **small onion, chopped**
- 1 **clove garlic, minced or pressed**
- 1 **teaspoon lemon juice**
- 1/4 **teaspoon chili powder**
- 1 **pound green beans, ends removed**
- 1/4 **cup** *each* **water and dry white wine**
- 1/2 **cup shredded sharp cheddar cheese**
  Salt

In a 10- to 12-inch frying pan over medium-high heat, stir almonds until lightly toasted, about 4 minutes; pour from pan and set aside.

In the pan, cook bacon over medium heat until evenly browned. Lift out bacon and drain on towels. When cool, crumble.

Discard all but 2 teaspoons drippings from pan. Add onion, garlic, lemon juice, and chili powder; stir often over medium heat until onion is limp, 7 to 10 minutes.

"He devised this combination to impress his bride."

As onion cooks, rinse beans and cut into 2-inch lengths. When onion is limp, add beans, water, and wine to pan. Cover and cook until beans are just tender to bite, 9 minutes. Mix bacon and almonds with beans, then sprinkle with cheese. Cover and heat just until cheese begins to melt, about 1 minute. Pour into a bowl. Season to taste with salt. Makes 4 to 6 servings.

PER SERVING: 134 calories, 6 g protein, 6.8 g carbohydrates, 9.2 g fat (3.3 g saturated), 15 mg cholesterol, 140 mg sodium

Floyd Paige

Petaluma, Calif.

IN NEW YORK CITY'S *happier days, lodges, political organizations, and neighborhood associations celebrated togetherness (and raised funds) through a type of banquet known simply as a "beefsteak." Tables were planks stretched on trestles, tablecloths were newspapers, and the meal consisted of beefsteak and sliced tomatoes. But what beefsteak! Whole beef tenderloins in staggering numbers were cooked rare and sliced at the table. Diners ate until they could hold no more.*

Jerry Robbins has his own beefsteak parties in Flagstaff, Arizona. He treats the tenderloin to a long bath in an elaborate citrus marinade, which later, after reduction, becomes a sauce.

ARIZONA BEEF À L'ORANGE

- 1/4 **teaspoon pepper**
- 1/2 **teaspoon dry thyme leaves**
- 1 **teaspoon grated orange peel**
- 2 **tablespoons olive oil**
- 1 **clove garlic, minced or pressed**
- 1/4 **cup sugar**
- 1/4 **cup honey**
- 1/2 **cup lime juice**
- 2/3 **cup dry red wine**
- 1 **cup orange juice**
- 1 **cup balsamic vinegar**
- 1 **beef tenderloin (4 to 5 lb.), fat trimmed**

In a bowl, mix together pepper, thyme, orange peel, oil, garlic, sugar, honey, lime juice, wine, orange juice, and vinegar.

Put beef in a pan about 9 by 13 inches; pour liquid mixture over meat. Roll to

"He treats the tenderloin to a long bath in a citrus marinade."

coat well, pricking all over with a cooking fork as you turn the meat. Cover and chill about 24 hours; rotate meat 3 or 4 times.

Lift out meat, draining liquid; save marinade. Set beef on a rack in a 10- by 15-inch pan. Pour liquid into a 10- to 12-inch frying pan. Boil on high heat until reduced to about 1 cup, about 25 minutes.

Meanwhile, fold thin end of roast under to make evenly thick; tie string securely around meat every 2 to 3 inches. Roast in a 425° oven until a meat thermometer inserted in thickest part registers 125° for very rare, about 40 minutes; or 135° to 140° for rare, 45 to 60 minutes. Baste several times with marinade.

Let roast stand for 10 minutes, then cut across the grain on a slight diagonal into 1/2-inch-thick slices. Offer remaining marinade to add to taste. Makes 12 to 14 servings.

PER SERVING: 385 calories, 23 g protein, 15 g carbohydrates, 25 g fat (9.7 g saturated), 81 mg cholesterol, 56 mg sodium

Jerry Robbins

Flagstaff, Ariz.

July Menus

CELEBRATE INDEPENDENCE *more than once in July with menus incorporating significant make-ahead steps. Our leisurely barbecue and serve-yourself fiesta will start the pre-fireworks festivities with style. For a second special treat, consider a weekend brunch that treats family like guests.*

FOURTH OF JULY FIESTA

Grilled Fish Tacos
Tomatillo Mayonnaise
Cilantro Slaw
Lean Refried Black Beans
Watermelon   Mixed Berries
Sparkling Lemonade   Margaritas

The grilled fish makes an easy-to-fix, light filling for tacos. Tuck the slaw into the tortillas with the fish or eat it separately as a salad.

You can make the tomatillo mayonnaise and the refried beans up to 2 days ahead of time. Marinate the fish and prepare the slaw up to 4 hours before serving.

For sparkling lemonade, mix equal parts of lemonade and carbonated water and pour into ice-filled glasses.

GRILLED FISH TACOS

1³⁄₄ to 2 pounds firm-textured, light-flesh fish, such as Chilean sea bass, swordfish, or sturgeon, about 2 inches thick

¹⁄₃ cup lime juice

3 tablespoons tequila (optional)

6 to 12 warm flour or corn tortillas (6 to 8 in. wide)

Tomatillo mayonnaise (recipe follows)

About 1 cup purchased salsa (optional)

Cilantro slaw (recipe follows)

Place fish in a wide, shallow bowl. Mix with lime juice and tequila; cover and chill at least 15 minutes or up to 4 hours.

Lay fish on a lightly oiled grill 4 to 6 inches above a solid bed of medium-hot coals (you can hold your hand at grill

Party for the Fourth of July features tacos filled with barbecued fish, black beans, cilantro slaw, and salsa. Complement the meal with summer fruits.

level for only 3 to 4 seconds). Cook, turning once or twice, until fish is lightly browned and opaque but still moist-looking in the thickest part (cut to test), about 10 minutes.

Place fish on a platter. To eat, cut off chunks of fish (removing the bones and skin) and enclose the pieces in tortillas, adding tomatillo mayonnaise, salsa, and slaw to taste. Also offer slaw as a side dish. Makes 6 servings.

PER SERVING: 201 calories, 26 g protein, 13 g carbohydrates, 4.6 g fat (0.7 g saturated), 54 mg cholesterol, 232 mg sodium

Tomatillo mayonnaise. Husk and rinse ¹⁄₂ pound **tomatillos.** Place in an 8- to 10-inch frying pan over medium-high heat, shaking pan often until tomatillos are tinged with brown and begin to soften, about 10 minutes. Pour into a blender or food processor and purée coarsely. Drain purée in a fine strainer, then stir tomatillo pulp into ¹⁄₃ cup **reduced-calorie** or regular **mayonnaise.** If made ahead, cover and chill up to 2 days. Makes about 1 cup.

PER TABLESPOON: 17 calories, 0.2 g protein, 0.9 g carbohydrates, 1.4 g fat (0.3 g saturated), 1.6 mg cholesterol, 26 mg sodium

CILANTRO SLAW

- ½ **pound green cabbage, very finely shredded (about 3 cups)**
- ½ **pound red cabbage, very finely shredded (about 3 cups)**
- 1 **cup firmly packed cilantro (coriander), minced**
- ¼ **cup lime juice**
- 1 **tablespoon salad oil**
- 1 **teaspoon sugar**
  Salt and pepper

Mix together cabbages, cilantro, lime juice, oil, and sugar. Serve or, if made ahead, cover and chill up to 4 hours. Add salt and pepper to taste. Makes about 6 cups.

PER CUP: 45 calories, 1 g protein, 5.8 g carbohydrates, 2.5 g fat (0.3 g saturated), 0 mg cholesterol, 13 mg sodium

LEAN REFRIED BLACK BEANS

- 1 **large (about ½ lb.) onion, chopped**
- 2 **cloves garlic, minced or pressed**
- 1½ **cups regular-strength chicken broth**
- 2 **cans (15 oz. each) black beans, drained**
- ½ **teaspoon ground cumin**
- ⅓ **cup packed feta cheese or queso fresco (available in Hispanic markets)**
  Cilantro (coriander) sprigs

In a 10- to 12-inch frying pan, combine onion, garlic, and ¾ cup broth. Boil over high heat, uncovered, until the liquid evaporates; stir often. When the browned bits stick in the pan, add 2 or 3 tablespoons of water and stir to release the browned bits. Repeat this boiling dry and deglazing step until the onion is a rich brown, about 3 times.

Stir in remaining broth to free browned bits; add beans and cumin. Remove from heat and coarsely mash beans with a large spoon or potato masher. If made ahead, cover and chill up to 2 days. Simmer over medium heat, stirring often, until beans are thick enough to mound, about 15 minutes. Spoon into a bowl and top with cheese and cilantro. Makes 6 servings.

PER SERVING: 181 calories, 11 g protein, 27 g carbohydrates, 3.3 g fat (1.9 g saturated), 10 mg cholesterol, 684 mg sodium

---

PATIO BRUNCH

Melon Crescents & Smoked Turkey
Hot, Crisp Waffles
Blueberry Buttermilk Sherbet
Orange Juice
Espresso & Hot Milk

Beat the heat of a warm weekend morning with crisp waffles topped with a memorable ice-cold sherbet.

Make the blueberry sherbet a day or up to a week before serving. Serve scoops on freshly baked waffles made from a favorite recipe. For a whimsical touch, bake the waffles in heart-shaped irons rather than the usual round or square ones.

Arrange alternating wedges of cantaloupe and honeydew melon on a platter. Ripple thinly sliced smoked turkey (allow about 3 oz. per serving) beside the fruit. Cover and chill platter while the waffles bake or, if made ahead, up to 2 hours.

For waffle toppings, buy lemon curd; heat and stir lemon curd to make it thinner and easier to pour. Also buy currant or blueberry syrup.

(Continued on next page)

Vivid blueberry sherbet, perched on warm waffles, gets topped with lemon curd and currant syrup. Melon and smoked turkey round out brunch.

BLUEBERRY BUTTERMILK SHERBET

2 cups fresh or unsweetened frozen blueberries
2 teaspoons grated lemon peel
2 tablespoons lemon juice
1/4 cup sugar
1 cup low-fat buttermilk

Rinse and drain blueberries; put in a 2- to 3-quart pan. Add lemon peel, lemon juice, and sugar. Stir often over medium-high heat until simmering and blueberries begin to pop, about 6 minutes. Chill until cool or up until next day. In a blender or food processor, purée the mixture with buttermilk until smooth.

Pour mixture into a 9- to 10-inch-square metal pan. Cover and freeze un-til solid, at least 4 hours. Break mixture into chunks; whirl in a food processor or beat with a mixer until smooth. Return to pan. Cover and freeze until ready to use, at least 30 minutes or up to 1 week. Let hard-frozen sherbet soften slightly before serving. Makes about 3 cups, 6 servings.

PER SERVING: 77 calories, 1.7 g protein, 17 g carbohydrates, 0.3 g fat (0.2 g saturated), 1.6 mg cholesterol, 47 mg sodium

AUGUST

Fajita Nachos (page 214)

Turn an informal summer-
time gathering into a festive affair by building your menu
around one of these festive themes: A simplified West Coast
version of a New England clambake—seafood and corn
cooked on the grill—at the beach, in a park, or
even at home in your garden. Or a south-of-the-border
menu featuring our super nachos. Or a walk-about
appetizer party with food you can eat with your fingers.
Other recipes to brighten August meals include
hearty seafood salads, berry-flavored Italian gelato, and
a low-fat cooky cheesecake.

A Pacific Clambake

SAVOR FRESH DEEP-SEA TREASURES *at this West Coast version of an Eastern clambake. Because seafood is grilled rather than buried in sand with hot rocks and seaweed, this picnic is easier and quicker to prepare—at the beach, in a park, even in your garden.*

Menu partners are tuna steaks, shrimp, clams, oysters, corn on the cob, and small potatoes. Enliven their flavors with freshly made salsas, and accompany with loaves of crusty bread and a dry Sauvignon Blanc or a crisp Chardonnay. Offer grapes and cookies for dessert.

You can cook on several small barbecues or 1 large one; or, if the recreation area has grills, make use of them. You'll need charcoal briquets for fuel and insulated chests to transport food and beverages.

Pluck out grilled oyster, season with salsa, and eat while supping the juices in the shell.

PACIFIC MIXED GRILL

 8 **large ears corn**
16 **to 24 jumbo (1 to 1½ lb. total) shrimp**
     Boiled potatoes (directions follow)
16 **to 24 medium-size oysters in shells, scrubbed**
16 **to 24 clams in shells, suitable for steaming, scrubbed**
 1 **to 1½ pounds ahi tuna or swordfish steaks, about 1 inch thick, rinsed**
     Green salsa (recipe follows)
     Red salsa (recipe follows)

Pull back corn husks to remove silk, then re-cover corn with husks and soak ears in water for 1 hour; drain. To devein shrimp, insert a toothpick beneath vein between joints on back of shell. Gently pull up and out to draw out vein; repeat as needed. If done ahead, cover and chill corn and shrimp until next day.

Cover barbecue grates with a solid layer of charcoal briquets. Mound briquets and ignite; when dotted with gray ash, in 20 to 30 minutes, spread coals level and place grills 3 to 6 inches above them. Unwrap pan of potatoes, add about 1 inch water, and set pan on a grill. Cook until potatoes are hot and tender when pierced, about 15 minutes. Set pan close to barbecue to keep potatoes warm as remaining foods cook.

To maintain steady heat 1 hour or longer (so you can cook foods a few pieces at a time), scatter about ¼ more briquets on hot coals 30 minutes after igniting them and every 30 minutes thereafter.

Lay corn, shrimp, oysters (cupped side down), clams, and tuna on grill over hot coals (you can hold your hand at grill level only 2 to 3 seconds).

Turn corn often until kernels are hot and turn more translucent, about 15 minutes.

Cook shrimp until just opaque in center (cut to test), about 10 minutes; turn once.

Cook oysters just until they open slightly, and clams until they pop open, 8 to 12 minutes.

Cook tuna until opaque on surface but still pink in center (cut to test), 6 to

8 minutes; turn once. Cook swordfish until opaque but still moist-looking in center (cut to test), 8 to 10 minutes; turn fish once.

Add salsa to seafood and vegetables to taste. Makes 8 servings.

PER SERVING SEAFOOD WITH VEGETABLES: 274 calories, 31 g protein, 32 g carbohydrates, 4 g fat (0.6 g saturated), 105 mg cholesterol, 126 mg sodium

Boiled potatoes. Scrub 24 small (1½- to 2-in. diameter) **thin-skinned red potatoes.** Put potatoes in a 5- to 6-quart pan and add **water** to barely cover.

Up to 6 hours before serving, bring potatoes to a boil. Cover and simmer until potatoes are barely tender when pierced, about 15 minutes; drain. To keep them warm up to 4 hours, carry in an insulated chest or wrap in about a 1-inch layer of newspapers.

Remove corn silk, then steam ear in its husk on the grill for an easy hand-held treat.

Take portable barbecues to the beach for grilling seafood, corn, and potatoes. If you prefer, cook in a park or even in your garden. Two lively salsas—one green, one red—enliven flavors. Crusty bread, white wine, and fresh fruit and cookies complete the picnic menu.

Green salsa. Mix 1 pound **tomatillos** (available in many supermarkets or at Mexican grocery stores), husked, cored, and chopped; 2 medium-size (about 1 lb. total) firm-ripe **avocados,** peeled, pitted, and diced; ½ cup thinly sliced **green onion;** ½ cup **lime juice;** ½ cup minced **fresh cilantro** (coriander); and ¼ cup minced **Spanish-style olives.** Add **salt** and **pepper** to taste. If made ahead, cover and chill up to 6 hours. Makes 4½ cups.

PER TABLESPOON: 12 calories, 0.2 g protein, 0.8 g carbohydrates, 1 g fat (0.2 g saturated), 0 mg cholesterol, 12 mg sodium

Red salsa. In a 6- to 8-inch frying pan, cook ¼ cup minced **garlic** in 1 tablespoon **salad oil** over low heat, stirring often, until soft and sweet, about 10 minutes. Mix garlic; 3 large (about 1½ lb. total) firm-ripe **tomatoes,** cored and chopped; 1 medium-size (about 6 oz.) **onion,** minced; ⅓ cup **lemon juice;** 1 or 2 tablespoons minced **canned chipotle chiles** (in some supermarkets or Mexican grocery stores); and **salt** to taste. If made ahead, cover and chill up to 6 hours. Makes 4 cups.

PER TABLESPOON: 7 calories, 0.2 g protein, 1 g carbohydrates, 0.3 g fat (0 g saturated), 0 mg cholesterol, 8.3 mg sodium

Walk-about Appetizer Party

AT THIS WALK-ABOUT *appetizer party for 12 (or lazy lunch for 6), you don't have to do a balancing act with glasses and plates. Instead, food you can eat with your fingers makes it easy to enjoy succulent morsels and beverages while strolling about to visit. For Stella and Sheldon Wilson of Chimney Rock Winery in Napa, California, it's a practical way to present food as guests sample their wines.*

The Wilsons offer hearty tidbits-on-the-bone or skewers from the barbecue, plus bite-size vegetables like cherry tomatoes, green onions, and cold cooked sugar-snap peas and tiny squash with dipping sauces (about 1 cup vegetables per person).

You can use a barbecue with gas or charcoal briquets for fuel. To maintain even heat with briquets, every 30 minutes add about ¼ of the original number of briquets used to start the fire.

Keep shellfish, raw meat, and poultry on a bed of ice until ready to grill. And have plenty of small paper napkins, with wastebaskets handy for scraps.

LAMB CHOPS WITH MINT PESTO

> 12 lamb rib chops, cut 1 inch thick (about 2½ lb. total)
> Mint pesto (recipe follows)
> Salt

With a small sharp knife, trim all fat from chops. Then cut a horizontal 1½-inch-wide pocket in each chop, starting at meaty rim and cutting to bone. Fill pockets equally with pesto. If made ahead, cover and chill up until next day.

Place lamb on grill above a solid bed of hot coals (you can hold your hand at grill level for only 2 to 3 seconds). Cook, turning to brown evenly, until done to taste; for medium-rare (pink in center; cut to test), allow 7 to 10 minutes. Add salt to taste. Makes 12 servings.

PER PIECE: 142 calories, 11 g protein, 1.3 g carbohydrates, 11 g fat (2.6 g saturated), 29 mg cholesterol, 57 mg sodium

Mint pesto. In a blender or food processor, smoothly purée 1 cup **fresh mint leaves,** ½ cup **pine nuts,** 3 cloves **garlic,** 3 tablespoons **olive oil,** and ¼ cup grated **parmesan cheese.** Makes ¾ cup.

SKEWERED SHRIMP

> 24 large (31 to 35 per lb., about 10 oz.) shrimp, shelled and deveined
> ¼ cup dry sherry or rice vinegar
> 1 tablespoon minced ginger
> 24 green onions (root ends trimmed), cut to 6 inches in length
> Salt

In a bowl, mix shrimp, sherry, and ginger. Cover; chill 1 hour or up until next day.

In a 10- to 12-inch frying pan, place onions in 1 inch of boiling water until limp, 15 to 30 seconds. Lift out and immerse in ice water until cool; drain. If made ahead, cover and chill up until next day.

Thread a slender skewer lengthwise into each shrimp, going almost, but not quite, all the way through. Lay an onion flat. Center a skewered shrimp across center of onion; tie onion around shrimp. If made ahead, cover and chill up to 4 hours.

Lay skewered shrimp on grill above a solid bed of hot coals (you can hold hand at grill level only 2 to 3 seconds). Cook, turning several times, until shrimp are opaque in center (cut to test), 2 to 4 minutes. Add salt to taste. Makes 12 servings.

PER PIECE: 31 calories, 4.7 g protein, 2.2 g carbohydrates, 0.4 g fat (0.1 g saturated), 31 mg cholesterol, 32 mg sodium

LEMON LAMB SKEWERS

> 1½ pounds boned and fat-trimmed lean lamb (leg or loin), cut into ¾-inch cubes
> Lemon marinade (recipe follows)

Mix lamb with lemon marinade in bowl. Cover and chill at least 1 hour or up to overnight; stir occasionally.

Divide meat into 12 equal portions. Thread each portion onto a slender skewer. Lay skewered lamb on grill

above a solid bed of hot coals (you can hold your hand at grill level only 2 to 3 seconds). Cook lamb, turning to brown evenly, until done to taste; for medium-rare (pink in center; cut to test), allow 6 to 8 minutes. Makes 12 servings.

PER SERVING: 106 calories, 12 g protein, 2.3 g carbohydrates, 5.1 g fat (1.4 g saturated), 38 mg cholesterol, 76 mg sodium

Lemon marinade. In a large bowl, mix ⅛ teaspoon **cayenne,** ½ teaspoon **salt,** 1 teaspoon *each* **ground coriander** and **ground turmeric,** 1 tablespoon **curry powder,** 2 tablespoons **apricot jam,** 3 tablespoons **salad oil,** ½ cup **lemon juice,** 2 cloves **garlic** (minced), and 1 large **onion** (minced).

CHINESE-STYLE QUAIL

> 6 quail (each about 4 oz.)
> 1 cup regular-strength chicken broth
> ½ cup dry vermouth or mirin (sweet rice wine)
> 1 tablespoon soy sauce
> 1 small lemon, thinly sliced
> 1 tablespoon minced fresh ginger
> 2 teaspoons Oriental sesame oil
> ¼ teaspoon white pepper

With poultry shears or kitchen scissors, snip off quail wing tips at joint. On each bird, cut parallel to each side of backbone, then cut in half lengthwise through breast. Rinse birds and pat dry; save scraps for another use, such as broth.

Place quail in a deep bowl. Add broth, vermouth, soy sauce, lemon, ginger, oil, and pepper. Cover and chill for 2 hours or up until next day; stir often. Lift from marinade and place on grill above a solid bed of hot coals (you can hold your hand at grill level only 2 to 3 seconds). Cook, turning to brown evenly, until breasts are still red but not wet-looking at the bone (cut from wing joint into breast to test), 7 to 10 minutes. Makes 12 servings.

PER HALF QUAIL: 113 calories, 10 g protein, 2.1 g carbohydrates, 7 g fat (1.8 g saturated), 0 mg cholesterol, 119 mg sodium

Sizzling on the grill, meats with handles make easy nibbling—lamb rib chops with mint pesto, marinated lamb and shrimp on skewers, quail halves with Chinese-style flavorings. All go with a colorful selection of raw vegetables for dipping.

Skinny Gelato

FOOL YOUR GUESTS *with this frozen dessert. Smooth, creamy, and intensely flavored, it tastes like egg-rich Italian gelato—but in reality, it's a low-fat version. We call it skinny gelato. Fruits with concentrated flavor, such as the season's fresh berries, work especially well.*

Like traditional gelato, this version starts with a cooked base. Our lean formula substitutes cornstarch for egg yolks and low-fat milk for richer milk. As milk and cornstarch cook, they form a thickened sauce much like a pudding. Stir in fruit purée to provide penetrating flavor and color. As gelato freezes, the cooked base works like sugar to keep the texture creamy, so you can use less sweetening.

Also, like Italian gelato, this version has a rather dense texture and expands very little as it freezes. The recipe makes about 1 quart, fitting in many of the frozen cylinders or other small ice cream freezers. For larger freezer containers, double the recipe if you like.

VERY BERRY SKINNY GELATO

- ½ cup sugar
- 3 thin strips lemon peel (yellow part only), each ½ by 3 inches
- 2 tablespoons cornstarch
- 2 cups extra-light or low-fat milk
  Berry purée (choices follow)
- 2 teaspoons vanilla

In a 2- to 3-quart pan, combine sugar and lemon peel; with a wooden spoon, press peel against sugar to release oils. Mix in cornstarch. Stir in milk. Stir over medium heat (with a whisk to remove any lumps) until sauce boils, about 5 minutes. When it boils, continue to stir 1 minute. Remove from heat. Lift out lemon peel; discard.

Stir berry purée and vanilla into hot pudding until smoothly blended. Cool, cover, and chill until cold, at least 1½ hours or up until next day.

Pour into a 1-quart or larger container of a frozen cylinder, self-refrigerated, or ice- and salt-cooled ice cream maker (use 1 part salt to 6 parts ice). Crank or process according to manufacturer's directions until gelato is softly frozen and hard to mix; remove dasher.

Serve or, to firm and mellow gelato, cover and freeze for 1 to 2 hours. Or cover ice- and salt-cooled container with plastic wrap, replace lid, and surround with 1 part salt to 4 parts ice; cover with several heavy towels and let stand for 1 to 2 hours. Serve gelato or store in freezer.

For the best flavor and texture, serve within 3 weeks.

To make hard-frozen gelato easier to scoop, let it soften at room temperature, 20 to 30 minutes for a full batch. Or soften in a microwave oven at half-power (50 percent), about 2 minutes for a full batch, checking at 1-minute intervals. Makes 3½ to 4 cups.

PER ½-CUP BLUEBERRY GELATO: 110 calories, 2.3 g protein, 24 g carbohydrates, 0.8 g fat (0.4 g saturated), 2.4 mg cholesterol, 34 mg sodium

PER ½-CUP RASPBERRY, BLACKBERRY, LOGANBERRY, OR BOYSENBERRY GELATO (ALL HAVE SIMILAR NUTRITIONAL DATA): 107 calories, 2.4 g protein, 23 g carbohydrates, 0.9 g fat (0.4 g saturated), 2.4 mg cholesterol, 31 mg sodium

PER ½-CUP STRAWBERRY GELATO: 102 calories, 2.3 g protein, 22 g carbohydrates, 0.8 g fat (0.4 g saturated), 2.4 mg cholesterol, 32 mg sodium

Blueberry purée. In a blender or food processor, combine 3 cups (about ¾ lb.) rinsed fresh or partially thawed frozen **blueberries** and 2 tablespoons **lemon juice;** whirl until berry skins are ground very fine. Makes about 2 cups.

Raspberry, blackberry, loganberry, or boysenberry purée. In a blender or food processor, purée 3 cups (about ¾ lb.) rinsed fresh or partially thawed frozen **raspberries,** blackberries, loganberries, or boysenberries and 1 tablespoon **lemon juice.** Pour purée into a fine strainer set over a bowl. With a spoon or flexible spatula, stir and press purée through strainer; discard seeds. Makes 1⅓ to 2 cups.

Strawberry purée. In a blender or food processor, purée 3½ cups (about 1 lb.) rinsed and hulled fresh or partially thawed frozen **strawberries** and 1 tablespoon **lemon juice.** Makes about 2 cups.

Purée fresh or frozen raspberries with lemon juice in a blender.

Pour berry purée into hot pudding base; stir to blend smoothly.

Freeze berry pudding in an ice cream maker until dasher stops.

Collection of vibrant-hued desserts includes (clockwise from far left) raspberry, blackberry, blueberry, strawberry, and loganberry gelato. Like egg-rich Italian gelato, this low-fat version is smooth, creamy, and intensely flavored, and has a rather dense texture.

Super Nachos

(Continued from page 214)

OUTH-OF-THE-BORDER FLAVORS _come together for two nacho dishes guaranteed to star at any summertime celebration. These colorful versions feature plenty of make-ahead steps to help cut down on last-minute preparation._

The first recipe combines the elements of fajitas; finish it on the barbecue for an outdoor family supper or a party appetizer. Another version pairs shredded turkey with white kidney beans for nachos that can be reheated in the oven.

For scooping up the savory mixtures, use oven-crisped flour tortilla chips or yellow or blue corn tortilla chips.

FAJITA NACHOS

- ¼ cup _each_ lime juice and olive oil
- ½ cup beer
- 2 cloves garlic, minced or pressed
- 1 teaspoon _each_ ground coriander and ground cumin
- 1 fresh jalapeño chili, stemmed, seeded, and minced
  Seasoned beans (recipe follows)
- 1 pound beef skirt or flank steak
  Mellow onions (recipe follows)
- 1 cup (4 oz.) shredded cheddar cheese
  Guacamole, purchased or homemade
  Lime salsa (recipe follows)
  About 8 cups flour tortilla chips (directions on page 216) or purchased corn tortilla chips

In a large heavy plastic bag, mix lime juice, oil, beer, garlic, coriander, cumin, and chili; remove 3 tablespoons marinade and set it aside for the beans. Place steak in bag and seal. Rotate bag and set

it in a large pan. Chill for at least 2 hours or up until next day; turn occasionally.

Place meat on a grill 4 to 6 inches above a solid bed of hot coals (you can hold your hand at grill level only 2 to 3 seconds). Grill until meat is brown and cooked to your liking, 3 to 5 minutes per side for rare steak (cut to test). Thinly slice meat crosswise, then cut each slice in half again.

Spread hot beans into a 10-inch round on a large ovenproof platter (protect dish by setting on a metal pan or platter if heating on the barbecue). Top evenly with onions and steak; sprinkle with cheese. Broil 4 to 6 inches below heat until cheese melts. Or set on the grill over medium coals (you can hold your hand at grill level only 4 to 5 seconds) and cover barbecue until cheese melts, 4 to 6 minutes.

Remove from oven and top with guacamole and salsa. Tuck about ⅓ of the tortilla chips around edges. Accompany with remaining chips and salsa. Scoop layered mixture onto chips to eat. Makes 6 main-dish or 10 to 12 appetizer servings.

PER MAIN-DISH SERVING: 600 calories, 31 g protein, 57 g carbohydrates, 26 g fat (8.6 g saturated), 58 mg cholesterol, 679 mg sodium

Seasoned beans. In a 2- to 3-quart heavy pan on medium-high heat, combine **reserved marinade** (see preceding), 2 cans (15 oz. each) drained **pinto beans,** and 1 cup **beer.** Stir often, using back of spoon or potato masher to coarsely mash beans, until mixture thickens slightly, 15 to 20 minutes; add **salt** to taste. Use hot.

If made ahead, cool, cover, and chill up until next day. Stir over low heat or medium-hot coals (you can hold your hand at grill level only 3 to 4 seconds) until hot.

Mellow onions. To a 10- to 12-inch frying pan over medium heat, add 1 tablespoon **olive oil** and 2 medium-size (about 1 lb. total) **onions,** chopped. Cook, partially covered, until onions are very limp and golden brown, stirring often, about 20 minutes. Use hot or cool. If made ahead, cool, cover, and chill up until next day.

Lime salsa. Mix 1 large (about ½ lb.) ripe yellow or red **tomato,** cored and finely diced; 2 large (about ½ lb. total) **tomatillos,** husks removed, chopped; ¼ cup minced **red bell pepper;** 2 tablespoons minced **red onion;** 1 teaspoon grated **lime peel;** and 1 tablespoon **lime juice.** Serve, or let stand, covered, up to 2 hours. Makes about 2½ cups.

CARNITAS NACHOS WITH WATERMELON-JICAMA PICO DE GALLO

- 1½ pounds skinned and boned turkey thigh
- 1 can (14½ oz.) regular-strength chicken broth
- 1 clove garlic, minced or pressed
- 1 dry bay leaf
- ½ teaspoon dry oregano leaves
- ¼ cup canned diced green chilies
- 2 tablespoons distilled white vinegar
  Beans (recipe follows)
- 1 cup (4 oz.) shredded jack cheese
  About 8 cups flour tortilla chips (directions follow) or purchased corn tortilla chips
  Pico de gallo (recipe follows)

(Continued on page 216)

Taking a cue from fajitas, seasoned hot beans, cooked onions, grilled beef steak, and shredded cheddar cheese are layered in a large oven-proof platter, then broiled just until cheese melts. Top with guacamole and lime salsa just before serving, and tuck tortilla chips around edge of platter.

Scoop up savory beans, tender braised turkey, and cheese with flour tortilla chips; serve with colorful watermelon-jicama pico de gallo.

cover and chill up until next day.) Bake, covered, in a 400° oven until hot in center, 15 to 25 minutes. Uncover and sprinkle with cheese. Bake, uncovered, until cheese melts, about 5 minutes.

Remove from oven. Tuck 1/3 of the tortilla chips around edges. Accompany with remaining chips and pico de gallo. Scoop layered mixture onto chips to eat. Makes 6 to 8 main-dish or 10 to 12 appetizer servings.

PER SERVING: 439 calories, 31 g protein, 45 g carbohydrates, 14 g fat (2 g saturated), 76 mg cholesterol, 578 mg sodium

Beans. In a 10- to 12-inch frying pan on medium-high heat, stir 1 tablespoon **olive oil** and 1 large (about 1/2 lb.) **onion,** chopped, until onion begins to brown, 8 to 10 minutes. Add 3/4 cup canned **diced green chilies** and 2 cans (15 oz. each) **cannellini** (white kidney) **beans,** drained. Stir often, using back of spoon or potato masher to coarsely mash beans, until mixture thickens slightly, about 5 minutes.

Pico de gallo. Mix 1 1/2 cups seeded, diced **watermelon;** 3/4 cup peeled, diced **jicama;** 2 teaspoons grated **orange peel;** 1 large (about 1/2 lb.) **orange** (cut off peel and white pith; cut between membranes to remove segments, then dice fruit); 1 fresh **jalapeño chili,** stemmed, seeded, and minced; 1 tablespoon *each* **lime juice** and minced **fresh cilantro** (coriander). Serve, or let stand, covered, up to 2 hours. Makes about 3 cups.

FLOUR TORTILLA CHIPS

Cut 8 **flour tortillas** (7 to 8 in. wide) into 8 wedges each. Measure out 2 tablespoons **salad oil.** Lightly oil 2 baking pans, each 10 by 15 inches. Fill pans with a single layer of tortilla wedges (place close together); brush tops lightly with oil.

Bake in a 500° oven until golden and crisp, 5 to 7 minutes. (If using 1 oven, switch pan positions after 3 minutes.) Pour out chips and repeat until all tortilla chips are baked.

Serve warm or cool; if made ahead, store cooled chips airtight at room temperature up until next day. Makes about 8 cups.

Cut turkey into 1 1/2-inch pieces and place in a 2- to 3-quart pan. Cook, covered, on medium heat to draw out juices, 8 to 10 minutes. Uncover; cook on high heat, stirring often, until liquid has evaporated and meat is well browned, 10 to 12 minutes.

Add broth, garlic, bay leaf, and oregano; stir to scrape browned bits free from pan. Bring to a boil, then reduce heat, cover, and simmer until meat is very tender when pierced, about 1 hour. Uncover; boil on high heat until all liquid has evaporated, 5 to 10 minutes. Add chilies and vinegar; stir to scrape browned bits free. Remove from heat. Shred meat, using 2 forks (or let cool and pull apart with fingers).

Spread beans into a 10-inch round on a large ovenproof platter. Top evenly with shredded turkey. (If made ahead,

Main-dish Seafood Salads

COOL GREENS AND SEAFOOD *join for refreshing main-dish salads. One mixes mizuna (a mild member of the mustard family), fresh fennel, and crab; the other pairs crisp romaine with smoked trout.*

MIZUNA, FENNEL & CRAB SALAD

Look for mizuna in Asian or specialty produce stores, and some supermarkets.

- ³/₄ **pound (about 1 large head) fennel**
- ²/₃ **pound mizuna, bare stems trimmed and yellow or bruised leaves discarded, rinsed and crisped**
- 1¹/₂ **pounds shelled cooked crab Mizuna dressing (recipe follows)**

Trim stems, root end, and core from fennel. Slice fennel thin to make 2 cups. Reserve feathery wisps of fennel and ³/₄ cup mizuna for dressing. Cut remaining mizuna into 2- to 3-inch-long pieces.

In a large bowl, mix fennel and mizuna. Mound crab on greens, placing the most attractive crab pieces on top. At the table, add dressing to greens and gently mix. Makes 6 entrée servings.

PER SERVING: 176 calories, 27 g protein, 7.1 g carbohydrates, 4.4 g fat (1.5 g saturated), 118 mg cholesterol, 475 mg sodium

Mizuna dressing. In blender or food processor, purée reserved ³/₄ cup **mizuna** (see preceding), ²/₃ cup **nonfat unflavored yogurt**, ¹/₄ cup **sour cream**, 2 tablespoons **lemon juice**, 1 tablespoon **Dijon mustard**, 1 tablespoon chopped **feathery wisps of fennel** (see preceding), 1 teaspoon **dry tarragon leaves**, and ¹/₂ teaspoon **sugar**. Pour into a bowl. Makes 1¹/₂ cups.

SMOKED TROUT & ONION SALAD

- 1 **medium-size (about 6 oz.) red onion, sliced thin**
- ¹/₄ **cup distilled vinegar**
- 1 **large head (about 1¹/₄ lb.) romaine lettuce, rinsed and crisped**
- ³/₄ **pound smoked trout, boned, skinned, torn into ¹/₂-inch pieces Fresh dill sprigs (optional) Dill dressing (recipe follows)**

Put onion in a deep bowl and cover with water. With your hands, squeeze slices until almost limp. Drain, rinse, and drain again.

In a bowl, combine onion, vinegar, and about 2 cups *each* ice cubes and water; let slices stand until crisp, about 15 minutes; drain well. Lift out onion.

Line each of 4 plates with 2 or 3 large lettuce leaves. Cut remaining lettuce crosswise in ¹/₄-inch-wide strips. In a large bowl, gently mix lettuce, trout, and onion.

Mound equal portions on each plate. Garnish with dill sprigs. Offer dill dressing to add to taste. Makes 4 entrée servings.

PER SERVING: 138 calories, 24 g protein, 7.2 g carbohydrates, 1.2 g fat (0.2 g saturated), 66 mg cholesterol, 662 mg sodium

Dill dressing. Blend ¹/₂ cup **regular** or light **sour cream**, 1 tablespoon **lemon juice**, 2 teaspoons **prepared horseradish,** and 1 tablespoon chopped **fresh dill** or 1 teaspoon dry dill weed.

PER TABLESPOON: 26 calories, 0.4 g protein, 0.7 g carbohydrates, 2.4 g fat (1.5 g saturated), 5.1 mg cholesterol, 7.6 mg sodium

For a warm-weather lunch or supper, team smoked trout, crisp red onion, and romaine lettuce. Garnish with sprigs of fresh dill. Offer a dill dressing to drizzle over individual servings.

Discovering Fresh Water Chestnuts

SURPRISINGLY SWEET AND CRISP, *fresh water chestnuts (ma tai in Chinese) bear little resemblance to the bland ones packed in cans. These mahogany-colored tufted corms (similar to bulbs) grow in shallow ponds and streams, sprouting a water grass. Most water chestnuts are imported from China.*

Used raw or cooked, fresh water chestnuts add a sweet crispness to any dish. You can find them year-round in Asian and specialty produce markets.

Don't confuse rough, thin-skinned water chestnut corms with water caltrops (Trapa bicornis, ling gok in Chinese); the two are not related, but both may be labeled water chestnuts. Ling gok are nuts with a hard, shiny black shell, shaped like a bat (the animal); they must be cooked.

Look for water chestnuts that are firm. Because they're high in sugar and water, they ferment readily if bruised; discard any with soft spots. Store loosely covered in the refrigerator up to a few days. If fresh and firm, they don't discolor when peeled. If you're not going to use peeled ones within an hour or two, cover with plastic wrap or water to prevent drying.

With a vegetable peeler, cut skin from fresh water chestnuts to reveal crisp white flesh.

WATER CHESTNUT & POTATO SALAD

- 1 pound (about 2 large) white thin-skinned potatoes, scrubbed
- 1/3 cup *each* unflavored yogurt and mayonnaise
- 2 tablespoons rice vinegar (or white wine vinegar plus 3/4 teaspoon sugar)
- 1 tablespoon minced fresh or 1 teaspoon dry basil leaves
- 2 cloves garlic, pressed or minced
- 1 pound (16 to 18 large) fresh water chestnuts, rinsed, ends trimmed, peeled, and quartered
- 2/3 cup thinly sliced green onion
  Salt and pepper

In a 3- to 4-quart pan, combine potatoes and about 1½ quarts water. Bring to a boil over high heat. Reduce heat, cover, and simmer until potatoes are tender when pierced, 25 to 35 minutes. Let cool. Cut potatoes into 3/4-inch cubes.

In a large bowl, mix yogurt, mayonnaise, vinegar, basil, and garlic. Add water chestnut wedges, potatoes, and green onion. Gently mix together. Add salt and pepper to taste. (If made ahead, cover and chill up to 24 hours.) Makes 4 servings.

PER SERVING: 336 calories, 5.2 g protein, 46 g carbohydrates, 15 g fat (2.3 g saturated), 12 mg cholesterol, 136 mg sodium

FRESH WATER CHESTNUTS WITH MINT

- 8 large (6 to 8 oz. total) fresh water chestnuts, rinsed, ends trimmed, and peeled
- 16 small (about 1/2-in. long) fresh mint leaves

Cut chestnuts in half crosswise. Place 1 leaf on each piece. Serve as after-dinner mints or palate refreshers. Makes 16.

PER PIECE: 12 calories, 0.2 g protein, 2.7 g carbohydrates, 0 g fat (0 g saturated), 0 mg cholesterol, 1.5 mg sodium

CURRIED WATER CHESTNUTS & SCALLOPS

- 2 tablespoons salad oil
- 1 small onion, chopped
- 2 tablespoons minced fresh ginger
- 2 cloves garlic, pressed or minced
- 1 teaspoon curry powder
- 1/2 teaspoon ground coriander
- 1/4 teaspoon crushed dried hot red chilies

Look-alike potatoes and water chestnuts surprise you with their contrasting textures in this salad.

- 3/4 pound sea scallops, rinsed and cut crosswise into 1/4-inch slices
- 1/2 pound (8 or 9 large) fresh water chestnuts, rinsed, ends trimmed, peeled, and sliced thin crosswise
  Sauce mixture (directions follow)
- 2 tablespoons fresh cilantro (coriander) leaves

Place a 10- to 12-inch frying pan over medium-high heat. Add oil, onion, ginger, and garlic; stir often until onion is tinged with brown, about 10 minutes. Add curry, coriander, and chilies; stir until curry becomes fragrant, about 1 minute.

Add scallops and water chestnuts; gently stir until scallops are almost opaque throughout (cut to test), about 2 minutes. Add sauce mixture and stir until it thickens. Pour onto a plate and sprinkle with cilantro. Makes 2 or 3 servings.

PER SERVING: 269 calories, 21 g protein, 21 g carbohydrates, 11 g fat (1.3 g saturated), 38 mg cholesterol, 202 mg sodium

Sauce mixture. Mix 1/2 cup **regular-strength chicken broth**, 1 teaspoon **cornstarch**, 1/2 teaspoon **cider vinegar**, and 1 teaspoon **fish sauce** (*nam pla* or *nuoc mam*) or soy sauce.

LIGHTENING UP SUNSET CLASSICS: Low-fat Cooky Cheesecake

DON'T BE DECEIVED *by the rich-tasting filling and sweet cookies that stud this cheesecake. It's leaner than it seems.*

In our popular cooky cheesecake recipe from May 1987, ingredients included cream cheese, whole eggs, and chocolate sandwich cookies for crust and filling. Here, we switch to neufchâtel (light cream) cheese, nonfat cottage cheese, egg whites, chocolate wafer cookies for the crust, and a satisfying number of sandwich cookies for the creamy filling (cookies may float or sink). The cake is not as dense or sweet as the original. But our tasters liked the flavors, and most couldn't tell they were eating a low-fat cheesecake.

LEAN CHOCOLATE COOKY CHEESECAKE

- 2 cups (1 carton, 16 oz.) nonfat large- or small-curd cottage cheese
- 2 packages (8 oz. each) neufchâtel (light cream) cheese, cut into chunks
- 6 large egg whites (3/4 cup)
- 1/4 cup all-purpose flour
- 2 teaspoons vanilla
- 1/2 to 3/4 cup sugar
  Lean chocolate crust (recipe follows)
- 1 package (5 1/4 oz., about 14) chocolate sandwich cookies, or 14 dark chocolate wafer cookies

In a blender or food processor, purée cottage cheese, neufchâtel, egg whites, flour, vanilla, and sugar (use 1/2 cup with sandwich cookies, 3/4 cup with wafer cookies) until smooth.

Pour 2/3 of the cheese mixture into crust. Break cookies in half and scatter over mixture, overlapping cookies, if needed. Pour remaining cheese mixture over and around cookies.

Set pan on a 10- by 15-inch baking pan. Bake in a 300° oven until filling jiggles only slightly in center when pan is gently shaken, 25 to 35 minutes. Remove pan from oven and carefully run a knife between cake and pan sides. Let cool in pan on a rack for 30 minutes. Cover and chill at least 4 hours or up to overnight (for firmest filling). Remove pan rim. Cut into wedges. Makes 12 to 16 servings.

PER SERVING: 255 calories, 9.4 g protein, 29 g carbohydrates, 11 g fat (4.2 g saturated), 24 mg cholesterol, 404 mg sodium

PER SERVING ORIGINAL CHOCOLATE COOKY CHEESECAKE (MAY 1987, PAGE 180): 502 calories, 8.1 g protein, 40 g carbohydrates, 35 g fat (16 g saturated), 158 mg cholesterol, 445 mg sodium

Chocolate sandwich cookies add sweetness to lightened-up cheesecake; cake's creamy texture comes from nonfat cottage cheese, neufchâtel cheese, and egg whites.

Lean chocolate crust. In a blender or food processor, whirl 1 package (9 oz.) **dark chocolate wafer cookies** to make fine crumbs (you should have about 2 1/2 cups). Whirl 1 **large egg white** in processor or whisk slightly with a fork, then whirl or mix in crumbs just until evenly moistened. Press crumbs over bottom and 1/2 inch up sides of a 9-inch cheesecake pan with a removable rim. Bake in a 300° oven until slightly firmer when pressed, about 20 minutes.

More August Recipes

OTHER AUGUST RECIPES *included a versatile parsley-based sauce and an elegant crème brûlée dessert tart.*

MULTIPURPOSE GREEN SAUCE

Five simple ingredients are all you need to create a versatile sauce that complements everything from poultry and seafood to salad greens and vegetables.

- 3¹/₂ **cups (about ¹/₄ lb.) parsley, stems trimmed**
- ¹/₂ **cup extra-virgin olive oil**
- 2 **to 4 cloves garlic**
- 1 **tablespoon drained capers**
- 3 **tablespoons lemon juice**

In a food processor or blender, whirl parsley, oil, garlic, capers, and lemon juice until smooth. Use as directed below. If made ahead, cover and chill up to 4 days. Makes about 1 cup.—*Fran Bigelow, Seattle.*

PER TABLESPOON: 64 calories, 0.2 g protein, 1 g carbohydrates, 7 g fat (1 g saturated), 0 mg cholesterol, 17 mg sodium

To use as a marinade. Arrange chicken, fish, shrimp, or pork in a shallow container. Add enough green sauce to coat all pieces generously (about ¹/₃ cup sauce per pound of meat). Cover and chill at least 1 hour or up to 6 hours. Grill or bake meat as desired.

To use as a sauce. Spoon room-temperature green sauce over grilled or baked chicken, fish, pork, or steamed vegetables. Use chilled sauce as a dressing for cold poached chicken or salmon.

To use as a salad dressing or dip. Mix ¹/₄ cup (or to taste) green sauce with 6 cups rinsed and crisped salad greens. Spoon sauce over sliced tomatoes and cucumbers. Offer as a dip for raw vegetables.

CRÈME BRÛLÉE TART

For pure indulgence, combine a classic crème brûlée custard with a buttery pastry crust, chocolate, and juicy berries.

Crisp broiled brown sugar crust tops custard tart with berries. You can make tart up to a day in advance, but prepare broiled sugar topping just before serving.

You can make this tart up to a day ahead, but make the broiled sugar topping just before serving; the sugar will melt if held more than an hour.

- 2 **cups raspberries or blackberries, rinsed and drained dry; or unsweetened frozen berries, thawed**
  Pastry crust (recipe follows)
- 3 **large eggs**
- ³/₄ **cup granulated sugar**
- ¹/₂ **cup light cream (half-and-half)**
- ¹/₂ **cup milk**
- 1 **teaspoon vanilla**
- ¹/₃ **cup firmly packed light brown sugar**
  Fresh mint sprigs (optional)

Arrange 1¹/₂ cups berries in the crust. Cover remaining berries and chill.

Beat to blend eggs, granulated sugar, cream, milk, and vanilla. Place pastry in a 300° oven and pour the egg mixture into it. Bake tart until center jiggles only slightly when gently shaken, about 1 hour. Cool slightly, then chill at least 4 hours or up until next day. (When tart is cold, wrap airtight.)

Press brown sugar through a fine strainer evenly over the custard. Broil tart 4 inches from heat until sugar melts slightly and is bubbling in a few places, 3 to 4 minutes. Chill until sugar hardens, 5 to 10 minutes or up to 1 hour. To serve, remove pan rim; garnish portions with reserved berries and mint. Makes 8 to 10 servings.

PER SERVING: 381 calories, 5.5 g protein, 55 g carbohydrates, 16 g fat (9.4 g saturated), 112 mg cholesterol, 106 mg sodium

Pastry crust. In a food processor or bowl, combine 1¹/₄ cups **all-purpose flour,** ¹/₂ cup **sugar,** and 6 tablespoons **butter** or margarine, in chunks. Whirl or rub with fingers until fine crumbs form. Add 1 **large egg yolk;** whirl or mix with a fork until dough holds together.

Press dough over bottom and up sides of a buttered and flour-dusted removable-rim 9-inch tart pan at least 1³/₄ inches deep. Bake in a 300° oven until pale gold, about 40 minutes. While the crust is hot, scatter into it 1 cup (5 oz.) coarsely chopped **semisweet** or bittersweet **chocolate** or whole semisweet chocolate baking chips. When chocolate softens, spread it with the back of a spoon evenly over the bottom and up the sides of crust to ¹/₂ inch below the rim. If made ahead, let crust cool, then wrap airtight and let stand up to 6 hours.

Chefs of 🍳 the West®

The Art of Cooking . . . by men . . . for men

IF A BED-AND-BREAKFAST INN *is worthy of its name, it should give you a quiet night's rest and a breakfast designed to spoil your appetite for lunch. Proprietors of such establishments have developed many a morning feast, largely in the area of hot breads and egg dishes. Earl Fraser sends us San Geronimo quiche from his inn in Taos, New Mexico, and it's hearty enough to fuel you for several hours of strolling through the thin, clean air of this picturesque mountain town.*

Fraser's crustless quiche—almost an omelet—has a regional flavor that comes from corn chips and salsa. We have taken the liberty of lightening it up a bit by eliminating ¼ cup butter.

SAN GERONIMO QUICHE

- ½ cup milk
- ¼ cup all-purpose flour
- 4 large eggs
- ¾ pound (3 cups) shredded sharp cheddar cheese
- 1½ cups small-curd cottage cheese
- ½ cup crushed corn chips
- 1 teaspoon *each* sugar and baking powder
  Prepared salsa

In a large bowl, smoothly stir milk into flour, then add eggs, cheddar cheese, cottage cheese, corn chips, sugar, and baking powder; beat mixture until well blended.

Pour into a 9- by 13-inch pan or baking dish. Bake, uncovered, in a 350° oven until quiche is slightly puffed and appears set when the pan is gently shaken, about 40 minutes. Let cool for 10 minutes, then cut into 12 equal rectangles. Transfer to plates using a wide spatula; add salsa to taste. Makes 12 servings.

PER SERVING: 203 calories, 13 g protein, 6 g carbohydrates, 14 g fat (7.8 g saturated), 106 mg cholesterol, 369 mg sodium

Earl Fraser
Taos, N.M.

TORN-APART SOUP *seems, on the face of it, to be an oxymoron—a contradictory statement akin to compulsory volunteer service or simplified tax form. Yet such a soup exists. It's called stracciatella, from the Italian verb stracciare, which means to tear apart.*

The name was derived from the appearance of the egg, which forms strands or shreds when immersed in the hot broth. If you have eaten Chinese egg-drop soup, you've seen this torn-apart look. Stracciatella is bolder in appearance, however, than the wispy Chinese version.

Of the many Italian egg soups, stracciatella is the simplest to prepare, and there are many ways of making it. Some recipes mix the cheese with the egg before serving; others insist that the broth not be stirred after adding the eggs. Roberto Lancellotti's version is straightforward and delicious.

STRACCIATELLA

- 4 to 5 cups regular-strength beef broth
- 3 tablespoons dry sherry
- ⅛ teaspoon ground nutmeg
- 1 tablespoon chopped parsley
- 4 large eggs
  Freshly ground pepper
  Freshly grated parmesan cheese

In a 2- to 3-quart pan, bring broth to a boil; add sherry, nutmeg, and parsley. In a small bowl, beat eggs to blend. Reduce heat so soup barely simmers, then slowly pour egg in a spiral into beef broth.

Ladle steaming soup into bowls; add pepper and cheese to taste. Makes 5 to 6 cups, 4 or 5 first-course servings.

PER SERVING: 83 calories, 5.9 g protein, 3 g carbohydrates, 4 g fat (1.3 g saturated), 170 mg cholesterol, 56 mg sodium

Roberto Lancellotti
Burlingame, Calif.

"Stracciatella is bolder in appearance than Chinese egg-drop soup."

Serve crisp vegetables and crackers with almond and coconut appetizer spread.

SPICY ALMOND BUTTER DIP OR SPREAD

¹/₂ **cup smooth almond or peanut butter**

¹/₂ **cup canned coconut milk**

3 **tablespoons lemon juice**

1 **clove garlic, minced or pressed**

¹/₈ **teaspoon crushed dried hot red chilies**

1 **teaspoon sugar (optional)**
Salt

1 **tablespoon thinly sliced green onion**
About 6 cups raw vegetables, such as cucumber slices, jicama sticks, or carrot sticks
Round butter crackers

In a blender or food processor, combine almond or peanut butter, coconut milk, lemon juice, garlic, and chilies; whirl to smoothly purée. Add sugar and salt to taste. Spoon the almond mixture into a small decorative crock or serving bowl. If made ahead, cover and chill up to overnight.

Bring almond mixture to room temperature before serving. Garnish with sliced green onion. Offer nut mixture to spread on raw vegetables and crisp crackers. Makes about 1 cup, enough for 12 to 16 appetizer servings.—*Carole Enmark, Weed, Calif.*

PER TABLESPOON: 78 calories, 1.8 g protein, 5.2 g carbohydrates, 6.2 g fat (1.8 g saturated), 0 mg cholesterol, 43 mg sodium

---

Mix red cabbage, carrots, radishes, red onion, and lemon for a lean slaw.

SPICY RED COLESLAW

6 **cups (about ³/₄ lb.) finely shredded red cabbage**

1 **cup thinly sliced radishes**

1 **cup shredded carrots**

¹/₄ **cup minced parsley**

1 **tablespoon finely chopped red onion**
Dressing (recipe follows)
Salt and pepper

6 **to 8 large green lettuce leaves, rinsed and crisped**

Place cabbage, radishes, carrots, parsley, and onion in bowl. Add dressing and gently mix. Cover and chill at least 30 minutes or up to 6 hours.

Mix again just before serving; add salt and pepper to taste. Arrange lettuce leaves on a shallow rimmed bowl or serving platter; mound slaw on leaves. Makes 6 servings.—*Lisa Miller, Berkeley.*

Dressing. In a bowl, beat to blend 3 tablespoons **olive oil**, 3 tablespoons **lemon juice**, 2 tablespoons **red wine vinegar**, 2 teaspoons **sugar**, 1 teaspoon **Dijon mustard**, ¹/₂ teaspoon **celery seed**, and ¹/₄ teaspoon **ground cumin.**

PER SERVING: 100 calories, 1.4 g protein, 9 g carbohydrates, 7.2 g fat (1 g saturated), 0 mg cholesterol, 47 mg sodium

---

Sweet, spiced sauce makes a flavorful condiment for baked or grilled chicken.

OLD SOUTHWEST SAUCE

1 **large onion, finely chopped**

3 **cloves garlic, minced or pressed**

1 **tablespoon butter or margarine**

3 **cans (8 oz. each) tomato sauce**

¹/₂ **cup firmly packed brown sugar**

¹/₄ **cup *each* lime juice and red wine vinegar**

2 **teaspoons chili powder**

2 **beef or chicken bouillon cubes**

¹/₂ **teaspoon *each* dry mustard and instant coffee powder**

¹/₈ **teaspoon liquid hot pepper seasoning**

¹/₈ **teaspoon liquid smoke (optional)**

In a 2- to 3-quart pan over medium-high heat, combine onion, garlic, and butter; stir often until onion is limp and golden, about 10 minutes.

To pan, add tomato sauce, brown sugar, lime juice, vinegar, chili powder, bouillon cubes, dry mustard, instant coffee powder, liquid hot pepper seasoning, and liquid smoke. Bring mixture to a boil; reduce heat and simmer, uncovered, until reduced to 3¹/₂ cups, about 30 minutes, stirring occasionally. If made ahead, cool, cover airtight, and chill up to 1 month. Makes 3¹/₂ cups.—*Evelyn Simco, Phoenix.*

PER TABLESPOON: 15 calories, 0.2 g protein, 3.2 g carbohydrates, 0.2 g fat (0.1 g saturated), 0.6 mg cholesterol, 105 mg sodium

HAM & SPINACH WHEELS

- 1 package (10 oz.) frozen chopped spinach, thawed
- 1 large package (8 oz.) neufchâtel (light cream) cheese or cream cheese
- 2 tablespoons prepared horseradish
- ⅛ teaspoon ground allspice
- ⅛ teaspoon ground pepper
- 6 flour tortillas (7 in. wide)
- ¾ pound thinly sliced cooked ham
- ¼ cup thinly sliced green onion (optional)

Press spinach firmly with the back of a spoon to remove excess moisture.

In a bowl, mix spinach, cheese, horse-radish, allspice, and pepper. Divide spinach mixture evenly among each of 6 tortillas. With a spatula, spread spinach mixture to cover tortilla evenly. Divide ham into 6 equal portions. Place 1 portion of ham on each tortilla, covering spinach mixture. Sprinkle with green onion (onion gets strong if held more than 4 hours).

Roll each tortilla tightly to encase filling. (If made ahead, cover airtight and chill up to overnight.) With a sharp knife, cut each tortilla diagonally into 4 equal slices. Makes 6 servings.—*Marilyn Swartz, Los Angeles.*

PER SERVING: 283 calories, 20 g protein, 16 g carbohydrates, 16 g fat (7.4 g saturated), 62 mg cholesterol, 1,182 mg sodium

Spinach, cheese, and thinly sliced ham swirl through center of sandwich wheels.

CHILE CON PAVO

- ½ cup Spanish-style olives or calamata olives
- 1 pound ground turkey or ground-turkey sausage
- 1 large (about 8 oz.) onion, chopped
- 1 fresh jalapeño chili, stemmed, seeded, and minced
- 1 tablespoon salad oil
- 3 tablespoons chili powder
- 1 can (7 oz.) diced green chilies
- 1 can (28 oz.) tomatoes
- 2 cans (15 oz. each) kidney beans
- ⅛ teaspoon ground cloves
  Toppings (choices follow)

Slice Spanish olives or cut flesh from cala-mata olives (discard pits); set aside. In a 4- to 5-quart pan over high heat, combine turkey, onion, jalapeño, and oil. Stir often until meat is crumbly and brown, about 20 minutes.

Stir in chili powder, green chilies, tomatoes (break up with a spoon) and juices, beans and liquid, cloves, and olives. Simmer, uncovered, to blend flavors, about 15 minutes. Serve in bowls; offer toppings to add to taste. Makes 5 or 6 servings.—*Sheryl Roberts, Las Vegas.*

Toppings. Corn chips, shredded **cheddar cheese,** chopped **cilantro** (coriander), **lime** wedges, unflavored **yogurt.**

PER SERVING WITHOUT TOPPINGS: 316 calories, 23 g protein, 34 g carbohydrates, 11 g fat (2.1 g saturated), 55 mg cholesterol, 1,292 mg sodium

Easy chili holds chunks of ground turkey and olives. Add condiments to taste.

C.J.'s FAVORITE LIME CHEESECAKE

- 1½ cups graham cracker crumbs
  About 1 cup sugar
- ¼ cup (⅛ lb.) butter or margarine
- 2 large packages (8 oz. each) neufchâtel (light cream) cheese or cream cheese
- 1 cup light or regular sour cream
- 3 large eggs
- 1 tablespoon grated lime peel
- ¼ cup lime juice
- 2 tablespoons all-purpose flour
  Topping (recipe follows)
  Thin lime slices

Mix crumbs, 2 tablespoons sugar, and butter. Press over bottom and ½ inch up sides of a 9-inch cheesecake pan with removable rim. Bake in a 350° oven until lightly browned, 10 minutes. Beat cheese, sour cream, eggs, remaining sugar, peel, juice, and flour until smooth; pour into crust. Bake in 350° oven until center jiggles only slightly when pan is gently shaken, 35 to 45 minutes. Cool; spread with topping. Cover and chill until cold, at least 4 hours or up to next day. Top with lime slices. Serves 12 to 16.—*Carrie-Casandra Stroble, Arcata, Calif.*

Topping. Mix 1 cup **light** or regular **sour cream** and 2 teaspoons *each* **sugar** and **lime juice.**

PER SERVING: 264 calories, 6.9 g protein, 25 g carbohydrates, 15 g fat (8.3 g saturated), 79 mg cholesterol, 224 mg sodium

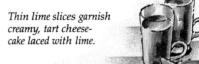

Thin lime slices garnish creamy, tart cheesecake laced with lime.

August Menus

WITH SOARING SUMMER *tempera-tures, cooks look for ways to mini-mize long, hot hours in the kitchen.*

Start with a breakfast that takes only minutes to prepare. Beat the midday heat with cool, make-ahead pasta salad served in a tomato shell. And for dinner, bring the cooking outdoors to the barbecue.

Spread the lean, fruit-flavored cheese on toast and fruit. The spread can be stored for several days.

APRICOT–RICOTTA CHEESE SPREAD

    ¼   cup chopped dried apricots
    3   tablespoons orange juice
        About 1 cup (1 carton, 8 oz.) part-skim milk ricotta cheese
    3   tablespoons honey
    ½   teaspoon ground coriander

In a small bowl, soak apricots in orange juice until soft, about 10 minutes.

In a food processor or blender, combine apricot-juice mixture, cheese, honey, and coriander; whirl until well blended. (If made ahead, cover and chill up to 3 days.)

Serve cheese spread cold or at room temperature. Makes about 1¼ cups, 4 or 5 servings.

PER TABLESPOON: 32 calories, 1.4 g protein, 4.7 g carbohydrates, 0.9 g fat (0.5 g saturated), 3.7 mg cholesterol, 15 mg sodium

Carry this cool lunch outdoors to enjoy by the pool or under a shady tree. The salad can be made up to a day ahead; mix together shortly before serving.

Lightly spread sliced cooked ham with mustard and roll up loosely; nestle in small to medium-size spears of rinsed and crisped romaine lettuce. Allow 3 to 4 ounces ham and 3 or 4 lettuce leaves for each serving.

For the beverage desserts, assemble tall glasses. Place a scoop of berry-flavor frozen yogurt in each of the glasses and fill

Cozy breakfast in bed features low-fat, high-protein apricot–ricotta cheese spread to slather on raisin toast and fresh fruit, such as nectarines, pears, and grapes. Make the spread in advance, if you like; it can be served cold or at room temperature.

with a chilled blend of berry juice and sparkling water.

HARVEST VEGETABLE PASTA SALAD

- 1 large (about 10 oz.) ear corn, husk and silk removed
- 1/4 pound green beans, ends trimmed
- 1 large (about 1/2 lb.) zucchini, ends trimmed
- 1/2 cup (3 oz.) dry rice-shaped or other small pasta
- 6 large (10 to 12 oz. each) firm-ripe tomatoes
  Tarragon dressing (recipe follows)
  Salt and pepper
  Fresh tarragon sprigs (optional)

In a 5- to 6-quart pan, bring about 3 quarts water to a boil. Add corn, beans, and zucchini. Cook until corn is hot and beans and zucchini are tender-crisp when pierced, about 5 minutes for corn and beans, 8 minutes for zucchini. Lift out of water as done and immerse in cold water. Add pasta to boiling water and cook until barely tender to bite, 7 to 12 minutes. Drain pasta and rinse with cold water.

Core and cut top 1/2 inch off tomatoes; set aside. With a spoon, scoop out insides of tomatoes; reserve for another use or discard. Drain tomato cups upside-down on towels. (If made ahead, cover and chill up until the next day.) Chop tomato tops. Cut corn off the cob. Thinly slice beans. Dice zucchini into about 1/2-inch pieces.

In a large bowl, mix pasta, corn, beans, zucchini, and chopped tomatoes. (If made ahead, cover and chill up until next day.) Mix in dressing. Add salt and pepper to taste. Fill tomatoes with pasta salad. Garnish with tarragon sprigs. Makes 6 servings.

PER SERVING: 194 calories, 5.5 protein, 29 g carbohydrates, 8 g fat (1.1 g saturated), 0 mg cholesterol, 103 mg sodium

Tarragon dressing. Mix 3 tablespoons *each* **olive oil** and **white wine vinegar,** 1 tablespoon chopped **fresh** or 1 teaspoon dry **tarragon leaves,** 1 tablespoon **water,** 1 tablespoon **Dijon mustard,** and 1 clove **garlic,** pressed or minced. (If made ahead, cover and chill up until the next day.)

Pasta salad with vegetables fills large tomato shell; accompany with ham rolls nestled in romaine spears, crusty bread, and a berry-flavored beverage.

SULTRY SUMMER SUPPER

Grilled Chicken Legs with Olives
Orange-Onion Escarole Salad
Sesame Rolls   Persian Melon Wedges
Dry Chenin Blanc   White Grape Juice

Chicken legs seasoned with a rosemary-scented olive mixture cook on the grill along with eggplant slices. Serve with a refreshing orange salad.

Tuck the olive mixture under the skin of chicken legs up to a day ahead. About 1 1/4 hours before serving, ignite the briquets. As you wait for the coals to heat, prepare salad ingredients. Just before serving, mix greens with dressing and arrange on plates alongside chicken and eggplant.

GRILLED CHICKEN LEGS WITH OLIVES

- 4 whole chicken legs with thighs attached (about 2 2/3 lb. total)
- 1/2 cup Spanish-style olives, chopped
- 1 clove garlic, pressed or minced
- 1 teaspoon minced fresh or 1/2 teaspoon crumbled dry rosemary leaves
- 1 medium-size (about 3/4 lb.) eggplant, cut crosswise into 3/4-inch-thick rounds
- 2 tablespoons olive oil
- 2 tablespoons orange juice
- 2 teaspoons honey

Rinse chicken and pat dry. Cut a slit just through skin at joint on outside of each chicken leg. Slide your fingers beneath

(Continued on next page)

skin to separate it from thigh and drumstick meat, but leave skin in place. Mix olives, garlic, and minced rosemary. Tuck ¼ of the olive mixture under skin on top side of each leg, pushing to distribute equally. (If made ahead, cover and chill up until the next day.)

Brush both sides of eggplant with oil. Mix orange juice and honey; set aside. Place chicken on a grill 4 to 6 inches above a solid bed of medium coals (you can hold your hand at grill level only 4 to 5 seconds). Cook for 20 minutes, turning often to avoid burning.

Add eggplant to grill. Turn chicken and eggplant to brown evenly, 15 to 25

minutes longer. Brush both with honey mixture. Cook, turning and basting often, until chicken is no longer pink at bone (cut to test) and eggplant is very soft when pressed, about 5 minutes longer. Transfer eggplant and chicken to 4 dinner plates. Makes 4 servings.

PER SERVING: 465 calories, 40 g protein, 9.6 g carbohydrates, 29 g fat (6.7 g saturated), 138 mg cholesterol, 542 mg sodium

ORANGE-ONION ESCAROLE SALAD

¼ cup white wine vinegar
2 tablespoons water
1 tablespoon sugar
½ cup thinly sliced sweet, mild onion
3 medium-size (about 1 lb. total) oranges
8 cups (about 7 oz.) bite-size pieces escarole, rinsed and crisped

In a small bowl, mix vinegar, water, and sugar. Add onion; mix to coat. Cover and chill 10 to 30 minutes.

Meanwhile, cut peel and white membrane off oranges. Thinly slice oranges crosswise. In a large bowl, mix onion and its marinade, oranges, and escarole. Makes 4 servings.

PER SERVING: 69 calories, 1.5 g protein, 17 g carbohydrates, 0.3 g fat (0 g saturated), 0 mg cholesterol, 13 mg sodium

SEPTEMBER

Nasturtium-Tarragon Pasta Salad (page 230)

Experiment with our unusual pastas, which capture the delicate beauty of fresh flowers and herbs between transparent, ready-made won ton or egg roll wrappers. Bring the flavors of Greece to your garden with an Aegean appetizer party; our menu suggests buy-and-serve dishes that make preparation easy on the cook. Other September articles offer three short-cut versions of minestrone, speedy pork and turkey entrées, recipes using packaged mixes for Middle Eastern specialties, and dishes showcasing late Bartlett or early winter pears.

Aegean Appetizers Alfresco

BENEATH A BRILLIANT SKY, *you're nibbling Aegean appetizers while sipping iced ouzo or wine. Sound like a scene from an exotic vacation? In a way, this Greek appetizer meal, or meze, is a cook's holiday. To create this garden party for 12, combine purchased foods with others that require little more than a splash of olive oil, some lemon juice, and a few herbs. A real plus: preparation takes only 2 hours, from grocery bags to the table.*

BUY & SERVE
MEZE FOR 12

Hummus   Crusty Bread
Favas with Herbs   Aegean Cheese
Marinated Shrimp
Radishes & Sardines
Raw Vegetable Tray   Olives
Pickled Vegetables
Stuffed Grape Leaves
Halvah   Honey & Nut Pastries
Melon & Grapes   Sparkling Water
Dry Sauvignon Blanc or Retsina
Ouzo

Delicatessens and international markets sell canned fava beans, halvah (a sesame seed candy sold canned or in bulk), and honey-soaked nut pastries such as baklava and burma. Suggested alternatives are in supermarkets. Buy anise-flavor ouzo (to pour over ice or mix with water) and retsina wines from a wine merchant.

Foods to buy and serve: About ³/4 pound canned **stuffed grape leaves** (called dolmathes, dolmades, or dolmas); ³/4 pound total **assorted olives** (calamata, dry salt-cured, niçoise, California ripe); 1 pound **giardiniera** (pickled vegetables); and ³/4 pound **marinated artichokes.** Drain foods before serving.

Also buy about 2¹/2 pounds *total* of **crusty bread** and **pocket bread,** 1 to 1¹/2 pounds **pastries** or butter cookies, 1 large (about 3¹/2 lb.) **cantaloupe,** and 1 pound **grapes.**

HUMMUS

- 2 cloves garlic
- 2 cans (15 oz. each) low-salt or regular garbanzos, drained
- ¹/3 cup tahini (sesame seed paste)
- ¹/3 cup lemon juice
- ¹/2 cup water
- 3 tablespoons olive oil
- ¹/4 teaspoon cayenne
  Salt

Drop garlic into a blender or food processor with motor running; whirl to mince. Add garbanzos, tahini, lemon juice, water, 2 tablespoons oil, and cayenne; whirl smooth. Scrape into a bowl; drizzle with remaining oil. Serve; or chill airtight up to 1 day, then bring to room temperature. Add salt to taste. Makes about 3 cups.

PER TABLESPOON: 33 calories, 1.1 g protein, 3.3 g carbohydrates, 1.9 g fat (0.2 g saturated), 0 mg cholesterol, 35 mg sodium

FAVAS WITH HERBS

- 2 cans (about 27 oz. each) fava beans, or 3 cans (15 oz. each) butter beans, drained
- ¹/3 cup minced red onion
- ¹/4 cup coarsely chopped fresh or 1¹/2 tablespoons dry oregano leaves
- 2 tablespoons olive oil
- ¹/4 cup red wine vinegar
  Salt and pepper

In a bowl, mix beans, onion, oregano, olive oil, vinegar, and salt and pepper to taste. Serve; or chill airtight up to 1 day, then bring to room temperature. Makes about 4²/3 cups, 12 servings.

PER ¹/3 CUP: 98 calories, 6 g protein, 14 g carbohydrates, 2.2 g fat (0.3 g saturated), 0 mg cholesterol, 495 mg sodium

AEGEAN CHEESE

Other regional cheeses to consider are halloumi, kasseri, manouri, or mizithra.

- 1 large clove garlic, minced
- 3 tablespoons olive oil
- 1 tablespoon fresh or 1 teaspoon dry thyme leaves
- 1¹/2 pounds feta cheese (from sheep's milk, if available), drained if in brine, and broken into chunks

In a bowl, mix garlic, olive oil, and thyme. Add cheese and mix gently. Serve; or chill airtight up to 1 day, then bring to room temperature. Makes 12 servings.

PER SERVING: 180 calories, 8 g protein, 2.5 g carbohydrates, 15 g fat (8.9 g saturated), 51 mg cholesterol, 633 mg sodium

MARINATED SHRIMP

- 1¹/2 pounds large (31 to 35 per lb.), shelled, cooked shrimp
- 3 tablespoons olive oil
- 3 tablespoons lemon juice
- 3 tablespoons chopped fresh dill or 1 tablespoon dry dill weed
- 3 tablespoons chopped fresh or 1¹/2 tablespoons crumbled dry mint leaves
- ³/4 teaspoon coarse-grind or cracked pepper
  Fresh dill sprigs (optional)

In a bowl, mix shrimp, oil, lemon juice, chopped dill, mint, and pepper. Chill airtight at least 30 minutes or up to 1 day. Transfer to a platter and garnish with dill sprigs. Makes 12 servings.

PER SERVING: 88 calories, 12 g protein, 0.5 g carbohydrates, 4 g fat (0.6 g saturated), 111 mg cholesterol, 128 mg sodium

RADISHES & SARDINES

- 3 cans (about 4 oz. each) brisling sardines, drained
- 2 or 3 thin onion slices, separated into rings
- 12 red radishes, each with a few unbruised leaves, rinsed and crisped
- 2 tablespoons red wine vinegar

Arrange sardines, onion, and radishes in a dish; sprinkle with vinegar. Serve, or chill airtight up to 1 day. Makes 12 servings.

PER SERVING: 54 calories, 6.1 g protein, 0.5 g carbohydrates, 2.8 g fat (0.4 g saturated), 35 mg cholesterol, 126 mg sodium

RAW VEGETABLE TRAY

- 1³/4 pounds romaine lettuce, cut through the core into 12 wedges
  About 1 pound red radishes, each with a few unbruised leaves
- 1 pound red or yellow cherry tomatoes, or a combination
- 1 medium-size (about 10 oz.) cucumber, cut into 12 wedges

Rinse and crisp lettuce and radishes. On a platter, arrange the lettuce, radishes, tomatoes, and cucumber. Serve, or chill airtight up to 1 day. Makes 12 servings.

PER SERVING: 27 calories, 1.7 g protein, 5.1 g carbohydrates, 0.4 g fat (0 g saturated), 0 mg cholesterol, 17 mg sodium

Simply seasoned foods need very little preparation: garbanzo-sesame dip; marinated shrimp; sardines and radishes; crisp vegetables and bowl of flavored fava beans; bread; herbed feta cheese; assorted olives; and a plate of marinated artichokes, pickled vegetables, and stuffed grape leaves.

Pasta Pictures

REMEMBER PRESSING FLOWERS *in a book to capture their delicate beauty? You can get the same effect with pasta by sandwiching fresh herbs and flowers between transparent, ready-made won ton or egg roll wrappers. The pasta pictures are not only visually appealing, they also have the herbs' fresh, lively pungency.*

The pasta is simple to assemble, stores well, and cooks in minutes. Recipes use nasturtium blossoms, and herbs and their flowers—buy them or harvest them from your garden; make sure they have been grown without pesticides. If you use flowers other than nasturtiums, be certain they are safe to eat.

FRESH HERB & FLOWER PASTA

Fresh herb leaves and flowers
(see recipes following for choices)
2 teaspoons cornstarch
Won ton skins or egg roll
wrappers (see recipes following)

Discard tough stems from herbs and flowers. Rinse leaves and blossoms; drain dry.

Mix cornstarch and 2 tablespoons water until smooth. Work with 2 pieces of pasta at a time (keep remaining pasta covered with plastic wrap). Brush 1 side of each piece of pasta with cornstarch mixture.

Arrange a single layer of a few herbs and flowers on top of 1 piece, leaving at least a ¼-inch border of uncovered pasta around edges. Place the other pasta piece over the first and press gently with a rolling pin to seal and expel air. If desired, cut edges with a fluted ravioli cutter. Repeat with remaining pasta, herbs, and flowers.

Lay pasta pieces slightly apart in a flour-dusted 10- by 15-inch pan and cover with plastic wrap; sprinkle with flour and layer more pasta on top. If made ahead, wrap airtight and chill up to 1 day. Or freeze in a single layer until solid, then package airtight and store in freezer up to 2 weeks.

To cook, fill a 5- to 6-quart pan ¾ full of water and bring to a boil over high heat. Add about half of the pasta at a time (do not thaw if frozen) and boil gently until barely tender to bite, about 2 minutes; occasionally push pasta under the boiling water. Lift out a couple of pieces at a time with a slotted spoon, draining, and gently mix in a bowl with seasonings as directed in the following recipes.

SAGE PASTA

Follow preceding recipe for **fresh herb and flower pasta,** using about 40 **fresh sage leaves** (each 2 to 3 in. long), 50 **fresh sage blossoms** (without stems), and 40 **won ton skins** (3¼-in. size; 9 oz. total).

Mix hot, drained pasta with 2 tablespoons melted **butter** or margarine. Transfer to warm plates and season pasta to taste with **salt, pepper,** and grated **parmesan cheese;** garnish with **fresh sage flowers** and **leaves.** Makes 4 servings.

PER SERVING: 227 calories, 8 g protein, 35 g carbohydrates, 6.3 g fat (3.6 g saturated), 16 mg cholesterol, 76 mg sodium

NASTURTIUM-TARRAGON PASTA SALAD

Follow preceding recipe for **fresh herb and flower pasta,** using 50 **tarragon leaves** (about 2 in. long), 20 **nasturtium flowers** (about 3 in. across; or use more tarragon), and 40 **won ton skins** (3¼-in. size; 9 oz. total). Mix hot pasta with 1½ teaspoons grated **lemon peel** and 6 tablespoons *each* **salad oil** and **lemon juice;** let cool.

On 4 plates, arrange 8 large (4 oz. total) **butter lettuce leaves,** rinsed and crisped; 2 cups lightly packed tender **nasturtium leaves,** or more lettuce, rinsed and crisped; and 1 cup thinly sliced, peeled **cucumber,** cut into matchstick slices.

Spoon dressing over greens; arrange pasta on top. Season with **salt** and **pepper;** garnish with **nasturtium flowers.** Makes 4 servings.

PER SERVING: 380 calories, 9 g protein, 39 g carbohydrates, 21 g fat (2.6 g saturated), 0 mg cholesterol, 35 mg sodium

Sage blossoms and leaves season and decorate easy-to-make pasta. Brush won ton skin with cornstarch paste, arrange herbs and flowers, and press another pasta skin on top. Roll to seal; cut fluted edges, if desired.

Fresh herb leaves and blossoms show through translucent cooked pasta. Season with butter and serve with chicken.

Nasturtium blossom and tarragon leaves sparkle inside translucent pasta. Dress tepid pasta with lemon vinaigrette and arrange on greens with matchstick slices of cucumber. Garnish with nasturtium flowers.

MIXED HERB PASTA TRIANGLES

Follow preceding recipe for **fresh herb and flower pasta,** using 8 **egg roll wrappers** (6-in. size; 6 oz. total) and mixed fresh herbs, such as 8 **fresh basil leaves** (about 2 in. long), 16 **fresh oregano leaves** (about 1 in. long), 24 **fresh rosemary leaves** (about ³/₄ in. long), and 1¹/₂ teaspoons **fresh thyme leaves.** Instead of sealing 2 pasta wrappers together, sprinkle herbs over half of each square and fold each wrapper into a triangle. Trim edges evenly.

Mix hot pasta with 2 tablespoons **olive oil.** Serve the pasta warm or cool. Place 2 pasta triangles on each plate.

Spoon chopped **firm-ripe tomatoes** (1 cup total) alongside pasta. Season pasta to taste with **salt, pepper,** and grated **parmesan cheese;** garnish with **fresh herb leaves.** Makes 4 servings.

PER SERVING: 186 calories, 5.7 g protein, 25 g carbohydrates, 7.2 g fat (0.9 g saturated), 0 mg cholesterol, 15 mg sodium

Minestrone Knows No Season

IN ITALY, MINESTRONE *comes in count-less variations, which can be eaten cool in the summer and hot in the winter. The base of this popular vegetable soup is usually a bean-thickened broth; these short-cut versions used canned beans to minimize cooking time. For a one-pot meal, add fresh vegetables and pasta, rice, or barley.*

All these soups taste good hot, cool, and in between. Accompany with a Soave, Gavi, Orvieto, or dry Sauvignon Blanc.

MINESTRONE GENOVESE

- 2 large (about 1¼ lb. total) leeks
- 3 quarts regular-strength chicken broth
- 2 large (about ½ lb. total) carrots, peeled and cut into ½-inch chunks
- 3 large stalks (about ½ lb. total) celery, sliced thin
- 2 cans (15 oz. each) cannellini (white kidney beans), drained
- 2 cups (4 oz.) dry elbow macaroni
- 1 pound (about 4 large) yellow crookneck squash or yellow zucchini, ends trimmed, cut into ½-inch chunks
- 1 large (about ½ lb.) red bell pepper, stemmed, seeded, and cut into ½-inch pieces
- 1 package (1 lb.) frozen petite peas
  Pesto (recipe follows)
  Salt and pepper

Trim root ends and green tops off leeks. Split leeks in half lengthwise and rinse thoroughly; thinly slice leeks crosswise.

In an 8- to 10-quart pan, combine leeks, broth, carrots, and celery; bring to a boil. Cover and simmer 10 minutes. Add beans, macaroni, squash, and bell pepper; cover and simmer until macaroni is just tender to bite, about 10 minutes. Add peas; bring to a boil. Stir ½ cup of pesto into soup. Serve hot or cold. (If made ahead, cool, cover, and chill up until next day. Warm to room temperature or reheat.) Offer remaining pesto, salt, and pepper to add to taste. Makes 10 to 12 servings.

PER SERVING WITHOUT PESTO: 220 calories, 12 g protein, 30 g carbohydrates, 6.3 g fat (1.6 g saturated), 3.2 mg cholesterol, 270 mg sodium

Pesto. In a food processor or blender, purée 2 cups (about 2 oz.) lightly packed **fresh basil leaves**, 1 cup **grated parmesan cheese**, ¼ cup **olive oil**, 2 tablespoons **pine nuts** or slivered almonds, and 1 to 2 cloves **garlic**. Add **salt** to taste. If made ahead, cover and chill up until next day. Warm to room temperature to use. Makes 1 cup.

PER TABLESPOON: 69 calories, 3.1 g protein, 1.8 g carbohydrates, 5.9 g fat (1.7 g saturated), 4.8 mg cholesterol, 114 mg sodium

MINESTRONE WITH CHARD & ROSEMARY

- 1 pound (about 5 large) Roma-type tomatoes
- 2 tablespoons olive oil
- 1 large onion, chopped
- 1 clove garlic, minced or pressed
- 2 stalks (about 6 oz. total) celery, diced
- 2 ounces thinly sliced prosciutto or cooked ham, cut into thin shreds
- 3 quarts regular-strength beef broth
- 2 large (about ½ lb. total) carrots, peeled and diced
- 1 tablespoon minced fresh or 1 teaspoon dry rosemary leaves
- ⅔ cup medium-grain white rice
- 1 pound Swiss chard, ends trimmed
- 3 cans (15 oz. each) pinto beans, drained
- ½ pound green beans, ends trimmed, cut into 1-inch lengths
- 1 pound (about 3 large) zucchini, ends trimmed, cut into ¾-inch chunks
  Freshly grated parmesan cheese
  Salt and pepper

In an 8- to 10-quart pan, bring about 1 quart of water to a boil. Drop in tomatoes and cook about 1 minute. Drain tomatoes and peel off skin. Core and chop tomatoes; set aside. Discard water in pan.

In the pan stir oil, onion, garlic, celery, and prosciutto over medium-high heat until onion is limp, about 8 minutes. Add broth, carrots, rosemary, and rice. Bring to a boil; cover and simmer 10 minutes.

Cut Swiss chard crosswise into ¼-inch strips. Mash 1 can pinto beans. Add mashed and whole pinto beans, green beans, tomato, and zucchini to pan. Cover and simmer 5 minutes longer. Stir in chard; simmer, uncov-

ered, until zucchini is tender to bite, 5 to 10 minutes longer. Serve hot or cool. (If made ahead, cool, cover, and chill up until next day; warm to room temperature or reheat.) Offer parmesan cheese, salt, and pepper to add to taste. Makes 10 to 12 servings.

PER SERVING: 175 calories, 8.9 g protein, 28 g carbohydrates, 3.5 g fat (0.5 g saturated), 2.8 mg cholesterol, 347 mg sodium

MINESTRONE WITH ESCAROLE

- 2 ounces pancetta or bacon, chopped
- 1 tablespoon olive oil
- 2 cloves garlic, pressed or minced
- 1 large (about ½ lb.) onion, chopped
- 2 quarts regular-strength chicken broth
- ½ pound (about 1 large) russet potato, peeled and diced
- ¾ cup pearl barley, sorted of debris and rinsed
- 2 tablespoons chopped fresh or 1 tablespoon dry mint leaves
- ½ teaspoon dry oregano leaves
- ¼ to ½ teaspoon crushed dry hot red chilies
- 2 cans (15 oz. each) garbanzos, drained
- 1½ pounds (about 8 large) Roma-type tomatoes, cored and diced
- 1 pound escarole, ends trimmed, rinsed and cut into 3-inch slivers
  Freshly grated parmesan cheese
  Salt and pepper

In a 5- to 6-quart pan over medium-high heat, mix pancetta with oil (omit oil if using bacon); stir frequently until lightly browned, about 5 minutes. Add garlic and onion; stir until onion is limp, about 5 minutes. Drain off fat.

Add broth, potato, barley, mint, oregano, and chilies. Bring to a boil, cover, and simmer until barley is tender to bite, about 30 minutes. Add garbanzos and tomatoes; bring to a boil. Stir in escarole; cook just until wilted, about 1 minute. Serve hot or cool. (If made ahead, cool, cover, and chill up until next day. Warm to room temperature or reheat.) Offer cheese, salt, and pepper to add to taste. Makes 6 to 8 servings.

PER SERVING: 235 calories, 11 g protein, 39 g carbohydrates, 4.7 g fat (4.7 g saturated), 1.7 mg cholesterol, 224 mg sodium

Basil pesto flavors all-vegetable minestrone genovese; canned beans minimize cooking time. Serve this thick, richly textured soup with crusty bread for a satisfying one-pot meal.

Building on Packaged Mixes

PACKAGED DRY MIXES for traditional Middle Eastern specialties form the base for these appealingly easy recipes. Boldly seasoned with the cuisine's characteristic herbs and spices—including lemon, garlic, sesame, cumin, and coriander—these mixes can quickly transform plain dishes into well-seasoned ones.

Hummus (made from ground garbanzos) and tahini (made from ground sesame seed) are most commonly served as dips for raw vegetables and bread. Tahini can also be thinned for use as a salad dressing.

Here we offer two more inventive uses for either of the mixes: as an ingredient in a rustic crusty bread and in a creamy, baked cheese-like custard. The garbanzos and sesame seed each contribute their own distinctive nutty flavors and dense, hearty textures to these choices.

We also built on a spiced rice pilaf mix by adding lamb and onion to make a quick one-pan meal; serve with a refreshing cucumber-yogurt-mint salsa.

Look for hummus, tahini, and rice pilaf mixes in supermarkets and natural-food stores in the section with rice and rice mixes or with the fancy foods. The mixes are sometimes also available by the pound in the bulk-foods section of some stores.

Purchased hummus mix endows this rustic quick bread with a scone-like texture and spicy flavor. Brush loaf with beaten egg just before baking.

HUMMUS OR TAHINI BREAD

- 2 large eggs
- 2/3 cup milk
- 1 package (6 oz.) hummus bean dip or tahini dip and dressing mix (about 1 1/2 cups)
  About 1 1/2 cups all-purpose flour
- 1 teaspoon baking soda
- 1/2 teaspoon baking powder

Lightly beat eggs; reserve 1 tablespoon. In a food processor or bowl, blend remaining eggs and milk. In another bowl, combine hummus or tahini mix and 1 1/2 cups flour, baking soda, and baking powder. Mix dry ingredients into liquid ingredients.

In a food processor or bowl, whirl or stir just until dough sticks together. If dough clings heavily to bowl, add flour, 1 tablespoon at a time, as needed. Working quickly, scrape dough onto a lightly floured board and shape into a smooth 6-inch round (dough dries out as it sits); place on an oiled 12- by 15-inch baking sheet. Brush loaf with reserved 1 tablespoon egg. Bake in a 350° oven until golden brown, 30 to 40 minutes. Makes 1 loaf (about 1 1/3 lb.).

PER OUNCE: 80 calories, 2.6 g protein, 8.1 g carbohydrates, 4 g fat (0.3 g saturated), 21 mg cholesterol, 59 mg sodium

LAMB PILAF

- 1 pound ground lean lamb
- 1 large (8 oz.) onion, coarsely chopped
- 1 package (6 to 8 oz.) rice pilaf mix with Middle Eastern seasonings
  Cucumber salsa (recipe follows)

In a 12-inch frying pan or 5- to 6-quart pan, cook lamb and onion over medium-high heat, stirring often, until meat is browned and onion is golden, about 15 minutes; discard any fat. Return to heat. When meat sizzles, add 1/4 cup water and stir to release browned bits;

when liquid evaporates, repeat this procedure twice.

To pan, add pilaf mix (including seasoning packet) and water amount specified on package directions for making entire mix. Bring to a boil, cover, and simmer until rice is tender to bite and liquid has evaporated, about 15 minutes. Transfer to a platter; serve with salsa. Makes 6 servings.

PER SERVING: 329 calories, 18 g protein, 35 g carbohydrates, 12 g fat (4.5 g saturated), 51 mg cholesterol, 563 mg sodium

Cucumber salsa. In a bowl, mix 1 pound (about 1 large) coarsely chopped **European cucumber,** 1 cup **unflavored non-fat yogurt,** 1/2 cup chopped **parsley,** 2 tablespoons chopped **green onion,** 2 tablespoons chopped **fresh mint,** 1 tablespoon **lemon juice,** 1 tablespoon drained **capers,** 2 teaspoons **olive oil,** and 1 clove **garlic,** minced or pressed. Makes 3 cups.

HUMMUS OR TAHINI CUSTARD WITH CONDIMENTS

1 1/2 **cups milk**
  1 **package (6 oz.) hummus bean dip or tahini dip and dressing mix (about 1 1/2 cups)**
  3 **large eggs**
    Condiments (suggestions follow)

In a blender, food processor, or large bowl, beat milk, hummus or tahini mix, and eggs until well blended. Pour into 8 greased custard or soufflé cups (each about 1/2 cup). Place cups in a larger baking pan in a 350° oven. Add boiling water to fill larger pan about 1 inch deep.

Bake until center is set and a knife inserted in center comes out clean, 15 to 25

Tahini mix flavors baked custard and gives it cheese-like consistency; here it's served as a first course with crisp greens and yogurt.

minutes. Remove cups from water; let cool 5 minutes. Run knife around edges and invert custards onto plates, or serve from cups. (If made ahead, cover and chill up until next day.) Serve hot, warm, or cool. Arrange with equal portions of condiments on 8 dinner plates. Makes 8 servings.

PER SERVING: 180 calories, 8.2 g protein, 8.5 g carbohydrates, 13 g fat (1.8 g saturated), 87 mg cholesterol, 200 mg sodium

Condiments. Offer 8 cups **salad greens** (rinsed and crisped); 2 small (about 8 oz. total) firm-ripe **tomatoes,** cored and cut into wedges; about 2/3 cup **unflavored yogurt;** 1/2 cup thinly sliced **green onion;** 1/3 cup **salt-cured olives;** and **lemon wedges.**

Fall Pears Steal the Show

FOR THE SHOWOFF INGREDIENT *in these two dishes, use the season's late Bartlett or early winter pears. The leg of lamb soaks in a piquant marinade, then grills with pears soaked in the same mixture. Dessert is a fragile hot souffléed pancake that bakes on butter-simmered pears.*

GRILLED BUTTERFLIED LEG OF LAMB & PEARS WITH ONION RELISH

> Onion relish marinade (recipe follows)
> 5 or 6 large (about 8 oz. each) firm-ripe pears, peeled, cut in half lengthwise, and cored
> 1 leg of lamb (about 6 lb.), boned
> Salt and pepper

Butterflied leg of lamb and pears were marinated in onion-orange mixture, then grilled; boil down marinade to make tart relish.

Bring onion marinade to boil on high heat. Add pears; reduce heat, cover, and simmer, turning fruit over occasionally, until pears are tender when pierced, 10 to 30 minutes, depending on ripeness.

With a slotted spoon, gently transfer pears to a bowl. Pour about ¼ of the liquid through a strainer onto the pears; return seasonings to pan. Cover pears; let stand up to 2 hours or chill up to overnight. Turn fruit over occasionally.

Rinse lamb and pat dry; trim excess fat. With boned side up, cut long, deep slashes through thickest sections and press apart to even the thickness of meat. Put meat in a large bowl with remaining marinade. Cover and chill for 2 hours or up until next day; turn meat over several times.

Lift lamb from marinade, shaking off seasonings; set aside. Return marinade from lamb and liquid from pears to pan; boil over high heat, uncovered, until reduced to about 2½ cups and most of liquid has cooked away, 10 to 15 minutes; stir often. Pour this onion relish into small bowl.

Lay lamb out flat, boned side up, on a grill over a solid bed of hot coals (you can hold your hand at grill level for only 2 to 3 seconds). Scatter 10 charcoal briquets onto coals. Cook until meat is evenly browned and done as you like in thickest part (cut to test); turn as needed. For medium-rare, allow about 45 minutes.

About 15 minutes before lamb is ready, thread pear halves, same sides up, onto parallel skewers (to keep the fruit from spinning). Lay pears on grill until warm, about 15 minutes, turning them several times. Transfer meat and pears to a large platter. Slice meat and serve with fruit and onion relish. Add salt and pepper to taste. Makes 10 to 12 servings.

PER SERVING: 317 calories, 32 g protein, 27 g carbohydrates, 9 g fat (3 g saturated), 97 mg cholesterol, 115 mg sodium

Onion relish marinade. With a vegetable peeler, pare 1 medium-size **orange,** removing only the orange part of the peel. Finely chop peel and put into a 4- to 5-quart pan. Cut off and discard remaining peel and white membrane. Holding fruit over pan, cut away membrane on sides of segments to release segments into pan. Squeeze juice from membrane into pan; discard membrane.

To pan add 1 large (about ¾ lb.) **red onion,** minced; 2 cups **dry red wine;** ½ cup **regular-strength beef broth;** ½ cup **golden** or dark **raisins;** ¼ cup *each* **raspberry vinegar** and **balsamic vinegar** (or all raspberry vinegar); 2 tablespoons minced **fresh ginger;** ¼ cup **sugar;** and 1 tablespoon **Dijon mustard.**

GOLDEN PEAR PANCAKE SOUFFLÉ

> 3 tablespoons butter or margarine
> ⅓ cup chopped pecans
> ¼ cup firmly packed brown sugar
> 1 tablespoon lemon juice
> 1 teaspoon ground cinnamon
> 3 large (about 8 oz. each) firm-ripe pears, peeled, cored, and cut lengthwise into thick slices
> Soufflé topping (directions follow)

Melt butter over medium heat in a 1½-quart shallow pan or 10-inch frying pan with ovenproof handle. Add pecans, sugar, lemon juice, and cinnamon; stir until bubbly. Add pears and cook, turning often with a spatula, until fruit is slightly tender when pierced, 5 to 10 minutes.

While pears are cooking, prepare soufflé topping. (If pears are ready first, keep them warm on lowest heat.) Pour topping over pears and jiggle pan to settle batter down around fruit; let cook about 30 seconds. Transfer to a 300° oven and bake until top is dark gold and center appears set when pan is jiggled, about 35 minutes. Spoon into bowls. Makes 6 servings.

PER SERVING: 356 calories, 7.2 g protein, 49 g carbohydrates, 16 g fat (6 g saturated), 196 mg cholesterol, 118 mg sodium

Soufflé topping. Whip 5 **large egg whites** and ¼ teaspoon **cream of tartar** in a deep bowl on high speed until foamy. Continue to beat, gradually adding ½ cup **granulated sugar,** until whites hold stiff peaks.

With unwashed beaters, beat 5 **large egg yolks** in a small bowl on high speed until about double in volume. Stir in ⅓ cup **all-purpose flour,** ¼ cup **half-and-half** (light cream), and 1 teaspoon **vanilla;** beat until mixed. Stir ¼ of the whites into yolks, then fold all together. Use at once.

LIGHTENING UP SUNSET CLASSICS: Chile Verde

THE POPULAR MEXICAN DISH *chile verde inspired this braised mixture laced with green chilies. It can be served as a stew or as a filling for tortillas.*

The original recipe (May 1974, page 186) used pork butt (shoulder). This lightened-up version instead uses chicken or turkey thighs, cutting calories by almost 30 percent and fat by just about two-thirds.

Rather than brown ingredients in fat, we use a no-fat browning technique we call braise-deglaze to develop a flavorful sauce base. Chopped onions boil in broth until the liquid evaporates, leaving a film of natural sugars from the onions that coats the pan.

Cooked further, these drippings turn a rich brown. The browned material, scraped free with the aid of more liquid, is absorbed by the onions. Repeated several times, this step builds up a rich taste that not only seasons sauces but also gives them an appetizing color.

LIGHTENED-UP BRAISED CHICKEN WITH GREEN CHILI SAUCE

- 3 pounds boned and skinned chicken or turkey thighs, lumps of fat pulled or trimmed off and discarded
- 1 large (about 8 oz.) onion, chopped
- 2 cloves garlic, pressed or minced
- 1 cup regular-strength chicken broth
- 1 teaspoon dry oregano leaves
- 1/2 teaspoon ground cumin
- 1 tablespoon wine vinegar
- 2 large (about 1 lb. total) green bell peppers, stemmed, seeded, and chopped
- 1/2 cup chopped fresh cilantro (coriander)
- 1 large can (7 oz.) diced green chilies
  Fresh cilantro sprigs
  Tomato wedges
  Nonfat unflavored yogurt or light sour cream
  Lime wedges
  Salt and pepper
  Hot cooked rice

Cut meat into 1-inch cubes; set aside.

In a 5- to 6-quart pan, combine onion, garlic, broth, oregano, and cumin. Boil, uncovered, on high heat until liquid evaporates and brown bits accumulate in pan, 10 to 15 minutes; stir often. To deglaze pan, add 2 tablespoons water and stir to release browned bits. Boil until more browned bits form, stirring often. Repeat deglazing step 2 or 3 times, or until onions are a rich brown color. Deglaze with vinegar and 1 tablespoon water.

When pan is dry, stir in chicken, peppers, chopped cilantro, chilies, and 1 tablespoon water. Cover and simmer over low heat until chicken is no longer pink in thickest part (cut to test), about 15 minutes; stir often. Skim off and discard fat.

Spoon into a bowl. Garnish with cilantro sprigs and tomatoes. Offer yogurt, lime, salt, and pepper to add to taste. Serve with rice. Makes 6 to 8 servings.

PER SERVING LIGHTENED UP BRAISED CHICKEN WITH GREEN CHILI SAUCE, WITHOUT ACCOMPANIMENTS: 237 calories, 35 g protein, 6.7 g carbohydrates, 7.2 g fat (1.8 g saturated), 141 mg cholesterol, 307 mg sodium

PER SERVING ORIGINAL BRAISED PORK WITH GREEN CHILI SAUCE, WITHOUT ACCOMPANIMENTS: 332 calories, 31 g protein, 6.4 g carbohydrates, 20 g fat (5.7 g saturated), 108 mg cholesterol, 865 mg sodium

For tacos, follow recipe for **braised chicken with green chili sauce** (preceding), except cut chicken into 3/4-inch chunks. With a slotted spoon, transfer cooked chicken to a bowl; keep warm. Boil juices, uncovered, over high heat until most liquid evaporates, 3 to 5 minutes. Mix with chicken.

Omit rice. Spoon chicken mixture onto **warm flour tortillas;** add tomatoes, sour cream, and lime juice; roll up to eat.

Spoon braised chicken thigh meat, mild chilies, and bell peppers onto flour tortillas. Embellish with tomato, yogurt, and lime; roll up to eat.

Speedy Ways with Pork

THE QUICK-COOKING *potential of pork is realized in these two dishes. In the first, couscous goes with pan-browned slender tenderloins in their own rich sauce. In the second, fat-trimmed meat from the shoulder or loin mixes with apples in a stir-fry.*

PORK TENDERLOIN WITH COUSCOUS

- 1½ **pounds (about 2) pork tenderloin**
- 2 **teaspoons sugar**
- 1 **tablespoon salad oil**
- 2⅓ **cups regular-strength beef broth**
- 1 **tablespoon** *each* **mustard seed and balsamic vinegar**
- 2 **teaspoons minced fresh or 1 teaspoon dry oregano leaves**
- 1 **tablespoon butter or margarine**
- 1 **cup (8 oz.) couscous**
- ½ **cup sliced green onions**
- ½ **cup dry red wine**
- 2 **teaspoons cornstarch mixed with 2 teaspoons water**
- ½ **pound asparagus, tough ends broken off**
  Salt and pepper

With a knife, trim fat and membrane from meat; sprinkle meat with sugar.

Pour oil into a 10- to 12-inch frying pan over medium-high heat; add pork and brown on all sides, about 4 minutes. Add ⅔ cup broth, mustard seed, vinegar, and oregano; cover and simmer over medium-low heat just until meat is no longer pink in center (cut to test), or until a thermometer in center of thickest part registers 155° to 160°, about 12 minutes.

Meanwhile, in a 2- to 3-quart pan over high heat, bring 1⅓ cups broth and butter to a boil. Stir in couscous. Cover, remove from heat, and let stand until liquid is absorbed, about 5 minutes; keep warm up to 15 minutes. Stir in onions with a fork.

Lift pork onto a platter; keep warm. To pan, add remaining ⅓ cup broth and wine; boil, uncovered, on high heat until reduced to ¾ cup, about 2 minutes. Stir in cornstarch mixture; stir until boiling.

While sauce reduces, bring ½ inch of water to a boil in another 10- to 12-inch frying pan over high heat. Add asparagus and cook, uncovered, just until it is barely tender when pierced, 4 to 5 minutes. Drain.

Slice meat and arrange on a platter. Mound couscous beside meat; top with asparagus. Spoon sauce onto meat. Add salt and pepper to taste. Makes 4 or 5 servings.

PER SERVING: 412 calories, 36 g protein, 41 g carbohydrates, 9.4 g fat (3 g saturated), 95 mg cholesterol, 100 mg sodium

PORK STIR-FRY WITH APPLE

- 1 **pound boned pork from the loin or shoulder (butt)**
  Teriyaki sauce (recipe follows)
- 2 **medium-size (about ¾ lb. total) red apples such as Red Delicious, cored and chopped**
- 2 **tablespoons lemon juice**
  About 2 tablespoons salad oil
- 1 **small onion, cut into thin wedges**
- 3 **cups hot cooked rice**
- 1 **or 2 medium-size oranges (peeled, if desired), sliced crosswise**
  Mint sprigs (optional)

Trim and discard fat and tough connective tissue from pork. Slice meat across the grain into 1/16- to 1/8-inch-thick strips about 2 inches long. In a small bowl, mix meat with teriyaki sauce; cover and chill at least 15 minutes, or up to overnight.

Mix apple with lemon juice; set aside.

Place a wok or 12-inch frying pan over high heat. When hot, add 1 tablespoon oil and onion. Stir-fry until onion is limp, about 2 minutes. Add apples with lemon juice; stir-fry until hot, about 1 minute. Spoon mixture into a bowl and set aside.

With a slotted spoon, lift ½ the meat into pan. Stir-fry until meat is lightly browned, about 2 minutes; add cooked meat to fruit. Repeat to cook remaining meat, adding more oil if needed. When lightly browned, add sauce and cooked meat and fruit to pan. Stir until boiling.

Mound rice onto a platter and pour meat mixture over rice; garnish with orange slices and mint sprigs. Makes 4 servings.

PER SERVING: 521 calories, 27 g protein, 65 g carbohydrates, 17 g fat (4 g saturated), 76 mg cholesterol, 91 mg sodium

Teriyaki sauce. Mix ½ cup **orange juice,** ¼ cup minced **fresh mint leaves,** 2 tablespoons **soy sauce,** 1 tablespoon minced **fresh ginger,** and 1 clove **garlic,** minced or pressed.

Serve pork-apple stir-fry over hot cooked rice. Orange slices echo flavors in the tangy teriyaki marinade. Mint sprigs make an aromatic garnish.

Turkey Saltimbocca

HOT FROM THE GRILL, *boneless turkey breast slices wrapped around a savory filling make a handsome entrée that's ideal for warm-weather dining. They are a lower-fat version of a traditional pan-sautéed Italian veal dish called saltimbocca.*

These two recipes for turkey rolls offer a choice of fillings. One features elements of a classic club sandwich, the other a robust combination of shiitake mushrooms, dried tomatoes, and cheese. The rolls, which can be assembled a day ahead, take only minutes to cook on the grill.

GRILLED TURKEY CLUB WITH TOMATO CHUTNEY

  8 **boned, skinned turkey breast slices or cutlets (each 2 to 3 oz. and about 3/8 inch thick), rinsed and patted dry**

  2 **tablespoons mayonnaise**

  1 **tablespoon coarse-grain Dijon mustard**

  2 **cups shredded romaine lettuce**
     Tomato chutney (recipe follows)

16 **thin slices pancetta or 8 slices bacon (6 to 7 oz. total)**

With a flat mallet, pound each turkey slice between sheets of plastic wrap until 1/8 inch thick. Peel off and discard plastic wrap.

Mix mayonnaise and mustard. Spread an equal amount of mayonnaise mixture evenly over each turkey slice. Mound 1/8 of the lettuce in the center of each piece; top with 1 tablespoon of chutney. Roll to enclose filling. Wrap 2 slices of pancetta (or 1 slice of bacon) around each roll. If made ahead, cover and chill up until next day.

Place rolls on a greased grill 4 to 6 inches above a solid bed of medium coals (you can hold your hand at grill level only 4 to 5 seconds). Cook, turning often to brown evenly, until meat is white in center of thickest part (cut to test), 8 to 11 minutes. Transfer rolls to plates. Offer remaining chutney to add to taste. Makes 6 to 8 servings.

PER SERVING: 151 calories, 16 g protein, 6.4 g carbohydrates, 6.7 g fat (1.7 g saturated), 42 mg cholesterol, 212 mg sodium

Tomato chutney. In a 2- to 3-quart pan over high heat, combine 1½ pounds (about 9 large) cored, chopped **Roma-type tomatoes;** ⅔ cup minced **shallots;** 2 tablespoons minced **fresh ginger;** ⅔ cup **sugar;** ⅓ cup **cider vinegar;** and ¼ teaspoon **crushed dry hot red chilies.**

Turkey rolls, made with meat pounded thin, grill in minutes and offer flavors of classic club sandwich. Wrap rolls in pancetta; filling includes tomato chutney and romaine.

Boil, uncovered, stirring often, until reduced to 2 cups, 45 to 55 minutes. Cool. Use, or cover and chill up to 3 weeks. Makes 2 cups.

PER SERVING: 23 calories, 0.3 g protein, 5.8 g carbohydrates, 0 g fat (0 g saturated), 0 mg cholesterol, 2.1 mg sodium

GRILLED TURKEY ROLLS WITH HERBED SHIITAKE-CHEESE FILLING

½ **pound fresh shiitake or common mushrooms, rinsed and drained**

  5 **teaspoons oil drained from oil-packed dried tomatoes and 2 tablespoons minced drained tomatoes**

  1 **clove garlic, minced or pressed**

  8 **boned, skinned turkey breast slices or cutlets (each 2 to 3 oz. and about 3/8 inch thick), rinsed and patted dry**

½ **pound fontina cheese, cut into 1/4-inch-thick sticks**

16 **large fresh or 1½ teaspoons dry sage leaves**

1½ **tablespoons minced fresh or 1½ teaspoons dry thyme leaves**

½ **cup grated asiago cheese**

Cut 4 mushrooms in half; coarsely chop remainder. In an 8- to 10-inch frying pan on medium-high heat, stir 2 tea-

spoons oil and mushroom halves until lightly browned, 6 to 8 minutes; remove from pan and set aside. Add remaining oil to pan with chopped mushrooms, tomatoes, and garlic. Stir often until mushrooms begin to brown, 6 to 8 minutes. Remove from heat and let cool.

With a flat mallet, pound each turkey slice between sheets of plastic wrap until 1/8 inch thick. Peel off and discard plastic wrap.

Lay 1/8 of the fontina cheese in center of each turkey slice; top equally with the mushroom mixture, sage, minced thyme, and asiago. Roll to enclose. If made ahead, cover and chill up until next day.

Place turkey rolls on a greased grill 4 to 6 inches above a solid bed of medium coals (you can hold your hand at grill level only 4 to 5 seconds). Cook, turning often to brown evenly, until meat is white in center of thickest part (cut to test), 8 to 11 minutes. Transfer rolls to plates and garnish with the reserved mushroom halves. Makes 6 to 8 servings.

PER SERVING: 223 calories, 24 g protein, 2.7 g carbohydrates, 13 g fat (7 g saturated), 73 mg cholesterol, 461 mg sodium

Quick & Light Fruit Drinks

THESE THICK BUT THINNING *drinks blend fruit with chunks of ice in minutes, forming a smooth, deceptively rich-tasting snack or dessert to enjoy frosty cool.*

BLUEBERRY FREEZE

2½ cups blueberries, fresh or frozen and partially thawed
1 cup low-fat lemon-flavor yogurt
2 tablespoons lemon juice
   About 1 tablespoon sugar
2 cups small ice cubes or crushed ice

In a blender, whirl berries, yogurt, lemon juice, and 1 tablespoon sugar until smoothly puréed. Add half the ice at a time, whirling after each addition, to make a fine, slushy texture. Add more sugar, if desired. Pour into tall glasses. Makes about 4 cups, 2 to 4 servings.

PER SERVING: 122 calories, 3.1 g protein, 27 g carbohydrates, 1.0 g fat (0.4 g saturated), 2.3 mg cholesterol, 40 mg sodium

PEACH DREAM

   Sugar
4 large (about 2 lb. total) ripe peaches
1 tablespoon lemon juice
1 small can (6 oz., ¾ cup) frozen pink lemonade concentrate
2 cups small ice cubes or crushed ice

Rub rim of 5 or 6 glasses (about 1-cup-size) with water, then dip in sugar to coat; set aside.

Peel and pit peaches; cut fruit in chunks into a blender.

To peaches, add the lemon juice and lemonade concentrate; whirl smooth. Add half the ice at a time, whirling after each addition, until mixture has a fine, slushy texture. Pour into sugar-rimmed glasses. Makes about 4½ cups, 5 or 6 servings.

PER SERVING: 127 calories, 0.9 g protein, 33 g carbohydrates, 0.2 g fat (0 g saturated), 0 mg cholesterol, 2.0 mg sodium

CAPPUCCINO-ORANGE SHAKE

1 cup orange juice
1 cup low-fat coffee-flavor yogurt
1 tablespoon orange marmalade or sugar

Deceptively rich-tasting, blueberry freeze makes a quick, light refreshment. Purée berries and yogurt in blender, then whirl with ice cubes to create thick, slushy texture.

2 cups small ice cubes or crushed ice
   Orange slices (optional)
   Candy coffee beans (optional)

In a blender, whirl the orange juice, coffee-flavor yogurt, and orange marmalade with half the ice until the mixture has a fine, slushy texture. Add remaining ice and repeat.

Pour the cappuccino mixture into tall glasses; garnish glass rims with orange slices and sprinkle a few candy coffee beans onto each drink. Makes about 4 cups, 2 to 4 servings.

PER SERVING: 89 calories, 3.2 g protein, 18 g carbohydrates, 0.7 g fat (0.5 g saturated), 2.8 mg cholesterol, 39 mg sodium

More September Recipes

OTHER SEPTEMBER RECIPES *included a refreshing sour orange dressing from Mexico and crisp-fried tortilla strips seasoned with flavored salt.*

SOUR ORANGE DRESSING

Seville oranges found in Yucatán are the base of a refreshing sour orange dressing freely splashed onto meats, fish, fruits, and vegetables as a flavor enhancement. Our own oranges are sweeter, but the juice, made tart-sweet with lime juice and sugar, approximates this eastern Mexico standard. Salt, sprinkled sparingly on the sour orange dressing just after it goes on foods, is essential to give the mixture its special zing.

The dressing often contains garlic, shallots, and pepper; you can add them if you like, for more gusto and variety.

Make up a batch and try it on the foods suggested above, on salads, and particularly on pork, which Yucatecans relish.

6	**tablespoons orange juice**
	About 5 tablespoons lime juice
1/8	**to 1/4 teaspoon sugar**
1	**clove garlic, minced or pressed (optional)**
1	**teaspoon minced shallots (optional)**
1/8	**teaspoon pepper (optional)**
	Salt

In a bowl, mix orange juice, 5 tablespoons lime juice (or enough to give orange juice a tart taste), sugar, garlic, minced shallots, and pepper. Use dressing to season foods suggested (preceding), adding salt to taste. Makes about 3/4 cup.

PER TABLESPOON: 5 calories, 0.1 g protein, 1.3 g carbohydrates, 0 g fat (0 g saturated), 0 mg cholesterol, 1.1 mg sodium

TORTILLA WHISKERS

Salted tortilla strips make irresistible nibbles. Strips are cooked briefly in oil until crisp, then seasoned with a flavored salt.

12	**corn or flour tortillas (7- to 10-in. diameter)**
	Salad oil
	Garlic-paprika salt or chili salt (recipes follow)

Stack 3 tortillas. With a long, sharp knife, cut stack into strips about 1/8 inch wide. Repeat to cut remaining tortillas.

Pour about 1 inch oil into a 4- to 5-quart pan over medium heat. When oil registers 350° on a thermometer, add 1/6 of tortilla strips; stir and cook until strips are lightly browned and crisp, 1 to 2 minutes. Transfer with a slotted spoon to paper towels to drain; while strips are warm, season to taste with flavored salt. Repeat to cook remaining tortilla strips.

Serve warm or cool. If made ahead, package cool strips airtight up until next day. To reheat, spread strips out in a paper towel–lined 10- by 15-inch pan; bake in a 300° oven until warm, about 10 minutes. Makes 10 to 12 servings.

PER SERVING: 88 calories, 2.1 g protein, 13 g carbohydrates, 3.4 g fat (0.2 g saturated), 0 mg cholesterol, 111 mg sodium

Garlic-paprika salt. Mix 1 tablespoon **garlic salt** with 1/4 teaspoon **paprika.**

Chili salt. Mix 1 tablespoon **salt** with 1/2 teaspoon **chili powder.**

Serve a golden haystack of tortilla whiskers for munching. Crisp-fried until lightly browned, thin tortilla strips are drained, then seasoned with flavored salt.

Warm, raisin-studded griddle cakes go with butter and jam as a breakfast or teatime treat.

WELSH GRIDDLE CAKES

- ½ cup sugar
- 1 cup all-purpose flour
- 1 teaspoon baking powder
- ¼ teaspoon ground nutmeg
- 6 tablespoons butter or margarine, cut into pieces
- ½ cup raisins or currants
- 1 large egg white
- 2 tablespoons milk
  Butter and jam

Set aside 1 tablespoon sugar. Mix together remaining sugar, flour, baking powder, and nutmeg. Add butter; rub with your fingers until fine crumbs form. Add raisins, egg, and milk; stir just until dough holds together. Roll dough ¼ inch thick on a lightly floured surface. With a 3-inch-wide cooky cutter, cut dough into rounds. Reroll dough scraps and cut rounds.

In a nonstick 12-inch frying pan or griddle on medium-low heat, place cakes slightly apart. Cook until bottoms are medium brown, 3 to 4 minutes. Turn cakes with a wide spatula and cook until bottoms are medium brown, about 3 minutes.

Sprinkle warm cakes with remaining sugar and serve with butter and jam. Makes about 10 cakes, 4 or 5 servings.—*Judy Pannunzio, Campbell, Calif.*

PER CAKE: 170 calories, 2.0 g protein, 25.5 g carbohydrates, 7.1 g fat (4.4 g saturated), 19 mg cholesterol, 121 mg sodium

---

CHICKEN BREASTS CALVADOS

- 1 large (about ½ lb.) Golden Delicious or Newtown Pippin apple
- ¼ cup apple brandy, brandy, or apple juice
- ¼ teaspoon ground nutmeg
- 2 boned and skinned chicken breast halves (about ¾ lb. total)
- 2 slices (about 1 oz. each) havarti cheese
  Minced parsley

Peel, core, and thinly slice apple. Divide between 2 shallow ovenproof ramekins (1½- to 2-cup size) the apple slices, brandy, and half the nutmeg. Cover ramekins tightly with foil. Bake apples in a 400° oven until tender when pierced, about 20 minutes.

Rinse chicken and pat dry. Put 1 breast half in each dish, basting surface of chicken with juices, then sprinkle with remaining nutmeg. Bake, uncovered, until chicken is no longer pink in center of thickest part (cut to test), about 12 minutes.

Top chicken with cheese. Broil 6 inches from heat until cheese is bubbling, about 2 minutes longer. Sprinkle with parsley. Makes 2 servings.—*Mickey Strang, McKinleyville, Calif.*

PER SERVING: 376 calories, 46 g protein, 24 g carbohydrates, 9.9 g fat (5.4 g saturated), 127 mg cholesterol, 324 mg sodium

Baked dinner for two is cheese-crusted chicken breast on a bed of nutmeg- and brandy-spiked apples.

INDIAN-SPICED CAULIFLOWER

Cauliflower, cooked Indian-style, is golden from ground turmeric. Green onions also season it.

- 1 tablespoon salad oil
- 1 medium-size head (1½ to 1¾ lb.) cauliflower, cut into bite-size flowerets, rinsed
- 3 tablespoons minced fresh ginger
- 2 cloves garlic, minced or pressed
- 4 green onions, ends trimmed
- ¾ pound (about 4 large) Roma-type tomatoes, cored and chopped
- ¼ cup dry white wine
- ½ teaspoon ground turmeric or paprika
  Salt

Combine oil, cauliflower, ginger, and garlic in a 10- to 12-inch frying pan over medium-high heat. Stir often until cauliflower is lightly browned, about 6 minutes.

Chop 3 of the onions; add half of them to cauliflower along with tomatoes, wine, turmeric, and ⅓ cup water; stir. Bring to a boil over high heat, then simmer, stirring often, until cauliflower is tender when pierced and liquid evaporates, about 10 minutes. Pour the vegetables into a bowl and sprinkle with remaining chopped onions. Garnish with whole green onion. Add salt to taste. Makes 4 to 6 servings.—*Jane C. Cross, Albuquerque.*

PER SERVING: 47 calories, 1.6 g protein, 5.9 g carbohydrates, 2.5 g fat (0.3 g saturated), 0 mg cholesterol, 12 mg sodium

CAJUN SCALLOPS & PASTA

1½ pounds bay scallops, rinsed and drained
1 tablespoon Cajun spice mix, or combine 1 teaspoon pepper, 1 teaspoon paprika, and ¼ teaspoon ground allspice
2 teaspoons salad oil
1 cup regular-strength chicken broth
1½ tablespoons cornstarch blended with ⅓ cup water
½ cup light sour cream or low-fat unflavored yogurt
6 cups hot, cooked spinach-flavor spiral pasta (1 lb. dry)

Mix scallops with spices to coat. Pour oil into a 10- to 12-inch pan over medium-high heat; when hot, add scallops and stir-fry until they are opaque but still moist-looking in the center (cut to test), 3 to 4 minutes. With a slotted spoon, transfer scallops to a bowl.

On high heat, boil pan juices, uncovered, until reduced to about ¼ cup. Add broth and bring to a boil. Stir cornstarch mixture into broth and continue to stir until liquid boils. Stir in sour cream and scallops. Ladle mixture over hot pasta on a platter or on plates. Makes 4 to 6 servings.—*Karen McQuilkin, South Ogden, Utah.*

PER SERVING: 440 calories, 31 g protein, 63 g carbohydrates, 6.1 g fat (1.8 g saturated), 44 mg cholesterol, 224 mg sodium

Temper heat of Cajun spices that season tiny bay scallops with a light cream sauce.

ASIAN-STYLE GREEN BEANS

1 large (about 10 oz.) onion, chopped
½ pound mushrooms, sliced
1 large (about ½ lb.) red bell pepper, stemmed, seeded, and cut into ¼-inch strips
1 clove garlic
3 tablespoons soy sauce
1½ tablespoons honey
1 pound tender, slender green beans, ends trimmed
¼ cup salted roasted peanuts, chopped

In a 10- to 12-inch frying pan over medium heat, combine onion, mushrooms, pepper, garlic, and ⅓ cup water. Boil over high heat until liquid evaporates; stir often. When browned bits form in pan, add ¼ cup water and stir to free them. Boil until liquid evaporates and brown bits form. Add ¼ cup water and repeat this step once or twice until mixture is a rich brown. Add soy sauce and honey; keep warm.

Meanwhile, on a rack in a covered pan over 1 inch of boiling water, steam beans just until tender-crisp, about 10 minutes. Arrange beans on a platter; spoon sauce on beans and sprinkle with peanuts. Makes 4 servings.—*Vicki Walton-Miller, Long Beach, Calif.*

PER SERVING: 164 calories, 7.2 g protein, 27 g carbohydrates, 5.1 g fat (0.7 g saturated), 0 mg cholesterol, 862 mg sodium

Top tender-crisp green beans with no-fat sauté of bell peppers, mushrooms, and crunchy peanuts.

WHOLE-WHEAT ORANGE BARS

1 cup whole-wheat flour
1 cup all-purpose flour
½ cup chopped pitted dates
2 tablespoons sugar
1 teaspoon baking soda
½ teaspoon baking powder
1 can (6 oz.) frozen orange juice concentrate, thawed
¼ cup (⅛ lb.) melted butter or margarine
2 large eggs
1 large (about ½ lb.) orange, peel and white membrane cut off, fruit cut into ½-inch chunks and seeded
Frosting (recipe follows)

Mix whole-wheat flour, all-purpose flour, dates, sugar, soda, and baking powder. Reserve 1 tablespoon concentrate; in a bowl, mix remaining concentrate with butter and eggs.

Add dry ingredients and orange; stir just to moisten evenly. Spread in a buttered 9-inch-square pan. Bake in a 350° oven until cake just pulls from pan sides, about 35 minutes. Frost hot; serve cool, cut into 12 pieces.—*Yvonne Douglas, Colorado Springs, Colo.*

Frosting. Beat until smooth ¾ cup **powdered sugar**, reserved **orange juice concentrate**, and 1 tablespoon **water**.

PER PIECE: 211 calories, 4.2 g protein, 38 g carbohydrates, 5.2 g fat (2.7 g saturated), 46 mg cholesterol, 139 mg sodium

Orange chunks and sweet bits of dates are scattered through hearty bar cookies. Orange glaze frosts them.

Chefs of the West®

The Art of Cooking . . . by men . . . for men

CATSUP, A SAUCE *often used to disguise the flavor of a hamburger, was originally spelled ketchup. But by one of those philological accidents that occur, this word was thought to be a proletarian mispronunciation of something more Anglo-Saxon, and so catsup was born. The word comes from Chinese ketsiap (meaning brine of pickled fish), which came from the Malay word kechap.*

Rodney Garside takes advantage of a large late-summer crop of tomatoes to make this catsup, or ketsiap, or kechap.

HOMEMADE CATSUP

10 pounds ripe tomatoes
1 large (about ¹/₂ lb.) onion, chopped
1 large (about ¹/₂ lb.) red bell pepper, stemmed, seeded, and chopped
1 teaspoon *each* celery seed, mustard seed, and whole allspice
1 cinnamon stick, about 2 inches long
³/₄ cup sugar
1 cup distilled white vinegar
1 tablespoon paprika
Salt

To peel tomatoes (if desired), immerse in boiling water for 4 to 5 seconds. Then remove from water and pull off skins. Core and quarter tomatoes into a 10- to 12-quart pan. Add onion and bell pepper. Bring to a boil over medium-high heat, stirring frequently. Reduce heat and simmer, uncovered, until tomatoes mash readily, 20 to 25 minutes.

Whirl tomato mixture, a portion at a time, in a blender or food processor until smoothly puréed. Return mixture to pan and continue to boil gently, uncovered, until volume is reduced by half, about 1 hour and 45 minutes; stir mixture occasionally.

Put celery seed, mustard seed, allspice, and the cinnamon stick on 2 stacked pieces of cheesecloth, each 6 inches square. Tie cloth to enclose spices; add to pan. Simmer 20 minutes. Remove spice bag and discard.

Stir in sugar, vinegar, and paprika; continue to simmer, stirring frequently, until catsup is reduced to about 4 cups, 40 to 50 minutes. Add salt to taste. Let cool and use, or store in covered containers in the refrigerator for up to 3 weeks. Freeze to store longer. Makes about 1 quart.

PER TABLESPOON: 25 calories, 0.7 g protein, 5.8 g carbohydrates, 0.2 g fat (0 g saturated), 0 mg cholesterol, 5.5 mg sodium

Rodney Garside

Tuolumne, Calif.

RICK EASTES' WILTED GREENS *with cilantro pesto is the apotheosis of greens: it snatches up edible but otherwise unremarkable foliage and creates a unique flavor.*

Once looked down upon as an element of the South's subsistence food, cooked or heated greens have become downright modish as a salad or a bedding for quail and other upscale comestibles in California cuisine.

WILTED GREENS WITH CILANTRO PESTO

1¹/₂ tablespoons Oriental sesame oil
1 tablespoon curry oil or salad oil
1¹/₂ teaspoons chili oil
³/₄ cup lightly packed fresh cilantro (coriander), rinsed and drained
1 clove garlic
2 mild or hot Italian sausages, about ¹/₂ pound total
¹/₂ pound red Swiss chard, rinsed, leaves and stems trimmed apart and each thinly sliced
1 medium-size (about 5 oz.) red bell pepper, stemmed, seeded, and cut into thin slivers
About ¹/₂ pound rapini (broccoli rabe) or Chinese broccoli (Chinese kale or gai laan), rinsed and drained, tough ends trimmed and thinly sliced

"Catsup was originally spelled ketchup. *The word comes from Chinese* ketsiap, *which came from the Malay word* kechap.*"*

4 **baby bok choy (about ³/₄ lb. total), ends trimmed, separated into leaves, rinsed and drained**
About ¹/₄ pound mâche or butter lettuce, separated into leaves, rinsed and drained
About ¹/₄ cup toasted nori slivers
Soy sauce
Lime wedges

In a blender or food processor, combine 1 tablespoon of the sesame oil with curry oil, chili oil, cilantro, and garlic. Whirl until puréed; set aside.

Remove sausage casings and crumble meat into a wok or a 5- to 6-quart pan. Stir often over high heat until sausage is well browned, about 10 minutes.

With a slotted spoon, transfer sausage to towels to drain. Discard drippings and wipe pan clean. Return pan to high heat. Add remaining sesame oil and swirl to coat pan. Add chard stems and red bell pepper; stir-fry 1 minute. Add chard leaves, rapini, and bok choy, stirring until greens are wilted (if pan gets full, stir until leaves begin to wilt, then add more), about 2 minutes. Mix in mâche.

Pour into a bowl and immediately add cilantro mixture; mix well. Scatter sausage and nori on top of vegetables; serve at once with soy sauce and lime juice added to taste. Makes 6 servings.

PER SERVING: 182 calories, 8.5 g protein, 6.3 g carbohydrates, 14 g fat (3.4 g saturated), 22 mg cholesterol, 393 mg sodium

Marina del Mar, Calif.

CAVIAR ON THE BUFFET *means serious, upwardly mobile entertaining—like having the boss for dinner—especially if the caviar you serve is the tiny gray or black kind, the priciest of foods, practically requiring a police escort home from the store.*

Chef Lauterbach has devised a way of serving caviar that appeals even to those who ordinarily shun it. Since he did not specify which kind to use, our testers, seeking both economy and heightened esthetic appeal, tried tobiko (flying fish eggs). This roe is a brilliant amber-orange, mild in flavor, and intriguingly crunchy. You may, of course, use any other caviar—alone, or combined to create a tiger-stripe effect.

"The priciest of foods practically requires a police escort."

CAVIAR TORTE

6 **hard-cooked large eggs, finely chopped**
3 **tablespoons reduced-calorie mayonnaise or mayonnaise**
1¹/₂ **cups chopped green onions, including tops**
1 **package (8 oz.) neufchâtel (light cream) cheese**
²/₃ **cup light sour cream**
1 **cup (about 8 oz.) tobiko (flying fish roe), rinsed in a fine strainer, drained, and chilled**
Parsley sprigs
Lemon slices
Crisp crackers or melba toast

With a fork, mix well the eggs, mayonnaise, onions, cheese, and sour cream. Spread mixture evenly in a 9-inch cheesecake pan with removable rim. Cover and chill at least 4 hours, or up until next day.

With a spoon, drop tobiko in small dollops evenly over cheese mixture. Gently spread in a smooth layer, using a long spatula. Remove pan rim; place torte on a platter. Garnish with parsley and lemon slices. To eat, spoon mixture onto crackers. Makes about 5 cups, 16 to 20 servings.

PER SERVING: 90 calories, 6.2 g protein, 1.8 g carbohydrates, 6.6 g fat (3 g saturated), 118 mg cholesterol, 76 mg sodium

Brewster, Wash.

WHY CALL IT GREEN CORN *quiche? One good reason is that the chilies are green, but another meaning lurks within, perhaps not even suspected by* John Perchorowicz, *who sends in this recipe from Tucson.*

The term "green corn" was used by earlier generations when they were talking about fresh, soft corn that could be roasted or boiled, as opposed to fully ripened, dry, hard corn that could be stored or ground into meal.

GREEN CORN QUICHE

1 **cup dehydrated masa flour (corn tortilla flour)**
¹/₂ **cup whole-wheat flour**
1 **teaspoon sugar**
1 **can (17 oz.) cream-style corn**
4 **large eggs**
1 **can (12 oz.) evaporated milk**
1 **tablespoon liquid hot pepper seasoning**
1 **teaspoon chili powder**
2 **cans (4 oz. each) diced green chilies**
1 **can (2¹/₄ oz.) sliced ripe olives, drained**
¹/₂ **cup *each* shredded jack cheese and sharp cheddar cheese**
1 **cup thinly sliced green onions, including tops**
Salt
Prepared salsa

In a bowl, mix masa flour, whole-wheat flour, sugar, and corn until well blended. Scrape into a greased 10-inch cheesecake pan with a removable rim. Spread or pat mixture evenly over the bottom and about 1¹/₂ inches up the side of the pan. Bake crust in a 425° oven for 10 minutes.

Meanwhile, beat eggs to blend with milk, hot pepper seasoning, chili powder, chilies, olives, jack cheese, cheddar cheese, and ¹/₂ cup of the onions.

Remove crust from oven; turn oven temperature to 375°. Pour filling into crust. Bake until filling is set when pan is gently shaken, 40 to 45 minutes. Let stand for 10 minutes, sprinkle with remaining onions, then cut into wedges. Add salt and salsa to taste. Makes 6 to 8 servings.

PER SERVING: 299 calories, 14 g protein, 36 g carbohydrates, 12 g fat (4.7 g saturated), 134 mg cholesterol, 632 mg sodium

Tucson

September Menus

A S WE SAY GOOD-BYE *to summer this month, take advantage of warm weather with suppers cooked on the barbecue, and carry breakfasts outside on a tray to eat in the garden.*

SUMMER SUPPER FROM THE GRILL

Honey-Mustard Ham Steak with Skewered Figs
Grilled Breadsticks
Cold Green Beans & Red Onion Slivers with Olive Oil & Balsamic Vinegar
Papaya Halves Filled with Frozen Vanilla Yogurt & Chopped Candied Ginger
Fumé Blanc   Sparkling Cider

This simple grilled menu goes together with ease in less than an hour.

Season breadsticks while the barbecue is heating. Grill ham and figs; toast bread just when meat comes off the grill.

HONEY-MUSTARD HAM STEAK WITH SKEWERED FIGS

  2 tablespoons *each* honey and Dijon mustard
  2 teaspoons cider vinegar
  1/4 teaspoon coarsely ground pepper
  16 small or 8 large ripe figs (1 to 1¼ lb. total), stems trimmed; cut large figs in half
  1 center-cut slice (about 1 lb.) cooked ham

Mix honey, Dijon, vinegar, and pepper to make glaze. Thread an equal number of figs on 4 slender skewers.

Place figs and ham on a grill 4 to 6 inches above a solid bed of medium-hot coals (you can hold your hand at grill level only 3 to 4 seconds). As meat cooks, brush several times with glaze and turn over at least twice. Turn figs to heat through; brush with glaze. When figs are hot and ham is lightly browned, 8 to 10 minutes total, transfer to a platter. Makes 4 servings.

PER SERVING: 356 calories, 24 g protein, 32 g carbohydrates, 15 g fat (5.2 g saturated), 61 mg cholesterol, 1,800 mg sodium

Shiny honey-mustard glaze flavors grilled ham steak and skewered green figs; accompany with herb-basted breadsticks and marinated green beans.

GRILLED BREADSTICKS

Combine ⅓ cup **olive oil,** 2 cloves minced **garlic,** and 1 teaspoon **dried thyme leaves.** Cut 2 **sourdough sandwich rolls** (each 6 in. long) lengthwise into quarters. Brush bread equally with seasoned oil. Lay wedges on a grill and lightly toast on all sides, 2 to 3 minutes total. Makes 8 pieces.

PER PIECE: 163 calories, 2.6 g protein, 16 g carbohydrates, 9.8 g fat (1.4 g saturated), 0.9 mg cholesterol, 165 mg sodium

---

PANCAKE BREAKFAST

Blackberry Soufflé Cakes
Lemon Curd or Lemon Yogurt
Blackberries
Herbal Tea   Pineapple Juice

Make soufflé cakes and serve at once—they settle upon cooling.

Offer berries separately or spooned onto warm pancakes; top both with homemade or purchased lemon curd, or, for a lean alternative, use low-fat lemon yogurt.

BLACKBERRY SOUFFLÉ CAKES

- ½ **cup all-purpose flour**
- ¾ **teaspoon baking powder**
- ½ **cup nonfat or low-fat milk**
- 5 **large eggs, separated**
- 1 **teaspoon vanilla**
- 1 **cup blackberries, rinsed and drained**
- ½ **teaspoon cream of tartar**
- 1 **tablespoon sugar**
  Melted butter or margarine

In a bowl, mix flour and baking powder. Add milk, yolks, and vanilla; whisk smooth. Gently stir in berries. In a large bowl, whip egg whites and cream of tartar until foamy; gradually whip in sugar until whites form stiff, moist peaks. Gently fold batter into whites.

Heat an electric griddle to 350°, or place a griddle over medium heat. When griddle is hot enough to make a

---

drop of water bounce, brush lightly with butter. For each pancake, spoon ⅓ cup batter onto griddle. When bottoms are browned, turn and cook until well browned on bottoms and edges feel dry, 8 to 10 minutes total. Makes about 18 cakes, 4 or 5 servings.

PER SERVING: 191 calories, 8.6 g protein, 18 g carbohydrates, 9.1 g fat (4 g saturated), 223 mg cholesterol, 179 mg sodium

---

ALFRESCO DINNER ON THE PATIO

Grilled Swordfish
with Rosemary Aïoli
Lentil & Bell Pepper Salad
Sliced Tomatoes
Melba Compote
Chardonnay   Sparkling Water

A splash of Mediterranean colors and robust flavors enhance this easy meal.

You can make the salad and aïoli ahead of time. While coals ignite, slice tomatoes and set the table.

For the finale, alternate fresh raspberries and peach slices in stemmed wine glasses. Drizzle fruit with blackberry-flavor liqueur for adults, berry-flavored syrup for youngsters.

GRILLED SWORDFISH WITH ROSEMARY AÏOLI

- 4 **swordfish steaks (1¼ to 1½ lb. total), cut 1 inch thick**
- 1 **tablespoon olive oil**
  Rosemary aïoli (recipe follows)
  Salt

Rinse fish steaks and pat dry, then brush oil on all sides. Place fish on a lightly greased grill 4 to 6 inches above a solid bed of hot coals (you can hold your hand at grill level only 2 to 3 seconds).

Top puffy blackberry pancakes with tart lemon curd and more berries.

Cook, turning once with a wide metal spatula, until fish is opaque but still moist-looking in thickest part, 7 to 10 minutes. Transfer fish on spatula to a warm platter. Add aïoli and salt to taste. Makes 4 servings.

PER SERVING: 201 calories, 28 g protein, 0 g carbohydrates, 9.1 g fat (2 g saturated), 55 mg cholesterol, 128 mg sodium

Rosemary aïoli. Combine 1 cup **mayonnaise,** 1½ tablespoons **lemon juice,** 4 cloves minced **garlic,** and 1½ teaspoons minced **fresh rosemary** or ¾ teaspoon dry rosemary. Cover and chill at least 1 hour or up to 2 days. Makes about 1 cup.

PER TABLESPOON: 100 calories, 0.2 g protein, 0.7 g carbohydrates, 11 g fat (1.6 g saturated), 8.1 mg cholesterol, 79 mg sodium

(Continued on next page)

LENTIL & BELL PEPPER SALAD

1½ cups (10 to 11 oz.) lentils

3 cups regular-strength chicken broth

1 *each* small (about 5 oz.) red and yellow bell pepper (or 2 of 1 color), stemmed, seeded, and diced

Dressing (recipe follows)

5 slices crisply cooked and well-drained bacon (about ¼ lb. uncooked)

Fresh basil sprigs

Salt and pepper

Sort and remove debris from lentils; rinse and drain, then put in a 3- to 4-quart pan. Add broth. Bring to boiling on high heat; cover and simmer until lentils are just tender to bite, 20 to 25 minutes. Drain well, reserving any liquid. Add bell peppers and dressing to lentils; mix well. Serve warm or cool, or cover and chill up until next day. If made ahead, you may want to moisten lentils slightly with reserved liquid. Crumble bacon over lentils and garnish with basil. Add salt and pepper to taste. Makes 4 servings.

PER SERVING: 388 calories, 25 g protein, 46 g carbohydrates, 13 g fat (2.7 g saturated), 6.7 mg cholesterol, 176 mg sodium

Dressing. Whisk together 6 tablespoons **raspberry** or red wine **vinegar,** ¼ cup chopped **fresh basil leaves** or 2 teaspoons dry basil leaves, 2 tablespoons **olive oil,** and 1 tablespoon minced **shallots.**

OCTOBER

Autumn fruit with cheese and wine (page 254)

Savor autumn's superb
fresh fruits this month. Pair them with an intriguing
selection of cheeses for a simple but elegant dessert
or tasting party, or feature them in colorful harvest soups.
Invite your favorite Halloween revelers to a
post-trick-or-treat sandwich party featuring bread shaped
to resemble a giant black widow spider.
Other October articles suggest dishes to complement
Chardonnay wines, cross-cultural entrées, and a selection
of simple, low-fat cookies to please nibblers of all ages.

Harvest Soups with a Sweet Surprise

FALL FRUITS ELEVATE *first-course soups to show-stopping first-class acts. Persimmons, pomegranates, and Asian pears add contrasting color, sweetness, texture, and surprise to the savory elements of these three composed soups.*

Yet for all their style and taste, these soups are easy to make. Each choice is based on a well-seasoned broth with poultry, seafood, or meat that you pour over vegetables and fruit attractively arranged in wide bowls. Served before guests, the soup becomes a dramatic first course.

Bring bowls with the arranged foods to the table. Cook the meat in the broth on a small portable burner at the table, or cook it in the kitchen and transfer it to a tureen. Carefully ladle the hot broth over the fruit and vegetables in the bowls.

GINGERED BROTH WITH PERSIMMON & CHICKEN

- 1/2 **pound boned and skinned chicken breasts, cut into paper-thin slices**
- 1 **tablespoon soy sauce**
- 1 **teaspoon Oriental sesame oil or toasted almond oil (optional)**
- 1 **large (about 8 oz.) firm Fuyu persimmon, peeled, stemmed, and cut into thin wedges**
- 20 **to 30 small (2 to 3 oz. total) edible-pod peas, strings removed**
- 1/3 **cup thinly sliced green onion Gingered broth (recipe follows)**

In a small bowl, mix chicken, soy sauce, and sesame oil. If made ahead, cover and chill up until next day.

In each of 6 wide, shallow bowls (about 1½-cup size), arrange equal portions of persimmon, peas, and onion; bring bowls to the table.

Asian pear, Fuyu persimmon, pomegranate contribute rich complexity to savory soups.

Heat gingered broth to boiling on the range or on a portable burner at the table. Stir in chicken; simmer just until chicken is opaque, 30 seconds to 1 minute. If cooking broth on range, pour into a tureen and bring to the table. Carefully ladle broth into each bowl over fruit and vegetables. Makes 6 first-course servings.

PER SERVING: 189 calories, 12 g protein, 18 g carbohydrates, 2.9 g fat (0.6 g saturated), 22 mg cholesterol, 254 mg sodium

Gingered broth. In a 3- to 4-quart pan, combine 1½ quarts **regular-strength chicken broth,** 1 cup **dry sherry,** 2 tablespoons minced **fresh ginger,** 1 **star anise** (or ½ teaspoon anise seed and 1 cinnamon stick, 3 in. long). Bring to a boil; cover and simmer for about 30 minutes. If desired, discard spices.

CHILI BEEF BROTH WITH PEAR

- 3/4 **pound boneless lean beef sirloin**
- 2 **tablespoons soy sauce**
- 2 **tablespoons sliced green onion**
- 1 **teaspoon Oriental sesame oil**
- 1 **teaspoon sugar**
- 1½ **cups (about 3½ oz.) finely shredded cabbage**
- 1 **large (9 oz.) Asian pear, cored and cut into thin slivers**
- 1 **large carrot, peeled and finely shredded**
- 1/2 **cup fresh cilantro (coriander) sprigs Chili broth (recipe follows)**

Trim fat off beef. Cut beef into thin slices about 3 inches long and mix with soy sauce, onion, sesame oil, and sugar. Cover and chill at least 15 minutes or up until the next day.

In each of 6 wide, shallow bowls (about 1½-cup size), arrange equal portions cabbage, pear, carrot, and cilantro sprigs; bring bowls to the table.

Heat chili broth to boiling on the range or on a portable burner at the table. Stir in beef; simmer to desired doneness, about 30 seconds for rare. If broth is cooked on range, pour into a tureen and bring to the table. Carefully ladle broth into each bowl over fruit and vegetables. Makes 6 first-course servings.

PER SERVING: 135 calories, 1.4 g protein, 12 g carbohydrates, 3.5 g fat (1 g saturated), 35 mg cholesterol, 391 mg sodium

Chili broth. In a 3- to 4-quart pan, combine 1½ quarts **regular-strength beef broth,** 1 cup **water,** 2 tablespoons

minced **fresh ginger,** 1 teaspoon minced **garlic,** and 1/4 teaspoon **crushed dry hot red chilies.** Bring to boil; cover and simmer about 30 minutes.

LEMON SEAFOOD BROTH WITH POMEGRANATE

- 1 **medium-size (about ½ lb.) pomegranate**
- 1/2 **pound boned and skinned mild white-flesh fish such as lingcod or orange roughy**
- 1/4 **pound shelled cooked tiny shrimp**
- 1/2 **cup finely shredded mizuna leaves or 1 cup small, tender watercress sprigs**
- 1 **large (8 oz.) firm-ripe avocado, peeled, pitted, diced, and coated in lemon juice Lemon broth (recipe follows)**

Cut crown end off pomegranate; lightly score rind lengthwise in several places. Immerse in a bowl of water for about 5 minutes. Holding pomegranate under water, break sections apart with your fingers, separating seeds from membrane. Seeds will sink; rind and membrane will float. Skim off and discard rind and membrane. Drain seeds; you need 3/4 to 1 cup. (If done ahead, cover and chill up until the next day.)

Cut fish into paper-thin slices about 2½ inches long. In each of 6 wide, shallow bowls (about 1½-cup size), arrange equal portions shrimp, mizuna, avocado, and pomegranate seeds; bring bowls to the table.

Heat broth to boiling on the range or on a portable burner at the table. Stir in fish; cook just until opaque, 30 seconds to 1 minute. If broth is cooked on the range, pour into a tureen and bring to table. Carefully ladle broth into each bowl over shrimp, fruit, and vegetables. Makes 6 first-course servings.

PER SERVING: 151 calories, 14 g protein, 9.5 g carbohydrates, 6.9 g fat (1.2 g saturated), 56 mg cholesterol, 125 mg sodium

Lemon broth. In a 3- to 4-quart pan, combine 1½ quarts **regular-strength chicken broth** and 1 cup **water.** In a piece of cheesecloth, tie to enclose 3 thin strips **lemon peel** (yellow part only, ½ by 3 in.), 1 tablespoon **white peppercorns,** 1 tablespoon **coriander seed,** and 1 teaspoon **cumin seed;** place in broth. Bring to a boil; cover and simmer 30 minutes. Lift out and discard packet of spices. Add 3 tablespoons **lemon juice.**

For dramatic presentation, bring wide bowls to table with arranged whole edible-pod peas, thin wedges of crisp Fuyu persimmon, and thinly sliced green onion; as your guests watch, carefully ladle ginger- and anise-scented broth with chicken over the fruit and vegetables.

Cross-cultural Cuisine

CROSS-CULTURAL COOKING comes easily to Jeanette Holley; she adds adventure to familiar foods, mixes flavors from different cuisines, and interprets Western foods with an Asian slant.

Holley's background contributes many influences. She was the child of a Japanese mother and African-American father, and she grew up in Japan and Korea. From Asia, she moved to Washington State University to study food chemistry and nutrition. Going beyond her early career as a dietitian, she trained at several innovative restaurants in the Los Angeles area and in France. Now her own culinary creativity comes into fascinating play at O'toto, a restaurant in Los Angeles.

If you don't find the ethnic ingredients for these recipes·in the supermarket, you'll need to shop at an Asian grocery store. Or use the suggested substitutes.

SHRIMP WITH RICE PAPER CRÊPES

If you can't find the rice papers, serve the shrimp with the rest of the ingredients as a salad; dress with the dipping sauce.

³/₄ **pound medium-size (43 to 50 per lb.) shrimp, shelled and deveined**

2 **teaspoons lime juice**

6 **cups (about 4 oz.) bite-size pieces mixed salad greens, such as mesclun, rinsed and crisped**
Sprigs of fresh mint, basil (anise, Indian, Opal, or Thai), cilantro (coriander), or shiso; use at least 3 different kinds

¹/₄ **cup long, fine shreds of carrot**

2 **tablespoons coarsely chopped roasted peanuts**

2 **tablespoons drained canned capers**

16 **rounds (6 to 8 in. wide) edible rice paper**
Dipping sauce (recipe follows)

Bring about 2 quarts of water to a boil in a 4- to 5-quart pan. Stir in shrimp, cover pan tightly, and remove from heat. Let stand until shrimp are opaque in thickest part (cut to test), 3 to 4 minutes. Drain well and mix with lime juice.

On each of 4 dinner plates, mound an equal portion of salad greens. Arrange herbs around salad. Spoon ¹/₄ of the shrimp onto each salad mound. Sprinkle with carrot, peanuts, and capers.

Just before serving, lightly brush both sides of rice papers with water. Place in a single layer on a wide platter; let stand briefly until soft. (If wet papers touch, they may stick and be difficult to separate without tearing.) Offer damp rice papers and dipping sauce with shrimp and greens.

To eat, mound about ¹/₄ shrimp and greens from each plate onto a damp rice paper. Top with herb sprigs; roll to enclose filling. To eat, dip in sauce. Makes 4 first-course servings.

PER SERVING WITHOUT RICE PAPER: 108 calories, 16 g protein, 3.2 g carbohydrates, 3.5 g fat (0.6 g saturated), 105 mg cholesterol, 218 mg sodium

Dipping sauce. Mix 6 tablespoons **water** or *dashi* (seaweed stock), 3 tablespoons **fish sauce** (*nuoc mam* or *nam pla*) or soy sauce, 2 tablespoons **lime juice,** 2 tablespoons **sugar,** and 1 teaspoon **Asian hot chili paste** or sauce or ³/₄ teaspoon crushed dry hot red chilies. Makes about ²/₃ cup.

PER TABLESPOON: 22 calories, 0.7 g protein, 3.6 g carbohydrates, 0.5 g fat (0.1 g saturated), 0 mg cholesterol, 0.5 mg sodium

Wrap shrimp, salad greens, and herbs in edible rice paper and dip in tangy sauce. Or if you prefer, serve shrimp with other ingredients as a salad, and dress with sauce.

BUCKWHEAT NOODLES WITH SCALLOPS & SESAME VINAIGRETTE

Hijiki, available in Japanese markets, is dried seaweed that looks like fine strands of black pasta. If it's unavailable, omit and make only half of the soy, mirin, and sake mixture; use mixture to marinate scallops.

The other Asian ingredients—mirin, sake, sesame oil, buckwheat noodles, daikon sprouts, rice vinegar, miso, and chili oil—have supermarket alternatives.

- 1 **tablespoon dry hijiki seaweed**
- 2 **tablespoons soy sauce**
- 2 **tablespoons mirin (sweet sake) or cream sherry**
- 2 **tablespoons sake (rice wine) or dry sherry**
- ³/₄ **pound bay scallops, rinsed**
- 1 **tablespoon Oriental sesame oil or salad oil**
- ¼ **cup dry sherry**
- 8 **ounces dry thin buckwheat noodles or angel hair pasta**
- 3 **green onions, ends trimmed**
  Sesame vinaigrette (recipe follows)
- 1 **cup julienne strips cucumber**
- ½ **cup (about 1 oz.) daikon sprouts, or long fine shreds of daikon**
- ½ **cup long fine shreds of carrot**
- 2 **tablespoons black sesame seed or toasted white (regular) sesame seed (for toasting in vinaigrette, see following recipe)**

Soak seaweed in water to cover until soft, about 20 minutes. Drain and rinse well.

In a small bowl, mix soy, mirin, and sake. In a 1- to 1½-quart pan, combine half the soy mixture, ¼ cup water, and hijiki. Simmer, covered, until seaweed is tender to bite, about 10 minutes. Cool. (If made ahead, cover and chill up until next day.) Drain.

Mix remaining soy mixture with scallops; marinate 5 minutes, stirring often. Drain scallops well; discard liquid.

Pour 2 teaspoons oil into a 10- to 12-inch frying pan and place over high heat. When oil is hot, add scallops, turning often, until they are barely opaque but still moist-looking in center

Dressed with sesame vinaigrette, buckwheat noodles, black seaweed, and marinated scallops have a Japanese heritage. Green onions add bright garnish.

(cut to test), about 2 minutes. Remove scallops from pan with a slotted spoon. Boil pan juices, uncovered, until they evaporate and brown in pan.

Add sherry; boil, uncovered, stirring to loosen browned bits, until reduced by half, about 1 minute. Pour reduced sherry over scallops. Cool, stirring occasionally. (If made ahead, cover and chill up to 4 hours.)

In a 5- to 6-quart pan, bring about 3 quarts water to a boil on high heat. Add noodles and cook, uncovered, just until barely tender to bite, 5 to 7 minutes. Drain and immerse in cold water with remaining 1 teaspoon oil; when cool, drain well.

Thinly slice 1 green onion; mix with cold noodles, sesame vinaigrette, and cucumber.

On each of 4 dinner plates, mound equal portions of noodles. Cut remaining onions diagonally into 3-inch lengths. Garnish salad with scallops, long diagonally sliced green onions,

seaweed, daikon sprouts, carrot, and sesame seed. Makes 4 servings.

PER SERVING: 592 calories, 26 g protein, 61 g carbohydrates, 25 g fat (3.3 g saturated), 28 mg cholesterol, 1,221 mg sodium

Sesame vinaigrette. In a 6- to 8-inch frying pan, stir 3 tablespoons **white** (regular) **sesame seed** over medium heat until golden, 5 to 7 minutes. Pour into a blender.

In the pan, stir ½ teaspoon minced **garlic** into 1 tablespoon **Oriental sesame** or salad **oil** over medium heat just until garlic is soft, about 1 minute. To the blender, add the garlic-oil mixture; whirl until a paste forms.

Add ¼ cup **rice vinegar** or cider vinegar, 3 tablespoons **mirin** (sweet sake) or cream sherry, 3 tablespoons **salad oil,** 1½ tablespoons **miso** or soy sauce, 1 tablespoon chopped **fresh ginger,** and ¼ to ½ teaspoon **chili oil** (to taste) or ⅛ to ¼ teaspoon cayenne. Whirl until blended. (If made ahead, cover and chill up until next day.) Makes ³/₄ cup.

Autumn Teammates: Fresh Fruit, Cheese & Wine

CHEESE AND FRUIT costar with ease as an elegant but simple end to a meal or, on a larger scale, as the heart of a quickly presented light party menu. And there is no better time to explore this combination than now; fall fruits are exceptionally suited to cheese partners.

Well-stocked supermarkets offer an extensive selection of precut or small whole cheeses; many also cut cheese to order. For more variety, check with cheese shops and delicatessens.

Options for presentation range from a single cheese and fruit to a variety of both.

An ounce of cheese and a piece of fruit make an adequate dessert, but chances are you'll want a more generous look, especially at a tasting party. Leftovers can always be enjoyed another day.

Grapes go well with most cheeses—here with creamy l'explorateur, quark, and mascarpone.

Offer a selection of wines, such as champagne, fruity late-harvest wine, and port. For guests who want to sample different wines, offer a dump bucket and a pitcher of water for rinsing.

CHEESES FOR DESSERT

Consider at least one cheese from each category; if a particular cheese is not available, ask for one that is similar.

Fresh cheeses. Instead of being aged, these are eaten when less than a month old. They are characterized by a delicate, clean flavor and are soft enough to spread. Serve in bowls or, if firm enough, swirled into mounds. Spread on unsalted crackers or slices of fruit. Often, a bit of apricot or plum jam enhances these cheeses.

Choices made from cow's milk include fine-grained **ricotta** (low-fat and whole-milk varieties), **quark** (like smooth cottage cheese with a little tang, sold in tubs or cartons), rich **mascarpone** (high fat, delicate tang; it spoils quickly—cheese should be fresh-smelling), and even **cream cheese.** There are also **fresh goat cheeses** (chèvres), some plain, some seasoned with herbs. All goat cheeses have a distinct piquancy.

Soft and semisoft cheeses. As these age and ripen, the texture softens and gets creamier, and flavors develop aromatic complexity. When ready to eat and at room temperature, they should feel soft when pressed and may be slightly runny. If firm when bought, let stand at room temperature for up to 2 days, then chill, if needed, to hold 1 or 2 days.

Readily available ones include rind-ripened **brie** made of cow's milk (there's also goat brie, which is sharper), **camembert, taleggio** (resembles brie in tex-

ture, but has a milder flavor), **port salut, teleme,** and stronger-flavored **livarot, reblochon,** and **Pont l'Évêque.**

Blue cheeses. These cheeses range from crumbly and sharp to smooth and subtle. **Roquefort** is the boldest; creamier blue cheeses include **blue castello, sweet gorgonzola** or regular **gorgonzola** (sharper flavor), and **saga blue** and **cambozola** (both have enough butterfat to fit the next category).

Triple-cream cheeses. These cheeses are about 70 percent butterfat and are extremely smooth and creamy. Examples are **Brillat-Savarin** (mild), **l'explorateur** and **St. André** (both slightly piquant), and **boursault.**

FALL FRUIT PARTNERS

Apples. Tarter varieties make a crisp contrast for triple creams; sweeter apples suit soft, semisoft, and blue cheeses.

Asian pears. Crisp, they are refreshing matched with soft, semisoft, and blue cheeses.

Figs. Their sweetness is best complemented by mascarpone or quark with a little sugar or tart jam.

Grapes. Versatile, they go well with all the preceding cheeses. But stronger-flavored cheeses go best with red flame grapes.

Pears. Their sweetness and buttery texture are particularly suited to soft and semisoft cheeses, especially the stronger ones, and blue cheeses.

Plums. Choose juicy red-skinned varieties; cut in half and top with mild fresh cheeses (with perhaps a dusting of sugar), especially mascarpone or cream cheese. Also try them with l'explorateur.

RICOTTA

QUARK

ST. ANDRE

BLUE CASTELLO

SWEET GORGONZOLA

BRILLAT - SAVARIN

TALE

GOAT BRIE

CAMBOZOLA BLUE

L'EXPLORATEUR

Green flags identify different cheeses, arranged with fresh autumn fruits for a tasting party or dessert. Unsalted crackers (plain or slightly sweet), a thick fruit jam, toasted nuts, and a selection of wines complete the picture.

When the Chardonnay Makers Have Lunch

IF YOU THOUGHT *that rules governing the use of certain wines with certain foods were hard and fast, you may find liberation in the way a group of California winemakers approached choosing foods to complement their Chardonnays. Some of the combinations may surprise you; we think all will please your palate.*

On these pages, you see a salad and three entrées served at one tasting, each with a companion Chardonnay. As you put together your own menu, select one dish, or make several if there are extra hands to handle the complexities.

Host Brice Jones of Sonoma-Cutrer Vineyards began with winning simplicity, offering a lobster salad dressed and served with his full-bodied, citrusy Chardonnay made by Bill Bonetti.

Smoke is a subtle taste element in wine contributed by the heat-shaped oak used to make wine barrels. Its gentle impression on Stephen Kistler's smooth Kistler Vineyards Chardonnay is delicately echoed in a smoked chicken filling for ravioli.

By contrast, Tom Selfridge emphasized the butter-oak tones of his mellower, fuller-bodied Kendall-Jackson Chardonnay by using the wood-like flavor of chanterelle mushrooms with chicken.

Zelma Long of Simi Winery capitalized on the fresh, crisp tropical fruit overtones of her wine to complement salmon; the wine also has enough rich feeling in the mouth to match the earthiness of a saffron mayonnaise.

Although each of the wines has its own style, many others have similar flavors and suit these foods. Advice from a good wine shop can help you expand your options.

LOBSTER SALAD

> 6 cups (about 5½ oz.) inner butter lettuce leaves, rinsed and crisped
> Cooked lobster (directions follow), shelled and sliced
> Chardonnay dressing (recipe follows)
> Salt and freshly ground pepper

Arrange the lettuce and lobster on 4 salad plates. Top with dressing, and add salt and pepper to taste. Makes 4 servings.

PER SERVING: 98 calories, 8.2 g protein, 2.1 g carbohydrates, 4.1 g fat (0.7 g saturated), 27 mg cholesterol, 147 mg sodium

Cooked lobster. Immerse 1 live Maine **lobster** (1½ to 2 lb.) in an 8- to 10-quart pan with 6 quarts rapidly boiling **water.** When boil resumes, reduce heat, simmer 15 minutes, drain, then let cool.

Chardonnay dressing. Mix together ¼ cup **Chardonnay** and 1 tablespoon *each* **extra-virgin olive oil** and **lemon juice.**

SMOKED CHICKEN RAVIOLI

> 6 dozen (14-oz. package) won ton wrappers
> Smoked chicken filling (recipe follows)
> 1½ tablespoons all-purpose flour smoothly mixed with ¼ cup water
> 1 cup regular-strength chicken broth, unsalted
> ¼ cup Chardonnay
> ¼ cup whipping cream
> 1 teaspoon cornstarch dissolved in 2 tablespoons water
> 2 tablespoons minced parsley
> Salt and pepper

Place 1 won ton wrapper on a flat surface. Spoon about 2 teaspoons filling onto center of wrapper. Brush edges lightly with flour-water mixture; align another wrapper over filling and press edges together firmly to seal. If desired, use a zigzag-rim ravioli cutter to decoratively trim edges of ravioli. Lay ravioli on a flour-dusted baking sheet; cover with plastic wrap to prevent drying.

Repeat to shape remaining ravioli. Lay them on the pan in a single layer, without touching. If made ahead, cover airtight and chill up until the next day. For longer storage, freeze in a single layer until firm, then transfer to an airtight container and freeze for up to 1 month.

In a 5- to 6-quart pan, bring 3 quarts of water to a boil over high heat.

Meanwhile, combine broth and wine in an 8- to 10-inch pan over medium-high heat. Boil, uncovered, until reduced to about ⅔ cup, about 10 minutes. Stir in cream and cornstarch mixture until sauce boils; keep warm.

When water is boiling, add ravioli and cook, uncovered, until heated through, 4 to 5 minutes (if frozen, 6 to 8 minutes).

Quickly transfer ravioli with a slotted spoon, draining briefly, to 4 to 6 warm dinner plates; top evenly with sauce. Sprinkle with parsley. Add salt and pepper to taste. Makes 36 ravioli—4 to 6 main-dish servings.

PER SERVING: 380 calories, 18 g protein, 34 g carbohydrates, 19 g fat (6.8 g saturated), 72 mg cholesterol, 560 mg sodium

Smoked chicken filling. Pour ¼ cup **hazelnuts** into an 8- to 9-inch-wide pan. Bake in a 350° oven until nuts are golden under skin (rub off some skin to test), about 15 minutes. Enclose nuts in a clean towel and rub cloth to remove skins.

Diners are offered two chicken entrées, each matched to a Chardonnay. Ravioli have a filling of smoked chicken; pan-browned chicken breast is served with chanterelle sauce.

Drop nuts into a food processor or blender; discard skins. Whirl nuts with 6 ounces diced **smoked chicken,** ¹/₂ cup (4 oz.) **neufchâtel** (light cream) **cheese** or cream cheese, and 2 tablespoons *each* **milk** and firmly packed **parsley** until mixture is smoothly puréed.

CHICKEN WITH CHANTERELLE-TARRAGON SAUCE

- ¹/₂ **ounce (about 1 cup) dry chanterelle mushrooms, or ¹/₂ pound thinly sliced fresh common mushrooms**
- 1 **tablespoon butter or extra-virgin olive oil**
- ³/₄ **cups regular-strength chicken broth**
- ¹/₄ **cup Chardonnay**
- 2 **teaspoons minced fresh or 1 teaspoon dry tarragon leaves**
- 4 **boned and skinned chicken breast halves (about 1¹/₄ lb. total)**
- 2 **tablespoons whipping cream**

Combine chanterelles and 1¹/₂ cups water in a 1¹/₂- to 2-quart pan. Bring to a boil over high heat; cover tightly and simmer gently until mushrooms are very tender when pierced, 30 to 40 minutes. Remove from heat and let stand 30 minutes. Lift chanterelles from water, squeezing liquid from them into pan; reserve water.

In a 10- to 12-inch nonstick pan over medium-high heat, melt half the butter.

Add chanterelles (or sliced mushrooms) to pan. Stir often until chanterelles are tinged a darker brown, about 5 minutes (8 to 10 minutes for sliced mushrooms). Carefully pour reserved cooking water into pan, taking care not to add any grit from mushrooms. Add broth, wine, and tarragon. Boil over high heat until liquid is reduced to ¹/₃ cup. Pour into a bowl.

Melt remaining butter in pan over medium-high heat. Add chicken and cook until lightly browned on both sides and meat is no longer pink in center of thickest part (cut to test), about 10 minutes total; transfer to plates and keep warm.

Return mushroom mixture to pan, add cream, and stir over high heat until bubbling. Spoon sauce evenly over chicken. Makes 4 servings.

PER SERVING: 220 calories, 34 g protein, 3.2 g carbohydrates, 7.3 g fat (3.6 g saturated), 98 mg cholesterol, 136 mg sodium

Vivid saffron mayonnaise seasons poached salmon; serve with fresh spinach leaves, wilted in butter, and hot cappellini topped with chopped pistachios.

POACHED SALMON WITH SAFFRON MAYONNAISE

- ¹/₃ **cup white wine vinegar**
- 1 **dry bay leaf**
- 10 **black peppercorns**
- 4 **salmon steaks (about 6 oz. each), ³/₄ to 1 inch thick**
- ¹/₂ **cup reduced-calorie or regular mayonnaise**
- ¹/₃₂ **teaspoon powdered saffron dissolved in 2 tablespoons of Chardonnay**
  Salt and pepper

In a 4- to 5-quart pan, combine 2 quarts water, vinegar, bay, and peppercorns. Bring to a boil over high heat, then cover and simmer for 15 minutes.

Return water to a rapid boil; add salmon, cover, and remove at once from heat. Let stand until fish is opaque but still moist-looking in the thickest part (cut to test), 10 to 12 minutes. Do not remove lid until you are ready to check for doneness; if needed, cover and let stand longer, testing every 2 minutes until done.

Meanwhile, mix mayonnaise and saffron mixture.

With a slotted spoon, lift fish from pan. Let stand until cool to touch. Gently peel off skin and set fish on plates; serve warm or cool with mayonnaise ladled onto portions. Add salt and pepper to taste. Makes 4 servings.

PER SERVING: 309 calories, 32 g protein, 2.5 g carbohydrates, 18 g fat (3.5 g saturated), 70 mg cholesterol, 208 mg sodium

Spider Bread for Halloween

USHER IN HALLOWEEN *with a giant black widow spider. This creature, made from purchased frozen dough, becomes an edible centerpiece on a party buffet for a dozen guests.*

Three loaves of dough form the easily shaped spider; a fourth loaf makes the "eggs." The spider is coated with black sesame seed (white sesame seed on the eggs) and then baked. Guests make their sandwiches from them.

To build a colorful salad resembling a haystack, mix about 3 quarts shredded carrots with about 1 cup orange juice; add honey and lemon juice to taste. Mound on a large rimmed platter and encircle with orange slices.

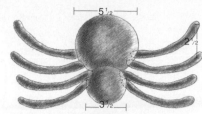

Shape loaves of purchased thawed frozen dough on a 14- by 17-inch baking sheet. Place legs first, then head and body.

SPIDER SANDWICH PARTY

Black Widow Bread
Haystack Salad
Cold Sliced Roast Beef, Turkey,
or Cured Meat
Fontina or Jack Cheese
Sliced Tomatoes
Mild Onion Slices
Butter Lettuce Leaves
Mustard
Mayonnaise
Cold Hard Cider or Sparkling Cider
Crisp Red Apples
Caramel Corn or Caramels

Shred carrots and slice oranges for salad the day of the party. The bread can be made well ahead and frozen.

You'll need a total of about 3 ounces cooked meat and cheese for each serving. You'll also need about 1 pound butter lettuce, rinsed and crisped; 1 to 1½ pounds

tomatoes, cored and thinly sliced; and 1 small mild red onion, thinly sliced.

For dessert, mound crisp red apples and caramels in a big basket or bowl.

BLACK WIDOW BREAD

You can buy black sesame seed in Asian markets, or use poppy seed.

4 loaves (1 lb. each) frozen whole-wheat or white bread dough, thawed
1 large egg, beaten to blend
3 tablespoons black sesame seed or poppy seed
2 tablespoons regular (white) sesame seed

The legs. On a floured board, divide 1 loaf into 8 equal pieces. Roll each portion into an 8-inch log. On a greased 14- by 17-inch baking sheet, place ends of 4 logs about 1½ inches to the right of the center of the length of the pan and centered in the middle part of the width of pan. Space outside ends 1½ to 2½

inches apart, curving them to fit pan and resemble spider legs (see drawing at left). Align remaining logs the same way, but to left of pan center, to make 4 pairs of legs.

The head. Divide 1 loaf in half. Knead 1 half on a floured board to make a smooth ball. Turn smooth side up. If wrinkled, pull top of dough under ball to make smooth; pinch ends to underside. Set ball on inner ends of 2 pairs of legs; gently flatten ball to make it 3½ inches wide.

The body. Knead remaining half-loaf with 1 whole loaf into a smooth ball, as directed above. Set ball, smooth side up, on inner ends of remaining 2 pairs of legs. Gently flatten ball to make it about 5½ inches wide (balls should touch). Keep body at least 1½ inches from pan edge; if it's too close, push it back, making balls more oval.

The eggs. Divide remaining loaf into 8 equal pieces. Shape each portion into a smooth ball; set smooth side up and slightly apart on a greased 12- by 15-inch baking sheet.

Cover dough lightly with plastic wrap; let rise in a warm place until puffy, 20 to 30 minutes. Brush dough with beaten egg; sprinkle spider with black seed, eggs with white seed. Bake in a 350° oven until bread is a rich gold color beneath seed and a toothpick inserted in thickest part comes out clean, 20 to 25 minutes for eggs, 40 to 45 minutes for spider. Serve warm, or cool on racks, package airtight, and hold up to 24 hours. Freeze to store longer (thaw, wrapped, about 4 hours at room temperature). Makes 1 loaf (about 3 lb.) and 8 buns (2 oz. each), 10 to 12 servings.

PER OUNCE: 82 calories, 2.4 g protein, 14 g carbohydrates, 1.9 g fat (0.4 g saturated), 4.7 mg cholesterol, 138 mg sodium

Seed-covered spider bread and rolls form creepy centerpiece for post-trick-or-treat sandwich supper. Guests build their own sandwiches from platters of cold sliced meats and cheeses, sliced tomatoes and onions, and butter lettuce. A colorful salad and crisp apples fill out the menu.

DUTCH MASHED VEGETABLES *are simple mashed potatoes glorified by the addition of other vegetables. They're called stamp pots (stamppotten).*

Our original recipes, published in October 1974 (page 152), added butter, bacon fat, or cream for flavor; our low-fat remodels use onions, braised and deglazed with only broth, for richness.

The first stamp pot, called hutspot, mashes carrots with the potatoes. For variations, try cabbage or escarole.

LIGHTENED-UP HUTSPOT

1½ **pounds (about 3 large) onions, chopped**
About 3 cups regular-strength chicken broth
1 **pound (about 4 large) carrots, peeled**
2 **pounds (about 4 large) russet potatoes**
Salt and pepper

In a 10- to 12-inch frying pan on high heat, boil onions and ¾ cup broth, uncovered, until liquid evaporates; stir often. When browned bits stick to pan, deglaze by stirring in ⅓ cup broth to release particles; boil and stir until pan is dry. Repeat deglazing step until onions are golden brown, about 4 times; keep warm.

Cut carrots into 1-inch chunks. In a 4- to 5-quart pan, bring about 1 quart water and carrots to a boil. Cover and simmer 10 minutes. Peel potatoes and cut into about 1-inch chunks. Add potatoes to carrots; simmer, covered, until both are very tender when pierced, about 20 minutes; drain.

Using a potato masher or an electric mixer, mash vegetables, adding about ⅓ cup broth for creamy consistency. Stir in onions. Add salt and pepper to taste. Makes 6 servings.

PER REVISED SERVING: 190 calories, 5.6 g protein, 40 g carbohydrates, 1.3 g fat (0.2 g saturated), 0 mg cholesterol, 59 mg sodium

PER ORIGINAL SERVING: 213 calories, 4 g protein, 32 g carbohydrates, 8 g fat (5 g saturated), 23 mg cholesterol, 116 mg sodium

Potatoes and onions form the base for low-fat mashed vegetable dishes; add carrots, cabbage, and escarole to vary color and flavor.

Stamp pot with cabbage. Follow recipe for **hutspot** (preceding), except omit carrots. After browning onions, remove from pan and add ½ cup **regular-strength chicken broth** and 8 cups chopped **cabbage** (about 2 lb.). Stir over high heat until cabbage wilts and all liquid evaporates, about 8 minutes. Stir into mashed potatoes with cooked onions. Makes 6 to 8 servings.

PER REVISED SERVING: 148 calories, 5 g protein, 31 g carbohydrates, 1 g fat (0.2 g saturated), 0 mg cholesterol, 47 mg sodium

PER ORIGINAL SERVING: 190 calories, 4 g protein, 25 g carbohydrates, 9 g fat (6 g saturated), 25 mg cholesterol, 119 mg sodium

Stamp pot with escarole. Follow recipe for **hutspot** (preceding), except omit carrots. After browning onions, remove from pan and add ½ cup **regular-strength chicken broth** and 8 cups chopped **escarole** (about 1 lb.). Stir over high heat until escarole wilts and liquid evaporates, about 8 minutes. Stir into mashed potatoes with the cooked onions. Makes 6 servings.

PER REVISED SERVING: 174 calories, 6 g protein, 36 g carbohydrates, 1.3 g fat (0.2 g saturated), 0 mg cholesterol, 52 mg sodium

PER ORIGINAL SERVING: 230 calories, 4.5 g protein, 27 g carbohydrates, 12 g fat (7.5 g saturated), 33 mg cholesterol, 148 mg sodium

Mixing Your Own Hot Cereal

A BOWL OF HOT *cereal gets the body running on a cold morning. Each of these two mixtures can serve a large family at one sitting or an individual for a week.*

BREAKFAST RICE, OATS & GRANOLA

    1 cup long-grain brown rice
    1 cup regular rolled oats
1 1/4 teaspoons ground cinnamon
    1 teaspoon vanilla
  1/2 teaspoon ground nutmeg
1 3/4 cups granola cereal
    Condiments (suggestions follow)

In a 1 1/2- to 2-quart pan, combine the rice and 2 1/2 cups water. Bring to a boil; cook, uncovered, over medium heat until most of the water evaporates, 15 to 20 minutes. Cover and cook over low heat until rice is tender to bite, about 15 minutes. Spoon rice into a large bowl; set aside.

In the same pan, bring 2 1/4 cups water to a boil; add oats, cinnamon, vanilla, and nutmeg. Stir over low heat until oats are tender to bite, about 5 minutes. Mix the cooked oatmeal and granola with rice.

Serve hot; or cool, cover, and chill up to 1 week. To reheat 1-cup portions, stir in a 1- to 1 1/2-quart pan over low heat about 10 minutes; add water if needed. In a microwave oven, reheat, covered, at full power (100 percent), about 1 1/2 minutes. Add condiments to taste. Makes 6 cups; serves 6 or 7.—*Carrie E. Wills, Pittsburg, Calif.*

PER PLAIN SERVING: 282 calories, 7.2 g protein, 47 g carbohydrates, 7.1 g fat (3 g saturated), 0 mg cholesterol, 15 mg sodium

Condiments. Choose from **milk, chopped dates, raisins,** chopped **nuts, honey, maple syrup, brown sugar,** diced **dried fruit,** and **peanut butter.**

SPICED BREAKFAST GRAINS

    1 cup quinoa, rinsed well and drained
    1 can (12 oz.) frozen apple juice concentrate
    1 teaspoon ground nutmeg
  1/2 teaspoon ground allspice
    1 cinnamon stick (about 3 in.)
    1 cup pearl barley, rinsed and drained
    1 cup millet, rinsed and drained
    Condiments (choices precede)

In a 4- to 5-quart pan, stir quinoa over medium heat until lightly browned, about 15 minutes. Remove from pan.

In pan, combine apple juice concentrate, 2 quarts water, nutmeg, allspice, and cinnamon; bring to a boil.

Stir in the barley; cover and simmer for 10 minutes. Add millet and quinoa; cover and simmer until the grains are tender to bite, 15 to 30 minutes.

Serve hot; or cool, cover, and chill up to 1 week. To reheat 1-cup portions, stir in a 1- to 1 1/2-quart pan over low heat about 10 minutes; add water if needed. In a microwave oven, reheat, covered, at full power (100 percent), about 1 1/2 minutes. Add condiments to taste. Makes 8 1/2 cups, 8 or 9 servings.

PER PLAIN SERVING: 313 calories, 7.4 g protein, 66 g carbohydrates, 2.6 g fat (0.5 g saturated), 0 mg cholesterol, 27 mg sodium

Add condiments to vary the texture and flavor of hot breakfast rice, oats, and granola. Package leftover cereal in 1-cup portions, refrigerate up to a week, and reheat as needed.

Simple, Low-fat Cookies

THESE SIMPLE, LOW-FAT *cookies are made without shortening or egg yolk. Cereal or ground almonds (which contribute some fat but no cholesterol) fill in for flour; egg white holds the dough together. All freeze well.*

Made without egg yolk or shortening, assorted cookies have a crisp and chewy, macaroon-like texture.

CHOCOLATE ALMOND COOKIES

    3/4 cup almonds
      1 large egg white
    1/8 teaspoon cream of tartar
   1 1/4 cups powdered sugar
      2 tablespoons unsweetened cocoa

In a blender or food processor, finely grind 1/2 cup almonds; set aside. Whirl remaining almonds until coarsely chopped; set aside.

In a bowl, mix egg white, cream of tartar, powdered sugar, and cocoa. Beat at high speed with a mixer until thick and smoothly blended. Stir in ground and chopped almonds.

Oil and flour 2 nonstick, 12- by 15-inch baking sheets (or lightly coat plain sheets with cooking oil spray, then flour). Drop dough in 1 1/2-teaspoon mounds 2 inches apart on pans.

Bake in a 375° oven until cookies are crisp outside but still soft inside (cut 1 to test), 10 to 12 minutes; switch pan positions after 5 minutes. Transfer cookies with a spatula to racks. Serve, or let cool and store airtight up to 3 days. Makes about 2 dozen cookies.

PER COOKY: 50 calories, 1 g protein, 7.3 g carbohydrates, 2.2 g fat (0.2 g saturated), 0 mg cholesterol, 2.8 mg sodium

GRAHAM CRACKER CRACKLE COOKIES

      1 large egg white
    1/8 teaspoon cream of tartar
   1 1/4 cups powdered sugar
      2 tablespoons malted milk powder
    1/2 cup finely crushed graham cracker crumbs
    1/4 cup semisweet chocolate baking chips

In a bowl, mix egg white, cream of tartar, sugar, and malted milk. Beat with a mixer on high speed until thick and smooth. Stir in crumbs.

Oil and flour 3 nonstick, 12- by 15-inch baking sheets (or lightly coat plain sheets with cooking oil spray, then flour). Drop dough on pans in 1 1/2-teaspoon mounds 3 inches apart. Lightly press chocolate chips equally into mounds.

Bake in a 375° oven until golden brown, 7 to 9 minutes. Alternate pan positions after 4 minutes. Cool the cookies on pans for 1 minute, then transfer them with a spatula to racks. Serve, or let cool and store airtight up to 3 days. Makes about 1 1/2 dozen cookies.

PER COOKY: 49 calories, 0.5 g protein, 9.9 g carbohydrates, 0.9 g fat (0.4 g saturated), 0.2 mg cholesterol, 26 mg sodium

NUGGET CRUNCH COOKIES

Follow directions for **graham cracker crackle cookies** (preceding), using 1/2 cup **crunchy nut-like cereal nuggets** instead of graham cracker crumbs. Also omit chocolate baking chips.

Bake in a 375° oven until golden brown, 7 to 9 minutes; alternate pan positions after 4 minutes. Cool cookies on pans for 1 minute, then transfer with a spatula to racks. Serve, or let cool and store airtight up to 3 days. Makes about 1 1/2 dozen cookies.

PER COOKY: 52 calories, 0.8 g protein, 12 g carbohydrates, 0.1 g fat (0.1 g saturated), 0.3 mg cholesterol, 34 mg sodium

CORN FLAKE CHEWS

      3 cups corn flake cereal
      1 large egg white
    1/8 teaspoon cream of tartar
   1 1/4 cups powdered sugar
      2 tablespoons malted milk powder

In a blender or food processor, whirl 2 1/2 cups cereal until finely ground; set aside. In a bowl, mix egg white, cream of tartar, sugar, and malted milk powder. Beat with a mixer on high speed until thick and smooth. Stir in ground cereal and cereal flakes.

Oil and flour 2 nonstick, 12- by 15-inch baking sheets (or lightly coat plain sheets with cooking oil spray, then flour). Drop dough in 1 1/2-teaspoon mounds 2 inches apart on pans.

Bake in a 375° oven until golden brown, 8 to 10 minutes; alternate pan positions after 4 minutes. Cool the cookies on pans for 1 minute; transfer them with a spatula to racks. Serve, or let cool and store airtight up to 3 days. Makes about 2 dozen cookies.

PER COOKY: 33 calories, 0.4 g protein, 7.6 g carbohydrates, 0.1 g fat (0 g saturated), 0.2 mg cholesterol, 37 mg sodium

FRUIT AND MEAT HAVE *been acquainted for centuries, but their relationship has blown hot and cold. In late medieval and Renaissance times, they frequently appeared together, and, in the form of mincemeat (which once actually had meat in it), they formed a perfect union.*

Over the years they grew apart and seldom saw each other except for the mandatory pineapple rounds on baked ham, the grapes in chicken Véronique, and the cranberry sauce with turkey. Of course, Polynesian cooking was different; South Sea islanders put fruit salad on everything, or so some restaurants believe.

Of late, modish cooking has rediscovered the meat-and-fruit combination, and we are only mildly surprised to find a veal chop resting in a blueberry purée or lamb with black currants. Falling right in step, Frank Doherty supplements the sweetness of his roast pork with figs and dates, as well as with the familiar apple.

ROAST PORK WITH DATE & FIG SAUCE

    1 boned pork shoulder roast, 3 to 4
       pounds
    1 clove garlic, halved
    1/2 teaspoon dry summer savory
       leaves
       Pepper
    1 cup finely chopped tart apple
    1/2 cup dry white wine
    1/2 cup firmly packed brown sugar
    1 cup pitted dates, cut into pieces
    6 dried figs, stem ends trimmed,
       coarsely chopped

Trim excess fat from pork, then rub meat all over with cut garlic. Place meat in a 9- by 13-inch pan and evenly sprinkle with savory and pepper.

Roast meat, uncovered, in a 375° oven until a thermometer inserted in center of thickest portion registers 155° (1½ to 1¾ hours). Transfer pork to a warm platter; keep warm.

Meanwhile, in a 2- to 3-quart pan, combine chopped apple with ¼ cup water. Cover and cook over medium heat until apple is soft when pressed, 4 to 5 minutes; set mixture aside.

Skim and discard fat from juices in pork pan; add wine to the pan and stir

over medium heat to loosen browned bits. Add apple mixture, sugar, dates, and figs; simmer, stirring, until mixture is hot, 3 to 5 minutes. Pour into a small bowl.

Slice pork and accompany with fruit sauce. Makes 9 or 10 servings.

PER SERVING: 291 calories, 21 g protein, 33 g carbohydrates, 8.7 g fat (3.3 g saturated), 72 mg cholesterol, 87 mg sodium

Frank Doherty

Las Vegas

THE PLUMP, OLEAGINOUS *duck is currently in fashion, both as breast slices artfully fanned over a pool of colorful sauce and as warm slivers in a salad of arugula, frisée, and other upwardly mobile greens. There are even designer ducks now—the brawny, aggressive Muscovy, which does not quack (it hisses), and the mullard, a hybrid between the Muscovy and the mallard, the green-headed wild ancestor of our common farmyard breed.*

One way of cooking a duck remains a time-honored classic: duck with orange flavor obtained from the citrus fruit itself or from some derivative of the fruit. Jay Nelson uses frozen orange juice concentrate and orange marmalade, along with orange slices for garnish.

ORANGE DUCKLING

    1 duck (4 to 5 lb.), thawed if frozen
    1 large onion, cut in half
    1 stalk celery, including
       some leaves
    1 can (12 oz.) frozen orange juice
       concentrate, thawed
    1/3 cup orange marmalade
       Belgian endive leaves or parsley
       sprigs
    1 large unpeeled orange, cut into
       wedges

Pull off and discard chunks of fat from duck; reserve giblets for other uses. Rinse duck and drain. With a fork, prick skin all over.

Tuck one half of the onion into the neck cavity and the other half into the body cavity. Cut the celery into pieces and tuck inside the body cavity. Place duck, breast down, in a 6- to 8-quart pan. Add orange juice concentrate and 2 cans water. Bring to a boil over high heat, cover, and reduce heat and simmer until duck is tender when pierced in thigh, about 1½ hours; turn duck over every 30 minutes.

Place duck, breast down, on a rack in a 12- by 14-inch roasting pan. Roast in a 400° oven until back is brown; then turn breast up and continue to roast until skin is brown, about 20 minutes.

Meanwhile, skim and discard fat from pan juices. On high heat, boil juices with marmalade, uncovered, until liquid is reduced to 1 cup, about 40 minutes.

Place duck on a platter and garnish with endive leaves and orange wedges. Carve and accompany with juices. Makes 3 or 4 servings.

PER SERVING: 781 calories, 35 g protein, 50 g carbohydrates, 49 g fat (17 g saturated), 145 mg cholesterol, 116 mg sodium

Salinas, Calif.

"South Sea islanders put fruit salad on everything, or so some restaurants believe."

Spoon tomato sauce over pan-browned chops; top with artichokes and feta; bake.

LAMB CHOPS WITH ARTICHOKES & FETA

- 1 jar (6 oz.) marinated artichoke hearts
- 6 lamb rib or loin chops (about 4 oz. each), cut 1 inch thick
- 1 clove garlic, minced or pressed
- 1 can (15 oz.) tomatoes
- 1/2 cup dry red wine
- 1/2 teaspoon dry rosemary
- 1/4 pound feta cheese, crumbled
- 1 tablespoon grated lemon peel
- 1/4 cup minced parsley

Drain marinade from artichokes into a 10- to 12-inch frying pan; chop artichoke hearts and set aside. Add chops to pan and cook on medium-high heat, turning as needed, until meat is well browned on both sides, 10 to 12 minutes total. Transfer lamb to a shallow 7- by 11-inch baking dish; set aside.

Drain off fat; discard. Add minced garlic, tomatoes, wine, and rosemary. Boil, uncovered, until reduced to 1 1/4 cups, 6 to 8 minutes; stir often, breaking up tomatoes with a spoon. Pour sauce over meat.

Mix artichokes, cheese, lemon peel, and parsley. Spoon equally onto chops. Bake in a 400° oven until cheese begins to brown, 12 to 15 minutes. Makes 6 servings.—*Rita C. Sugarman, Palo Alto, Calif.*

PER SERVING: 415 calories, 16 g protein, 6.8 g carbohydrates, 35 g fat (15 g saturated), 80 mg cholesterol, 517 mg sodium

Season vibrant array of cool vegetables with a mint-freshened vinaigrette.

GREEN BEAN & BELL PEPPER SALAD

- 1 pound green beans, ends trimmed
- 1 can (15 1/2 oz.) garbanzos, drained and rinsed
- 1 *each* small (about 1/4-lb. size) red and yellow bell pepper, stemmed, seeded, thinly sliced
- 1/2 cup sliced red onion (optional)
  Fresh mint sprigs
  Vinaigrette (recipe follows)

In a 10- to 12-inch frying pan, bring 1 inch water to boiling. Add green beans; cook, uncovered, until barely tender when pierced, 7 to 8 minutes. Drain, immerse in ice water until cold, then drain again.

Mound green beans, garbanzos, peppers, and onion separately on a platter. Garnish with mint. Pour vinaigrette over vegetables and mix. Makes 6 servings.

Vinaigrette. In a small bowl, whisk together 1/4 cup **sherry** or red wine vinegar, 1/4 cup minced **fresh mint leaves** or 1 tablespoon dry mint leaves, 3 tablespoons **olive oil**, 2 tablespoons **Dijon mustard**, and 1/4 teaspoon **pepper**.—*Louise Ross, Elk Grove, Calif.*

PER SERVING: 146 calories, 4.1 g protein, 15 g carbohydrates, 8.4 g fat (0.9 g saturated), 0 mg cholesterol, 236 mg sodium

Bake zucchini-carrot crust until brown and crisp; embellish with toppings.

ZUCCHINI-CARROT PIZZA CRUST WITH TOPPINGS

- 2 to 3 slices (about 2 oz. total) sourdough bread, torn up
- 1 tablespoon olive oil
- 2 cloves garlic, minced or pressed
- 2 large eggs
- 2 tablespoons all-purpose flour
- 1/4 teaspoon pepper
- 1 teaspoon dry basil leaves
- 1 cup shredded carrot
- 1 cup shredded zucchini
- 1 1/2 cups (6 oz.) shredded jack cheese
  Toppings (suggestions follow)

In a blender or food processor, whirl bread to make 1 cup crumbs. In an 8- to 10-inch frying pan on medium-high heat, stir crumbs, oil, and garlic until crumbs are crisp, 6 to 8 minutes; set aside.

Beat eggs with flour, pepper, basil, carrot, zucchini, and crumbs. Spread evenly in a well-oiled 12-inch pizza pan. Bake in a 400° oven until crust is browned, 20 to 25 minutes. Sprinkle with cheese and 1 to 3 toppings; bake until hot, 10 to 12 minutes. Use a spatula to loosen; crust tends to stick. Makes 4 servings.

Toppings. 1 cup thinly sliced **mushrooms**, 1 cup sliced **black ripe olives**, 1/4 pound thinly sliced **dry Italian salami**.—*Jeannine Johnson, Culver City, Calif.*

PER SERVING WITH MUSHROOMS: 266 calories, 14 g protein, 17 g carbohydrates, 16 g fat (7.0 g saturated), 140 mg cholesterol, 284 mg sodium

MINIATURE HONEY WHEAT LOAVES

1 package active dry yeast
2 cups warm water (110°)
¾ cup honey
3 tablespoons salad oil
1 teaspoon salt
2 cups regular rolled oats
1 cup multigrain cereal
3 cups whole-wheat flour
   About 3¼ cups all-purpose flour

In a large bowl, mix yeast with warm water; let stand about 5 minutes. Stir in honey, oil, and salt. Beat in oats, cereal, and whole-wheat flour.

Gradually stir in 3 cups all-purpose flour. On a floured board, knead dough until smooth, about 10 minutes, adding flour as required to prevent sticking. Place dough in greased bowl.

Cover bowl with plastic wrap; let rise in warm place until dough doubles, about 1 hour. Punch dough down; divide into sixths. Shape each section into a loaf and place each in a greased 3- by 5½-inch loaf pan. Cover with plastic wrap; let rise in a warm place until almost doubled, about 30 minutes.

Place pans on a 12- by 15-inch baking sheet. Bake in a 375° oven until richly browned, 25 to 30 minutes. Remove from pans; cool on racks. Makes 6 loaves, each about ½ pound.—*Mary Jane Campbell, Geyserville, Calif.*

PER OUNCE: 83 calories, 2.2 g protein, 17 g carbohydrates, 1.1 g fat (0.2 g saturated), 0 mg cholesterol, 42 mg sodium

Wrap mini-loaves airtight and freeze up to 2 weeks; thaw and reheat to serve.

CHUNKY SPLIT-PEA SOUP WITH HAM HOCKS

1½ pounds meaty ham hocks
1½ teaspoons black peppercorns
½ teaspoon whole cloves
1½ teaspoons dry rosemary
1 quart *each* regular-strength beef broth and water
1 cup green split peas
1 large (about 8 oz.) onion, coarsely chopped
1 large (about ¾ lb.) russet potato, peeled and diced
2 large (about 10 oz. total) carrots, peeled and thinly sliced
¼ cup minced parsley

In a 5- to 6-quart pan, combine ham, peppercorns, cloves, rosemary, broth, and water. Bring to a boil, cover, and simmer, stirring occasionally, until meat pulls easily from bone, about 2 hours. Lift out ham. Skim fat from soup. Discard spices with a slotted spoon. Simmer soup, covered, on low heat.

Sort peas and discard debris; rinse and drain. Pull meat off bone; discard bone, skin, and fat. Tear meat into bite-size pieces. Add meat, peas, onion, potato, and carrots to soup. Simmer, uncovered, until peas are soft enough to mash, 45 to 55 minutes. Sprinkle with parsley. Makes 5 or 6 servings.—*Lita J. Verts, Corvallis, Ore.*

PER SERVING: 267 calories, 15 g protein, 37 g carbohydrates, 7.0 g fat (2.3 g saturated), 15 mg cholesterol, 380 mg sodium

Hearty soup of split peas, potatoes, carrots, and bits of ham makes a meal.

PEANUT BUTTER MOUSSE PIE

½ cup chunky peanut butter
¾ cup sugar
1 large package (8 oz.) neufchâtel (light cream) or cream cheese, at room temperature
2 tablespoons milk
1 cup whipping cream
   Chocolate crust (recipe follows)
   Chocolate curls (optional)

In a large bowl, beat peanut butter, sugar, cheese, and milk with an electric mixer until smoothly blended. In another bowl, whip cream until it holds soft peaks, then gently fold into peanut butter mixture. Spoon into crust. Chill until filling is set, about 4 hours or, covered, up until next day. Garnish with chocolate curls. Cut into wedges. Makes 8 servings.

Chocolate crust. In a blender or food processor, whirl 22 **chocolate wafers,** broken into pieces, to make 1 cup fine crumbs; pour into a 9-inch pie pan. Stir in ⅓ cup finely chopped **unsalted peanuts** and 3 tablespoons melted **butter** or margarine; mix. Press mixture firmly over bottom and up sides of pan. Bake in a 350° oven until darker brown at rim, 8 to 10 minutes. Cool.—*Sandra Krist, Bainbridge Island, Wash.*

PER SERVING: 474 calories, 10 g protein, 37 g carbohydrates, 34 g fat (15 g saturated), 67 mg cholesterol, 358 mg sodium

To create curls, pull a vegetable peeler across a bar of barely warm chocolate.

October Menus

A S FROSTIER DAYS AND NIGHTS *arrive, put your oven to work to create speedy, handsome, warming meals. Menus focus on autumn produce and heartier fare. Inspiration comes from the West's rich culinary heritage, blending the flavors of Asia, the Americas, and Europe.*

CITY LIGHTS SUPPER

Glazed Game Hens
Sweet Dumpling Squash with Peas
Green Salad
Onion Brushes
Tortilla Sticks
Sake
Baked Pears in Ginger Syrup

Let the oven do the lion's share of the work for this menu. First bake rolled flour tortillas to crisp.

Game hens and dessert pears share the oven next, while miniature squash steam on the range; give the squash a 10-minute head start. The pears finish baking as you eat dinner.

While foods cook, anoint purchased mesclun salad mix with your favorite dressing and make onion brushes. Cut 12 green onions into 4-inch lengths. Make narrow, parallel cuts about 2 inches long from the bulb end. Small Japanese lunch boxes—lacquered, plastic, or metal—make attractive salad containers.

Pour warm or chilled sake from a pot or bottle; sip from cups or traditional boxes.

GLAZED GAME HENS

- **6 small (1¼ to 1½ lb. each) Rock Cornish game hens**
- **2½ teaspoons grated tangerine or orange peel**
- **2 cups tangerine or orange juice**
- **2 tablespoons cornstarch**
- **3 tablespoons hoisin sauce or soy sauce**
- **½ teaspoon crushed dry hot red chilies**

Remove giblets from hens and save for other uses. Rinse birds and pat dry. Place birds breast up in a shallow 12- by 15-inch pan.

Just 30 minutes in the oven and glazed game hens are ready to serve. Elegant but easy meal for six features Asian-style foods cooked simply.

Mix tangerine peel, juice, cornstarch, hoisin, and chilies; pour evenly over birds. Bake in a 450° oven, basting every 10 to 15 minutes, until meat is no longer pink at thighbone (cut to test), 30 to 40 minutes. Place birds on warm plates. Skim fat from sauce; pour sauce into a bowl. Spoon onto birds to taste. Makes 6 servings.

PER SERVING: 655 calories, 69 g protein, 13 g carbohydrates, 34 g fat (9.5 g saturated), 220 mg cholesterol, 461 mg sodium

SWEET DUMPLING SQUASH WITH PEAS

Season vegetables with some of the game hen sauce.

- **6 sweet dumpling squash (8 to 10 oz. each)**
- **2 packages (10 oz. each) frozen petite peas**

Deeply pierce squash in several spots. Set on a rack above about 1 inch water in a wok or 6- to 8-quart pan. Cover pan and bring water to a boil; steam until squash are tender when pierced, 20 to 30 minutes.

Place peas and ¼ cup water in a 1½- to 2-quart pan. Stir often over high heat until hot, 5 minutes. Drain; keep warm. Protecting hands, cut off squash tops. Scoop out seeds; fill with peas. Set tops on peas if desired. Makes 6 servings.

PER SERVING: 131 calories, 5.8 g protein, 29 g carbohydrates, 0.5 g fat (0 g saturated), 0 mg cholesterol, 132 mg sodium

TORTILLA STICKS

12 flour tortillas (10-in. size, 20 oz. total)
Salt

Dip tortillas, 1 at a time, in water and drain briefly. Season to taste with salt. Loosely roll each into a cylinder and fasten with toothpicks.

Place tortillas on 2 greased baking sheets, each 12 by 15 inches. Bake in a 500° oven until bottoms are golden, 4 to 6 minutes. Turn tortillas over, switch positions of pans, and bake until tortillas are crisp and deep golden, 3 to 5 minutes longer. Remove toothpicks. Serve warm or cool. Makes 12.

PER PIECE: 150 calories, 4.3 g protein, 31 g carbohydrates, 0.4 g fat (0 g saturated), 0 mg cholesterol, 275 mg sodium

BAKED PEARS IN GINGER SYRUP

6 medium-size (2½ lb. total) firm-ripe Bosc or Bartlett pears
¾ cup water
1 tablespoon lemon juice
2 tablespoons sugar
⅓ cup minced crystallized ginger

Trim bottoms of pears, if needed, so they will sit upright. Fit pears snugly in a shallow 1½- to 2-quart baking dish, such as an 8-inch square pan. Mix water and lemon juice; pour over pears. Sprinkle fruit with sugar.

Bake in a 450° oven for 30 minutes. Baste pears with pan juices and sprinkle with ginger. Continue baking pears at 400°, basting occasionally, until they are tender when pierced and richly browned, 30 to 45 minutes longer. Offer warm or cool. Makes 6 servings.

PER SERVING: 167 calories, 0.7 g protein, 43 g carbohydrates, 0.7 g fat (0 g saturated), 0 mg cholesterol, 9 mg sodium

---

PORK DINNER BRAZILIAN-STYLE

Spiced Pork Roast
Wilted Kale
Hasty Hominy
Ale or Orange Juice
Vanilla Ice Cream
Pineapple

Typically Brazilian seasonings of garlic, cumin, and oregano coat this pork roast. It cooks unattended, leaving you plenty of time to prepare the kale and hominy.

Rinse and chop the kale, wilt it briefly in a big pan, and stir in green olives and onions. The hominy couldn't be simpler —just warm it out of the can with herbs and a little olive oil.

Ice cream with fresh or canned unsweetened pineapple makes a satisfying, sweet-tart dessert.

SPICED PORK ROAST

1 small, boned center-cut pork loin roast, 2 to 2½ pounds
1 tablespoon cumin seed
1 teaspoon black peppercorns
1 tablespoon dry oregano leaves
3 large cloves garlic, minced or pressed
Wilted kale (recipe follows)

Trim most of the fat from pork, leaving a thin layer. With a mortar and pestle or in a blender, coarsely crush cumin seed and peppercorns with oregano. In mortar or a bowl, combine seasonings with garlic. Pat mixture all over pork. Shape meat into a neat log, then tie securely in several places with cotton string.

Place the roast, fat side up, on a rack in a 12- by 15-inch roasting pan. Roast in a 375° oven until a thermometer inserted in the thickest part of the meat registers 155°, 45 to 55 minutes. Put the meat on a platter. Remove strings and keep the roast warm.

Remove pan rack. Skim and discard fat from drippings. Add ½ cup boiling water to pan; stir to loosen browned bits, then add juices to kale. Offer meat with kale. Makes 6 servings.

PER SERVING: 251 calories, 34 g protein, 1.8 g carbohydrates, 11 g fat (3.8 g saturated), 95 mg cholesterol, 102 mg sodium

---

Easy-to-carve roast pork, served with wilted kale and oregano-seasoned golden hominy, can be prepared quickly on a busy weeknight.

WILTED KALE

¾ pound kale, rinsed and drained
½ cup thinly sliced green onions
½ cup drained Spanish-style pimento-stuffed olives, sliced
Meat juices from roast pork (recipe precedes)

Trim tough stems from kale, then coarsely chop leaves. Place kale in a 5- to 6-quart pan with ½ cup water. Cover and bring to a boil over high heat. Reduce heat and simmer until kale is wilted, about 3 minutes.

Stir in onions, olives, and meat juices. Makes 6 servings.

PER SERVING: 44 calories, 2.2 g protein, 6.3 g carbohydrates, 1.8 g fat (0.2 g saturated), 0 mg cholesterol, 297 mg sodium

HASTY HOMINY

3 cans (15 oz. each) hominy, drained
2 tablespoons olive oil
1 teaspoon dry oregano leaves
Salt and pepper

(Continued on next page)

In a 10- to 12-inch frying pan over medium-high heat, frequently stir hominy, oil, and oregano until the hominy is hot, 3 to 5 minutes. Add salt and pepper to taste. Makes 6 servings.

PER SERVING: 194 calories, 3.2 g protein, 30 g carbohydrates, 6.4 g fat (0.9 g saturated), 0 mg cholesterol, 447 mg sodium

BREAD PUDDING BREAKFAST

Cinnamon Bread Pudding with Pumpkin Custard
Pork Sausages
Golden Delicious Apples
Earl Grey Tea

Sweetly spiced bread pudding bakes with just enough egg and milk to hold it together. While the pudding cooks, stir pumpkin custard in a double boiler, brown sausages, and make tea.

CINNAMON BREAD PUDDING WITH PUMPKIN CUSTARD

8 to 10 ounces day-old crusty sour-dough bread, unsliced
1/4 cup (1/8 lb.) melted butter or margarine
3/4 cup sugar
2 teaspoons ground cinnamon
3 large eggs
2 3/4 cups milk
1/2 cup pecan halves
1 can (1 lb.) pumpkin
1/2 teaspoon ground nutmeg
1 teaspoon vanilla

Tear bread into 1-inch chunks; you should have about 6 cups.

In a bowl, mix bread with butter. Combine 1/4 cup sugar and cinnamon; sprinkle over bread and mix. In a small bowl, beat 1 egg and 3/4 cup milk; gently mix with bread.

Spoon bread mixture into a buttered 1 1/2- to 2-quart shallow baking dish. Bake in a 375° oven 15 minutes. Scatter pecans over bread; bake until deeply browned and crisp, about 15 minutes more.

Meanwhile, in the top of a 2- to 3-quart double boiler, beat remaining sugar, eggs, and milk with pumpkin, nutmeg, and vanilla. Stir often over simmering water until custard is steaming and thickly coats a metal spoon, about 12 minutes. Pour into a pitcher.

Pour custard into bowls and spoon warm bread pudding on top. Makes 6 servings.

PER SERVING: 498 calories, 13 g protein, 65 g carbohydrates, 22 g fat (8.8 g saturated), 144 mg cholesterol, 443 mg sodium

NOVEMBER

Thanksgiving turkey with trimmings (pages 273, 274, 276, 288)

Ring in the holidays with our special section of festive, well-trimmed menus and party dishes. At this time of year, overindulgence is no longer inevitable. Our goal has been to reduce the fat without spoiling the fun in holiday foods. Let our lavish appetizers, showy vegetables and grains, even desserts and beverages offer inspiration for your grand dinners and holiday entertaining from Thanksgiving to Christmas. Experiment with dried fruits in cordials and cake. You'll also find easy, time-saving entrées to help you get through the busy workweek.

ABUNDANCE IS THE HALLMARK *of Thanksgiving, and this menu carries on the tradition in a generous spirit. In keeping with other recipes throughout this holiday bonus section, many of the ones in this menu are low in fat (but don't taste like it), and most have make-ahead steps. So, with the joy of feasting comes the pleasure of knowing you're enjoying better balance, in both nutrition and time, during the holidays.*

A GRAND THANKSGIVING FEAST FOR 10 TO 12

Red or White Belgian Endive
with Smoked Salmon
& Mustard Sauce

Buttered Toast Triangles

Roast Turkey (page 288)

Giblet Gravy

Cranberry Chipotle Relish

Steamed Mini-pumpkins
with Fresh Raisin Chutney (page 273)

Red Bell Peppers
& Caper Rice (page 273)

Green Beans
& Butter-browned Onions

Wild Rice with Aromatics (page 274)

Fila-wrapped Rum Cake
Bundles (page 276)

Chardonnay

Sparkling Apple Juice

RED OR WHITE BELGIAN ENDIVE WITH SMOKED SALMON & MUSTARD SAUCE

---

3 heads (about $3/4$ to 1 lb. total) red
   or white Belgian endive, rinsed
   and crisped
   About $3/4$ pound thinly sliced
   smoked salmon
   Mustard sauce (recipe follows)
   About 3 tablespoons drained
   canned capers

Break outer leaves from endive and arrange on each of 10 to 12 salad plates (reserve small leaves for other uses). Drape salmon slices equally over endive. Mound mustard sauce equally onto salmon; sprinkle with capers. Makes 10 to 12 servings.

PER SERVING: 114 calories, 5.5 g protein, 4.2 g carbohydrates, 8.2 g fat (1 g saturated), 6.5 mg cholesterol, 730 mg sodium

Mustard sauce. In a bowl, mix $3/4$ cup **Dijon mustard**, $1/3$ cup **salad oil**, 1 tablespoon **white wine vinegar**, 1 tablespoon firmly packed **brown sugar**, and 1 tablespoon **dried dill weed**. If made ahead, cover and chill up to 1 week. Makes about $11/4$ cups.

CRANBERRY CHIPOTLE RELISH

---

1 dried chipotle chili, about $21/2$
   inches long, rinsed; or 1 fresh
   jalapeño chili, rinsed, stemmed,
   seeded, and minced
1 small (5 oz.) orange or tangerine,
   rinsed
3 cups (12 oz.) fresh or frozen
   cranberries, rinsed
$1/2$ cup packed fresh cilantro
   (coriander)
1 tablespoon chopped fresh ginger
2 tablespoons lime juice
2 tablespoons sugar
2 tablespoons orange-flavor liqueur
2 tablespoons tequila
   Salt
   Cilantro sprigs and lime slices

Remove and discard stems and seeds from chipotle. Break chili into a food processor. Cut orange (with peel) into chunks; discard seeds.

Put orange, cranberries, the $1/2$ cup cilantro, and ginger into processor; whirl until finely chopped (or grind ingredients with a food chopper). Add lime juice, sugar, liqueur, tequila, and salt to taste. Serve, or cover and chill up to 1 week. Garnish with cilantro sprigs and lime slices. Makes about $22/3$ cups.

PER TABLESPOON: 12 calories, 0.1 g protein, 2.4 g carbohydrates, 0 g fat, 0 mg cholesterol, 0.3 mg sodium

Roast turkey, centerpiece of Thanksgiving dinner, is surrounded by tiny pumpkins filled with raisin chutney, and roasted red peppers stuffed with caper rice. Wild rice, cranberry chipotle relish, green beans and butter-browned onions, and fila-wrapped rum cakes wrap up the feast, which begins with a handsome salad.

ADORN YOUR *holiday roast platter* with attractive, complementary vegetable and fruit side dishes. Here are five colorful choices, featuring cranberries, carrots, tiny edible pumpkins, bell peppers, and artichokes. They all can be made in advance, and some of them improve with reheating.

To reheat in a microwave oven, set foods slightly apart on a microwave-safe plate. Drape with plastic wrap and cook on full power (100 percent) for 2 minutes. Rotate plate to reverse position of foods. Continue heating, 1 minute at a time, rotating plate ¼ turn each time, until vegetables are hot. For these quantities, allow at least 10 minutes.

CRANBERRY-TOMATO RELISH IN LEMON SHELLS

> 4 or 5 lemons (each about 5 oz. and about 3½ in. long), or ½ cup lemon juice
>
> 1 can (28 oz.) tomatoes
>
> 1 large (½ lb.) onion, finely chopped
>
> 1 cup sugar
>
> 2 tablespoons minced fresh ginger
>
> 1 package (12 oz., 3 cups) fresh or frozen cranberries

To use lemons for serving containers, cut lemons (decoratively, if desired) in half crosswise. Ream juice, reserving ½ cup. Scoop out and discard pulp and membrane. Trim a thin slice off base of each lemon so it will sit steadily upright. Wrap shells in a towel, put in a plastic bag, and refrigerate. Use within 2 days. If not using lemons, see below.

Pour ½ cup lemon juice into a 10- to 12-inch frying pan or 5-quart pan; add tomatoes and liquid (break tomatoes apart with a spoon), onion, sugar, and ginger. Boil on medium-high heat, stirring often, for 20 minutes.

Add cranberries and stir often until reduced to 3½ cups, about 30 minutes longer. As mixture thickens, watch carefully and stir more often to avoid scorching. Cool. Use, or cover relish and chill up to 3 weeks.

Divide relish evenly among lemon halves; otherwise serve in small cups or bowls (about ⅓-cup size) and arrange on a large platter around an entrée. Makes 8 to 10 servings.

PER SERVING: 142 calories, 1.2 g protein, 36 g carbohydrates, 0.3 g fat (0 g saturated), 0 mg cholesterol, 0 mg sodium

CARROT & ONION BUNDLES

> 5 or 6 green onions with tops, root ends trimmed
>
> 6 to 8 large (1½ to 2 lb. total) carrots, peeled and cut into ⅛-inch-thick sticks, each about 3 inches long

Cut each onion in half lengthwise. In a 4- to 5-quart pan, bring 2 inches water to boiling; add carrots. Cover and cook until carrots are barely tender to bite, about 3 minutes. Lift out with a slotted spoon and immerse in ice water to stop cooking. When cool, drain and divide into 10 to 12 equal portions.

Return the cooking water to boiling and push a few onions at a time beneath the surface. Cook just until onions are limp. Transfer them to ice water to cover. Drain thoroughly.

To make bundles, lay an onion piece out flat. Neatly align a portion of carrots on onion to make a cross. Tie onion gently but snugly around carrots. Trim ends of onion to make a tidy-looking bundle. If made ahead, set bundles side by side, cover airtight, and chill up until next day.

Serve cold, at room temperature, or reheated in a microwave oven (see directions preceding). Place bundles on a large platter around an entrée. Makes 10 to 12 servings.

PER SERVING: 23 calories, 0.6 g protein, 5.5 g carbohydrates, 0.1 g fat (0 g saturated), 0 mg cholesterol, 18 mg sodium

Carrot and onion bundles and lemon shells filled with cranberry, tomato, and lemon relish make attractive, tasty additions to roast beef platter.

STEAMED MINI-PUMPKINS WITH FRESH RAISIN CHUTNEY

10 to 12 miniature pumpkins (7 to 8 oz. each), such as Jack Be Little or Munchkin

Fresh raisin chutney (recipe follows)

10 to 12 nontoxic green leaves, slightly larger than pumpkins, rinsed and dried (optional)

10 to 12 small clusters green grapes, rinsed and drained (optional)

Rinse pumpkins and set on a rack (they can be stacked loosely) over 1 inch boiling water in a 6- to 8-quart pan. Cover and steam over medium-high heat until pumpkins are tender when pierced, about 20 minutes.

Lift pumpkins from rack and let stand until cool. Slice off top ¼ of each pumpkin. With a spoon, gently scoop out seeds; take care not to break through shell. If cooked ahead, replace lids, cover, and chill up until next day; reheat pumpkins by steaming about 8 minutes in a single layer (you'll need 2 pans), or use a microwave oven (see instructions on facing page).

Spoon warm chutney equally into each pumpkin and replace lids. Arrange pumpkins on leaves on the rim of a large platter around an entrée. Garnish with grapes. If tender to bite, shells of pumpkins are also edible. Makes 10 to 12 servings.

PER SERVING: 159 calories, 2.2 g protein, 40 g carbohydrates, 0.6 g fat (0.2 g saturated), 0 mg cholesterol, 7.3 mg sodium

Fresh raisin chutney. In a 12-inch frying pan or 5- to 6-quart pan, braize-deglaze (see page 275) 2 large (about 1 lb. total) finely chopped **onions** with **water** until mixture is deep brown. Add 2 large (1 lb. total) cored, peeled, finely chopped tart **apples** (Newtown Pippin or McIntosh), 4 cups **seedless green grapes**, 1 cup **water**, ¾ cup **red wine vinegar**, ¾ cup firmly packed **brown sugar**, and ¼ teaspoon **pepper**. Bring to a boil on high heat; cover and simmer until grapes begin to split, 10 to 15 minutes.

Cook uncovered, stirring often, until mixture is thick and no longer has any free-flowing liquid; as mixture thickens, stir more often to prevent scorching. Add **salt** to taste. If made ahead, cover and chill up to 3 days; reheat to use. Makes about 4 cups.

RED BELL PEPPERS & CAPER RICE

If you can't find small peppers, use medium-size ones cut down in size. After cutting off the top, trim the cut edges of both pieces so the pepper is 2 to 3 inches tall when reassembled.

10 to 12 small (each 2 to 3 oz. and 2 to 3 in. tall) red, yellow, or orange bell peppers

8 slices bacon

1 cup short- or medium-grain rice

4 teaspoons grated lemon peel

¼ cup drained canned capers

¼ cup seasoned rice vinegar (or ¼ cup rice vinegar and 4 teaspoons sugar)

Cut off top ⅓ of each pepper; set tops aside. With a small spoon, scoop out seeds and white membrane from pepper bases and tops; rinse and drain both. If needed, trim pepper bases so they will sit steadily.

In a 2- to 3-quart pan over medium heat, stir bacon often until crisp, about 10 minutes. With a slotted spoon, transfer bacon to towels; let drain. When cool, finely crumble. Discard drippings; wipe pan clean.

To pan, add rice, lemon peel, and 2½ cups water. Bring to boiling over high heat. Stir; then cover and simmer until liquid is absorbed, about 20 minutes. Uncover; with a fork, stir in bacon, capers, and vinegar.

Set pepper shells upright and apart in a rimmed 10- by 15-inch pan. Mound rice equally into shells; set tops on peppers. If made ahead, cover and let stand up to 4 hours. Bake, uncovered, in a 450° oven until peppers blister and rice is hot in center, 8 to 12 minutes. (Or bake up to 4 hours ahead, let stand, then reheat in a microwave oven; see facing page.) Set peppers on platter around an entrée. Makes 10 to 12 servings.

PER SERVING: 114 calories, 3.2 g protein, 20 g carbohydrates, 2.6 g fat (0.8 g saturated), 3.6 mg cholesterol, 218 mg sodium

ARTICHOKES WITH PARSLEY PESTO

⅓ cup cider vinegar

1 tablespoon cumin seed

1 tablespoon minced fresh ginger

About 1½ tablespoons drained canned green peppercorns

4 or 5 artichokes, 4 to 4½ inches wide (about ¾ lb. each)

Parsley pesto (recipe follows)

In an 11- to 12-quart pan, combine 5 quarts water, vinegar, cumin seed, ginger, and 1 tablespoon peppercorns. Cover and bring to a boil over high heat.

Meanwhile, break off coarse outer leaves from artichokes and trim stems even with bases. With a sharp knife, cut off top ⅓ of each artichoke. With scissors, trim thorny tips from remaining leaves. Immerse artichokes in cool water and swish back and forth; shake out water.

Place artichokes in pan. Reduce heat, cover, and boil gently until bottoms are tender when pierced, 30 to 40 minutes. Lift out artichokes and drain upside-down. If desired, pour cooking liquid through a strainer and reserve seasonings. Pull small center leaves from artichokes; with a small spoon, go down through opening and scrape out fuzzy choke. Slice artichokes in half lengthwise. If cooked ahead, cover and chill up until next day. To reheat, place in a microwave oven (see facing page), or immerse in simmering water to cover for about 5 minutes, then drain well.

Set artichokes cup side up on a large platter around an entrée. If desired, scatter artichokes with reserved seasonings; mound pesto equally into each. Sprinkle pesto with remaining peppercorns. Makes 8 to 10 servings.

PER SERVING: 130 calories, 2.8 g protein, 10 g carbohydrates, 9.7 g fat (1.2 g saturated), 0 mg cholesterol, 82 mg sodium

Parsley pesto. In a blender or food processor, whirl ¼ cup **roasted salted almonds** to a fine powder. Add 2 cups lightly packed **parsley**, ⅓ cup **olive oil**, 3 tablespoons **cider vinegar**, and 1 tablespoon drained **canned green peppercorns**; smoothly purée. If made ahead, cover and chill up until next day. Makes about 1 cup.

Artichoke half makes ample cup to hold dipping sauce of parsley pesto.

HOLIDAY ENTERTAINING: Low-fat Side Dishes

THE SECRET OF LEANER *eating, regardless of the season, is to replace fattening steps in recipes with fat-free alternatives, using everyday ingredients that produce equally good if not better-tasting results. For three of these delicious companion dishes—a pilaf, wild rice, and scalloped root vegetables—we used braise-deglazing to brown vegetables without adding fat. We think you'll find the results remarkably flavorful. Even Yorkshire pudding can take a trimming with no loss of appetite appeal.*

Other recipes throughout this holiday section also use the braise-deglaze cooking technique.

BARLEY & BROWN RICE PILAF

> 2 large (about 1 lb. total) onions, chopped
> 4½ cups regular-strength chicken broth
> 1 cup long-grain brown rice
> 1 cup pearl barley
> ½ teaspoon dry thyme leaves
> ¼ cup dry sherry (optional)
> Salt

In a 3- to 4-quart pan, braise-deglaze onions until richly browned (see directions on facing page); start with ½ cup broth, then use water. With last addition of water, scrape onions from pan. Rinse and dry pan.

Rinse and drain rice and barley. Add to pan and stir over medium-high heat until grains are dry and smell toasted. Add remaining 4 cups broth, braise-deglazed onions, and thyme. Bring to a boil on high heat, then cover and simmer gently until grains are tender to bite, 40 to 50 minutes. Stir in sherry and heat until boiling. Serve or, if made ahead, cover and chill up until next day; to reheat, use the directions below. Add salt to taste. Makes about 5 cups, 6 to 8 servings.

PER SERVING: 210 calories, 6.2 g protein, 42 g carbohydrates, 2 g fat (0.4 g saturated), 0 mg cholesterol, 35 mg sodium

To reheat pilaf or wild rice (following), pour rice into a microwave-safe bowl and heat in a microwave oven on full power (100 percent) for 3 minutes. Continue to heat and stir, 1 minute at a time, until hot. Or add about ½ cup broth to pan and stir over medium heat until hot, about 15 minutes.

WILD RICE WITH AROMATICS

> 3 tablespoons mustard seed
> 1 teaspoon coriander seed
> ½ teaspoon cumin seed
> ½ teaspoon whole allspice
> ¼ teaspoon cardamom seed (pod removed)
> 1 teaspoon dried thyme leaves
> 2 tablespoons minced fresh ginger
> 2 large (about 1 lb. total) onions, chopped
> 8 cups regular-strength chicken broth
> 3 cups (1¼ lb.) wild rice, rinsed and drained
> Salt

In a 5- to 6-quart pan on medium-high heat, stir mustard seed, coriander seed, cumin seed, allspice, and cardamom until seeds become very aromatic, about 1 minute. Add thyme, ginger, onions, and ½ cup of the broth. Braise-deglaze onions until richly browned (see facing page), using water for each deglazing step.

Stir in remaining broth and rice. Bring to boil on high heat; cover and simmer gently until rice is tender to bite and grains begin to split open, 45 to 55 minutes. Drain, reserving liquid for reheating or another use. If made ahead, chill rice and broth separately up until next day. Reheat as directed, preceding. Add salt to taste. Makes about 11 cups, 12 to 14 servings.

PER SERVING: 186 calories, 8.3 g protein, 35 g carbohydrates, 2.1 g fat (0.3 g saturated), 0 mg cholesterol, 34 mg sodium

LEAN YORKSHIRE PUDDING

> 1 large egg
> 1 large egg white
> ½ cup all-purpose flour
> ½ cup nonfat milk
> 1 teaspoon sugar
> ¼ teaspoon salt
> 1 tablespoon butter or margarine

In a blender or with a whisk, smoothly combine egg, egg white, flour, milk, sugar, and salt. If made ahead, cover batter and chill up until next day; stir before using.

In an 8- to 9-inch by 11- to 12-inch oval pan or 10- to 11-inch frying pan with

Rumpled Yorkshire pudding uses lean ingredients and little fat. Bake in oven until golden brown, then cut in wedges in pan.

How to Braise-Deglaze Vegetables

TO MAKE *a flavorful, richly browned, no-fat seasoning base for soups, stews, pilafs, and casseroles, use this braise-deglaze technique.*

Choose vegetables that are typically sautéed, such as carrots, celery, fennel, leeks, mushrooms, onions, and firm vegetables like rutabagas and turnips.

With this method, you combine chopped vegetables with a little water or broth in a pan and cook until a rich brown color develops. As the liquid boils away, browned bits or a film (from sugar and starches cooked out of vegetables) forms in the pan. Deglaze the pan by adding liquid and boiling again, stirring to free browned bits. Repeat the deglazing step until vegetables soak up rich flavor and brown color.

We use this technique often in recipes. The following directions will guide you through the process.

To braise-deglaze, use the pan specified in recipe or a 10- to 12-inch frying pan or 5- to 6-quart pan (a heavy non-stick pan works particularly well; use wider-diameter pan for larger quantity). Combine chopped **vegetables** as specified in recipe and **regular-strength chicken broth** or water (amount specified in recipe or about 1/4 cup for 1/2 to 1 lb. vegetables, 1/2 cup for 1 to 3 lb.).

Cook uncovered over high heat, stirring occasionally, until liquid evaporates and browned vegetable bits stick in the pan or a rich brown film forms.

Deglaze pan by adding 2 to 4 tablespoons **water** or unsalted broth (use larger amount with larger quantity of vegetables). Stir or scrape to free browned bits or film. Stir often until liquid evaporates and browned bits

form again. Repeat deglazing and cooking dry until a rich brown color develops.

You can substitute braise-deglazed onions for sautéed onions in your own recipes. The technique often takes longer than sautéing, so you might want to make big batches at a time to store in the freezer.

Home recipes with braise-deglazed onions. Follow preceding directions for braise-deglazing, using **onions.** To make 1/3 cup braise-deglazed onions, start with 1 large (about 1/2 lb.) onion; to make 2/3 cup, start with 2 large (about 1 lb. total) onions; to make 1 cup, start with 3 large (about 1 1/2 lb. total) onions; to make 2 cups, start with 6 large (about 3 lb.) onions. Use or, if made ahead, cover and chill up to 3 days or freeze in small portions up to 1 month.

---

ovenproof handle, melt butter over medium-high heat until it just begins to brown slightly. At once, pour batter into pan and place in a 425° oven. Bake until pudding is richly browned, about 25 minutes. Cut into wedges in pan. Makes 4 to 6 servings.

PER SERVING: 3.4 calories, 3.4 g protein, 9.8 g carbohydrates, 2.9 g fat (1.5 g saturated), 41 mg cholesterol, 140 mg sodium

ALSATIAN GRATIN OF ROOTS

3 large (about 1 1/2 lb. total) onions, finely chopped

4 large (about 1 lb. total) carrots, finely chopped

3 cups regular-strength chicken or beef broth

3 pounds (about 6 large) thin-skinned potatoes

1 pound (about 2 medium-size) rutabagas

1/2 cup minced parsley
  About 1/2 teaspoon freshly grated nutmeg

3/4 cup shredded light Jarlsberg cheese or fontina cheese
  Salt and pepper

In a 5- to 6-quart pan, braise-deglaze onions and carrots (see above); start with 1/2 cup broth, then add another 1/2 cup broth in 2- or 3-tablespoon portions to deglaze. Continue deglazing with water until vegetables are richly browned. When deglazing the last time, do not cook vegetables dry. If made ahead, cover and chill up to 3 days.

Peel and very thinly slice potatoes and rutabagas. In a shallow 4-quart casserole, arrange layers of potatoes, rutabagas, braise-deglazed onions and carrots, parsley, and a light sprinkling of nutmeg; start and end with potatoes. Pour 2 cups broth into the dish and cover tightly with a piece of lightly oiled foil, greased side down.

Bake in a 425° oven until vegetables in the center of casserole are very tender when pierced, 1 hour and 30 minutes to 1 hour and 45 minutes. Uncover, sprinkle with cheese, and dust lightly with nutmeg.

Broil about 8 inches from heat until cheese is bubbling and lightly browned. Casserole is very hot; if kept in a warm place, it holds well up to 45 minutes. Add salt and pepper to taste. Makes 10 to 12 servings.

PER SERVING: 170 calories, 6.2 g protein, 32 g carbohydrates, 1.9 g fat (0.1 g saturated), 3.2 mg cholesterol, 74 mg sodium

Bubbling gratin of roots has only a dusting of cheese and nutmeg.

BEHIND EACH OF *these beautiful desserts is one recipe for a fine-grain, tender-textured cake. You bake the batter in muffin cups for the dessert bundled in fila to make a gift package to end a meal. For another dessert, you add a little cornmeal to the batter and bake it in cornbread-stick pans to make a crunchy cooky-cake just right for dunking in hot chocolate. For the last dessert, you bake the batter in little rectangular pans, then wrap the cake in pink marzipan with a marzipan bow.*

FILA-WRAPPED RUM CAKE BUNDLES

½ cup finely chopped salted
  macadamia nuts
1 recipe pound cake batter
  (directions follow)
  Rum syrup (directions follow)
24 sheets fila dough, each about
  11 by 17 inches (⅓ to ½ lb. total)
½ cup (¼ lb.) butter or margarine,
  melted
  Cotton string
  About 6 yards ½-inch-wide satin
  or grosgrain ribbon, cut into 12
  equal pieces

Stir nuts into cake batter, then spoon batter equally into 12 buttered and floured 2½-inch muffin cups. Bake in a 300° oven until a toothpick inserted in center of cakes comes out clean, about 25 minutes. Cool cakes in pan on a rack for about 5 minutes. Run a knife between each cup and cake and invert pan to release cakes.

Set warm cakes close together on a rimmed plate or pan. With a fork or slender skewer, pierce holes about 1 inch deep and about ¼ inch apart all over tops of cakes. Immediately pour an equal amount of rum syrup over each cake. Let cakes stand until cool, about 30 minutes.

Lay 1 fila sheet flat; brush lightly with butter. Keep remaining fila covered with plastic wrap to prevent drying. Top buttered fila with another fila sheet; brush lightly with butter. Cut buttered sheets in half crosswise. Set 1 section on top of the other to form a cross.

Ruffles of fila, decorated with wired ribbon, enclose rum-soaked macadamia nut cake. Batter is baked in muffin cups; warm cakes are pierced, then soaked in rum syrup.

Place 1 rum-soaked cake in center of fila cross. Gently lift fila up and around cake, gathering at the top; tie pastry with a piece of string to hold it around cake. Set cake bundle in a buttered 10- by 15-inch rimmed pan.

Repeat to shape remaining cake bundles, setting them slightly apart in pan. At this point you can cover them airtight with plastic wrap and chill up to 1 day.

Cut 12 pieces of foil, each 6 inches square. Loosely cup a foil piece over ruffled top of each bundle. Bake on the lowest rack in a 350° oven for 10 minutes; gently remove foil caps and continue baking until ruffles are browned, about 5 minutes longer. Let cool 10 minutes. At once, with a wide spatula,

transfer bundles to a platter or dessert plates. Tie ribbons in bows below fila ruffles. Serve warm or let stand up to 1 day. Makes 12.

PER PIECE: 472 calories, 4.4 g protein, 53 g carbohydrates, 25 g fat (13 g saturated), 105 mg cholesterol, 300 mg sodium

Pound cake batter. In a large bowl with a mixer, beat ¾ cup (⅜ lb.) **butter** or margarine until creamy. Add 1¾ cups sifted **powdered sugar;** stir to mix, then beat until mixture is fluffy. Add 3 **large eggs,** 1 at a time, beating well after each addition. Add ½ teaspoon **vanilla** and 1¼ cups sifted **cake flour;** stir to mix, then beat to blend well.

Rum syrup. In a 1½- to 2-quart pan, combine 1 cup **sugar,** ¼ cup **light corn syrup,** and 6 tablespoons **water.** Stir over medium-high heat until mixture simmers. Continue heating, without stirring, until mixture boils. Cover and boil until sugar dissolves and liquid is clear, about 1 minute. (If you don't cover pan and do stir boiling syrup, crunchy sugar crystals will form in cake.)

Remove from heat and uncover; let stand 5 minutes. Stir in 10 tablespoons **rum.** Use hot or reheated; if made ahead, cover and let stand up to 1 day. Makes 1¾ cups.

CORN CAKE STICKS IN CORNHUSKS

> About ¼ cup yellow cornmeal
> 1 recipe pound cake batter (directions on facing page)
> Cooking oil spray
> 1 tablespoon unsweetened cocoa
> About 42 dry cornhusks (6 to 8 in. long)

Stir ¼ cup cornmeal into cake batter. With oil spray, lightly coat cornstick pans with molds about 5½ inches long. (You will need to bake about 19 cakes total, but batter can stand if you have only 1 pan and bake cakes in sequence.) Sprinkle cornmeal lightly into molds; shake out excess. Spoon 2½ tablespoons batter into each mold.

Bake in a 300° oven until a toothpick inserted in center comes out clean, 30 to

Dry corn husks cradle cocoa-dusted cornstick cakes to eat with hot chocolate.

35 minutes. Cool 5 minutes. Then, with the tip of a small knife, loosen sticks from pans; invert onto racks and cool completely. (If reusing pan, wash, dry, oil, and dust with cornmeal after each batch.)

Lightly dust the patterned side of the cakes with cocoa. Overlap 2 cornhusks lengthwise; set a cake in the center of the length of the husks. Fold husk around cake, overlapping, then tie cut end of husks with a thin strip of more husk. Repeat to wrap remaining cakes. If made ahead, cover airtight and hold up to 1 day. Makes 19.

PER PIECE: 144 calories, 1.8 g protein, 16 g carbohydrates, 8.5 g fat (4.9 g saturated), 53 mg cholesterol, 85 mg sodium

MINIATURE MARZIPAN GIFT BOXES

> 1 recipe pound cake batter (directions on facing page)
> ¼ cup raspberry preserves
> 2 tablespoons black raspberry–flavor liqueur
> Powdered sugar
> Tinted marzipan (directions follow)
> ⅔ cup packed (6 to 7 oz.) marzipan

Butter and flour-dust 6 miniature loaf pans, each about 2½ by 4 inches. Spoon cake batter equally into pans; spread batter smooth.

Bake in a 300° oven until a toothpick inserted in center of cakes comes out clean, 30 to 35 minutes. Set pans on a rack for 5 minutes. Run a knife between each cake and pan; invert cakes onto racks to cool.

With a serrated knife, slice each cake in half horizontally. Combine preserves and liqueur; equally spread mixture on cut surface of each cake bottom. Set cake tops (cut down) on jam. If made ahead, wrap each cake airtight and hold at room temperature up until next day.

Lightly coat a sheet of waxed paper (at least 12 by 15 in.) with powdered sugar. Form ⅙ of the tinted marzipan into a flat, square patty and set on sugar. Sprinkle marzipan lightly with more sugar, then cover with another sheet of waxed paper. Roll marzipan to form a rectangle about 5½ by 7 inches. If paper wrinkles and gets embedded in marzipan, peel off and replace paper.

Peel top paper off rolled marzipan. Gently pull and lift marzipan from

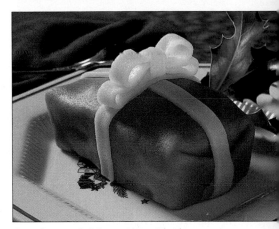

Smooth wrap of pink marzipan with a bow makes a gift of cake with raspberry filling.

bottom paper. Carefully center marzipan atop a cake and drape edges over cake sides. At narrow ends, fold marzipan to fit snugly against cake; trim edges flush with cake. Repeat to wrap remaining cakes.

Roll plain marzipan between sheets of sugar-dusted waxed paper to form a 9-inch square. Peel off top paper; cut marzipan into 18 equal strips. To create a "ribbon" on each cake, gently lift 1 marzipan strip and lay it lengthwise on center of a cake, pressing lightly to stick to tinted marzipan. Drape a second strip of plain marzipan across the center of the first, pressing gently into place. Trim edges flush with cake base.

To make a bow, cut 1 strip into a 6-inch piece and a 3-inch piece. Loop ends to the center of each strip. Center small loop on top of the big one, then center on top of the cake. Repeat to put bows on remaining cakes.

Gather plain scraps and reroll between sugared waxed paper; cut 6 strips about ¼ inch by 1½ inches. Fold each strip around the center of the bow to cover the joint. Serve, or cover airtight slightly apart up to 1 day. Makes 6; each cake serves 2.

PER SERVING: 392 calories, 4.5 g protein, 61 g carbohydrates, 15 g fat (7.7 g saturated), 85 mg cholesterol, 140 mg sodium

Tinted marzipan. Put 1 cup packed (about 12 oz.) **marzipan** in a bowl. Add **red food coloring,** kneading in 1 drop at a time, until mixture is an even-colored pale pink. If made ahead, chill airtight up to 2 days. Use at room temperature.

READY AND WAITING: *that's how this walkabout party is organized. There are stations for hot foods, several for cold dishes, one for beverages, and one for sweets. Without the distraction of having to balance plates, forks, and glasses, conversation flows easily as the guests meander from one station to another.*

Broadly represented, but well disguised by satisfying flavors, are many dishes that are significantly low in fat. All the foods hold up well over several hours. Use a warming tray to keep the meats steaming hot. Present a range of beverages so guests can make their own choices (see page 283).

Set out plenty of wastebaskets, and offer paper napkins at each station.

WALKABOUT HOLIDAY PARTY FOR 24

SLIM PICKINGS:

Lentils with Green Herbs

Roasted Fennel & Carrots with Belgian Endive

Falafel Pizza (page 282)

CRISP BITES:

Parmesan Cream Dip with Vegetables

HOT SPOT:

Faux Squab Wings

Roasted Sausages & Onions, Italian-style

Norwegian Meatballs

COOKY STOP (page 284):

Snow-frosted Rye Cutouts

Oatmeal Thumbprints

Wheat Germ Shortbread

Whole-wheat Crisps

CHOOSE YOUR SIPPING
(regular or nonalcoholic):

Dry White & Red Wines

Sparkling Wine   Beer

Mineral Water   Fruit Juices

LENTILS WITH GREEN HERBS

2   **large (about 1 lb. total) onions, finely chopped**

5   **cups regular-strength chicken broth**

1   **can (7 oz.) diced green chilies**

2   **tablespoons mustard seed**

1   **teaspoon coriander seed**

1   **teaspoon grated lemon peel**

1/2   **teaspoon cumin seed**

1   **package (12 oz. or 1 3/4 cups) lentils, sorted for debris and rinsed**

3/4   **cup lightly packed fresh cilantro (coriander)**

3/4   **cup lightly packed fresh mint leaves (or parsley and 1/4 teaspoon mint extract)**

1/4   **cup lime juice**
     Salt
     Thin lime slices and fresh cilantro sprigs
     About 1 1/2 dozen miniature pocket bread rounds (about 3 in. wide), cut in half
     About 1 cup unflavored nonfat yogurt

In a 5- to 6-quart pan, braise-deglaze onions (see page 275), starting with 1 cup broth, then adding water, until onions are richly browned. Add remaining 4 cups broth, chilies, mustard, coriander, lemon peel, cumin, and lentils. Bring to a boil on high heat; cover and simmer until lentils are tender to bite, 35 to 40 minutes.

Drain off and save liquid. Let lentils cool; if made ahead, cover and chill cooking liquid and lentils up to 3 days.

In a food processor, whirl 3/4 cup cilantro and 3/4 cup mint until finely chopped (or mince with a knife). Mix herbs and lime juice with lentils; add a little of the cooking liquid if you want moister lentils (use remaining liquid in soups), and salt to taste.

Pour into a bowl and garnish with lime slices and cilantro sprigs. Spoon mixture into pocket bread halves and add yogurt to taste. Makes 6 cups, 24 appetizer servings.

PER SERVING: 139 calories, 7.6 g protein, 25 g carbohydrates, 1 g fat (0.1 g saturated), 0.2 mg cholesterol, 207 mg sodium

(Continued on page 280)

Light but filling foods include falafel pizza cut into slim wedges, savory herb-seasoned lentils to eat in pocket bread, and braise-deglazed vegetable dip served with Belgian endive. Foods located at various stations encourage guests to circulate.

Guests serve themselves hot foods, cold dishes, sweets, and beverages at various food stations. Pick-up foods eliminate plates; offer paper napkins at each table.

mound in a small bowl, garnish with fennel tops, and set on a platter. Break endive leaves from heads and arrange on platter around vegetable mixture. Spoon onto leaves to eat. Makes 4 cups vegetables, 24 appetizer servings.

PER PORTION: 40 calories, 1.7 g protein, 7.3 g carbohydrates, 0.6 g fat (0.1 g saturated), 0 mg cholesterol, 54 mg sodium

PARMESAN CREAM DIP WITH VEGETABLES

For another dipper, wrap blanched Chinese pea pods (split in half) around shelled, cooked tiny shrimp.

- 1 **cup light or regular sour cream**
- 1/2 **cup freshly grated parmesan cheese**
- 3 **tablespoons red wine vinegar**
- 1 **teaspoon Dijon mustard**
- 1 **clove garlic, minced or pressed**
- 1 **to 2 teaspoons sugar**
  About 1 tablespoon minced parsley
- 4 **or 5 large (about 7 oz. each) yellow, red, or green bell peppers, rinsed and drained**
- 2 **to 3 quarts small inner romaine lettuce leaves, rinsed and crisped**
  About 3 pounds (8 to 9 cups total) firm-ripe yellow or red cherry tomatoes, rinsed and drained

Stir together sour cream, cheese, vinegar, mustard, garlic, and sugar to taste. If made ahead, cover and chill up until next day. Pour into a small bowl and sprinkle with parsley.

Set peppers on stem ends. Cut down but not through peppers, dividing each into about 8 wedges. Place cut ends up in a large basket along with lettuce and tomatoes. If prepared ahead, cover vegetables airtight and chill up to 4 hours. Serve with dip. Makes 1½ cups dip, 2 dozen appetizers.

PER APPETIZER WITH 1 TEASPOON DIP: 49 calories, 2.6 g protein, 5.5 g carbohydrates, 2.2 g fat (1.1 g saturated), 4.9 mg cholesterol, 51 mg sodium

FAUX SQUAB WINGS

- **About 2 pounds (24 pieces) chicken wings, shoulder and middle sections only, cut apart**
- 1/4 **cup soy sauce**
- 1/4 **cup dry sherry**

ROASTED FENNEL & CARROTS WITH BELGIAN ENDIVE

Be sure to use unsalted homemade broth or canned reduced-sodium broth; salted broth concentrated this much will over-season the dip.

- 2 **medium-size (each about 1 lb.) heads fennel, rinsed and drained**
- 5 **cups (about 2 lb.) finely chopped carrots**
- 2 **large (about 1 lb. total) onions, finely chopped**
- 2 **teaspoons** *each* **cumin seed and mustard seed**
- 4 **cloves garlic, minced or pressed**

- 5¼ **cups unsalted regular-strength chicken broth, or 4 cans (10 oz. each) low-sodium chicken broth**
  Salt and pepper
- 6 **heads (about 1 lb. total) Belgian endive, rinsed and crisped**

Trim stems, root ends, and any bruised spots from fennel. Finely chop fennel and set aside. Wrap feathery tops in a damp towel, enclose in a plastic bag, and chill.

In a 5- to 6-quart pan over high heat, combine chopped fennel, carrots, onions, cumin, mustard, and garlic. Braise-deglaze (see page 275), starting with ½ cup broth and deglazing with ¼ cup broth each time, until vegetables are richly browned and all broth is used, about 50 minutes.

Add salt and pepper to taste. Serve warm or at room temperature. If made ahead, cover and chill up to 3 days;

2 tablespoons Oriental sesame oil
1 tablespoon honey
1 teaspoon five spice (or ¼ teaspoon *each* ground cinnamon, ground cloves, ground ginger, and anise seed)

In a bowl or heavy plastic bag, combine wings, soy, sherry, oil, honey, and five spice; mix well. Cover and chill 1 hour or up until next day.

Drain and save marinade. Arrange wings in a single layer in a 10- by 15-inch rimmed pan. Bake in a 475° oven, basting often the first 20 minutes with reserved marinade. Turn wings over, baste again, and bake until dark brown, 10 to 15 minutes longer.

Serve or, if made ahead, let cool, cover, and chill up until next day. To reheat, return wings to washed pan and bake at 350° until hot, about 10 minutes. Makes 24 pieces, 24 appetizer servings.

PER SERVING: 49 calories, 3.9 g protein, 0.6 g carbohydrates, 3.3 g fat (0.9 g saturated), 12 mg cholesterol, 101 mg sodium

ROASTED SAUSAGES & ONIONS, ITALIAN-STYLE

1½ pounds mild Italian sausages, cut into 1-inch lengths
2 large (about 1 lb. total) onions, cut into wedges
7 tablespoons balsamic vinegar
   About 1½ dozen miniature pocket bread rounds (about 3 in. wide), cut in half

Dip pea pod–wrapped shrimp and raw vegetables in parmesan cream dip.

Combine sausages, onions, and 6 tablespoons vinegar in a 10- by 15-inch rimmed pan. Bake in a 425° oven until meat is well browned and liquid evaporates, about 1 hour. Turn meat and onions occasionally with a wide spatula.

Remove from oven and push contents to 1 side; tilt pan to drain fat into a corner. Spoon out and discard fat, blotting pan with towels to remove as much as possible of the remaining fat. Mix remaining tablespoon vinegar and 1 tablespoon water in pan. Let stand about 5 minutes, then stir to free browned bits.

If made ahead, cover and chill up until next day. To reheat, place in a 375° oven for about 10 minutes. Transfer to a serving dish and keep hot on a warming tray. Spoon mixture into pocket bread halves. Makes about 3 cups, 24 appetizer servings.

PER SERVING: 155 calories, 6.3 g protein, 16 g carbohydrates, 7.3 g fat (2.5 g saturated), 19 mg cholesterol, 336 mg sodium

NORWEGIAN MEATBALLS

¼ cup regular-strength chicken broth or water
6 tablespoons all-purpose flour
2 pounds skinned and boned ground chicken or turkey breast or thigh (or a combination)
2 large egg whites
1 teaspoon dried rubbed sage
1 teaspoon pepper
½ teaspoon fennel seed
½ teaspoon salt
   Gjetost sauce (recipe follows)

In a bowl, smoothly mix broth with flour, then add chicken, egg whites, sage, pepper, fennel, and salt. Mix well with a fork. Make 1-tablespoon-size mounds of the meat and set slightly apart in 2 nonstick or lightly oiled 10- by 15-inch rimmed pans.

Bake in a 500° oven for 10 minutes. Turn meatballs over with a wide spatula. Continue baking until well browned and no longer pink in center (cut to test), 2 to 5 minutes longer. Use or, if made ahead, let meatballs cool, cover, and chill up to 2 days.

To serve, add to warm gjetost sauce (if meatballs are cold, first stir over low heat to warm); keep hot on a warming

Warming tray, draped with bay leaves, holds wings, sausages, and meatballs.

tray. Spear meatballs with small skewers to eat. Makes about 5 cups sauce and 4 dozen meatballs, 24 appetizer servings.

PER SERVING: 82 calories, 10 g protein, 5.1 g carbohydrates, 2 g fat (1.1 g saturated), 22 mg cholesterol, 110 mg sodium

Gjetost sauce. In a 10- to 12-inch frying pan, braise-deglaze 1 large (8 oz.) chopped **onion** with ½ cup **regular-strength chicken broth** total (see page 275 for braise-deglaze instructions). Add 2 tablespoons **cornstarch** to pan and smoothly mix in an additional 2 cups **regular-strength chicken broth.** On high heat, stir until boiling rapidly. Turn heat to low and add 1 cup (4 oz.) shredded **gjetost cheese;** stir until cheese melts. Pour into serving bowl; use hot (sauce thins if reheated).

HOLIDAY ENTERTAINING: Showpiece Appetizers

BIG, HANDSOME, *and make-ahead: those attributes make these showpiece appetizers ideal for entertaining. The first dish is a savory cheesecake pungent with the bite of Roquefort cheese but lightened up with a ricotta base. Spread it onto crisp radishes or crackers. The pastrami torte is assembled in layers in a little loaf pan; inverted and sliced, it reveals pepper cheese and pink ribbons of pastrami. Enjoy the torte in small portions on thin toasted bagel slices. And for a wild twist on pizza, bake falafel mix in a precooked crust. Cut the pizza into thin wedges to pick up and eat, warm or cool, with yogurt. The aromatically seasoned garbanzo flour in the falafel has a substantial character that many mistake for meat.*

RICOTTA ROQUEFORT CHEESECAKE

- 2 **cartons (15 oz. each, about 2 cups) part-skim or whole-milk ricotta cheese**
- 1 **cup packed (6 oz.) Roquefort cheese**
- 1 **teaspoon freshly ground pepper Salt**
- 6 **large egg whites**
- 1/4 **cup fresh, thinly shredded parmesan cheese**
- 3 **to 4 dozen red radishes, ends trimmed, rinsed and drained Parsley sprigs Crisp crackers**

Crisp radishes and crackers go with Roquefort cheesecake.

In a food processor or bowl, whirl or mix ricotta, Roquefort, pepper, and salt to taste. Beat in egg whites. Scrape mixture into a 10-inch cheesecake pan with removable rim. Sprinkle evenly with parmesan cheese.

Bake, uncovered, in a 325° oven until cheesecake is firm in center when pan is gently shaken, 35 to 45 minutes. Cool, cover, and chill at least 2 hours or up until next day.

Pinch all but 1 or 2 pretty leaves from each radish. Wrap in a damp towel; enclose in a plastic bag. Chill at least 30 minutes or up until next day.

Remove pan rim and set cake on a platter. Surround and garnish with radishes and parsley, and accompany with crackers. Spread cake by the spoonful onto radishes or crackers. Makes 16 to 18 servings.

PASTRAMI TORTE

- 1/4 **pound very thinly sliced pastrami**
- 3 **packages (4 oz. each, about 1½ cups total) fresh pepper or herb cheese**
- 3 **tablespoons minced parsley Toasted bagel slices or unsalted crackers**

Line bottom and sides of a 3- by 5½-inch loaf pan with a single, slightly overlapping layer of pastrami slices that extends a little over pan rim. Spoon ⅙ of the cheese in dollops evenly into pan. Press cheese into an even layer, holding meat in place (it wants to slide around); sprinkle with about ⅙ of the parsley. Cover cheese with a layer of pastrami, pressing level. Repeat layers, using all the cheese and parsley.

Tap pan sharply against counter to settle loaf firmly into pan. Fold overhang of pastrami onto cheese, then cover cheese with remaining pastrami, patting in place. Cover and chill until loaf feels firm when pressed, at least 4 hours or up until next day.

Run a thin knife between pastrami and pan sides, then invert loaf onto a platter. Slice, then cut portions of each slice to eat on toasted bagel slices. Makes 12 to 14 servings.

Curls of green onion top falafel pizza. Offer yogurt as a topping or dip.

FALAFEL PIZZA

- 3 **large eggs**
- 3/4 **cup milk**
- 1 **small can (4 oz.) diced green chilies**
- 1 **package (6 to 8 oz., about 1½ cups) falafel mix**
- 1 **package (16 oz.) prebaked refrigerated or frozen cheese crust (about 12 in. wide) Thinly sliced green onion**
- 1 **to 1½ cups unflavored nonfat yogurt**

In a large bowl, beat eggs, milk, chilies, and falafel to mix well. Cover and let stand to allow falafel mix to absorb moisture, about 10 minutes.

Place crust, cup side up, on a 14- by 17-inch baking sheet (or large sheet of foil). Scrape falafel mixture into center of crust and spread smoothly to fill hollow. Bake in a 350° oven until center feels firm when pressed lightly, 35 to 45 minutes. Garnish with green onion. Serve warm or at room temperature; cut wide wedges to eat with fork, thin wedges to pick up and eat. Offer yogurt as topping or dip. Makes 32 thin wedges, about ¾ inch at rim.

BEVERAGES ARE A *significant part of menu and party planning this time of year, and choice is the word of the day. For those who want somewhat lighter punches, here are three from cool to hot. To help you select sparkling wines to suit the occasion, we present a guide assembled by Sunset's wine consultant, Bob Thompson. You can also choose from a range of nonalcoholic wines and beers.*

Holiday Punches

ROSY SUNRISE

In a pitcher, mix 6 cups **orange juice,** 2 to 4 tablespoons **black raspberry–** or cassis-flavor **liqueur,** and ¹/₂ to ³/₄ cup **vodka.** Serve in ice-filled glasses. Makes 6¹/₂ to 7 cups.

PER ½-CUP SERVING: 78 calories, 0.8 g protein, 13 g carbohydrates, 0.1 g fat (0 g saturated), 0 mg cholesterol, 1.2 mg sodium

SOUTHERN CIDER

Cut 3 thick center slices **orange** into quarters; stud with 6 to 8 **whole cloves.** In a 1¹/₂- to 2-quart pan, heat orange pieces, 4 cups **apple juice,** and 1 **cinnamon stick** (about 3 in.) to simmering. Add ¹/₂ cup **bourbon.** Ladle into mugs. Makes about 4¹/₂ cups.

PER ½-CUP SERVING: 83 calories, 0.1 g protein, 13 g carbohydrates, 0.1 g fat (0 g saturated), 0 mg cholesterol, 3.5 mg sodium

SMOOTH SLIM RUM EGGNOG

2 cups nonfat milk
1 tablespoon cornstarch
   About ¹/₄ teaspoon freshly grated nutmeg
2 large egg whites
¹/₄ cup sugar
¹/₄ cup rum

Smoothly blend milk with cornstarch and ¹/₈ teaspoon nutmeg in a 1- to 1¹/₂-quart pan; set aside.

With a mixer, whip whites until foamy. Beating at high speed, gradually add sugar until whites hold short peaks. Stir milk mixture over high heat until just boiling. With mixer on medium speed, at once pour hot milk into whites, scraping down bowl sides. Let stand at least 4 minutes (boiling milk kills salmonella).

Add rum to eggnog; serve hot or cover and chill until cold, about 3 hours or up to 8. Pour mixture through a fine strainer into glasses. Dust with nutmeg. Makes 4¹/₂ cups.

PER ½-CUP SERVING: 62 calories, 2.6 g protein, 9.1 g carbohydrates, 0.1 g fat (0.1 g saturated), 1.1 mg cholesterol, 41 mg sodium

Sparkling Wines

IN THE FRENCH STYLE

The key qualities of sparkling wines styled after French Champagne are understated fruit flavors and dry, crisp, cleansing textures. Blanc de Noirs (mostly or all Pinot Noir grapes) are typically fuller-bodied and grapier-tasting than Blanc de Blancs (mostly or all Chardonnay grapes). Wines labeled only as Brut (blended Pinot Noir and Chardonnay) fall in between.

In the luxury class (limited production; $20 and up): Chandon Napa Valley Reserve (Brut) • Gloria Ferrer Carneros Cuvée (Brut) • Iron Horse Sonoma–Green Valley Blanc de Noirs, Blanc de Blancs • Mumm Napa Valley Vintage Reserve (Brut), Napa Valley–Winery Lake (Brut) • S. Anderson Napa Valley Blanc de Noirs • Schramsberg Napa Valley Blanc de Noirs, Brut, Napa Valley Reserve (Brut).

Medium-priced ($10 to $19): Chandon Carneros Blanc de Noirs, Napa Valley Brut • Culbertson California Brut • Domaine Carneros Carneros Brut • Gloria Ferrer Carneros (Brut), Carneros Royal Cuvée (Brut) • Gruet New Mexico Brut • Maison Deutz Arroyo Grande Brut • Mumm Napa Valley Brut Prestige • Piper-Sonoma Brut • Roederer Estate Anderson Valley Brut • S. Anderson Napa Valley 'Tivoli' (Brut) • Scharffenberger Mendocino Blanc de Blancs, Mendocino Rosé (Brut), Mendocino Brut • Shadow Creek California Brut.

POPULARLY PRICED BUBBLES

Wines priced to be mixed into punches or served at receptions are overtly fruity and sweet. Most such wines are made by a fast, money-saving method called charmat or bulk process. Prices run $4 to $7.50.

André California Brut • Cook's California Brut, California Extra Dry • Tott's California Brut.

CALIFORNIA ORIGINALS

Some producers include Chenin Blanc, French Colombard, Riesling, or other grapes; the result is sparkling wine with riper, more distinctively fruity flavors.

These wines may be made by methods other than classic méthode champenoise. Prices run $7 to $12.

Chateau de Baun Symphony Sonoma Brut • Domaine Masson • Korbel California Brut.

ASTI SPUMANTE–STYLE WINES

A handful of California producers make intensely fruity, dessert-sweet sparkling Muscats similar to Asti spumantes. Prices run about $4 to $10.

Ballatore California Spumante • Chateau de Baun Sonoma Symphony 'Romance' • Cook's California Spumante.

Nonalcoholic Wines & Beers

For those who enjoy the flavors of wine and beer but want alternatives without alcohol, there is a growing selection to bridge the interests.

WINES

Prices range from $5 to $15 for blends and varietals, $6 to $22 for sparkling wines.

Ariel (Blanc, Blanc de Noirs, Brut, Cabernet Sauvignon, Chardonnay, Riesling) • St. Regis (Blanc, California Champagne, Chardonnay, Red, White Zinfandel).

BEERS

Many are made by well-known brewers. Six bottles cost $3.75 to $7.

Buckler (Heineken) • Cheers • Clausthaler (Marke) • Firestone • Goetz Pale Near Beer • Haake Beck (Beck's) • Kaliber (Guinness) • Kingsbury • Moussy • O'Doul's (Anheuser-Busch) • Paulaner ThomasBräu • Sharps (Miller) • Texas Light (regular, dark).

WHOLESOME FLAVORS *from hearty flours give this assortment of cookies special personalities. Masa flour gives masa toffee bars the unmistakable imprint of corn tortillas, but with orange peel, chocolate, and pine nuts, the bars also make a Southwestern statement. Dark rye flour, favored by Finnish cooks, makes thin, crisp cutout wafers—good plain or as cooky sandwiches. Oatmeal gives jellied thumbprints a new dimension. Plain wheat germ develops toasted taste and aroma as it bakes in chewy-crisp shortbread. Whole-wheat flour lends a different toasted flavor to crisp rounds. The adventurous cook will find blue cornmeal cookies an amusing experiment in food chemistry—lemon juice turns the dough an earthy pink.*

To store cookies, *package each kind separately in rigid, airtight containers. If cookies have frostings or toppings or are inclined to stick together, separate layers with waxed paper. If held longer than 1 day at room temperature, cookies begin to soften and taste stale. Freezing preserves freshness best, even if cookies are to be kept only a few days; you can serve them directly from the freezer.*

MASA TOFFEE BARS

- 1   **cup pine nuts**
- 1½   **cups** *each* **dehydrated masa flour (corn tortilla flour) and all-purpose flour**
- 2   **teaspoons ground cinnamon**

Pine nuts embedded in chocolate top corn masa cookies with orange peel.

- 1   **cup (½ lb.) butter or margarine, cut into chunks**
- 1½   **cups firmly packed dark brown sugar**
- 2   **large eggs**
- 2   **tablespoons grated orange peel**
- 1   **large package (12 oz., 1½ cups) semisweet chocolate baking chips, or 12 ounces semisweet baking chocolate, chopped**

In a 6- to 8-inch frying pan over medium-low heat, shake pine nuts frequently until golden, about 10 minutes. Pour from pan and set aside.

Stir together masa, all-purpose flour, and cinnamon.

In a food processor or with a mixer, whirl or beat butter, sugar, eggs, and orange peel until creamy. Whirl or stir in masa mixture until dough holds together. Pat dough evenly into a 10- by 15-inch rimmed pan.

Bake in a 300° oven until golden brown, about 1 hour. Remove from oven and immediately scatter chocolate over hot cooky; when chips soften, spread evenly with a spatula, then sprinkle pine nuts onto chocolate. With a clean, wide spatula, lightly press nuts into chocolate.

Let cool until chocolate is just firm to touch. With a sharp knife, cut cookies into bars about 1½ by 2 inches. Remove from pan with a spatula. Serve or store (see at left). Makes about 4 dozen.

PER BAR: 144 calories, 2 g protein, 17 g carbohydrates, 8 g fat (2.7 g saturated), 19 mg cholesterol, 44 mg sodium

SNOW-FROSTED RYE CUTOUTS, SINGLES OR SANDWICHES

- ½   **cup (¼ lb.) butter or margarine, at room temperature**
- ¾   **cup granulated sugar**
- 1   **large egg**
- 2   **cups rye flour**
  Snow frosting (recipe follows)
  About ½ cup fruit jam (optional)

In a food processor or with a mixer, whirl or beat butter, sugar, and egg until well mixed. Add rye flour; whirl or stir to mix, then beat until dough holds together. Gather dough into a ball, wrap airtight, and chill until firmer, at least 1 hour or up until next day.

Cut dough into 4 equal portions. On a lightly floured board (use rye or all-

Jam dot is optional finish for frosted rye cutout cookies.

purpose flour), roll 1 portion to about ¹⁄₁₆ inch thick. With a flour-dusted cooky cutter 2 to 2½ inches wide, cut out cookies and place slightly apart on 2 lightly greased 12- by 15-inch baking sheets. Bake in a 300° oven until slightly darker, 12 to 15 minutes. With a spatula, transfer to racks to cool.

Spread a thin layer of frosting on all or half the cookies. Let stand until frosting is dry to touch, about 1 hour. Serve or store (see at left). Up to 4 hours before serving, make sandwich cookies by spooning about ½ teaspoon jam on each unfrosted cooky, then setting a frosted cooky on top. Dot tops with jam. Makes about 6 dozen single cookies, 3 dozen filled.

PER FROSTED COOKY: 43 calories, 0.4 g protein, 7.6 g carbohydrates, 1.4 g fat (0.8 g saturated), 6.4 mg cholesterol, 14 mg sodium

PER SANDWICH COOKY: 92 calories, 0.7 g protein, 17 g carbohydrates, 2.8 g fat (1.6 g saturated), 13 mg cholesterol, 28 mg sodium

Snow frosting. To frost all the rye cutouts, stir together 2 cups **powdered sugar** and 3 to 4 tablespoons **milk** until smooth; to frost half the cookies, use 1 cup powdered sugar and 1½ to 2 tablespoons milk.

OATMEAL THUMBPRINTS

- 1   **cup (½ lb.) butter or margarine, at room temperature**
- ½   **cup firmly packed brown sugar**
- 1   **large egg, separated**
- 1½   **teaspoons vanilla**
- 1   **cup all-purpose flour**
- 2   **cups regular rolled oats**
  About 1½ cups finely chopped walnuts or almonds
  About ½ cup fruit jam

In a food processor or with a mixer, whirl or beat butter, sugar, egg yolk, and vanilla until smoothly blended. Whirl or stir in flour until mixed, then stir in oats.

Shape dough into 2-teaspoon-size balls. Beat egg white and 2 teaspoons water with a fork. Dip balls into egg white, drain briefly, then roll them in nuts. Set balls about 1 inch apart on an ungreased 12- by 15-inch baking sheet. With your thumb, press a well in the center of each ball.

Bake cookies in a 300° oven for 15 minutes. Remove from oven and re-shape each thumbprint by pressing the hollow down with rounded end of a wooden spoon. Quickly spoon about ½ teaspoon jam into each hollow (jam should not flow over rim). Return to oven and bake until cookies are golden brown and jam has melted, about 15 minutes longer.

With a spatula, transfer cookies to racks to cool. Serve or store (see facing page). Makes about 4 dozen.

PER COOKY: 92 calories, 1.3 g protein, 9.3 g carbohydrates, 5.7 g fat (2.6 g saturated), 15 mg cholesterol, 42 mg sodium

WHEAT GERM SHORTBREAD

¼ **cup pecans**
½ **cup** *each* **plain wheat germ and all-purpose flour**
½ **cup firmly packed brown sugar**

Round whole-wheat crisps get impressed by distinctive design of a potato masher.

½ **teaspoon ground cinnamon**
⅓ **cup butter or margarine, cut into chunks**
1 **teaspoon vanilla**
1 **to 2 tablespoons powdered sugar (optional)**

In a food processor, whirl pecans to a fine powder (or mince). Mix in wheat germ, flour, brown sugar, and cinnamon. Add butter and vanilla; whirl or rub mixture with fingers until dough holds together.

Scrape dough into a 9-inch cake pan with removable rim; pat the dough flat with lightly floured hands.

Bake in a 325° oven until cooky is darker brown and smells toasted, 25 to 30 minutes. For a decorative rim, firmly press tines of a floured fork around edge of warm cooky, then cut cooky into 10 to 12 wedges. Let cool, remove pan rim, and rub powdered sugar through a fine strainer onto cookies. Serve or store (see facing page). Makes 10 to 12.

PER WEDGE: 123 calories, 2.1 g protein, 16 g carbohydrates, 6.1 g fat (2.7 g saturated), 11 mg cholesterol, 44 mg sodium

WHOLE-WHEAT CRISPS

1 **cup whole-wheat flour**
½ **cup cornstarch**
About ½ **cup powdered sugar**
¾ **cup (⅜ lb.) butter or margarine, cut into chunks**
1 **teaspoon vanilla**

In a food processor or bowl, mix flour, cornstarch, and ½ cup powdered sugar. Add butter and vanilla; whirl or rub until dough holds together compactly.

Shape dough into 1-tablespoon-size balls. Place 2 inches apart on 2 ungreased 12- by 15-inch baking sheets. Dip a potato masher, slotted spoon, or fork in powdered sugar, then press each ball to flatten to about 1¾ inches in diameter.

Bake in a 325° oven until richly browned, 25 to 35 minutes. If using 1 oven, switch pan positions halfway through baking. Transfer cookies to racks with a spatula and let cool. Dust lightly with more powdered sugar, if desired. Serve or store (see facing page). Makes about 2 dozen.

PER COOKY: 89 calories, 0.7 g protein, 8.6 g carbohydrates, 5.9 g fat (3.3 g saturated), 16 mg cholesterol, 60 mg sodium

Pink cookies start with blue cornmeal; lemon juice contributes to color change.

SKY BLUE TO PINK COOKIES

Blue cornmeal (found in fancy food stores), like red cabbage, turns pink or brighter red when acid is added. In these earthy-flavor blue corn cookies, lemon juice contributes not only a pleasant tartness, but also a curious pink color.

1½ **cups blue cornmeal**
1 **cup all-purpose flour**
½ **cup sugar**
½ **cup (¼ lb.) butter or margarine**
1 **large egg white**
1 **tablespoon grated lemon peel**
⅓ **cup lemon juice**
Lemon icing (recipe follows)

In a food processor or large bowl, whirl or stir together blue cornmeal, flour, and sugar. Add butter and whirl or rub with fingers until mixture forms fine crumbs. Add egg white, lemon peel, and lemon juice; whirl or stir until well mixed.

Shape dough firmly into 4 ropes about ¾ inch in diameter and as long as a 12- by 15-inch baking sheet. Lay ropes about 2 inches apart on pan. With your thumbs, press ridges diagonally down the length of each rope (be careful not to press all the way to the pan).

Bake in a 300° oven until ropes are lightly browned at edges, 25 to 30 minutes. While ropes are hot, cut them at a 45° angle into 1-inch lengths across thumbprint ridges. Cool, then drizzle with lemon icing. Serve or store (see facing page). Makes about 4 dozen.

PER COOKY: 66 calories, 0.7 g protein, 11 g carbohydrates, 2.4 g fat (1.4 g saturated), 5.9 mg cholesterol, 24 mg sodium

Lemon icing. Stir together until smooth 1 cup **powdered sugar** and 1 tablespoon *each* **lemon juice** and **water.**

SIT DOWN TO A *cool, crisp shrimp and celery root salad with beef and roasted vegetables ready to serve. Well ahead, you can prepare the salad, the vegetables, the barley and brown rice pilaf, and the zingy grapefruit dessert.*

ELEGANTLY TRIM CHRISTMAS DINNER

Shrimp & Celery Root Salad
Black Bean Beef Fillet
Roasted Fennel, Tomatoes & Mushrooms
Sugar Snap Peas
Barley & Brown Rice Pilaf (page 274)
Winter Grapefruit Tart
Dry Sauvignon Blanc
Cabernet Sauvignon

SHRIMP & CELERY ROOT SALAD

- 1 to 1¼ **pounds celery root**
- ¼ **cup white wine vinegar**
- ½ **pound shelled cooked tiny shrimp**
- 3 to 4 **cups watercress sprigs, rinsed and crisped**
  Dressing (recipe follows)

Scrub and peel celery root and finely shred it into a bowl of water. Bring vinegar and about 2 quarts water to a boil. Drain celery root and add to boiling water; cook about 1 minute (to stop darkening caused by air). Drain; rinse with cold water and drain well. If made ahead, wrap airtight and chill up until next day. Arrange celery root, shrimp, and watercress equally on 6 salad plates. Moisten evenly with dressing. Makes 6 servings.

PER SERVING: 90 calories, 10 g protein, 11 g carbohydrates, 1.2 g fat (0.2 g saturated), 74 mg cholesterol, 168 mg sodium

Dressing. Mix ¼ cup **rice vinegar** with 2 tablespoons **fish sauce** (*nuoc mam* or *nam pla*) or soy sauce, 2 teaspoons **sugar,** and ¼ teaspoon **crushed dried hot red chilies.**

BLACK BEAN BEEF FILLET

- About 1¾ **pounds narrow end section beef tenderloin, fat trimmed**
- 2 **tablespoons salted, fermented black beans, sorted of debris and rinsed**
- 1 **clove garlic**
- 1 **tablespoon Oriental sesame oil**
- 1 **teaspoon minced fresh ginger**

Fold narrow end of beef under to make meat evenly thick. Tie snugly every 1½ inches with cotton string.

Mash beans with garlic until smooth (use food processor or mortar and pestle); mix with oil and ginger. Smear over beef; if made ahead, cover and chill up until next day.

Place meat on a rack in a 9- by 13-inch pan. Roast at 450° until a thermometer in center registers 125° for rare, 20 to 30 minutes. Let stand at least 10 minutes, then slice, discarding string. Makes 6 servings.

PER SERVING: 189 calories, 21 g protein, 0.5 g carbohydrates, 11 g fat (3.5 g saturated), 61 mg cholesterol, 190 mg sodium

ROASTED FENNEL, TOMATOES & MUSHROOMS

- 4 **heads (about 2 lb. total untrimmed) fennel**
- 6 **medium-size (about 1 lb. total) Roma-type tomatoes**
- 12 **large (2½- to 3-in.-wide caps, about 1 lb.) mushrooms**
  About 2 teaspoons olive oil
- ¼ **cup regular-strength chicken broth**
  Salt and pepper

Rinse and drain fennel, tomatoes, and mushrooms. Trim discolored bases, bruises, and stems from fennel. Cut fennel heads in half vertically. Cut tomatoes in half lengthwise.

Lightly oil a 10- by 15-inch rimmed pan. Lay fennel cut side down and tomatoes cut side up in pan. Rub fennel tops lightly with oil. Bake in a 450° oven for 10 minutes.

Meanwhile, trim stems of mushrooms flush with caps. Rub tops of mushrooms very lightly with oil. After fennel has cooked 10 minutes, set mushrooms, stems down, close together in pan with fennel. (If pieces won't sit flat, put extras in another pan, 8 to 9 in. square.)

Bake until fennel turns dark brown on bottom sides and mushrooms are browned, about 25 minutes longer. Turn both over with a spatula. Continue cooking until fennel is tender when pierced, tomatoes are tinged with brown, and mushrooms are browned, about 10 minutes longer.

Remove cooked vegetables from the oven and add broth to the hot pan, tilting to moisten brown drippings. Serve vegetables hot, warm, or at room temperature. If made ahead, let stand up to 4 hours and reheat in a 450° oven for 5 to 8 minutes; add 3 tablespoons water to the hot pan after removing it from oven. Transfer vegetables with a spatula to a platter; use the spatula to scrape browned drippings into pan liquid, then drizzle liquid over vegetables. Serve with salt and pepper to add to taste. Makes 6 servings.

PER SERVING: 65 calories, 3.6 g protein, 9.7 g carbohydrates, 2.1 g fat (0.3 g saturated), 0 mg cholesterol, 120 mg sodium

WINTER GRAPEFRUIT TART

- 1 **cup all-purpose flour**
- ½ **cup powdered sugar**
- 6 **tablespoons butter or margarine, in chunks**
  Fruit topping (recipe follows)

In a food processor or with your fingers, whirl or rub together flour, sugar, and butter until the mixture holds together. Pat compactly in a 9-inch cake pan with removable rim. Bake in a 300° oven until tart turns a rich golden brown, about 30 to 40 minutes.

While the pastry is warm, pour syrup from topping over it. If made ahead, cover and chill up until the next day. Arrange grapefruit segments from the topping neatly on pastry and then scatter peel from topping over the fruit. Remove pan rim and put the tart on a platter; it can stand up to 3 hours. Cut into wedges. Makes 6 servings.

PER SERVING: 320 calories, 3 g protein, 48 g carbohydrates, 12 g fat (7.2 g saturated), 31 mg cholesterol, 119 mg sodium

Fruit topping. With a vegetable peeler, cut yellow part only from 1 large (1 lb.) **grapefruit.** Ream juice from fruit; set aside. Cut peel into very thin slivers. In a 1½- to 2-quart pan, cover peel with **water;** bring to a boil. Drain off water; repeat step.

Add to peel 2 tablespoons **honey,** 2 tablespoons **sugar,** and ¼ cup **water.** Boil uncovered, on high heat, watching closely, until liquid is almost gone and syrup forms big, shiny bubbles, about 10 minutes. At once, add reserved juice; set aside.

Using a sharp knife, cut peel and white membrane from 2 more large (2 lb. total) **grapefruit** and discard. Into a strainer set over a bowl, cut segments

Salute the dinner! Abundant in tastes, miserly in fat, this Christmas dinner offers a great new way to celebrate. Shrimp and celery root salad with watercress precedes elegant entrée: black bean beef fillet served with roasted vegetables and savory pilaf.

free from internal membrane. Squeeze juice from membrane into bowl; discard membrane.

Combine juice and ¼ cup **orange-** **flavor liqueur** with peel mixture in pan. Boil uncovered, over high heat, stirring until reduced to ½ cup, 12 to 15 minutes. Pour syrup through a strainer; use syrup warm, or reheat if made ahead. Spread peel out on a plate. Cover and chill fruit and peel separately up until next day.

THE STAR OF MOST *holiday dinners is the roast, whether it be a big whole turkey for a crowd or a small boneless lamb loin for 6. Here we give you charts and guidelines for basic roasting. Cook roasts plain or—when very lean or trimmed of fat—brush them with a little oil or melted butter. Add flavor by brushing with a baste (to avoid burning, use sauces with sweetness only during the last quarter of cooking) or rubbing with herbs, seeds, or spices.*

ROAST TURKEY

For best results, use a meat thermometer. Because birds of the same weight often have different conformations, cooking times are only a guide (for example, unstuffed 10-lb. birds can take a little longer to cook than unstuffed 12-lb. birds). Be sure to check birds under 12 pounds at least 30 minutes before the time given at left. Check larger birds at least 1 hour ahead, then every 15 minutes.

Stuffing adds to cooking times; small birds take up to 30 minutes longer, larger ones up to 50 minutes longer. You can make stuffings ahead, but to avoid food poisoning *never* stuff a bird until ready to roast; and *never* let stuffing cool in bird—remove stuffing while bird is still hot.

Pull off fat lumps and discard. Release legs if trussed. Remove giblets, rinse bird, and pat dry. Fold wing tips under turkey back. Stuff if desired, filling breast and body cavity (see chart at left for amounts); skewer shut.

Set on a V-shaped rack in a rimmed pan at least 2 inches larger on all sides than bird. Brush with melted butter or olive oil; add salt and pepper before or after cooking.

If you start roasting the turkey breast down, the back will have better color and flavor; some find the breast moister. A hot turkey is slippery and heavy, so have help when you turn the bird over to finish roasting breast up.

Let the cooked bird rest at least 20 minutes before carving.

These cooking times produce moist breast meat, but thighs may be pinker at hip joint than you like. Cut and check when you first take the bird from the oven. If desired, cut off the legs now or when you carve at the table; put them in a pan and bake in a 450° oven for 10 to 15 minutes more, then carve and serve.

Roasting a Whole Turkey

Whole turkey with giblets	Oven temp.	Internal temp.*	Cooking time	Amount of stuffing
10 lb.	350°	160°	1¾ to 2¼ hr.	4 cups
12	350°	160°	1½ to 2¼	5 cups
14	325°	160°	2½ to 3	5 cups
16	325°	160°	2½ to 3	6 cups
18	325°	160°	2½ to 3	6 cups
20	325°	160°	2½ to 3	7 cups
22	325°	160°	3 to 3½	7 cups
24	325°	160°	3¼ to 3½	8 cups
26	325°	160°	3¼ to 3¾	8 cups
28	325°	160°	3½ to 4	9 cups
30	325°	160°	3¾ to 4½	9 cups

*Insert thermometer at breast bone in thickest part.

Other Holiday Roasts

Meat and cut	Oven temp.	Internal temp.	Cooking time	Rimmed pan size
Center cut pork loin (about 4 lb.), bone in; serves 5 or 6	325°	160°**	1½ to 1¾ hr.	12 by 15 in. (set bone-side down)
Pork loin, boned center cut, rolled and tied (3 to 4 lb. meat); serves 8 to 12	375°	155°*	50 to 65 min.	12 by 15 in.
Whole beef tenderloin (4 to 5 lb.), narrow tip folded under and tied to make evenly thick; serves 10 to 12	450°	125° rare* 135° medium* 145° well done*	20 to 25 min. About 35 min. About 45 min.	12 by 17 in.
Center cut beef standing rib (about 8 lb.); serves 10 to 16	325°	135° rare** 155° medium** 160° well done**	About 2½ hr. 2¾ hr. About 3 hr.	12 by 17 in. (set bone-side down)
Boned lamb loin, rolled and tied (about 1½ lb.); serves 5 or 6	475°	140° rare*	30 to 40 min.	9 by 13 in.

*Insert thermometer in center of thickest part.
**Insert thermometer through thickest part until it touches bone.

ROASTS

Trim roasts of fat and tie, if specified, for uniform shapes that roast evenly. To determine temperature for boneless roasts, insert a thermometer in the middle of the thickest section of meat. For bone-in roasts, insert the thermometer through the thickest part until it touches the center bone. Always check after about half the estimated cooking time, in case your oven is running hotter than the thermostat indicates.

Rinse meat; pat dry. Season as desired. Place on rack, fattiest side up.

Let roasts stand at least 20 minutes before carving so hot juices can settle.

Cooking with Fall Pistachios

WHEN THE FALL *harvest of California's pistachios is tallied, it comes in second among the world's supplies of the subtle green nuts. These Western favorites have a tender crunch and a slightly floral-peach flavor.*

It's this sensual balance that makes pistachios compatible with fruit, herbs, and cheese, in both sweet and savory combinations. Mixed with onion, chilies, and cilantro, pistachios make a refreshing sauce to go with fish; with cheese, the nuts make a flavorful spread. For a dessert in shades of green, try pistachios and green grapes with a caramel glaze.

BAKED FISH WITH PISTACHIO SALSA

- ¼ cup *each* minced green onion and lime juice
- 2 tablespoons diced canned green chilies
- 1 tablespoon minced fresh cilantro (coriander)
- ½ cup chopped roasted, salted pistachios
  Baked fish (recipe follows)
  Salt and pepper

Mix together onion, lime juice, chilies, and cilantro; if made ahead, cover and chill up to 4 hours. Stir pistachios into onion mixture. Spoon sauce onto portions of hot fish and add salt and pepper to taste. Makes 4 servings.

PER SERVING: 263 calories, 35 g protein, 5.6 g carbohydrates, 11 g fat (2 g saturated), 70 mg cholesterol, 214 mg sodium

Baked fish. Rinse and pat dry about 1½ pounds boned and skinned **firm-texture white-flesh fish** (such as Chilean sea bass, halibut, or sole); cut steaks about 1 inch thick or fold fillets to make 1 inch thick. Divide into 4 portions and lay them slightly apart in a lightly oiled 9- by 13-inch pan. Bake in a 450° oven until fish is opaque but still moist-looking in center of thickest part (cut to test), 8 to 10 minutes.

PISTACHIO-ONION CHEESE

- 1½ pounds (about 3 large) onions, chopped
  About 1¾ cups regular-strength chicken broth

- 1 package (8 oz.) neufchâtel (light cream) cheese
- 1 cup chopped roasted, salted pistachios
  Crackers or baguette slices

In a 10- to 12-inch frying pan over high heat, boil onions and ¾ cup broth, uncovered, until liquid evaporates and onions start to brown; stir often. Stir in ¼ cup broth to release browned onion bits, and boil dry again. Repeat until onions are a rich brown, 2 or 3 more times; cool.

Mix the onions with cheese and nuts. If made ahead, cover and chill up to 4 days. Spread on crackers. Makes 2 cups.

PER TABLESPOON SPREAD: 100 calories, 3.8 g protein, 5.6 g carbohydrates, 7 g fat (2.6 g saturated), 11 mg cholesterol, 97 mg sodium

PISTACHIO & GRAPE CARAMEL TART

- 2 cups seedless green grapes
  Graham cracker crust (recipe follows)
- 1 cup shelled roasted, salted pistachios
- 1 cup sugar
- ½ cup water
  About 6 tablespoons whipping cream
- 2 teaspoons grated orange peel

Spread grapes level in crust, then scatter pistachios onto fruit.

In a 1½- to 2-quart pan, stir together sugar and water. Cook over medium-low heat until syrup is clear, 15 to 18 minutes; do not stir. As syrup cooks, frequently wash off sugar crystals that form on pan sides with a wet brush. Turn heat to high and boil syrup, uncovered, until the color is golden brown (about 360° on a thermometer), 5 to 7 minutes; do not wash pan sides.

Remove from heat and smoothly stir in 6 tablespoons cream, then add peel. Caramel should have the consistency of corn syrup. If thicker, add a little more cream; if thinner, stir over low heat until it thickens. Pour warm glaze evenly over grapes and nuts. Let cool until firm enough to cut, at least 2 or up to 6 hours (glaze melts slowly). Remove pan rim. Makes 8 to 10 servings.

PER SERVING: 367 calories, 4.5 g protein, 49 g carbohydrates, 18 g fat (7.4 g saturated), 32 mg cholesterol, 239 mg sodium

Graham cracker crust. Mix 1½ cups **graham cracker crumbs** (about 24 squares), ¼ cup **sugar**, and 2 tablespoons **all-purpose flour**. Add 7 tablespoons melted **butter** or margarine; stir until well mixed. Press over bottom and sides of a 9-inch tart pan with removable rim. Bake in a 350° oven until it turns a slightly darker brown, about 15 minutes. Let cool; if made ahead, cover and chill up until next day.

Pistachios and green grapes sparkle through caramel glaze; glaze holds filling in place.

Extra-long Loaves

LONG LOAVES of flatbread dressed with special seasonings can add big-size drama to the table. While our breads are limited to 17 inches (the length of a baking sheet), loaves baked in traditional wood-burning ovens, as we observed in Italy, can exceed 10 feet.

Each of these recipes begins with a basic dough flattened on rimless baking sheets; the dough's thickness and the dressing and seasonings determine each bread's character. You can choose from a sesame-speckled loaf; crisp whole-wheat sage crackers; and thin, chewy focaccia.

Both the sesame loaf and the Roman focaccia are best eaten within 8 hours of baking. To store them longer, wrap airtight and freeze. Reheat frozen loaves, lightly covered, in a 350° oven until warm, 15 to 25 minutes. The cracker bread can be stored airtight at room temperature up to 3 days.

SESAME BOARD

- 1 package active dry yeast
- 2 cups warm water (about 110°)
- 2 tablespoons sugar
- 1 teaspoon salt
- 2 tablespoons Oriental sesame oil or salad oil
- 5$\frac{1}{3}$ to 5$\frac{3}{4}$ cups all-purpose flour
  About 1 tablespoon beaten egg
- 3 tablespoons white or black sesame seed

In a large bowl, soften yeast in water, about 5 minutes. Stir in sugar, salt, and oil. Add 3 cups flour, then beat with a heavy-duty electric mixer on high speed until dough is stretchy and glossy, about 5 minutes. Stir in 2$\frac{1}{3}$ cups more flour.

To knead with a dough hook, beat dough on medium speed until it pulls away from bowl sides and is smooth and no longer sticky, about 5 minutes; if sticky, add flour 1 tablespoon at a time. Remove dough hook; cover bowl with plastic wrap.

To knead by hand, turn dough out onto a floured board, then knead until smooth and no longer sticky, about 8 minutes; add flour, as required, to prevent sticking. Return dough to bowl; cover with plastic wrap.

Set dough in a warm place and let rise until doubled—about 1 hour—or let rise overnight in the refrigerator. Punch dough down and turn onto a floured board. Knead until smooth.

Grease a rimless 14- by 17-inch or 12- by 15-inch baking sheet. On a lightly floured board, shape dough into a 14-inch-long log. Then roll dough into a $\frac{1}{2}$-inch-thick strip about the length of baking sheet. Lay dough on sheet, then roll to a $\frac{1}{3}$-inch thickness. With a pizza cutter or knife, make cuts down length of dough about $\frac{1}{2}$ inch apart and to within $\frac{1}{2}$ inch of ends and sides.

Cover lightly with plastic wrap and let rise in a warm place until puffy, 20 to 30 minutes. Brush with egg and sprinkle evenly with sesame seed. Bake in a 400° oven until richly browned, about 30 minutes. Cool on rack. Serve warm or cool. Makes 1 loaf, about 2 pounds.

PER OUNCE: 92 calories, 2.4 g protein, 17 g carbohydrates, 1.5 g fat (0.2 g saturated), 2 mg cholesterol, 69 mg sodium

SAGE CRACKER BREADS

Make dough for **sesame board** (preceding) except use **olive oil** instead of Oriental sesame oil, and 2$\frac{1}{3}$ cups **whole-wheat flour** for the second addition of all-purpose flour. Also add 2 tablespoons minced **fresh sage leaves** or 1 tablespoon dry sage leaves to the dough.

For a dramatic appetizer, break pieces of crisp pan-size cracker bread to eat with cheese. Fresh sage leaves embedded in bread season and decorate it.

Grease 3 rimless baking sheets, each 14 by 17 inches. Dust each of the baking sheets with **wheat germ.**

Shape dough into 3 equal logs about 14 inches long. Roll each to ¹/₂ inch thick and lay down the length of 1 pan. Sprinkle lightly with **coarse salt.** Lay 12 to 16 damp **fresh sage leaves** randomly over each dough strip, or sprinkle evenly with 1 teaspoon dry sage leaves. With a lightly floured rolling pin, roll the strips ¹/₈ inch thick. (Don't let rise, cut, or brush with egg, and omit the sesame seed.) If you can't bake all the loaves at 1 time, stagger the shaping procedure, so each loaf can go into the oven as it's completed.

Bake in a 375° oven (changing pan positions after 8 minutes if using 1 oven) until browned and crisp throughout, 15 to 20 minutes. Cool on racks. Cool loaves should be crisp like a cracker; if not, return cracker bread to oven for a few minutes to dry completely. If made ahead, wrap airtight and store at room temperature up to 3 days. Makes 3 loaves, each about 9 ounces. Break into pieces to eat.

PER OUNCE: 102 calories, 3.2 g protein, 19 g carbohydrates, 1.5 g fat (0.2 g saturated), 2.4 mg cholesterol, 83 mg sodium

ROMAN THIN FOCACCIA

Make dough for **sesame board** (preceding), but substitute **olive oil** for the Oriental sesame oil. Grease 2 rimless 14- by 17-inch or 12- by 15-inch baking sheets. Dust sheets lightly with **wheat bran** or cornmeal.

Shape dough into 2 equal logs about 14 inches long. Roll each to ¹/₂ inch thick and lay down the length of 1 pan. Drizzle 1 tablespoon **extra-virgin olive oil** over each loaf. With your fingertips, press all over dough surface, flattening dough to a ¹/₄-inch thickness. Sprinkle lightly with **coarse salt** and **pepper;** let stand, uncovered, at room temperature until slightly puffy, 15 to 20 minutes. (Do not cut dough, brush with egg, or sprinkle with seed.)

Bake in a 400° oven (changing pan positions after 8 minutes if using 1 oven)

Baker at Il Fornaio in Albano Laziale, south of Rome, proudly displays focaccia baked in 12-foot-long oven. Customers enjoy the olive oil–anointed bread plain or in sandwiches.

until golden brown all over, 15 to 20 minutes. Cool on racks. Just before serving, brush each loaf with 1¹/₂ to 2 tablespoons **extra-virgin olive oil.** Cut crosswise into individual pieces. Serve warm or cool. Makes 2 loaves, each about 1 pound.

PER OUNCE: 107 calories, 2.3 g protein, 17 g carbohydrates, 3.3 g fat (0.5 g saturated), 2 mg cholesterol, 71 mg sodium

Getting You through the Workweek

As OUR LIVES BECOME *busier, it's often difficult to find time to cook a good dinner. Supermarkets recognize the time crunch that many people face and offer a wide choice of foods suited to preparing speedy and convenient meals at home.*

Here we offer five entrées, each with menu suggestions, to get you through the workweek. Recipes are designed for two or three but can be easily doubled for a larger group. Most require only one pan for cooking, minimizing cleanup.

Monday. Salsa Fish Chowder. Meal in a bowl features fish and corn in salsa broth. Serve with vegetables to dip in guacamole.

Tuesday: Fettuccine Cambozola. Pasta with peas has a sauce of blue-veined cheese. Serve it with breadsticks, fresh and marinated vegetables.

In many supermarket produce sections and salad bars, you'll find vegetables and fruit already washed, trimmed, cut, and ready to eat raw or cooked. When you buy this produce, check carefully for freshness. Once cut, most vegetables and fruit deteriorate rapidly; it's best to buy only what you plan to use within a day or two.

Frozen vegetables are another fresh-tasting alternative. They're ready to use (without last-minute shopping) at a moment's notice.

At the meat and poultry counters, many selections are trimmed, boned, and thinly sliced for quick sautés and stir-fry dishes. Some meat, poultry, and fish also come marinated. Throughout the store, quality sauces, dressings, oils, vinegars, cheeses, spices, and herbs add instant flavor to many dishes.

Keep in mind convenience costs. If you're willing to spend time to clean and cut vegetables and slice meat, you'll find these dishes are still easy to prepare but at a lower price than if you used presliced ingredients.

SALSA FISH CHOWDER

Precede or accompany whole-meal chowder with crisp raw vegetables to dip in purchased guacamole. Offer toasted corn tortillas (available in the Mexican section) or tortilla chips to eat with the avocado dip, or crumble the tortillas into the broth. For dessert, fill seeded ripe papaya or small cantaloupe halves with vanilla ice cream or lime sorbet.

- 3 cups homemade or canned regular-strength chicken broth
- 1/3 cup regular or quick-cooking long- or short-grain rice
- 1 cup frozen corn kernels
- 1/2 pound boned and skinned mild white-flesh fish, such as rockfish or lingcod, cut into 1-inch chunks
- 1/2 cup refrigerated or canned tomato-based chunk-style salsa or canned Mexican-style stewed tomatoes
  Lime wedges

In a 2- to 3-quart pan over high heat, bring broth and rice to a boil. Cover and simmer until rice is tender to bite, about 15 minutes (5 minutes for quick-cooking). Add corn, fish, and salsa; cover and simmer until fish is just opaque in thickest part (cut to test), about 5 minutes. Ladle into bowls; add lime to taste. Makes 2 servings.

PER SERVING: 352 calories, 29 g protein, 48 g carbohydrates, 4.9 g fat (1.2 g saturated), 48 mg cholesterol, 512 mg sodium

FETTUCCINE CAMBOZOLA

Creamy cambozola or gorgonzola cheese forms a flavorful sauce as it melts on hot strands of pasta. Serve it with breadsticks and sliced tomatoes or crisp salad greens dressed with olives and marinated artichoke hearts. Conclude the meal with wedges of honeydew with lime.

- About 8 ounces fresh fettuccine
- 1 package (10 oz.) frozen peas
- 6 ounces (about 1 cup packed) cambozola or gorgonzola cheese, diced
  Freshly ground pepper

In a 5- to 6-quart pan, bring about 3 quarts water to boiling. Add fettuccine and cook until barely tender to bite, 3 to 4 minutes. Stir in peas. Drain.

Return pasta and peas to pan. Add cheese and 2 tablespoons hot water. With 2 forks, gently mix over low heat until cheese melts and coats pasta, 2 to 3 minutes. Lift onto 2 or 3 warm dinner plates. Add pepper to taste. Makes 2 or 3 servings.

PER SERVING: 492 calories, 27 g protein, 56 g carbohydrates, 18 g fat (11 g saturated), 131 mg cholesterol, 918 mg sodium

MU SHU SANDWICHES

For supper sandwiches, tuck a quick stir-fry of meat and vegetables into pocket bread halves. Add pickled ginger and scallions if you like. Look for the pickles as well as the hoisin or oyster sauce in the Asian section of your supermarket. If desired, serve with hot canned broth seasoned with green onions, mushrooms, and more ginger. For dessert, try canned litchis, including their syrup, over ice cream.

2 **tablespoons salad oil**

1½ **cups (about 9 oz.) thinly sliced onion**

1 **cup (about 4 oz.) thinly sliced green or red bell pepper**

½ **pound boned and skinned turkey or chicken, or beef, pork, or lamb, cut into thin, bite-size strips**

2 **tablespoons hoisin or oyster sauce**
   Whole green onions (optional)

2 or 3 **pocket bread rounds (6 to 7 in. wide), cut crosswise**
   Pickled scallions and pickled sliced ginger (optional)

Place a wok or 12-inch frying pan over high heat. When pan is hot, add 1 tablespoon oil, sliced onion, and bell pepper; stir-fry until vegetables are lightly browned, about 2 minutes. Remove from pan and add 1 more tablespoon oil to pan. When pan is hot, add meat strips and stir-fry until meat is lightly browned, 2 to 3 minutes. Add hoisin sauce and cooked vegetables; stir to mix well.

Pour into a bowl; garnish with green onions. Offer pocket bread halves (warm, if desired), scallions, and ginger alongside. Fill bread halves, as desired, to make sandwiches. Makes 2 servings.

PER SERVING: 338 calories, 22 g protein, 36 g carbohydrates, 12 g fat (1.9 g saturated), 52 mg cholesterol, 640 mg sodium

SAUSAGES WITH HOT SLAW

Brown sausages to eat with a warm slaw; serve with buttered rye toast. For a cool ending, offer grapes.

2 **Polish (kielbasa) sausages (about ½ lb. total)**

1 **tablespoon salad oil**

¼ **cup cider vinegar**

1 **tablespoon sugar**

½ **teaspoon cumin seed or caraway seed**

½ **cup (3 oz.) thinly sliced red onion**

2 **cups (¼ lb.) shredded green or red cabbage**

1 **cup (⅛ lb.) shredded carrot or more shredded cabbage**
   Coarse-grain or Dijon mustard

Slash sausages several times on each side. Pour oil into a 10- to 12-inch frying pan over medium heat. Add sausages and cook, turning often, until hot in

thickest part (cut to test), 5 to 8 minutes. Lift out of pan and keep warm on a serving plate.

Add vinegar, sugar, cumin, and onion to pan; bring to a boil. Remove from heat and stir in cabbage and carrot. Place alongside sausages. Offer mustard to add to taste. Makes 2 servings.

PER SERVING: 501 calories, 18 g protein, 19 g carbohydrates, 40 g fat (13 g saturated), 80 mg cholesterol, 1,017 mg sodium

HOT STEAK SALAD

Bite-size pieces of salad greens form the base for this main dish. Extra-virgin olive oil and vinegar or a good bottled dressing flavors broiled beef or chicken and the crisp, cool greens. Serve with a crusty baguette or roll. For a no-fuss dessert, offer whole strawberries to dip into powdered sugar.

2 **beef loin steaks (each 6 oz. and about 1 in. thick), or 2 boned and skinned chicken breast halves (each 4 oz.)**
   About ⅓ cup extra-virgin olive oil or ½ cup bottled vinaigrette-type salad dressing

5 **cups (about 5 oz.) rinsed and crisped bite-size pieces mixed salad greens (mesclun)**

6 to 10 **cherry tomatoes, stemmed**
   About 3 tablespoons balsamic or red wine vinegar (only if olive oil is used)
   Salt and pepper

Brush beef or chicken with 1 to 2 tablespoons of the oil or dressing. Place chicken or beef on a rack in a 12- by 14-inch broiler pan. Broil 3 to 4 inches from heat, turning once, until beef is browned on outside but pink in thickest part (cut to test), 8 to 10 minutes, or until chicken is white in thickest part (cut to test), 10 to 12 minutes.

Divide greens between 2 dinner plates. Set hot meat next to or on lettuce. Garnish with tomatoes. Drizzle meat and greens with olive oil and vinegar or bottled dressing and add salt and pepper to taste. Makes 2 servings.

PER SERVING WITH BEEF: 682 calories, 32 g protein, 6 g carbohydrates, 60 g fat (17 g saturated), 107 mg cholesterol, 89 mg sodium

Wednesday: Mu Shu Sandwiches. Stir-fry sliced meats with vegetables and hoisin sauce to make a hot filling for pocket bread.

Thursday: Sausages with Hot Slaw. Brown the sausages, then mix cabbage and vinegar in pan for slaw. Serve with rye toast.

Friday: Hot Steak Salad. Pair broiled steak with salad greens. Use bottled dressing or extra-virgin olive oil as meat baste and salad dressing.

Fresh Ideas with Dried Fruits

NEWS IN PRODUCE *isn't always fresh; in this case it's dried. Enlarging the spectrum of dried fruits available in Western markets are exotic tropicals.*

Here we explore ways to take advantage of the flavors and textures of some of these fruits and old standards—in particular, dried banana, mango, papaya, pineapple, star fruit, and cherries.

Except for cherries, the dried fruits are commonly found in Asian (especially Southeast Asian) markets. You may also

Dried fruits include (top row, from left) mango, papaya, and banana and (bottom row) cherries, pineapple, and star fruit.

Soak dried pineapple in a mixture of wine, brandy, and sugar to enhance both fruit and cordial.

find a surprisingly large assortment of dried fruit in health food stores and at snack stands.

With the exception of mango and banana, the dried fruits called for in the following recipes don't taste much like their fresh counterparts. Some, like the papaya, appear to be glazed and rather translucent. Some, like the pineapple, suggest a cross between dried and candied fruit (but candied fruits are much sweeter). Others, like the banana, cherries, and star fruit, are quite shriveled and leathery to look at and touch. (Crisp chips, like those made from bananas and apples, won't work in these recipes.)

To make intensely flavored, long-lasting fruit cordials, and to infuse the dried fruit with a moist succulence that brings out its fresher side, mix fruit with a fruity white wine, sugar, and a spirit, such as brandy; then let the mixture stand several days to several months.

You can sip the sweet liquid and use the plumped fruit as a topping for desserts such as ice cream, sherbets, or sorbets; but keep in mind that as you pour out the cordial mixture, fruit that surfaces and is exposed to air will deteriorate and should be used within 2 or 3 days.

Presented in decorative glass containers, cordials make handsome gifts. The small, long-lasting fruit cakes also are attractive make-ahead offerings when sealed in foil and wrapped in colored cellophane or tissue paper.

DRIED PINEAPPLE CORDIAL

- 1½ **cups fruity Chenin Blanc**
- ½ **cup brandy or vodka**
- 1 **cup sugar**
- ¼ **pound dried pineapple rings, halved**

In an attractive bottle or jar about 1-quart size, combine wine, brandy, and sugar, stirring well. Add pineapple (cut pieces if needed to fit into container). Cover airtight and let stand at room temperature at least 2 days for flavors to blend, or until fruit begins to fall apart, about 3 months. Stir occasionally until sugar dissolves.

Serve soaked fruit as dessert topping; sip cordial from small glasses, either at room temperature or over ice. Makes about 3 cups.

PER ¼ CUP FRUIT AND CORDIAL: 122 calories, 0 g protein, 21 g carbohydrates, 0 g fat, 0 mg cholesterol, 9.3 mg sodium

DRIED MANGO CORDIAL

Follow directions for **dried pineapple cordial** (preceding), but omit Chenin Blanc and pineapple. Instead, use 1½ cups fruity **Johannisberg Riesling** and ½ pound **dried sliced mango**.

PER ¼ CUP FRUIT AND CORDIAL: 114 calories, 0.2 g protein, 20 g carbohydrates, 0.1 g fat (0.1 g saturated), 0 mg cholesterol, 1.9 mg sodium

DRIED STAR FRUIT CORDIAL

Follow directions for **dried pineapple cordial** (preceding), but omit pineapple and use ½ pound **dried sliced star fruit**.

PER ¼ CUP FRUIT AND CORDIAL: 114 calories, 0.2 g protein, 20 g carbohydrates, 0.1 g fat (0 g saturated), 0 mg cholesterol, 1.9 mg sodium

DRIED BANANA CORDIAL

Follow directions for **dried pineapple cordial** (preceding), but omit Chenin Blanc and pineapple. Instead, use 1½ cups fruity **Johannisberg Riesling** and ½ pound **dried bananas** (the brown fruit, not the crisp chips). As an alternative for brandy, **dark rum** is also complementary.

PER ¼ CUP FRUIT AND CORDIAL: 119 calories, 0.3 g protein, 22 g carbohydrates, 0.1 g fat (0.1 g saturated), 0 mg cholesterol, 1.7 mg sodium

DRIED CHERRY CORDIAL

Follow directions for **dried pineapple cordial** (preceding), but omit Chenin Blanc and pineapple; instead, use 1½ cups fruity **Johannisberg Riesling** and ½ pound **dried pitted cherries.**

PER ¼ CUP FRUIT AND CORDIAL: 114 calories, 0 g protein, 20 g carbohydrates, 0 g fat, 0 mg cholesterol, 1.7 mg sodium

TROPICAL FRUIT CAKE

   ⅔ **cup firmly packed dark brown sugar**
   ½ **cup (¼ lb.) butter or margarine, at room temperature**
   3 **large eggs**
  1¼ **cups all-purpose flour**
   ½ **teaspoon baking powder**
   ½ **teaspoon ground cinnamon**
   ¼ **teaspoon ground mace**
   ⅛ **teaspoon ground cloves**
      Tropical fruit and nut mix (following)
      Dried papaya, cut into thin slivers
      About 1½ cups dark rum

In a large bowl, beat sugar and butter with a mixer until well blended, then beat in eggs, 1 at a time. Stir together flour, baking powder, cinnamon, mace, and cloves. Add to egg mixture; stir, then beat to blend well. Stir in fruit and nut mix.

Spoon batter equally into 10 greased 2½- by 4-inch (1½-in.-deep) individual

Bright orange dried papaya decoration offers a preview of the subtle tropical flavors of these miniature fruitcakes. Cakes can be made ahead for holiday gifts.

loaf pans (if you have fewer pans, let batter stand as cakes bake in sequence). Spread batter evenly and smooth top. Decorate each cake with slivers of papaya.

Bake in a 300° oven until a toothpick inserted in centers comes out clean and cakes are firm when lightly pressed in center, 45 to 60 minutes. Cool in pans on a rack for 10 minutes, then invert onto rack to cool completely.

Set the cakes in a single layer in a 9- by 13-inch baking dish or pan, or set each cake on a rectangle of foil large enough to seal the cake airtight. Spoon 2 tablespoons of rum onto each cake slowly enough to let it seep in. Then wrap the dish or the individual cakes airtight in foil.

Store at room temperature at least 8 hours or up to 2 weeks; freeze to store up to 2 months. Makes 10 cakes, each about 5 ounces.

PER OUNCE: 101 calories, 1.3 g protein, 13 g carbohydrates, 3.8 g fat (1.5 g saturated), 18 mg cholesterol, 29 mg sodium

Tropical fruit and nut mix. Combine 1 cup **muscat** (or golden) **raisins**; ½ cup *each* **golden raisins,** coarsely chopped **dried papaya,** coarsely chopped **dried mango,** and coarsely chopped **dried pineapple;** ½ cup *each* **salted macadamia nuts** and **salted pistachios.**

LIGHTENING UP SUNSET CLASSICS: Tamale Pie

ONE OF THE TRICKS to lightening up your favorite recipes, aside from simply reducing the fat, is to change the flavor as little as possible. This can be difficult, especially with recipes that need major overhauls to lower fat and calorie content.

Such was the case with our mucbil-pollo, the Yucatán tamale pie featured on page 104 of the May 1980 Sunset. With 1⅓ cups of lard in the thick masa crust, the recipe weighed in at a whopping 1,300 calories per serving!

We eliminated the lard and put the crust on top of the filling instead of around it. The result, which is 75 percent leaner, looks more like a cobbler than a tamale pie. But, by keeping the achiote condiment in the filling and the masa flour in the crust, the updated dish retains much of its authentic flavor.

Accompany the pie with a lean, refreshing salad of grapefruit segments and orange and apple slices, dressed to taste with lime juice, minced cilantro, and salt.

LIGHTENED-UP YUCATÁN TAMALE PIE

Buy the rust-hued achiote condiment in Hispanic markets, or use the substitute.

- 3 ounces achiote condiment or achiote substitute (recipe follows)
- 2 cups regular-strength chicken broth
- 2 tablespoons minced fresh or 1 teaspoon dried mint leaves
- ⅛ teaspoon anise seed
- 3 cups skinned and boned cooked chicken, cut into bite-size pieces
- 2 large (about 1¼ lb. total) onions, chopped
- 2 large (about 1 lb. total) tomatoes, cored and cut into wedges
- 2 tablespoons cornstarch mixed with ¼ cup water
- Masa topping (recipe follows)
- Cilantro (coriander) sprigs

In a 1½- to 2-quart pan, combine the achiote condiment with ½ cup broth. With a heavy spoon, work into a smooth paste. Stir in remaining broth, mint, and anise. Bring to a boil over high heat, then simmer, uncovered, for 5 minutes; stir often to prevent sticking. If made ahead, cool, cover, and chill up until next day.

Mix achiote sauce, chicken, onions, tomatoes, and cornstarch mixture. Spoon into a 2- to 3-quart deep casserole and spread into an even layer. Spoon dollops of masa topping over filling.

Bake on the bottom rack of a 400° oven until filling is bubbling in center and topping is well browned, 45 to 55 minutes. Remove from oven and let stand 5 minutes before serving. Garnish with cilantro sprigs. Makes 6 servings.

PER SERVING: 320 calories, 26 g protein, 31 g carbohydrates, 10 g fat (2.2 g saturated), 63 mg cholesterol, 214 mg sodium

PER SERVING OF ORIGINAL PIE: 1,300 calories, 39 g protein, 51 g carbohydrates, 105 g fat (38 g saturated), 295 mg cholesterol, 976 mg sodium

Achiote substitute. Mix together until well blended 3 tablespoons **paprika**, 2 tablespoons **distilled white vinegar**, 1½ teaspoons dried **oregano** leaves, 3 cloves **garlic** (minced), and ½ teaspoon ground **cumin**.

Masa topping. In a bowl, combine ½ cup **masa harina** (dehydrated masa flour), ½ cup **all-purpose flour**, and 1½ teaspoons **baking powder**. Mix in 1 large **egg white**, 1½ tablespoons **salad oil**, and ½ cup **nonfat milk** until just blended.

Masa biscuits top rich-tasting chicken filling in lean, deep-dish version of tamale pie. Serve with a refreshing fruit salad dressed with lime juice and minced cilantro.

Western Sushi

BRILLIANT PINK SUSHI *merges traditional Japanese sushi with Western ingredients. Juice from canned pickled beets dyes the sweet-tart rice mixture pink, and diced beets add texture and earthy flavor.*

Present the rice with nori and a colorful collection of East-West condiments.

PICKLED BEET SUSHI

Look for the Japanese ingredients at well-supplied supermarkets or Asian stores.

6 sheets (about 8 in. square) plain or seasoned nori
Pink sushi rice (recipe follows)
Condiments (choices follow)
Soy sauce
Prepared horseradish

If nori is pretoasted and package is just opened, use as is. If not, toast or re-crisp nori:

Over a gas burner, hold each sheet of nori with tongs and pass 1 side 1 inch above flame until nori goes limp, 5 to 10 seconds.

Over an electric burner, cook 1 sheet at a time in a 10- by 12-inch frying pan over medium heat just until nori bubbles slightly, 5 to 10 seconds.

Cut toasted nori into 4- to 5-inch squares. (If you do this step ahead, wrap nori airtight up until the next day.)

To serve, stack nori in a basket. Serve rice on a large platter. Present condiments, soy sauce, and horseradish in containers.

To assemble sushi, place a piece of nori in the palm of your hand. Spoon about 1/4 cup rice into center; add condiments to taste.

Overlap corners of nori to enclose filling. Dip in soy sauce (flavored with horseradish, if desired). Makes 8 to 10 appetizer or 4 main-dish servings.

PER APPETIZER SERVING WITHOUT CONDIMENTS: 150 calories, 3.3 g protein, 33 g carbohydrates, 0.2 g fat (0.1 g saturated), 0 mg cholesterol, 218 mg sodium

Pink sushi rice. Drain 1 small can (about 8 oz.) **sliced pickled beets;** reserve juice. To juice, add enough **water** to make 1 3/4 cups. Finely dice beets and set aside.

In 2- to 3-quart pan, cover 1 1/2 cups **short-grain (pearl) rice** with water; stir, then drain. Repeat until water is clear; drain. Add beet juice mixture to rice. Cover; bring to a boil over high heat. Reduce heat to low; cook, without stirring, until liquid is absorbed, 10 to 15 minutes.

Gently stir in 1/4 cup **seasoned rice vinegar** (or 1/4 cup distilled vinegar with 2 tablespoons sugar and salt to taste).

Spread rice in a 10- by 15-inch baking pan. Let cool to room temperature. (If made ahead, cover and store at room temperature up to 6 hours. Do not refrigerate.)

Mix rice, beets, 1/2 cup sliced **pickled scallions** or cocktail onions, and 1 cup thawed **frozen petite peas.**

Condiments: 1/2 to 3/4 pound **shelled cooked tiny shrimp** and about 1/4 cup *each* **unflavored yogurt, sliced** or slivered **pickled ginger,** and **seasoned rice vinegar** (or 1/4 cup distilled vinegar with 2 tablespoons sugar and salt to taste).

Pickled beets, scallions, and petite peas combine in pink sushi rice; accompany with nori for wrappers (top right), and yogurt, ginger, horseradish, shrimp, soy, vinegar.

The Surprise: A Sweet Spice

THE SWEETER SPICES, *such as allspice, cinnamon, cloves, and nutmeg, needn't be limited to desserts and baked goods. When used in savory dishes, as in the following recipes, they add an exotic richness and depth of flavor.*

LAMB STEW WITH WHITE BEANS, ANISE & ALLSPICE

1½ **pounds boneless lamb stew meat, excess fat trimmed**

1 **large (about 10 oz.) onion, chopped**

2½ **cups regular-strength beef broth**

1 **tablespoon minced fresh ginger or 1 teaspoon ground ginger**

1 **tablespoon grated orange peel**

2 **teaspoons anise seed**

½ **teaspoon ground allspice**

¼ **teaspoon cayenne**

3 **large (about ⅔ lb. total) carrots, peeled and cut diagonally into thin slices**

3 **cans (15 oz. each) cannellini beans, rinsed and drained**

1 **tablespoon cornstarch dissolved in ¼ cup water**

3 **tablespoons minced fresh cilantro (coriander)**

Fresh cilantro (coriander) sprigs

Place lamb in a 5- to 6-quart pan with onion and ¼ cup water. Cover and bring to a boil over high heat, then simmer 30 minutes. Uncover pan and boil over high heat until liquid evaporates, about 10 minutes. When meat sizzles, add ¼ cup water; stir to release browned bits. When the liquid evaporates, repeat procedure once.

To pan, add broth, ginger, orange peel, anise, allspice, and cayenne; stir to free browned bits from pan bottom. Bring the mixture to a boil, then cover tightly and simmer until meat is very tender when pierced, 1 to 1¼ hours. Add the carrots and simmer until carrots are tender when pierced, about 20 minutes longer.

Add beans to pan. Bring to a boil over high heat. Add cornstarch mixture; stir until stew returns to a boil. Mix in minced cilantro. Transfer stew to a serving dish. Garnish with fresh cilantro sprigs. Makes 6 servings.

PER SERVING: 502 calories, 32 g protein, 35 g carbohydrates, 25 g fat (11 g saturated), 80 mg cholesterol, 354 mg sodium

SWEET-SPICED SHREDDED PORK

1¼ **pounds boneless pork shoulder or butt, excess fat trimmed**

1 **large (about 10 oz.) onion, chopped**

2 **cloves garlic, minced or pressed**

1 **can (28 oz.) tomatoes, undrained**

1 **cup regular-strength beef broth**

1 **can (4 oz.) diced green chilies**

¼ **cup raisins**

2 **tablespoons cider vinegar**

1 **cinnamon stick (about 2½ in. long) or 1 teaspoon ground cinnamon**

½ **teaspoon ground cloves**

½ **teaspoon pepper**

8 **flour tortillas (6 to 8 in. wide)**

Salt

Cut pork into 1½-inch pieces. Place meat in a 4- to 5-quart pan with onion and garlic. Cover and cook over medium-high heat until meat and onion exude juices, 10 to 12 minutes. Uncover and stir often until liquid evaporates and meat and onion are browned, about 15 minutes.

To pan, add the tomatoes and their liquid, broth, green chilies, raisins, vinegar, cinnamon, cloves, and pepper. Stir to release browned bits from pan bottom. Cover pan and simmer until meat is very tender when pierced, 1¼ to 1½ hours. Uncover and, over high heat, boil mixture until excess liquid evaporates, about 10 minutes. Using two forks, coarsely shred meat.

If made ahead, cool, cover, and chill up to 2 days. To reheat, place mixture over medium heat, stirring occasionally, until hot throughout, about 10 minutes.

Meanwhile, wrap tortillas in foil; bake in a 350° oven until warm, 15 to 20 minutes. (Or wrap in plastic wrap and cook in a microwave oven at full power—100 percent—until warm, about 1 minute.)

Transfer meat to serving container. To eat, spoon mixture into warm tortillas. Season to taste with salt. Makes 4 servings.

PER SERVING: 637 calories, 31 g protein, 49 g carbohydrates, 37 g fat (12 g saturated), 102 mg cholesterol, 871 mg sodium

Anise and allspice lend an unusual sweet note to hearty lamb and bean stew. Ginger, orange peel, and cilantro also add their intriguing flavors.

Onward with Spaghetti Squash

CHEERFUL YELLOW *strands of the curious spaghetti squash, known for its tender-crisp texture, are the base of a low-fat salad and ginger-spiked pancakes.*

To start, either bake the squash or cook it in a microwave oven. A medium-size squash yields 5 to 7 cups of strands.

To bake. *Pierce shell of 1 medium-size (3- to 4-lb.) spaghetti squash in several places. Set squash on a sheet of foil and bake in a 350° oven for 45 minutes. Turn it over and bake until shell gives to pressure, 15 to 25 minutes longer. When cool, cut squash in half horizontally, discard seeds, and scrape out strands of squash with a fork.*

To cook in a microwave. *Cut 1 medium-size (3- to 4-lb.) spaghetti squash in half horizontally. Place cut sides up in a 9- by 13-inch microwave-safe dish with ¼ cup water. Cover with plastic wrap and cook in a microwave oven on full power (100 percent) until shell gives to pressure, 15 to 20 minutes; rotate dish after 5 minutes. Let stand 5 minutes; uncover. When cool, discard seeds and scrape out strands of squash with a fork.*

To store cooked squash. *Cover and chill up to 4 days.*

Lean, light, and tender-crisp spaghetti squash salad with bright broccoli is delicately flavored with orange peel and rice wine vinegar.

SPAGHETTI SQUASH & BROCCOLI SALAD

- ½ **cup walnuts or pecans, coarsely chopped**
- 2 **cups broccoli flowerets**
- 4 **to 5 cups cooked spaghetti squash (see preceding), at room temperature or chilled**
- 2 **tablespoons grated orange peel**
- ½ **cup seasoned rice vinegar (or ½ cup rice vinegar with 1 teaspoon sugar)**
  Butter lettuce leaves, rinsed and crisped
  Salt

In a 6- to 8-inch frying pan, stir nuts over medium-high heat until lightly toasted, about 7 minutes. Pour from pan and set aside.

In a 1½- to 2-quart pan, bring 3 cups water to boiling over high heat. Add broccoli and cook, uncovered, until just tender when pierced, about 2 minutes.

Drain and immediately immerse broccoli in ice water; when cold, drain thoroughly.

In a bowl, combine broccoli, squash, and orange peel. If made ahead, cover squash mixture and nuts; chill up until next day. Add vinegar to squash and mix well. Arrange lettuce leaves on 6 salad plates. Mound salad on lettuce and sprinkle with nuts. Season to taste with salt. Makes 5 or 6 servings.

PER SERVING: 129 calories, 3 g protein, 16 g carbohydrates, 6.5 g fat (0.6 g saturated), 0 mg cholesterol, 33 mg sodium

GINGER, GREEN ONION & SPAGHETTI SQUASH PANCAKES

- 2 **large eggs**
- 3 **cups cooked spaghetti squash (see directions preceding)**
- 2 **tablespoons grated fresh ginger**
- 1 **cup minced green onion (including tops)**
- 2 **tablespoons salad oil**
  Soy sauce

In a bowl, beat eggs to blend. Add squash, ginger, and green onion; mix gently.

Pour 1 tablespoon oil into a 10- to 12-inch nonstick frying pan on medium-high heat. When oil is hot, add squash mixture in ¼-cup mounds, spacing about 3 inches apart. With the back of a spoon, spread mounds to make cakes that are about 3 inches in diameter.

Cook until golden brown on bottoms, 2 to 3 minutes. Carefully turn with a wide spatula and cook other sides until golden brown, about 2 minutes.

Transfer cakes to a platter and keep warm. Repeat to cook remaining squash, adding oil as needed to promote browning. Add soy sauce to taste. Makes 12 pancakes, 3 main-dish or 6 vegetable servings.

PER PANCAKE: 47 calories, 1.4 g protein, 3.2 g carbohydrates, 3.2 g fat (0.6 g saturated), 35 mg cholesterol, 17 mg sodium

Puebla's Anytime, Anywhere Snack

HOT CHILIES, SWEET *spices, and tender shreds of simmered flank steak unite in tinga, a beef mixture from Puebla, Mexico. There, tinga is enjoyed as a street snack, wrapped in tortillas, and as a supper entrée.*

Look for canned chipotle chilies in Mexican markets. The chilies are hot but have a unique smoky flavor.

PUEBLA SIMMERED SPICED BEEF
(*Tinga*)

Serve tinga in warm tortillas or crusty rolls with shredded lettuce, sliced avocado, and crumbled feta cheese.

- 2 **pounds beef flank steak**
- 3 **medium-size (about 1¼ lb. total) onions, chopped**
- 12 **cloves garlic, minced or pressed**
- 4 **large dried bay leaves**
- 1 **cinnamon stick (3 in.)**
- 10 **whole cloves**
- 1 **teaspoon *each* dried marjoram leaves and dried thyme leaves**
- 2½ **pounds medium-size firm-ripe tomatoes**
- ½ **pound firm-texture chorizo sausage, casings removed**
- 2 **to 4 tablespoons minced canned chipotle chilies in adobado sauce**
- ⅓ **cup cider vinegar**
- 2 **tablespoons firmly packed brown sugar**

Trim and discard excess fat from meat. Cut meat into 2-inch chunks. In a 5- to 6-quart pan, combine meat, 1 onion, garlic, bay leaves, cinnamon, cloves, marjoram, thyme, and 6 cups water. Bring to a boil over high heat; cover, reduce heat, and simmer until meat is tender when pierced, about 2 hours.

Meanwhile, lay tomatoes in a 10- by 15-inch pan. Bake in a 450° oven until skins split and are tinged brown, about 20 minutes. Cool tomatoes; remove and discard skins and cores. Coarsely chop remaining tomato.

Break sausage into small pieces and add to a 10- to 12-inch frying pan over medium-high heat. Cook, stirring, until lightly browned, about 15 minutes; discard excess fat.

Add tomato, remaining onions, 2 tablespoons chipotle chilies (or more to taste), vinegar, and sugar. Simmer, uncovered, stirring often, until sauce is reduced by about ¼, about 30 minutes.

When beef is done, transfer with a slotted spoon to a bowl. Pour cooking liquid into a strainer over a bowl; press to remove liquid, then discard residue. Return liquid to pan and boil over high heat until reduced to 1½ cups; add to chorizo mixture.

Tear beef into shreds; add to chorizo mixture. (If made ahead, cover and chill up to 3 days.) Stir often over medium heat until hot. Makes about 4 cups, 8 servings.

PER ½-CUP SERVING: 314 calories, 29 g protein, 19 g carbohydrates, 14 g fat (5.3 g saturated), 73 mg cholesterol, 240 mg sodium

Spoon tender shreds of flank steak laced with roasted tomatoes, chorizo sausage, and smoky chipotle chilies onto shredded lettuce in a soft, warm corn tortilla; top with avocado slices and a squeeze of lime.

Chocolate Takes the Cake

CHOCOLATE, CHOCOLATE, *and more chocolate give a spectacularly rich flavor to this sweet, dark, moist special-occasion cake.*

Cocoa and ground semisweet chocolate baking chips contribute a fudge flavor. Whole chocolate chips add dots of creaminess to the fine-textured interior.

Serve this cake warm or cool, plain or topped with vanilla ice cream. Offer hot coffee or tea.

CHOCOLATE CHIP CAKE

1 large package (12 oz.) or 2 cups semisweet chocolate baking chips
1 cup (½ lb.) butter or margarine, cut into chunks
2½ cups firmly packed brown sugar
4 large eggs
1 cup milk
1 cup sour cream
1 teaspoon vanilla
2 cups sifted cake flour
   About ¾ cup unsweetened cocoa
1 teaspoon *each* baking soda and baking powder
1 tablespoon powdered sugar

In a blender or food processor, whirl 1 cup chocolate chips until finely ground; remove from blender and set aside.

In a large bowl, beat butter and brown sugar with an electric mixer until creamy and blended. Beat in eggs until fluffy. Stir in milk, sour cream, vanilla, and ground chocolate until blended.

In a small bowl, mix flour, ¾ cup cocoa, baking soda, and baking powder; add to butter mixture and blend thoroughly. Stir in remaining whole chocolate chips.

Pour batter into a well-greased and floured 12- to 14-cup fluted tube pan (batter fills pan almost to rim). Bake in a 350° oven until a toothpick inserted in center comes out clean and cake begins to pull away from pan sides, about 1 hour. Cool in pan on a rack for 30 minutes. Invert cake onto a rack to cool, or onto a plate to serve warm.

If made ahead, wrap airtight when cool and store at room temperature up until next day (or freeze up to 2 months; thaw wrapped).

Sift about 1 tablespoon cocoa, then the powdered sugar, onto cake; cut into wedges. Makes 16 servings.

PER SERVING: 460 calories, 5.8 g protein, 61 g carbohydrates, 23 g fat (10 g saturated), 93 mg cholesterol, 237 mg sodium

Candle forest tops cake that's a chocolate lover's wish come true. Serve it warm or cool, plain or topped with vanilla ice cream.

INDONESIAN BROWN RICE SALAD

Mix brown rice with vegetables, raisins, and lime dressing for salad.

- 2 cups long-grain brown rice
- 1 medium-size (about 6 oz.) red or green bell pepper
- 1/3 pound Chinese pea pods, strings removed
- 5 green onions, ends trimmed
- 1 can (about 8 oz.) water chestnuts, drained and chopped
- 1/4 cup chopped fresh cilantro (coriander)
- 1/4 cup raisins (optional)
  Lime dressing (recipe follows)

In a 2½- to 3-quart pan, combine rice and 4½ cups water. Bring to a boil; cover and cook on low heat until rice is tender to bite, about 45 minutes. Cool.

Stem, seed, and chop the bell pepper. Thinly slice the peas and onions. In a large bowl, combine bell pepper, peas, onions, water chestnuts, cilantro, raisins, rice, and dressing. Mix to blend. Spoon salad into a shallow bowl. Makes 8 servings.—*Carla Van Dyke, Ketchum, Idaho.*

Lime dressing. Mix 2/3 cup **rice** or cider **vinegar**, 2 tablespoons reduced-sodium **soy sauce**, 2 tablespoons **lime juice**, 1 tablespoon minced **fresh ginger**, 2 teaspoons minced **garlic**, and 1 teaspoon **Oriental sesame oil** or salad oil.

PER SERVING: 213 calories, 5 g protein, 44 g carbohydrates, 2 g fat (0.4 g saturated), 0 mg cholesterol, 158 mg sodium

---

HOT ARTICHOKE DIP

Scoop up hot artichoke-cheese dip with baguette slices or artichoke leaves.

- 1 cup grated parmesan cheese
- 1 large package (8 oz.) neufchâtel (light cream) cheese, at room temperature
- 1 cup light sour cream or reduced-calorie mayonnaise
- 1/8 teaspoon dry dill weed
- 1 large can (13¾ oz.) artichoke hearts, drained and chopped
  Whole cooked artichokes (optional)
  Toasted baguette slices

Set aside 1 tablespoon parmesan cheese. In a bowl with a mixer, beat the remaining parmesan, neufchâtel cheese, sour cream, and dill weed until well blended and creamy. Stir in chopped artichoke hearts until blended. Spoon mixture into an attractive shallow 3- to 4-cup baking dish. Sprinkle with the reserved 1 tablespoon parmesan cheese. (If made ahead, cover and chill up until the next day.)

Bake, uncovered, in a 325° oven until lightly browned and hot in center, 30 to 45 minutes. Scoop up mixture with artichoke leaves and bread slices. Makes 3 cups, 16 to 18 appetizer servings.—*Doris Keyes, San Juan Capistrano, Calif.*

PER SERVING: 81 calories, 4.4 g protein, 2.6 g carbohydrates, 6.1 g fat (3.6 g saturated), 18 mg cholesterol, 140 mg sodium

---

TURKEY & LIMA STEW

Serve turkey and lima stew with egg noodles and jellied cranberry relish.

- 1 large (½ lb.) onion, chopped
- 2 cups (6 oz.) sliced mushrooms
- 1 cup thinly sliced carrots
- 1 teaspoon dry thyme leaves
  About 3 cups regular-strength chicken broth
- 2 tablespoons lemon juice
- 2 pounds skinned and boned turkey or chicken thigh, fat trimmed, cut into 1-inch pieces
- 1 tablespoon cornstarch
- 1 package (10 oz.) frozen baby lima beans

In a 5- to 6-quart pan, combine onion, mushrooms, carrots, thyme, and 1 cup broth. Boil, uncovered, on high heat until liquid evaporates and brown bits form in pan, 10 to 15 minutes; stir often.

To deglaze pan, add 1/4 cup broth and stir to release bits. Boil, uncovered, until browned bits form; stir often. Deglaze 2 or 3 more times or until mixture is a rich brown. Deglaze with lemon juice.

When pan is dry, stir in turkey and 1/2 cup broth. Cover; simmer over low heat until turkey is tender, 40 to 50 minutes (25 to 30 minutes for chicken). Skim fat. Mix 3/4 cup broth and cornstarch; add with limas to pan and stir over medium-high heat until sauce boils. Makes 6 servings.—*Lita J. Verts, Corvallis, Ore.*

PER SERVING: 298 calories, 36 g protein, 20 g carbohydrates, 7.4 g fat (2.3 g saturated), 114 mg cholesterol, 182 mg sodium

DRIED BEEF CLAM CHOWDER

- 4 cans (6½ oz. each) chopped clams
- 2 tablespoons butter or margarine
- 2 tablespoons all-purpose flour
- 1 pound (about 2 large) thin-skinned red potatoes, diced
- 1 jar (2½ oz.) dried beef, chopped
- 3 cups milk or half-and-half (light cream)
- 1 package (10 oz.) frozen corn kernels
- ½ cup thinly sliced green onion
  About 1 teaspoon pepper

Drain liquid from clams and measure it. Add water to make 3 cups.

In a 5- to 6-quart pan on low heat, melt butter. Add flour and stir until blended. Stir in clam juice mixture. Add potatoes; bring to a boil on high heat.

Cover and simmer gently until potatoes are tender when pierced, 20 to 25 minutes. Meanwhile, rinse and drain beef. Add beef, milk, corn, onion, clams, and 1 teaspoon pepper to pan.

Heat, uncovered, stirring occasionally just until soup is hot. Ladle into a tureen or bowls. Add more pepper to taste. Makes 6 or 7 servings.—*Lois Dowling, Tacoma, Wash.*

PER SERVING: 290 calories, 23 g protein, 30 g carbohydrates, 8.7 g fat (4.5 g saturated), 60 mg cholesterol, 504 mg sodium

Flecks of dried beef and corn enrich flavor and texture of clam chowder.

GARLIC BEEF

- 3½ pounds beef chuck, fat trimmed, cut into 1½-inch chunks
- 1 tablespoon soy sauce
- 1⅓ cups regular-strength beef broth
- 30 cloves (about 6 oz.) garlic
- 1⅓ cups dry red wine (or more broth)
  Chopped parsley
  Salt

In a 5- to 6-quart pan, combine beef and soy sauce. Cover tightly and bring to a boil over medium heat; let meat simmer in its own accumulated juices for 30 minutes.

After beef has cooked 30 minutes, uncover; boil over high heat until juices have evaporated, 10 to 15 minutes. When meat starts to sizzle, stir often until richly browned. Add broth and stir well, then add garlic and wine. Cover and simmer until meat is very tender when pierced, about 1½ hours; garlic may disintegrate and thicken sauce slightly.

Skim off and discard fat. Transfer to serving dish. Garnish with parsley. Add salt to taste. Makes 6 servings.—*Peg Roberts, Santa Barbara, Calif.*

PER SERVING: 312 calories, 45 g protein, 11 g carbohydrates, 9 g fat (3.2 g saturated), 121 mg cholesterol, 315 mg sodium

Crush 30 cloves garlic with side of cleaver; peel and simmer with beef.

APRICOT BRANDY POUNDCAKE

- 1 cup (½ lb.) butter or margarine, at room temperature
- 2½ cups sugar
- 6 large eggs
- 1 cup light or regular sour cream
- ½ cup apricot brandy, orange-flavor liqueur, or sour cream
- 1 teaspoon vanilla
- ½ teaspoon lemon extract
- ¼ teaspoon almond extract
- 3 cups all-purpose flour
- ½ teaspoon baking soda

In a large mixer bowl, beat butter until creamy. Gradually add sugar, beating until mixture is light and fluffy. Add eggs, 1 at a time, beating well after each addition. Add sour cream, brandy, vanilla, lemon extract, and almond extract; mix until well blended. Mix flour and baking soda; gradually add to butter mixture, mixing until well blended. Scrape batter into a well-buttered and floured 10-inch (12-cup) tube pan.

Bake in a 325° oven until a toothpick inserted in thickest part comes out clean, 1¼ to 1½ hours. Set pan on a rack for about 10 minutes. Just at top of pan, run a knife between cake and rim. Invert onto rack; cool. Makes 16 to 18 servings.—*Carmela Meely, Walnut Creek, Calif.*

PER SERVING: 340 calories, 5.2 g protein, 47 g carbohydrates, 14 g fat (7.8 g saturated), 103 mg cholesterol, 149 mg sodium

Thinly slice poundcake flavored with apricot brandy for fall dessert.

THE TRUE MEANING *of haute cuisine,* *Julia Child tells us, is "Never let anything alone." Gerald Gardner might not have been aware of Child's dictum when he confronted his hash browns one morning, but his instincts were right. Adding apples to the potatoes was a bold stroke, and common sense prompted him to throw in the cheddar cheese. Adding the chili powder, however, was beyond common sense; let's just call it poetry.*

Indulge in these potatoes at your next breakfast, and you'll be fueled up till dinner.

CHEESE & APPLE HASH BROWNS

- ¼ **cup (⅛ lb.) butter or margarine**
- 4 **medium-size (2 to 2¼ lb. total) russet potatoes, peeled and cut into ¼-inch cubes**
- 1 **medium-size (about 6 oz.) onion, chopped**
- 1 **medium-size (about 5 oz.) red bell pepper, stemmed, seeded, and diced**
- 2 **medium-size (about ¾ lb. total) Golden Delicious apples, cored, peeled, and chopped**

- 1 **teaspoon chili powder**
- ¼ **cup chopped parsley**
- 1 **cup (4 oz.) shredded sharp cheddar cheese**
  Salt and pepper

Melt butter in a 10- to 12-inch nonstick frying pan over medium-high heat; add potatoes, onion, and bell pepper. Turn frequently with a wide spatula until potatoes are browned and tender when pierced, about 25 minutes. Stir in apples, chili, and parsley; cook until apples are tender when pierced, about 5 minutes longer.

Sprinkle cheese over potato mixture; stir until melted, then spoon onto plates. Season to taste with salt and pepper. Makes 6 or 7 servings.

PER SERVING: 257 calories, 6.9 g protein, 30 g carbohydrates, 13 g fat (7.7 g saturated), 35 mg cholesterol, 184 mg sodium

Gerald M. Gardner

Bellevue, Wash.

SHORT OF COMPLETE *collapse, the worst thing that can happen to a cake is that it be dry. A moist texture is absolutely guaranteed in Martine Saunier's Orange Cake. Drawing on her background in French wine and food, she ensures moistness by anointing the cake* *with a syrup of sugar, orange juice, and orange liqueur. And if there were any doubt that it is an orange cake, orange peel in the batter and a topping of orange sections should allay it.*

ORANGE CAKE

- 2 **large eggs**
- ¾ **cup sugar**
- ¾ **cup all-purpose flour**
- 1½ **teaspoons baking powder**
- 2 **tablespoons grated orange peel**
- ¼ **cup (⅛ lb.) melted butter or margarine, cooled**
  Orange syrup (recipe follows)
- 2 **large (about 1 lb. total) oranges, peel and white membrane cut off, and fruit sections cut from inner membrane**

With a mixer, beat eggs and ½ cup of the sugar in a bowl until thick and lemon colored. Add flour, baking powder, orange peel, and butter; beat until mixed thoroughly. Scrape batter into a greased and flour-dusted 9-inch-diameter cake pan.

Bake in a 375° oven until cake just begins to pull from sides of pan and center springs back when lightly pressed, about 20 minutes. Let stand for 10 minutes, then invert onto a rack; holding rack and pan together, invert to return cake to pan.

Pierce cake all over with a fork. Slowly pour warm syrup over warm cake; let cool (if made ahead, cover airtight up until next day). Lay a rimmed serving plate, top down, on cake pan; hold together and invert to release cake. Garnish cake with orange sections.

No more than 4 hours before serving, place remaining ¼ cup sugar in a 6- to 8-inch frying pan over high heat; tilt and shake pan to mix melting sugar with dry sugar until sugar is melted and caramel colored, 3 to 4 minutes. Watch carefully to avoid burning. Pour hot

"Adding apples to hash brown potatoes was a bold stroke; adding chili powder is poetry."

"The worst thing that can happen to a cake is that it be dry."

syrup in a thin stream, rippling it back and forth over the top of cake and fruit. Makes 8 or 9 servings.

PER SERVING: 247 calories, 3.2 g protein, 44 g carbohydrates, 6.6 g fat (3.7 g saturated), 62 mg cholesterol, 140 mg sodium

Orange syrup. In a 1½- to 2-quart pan, mix ⅓ cup *each* **sugar** and **water,** and 2 cups **orange juice.** Bring to a boil over high heat and boil, uncovered, until reduced to about 1½ cups, about 10 minutes. Remove from heat and stir in 2 tablespoons **orange-flavored liqueur.** Use syrup warm. If made ahead, cover and chill up until next day, then reheat to use.

San Rafael, Calif.

Living high on the *hog, in the picturesque idiom of the South, means the good life—eating loin chops or ham instead of the poor folks' cut referred to as sowbelly, white bacon, or simply salt pork. Eating low on the lamb—the shank instead of the loin—can be pleasurable, but only if you remember that this cut,*

which comes from the foreleg, needs long, slow braising. When the young lambs bound as to the Wordsworthian tabor's sound, they are toughening their leg muscles. You will have to apply slow, moist heat to make these muscles tender.

Steven Brown and his wife are lovers of lamb, but their children are not. The children, however, actually ask for his Honey Delight Lamb Shanks.

HONEY DELIGHT LAMB SHANKS

- 4 lamb shanks (about 4 lb. total), bones cracked
- 1 tablespoon olive oil or salad oil
- 3 cloves garlic, minced or pressed
- 1 large onion, chopped
- ¼ cup honey
- 1 cup rosé wine or white or blush Zinfandel
- 1 large can (15 oz.) tomato sauce
- ¼ teaspoon *each* dried basil leaves, dried oregano leaves, and pepper
  Hot cooked rice
  Salt

In a 5- to 6-quart pan over medium-high heat, brown lamb on all sides in oil (about 25 minutes). Add garlic and onion; stir often until onion is limp, about 10 minutes. Add honey, wine, tomato sauce, basil, oregano, and pepper; bring to boil. Cover and simmer until meat is very tender when pierced, about 1½ hours.

"You will have to apply slow heat to make these muscles tender."

Transfer lamb to a serving dish; keep warm. Skim and discard fat from pan juices. If needed, boil juices, uncovered, over high heat until reduced to about 2 cups. Spoon some juices over lamb; offer remaining to spoon over individual portions and rice. Add salt to taste. Makes 4 servings.

PER SERVING: 527 calories, 64 g protein, 30 g carbohydrates, 16 g fat (5 g saturated), 195 mg cholesterol, 834 mg sodium

Union City, Calif.

They've come a long *way from rumaki, but Robert Decker's baby corn appetizers probably owe their origin to that Japanese-Hawaiian delicacy. In the original recipe, bacon is wrapped around water chestnuts and chicken livers, and then soaked in a soy marinade before grilling. Decker's appetizers get the crunch from baby corn.*

BABY CORN APPETIZERS

The number of corn ears in a can varies; use ½ slice of bacon per ear.

- About 12 slices (about 10 oz. total) bacon
- About ½ cup firmly packed brown sugar
- 1 can (15 oz.) baby corn, drained

Cut bacon slices in half crosswise. Coat both sides in sugar, then spiral-wrap each piece around an ear of corn. Lay corn, with ends of bacon beneath, slightly apart on a rack in a foil-lined broiler pan (about 12 by 14 in.). Bake in a 400° oven until bacon is crisp on all sides, about 25 minutes. Serve hot. Makes about 24.

PER PIECE: 40 calories, 1.3 g protein, 5.1 g carbohydrates, 1.6 g fat (0.6 g saturated), 2.8 mg cholesterol, 56 mg sodium

Menlo Park, Calif

November Menus

Restore body and soul with quiet meals at home before the madness of holiday activities arrives. By the fire, enjoy a turkey soup like Grandma used to make. For a lazy meal, bake beans and sausage in the oven as you relax. Dinner and movies come home with sandwiches in front of the VCR.

ahead or baked during dinner to serve warm. While the turkey meat heats in the soup, bake the decorated bread slices. Cut out stencils or use doilies or leaves to create patterns on bread and gingerbread. To make orange blossoms, score skin of each orange into 5 sections; pull peel back and roll ends in for blossom shape.

In a 6- to 8-quart pan, combine carrot, celery, onion, tomatoes, rice, and broth. Bring to a boil. Cover and simmer until carrot is tender to bite, about 20 minutes. Add turkey (reserved from broth); simmer until hot, about 5 minutes. Add salt and pepper to taste. Transfer soup to a container. Makes 6 to 8 servings.

Per Serving: 247 calories, 26 g protein, 24 g carbohydrates, 5.3 g fat (1.5 g saturated), 54 mg cholesterol, 314 mg sodium

---

POST-THANKSGIVING SUPPER

Grandma's Turkey Soup
Leaf-embossed Toast
Orange Blossoms
Warm Gingerbread
Milk or Beaujolais Nouveau

Use the Thanksgiving turkey for this soup. Reserve meat and make a broth from the carcass up to 2 days ahead. Once the broth is done, the menu goes quickly.

The gingerbread can be made a day

GRANDMA'S TURKEY SOUP

To serve soup in a large, hollowed-out pumpkin, fill pumpkin with boiling water; let stand about 10 minutes. Empty shell; fill with soup.

1½ cups thinly sliced carrot
1½ cups thinly sliced celery
1 cup chopped onion
1 can (14½ oz.) stewed tomatoes, chopped
⅓ cup long-grain white rice
Turkey broth and meat (recipe follows)
Salt and pepper

Turkey broth and meat. Pull meat off a **roast turkey carcass;** reserve meat (you need 3 to 4 cups bite-size pieces to use in soup, preceding). If done ahead, wrap and chill meat up to 2 days.

Break carcass into quarters; gather in cheesecloth and tie shut. Place in an 8- to 10-quart pan. Add 2 quarts **regular-strength chicken broth;** 2 medium-size (about 1 lb. total) **onions,** chopped; 2 large stalks (about 6 oz. total) **celery,** chopped; 2 large (about ½ lb. total) **carrots,** chopped; 1 tablespoon *each* **dried rubbed sage** and **dried marjoram leaves;** 4 cloves **garlic,** minced or pressed; 3 **dried bay leaves;** and ½ teaspoon **pepper.**

Bring broth to a boil. Cover and simmer for about 3 hours. Lift carcass from broth; drain and cool. Remove cloth and separate meat from bones. Add meat to reserved turkey to use in soup; discard bones. (If made ahead, cover and chill meat up to 2 days.)

Pour remaining broth through a colander set over a large bowl; discard vegetables. Skim fat. If needed, add water or boil, uncovered, to make 2 quarts. (If made ahead, cool broth, cover, and chill up to 2 days. Spoon off any fat.)

LEAF-EMBOSSED TOAST

6 to 8 slices dark rye bread
About 2 tablespoons olive oil
About ⅓ cup grated parmesan cheese

On piece of paper about the size of a slice of bread, cut out a leaf shape.

Enjoy this easy post-Thanksgiving supper by the fireplace with Grandma's turkey soup, leaf-stenciled bread slices, gingerbread, and juicy oranges.

Lay bread in a single layer on 12- by 15-inch baking sheets. Brush tops lightly with oil. Set leaf stencil on bread and sprinkle cheese generously over cutout. Carefully lift off stencil. Repeat for remaining slices.

Bake in a 450° oven until bread is crisp, about 5 minutes (watch closely to prevent burning). Serve warm. Makes 6 to 8 pieces.

PER SERVING: 123 calories, 4 g protein, 13 g carbohydrates, 6 g fat (1.8 g saturated), 4.2 mg cholesterol, 232 mg sodium

WARM GINGERBREAD

For stencil patterns, see suggestions on facing page.

- $^1/_4$ cup ($^1/_8$ lb.) butter or margarine, at room temperature
- $^1/_4$ cup granulated sugar
- 1 large egg
- $^1/_2$ cup light molasses
- 1$^1/_4$ cups all-purpose flour
- 1 teaspoon baking soda
- $^1/_4$ teaspoon *each* ground nutmeg and salt
- 1 teaspoon ground ginger, or 1 tablespoon minced fresh ginger, or 3 tablespoons minced crystallized ginger
- $^1/_2$ cup hot water
  About 1 tablespoon powdered sugar

Cream butter, granulated sugar, and egg until blended. Beat in molasses. Mix flour, soda, nutmeg, salt, and ginger. Add to egg mixture alternately with water. Mix until smooth. Spread into a greased and floured 8- to 9-inch-diameter cake pan.

Bake in a 350° oven until a toothpick inserted in center comes out clean, 25 to 30 minutes. Cool in pan on a rack until just warm to touch, about 15 minutes. Turn cake out onto a rack. Set serving plate over cake and invert together so top of cake is up. Just before serving, sift powdered sugar over stencils to create decorative pattern on cake. Lift off stencils. Serve cake warm or cool. Makes 6 servings.

PER SERVING: 285 calories, 3.8 g protein, 48 g carbohydrates, 9 g fat (5 g saturated), 57 mg cholesterol, 324 mg sodium

LAZY WEEKNIGHT OVEN SUPPER

Baked Beans with Sausages
Mixed Green Salad with Vinaigrette
Milk or Hard Cider
Oatmeal Cookies

You can start the beans and sausage the night before for a simple just-heat meal the next day, or make it from scratch in one night. Both the beans and the sausage cook unattended in the oven, giving you time to relax.

For the salad, mix a tangy vinaigrette with rinsed and crisped greens or purchased mesclun.

BAKED BEANS WITH SAUSAGES

- 1 large (about 12 oz.) red onion, chopped
- 3 cans (15 oz. each) pinto beans, drained and rinsed
- 1 can (20 oz.) pineapple chunks, drained, or 1$^1/_2$ cups bite-size pieces peeled, cored fresh pineapple
- 1 tablespoon mustard seed
- 1 teaspoon coriander seed
- 4 cloves garlic, minced or pressed
- $^1/_2$ cup light molasses
- $^1/_3$ cup *each* catsup and firmly packed brown sugar
  About 2 pounds mild or hot Italian sausages
  Fresh pineapple slices and chopped red onion (optional)

In a 2$^1/_2$- to 3-quart shallow baking dish, mix chopped onion, beans, pineapple chunks, mustard seed, coriander seed, garlic, molasses, catsup, and sugar. Cover dish. Place sausages in a 9- by 13-inch baking pan. In a 350° oven, bake beans and sausages for 1 hour. Turn sausages occasionally to brown evenly, then drain off excess fat.

Uncover beans and nestle sausages into beans. (If made ahead, cool, cover,

Beans and sausages bake together for a sit-and-wait casserole supper. Serve with mixed greens and oatmeal cookies.

and chill up until next day.) Cover and continue baking for 1 hour (add 15 minutes if made ahead); uncover the last 5 minutes to brown sausage. Let dish cool for about 10 minutes. If desired, garnish with pineapple slices and red onion. Makes 6 to 8 servings.

PER SERVING: 517 calories, 24 g protein, 56 g carbohydrates, 23 g fat (7.6 g saturated), 65 mg cholesterol, 1,139 mg sodium

(Continued on next page)

STEAKWICHES AT THE MOVIES

Steakwiches with Slaw
Celery & Olives
Winter Pears
Almonds & Walnuts
Milk or Beer

Try this casual, hands-on meal while watching movies at home.

One marinade seasons meat and slaw. You can marinate the meat up to a day before. To assemble the sandwiches, quickly broil the beef, mix the slaw, and toast the rolls. Offer celery and olives to eat with sandwiches.

STEAKWICHES WITH SLAW

1½ **pounds boneless beef sirloin steak, about 1 inch thick, fat trimmed**
   Marinade (recipe follows)
6 **onion sandwich rolls**
2 **cups** *each* **finely shredded red cabbage and turnip**
6 **lettuce leaves, rinsed and crisped**

In a heavy plastic bag, coat steak with ¾ cup marinade; seal bag. Chill at least 1 hour or up until next day, turning occasionally. Reserve remaining marinade for the cabbage-turnip slaw.

Lift steak from bag, draining off and discarding excess marinade. Place the steak on a rack in a 10- by 15-inch broiler pan. Broil 4 inches from the heat, turning once, until meat is done to your liking in the thickest part (cut to test), about 12 minutes total for medium-rare.

Split rolls; place, cut sides up, on a 12- by 15-inch baking sheet. Broil about 4 inches from heat until lightly toasted, about 1 minute.

Mix cabbage, turnip, and reserved marinade for slaw.

Cut steak crosswise into very thin slices. Set rolls on plates, toasted sides up. Lay ⅙ of the lettuce, slaw, and beef on each roll bottom. Cover with roll tops. Makes 6 servings.

PER SERVING: 430 calories, 32 g protein, 36 g carbohydrates, 17 g fat (4 g saturated), 78 mg cholesterol, 478 mg sodium

Marinade. Whisk together ½ cup *each* **olive oil** and **balsamic** or red wine **vinegar,** ¼ cup **lemon juice,** 2 tablespoons **Dijon mustard,** and 2 teaspoons **prepared horseradish.**

Festive soup buffet (page 310)

E

njoy the holidays
with gatherings planned for informal sociability, self-
service by guests, and easy cleanup. A festive soup buffet
features substantial chowder and a walk-around salad.
Celebrate Sweden's traditional St. Lucia holiday or
invite young guests to decorate graham cracker houses.
For Hanukkah, we suggest a new way to cook latkes.
You'll find recipes for handsome assembly-line appetizers,
one-dish party entrées, and lean but glamorous holiday
desserts, as well as ideas for decorative chili
wreaths and gifts for cooks.

309

A Festive Soup Buffet

"LET'S GET TOGETHER *around the holidays"* *is an easy invitation to extend when you have the right menu. This festive soup meal—geared for a large, informal party—suits all ages and adapts well to self-service. It also uses few utensils, making for easy cleanup.*

A filling but lean chowder, packed with seafood and corn, provides the base for the casual buffet meal. Ladled into mugs, the potato-thickened soup is easy to eat standing up. Breadsticks and a walk-around salad complete the simple menu. Serve Christmas cookies and seasonal fruit for dessert.

SOUP SUPPER FOR A DOZEN

Walk-around Salad
Crowd-pleasing
Seafood Corn Chowder
Breadsticks
Sauvignon Blanc
Cranberry Punch
Christmas Cookies
Winter Fruits

For a no-fork-needed salad, offer raw vegetables (5 to 6 lb. total) such as bell peppers, carrots, celery, cherry tomatoes, green onions, and Belgian endive to dip into homemade or purchased dressing (1½ to 2 cups). Up to a day ahead, rinse, trim, cover, and chill vegetables.

For an easy-to-eat party entrée, sip mugs of low-fat seafood corn chowder.

Most of the chowder can be made a day ahead. Shortly before serving, thicken soup and add seafood.

CROWD-PLEASING SEAFOOD CORN CHOWDER

2 medium-size (about ¾ lb. total) onions, finely chopped
  About 11 cups regular-strength chicken broth
2 cloves garlic, minced or pressed
1 teaspoon pepper
½ teaspoon dried thyme leaves
6 cups (about 2½ lb.) peeled and shredded thin-skinned potatoes
3 tablespoons cornstarch blended smoothly with 3 tablespoons water

5 cups nonfat or whole milk
3 packages (10 oz. each) frozen corn kernels
1 jar (10 oz.) shucked fresh oysters, cut into bite-size pieces, and juices; or 2 cans (6½ oz. each) chopped clams and juices
1 pound cooked shelled crab or tiny cooked shelled shrimp
2 tablespoons minced parsley

In an 8- to 10-quart pan, combine onions and ½ cup broth. Boil uncovered on high heat, stirring often, until liquid evaporates and onions start to brown, 12 to 15 minutes. To deglaze, add ⅓ cup broth, then stir to release browned bits. Stir occasionally until liquid evaporates and mixture begins to brown again, 1 to 3 minutes. Repeat deglazing step until onions are richly browned, about 3 more times.

Add 3 cups broth, garlic, pepper, and thyme. Boil on high heat, uncovered, until mixture is reduced to 3 cups, about 25 minutes; stir often. Add potatoes; simmer uncovered, stirring often, until tender to bite, about 30 minutes. If made ahead, cover and chill up until next day.

Stir in 6 cups broth, cornstarch mixture, milk, and corn; stir often on medium-high heat just until boiling, 10 to 20 minutes. Remove from heat, then add oysters and crab. Pour into a tureen; sprinkle with parsley. Makes 6 quarts, 12 to 14 servings.

PER SERVING: 237 calories, 16 g protein, 37 g carbohydrates, 3.1 g fat (0.7 g saturated), 45 mg cholesterol, 210 mg sodium

Party menu satisfies guests of all ages. Serve lean but filling chowder, breadsticks, vegetables to dip in dressing, fresh fruit, and decorated cookies. Self-service meal simplifies serving and cleanup.

Assembly-line Appetizers

USING A VARIETY of toppings, garnishes, and bases, you can prepare these eight appetizers quickly. Use the combinations shown here, or, to simplify shopping and preparation, use the same base for all.

ASSEMBLY-LINE APPETIZERS

For the bases, use **crackers,** 1/4-inch-thick slices European cucumber, or peeled bite-size pieces jicama. Or use toasted bread slices such as raisin, pumpernickel, rye, or baguette. To toast bread, cut into bite-size pieces (remove crusts, if desired) and place on a 12- by 15-inch baking sheet. Broil about 8 inches from heat until golden, about 1½ minutes. Toast other side, about 45 seconds. Cool.

Spread with **cream cheese** (plain or chive), neufchâtel (light cream) cheese, herb cheese, or sour cream. Add **toppings** as shown, or design your own combinations. If you prepare appetizers ahead, cover and chill vegetable- and toast-base ones up to 2 hours. Prepare cracker-base appetizers just before serving; crackers soften quickly.

Below are combinations shown on the tray at right:

1 Cream cheese, basil, and dried tomato packed in oil (drained) top toasted baguette.

2 Sour cream, apple slice (coated in lemon juice), smoked chicken, and green onion crown raisin toast.

3 Herb cheese, red onion, and smoked salmon rest on cucumber slice.

4 Cream cheese, purchased olive tapenade, and Italian parsley decorate rye toast triangle.

5 Herb cheese, tiny shrimp, and dill top cracker.

6 Sour cream, brisling sardine, and lemon zest adorn jicama slice.

7 Sour cream, pickled herring, and beet horseradish crown cucumber slice.

8 Cream cheese and flying fish roe (tobiko—rinse and drain in a fine strainer) top pumpernickel toast.

1   2   3

Tray filled with handsome appetizers sets festive tone for holiday entertaining. Efficient shopping simplifies preparation with use of purchased bases, varied toppings, and colorful garnishes.

Making Chili Wreaths

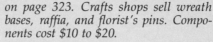

EVOKE THE SPIRIT *of the Southwest this holiday season with a dried chili wreath. The firecracker wreath below contains fiery de arbol chilies and medium-hot cascabels. Chilies in the starburst wreath at right are mild to medium-hot, reddish black Anaheim (also called New Mexico or California) and mild, black pasilla (also called negro).*

Look for chilies and cornhusks at supermarkets and Latino grocery stores, or order chilies by mail from a source listed on page 323. *Crafts shops sell wreath bases, raffia, and florist's pins. Components cost $10 to $20.*

To use chilies after the holidays, break or snip them off and wipe them clean. Stem them and—for milder flavor—shake out seeds.

You can add whole dried chilies to simmering soups or stews. Or break chilies in pieces and whirl to finely grind in a blender to make chili powder for cooking. Store powders airtight in jars.

Assemble components for wreath: dried chilies, rosemary, wreath base, needle and thread, and florist's pins.

FIRECRACKER WREATH

String dried **de arbol chilies***, piercing beneath stem, with slim **needle and thread.** Make into a circle to fit a 6½-inch **twig** or straw **wreath base;** knot thread. Repeat for second chili circle. Stack circles on wreath base; secure with **florist's pins** and **raffia.** String 3 dried **cascabel chilies;** tie to **rosemary sprigs.** Pin to base.

*Buy 5 ounces perfect de arbol chilies (fruit and stems intact) for a 6½-inch wreath. Buy 10 ounces if you can't cull chilies first.

STARBURST WREATH

Soak 2 ounces **cornhusks** in hot water to soften; separate. Wrap a 9½-inch **foam** or straw **wreath base** with some husks; fasten with **florist's pins.** Attach flat husks (pointed ends out) to back and front of base. On top of wreath, alternate large dried **Anaheim chilies** and large dried **pasilla chilies***; overlap slightly, stems facing in. Pin through pods to base.

*Buy 7 ounces Anaheim chilies, 2½ ounces pasillas.

Fiery de arbol chilies are paired with medium-hot cascabels in this colorful wreath. Green sprigs of fresh rosemary add a festive contrast.

Create Southwestern holiday spirit for your home with starburst wreath of reddish black, mild to medium-hot dried Anaheim chilies paired with mild, dried black pasilla (or negro) chilies atop a circle of dried cornhusks. After the holidays, you can use chilies for cooking.

Sweden's Holiday Tradition

ST. LUCIA, SAINT OF *light, ushers in the Swedish holiday season with the festival of lights. At daybreak on December 13, the youngest daughter dons a wreath crown and serves her family S-shaped cardamom buns.*

The Ritter family of Mill Valley, California, celebrates this ritual by sharing with friends a buffet breakfast featuring St. Lucia buns.

You can adapt this Swedish tradition for your family by serving the buffet as a breakfast, brunch, or supper. You can even consider the party for a weekday, as most of the steps can be done ahead.

ST. LUCIA CELEBRATION

St. Lucia Buns

Sausage (or Vegetable) & Cheese Bread Custard

Apples, Sliced Pineapple & Bananas

Hot Chocolate or Coffee

Make the buns up to 3 weeks ahead. Assemble the meat or vegetable casserole at least 8 hours ahead.

ST. LUCIA BUNS

- 1 package active dry yeast
- 1 cup warm milk (110°)
- 2/3 cup sugar
- 1/3 cup butter or margarine at room temperature
- 2 large eggs
- 1/2 teaspoon salt
- 2 teaspoons ground cardamom or crushed, hulled cardamom seed
  About 3 3/4 cups all-purpose flour
  About 1/4 cup raisins

In a bowl, combine yeast and milk; let stand 5 minutes to soften. Blend in sugar, butter, 1 egg, salt, and cardamom. Stir in 3 1/2 cups flour to form a stiff dough.

To knead with a dough hook, beat at high speed until dough pulls cleanly from sides of bowl, about 6 minutes. If dough still sticks, add flour, 1 tablespoon at a time, until dough pulls free.

To knead by hand, scrape dough onto a floured board. Knead until smooth and elastic, about 10 minutes, adding as little flour as possible to prevent sticking. Place dough in a greased bowl.

Cover bowl with plastic wrap and let dough rise in a warm place until doubled, about 1 1/2 hours.

Punch down dough, turn out onto a board, and knead lightly. Pinch off 1 1/2-inch balls of dough; roll each into a smooth rope about 10 inches long. On lightly greased 10- by 15-inch baking sheets, form each rope into an S by snugly coiling ends in opposite directions. Put a raisin in center of each coil; set buns 2 inches apart.

Cover buns lightly with plastic wrap and let rise in a warm place until almost doubled, about 25 minutes. Beat remaining egg; brush buns evenly with egg.

Bake in a 350° oven until golden, 15 to 20 minutes. (If using 1 oven, switch pan positions halfway through baking.) Transfer to a rack. Serve warm or cool.

(Continued on page 318)

Continuing a family tradition, mother and daughter make S-shaped buns (sometimes called Christmas pigs or boars).

Wearing traditional Swedish costume, Emily offers Ben a St. Lucia bun to begin the holiday season. S-shaped cardamom buns are usually served at daybreak on December 13. Our buffet menu goes equally well for breakfast or a winter supper.

If made ahead, wrap and store at room temperature up until next day or freeze up to 3 weeks. Thaw frozen buns unwrapped. To heat, wrap in foil and bake in a 350° oven until warm, about 15 minutes. Makes 3 dozen buns, about 1 ounce each.

PER BUN: 89 calories, 2 g protein, 15 g carbohydrates, 2.3 g fat (1.3 g saturated), 17 mg cholesterol, 55 mg sodium

SAUSAGE & CHEESE BREAD CUSTARD

2 **pounds hot or mild Italian sausage, casings removed**

About 1 loaf (1-lb. size, with ½-inch-thick slices) firm white bread

½ **pound cheddar cheese, shredded**

7 **large eggs**

5 **cups milk**

1 **tablespoon Dijon mustard**

½ **teaspoon pepper**

In a 10- to 12-inch frying pan, stir sausage over medium-high heat until crumbly and brown, about 15 minutes. Drain and discard fat.

Cut bread into 1-inch pieces. Evenly spread ½ the bread cubes in a buttered shallow baking dish (about 9 by 13 in.). Top with ½ the cheddar cheese and ½ the sausage. Layer remaining bread, sausage, and cheddar cheese.

With a whisk, blend eggs, milk, mustard, and pepper; pour over layered casserole. Cover and chill at least 8 hours or until next day.

Bake casserole, uncovered, in a 350° oven until edges are golden brown and the center is firm, 45 to 55 minutes. Cool 15 minutes on a rack. Cut into rectangles and serve. Makes 8 to 10 servings.

PER SERVING: 557 calories, 31 g protein, 31 g carbohydrates, 34 g fat (15 g saturated), 243 mg cholesterol, 1,132 mg sodium

Accompanying the buns, sausage and cheese bread custard completes the main course for this Swedish holiday menu; serve with pineapple, bananas, and apples.

VEGETABLE & CHEESE BREAD CUSTARD

Follow recipe for **sausage and cheese bread custard** (preceding), except omit sausage. Pour 1 tablespoon **salad oil** in frying pan. Add 2 medium-size (about 1 lb. total) **red** or green **bell peppers,** cored, seeded, and chopped; 1 medium-size (8 oz.) **onion,** chopped; and ¾ pound **mushrooms,** rinsed and sliced. Cook until onion is golden, about 20 minutes.

Layer vegetable mixture and 1 large package (8 oz.) **cream cheese,** cut into ½-inch cubes, with bread and cheddar cheese. Makes 8 to 10 servings.

PER SERVING: 452 calories, 21 g protein, 34 g carbohydrates, 26 g fat (14 g saturated), 216 mg cholesterol, 589 mg sodium

Ideas for Party Planners

GIVING A HOLIDAY PARTY? *Here are some menu ideas and serving tips to make planning and hosting easier.*

For parties including children, provide activities such as wreath making, cooky decorating, or caroling to make it more enjoyable for all ages.

PLANNING THE MENU

Following are some basic menu concepts to consider. Offer a selection of beverages, including nonalcoholic choices; allow 2 to 4 cups per person.

One big whole-meal dish. Focus on one main dish such as soup, chili, stew, or salad. Choose a recipe that can be prepared ahead and holds up well on a buffet table. If applicable, offer condiments for guests to add to taste. Accompany with breads, raw vegetables, holiday cookies, and fruit. For each serving, allow 1½ to 2 cups of the main dish.

Basic meat, starch, vegetable meal. This straightforward menu adapts to everything from make-ahead buffets to fancy sit-down dinners. For buffets, consider foods that hold up well as they stand and are easy to eat without sitting at a table. Consider boneless, easy-to-slice (and to eat) roasts, make-ahead vegetable casseroles, grain salads or pilafs, or marinated vegetables. Sit-down meals allow you more flexibility in food, but this method depends on the tastes of your guests, the size of the group, and whether you have help in the kitchen.

Allow about ¼ pound boneless meat or fish or ¾ pound bone-in poultry, meat (such as ribs), or shellfish; about ¼ pound ready-to-serve vegetable; and about ⅓ pound cooked starch per guest.

Appetizer party. This works for any size group. Offer an assortment of bite-size, easy-to-manage foods. For a large party, place foods at different stations, so guests circulate and have easier access. For small pieces of food, napkins are adequate. As a meal, allow 10 to 15 pieces or about ¼ pound cheese or meat per serving; for a predinner party, use about a third of these amounts.

Dessert party. For a late-evening party, consider a selection of desserts. Choose a variety of sweets, from small chocolates to lavish cakes. Also include fresh fruit and cheese. For each serving, allow 2 to 4 small pieces of dessert, 1 to 2 ounces cheese, and 3 to 6 bite-size pieces of fruit. Serve with fruity sparkling wine and coffee.

HOW TO HANDLE THE FOOD

Buy and serve. Ready-to-eat foods attractively arranged make an easy, quick party. Order several days ahead to make sure you get what you want. This kind of party can be pricey, but it's usually less costly than hiring a caterer. You can share costs by asking guests to bring specific items from the delicatessen.

Cook it yourself. Plan ahead with an easy-to-prepare menu that you can handle in your kitchen. Cook as much as possible before the party. Foods that don't need reheating minimize last-minute details.

Share the cooking. Ask guests to bring one dish of their choice or one batch of a specified recipe that you can combine with others.

Host a cooking contest. Ask contestants to bring their best appetizer, judge them, and give awards—then everyone eats the entries. Or, for a small party, make cooking together the focus of the evening; eating the meal is the delicious result.

Catered event. Easiest, but most expensive, is hiring a caterer to do the whole job for you. To cut costs, have the caterer prepare the food, then you take care of serving it. Consider a buffet or hiring students to help.

Bite-size appetizers are served with beverage before meal. Build party menu around one whole-meal dish, such as our self-serve soup buffet.

One-dish Entrées for Holiday Entertaining

ONE CHALLENGE OF *holiday entertaining is how to spend time with your guests rather than in the kitchen. These make-ahead entrées offer a solution by getting all the major steps out of the way a day or two before.*

Choose from a black bean cassoulet or a handsome sauerbraten beef pie. Once the few *time-consuming steps are finished, final assembly proceeds quickly; both casseroles can be fully completed up to a day ahead.*

On party night, allow an hour to reheat the casserole. Just add a salad, crusty bread, and wine or milk to complete either meal, and you're free to enjoy your guests.

Cassoulet of black beans and turkey with tortilla arrows is a make-ahead choice for holiday entertaining. Serve with tortilla whiskers, a big salad, bread, wine, and milk.

SOUTHWEST CASSOULET

1 tablespoon canned chipotle chili with adobo sauce; or 1 dried chipotle chili (2 to 3 in.), rinsed, stemmed, seeded, and crumbled; or 1 fresh jalapeño chili, stemmed and minced

1 teaspoon *each* ground cinnamon, ground cumin, and dried oregano leaves

2 large (about 1 lb. total) onions, chopped

About 8 cups regular-strength chicken broth

1½ pounds (3¾ cups) dried black beans, sorted for debris and rinsed

Mexican-seasoned turkey (recipe follows)

1 jar (15 oz.) roasted red peppers, thinly sliced

1 can (7 oz.) whole green chilies, thinly sliced

Tortilla arrows and whiskers (recipe follows)

In an 8- to 10-quart pan, combine chipotle chili, cinnamon, cumin, oregano, onions, and ½ cup broth. Boil, uncovered, on high heat, stirring occasionally, until liquid evaporates and onions start to brown, 12 to 15 minutes.

To deglaze, stir in ⅓ cup broth to release browned bits. Stir occasionally until liquid evaporates and mixture begins to brown again, 1 to 3 minutes. Repeat deglazing step 3 more times, until mixture is richly browned.

Add to onions the beans, 6 cups broth, and 6 cups water. Cover and bring to a boil on high heat. Reduce heat and simmer, stirring occasionally, until beans are just tender to bite, about 1 hour. Add turkey; simmer until meat is no longer pink at bone in thickest part (cut to test), about 1 hour.

Remove pan from heat; lift out turkey. When turkey is cool enough to touch, pull meat from bones and cut into bite-size pieces.

Drain beans, reserving liquid; set beans aside and return liquid to pan. Boil liquid on high heat until reduced to 2 cups.

In a shallow 5-quart casserole, mix beans, cooking liquid, turkey, red peppers, and green chilies. If made ahead, cover and chill up until next day.

Bake, uncovered, in a 350° oven until casserole is hot in center, about 45 minutes (1 hour if chilled). Lay tortilla arrows on casserole; serve whiskers to scatter onto portions to taste. Makes 10 to 12 servings.

PER SERVING WITHOUT TORTILLA WHISKERS: 338 calories, 30 g protein, 43 g carbohydrates, 5.4 g fat (1.5 g saturated), 57 mg cholesterol, 780 mg sodium

Mexican-seasoned turkey. Combine 2 tablespoons **salt** and 1 tablespoon **chili powder;** rub evenly over 2 or 3 skinned **turkey thighs** (about 3½ lb. total). Place meat in a heavy plastic bag or noncorrodible bowl (glass, ceramic, or stainless steel). Cover and chill 6 hours (for minimum salt flavor) to 8 hours (for full salt flavor).

Rinse meat under cold running water, rubbing lightly to extract as much salt as possible; pat dry. If made ahead, cover and chill turkey thighs up to 2 days; rinse before using.

Tortilla arrows and whiskers. You will need 12 **corn tortillas** (about 7 in.). With a sharp knife, cut large decorative arrows from 4 of the tortillas. Stack remaining tortillas (3 or 4 at a time) and scraps; cut into strips about ⅛ inch wide.

Pour about ½ inch **salad oil** into a 4- to 5-quart pan over medium-high heat. When oil reaches 350° on a thermometer, turn heat down to maintain temperature. Add ⅓ of the tortilla strips at a time; stir until strips are lightly browned and crisp, about 1½ minutes. With a slotted spoon, transfer strips to paper towels to drain; while warm, sprinkle lightly with **salt** or chili-seasoned salt. Also fry tortilla arrows until crisp, about 1½ minutes; drain on paper towels.

Serve warm. If made ahead, let cool, then package arrows and whiskers separately and airtight. Chill up to 2 days. To reheat, spread whiskers in a paper towel–lined 10- by 15-inch rimmed pan. Bake at 300° until warm, about 10 minutes. Then, on same pan, reheat arrows until crisp, about 10 minutes. Makes 4 arrows and about 8 cups whiskers.

PER CUP: 88 calories, 2.1 g protein, 13 g carbohydrates, 3.4 g fat, 0 mg cholesterol, 111 mg sodium

SAUERBRATEN BEEF PIE

4½ **pounds boned blade-cut beef chuck**

2 **large (about 1 lb. total) onions, chopped**

2 **tablespoons minced fresh ginger**

1 **tablespoon mustard seed**

½ **teaspoon pepper**

¼ **teaspoon ground cloves**

1 **cup red wine vinegar**

2 **cups regular-strength beef broth**

1½ **cups dry red wine**

2 **tablespoons firmly packed brown sugar**

2 **pounds (about 9 large) carrots, thinly sliced diagonally**

1 **cup pitted dried prunes, quartered**

½ **cup raisins**

1 **tablespoon cornstarch**
   Cream cheese pastry (recipe follows)

1 **large egg, beaten to blend**

Trim and discard fat from beef; cut meat into 1-inch chunks. Combine meat, onions, ginger, mustard seed, pepper, cloves, and ¾ cup water in a 5- to 6-quart pan; cover tightly. Bring to a boil over high heat; reduce heat and simmer for 30 minutes.

Uncover and boil on high heat until liquid evaporates and meat begins to sizzle in its own drippings; stir often until drippings in pan are richly browned. Add ¼ cup water and boil, stirring often, until the drippings are again richly browned. Spoon out any fat. Add vinegar and stir to free the browned drippings.

Add broth, wine, and sugar. Lay carrots over meat. Cover pan tightly and bring liquid to boiling on high heat. Reduce heat and simmer until the meat is very tender when pierced, about 1 hour.

With a slotted spoon, transfer meat and vegetables to a shallow 3-quart casserole (about 2 in. deep and about 8 by 12 in.). Mix the prunes and raisins in with the meat.

Over high heat, boil liquid left in pan, uncovered, until reduced to 1 cup, about 15 minutes; remove from heat. Meanwhile, smoothly blend cornstarch with 2 tablespoons water. Stir into pan juices, then pour over meat and vegetables. If made ahead, cover tightly and chill up to 2 days.

Lay pastry rectangle over meat mix-

ture, folding edges under; flute firmly against the casserole rim. Set reserved pastry cutouts decoratively on top. Cut slits in crust. If made ahead, cover casserole and chill up to 1 day (meat holds only 2 days total).

Brush pastry lightly with beaten egg. Bake in a 400° oven on the lowest rack until pastry is well browned and filling is bubbling, 40 to 55 minutes. If pastry rim or cutouts begin to darken excessively before center is brown, drape these areas with foil.

You can also bake the pie ahead, chill, then cover airtight up to 1 day (meat holds 2 days maximum). Reheat, uncovered, in a 350° oven until filling is hot to touch in center, about 40 minutes. (If edges of crust darken during baking, cover with foil.) Makes 8 to 10 servings.

PER SERVING: 783 calories, 48 g protein, 59 g carbohydrates, 40 g fat (20 g saturated), 238 mg cholesterol, 464 mg sodium

Cream cheese pastry. In a food processor or bowl, combine 2½ cups **all-purpose flour;** 1 cup (½ lb.) **butter** or margarine, cut into chunks; and ⅔ cup (about 6 oz.) **neufchâtel** (light cream) **cheese.** Whirl or rub with fingers until coarse crumbs form. Add 1 **large egg;** whirl or stir with fork until dough holds together. Reserve ½ cup dough for decorations. Pat each portion of pastry dough into a ball. If made ahead, chill airtight up to 3 days. On a lightly floured board, roll large ball of pastry in a rectangle to match dimensions of the casserole plus 1 inch on all sides.

Roll reserved ½ cup pastry about ⅛ inch thick and cut designs, such as poinsettia leaves; place on top of crust.

Handsomely decorated cream cheese crust caps hearty pie with sauerbraten filling.

Gifts for or from a Cook

IS THERE A FOOD *lover on your holiday gift list? Consider offering a food discovery package. The ones shown here require only brief assembly. Once prepared, they'll keep several months to up to a year. Copy the information and use it as a gift tag to guide the receiver in his or her culinary experimentation.*

Gourmet stores sell most ingredients —vanilla beans ($1.50 to $3 per bean), truffle oil ($15 to $20 for a 2- to 3-oz. bottle), cob popcorn (30 cents to $1 apiece), and dried mushrooms ($3 to $13 per oz.). These items and the dried chilies featured on page 314 are also available by mail order (see facing page).

VANILLA BEAN

Use the strongly aromatic beans whole, or split them to get more flavor from the thousands of tiny seeds inside. After using whole or split beans, rinse, pat dry, and store in a cool, dark place to reuse. Fresh and reused beans will keep indefinitely immersed in alcohol or stored airtight.

Vanilla sugar. Put 1 or 2 **vanilla beans** into a jar; fill with **granulated** or powdered **sugar** to cover. Seal tightly; shake jar every few days for about 1 month. (To speed up the process, whirl chopped vanilla beans and sugar in a blender; store for at least 1 week, then sift sugar.) Use sugar over fruit and in desserts. Replace sugar as used.

Vanilla extract. Place 1 **vanilla bean** (split, if desired) into a narrow bottle. Fill bottle with **brandy,** vodka, or rum to completely cover bean. Seal airtight; let stand about 1 month in a cool, dark place, shaking bottle occasionally. Use to flavor desserts, or as called for in recipes.

TRUFFLE OIL ON POPCORN OR PASTA

Olive oil infused with the essence of crushed white truffles takes on the distinctive musky smell and flavor of the highly valued fungus. Use sparingly as a seasoning oil; long cooking dissipates flavor. Imported oils, especially those from Italy, seem to have the strongest scent. Store in a cool, dark place up to a few months.

Truffled popcorn. Mix 1 to 2 teaspoons **truffle oil** with 1 quart **popped corn.** Add **salt** to taste.

To pop cob popcorn, place 1 **cob popcorn** (6 to 8 in.) in a brown paper lunch bag. Fold top over several times and set bag in the middle of a microwave oven. Set time for 4 minutes at full power (100

Aromatic vanilla beans make an intriguing gift for a cook, whether whole (bottom), adding flavor to sugar (left), or flavoring brandy to make vanilla extract (right).

percent). Cook until popping slows to 2 to 3 seconds between pops, 2 to 4 minutes. Listen closely; do not overcook. Makes about 1 quart.

Truffled pasta. Mix 1 to 2 tablespoons **truffle oil** with 4 cups hot cooked **pasta.** Add freshly grated **parmesan cheese** and **pepper** to taste.

MUSHROOMS IN A BASKET

Drying concentrates mushrooms' rich flavor. Your woodland basket may hold these choices: *Morels* are deeply cratered and have elongated dark brown caps and earthy flavor. *Chanterelles* are golden brown with pronounced gills; flavor is mild and nutty. *Porcini* (cêpes), in dark brown slices, have intense, pungent aroma and flavor. *Shiitakes* have wrinkled dark brown caps and intense, rich flavor.

To use mushrooms. Soak mushrooms in hot water to cover until soft, 20 to 30 minutes. Rub with fingers in liquid to remove grit; lift from liquid. Discard stems, if tough. You can also use the flavorful soaking liquid; carefully pour off water, leaving the gritty sediment. Use mushrooms (whole, sliced, or chopped) and liquid in pasta sauces and rice dishes, and with poultry and meats. One ounce dried mushrooms is enough to season 6 servings. Store airtight in a dark place at room temperature for up to 1 year.

MAIL-ORDER SOURCES

Corti Brothers, 5810 Folsom Blvd., Sacramento 95819; (916) 736-3800. Vanilla, oil, mushrooms, chilies.

De Laurenti Specialty Food Markets, 1435 First Ave., Seattle 98101; (206) 622-0141. Vanilla, oil, mushrooms, chilies.

G.B. Ratto, 821 Washington St., Oakland 94607; (800) 325-3483. Vanilla, oil, mushrooms, chilies.

Mushrooms in a moss-lined basket bring hints of the woodland to cooked foods. Before using, soak dried mushrooms in hot water for 20 to 30 minutes.

Irvine Ranch Market, 142 S. Vincente Blvd., Los Angeles 90048; (213) 657-1931. Vanilla, oil, popcorn, mushrooms, chilies.

Patricia Rain Specialty Foods, (408) 458-3103. Vanilla.

Strohecker's, Inc., 2855 S.W. Patton Rd., Portland 97201; (503) 223-7391. Vanilla, popcorn, mushrooms, chilies.

Wally's West, 2107 Westwood Blvd., Los Angeles 90025; (213) 475-0606. Vanilla, oil, popcorn, mushrooms, chilies.

Lean but Glamorous Holiday Desserts

REFRESHING CITRUS *accents these cool desserts. Their glamorous appearance and palate-pleasing flavors belie their relatively lean composition and offer little threat to your waistline.*

FOUR-ORANGE CUSTARD

1 **envelope unflavored gelatin**
¼ **cup milk**
7 **to 9 large (about 4 lb. total) oranges**
1 **package (8 oz.) neufchâtel (light cream) cheese, at room temperature, cut up**
¾ **cup powdered sugar**

About ¼ **cup orange-flavor liqueur (optional)**
Chocolate sauce (recipe follows)

Sprinkle gelatin over milk; let soften about 5 minutes.

Ream about 3 oranges to make 1⅓ cups juice. If desired, pour juice through a fine strainer to remove pulp for discard. In a 1- to 1½-quart pan, bring juice to a boil. Add gelatin mixture; stir over low heat until gelatin dissolves. In blender or food processor, whirl juice mixture, cheese, and sugar until smooth.

Pour mixture into an 8-inch-square cake pan. Cover pan without touching custard and chill until firm, at least 4 hours, or up to 4 days.

To unmold, quickly dip pan in hot water to within ½ inch of pan rim. Set plate over pan; holding them together, invert custard onto plate. (If done ahead, chill custard up until next day.)

Up to 4 hours before serving, finely shred enough peel from oranges to make 1 tablespoon. Cut remaining peel and membrane off oranges. Thinly slice fruit crosswise to make about 24 slices; remove seeds. Cover and chill slices and peel separately until serving.

To serve custard, arrange about 3 orange slices on each of 8 dessert plates. Pour liqueur over slices to taste. Cut custard into 4-inch triangles; place on plates. Drizzle with chocolate sauce and garnish with shredded orange peel. Makes 8 servings.

PER SERVING: 230 calories, 5 g protein, 33 g carbohydrates, 10 g fat (6 g saturated), 23 mg cholesterol, 120 mg sodium

Chocolate sauce. Seal 4 tablespoons **semisweet chocolate baking chips** and 2 teaspoons **nonfat milk** in a small (not pleated) zip-lock plastic bag. Set in top of double boiler over simmering water; heat until chocolate softens. Through plastic, blend chocolate and milk with fingers until smooth.

To use, trim a corner from bag to make an ⅛-inch hole. Pipe chocolate from bag.

RUBY GRAPEFRUIT TERRINE WITH TEA SAUCE

8 **to 9 large (about 1 lb. each) ruby grapefruit**
3 **tablespoons orange juice concentrate, thawed**
1 **tablespoon sugar**
3 **teaspoons (about 1½ envelopes) unflavored gelatin**
Tea sauce (recipe follows)
Citrus leaves, rinsed

Cool custard streaked with chocolate tops orange slices splashed with liqueur. Refreshing citrus flavors offer pleasing end to a meal.

Cut peel and membrane from 8 grapefruit. Over bowl, cut fruit between inner membranes to free segments. Carefully drain juice from bowl and measure. You need 2½ cups juice and 6 cups segments. If needed, segment or ream another fruit. Cover and chill 8 to 10 good-looking segments until ready to serve.

In a 4½- by 8-inch metal loaf pan, neatly layer remaining segments to within ½ inch of pan rim.

In a 1- to 2-quart pan, mix together 1 cup grapefruit juice (reserve remainder for sauce), orange concentrate, sugar, and gelatin. Let gelatin soften about 5 minutes. Stir over medium heat until all gelatin dissolves. Pour over segments.

Cover terrine and chill at least 8 hours or up to 1 day. To serve, dip chilled terrine briefly in hot water to within ½ inch of pan rim. Uncover and place platter over pan; holding them together, invert terrine onto platter.

Pour equal portions of tea sauce on 8 to 10 dessert plates. With a sharp knife, carefully cut terrine into 8 to 10 equal slices. Set slices on sauce. Garnish with reserved segments and leaves. Makes 8 to 10 servings.—*The Donatello, San Francisco.*

PER SERVING: 84 calories, 2 g protein, 20 g carbohydrates, 0.2 g fat (0 g saturated), 0 mg cholesterol, 3.3 mg sodium

Tea sauce. In a 2- to 3-quart pan, stir together 1½ cups **grapefruit juice** (reserved from terrine) and 2 tablespoons **sugar**. Over medium-high heat, bring mixture to a boil. Add 1 tablespoon **black tea leaves;** simmer, covered, for 5 minutes. Pour mixture through a fine wire strainer. (If made ahead, cool, cover, and chill up to 3 days.)

Mix 1 tablespoon **cornstarch** with 2 tablespoons **water** and stir into grapefruit mixture; bring to a boil over medium-high heat. Let cool.

SAGE & GIN SHERBET

2½ cups water
2 cups sugar
1 cup (about ½ oz.) lightly packed fresh sage leaves, chopped; or 1 tablespoon dried sage leaves
About 2 tablespoons chopped lemon peel (yellow part only)
½ cup lemon juice
About ⅓ cup gin, chilled in freezer
Fresh sage leaves or thin lemon slices

In a 2- to 3-quart pan, stir water and sugar over high heat until mixture boils and sugar dissolves. Pour over chopped sage and lemon peel; cover and steep about 4 hours. Chill until cold, about 2 hours or up until next day. Pour syrup through a fine strainer; discard sage and peel. Add lemon juice to syrup.

Freeze syrup in a 1-quart or larger ice cream freezer container (self-refrigerated, frozen cylinder, or with ice and salt), following the manufacturer's directions.

Or use your freezer. Pour mixture into a metal pan (8 to 9 in. square or 9 by 13 in.); cover and freeze until solid, at least 4 hours or up to 1 month. Break into small chunks and whirl in a food processor or beat with a mixer until a smooth slush forms.

Serve, or cover and freeze up to 1 month. If mixture becomes hard, beat to soften before serving.

To serve, scoop sherbet into 6 to 8 martini or wine glasses and drizzle with gin to taste. Garnish with sage leaves. Serve immediately. Makes 6 to 8 servings.—*The Donatello, San Francisco.*

PER SERVING: 221 calories, 0.1 g protein, 51 g carbohydrates, 0.1 g fat (0 g saturated), 0 mg cholesterol, 4 mg sodium

Ruby grapefruit terrine floats in a pool of citrus-tea sauce for a refreshing dessert.

Icy sherbet flavored with sage and lemon swims in bath of cold gin.

Give a Dog a Bone

ERE'S A HOLIDAY GIFT *for Fido that children can have the fun of making themselves.*

While you're gearing up for preholiday baking, add a batch of homemade bones to your list. The crunchy treats won high marks with our canine tasters and are chock-full of ingredients approved by a veterinary nutritionist. Even the eggshells are included to provide additional calcium.

Once the dough is made, children can roll it out and make bones with a bone-shaped cooky cutter or a homemade template. Or simply pinch the dough into bone shapes by hand.

To reduce moisture content in the dense bones, we baked them a long time at a low temperature. Bones that aren't thoroughly dried may develop harmless mold at room temperature, so it's best to store them in the refrigerator or freezer.

CANINE BONES FOR CHRISTMAS

- 1 **pound beef liver**
- 2 **large eggs, shells washed**
- 1 **cup low-fat cottage cheese**
- 1½ **cups wheat germ**
  About 3½ cups whole-wheat flour

Rinse liver and cut into 1-inch chunks. Put in a 1½- to 2-quart pan with 1 cup water. Bring to a boil on high heat; cover, reduce heat, and simmer gently until liver is no longer pink in center of thickest piece (cut to test), about 5 minutes. Drain liquid into a 1-cup glass measure; if needed, add more water to make 1 cup.

Put liver in a blender or food processor; break in eggs, including shells. Whirl to purée, adding reserved liquid as needed to keep mixture moving; scrape sides of container often. Scrape mixture into a bowl; add remaining cooking liquid, cottage cheese, wheat germ, and 3 cups flour. Stir until evenly moistened.

Scrape dough onto a well-floured laminate counter or large plastic cutting board (wood is apt to pick up liver odor); knead until dough no longer feels sticky, adding more flour as required to prevent sticking.

Shape dough into a ball and set aside. Scrape counter clean and coat lightly with more flour. Set dough on flour, dust ball with flour, then roll out until ½ inch thick. Cut with a floured bone-shaped cooky cutter (sold in cookware shops), or lay a floured bone-shaped template (made of firm cardboard and about 3½ in. long) on dough and cut around it with a short-bladed knife.

(Or don't roll out dough; instead, pinch 2-tablespoon lumps of it into bone shapes.) Set bones slightly apart on greased 12- by 15-inch baking sheets.

Bake in a 300° oven until bones are tinged darker brown and feel firm to touch, about 1 hour. Transfer to racks to cool. (Once cool, bones should be hard when pressed; if not, return to 300° oven and bake 10 minutes longer; cool.) To store, package airtight in refrigerator or freezer. Makes about 4½ dozen 3½-inch-long bones.

PER BONE: 41 calories, 3.2 g protein, 5.5 g carbohydrates, 0.7 g fat (0.2 g saturated), 28 mg cholesterol, 19 mg sodium

Charley's good manners are put to the test by an offer of a Christmas bone from a jarful made especially for him.

Graham Cracker Houses

EASY-TO-ASSEMBLE *graham cracker houses provide a time-saving alternative to the homemade gingerbread versions. A simple sugar icing cements the houses together and holds decorations in place. To apply frosting, use mock pastry bags made from small unpleated zip-lock plastic bags with tip (about ⅛ in.) of one corner cut off.*

For an activity-oriented holiday party, Nyla Witmore of Boulder, Colorado, assembles the houses ahead of time, then lets guests decorate them. She provides the houses (one per guest) and bags of icing, and each guest brings a bag of candy, pretzels, or cereal to put into a decoration collection for all to use. (Note: after several hours, colored hard candies may bleed coloring into icing.)

To make the icing, beat together 2 large **egg whites,** ⅛ teaspoon **cream of tartar,** and 2 teaspoons **water** until frothy. Gradually beat in 2½ to 3 cups **powdered sugar** until mixture is smooth and resembles stiff paste. Spoon into unpleated zip-lock plastic bags and seal airtight. Use, or chill up until next day. Each batch makes enough icing to assemble *or* decorate 6 to 8 houses.

Assemble graham cracker houses on foil-covered cardboard bases up to 3 days ahead. A house requires 6 double crackers; create peaked roofs on double crackers with a long knife and a swift motion.

Squeeze on icing using plastic "pastry" bags, then decorate with a variety of candy, pretzels, and cereals.

Lighter, Quicker Latkes

BY TRADITION, LATKES *(golden fried potato pancakes) are eaten during Hanukkah, the Jewish festival of lights.*

Instead of the calorie-raising and time-consuming task of frying individual cakes, we bake the potato mixture on large pizza pans. Baking turns them crisp, and the absence of oil makes them lighter and leaner than their traditional counterparts.

The recipe includes convenient make-ahead steps, so you can make several and reheat them for a large group.

Serve latkes as you would pizza, in big wedges. To each serving, add applesauce and sour cream to taste.

PIZZA LATKES

- 5 slices (5½ oz. total) sourdough sandwich bread, torn up
- 1 tablespoon olive oil
- 4 cloves garlic, minced or pressed
- 5 large eggs
- 2 teaspoons dried rubbed sage
- ½ teaspoon pepper
- 3 large (about 1½ lb. total) russet potatoes
- 2 large (about 1 lb. total) onions, minced
  Salt
- 1 cup light or regular sour cream
- 2 to 3 cups applesauce

In a blender or food processor, whirl enough bread to make about 2¾ cups fine crumbs. In a 10- to 12-inch frying pan on medium-high heat, stir crumbs, oil, and garlic until crumbs become crisp, 8 to 10 minutes; set aside. If crumbs are made ahead, cool and cover airtight up to 2 days.

Grease well and flour-dust 2 nonstick pizza pans (each about 12-in. diameter); set aside.

Baked on a large pizza pan, crisp latke is cut into wedges like pizza to serve. Top individual servings with applesauce and sour cream.

In a large bowl, beat to blend eggs, sage, and pepper. Peel and shred potatoes. Add potatoes, onions, and crumbs to egg mixture; stir well to combine. Spread ½ of the potato mixture evenly into each pan (be sure edges and middle are equally thick, or edges will burn).

Bake in 400° oven until crust is crisp and browned, 45 to 55 minutes; cover pancake edges with foil if they begin to darken too much. If using 1 oven, change pan positions halfway through baking. With a spatula, loosen crust from pan. If made ahead, cool, cover, and chill up until the next day.

To reheat, bake latkes on original pizza pans or on 12- by 15-inch baking sheets, uncovered, in a 425° oven until sizzling hot, 8 to 12 minutes; cover with foil if latkes darken too much.

Cut into wedges. Add salt, sour cream, and applesauce to taste. Makes 8 servings.

PER SERVING: 301 calories, 10 g protein, 44 g carbohydrates, 9.8 g fat (3.3 g saturated), 143 mg cholesterol, 162 mg sodium

Stretching Crab Elegantly

'T IS THE SEASON *to enjoy one of the West Coast's special delicacies— Dungeness crab. But even at its peak time, shelled cooked crab can be costly for entertaining. These two elegant entrées stretch a small amount of crab among several guests.*

CRAB WITH EMERALD SAUCE

- 1/2 **pound fresh basil, rinsed (or 6 oz. spinach and 1/4 cup dried basil)**
- 1/4 **pound fresh cilantro (coriander), rinsed**
- 8 **ounces dry angel hair pasta**
- 1/4 **cup seasoned rice vinegar (or 1/4 cup rice vinegar mixed with 1 teaspoon sugar)**
- 1 **tablespoon Oriental sesame oil**
- 1 **tablespoon minced lemon peel**
- 3/4 **cup regular-strength chicken broth**
- 2 **tablespoons salad oil**
- 1/3 **to 1/2 pound shelled cooked crab, rinsed and drained**

Reserve 4 of the prettiest basil or cilantro sprigs for garnish; cover and chill.

Bring 3 quarts water to a boil in a 5- to 6-quart pan over high heat. Gather half the remaining fresh basil or spinach into a bunch. Holding with tongs by stem ends, dip leaves into boiling water just until they turn bright green, about 3 seconds. At once plunge basil into ice water. Repeat with remaining basil and cilantro.

Add pasta to water and cook, uncovered, until tender but still firm to bite, about 3 minutes. Drain, rinse with cold water, then drain well. Place pasta in a bowl. Add vinegar, sesame oil, and peel; mix well.

Drain basil and cilantro; blot dry. Cut leaves from stems; discard stems. Place leaves in a blender or food processor with dried basil (if spinach is used), broth, and oil; whirl until very smooth.

Divide sauce among 4 wide, rimmed plates; spread it out to rim. Mound 1/4 of the pasta and crab on each plate. Garnish with reserved sprigs. Makes 4 servings.

PER SERVING: 378 calories, 18 g protein, 49 g carbohydrates, 13 g fat (2 g saturated), 37 mg cholesterol, 164 mg sodium

CRAB LASAGNA WITH ROASTED FENNEL

- 2 1/4 **pounds (about 2 large heads) fennel, ends trimmed**
- 2 **large (about 1 lb. total) onions, thinly sliced**
- 3/4 **pound mushrooms, sliced**
- 2 **cups regular-strength chicken broth**
- 8 **ounces dry lasagne noodles**
- 2 **cups low-fat milk**
- 1/4 **cup dry sherry**
- 1/4 **cup cornstarch mixed with 1/3 cup water**
- 1/2 **pound (about 2 cups) shredded fontina cheese**
- 3/4 **to 1 pound cooked shelled crab, rinsed and drained**

Thinly slice fennel crosswise; reserve feathery tops. In a 12- by 14-inch roasting pan, mix fennel, onions, and mushrooms. Roast, uncovered, in a 475° oven, stirring occasionally, until browned bits form on pan bottom, about 45 minutes.

Add 1/2 cup broth, stir to scrape browned bits free, and continue roasting until browned bits again form in pan, about 20 minutes. Repeat process once more until vegetables are well browned. Add 1/2 cup broth and stir to loosen browned bits; keep warm. (Or, if made ahead, cool, cover, and chill up until next day. Reheat, uncovered, in a 400° oven until vegetables are hot, 5 to 10 minutes.)

Meanwhile, bring 3 quarts water to a boil in a 5- to 6-quart pan over high heat. During vegetables' last 10 minutes of roasting, add noodles to water and cook until just tender to bite, about 10 minutes. Drain well; blot dry.

Mince 1/4 cup reserved fennel tops; save remaining for garnish or discard. In a 10- to 12-inch pan, combine minced fennel, 1/2 cup broth, milk, and sherry. Bring to a boil over high heat. Add cornstarch mixture; stir until sauce boils. Remove from heat, add half the cheese, stir until smooth, and keep hot.

Cover bottom of a 9- by 13-inch baking dish with 1/3 of noodles. Spread with vegetables and 1/2 of sauce. Cover with 1/3 of noodles, top with all the crab and all but 1/2 cup sauce; cover with remaining noodles. Top with rest of sauce and remaining cheese.

Bake in a 450° oven until bubbling, about 10 minutes. Broil 4 to 6 inches from heat until cheese is browned, 4 to 5 minutes. Let stand 5 minutes. Garnish with fennel tops. Makes 6 to 8 servings.

PER SERVING: 364 calories, 25 g protein, 38 g carbohydrates, 11 g fat (6 g saturated), 78 mg cholesterol, 487 mg sodium

Delicate Dungeness sits atop cool pasta dressed with rice vinegar, lemon peel, and sesame oil. Green sauce starts with basil and cilantro, blanched to keep them green.

Lightening Up Sunset Classics: Cocoa Sigh Cake

UNSWEETENED COCOA *is the star of this lightened-up version of a Sunset favorite, Chocolate Sigh. The original cake was calorie-laden chocolate inside and out.*

Cocoa, lighter and leaner than chocolate, lends intense flavor to this cake and pudding-like frosting. Switching from butter and whole eggs to nonfat milk and egg whites also reduces calories. A garnish of candied violets (available in fancy food stores) and green leaves replaces the original garnish of chocolate leaves.

The 1991 variation looks as luscious as the full-fat counterpart. Its texture is slightly denser, and the flavor has bittersweet overtones.

The cake, as its name implies, puffs up when baking, then sinks on cooling.

COCOA SIGH

- 1 **cup sifted cake flour**
- 3/4 **cup unsweetened cocoa**
- 1 1/2 **teaspoons** *each* **baking powder and baking soda**
- 1 1/4 **cups sugar**
- 1 **cup nonfat milk**
- 2 **teaspoons vanilla**
- 6 **large egg whites**
  Cocoa frosting (recipe follows)
  Candied violets (optional)
- 2 **or 3 nontoxic leaves (such as citrus or camellia), rinsed and dried, optional**

In a small bowl, mix flour, cocoa, baking powder, and baking soda. In a large bowl, beat 3/4 cup sugar, milk, and vanil-la until well blended. Stir in flour mixture and beat until evenly moistened.

In another large bowl and using clean, dry beaters, whip egg whites on high speed until frothy; gradually beat in remaining 1/2 cup sugar (1 tablespoon at a time) until stiff, moist peaks form. Immediately add to cocoa mixture, gently folding in with a wire whisk until evenly blended.

Pour batter into a lightly oiled and floured 9-inch cheesecake pan (at least 3 in. deep) with removable rim. Gently zigzag a spatula through batter to remove air pockets; smooth top.

Bake in a 350° oven until a toothpick inserted in center of cake comes out clean, about 45 minutes. Cool on a rack (as cake cools, it settles and sinks slightly in center).

Remove pan sides. Spread cake top and sides evenly with cocoa frosting. If made ahead, cover with a large bowl and chill up until next day. If desired, garnish just before serving with candied violets and leaves. Cut into wedges. Makes 12 to 16 servings.

PER REVISED SERVING: 155 calories, 4.2 g protein, 35 g carbohydrates, 1.5 g fat (0.8 g saturated), 0.6 mg cholesterol, 154 mg sodium

PER ORIGINAL SERVING (FIRST APPEARED FEBRUARY 1982, PAGE 152 NORTH EDITION, PAGE 154 SOUTH AND DESERT EDITIONS): 370 calories, 5.5 g protein, 56 g carbohydrates, 16 g fat (9.1 g saturated), 89 mg cholesterol, 141 mg sodium

Cocoa frosting. In a 1- to 2-quart pan, stir together 2/3 cup sifted **unsweetened cocoa** and 1/2 cup **sugar.** In a small bowl, mix 1/3 cup **cornstarch** and 1 cup **nonfat milk** until well blended and free of lumps. Whisk cornstarch mixture into cocoa mixture until well blended.

Cook over medium heat, stirring constantly and scraping pan bottom and sides with a whisk, until glossy and thick, about 7 minutes.

Remove pan from heat; add 1/4 teaspoon **vanilla;** beat to remove lumps. Cool completely; stir occasionally. If made ahead, cover and chill up until next day. Just before using, bring to room temperature (if cold) and beat until smooth. If desired, use a whisk to push frosting through a fine wire strainer to remove any lumps.

Shiny frosting cloaks lean cocoa-based cake; garnish with green leaves and candied violets. Cake puffs up while baking, then sinks as it cools.

More December Recipes

OTHER ARTICLES IN *December feature sautéed veal pungently flavored with salty olives and dried tomatoes, and a crisp noodle pancake that comes from Hong Kong.*

VEAL WITH OLIVES & DRIED TOMATOES

Pungent flavors accent tender, pounded veal in this sautéed dish. Serve with a blend of salty olives and dried tomatoes packed in oil. Each step offers a make-ahead option.

1¼	**pounds boneless veal leg, cut across the grain into 8 equal slices**
¾	**cup fine dry bread crumbs**
1	**tablespoon chopped parsley**
¾	**teaspoon pepper**
1	**large egg**
½	**cup milk**
	Olives and dried tomatoes (recipe follows)
2	**tablespoons melted butter or margarine**
	Salt

Trim and discard tough membrane from meat. Place meat between sheets of plastic wrap. With a flat mallet, gently pound meat until it is ⅛ inch thick. (If made ahead, wrap in plastic and chill up to overnight.)

Mix crumbs, parsley, and pepper on waxed paper. In a shallow pan, beat egg with milk. Dip meat into egg mixture, then coat with crumbs. Lay slices in 1 layer; if made ahead, cover and chill up to 30 minutes.

Drain oil from olive and tomato mixture; put ½ the oil and ½ the butter in a 10- to 12-inch frying pan on medium-high heat. When pan is hot, add veal without crowding; brown on each side, 4 to 5 minutes total. Keep cooked meat warm while browning remainder with remaining oil and butter. Top veal with olive mixture; add salt to taste. Makes 4 to 6 servings.

PER SERVING: 342 calories, 24 g protein, 12 g carbohydrates, 22 g fat (5.5 g saturated), 123 mg cholesterol, 652 mg sodium

Olives and dried tomatoes. In an 8- to 10-inch frying pan over low heat, stir 2 tablespoons **salad oil,** 2 tablespoons **olive oil,** ¼ cup chopped **dried tomatoes packed in oil,** and ¼ cup chopped **oil-cured black ripe olives** until oil is flavored, about 10 minutes. Use warm or at room temperature (if made ahead, cover and let stand up to overnight).

Sugar and vinegar add surprising and refreshing taste to crisp noodle pancake. Serve noodles as a palate refresher, or as a first course or snack.

CRISP NOODLE PANCAKE

The combination sounds odd, but sugar and vinegar over a crisp noodle pancake create a delightful contrast of flavors. The recipe is a specialty of Hong Kong restaurants serving Chiu Chow cuisine (a regional style).

In a multicourse meal, the noodles come near the end to refresh the palate. You might serve them with tea, as a first course, or as a snack.

The Chinese serve the noodles with aged black vinegar made from sweet glutinous rice; it's available here at some Asian markets.

½	**pound fresh thin egg noodles, Chinese-style or capellini**
1	**tablespoon Oriental sesame oil**
1	**tablespoon salad oil**
	Rice, balsamic, or wine vinegar
	Sugar

In a 5- to 6-quart pan, bring about 3 quarts water to a boil. Stir in noodles; cook just until barely tender to bite, 2 to 3 minutes. Drain well. Mix noodles with sesame oil.

Place a 12-inch pizza pan in oven while it heats to 500°. When pan is hot, about 5 minutes, pour in salad oil; tilt pan to coat surface. Spread noodles in an even layer in pan. Bake on lowest rack, uncovered, until golden on top and bottom, 20 to 25 minutes. Slide noodles onto a plate. Cut into wedges. Add vinegar and sugar to taste. Makes 8 to 10 servings.

PER SERVING: 90 calories, 2.6 g protein, 12 g carbohydrates, 3.2 g fat (0.4 g saturated), 17 mg cholesterol, 5.9 mg sodium

Chopped apple, raisins, and cinnamon embellish satisfying oat waffles.

APPLE OATMEAL WAFFLES

1 cup regular rolled oats
1²/₃ cups all-purpose flour
2¹/₂ teaspoons baking powder
1 teaspoon ground cinnamon
¹/₂ teaspoon salt (optional)
1 cup nonfat milk
¹/₄ cup maple syrup
¹/₄ cup orange or apple juice
1 large egg
3 large egg whites
³/₄ cup chopped tart apple
¹/₂ cup raisins

Place oats in an 8- to 9-inch cake pan and bake in a 350° oven until golden, stirring occasionally, 12 to 15 minutes.

In a bowl, stir oats, flour, baking powder, cinnamon, and salt. In another bowl, beat milk, syrup, juice, egg, and egg whites; add apple and raisins, then stir into flour mixture until evenly moistened.

Preheat a waffle iron according to manufacturer's directions. Grease iron, then fill ³/₄ full of batter. Bake until golden and crisp, 6 to 8 minutes. Keep warm on rack in a 200° oven while making remaining waffles. Makes 12 waffles, about 4 inches square. —*Barbara Keenan, Fort Morgan, Colo.*

PER WAFFLE: 152 calories, 5.2 g protein, 30 g carbohydrates, 1.6 g fat (0.2 g saturated), 18 mg cholesterol, 120 mg sodium

---

Top wholesome soup of spinach and chard with croutons and parmesan.

ROBUST GREENS SOUP

¹/₃ cup (about 3 oz.) chopped bacon
2 cups chopped onions
1 tablespoon dried basil leaves
1 teaspoon dried rosemary
1 pound Swiss chard
³/₄ pound spinach
1 quart regular-strength chicken broth
1 can (14 oz.) Italian-style tomatoes, cut up
Salt and pepper
Croutons and grated parmesan cheese, optional

In a 5- to 6-quart pan, stir bacon often over medium-high heat until brown, 5

to 8 minutes. Add onions, basil, and rosemary to pan, crumbling the herbs. Stir often until onions are limp, about 10 minutes.

Meanwhile, trim tough stems and roots from chard and spinach. Rinse greens, drain, and chop. Add greens and broth to pan. Cover, bring to a boil over high heat, then simmer until greens are wilted, about 3 minutes. Stir in tomatoes and cook about 1 minute more.

Serve soup with salt and pepper, croutons, and cheese to add to taste. Makes 2 quarts, about 6 servings.—*Julie Brown Lee, Langley, Wash.*

PER SERVING: 155 calories, 6.5 g protein, 12 g carbohydrates, 9.8 g fat (3.3 g saturated), 9.5 mg cholesterol, 422 mg sodium

---

A quarter cup each of three legumes and barley gives stew its name.

FOUR QUARTERS BEAN & BARLEY STEW

¹/₄ cup *each* dried kidney beans, pinto beans, black-eyed peas, and pearl barley
5 to 6 cups regular-strength chicken broth
1 medium-size (about 7 oz.) onion, chopped
1 cup chopped celery
2 cups sliced carrots
2 teaspoons curry powder
1 teaspoon ground turmeric
1¹/₂ tablespoons cider vinegar
Salt and pepper

Sort kidney beans, pinto beans, black-eyed peas, and barley for debris, then rinse. Place beans, peas, and barley in a 4- to 5-quart pan with water to cover by 1 inch. Boil, uncovered, over high heat for 2 minutes. Cover and let stand for 1 hour; drain well.

In pan, mix bean mixture, 5 cups broth, onion, celery, carrots, curry, and turmeric. Cover, bring to a boil over high heat, and simmer until beans are tender to bite, about 45 minutes. If too thick, add more broth. Add vinegar; simmer 5 minutes more. Season to taste with salt and pepper. Makes 4 servings.—*Marie Mitchell, Lake Oswego, Ore.*

PER SERVING: 248 calories, 13 g protein, 44 g carbohydrates, 2.8 g fat (0.6 g saturated), 0 mg cholesterol, 121 mg sodium

BAKED SWEET & SOUR CABBAGE & MEATBALLS

1½ pounds ground extra-lean beef
½ cup uncooked white long- or short-grain rice
1 large egg
1 jar (32 oz.) marinara sauce
2 medium-size (7 oz. each) onions
1 medium-size (1½ lb.) head red cabbage
⅓ cup lemon juice
¼ cup firmly packed brown sugar
   Parsley sprigs

In a bowl, mix beef, rice, egg, and ½ cup of the marinara sauce. Chop 1 onion; mix into meat. Shape meat mixture into 2-inch balls.

Cut cabbage in thin shreds and slice remaining onion; combine in a deep 12-by 15-inch roasting pan and tuck in meatballs. Combine remaining marinara, lemon juice, and sugar; pour evenly over cabbage and meatballs.

Cover pan very tightly with foil and bake in 350° oven for 1 hour. Stir gently and bake, uncovered, until meat and cabbage are glazed and browned, about 45 more minutes. Transfer mixture to serving dish. Garnish with parsley. Makes 6 servings.—*Loretta Woolman, Huntington Beach, Calif.*

PER SERVING: 527 calories, 28 g protein, 49 g carbohydrates, 26 g fat (8.8 g saturated), 114 mg cholesterol, 1,057 mg sodium

Present baked meatballs and cabbage in marinara sauce for hearty supper.

SAVORY LEMON CHICKEN IN A POUCH

   Cooking parchment or foil
4 chicken breast halves (2 lb. total), skinned, rinsed, and patted dry
8 medium-size (about 8 oz. total) green onions, ends trimmed
1 large (about 8 oz.) red bell pepper, stemmed and seeded
1½ cups thinly sliced carrots
⅓ cup lemon juice
1½ tablespoons minced fresh ginger
1 tablespoon soy sauce
1 teaspoon dried thyme leaves
⅛ teaspoon cayenne

Cut cooking parchment or foil into 4 pieces, each 15 by 24 inches. Place a breast half in the center of each. Cut onions and pepper into 4-inch slivers. Divide onions, pepper, and carrots over chicken. Mix juice, ginger, soy, thyme, and cayenne; spoon over vegetables.

To seal each packet, bring together short ends of paper and fold over 1 inch three times; fold each remaining end under 1 inch twice and tuck under chicken. Lift to a 12- by 15-inch baking sheet.

Bake in a 425° oven until chicken is white in center of thickest part (open; cut meat to test), about 30 minutes. Serve from packets, if desired. Makes 4 servings.—*V.G. Madsen, Albuquerque.*

PER SERVING: 215 calories, 36 g protein, 12 g carbohydrates, 2.2 g fat (0.5 g saturated), 86 mg cholesterol, 376 mg sodium

Wrap chicken and vegetables in a parchment or foil package for baking.

HOLIDAY JEWEL TART

1½ cups all-purpose flour
6 tablespoons sugar
6 tablespoons butter or margarine
1 large egg
½ cup dried figs, stemmed
½ cup moist, pitted prunes
½ cup moist, dried apricot halves
¼ cup orange juice
6 ounces cream cheese
¾ cup unflavored yogurt
2 teaspoons grated orange peel
2 tablespoons chopped pistachios

In a bowl, rub flour, 2 tablespoons sugar, and butter with fingers until fine.

Stir in egg thoroughly; press into a smooth ball. Press over bottom and halfway up side of a greased 10- to 11-inch tart pan with removable rim. Bake in a 300° oven until golden, about 40 minutes; cool.

Halve figs and prunes; mix with apricots and juice. Let stand until juice is absorbed, about 30 minutes; stir occasionally. Beat cheese, yogurt, remaining sugar, and peel. Spread crust with cheese mixture; arrange fruit on top. Cover and chill at least 2 hours or up to 1 day. To serve, sprinkle with pistachios and remove rim. Makes 8 to 10 servings.—*Roxanne Chan, Albany, Calif.*

PER SERVING: 308 calories, 5.9 g protein, 40 g carbohydrates, 15 g fat (8.5 g saturated), 60 mg cholesterol, 141 mg sodium

Dried fruit and pistachios decorate orange-flavored cream cheese tart.

MANICOTTI IS ITALIAN *for muffs—those puffy, fur-covered, silk-lined tubes that ladies once stuffed their hands into to keep them warm while riding in a carriage or touring car. Some of us may remember that our mothers or grandmothers had them, and opera lovers will remember that Mimi's last wish in La Bohème was for a manicotto to warm her icy hands.*

Culinary manicotti are neither fur-covered nor silk-lined, but they are tubes into which the cook may stuff a wide variety of fillings. Manicotti may be smooth or ridged; there is no difference in flavor, but some people think that the ridged kind will hold more sauce.

Barry Schoenfeld uses a spinach-ricotta stuffing, perked up with a bit of feta cheese. For convenience, he uses a prepared Italian-style pasta sauce. There are many on the market now, and they are quite good, but if you are the sort of cook who likes to listen to the rustic music of bubbles bursting in a long-simmered pot of sauce, feel free to make your own.

STUFFED MANICOTTI ALLA FIORENTINA

2 tablespoons olive oil

1 large (8 oz.) onion, chopped

1 medium-size (about 6 oz.) red bell pepper, stemmed, seeded, and chopped

3/4 cup (about 5 oz.) packed feta cheese, crumbled

1 cup (1/2 lb.) ricotta cheese

1/2 pound spinach, stems and wilted leaves discarded; rinse leaves well, drain, and finely chop

Freshly ground pepper

1 jar (30 oz.) Italian-style pasta sauce

1 package (8 oz.) large dry manicotti

1 large (8 to 10 oz.) firm-ripe tomato, cored, seeded, and chopped

3 tablespoons freshly grated parmesan cheese

In a 10- to 12-inch frying pan over medium heat, combine oil, onion, and bell pepper; stir often until vegetables are limp, about 10 minutes. Let cool.

In a bowl, stir together feta, ricotta, spinach, and onion mixture; season to taste with pepper.

Spoon about 1/2 the pasta sauce into a 9- by 13-inch pan. Divide spinach mixture in equal portions to match the number of manicotti pieces. One at a time, rinse manicotti with cool water, shake off excess moisture, and push a portion of the spinach mixture into center of pasta with your fingers.

Lay stuffed pasta in a single layer in sauce; spoon remaining sauce over pasta. Cover and bake in a 400° oven for 45 minutes; uncover and continue baking until pasta is tender when pierced, 10 to 15 minutes longer. Let stand 5 to 10 minutes. Sprinkle with tomato, then cheese. Makes 6 servings.

PER SERVING: 450 calories, 18 g protein, 51 g carbohydrates, 21 g fat (8.7 g saturated), 43 mg cholesterol, 1,272 mg sodium

Los Angeles

SO MANY FLAVORS, *so few words to describe them—that is the food writer's curse. Worse, these few words are used so often that they grate on the mind. Let's forget zesty and tangy and look for a new word to describe Rachel Craven's cocktail. One that comes to mind is grateful, an old-fashioned word that could stand reviving. The Oxford English Dictionary defines it as "pleasing to the mind or the senses, agreeable, acceptable, welcome."*

Grateful was once used to convey a sense of refreshment in warm weather or after exertion: shade is grateful after a hike through the desert; a glass of cold cider is grateful during a break in the afternoon's threshing. And Rachel's Cocktail, combining the proverbial coolness of cucumber and mint with the wake-up sharpness of grapefruit, is grateful, sharpening the palate before a meal or refreshing it between courses.

"Manicotti are tubes into which the cook may stuff a wide variety of fillings."

"It combines the coolness of cucumber and mint with the wake-up sharpness of grapefruit."

RACHEL'S COCKTAIL

- 1 large (about 12 oz.) cucumber
- 3 medium-size (about 1 lb. each) grapefruit
- 2 tablespoons minced fresh mint leaves
  Fresh mint sprigs

Peel and dice cucumber; place in a medium-size bowl.

Cut off all peel and white membrane from grapefruit. Holding grapefruit over the bowl to catch the juice, cut between membranes to remove sections; add to cucumber. Squeeze juice from membrane into bowl; discard membrane. Stir in minced mint. Cover and chill until cold, about 1½ hours, or up to 4 hours.

Spoon fruit mixture into 5 or 6 stemmed glasses; drizzle with juices. Garnish with mint sprigs. Makes 5 or 6 servings.

PER SERVING: 43 calories, 1 g protein, 11 g carbohydrates, 0.2 g fat (0 g saturated), 0 mg cholesterol, 2.9 mg sodium

Cupertino, Calif.

F**ISH FILLETS ANOINTED** *with butter and lemon juice; scented with savory, shallots, and parsley; and sealed to bake to moist opacity need little or no further flavor enhancement.*

Without breading and frying, they do, however, have a deplorably naked look that calls out for clothing, or at least adornment. The trick is to furnish this touch without obscuring the delicate flavor of the fish.

James Kircher's solution? He dresses his fish in a mushroom sauce with white wine, chicken broth, and a whiff of Beau Monde seasoning. It qualifies him for a chef's toque and the honorary degree of saucier's apprentice.

BAKED FISH WITH MUSHROOM SAUCE

- 2 pounds boned and skinned white-flesh fish such as Chilean sea bass, lingcod, or halibut, cut 1 inch thick
  Salt and pepper
- 1 tablespoon finely chopped shallots
- 1 teaspoon dried summer savory
- 1 tablespoon chopped parsley
- 4 teaspoons butter or margarine
- 2 tablespoons lemon juice
- ½ pound mushrooms, thinly sliced
  About ⅓ cup *each* regular-strength chicken broth and dry white wine
- 1 tablespoon cornstarch mixed with 1 tablespoon water
- 1 teaspoon Beau Monde seasoning powder or dried thyme leaves

"He dresses his fish in a mushroom and wine sauce."

Rinse fish and pat dry; arrange in a single layer in a 9- to 10-inch-square pan. Lightly sprinkle with salt and pepper, then evenly top with shallots, savory, and parsley. Cut 2 teaspoons butter into small pieces and scatter on top of fish. Drizzle with lemon juice and seal pan with foil. Bake in a 350° oven until fish is opaque and moist-looking in thickest part (cut to test), about 20 minutes.

Meanwhile, melt remaining 2 teaspoons butter in a 10- to 12-inch frying pan over medium heat. Add mushrooms and stir often until lightly browned, about 5 minutes. With a slotted spatula, lift fish to a warm serving platter; keep warm. Pour fish juices into a glass measure and add equal parts of broth and wine to make 1 cup *total*. Smoothly stir cornstarch mixture and Beau Monde into broth mixture. Return to pan and stir over high heat until sauce boils. Serve fish with sauce to add to taste. Makes 4 servings.

PER SERVING: 298 calories, 43 g protein, 6.3 g carbohydrates, 8.8 g fat (3.6 g saturated), 103 mg cholesterol, 392 mg sodium

Burley, Idaho

December Menus

DURING THIS BUSY *entertaining season, be kind to the cook with simple but special meals for all to enjoy. Offer cheddar scones and warm apples with frozen yogurt for breakfast. Or celebrate with a festive but easy meal of roast beef. Bake sausages and pasta in one pan for supper.*

CHRISTMAS BREAKFAST

Cinnamon Apples with Molded Frozen Yogurt
Cheddar Scone Cutouts
Butter & Jalapeño Jelly
Crisp Bacon
Hot Cranberry Cider

For a festive breakfast on Christmas morning, serve this meal with special treats and fanciful shapes of molded frozen yogurt and butter, and scones designed with a cooky cutter.

Mold frozen yogurt and butter up to a few days ahead. In the morning, bake apples; let them cool as you make the scones and cook the bacon. Heat cider; add thin strands of orange peel for flavor and garnish.

To shape butter. *Chill wooden butter molds or paddles in ice water for 10 minutes. Fill molds with softened butter or margarine; smooth top. Chill or freeze until firm, then release butter from mold. Or roll cubes or sticks of butter between paddles to form balls or logs, then immerse in ice water. Chill shaped butter airtight up to 4 days.*

CINNAMON APPLES WITH MOLDED FROZEN YOGURT

- 1 to 2 pints vanilla frozen yogurt or ice cream, slightly softened
- 1/4 cup (1/8 lb.) butter or margarine, cut up
- 1/2 cup firmly packed brown sugar
- 1 tablespoon lemon juice
- 1 teaspoon ground cinnamon
- 4 large (about 2 lb. total) Golden Delicious apples

Solidly pack frozen yogurt into molds (about 1/3-cup size), level, and freeze until yogurt is firm, at least 3 hours or up to 4 days.

To unmold, quickly dip mold in hot water; open and remove yogurt (pry loose, if needed). Serve or freeze, airtight, in a single layer up to 2 days. Or instead of molds, scoop frozen yogurt to make balls.

Melt butter in a 10- by 15-inch baking pan in a 400° oven, about 1 1/2 minutes. Stir in 2 tablespoons water, sugar, juice, and cinnamon.

Peel, core, and thinly slice apples; add to pan and stir to coat with sugar mixture. Bake until fruit is slightly tender when pierced, 20 to 30 minutes. Cover to keep warm. Serve apples and juices slightly warm or at room temperature with frozen yogurt. Makes 4 servings.

PER SERVING: 433 calories, 4 g protein, 78 g carbohydrates, 14 g fat (8 g saturated), 36 mg cholesterol, 131 mg sodium

CHEDDAR SCONE CUTOUTS

- About 2 cups all-purpose flour
- 1 1/2 cups (5 oz.) shredded sharp cheddar cheese
- 1 tablespoon sugar
- 2 teaspoons baking powder
- 1 1/2 teaspoons cumin seed
- 3/4 cup sour cream
- 1/4 cup salad oil
- 1 large egg

In a large bowl, mix flour, cheese, sugar, baking powder, and cumin. In a small bowl, beat sour cream, oil, and egg to blend. Add egg mixture to flour mixture; stir just enough to moisten evenly. Scrape dough onto a lightly floured board and knead lightly 10 turns.

On a greased and lightly floured 12- by 15-inch baking sheet, pat dough into

For Christmas breakfast, gather the family and enjoy a meal of whimsical cooky-cutter scones and molded frozen yogurt. Eat with spiced apples, bacon, and cranberry cider.

an 8- by 12-inch rectangle. Dip cooky cutter (2 to 3-in. size) in flour, then cut out dough. Carefully lift cutout with cutter, to preserve the shape (use a spatula, if needed). Transfer cutout to a second greased and floured 12- by 15-inch baking sheet. Carefully push dough from cutter. Repeat to make 6 cutouts, about 1½ inches apart on dough (set cutouts on second pan at least 1½ in. apart).

Bake both pans in a 350° oven until richly browned, 30 to 40 minutes (remove individual scones if they begin to darken too much). If using 1 oven, switch pan positions halfway through baking. Transfer loaf and small scones to basket and serve hot, warm, or at room temperature. Makes 1 pound of scones (loaf and cutouts), about 6 servings.

PER OUNCE: 162 calories, 5 g protein, 14 g carbohydrates, 9.7 g fat (4.2 g saturated), 29 mg cholesterol, 130 mg sodium

---

HOLIDAY ROAST DINNER

Green & Red Salad
Beef Tri-tip Roast with Couscous & Peas
Cabernet Sauvignon
Chocolate Cake

Serve this easy but company-worthy dinner for family or friends.

Red wine, Chinese hoisin sauce, garlic, and coriander coat this beef roast and season the couscous. The roast cooks in less than 45 minutes. Meanwhile, make the salad. When roast is done, transfer meat to a board; keep warm. Use roasting pan to prepare couscous.

Chocolate cake, purchased or homemade, adds a sweet finish.

GREEN & RED SALAD

2 large (about 2½ lb. total) European cucumbers, rinsed, ends trimmed
  About ½ pound radishes, rinsed, stems and leaves removed
  Vinaigrette (recipe follows)
4 to 8 large leaf lettuce leaves, rinsed and crisped
  Salt and pepper

Finely shred cucumbers, then radishes (keep separate); drain well. Pour ⅔ of vinaigrette over cucumbers and remaining ⅓ over radishes; mix to coat.

Line each of 4 plates with 1 or 2 lettuce leaves. Mound equal portions of cucumber on each plate. Top with radishes. Add salt and pepper to taste. Makes 4 to 6 servings.

PER SERVING: 102 calories, 1.4 g protein, 8.8 g carbohydrates, 7.5 g fat (1 g saturated), 0 mg cholesterol, 163 mg sodium

Vinaigrette. In a bowl, beat to blend ¼ cup **white wine vinegar,** 3 tablespoons **olive oil,** 2 tablespoons **Dijon mustard,** 2 teaspoons **dried tarragon leaves,** and 1 teaspoon **sugar.**

BEEF TRI-TIP ROAST WITH COUSCOUS & PEAS

1¾ **pounds boneless beef triangle tip (tri-tip) or top round roast**
½ **cup dry red wine**
2 **tablespoons hoisin or soy sauce**
2 **cloves garlic, minced or pressed**
½ **teaspoon ground coriander**
  About 2¼ cups regular-strength beef broth
1½ **cups couscous**
1 **package (10 oz.) frozen petite peas, thawed**
¼ **cup sliced green onion**
  Fresh parsley sprigs
  Salt and pepper

Trim and discard any excess fat from roast; rinse meat and pat dry. Set meat in an 8- by 12-inch metal roasting pan.

In a bowl, combine wine, hoisin, garlic, and coriander. Brush wine mixture evenly over roast. Bake in a 425° oven, brushing 4 times with mixture (if pan drippings begin to burn, add 4 to 6 tablespoons water to pan and scrape browned bits free). Reserve any remaining wine mixture. Roast until a thermometer inserted in thickest part registers 125° for rare, 35 to 45 minutes. After 25 minutes, check temperature every 5 to 10 minutes.

Serve thin slices of roast beef with couscous flavored by beef juices and basting sauce.

Transfer meat to a board; reserve all meat juices. Let roast stand, loosely covered.

Measure meat juices and remaining wine mixture; add broth to make 2¼ cups total. Pour into roasting pan; bring to a boil over medium-high heat; stir and scrape browned bits free.

Add couscous; stir until boiling. Cover pan very tightly with foil. Let stand until liquid is absorbed, about 5 minutes. Stir in peas, onion, and any juices on the board that have accumulated from the roasting meat.

Arrange meat and couscous on platter. Garnish with parsley. Add salt and pepper to taste. Makes 4 to 6 servings.

PER SERVING: 388 calories, 39 g protein, 44 g carbohydrates, 4.9 g fat (1.6 g saturated), 76 mg cholesterol, 311 mg sodium

(Continued on next page)

ONE-PAN
PASTA SUPPER

One-pan Tomato &
Sausage Pasta
Spinach Salad
Sourdough Bread with
Fruity Olive Oil
Sparkling Water
or Chianti
Tangerines
Amaretti or Crisp
Almond Cookies

For a simple meal, bake sausage and onions to brown and develop flavor. Then add tomatoes, broth, and pasta; cover and return to oven until pasta is tender, then top with cheese.

Warm bread as casserole bakes. Meanwhile, make your favorite spinach salad.

For dessert, offer fruit and crisp Italian cookies.

ONE-PAN TOMATO & SAUSAGE PASTA

1 can (28 oz.) tomatoes
  About ¾ cup regular-strength beef broth
1 pound mild Italian sausages, cut into ¼-inch-thick slices
2 large (about 1 lb. total) onions, minced
2 teaspoons dried basil
¾ pound (about 1½ cups) dry rice-shape or other tiny pasta
¼ to ½ cup shredded mozzarella cheese

Break tomatoes with a spoon, then drain juice well from tomatoes into a 1-quart measure; reserve tomatoes. Add broth to juice to make 3 cups; set aside. Place sausages and onions in a shallow 2½- to 3-quart casserole. Bake in a 450° oven, stirring and scraping browned bits occasionally, until sausages and onions are well browned, 1 to 1½ hours; drain off fat.

Remove dish from oven and add tomatoes, broth mixture, and basil. Stir and scrape to release any browned bits. Continue baking until mixture boils, about 10 minutes. Add pasta; stir to moisten. Cover dish tightly with foil; bake until liquid is absorbed and pasta is tender, about 15 minutes. Sprinkle with cheese. Makes 4 to 6 servings.

PER SERVING: 457 calories, 22 g protein, 55 g carbohydrates, 17 g fat (5.8 g saturated), 47 mg cholesterol, 750 mg sodium

Articles Index

Index of Recipe Titles

General Index

Photographers

Douglas Bond: 4, 5 (center, bottom), 36. **Glenn Christiansen:** 7, 9, 10, 11 (bottom left), 14, 15, 16, 17, 18 (bottom left), 19, 20, 21, 22, 42, 48, 70, 71, 78, 92, 128, 129, 151, 152, 153, 154, 155, 157, 159, 160, 162, 170, 172, 173, 194, 195, 207, 216, 266, 267, 291, 316, 317, 336. **Peter Christiansen:** 5 (top), 23, 26, 35, 37, 38, 44, 45, 49, 50, 53, 65, 66, 67, 80, 88, 89, 91, 94 (top right, bottom right), 95, 98, 99, 104, 105, 106, 110, 118, 119, 131, 133, 136, 137, 145, 149, 156, 164, 165, 182, 191, 196, 199, 212, 213, 215, 219, 220, 234, 235, 236, 239, 230, 231, 246, 247, 250, 251, 252, 253, 256, 257, 259, 260, 276, 277, 289, 292, 293, 296, 297, 298, 299, 300, 306, 309, 310, 311, 312–313, 314 (left), 315, 318, 319, 320, 325, 328, 329, 330, 331. **Frederica Georgia:** 146. **Renee Lynn:** 96, 97, 124, 125. **Norman A. Plate:** 11 (top right), 121, 122, 123, 126, 127, 168, 169, 181, 185, 186, 188, 217, 237, 326. David Stubbs: 81. **Darrow M. Watt:** 1, 2, 6, 12, 18 (top right), 24, 25, 27, 32, 33, 39, 41, 46, 47, 51, 52, 54, 55, 60, 61, 63, 69, 72, 73, 75, 76, 77, 79, 82, 83, 93, 100, 101, 102, 107, 108, 109, 111, 112, 113, 132, 134, 135, 142, 143, 158, 161, 163, 166, 167, 178, 179, 193, 204, 205, 208, 209, 211, 218, 224, 225, 227, 229, 230, 231, 233, 238, 249, 254, 255, 261, 262, 269, 270–271, 272, 273, 274, 275, 278–279, 280, 281, 282, 284, 285, 287, 290, 294, 295, 301, 307, 314 (top right), 321, 322, 323, 324, 327, 337. **Doug Wilson:** 94 (bottom left). **Tom Wyatt:** 197.